595

FIVE
CENTURIES
OF
KEYBOARD
MUSIC

FIVE CENTURIES OF KEYBOARD MUSIC

An Historical Survey
of Music for Harpsichord and Piano

JOHN GILLESPIE

Professor of Music, University of California

DOVER PUBLICATIONS, INC.

NEW YORK

This Dover edition, first published in 1972, is an unabridged republication of the work originally published in 1965. This new edition has been reprinted by special arrangement with Wadsworth Publishing Company, Inc., Belmont, California, publisher of the original edition.

International Standard Book Number: 0-486-22855-X
Library of Congress Catalog Card Number: 75-188812

Manufactured in the United States of America
Dover Publications, Inc.
180 Varick Street
New York, N. Y. 10014

To my wife
ANNA
whose inspiration, encouragement, and help
made this book possible

PREFACE

As a practicing harpsichordist and pianist, I have felt the need for a book that would provide a frame of reference for the music I play and also supply new ideas for additional repertoire. As a professor of music history and literature of keyboard music, I have wished for a book that might furnish suitable material for such courses. Finally, as one who has a great admiration for both piano and harpsichord music, I have looked for a book that might unfold a progressive panorama of keyboard music as it developed through the ages. There seemed to be no one book to fill these needs.

In this work I have endeavored to satisfy a wide range of interests. For the serious student of clavier literature, I have tried to give an idea of the different phases of keyboard development and to quote original sources whenever possible. For the musical amateur with a limited technical vocabulary, I have kept the text as simple as possible; since many terms are not necessarily self-explanatory, I have added a Glossary of pertinent musical terms. The more important musical forms—sonata, suite, fugue—are discussed more fully in the text (Chapters 3 and 11).

The main content of the book is limited to harpsichord (also clavichord) and piano music. Organ music has its own niche and requires a separate volume. Therefore, the word keyboard is used to designate all stringed keyboard instruments, excluding the organ. The principal purpose of this book is to present a summary of music for *solo* keyboard. Ensemble music and compositions for keyboard and orchestra are also important and interesting; yet a thorough coverage of these would involve a separate book for each. The concerto form in general has been admirably explored by such writers as Abraham Veinus (London: Cassell & Co., Ltd., 1948) and Ralph Hill (Baltimore: Penguin Books, 1961), each in a book titled *The Concerto.*

For the pianist or harpsichordist—professional and amateur—who wishes to obtain the music discussed, I have indicated in the notes to each chapter where the compositions of each outstanding composer are published. At the end of the book is a list of the most important keyboard music publishers. Since it is impossible to maintain a current list of books and music in print, the reader is referred to the larger municipal and university libraries and to publishers' catalogs for the most up-to-date listings. I have also included recent and unpublished dissertations as an important source of material; these are usually available on microfilm or in Xerox copies.

In a book of this scope it is impossible to discuss all the works of one specific composer, or to mention every composer who wrote a piano piece. I have tried to bring into focus composers who have written unusually attractive music or influenced the course of keyboard literature. Minor composers are introduced to complete the narrative.

My principal interest regarding the individual composers centers around their place of activity rather than their nationality. For example, Johann Schobert, a German-born composer, is placed in the chapter on France, since he worked mostly in that country.

Wherever feasible, I have tried to provide the compositions with original titles plus an English translation. And I have supplied English versions to all excerpts that originated in a foreign tongue.

For their help with some translations and proofreading, I want to thank Mr. and Mrs. Eduard Schmutzer. I also give my grateful thanks to Dr. Wendell Nelson and Dr. Roger Nyquist for their kindness in reading the manuscript; to Dr. Dolores Menstell Hsu for her careful study of the text and her helpful suggestions; and to the eminent Dr. Karl Geiringer for his final reading of the completed manuscript. A special note of gratitude goes to Mr. John de Keyser, owner of the de Keyser music shop in Hollywood, California, for his patient and knowledgeable assistance in searching out the vast repertoire of keyboard music.

CONTENTS

Part V

Ill. 1. CLAVICHORD from the *Weimarer
Wunderbuch, ca.* 1440.

Ill. 2. FRETTED GERMAN CLAVICHORD,
18th century (close-up of action). Courtesy
The Smithsonian Institution. Photograph by
Robert Lautman.

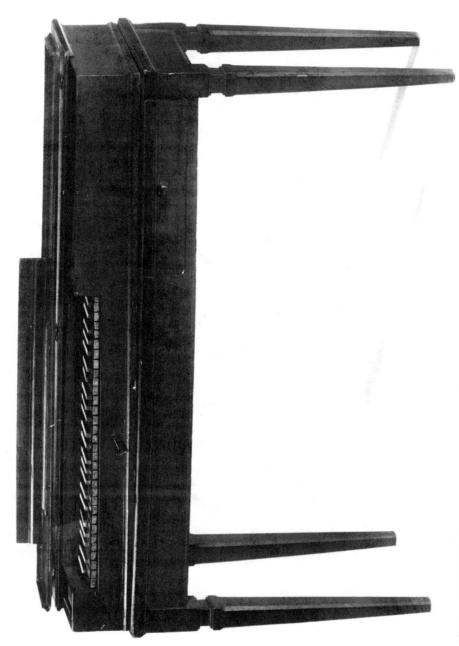

Ill. 3. FRETTED GERMAN CLAVICHORD, 18th century.
Courtesy The Smithsonian Institution.

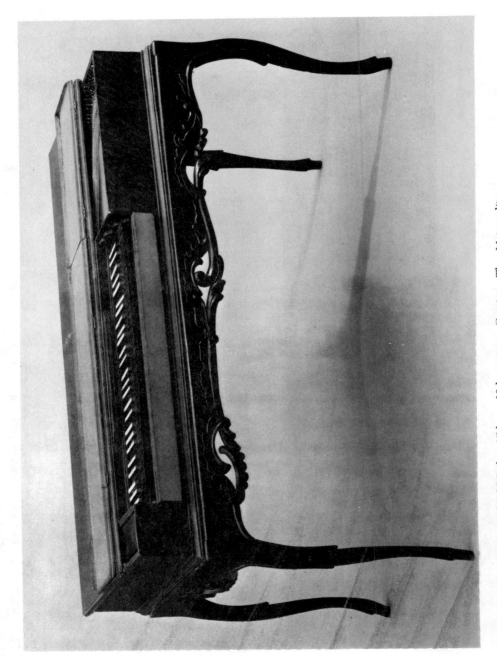

Ill. 4. UNFRETTED CLAVICHORD, late 17th or 18th century. Courtesy The Metropolitan Museum of Art, The Crosby Brown Collection of Musical Instruments, 1889.

Ill. 5. HARPSICHORD from the *Weimarer Wunderbuch, ca.* 1440.

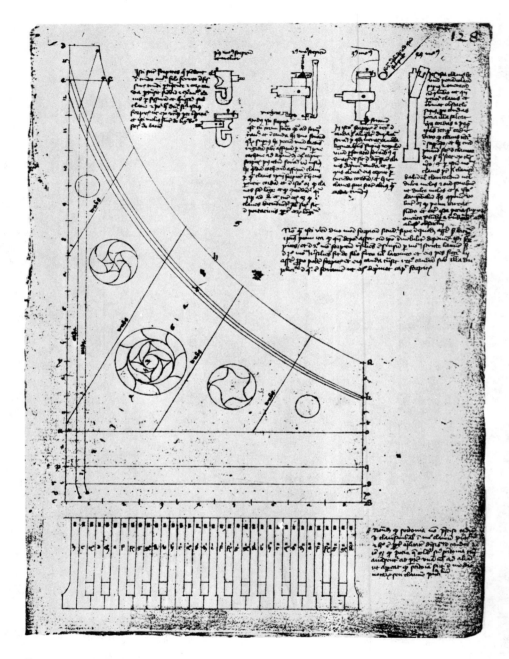

Ill. 6. DIAGRAM OF A HARPSICHORD by
Henri Arnault de Zwolle, *ca.* 1440. Photograph
courtesy The Library of Congress, Washington, D.C.

Ill. 7. ITALIAN HARPSICHORD, made in 1643. Inscribed on nameboard: "Horatius Albana f. Anno MDCXXXIII." Courtesy The Smithsonian Institution.

Ill. 8. TWO-MANUAL HARPSICHORD, made by Burkat Shudi, England, in 1747. Courtesy Hugo Worch Collection, The Smithsonian Institution.

Ill. 9. TWO-MANUAL HARPSICHORD, made
by Johannes Daniel Dulcken, Belgium, in 1745.
Courtesy Hugo Worch Collection, The Smithsonian Institution.

Ill. 10. HARPSICHORD JACK. Photo courtesy
The Metropolitan Museum of Art, The Crosby
Brown Collection of Musical Instruments, 1889.

Ill. 11.   TWO-MANUAL HARPSICHORD,
made by Johannes Couchet, *ca.* 1650. Courtesy
The Metropolitan Museum of Art, The Crosby
Brown Collection of Musical Instruments, 1889.

Ill. 12. PIANOFORTE, made by Bartolomeo Cristofori, Italy, in 1720. Courtesy The Metropolitan Museum of Art, The Crosby Brown Collection of Musical Instruments, 1889.

Ill. 13. GRAND PIANO, made by Johann Andreas Stein, Augsburg, Germany, 1773. Courtesy Hugo Worch Collection, The Smithsonian Institution.

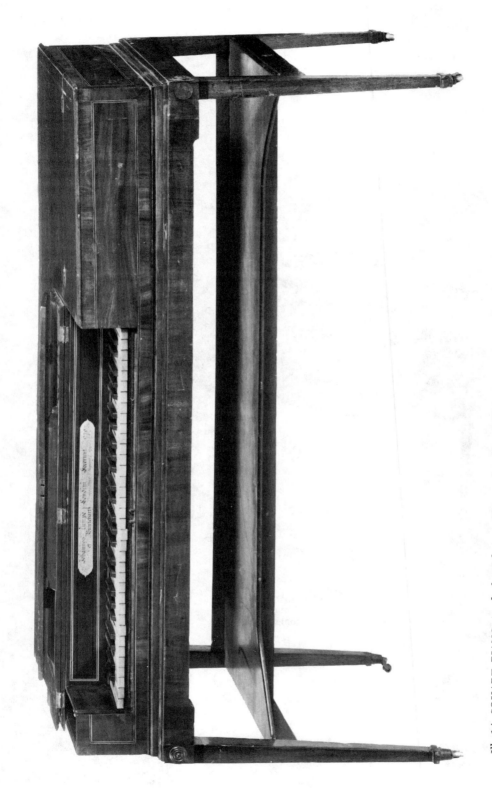

Ill. 14. SQUARE PIANO, made by Johannes Zumpe, London, 1770.
Courtesy Hugo Worch Collection, The Smithsonian Institution.

Ill. 15. PIANOFORTE, made by John Broadwood, London, 1789.
Courtesy Mrs. MacKinley Helm.

Ill. 16. GRAND PIANO, made by Robert Stodart, London, 1790. Courtesy Hugo Worch Collection, The Smithsonian Institution.

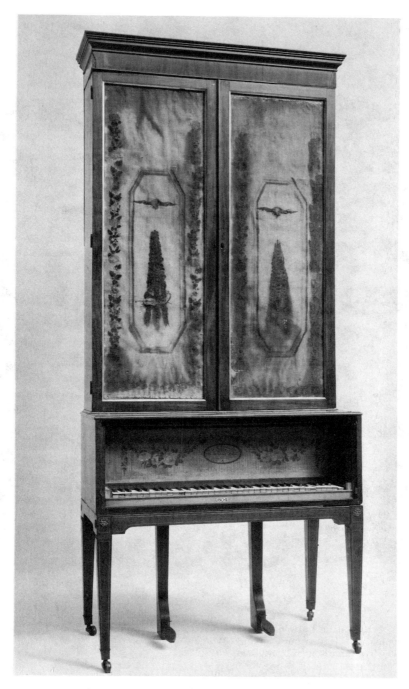

Ill. 17. UPRIGHT GRAND PIANOFORTE,
made by William Stodart, London, 1801. Cou
tesy The Metropolitan Museum of Art, Th
Crosby Brown Collection of Musical Instruments, 1889.

Ill. 18. PIANO, made by John Isaac Hawkins,
Philadelphia, Pa., 1801. Courtesy Hugo Worch
Collection, The Smithsonian Institution.

Ill. 19. SQUARE PIANO, made by Alpheus Babcock at "William Swift's Piano Forte Manufactory," Philadelphia, *ca.* 1835. Courtesy Hugo Worch Collection, The Smithsonian Institution.

Ill. 20. SQUARE PIANO, made by Alpheus Babcock, *ca.* 1835 (view of action). Courtesy Hugo Worch Collection, The Smithsonian Institution.

Ill. 21. UPRIGHT PIANO, *Giraffen Flügel,*
made by Andreas Stein, Vienna, Austria, *ca.*
1810. Courtesy Hugo Worch Collection, The
Smithsonian Institution.

Ill. 22. DOUBLE ESCAPEMENT MECHANISM. Courtesy Steinway & Sons.

PART

I

1

STRINGED KEYBOARD
INSTRUMENTS: THEIR ORIGINS
AND DEVELOPMENT

Clavichord, harpsichord, piano—each is a stringed keyboard instrument, yet each instrument as it appears in various shapes and sizes possesses its own merit and strength as well as its weaknesses. A flowing melodic line is most beautifully expressed by the clavichord, whose strings are activated by gentle pressure strokes from metal tangents; but at the same time lack of tonal power limits its enjoyment to a small circle of admirers. The harpsichord, whose strings are *plucked*, is admirably suited to the quasi-polyphonic lines of Baroque music; however, the more lyric pieces of the early eighteenth century are less effective on the harpsichord due to its lack of flexibility in creating nuances. The piano—that dynamic instrument whose strings are *struck* by hammers—possesses extraordinary expressive possibilities, but lacks the clarity of the harpsichord. These three instruments, together with their more pompous companion the pipe organ, form a keyboard dynasty that remains unchallenged.

ECHIQUIER

Despite the fact that all types and sizes of early clavichords and harpsichords have been preserved, as well as information concerning their construction, the earliest stringed keyboard instrument continues to be somewhat of an enigma. In a manuscript titled *Les Enseignemens* (Instructions, 1483)[1] Imbert Chandelier reveals his favorite pastime:

> *Never do I suffer from melancholy,*
> *Incessantly I play the echiquier....*

[1] *Jamais ne seuffre en moy merencolie,*
Incessamment je joue de l'eschiquier,
De fleustes, d'orgues, en menant doulce vie,
Comme voiez en l'istoire au premier.
Imbert Chandelier, *Les Enseignemens* (Bibliothèque Nationale de Paris, ms. fr. 1673, fol. 1–1483). Quoted in André Pirro, *Les Clavecinistes* (Paris: Henri Laurens, 1925), p. 7.

What was this elusive *echiquier* (there are several spellings for the word) so often mentioned by the chroniclers but never clearly described? The instrument was in use at an early date, for even in Chandelier's time it had been known for well over a hundred years. In the year 1360, King Edward III of England presented to his prisoner King Jean le Bon of France an *echequier* made by a certain Jehan Perrot.[2] This transaction could indicate a possible English origin for the keyboard instrument, a conjecture strengthened by the poet-musician and man of the Church Guillaume de Machaut (*ca.* 1300–1377). In his grandiose poem *La Prise d'Alexandrie* (The Capture of Alexandria),[3] Machaut lists an *exchaquier d'Engleterre* in an enumeration of musical instruments.

But there is something more to be learned about the *echiquier* than what is revealed in casual literary reference. *Echiquier* performers were in demand in their day and well paid for their services. An anonymous minstrel who played for Philippe le Hardi, Duke of Burgundy, in 1376, received a fee of six francs.[4] Two years later the French poet Eustache Deschamps wrote about one Platiau who could play the *echiquier* as well as the harp. Deschamps himself declared that he had never undertaken anything so difficult as learning to play the *echiquier*.[5]

The French term *echiquier* (chessboard) was not the only name applied to this early instrument. In England it was called the chekker. In 1393 a Bishop Braybroke of London paid 3s/4 "to one playing on the chekkers at Stepney."[6] The German poet Eberhardus Cersne von Minden in *Der Minnen Regelen* (The Rules of Love, 1404)[7] mentions not only the *clavicymbolum* (harpsichord) and *clavichordium* (clavichord) but also the *Schachtbret*, probably the German equivalent of the French word *echiquier*.

One of the few references to the instrument's construction comes from the year 1388 when King John I of Aragon wrote to the Duke of Burgundy to request the services of the minstrel *Johan dels orguens* who was, according to the letter, able to play the *echiquier*, an instrument described as *similar to the organ* but which sounded *by means of strings*.[8]

Some authorities consider the *echiquier* to be a type of clavichord with a primitive hammer action. Others believe that it is an early ancestor

[2] Pirro, *ibid.*, p. 5.

[3] Guillaume de Machaut, *La Prise d'Alexandrie* (Genève: Imprimerie Jules-Guillaume Fick, 1877), p. 36.

[4] Pirro, *op. cit.*, p. 5.

[5] Eustache Deschamps, *Oeuvres Complètes* (Paris: Firmin Didot, 1878–1900), VIII, 34–36.

[6] See the article by W. H. Grattan Flood titled "Chekker," *Grove's Dictionary of Music and Musicians*, fifth edition, pp. 194–195.

[7] Eberhardus Cersne von Minden, *Der Minnen Regelen*. In *Deutsche National-Litteratur*, ed. J. Kürschner (Berlin and Stuttgart: W. Spemann, 1887), X, 202.

[8] Pirro, *op. cit.*, p. 6.

of the harpsichord. To support the latter theory, it has been suggested that the sight of the jacks—the wooden pieces that housed the plucking mechanism—lined up along the keyboard could have reminded someone of chessmen, thus calling forth the name *echiquier*.[9] Whatever the construction principle, it is obvious that stringed keyboard instruments were popular as early as the fourteenth century. Alain Chartier (*ca.* 1392–*ca.* 1430), who writes poetically about the battle of Agincourt in his *Livre des Quatre Dames* (Book of the Four Ladies, 1416),[10] mentions the *echiquier;* and the *Naufrage de la Pucelle* (Shipwreck of the Virgin)[11] by Jean Molinet (1435–1507) enumerates *bons eschequiers et les doucemelles*. The name *echiquier,* whatever it may have been, disappears from literary sources in the late fifteenth century. Public attention then turned to the clavichord.

CLAVICHORD

The clavichord is the earliest type of stringed keyboard instrument about which there is specific information available. Its known ancestry goes back to the sixth century B.C. when Pythagoras used a monochord for his experiments in musical mathematics. The monochord consisted of an oblong hollow box—the sounding board—above which stretched a string tuned by means of a peg. A movable bridge or fret made it possible to vary the length of the string. Later on, more strings were added.

Another precursor of the clavichord was the dulcimer, an instrument in which a series of strings were fitted over two stationary bridges and tuned by movable pins. The dulcimer was played by means of hammers striking the strings from above. This instrument still exists as the Hungarian *cimbalom*.

About the eleventh or twelfth century a stringed instrument was provided with a row of keys. Each key had a metal tangent at its tip (Fig. 1); when a key was struck, its tangent produced a small delicate tone capable of some dynamic variation. One string could be used for several keys, the various tangents striking a given string at different places. One of the first pictorial representations of this clavichord appears in the *Weimarer Wunderbuch* (Weimar Wonderbook), dated about 1440 (Ill. 1).

By the mid-fifteenth century, the clavichord competed with the *echi-*

---

[9] Curt Sachs (*The History of Musical Instruments*, 1940, pp. 336–337) sees the *echiquier* as a portable upright harpsichord while Francis Galpin (*A Textbook of European Musical Instruments*, 1937, p. 119) considers it to be a type of clavichord.

[10] The complete works of Chartier were edited in Paris by A. Duchesne (1617).

[11] *Les Faictz et Dictz de Jean Molinet,* ed. Noël Dupire (Paris: Société des Anciens Textes Français, 1936), I, 90.

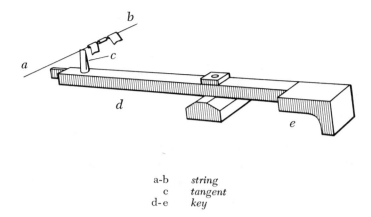

a-b   *string*
c   *tangent*
d-e   *key*

Fig. 1. Clavichord Mechanism

Reproduced by permission. Karl Geiringer. Musical Instruments. *New York: Oxford University Press, 1945.*

quier for popular favor. When one Jean-Ulrich Surgant studied at the Sorbonne about the year 1472, he reported that the scholars there amused themselves by singing in parts and playing the lute or the clavichord.[12] The English also liked this intimate keyboard instrument with its silvery sound. In 1477, William Horwood, master of choristers at Lincoln Cathedral, was appointed to teach the boys "playing on the clavychordes."[13] And in his satirical poem "Against a Comely Coistrown," England's poet laureate John Skelton (*ca.* 1460–1529) exclaims:

> *Comely he clappeth a pair of clavichordes;*
> *He whistleth so sweetly, he maketh me to sweat;*
> *His descant is dashed full of discordes;*
> *A red angry man, but easy to entreat.*[14]

Among the earliest clavichord performers are Pierre Beurse in the late fifteenth century and Henry Bredemers (1472–1522), a Flemish teacher. In Paris in 1485, the nobleman René de Lorraine paid a service fee to a performer on the *manichordion* (clavichord).[15]

[12] Pirro, *op. cit.*, p. 13.
[13] W. H. Grattan Flood, "The Eschiquier Virginal," *Music and Letters* (April, 1925), p. 152.
[14] *The Complete Poems of John Skelton,* ed. Philip Henderson (London: J. M. Dent & Sons, Ltd., 1959), p. 35.
[15] Pirro, *op. cit.*, p. 13.

The clavichord is not conspicuous in sixteenth-century records, although it was used. Scotland's King James IV (reigned 1488–1513) entertained his bride, Margaret of England, by playing the lute and clavichord. Isabella d'Este (1474–1539), protectress of Raphael and Mantegna and known in her own time as a living example of Renaissance ideals, received clavichord lessons as a young girl. After her sister Beatrice acquired a handsome clavichord made by Lorenzo Gusnasco, Isabella ordered a similar instrument but requested a more supple keyboard.[16]

The so-called fretted clavichord—one string for several keys or notes —was satisfactory as long as the music itself remained simple (Ill. 2–3). However, with the advent of more complicated instrumental writing during the second half of the seventeenth century, the clavichord was gradually supplied with one string for each key and sometimes even a pair of strings for each key. Also in that century, the term clavichord came into more general use. Previously, the old term monochord and its various modifications (monachord, manichord, and manichordion) had been used more often.

By the seventeenth century, the clavichord had achieved its classic form. The mechanism was enclosed in an oblong case three to four feet long and two feet wide. The sound was produced by means of small metal tangents attached to the ends of the keys; these tangents gently *struck* the strings from below. A certain nuance was possible, but only within a limited range. One technique peculiar to this instrument was the *Bebung* or tremolo, which produced a slight vibrato or fluctuation in pitch. The clavichord served throughout western Europe during the sixteenth and seventeenth centuries but seemed to go out of fashion during the eighteenth century, except in Germany where it remained a favorite until the close of that century (Ill. 4).

HARPSICHORD

The harpsichord (the French *clavecin*, the Italian *cembalo* or *clavicembalo*) played a primary role in the music of the eighteenth century; it assumed a position similar to that of the concert grand piano during the nineteenth and twentieth centuries. Yet today the harpsichord is not considered an obsolete instrument; it has undergone an unprecedented revival during the present century, and harpsichord factories are now flourishing.

The harpsichord has had a brilliant career. From the fifteenth century to about 1750, it reigned, so to speak, as the king of keyboard instruments; its renown was due in great part to Antwerp's master harpsichord builders,

[16] *Ibid.*, p. 14.

the Ruckers family, famous in the seventeenth century for building fine instruments. Harpsichord history can be traced at least as far back as the Middle Ages when the psaltery, a stringed instrument similar to the modern zither, appeared in various shapes; the strings were *plucked* by the fingers. It was comparatively simple to adjust a primitive keyboard to the psaltery and in turn to supply each key with a plucking mechanism.

From the records it seems clear that by the fifteenth century the harpsichord had passed the experimental stage and was commonly used. The previously mentioned *Weimarer Wunderbuch* contains a drawing of a simple harpsichord (Ill. 5). About 1440 Henri Arnault de Zwolle, astronomer at the Burgundian court, described and diagramed a large *clavicymbalum* (harpsichord—Ill. 6).[17] In his manuscript Arnault explains several methods of plucking the strings and indicates that quill was used as the plucking medium. Then by 1500 a second set of strings was added to the harpsichord, and sometime before 1579 a set of "four-foot" strings (where the pitch sounds an octave higher than the key pressed) was also included in some instruments. The range, originally limited to some twenty notes, was increased toward the lower regions. The outward appearance was transformed from its earlier rectangular shape to the present familiar outlines of the horizontal harp or wing. In fact, the Germans adopted their word *Flügel* (wing) to designate the harpsichord. For playing convenience, the instrument was mounted on four legs and at the same time it became fashionable to decorate the cases with lacquer paintings.

Thus improved, the harpsichord was ready to impose itself upon society. During the seventeenth century it competed successfully with the lute, which for so long had been the favorite secular instrument in many European countries. The harpsichord rapidly dominated the musical scene throughout Europe. It influenced music composition and produced master musicians like Chambonnières and Louis Couperin, two French composers who wrote especially for the regal instrument. These were the beginnings of the glorious French *clavecin* school that existed during the seventeenth and eighteenth centuries—the school that fostered the musical dynasty of the Couperins and the talent of Jean-Philippe Rameau (see Chapter 6). Inspired by the harpsichord's refinement, members of the Bach family created their rich musical legacy for Germany, and in Spain the transplanted Neapolitan composer Domenico Scarlatti wrote his scintillating pieces especially for this instrument.

During the seventeenth and eighteenth centuries the harpsichord held first place among all musical instruments. Apart from its virtuoso role, it was indispensable as a sustaining and accompanying medium: it was heard

[17] *Les Instruments de Musique du XVe Siècle. Les Traités d'Henri Arnault de Zwolle et de divers Anonymes*, eds. Le Cerf and Labande (Paris: Editions Picard, 1932).

in church, lending its support to the choir; it was seen in the salon, where it accompanied sonatas and played an important part in other chamber music; and it was found in the orchestra as an integral part of the orchestral apparatus.

During its golden age, from 1650 to 1750, the harpsichord varied from six to eight feet in length and ideally had two keyboards, each with about five octaves (Ill. 7–9). There were three or four sets of strings sounded by means of small quills or leather plectra hinged on wooden jacks (Fig. 2; Ill. 10). Each set of strings varied in pitch and tone quality. These

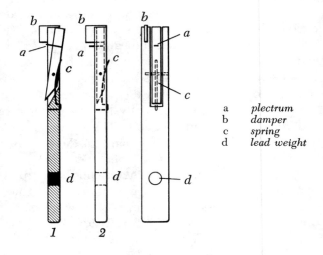

a	*plectrum*
b	*damper*
c	*spring*
d	*lead weight*

Fig. 2. Harpsichord Jack

Reproduced by permission. Karl Geiringer. Musical Instruments. New York: Oxford University Press, 1945.

strings were operated by means of stops placed above the keyboard. Frequently there was a lute stop, a device that dampened a given set of strings by means of small pieces of cloth or felt in order to imitate the lute sound. Since crescendo and diminuendo were impossible on this plucked instrument, it was necessary to have different timbres or tone colors produced by the sets of strings.

One important reason for the harpsichord's popularity and development was that its construction was so greatly improved by the Ruckers family. Hans Ruckers, the first master builder, began making harpsichords in Antwerp about 1579, and the family firm continued until after 1667. Prior to the Ruckers period there were isolated examples of harpsichords with two keyboards, a "four-foot" and an "eight-foot" register, and stops for coupling and manipulating the different registers. But it was the Ruckers family that standardized the use of these principles and improved upon them. Ruckers harpsichords were considered by contemporary musicians to possess the most beautiful tone of any such instrument in existence (Ill. 11).[18]

Later manufacturers modeled their harpsichords after the classic Ruckers examples. German builders introduced a "sixteen-foot" stop (an octave below standard pitch), thus providing an expansive sonorous range. A pedal keyboard—similar to the organ pedal board—was occasionally used with the harpsichord or clavichord. In an era when the organ had to be pumped by hand, the pedal keyboard made it possible for the organist to practice his organ repertoire on a harpsichord or clavichord without having to hire an assistant to pump the organ. (Bach is supposed to have owned a pedal keyboard.) In the eighteenth century, the English harpsichord firms Shudi and Kirkman likewise used Flemish models. Some English builders substituted foot pedals for the hand-operated stops, thereby facilitating the changing of registers. Some English instruments also contained a mechanism called the Venetian swell, which enabled the lid of the instrument to be opened and closed, producing a degree of dynamic change.

There were other types of plucked-string instruments. The *spinet* was a modest harpsichord, usually in a triangular or pentagonal case, with its strings strung at acute angles to the keyboard. The *virginal* (sometimes called virginals or pair of virginals) was the preferred instrument in England during the sixteenth and early seventeenth century; during the latter century it was replaced by the larger continental-type harpsichord. A small rectangular instrument, the virginal had only one set of "eight-foot" strings, which were strung parallel to the keyboard.

PIANOFORTE

The large harpsichord had sparkling clarity yet lacked expressive power. As the keyboard manufacturers learned how to make instruments capable of greater nuance, the harpsichord began to lose favor. In 1709 the Florentine instrument maker Bartolomeo Cristofori realized a significant objective—a harpsichord with hammers. The Italian gave his instrument the shape of a large harpsichord and called it a *gravicembalo col piano e forte* (harpsichord with soft and loud). So began the era of the piano.

[18] See Dr. Burney's evaluation of the Belgian harpsichord builders in *Dr. Burney's Musical Tours in Europe*, ed. Percy A. Scholes (London: Oxford University Press, 1959), II, 16.

Cristofori's invention of an escapement mechanism for his new harpsichord with hammers brought about a major transformation in keyboard instruments (Fig. 3). In the harpsichord, the jack—under pressure from

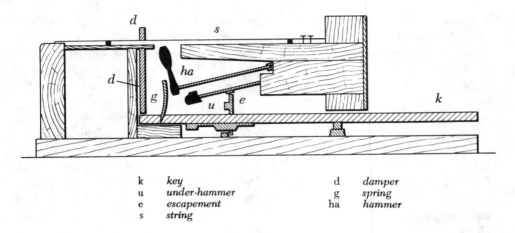

k	key	d	damper
u	under-hammer	g	spring
e	escapement	ha	hammer
s	string		

Fig. 3. Cristofori's Escapement Mechanism

Reproduced by permission. Karl Geiringer. Musical Instruments. New York: Oxford University Press, 1945.

the key—attacks the string with the tip of its plectrum, thus producing a metallic sound that almost immediately is extinguished by a damper attached to the jack. Cristofori substituted a little hammer for the jack and added more strings to reinforce the sound. Under the pressure of the key, this hammer is lifted by means of a lever (or under-hammer), which transmits to the hammer an impulse made possible by a mobile piece called an escapement—so called because after contact has been made, the mechanism escapes, permitting the hammer to fall back to the bed of the key, ready to receive a new impulse and to give a new stroke. As the hammer returns to the bed, a damper rises to stifle the vibrating string.

In 1720 Cristofori improved the striking action of his instrument and also provided it with a side-slip. This device, activated by a hand stop, shifted the mechanism so that only one string was struck. This is the origin of our soft or *una corda* pedal. There are in existence two, possibly three, such instruments attributed to Cristofori (Ill. 12); but it appears that in his own time the invention did not attract much attention, and production of the new instrument was limited.

Cristofori's admirers and followers—Gottfried Silbermann (1683–1753) in Germany and a pupil of Silbermann named Johannes Zumpe in England—preserved the general principles of his invention. In 1716 a Frenchman named Jean Marius designed models of harpsichords with hammers, some models with the hammers striking down onto the strings from above and other models with the hammers striking upward from below the strings. Marius may have been somewhat influenced by Pantaleon Hebenstreit, for about 1705 this German inventor delighted the court at Versailles by playing directly with two single hammers on huge dulcimers. He called his invention a *pantaleon* (after his own first name) and handled the instruments with amazing virtuosity. His success doubtlessly stimulated imaginations in France and Germany, for the piano itself is basically a keyed dulcimer. In Germany, the harpsichordist Cristoph Gottlieb Schröter (1699–1782), who had witnessed Hebenstreit's pantaleons in Dresden, became convinced that a keyboard instrument could be constructed in a similar manner. Marius and Schröter never got past the experimental stage. Their ideas were not enthusiastically received by the harpsichord performers, who for a long period thereafter continued to prefer the classic instrument with its plucked strings.

The new harpsichord with hammers was baptized at the court of Saxony, where two instruments made by Gottfried Silbermann in 1726 came to the attention of Johann Sebastian Bach. Aided by Bach's helpful advice, Silbermann, in 1745, built the first pianoforte with a sonority perfectly equal along its range of keys. Silbermann was the first builder to exploit the commercial possibilities of the new instrument. The striking action that he used for his pianos became known as "English" action.

However, despite the activity in piano construction, there had to be a gestation period of some twenty years before any consistent piano literature emerged. It began with the Clementi sonatas published in 1770.[19] Even then the older instruments did not disappear. England's Dr. Burney, traveling throughout Europe in 1770 and 1772, observed that all three instruments—harpsichord, clavichord, and piano—were still in use.

Muzio Clementi (1752–1832), a composer and virtuoso keyboard performer, founded a piano factory in London and became one of the first pianists. Joseph Haydn composed for the early piano, and in 1777 Wolfgang Mozart became a permanent convert to the instrument when he played a piano made in Vienna by the German Johann Stein, an apprentice of Silbermann (Ill. 13). In addition to having superb action, the Stein pianos built after 1789 used a foot pedal to raise the dampers from the keys (*sostenuto*). Previous to this period, the builder had employed knee stops. The square

---

[19] There are isolated instances of earlier compositions for piano. See Lodovico Giustini, *Sonate da Cimbalo di Piano, e Forte* (Florence, 1732), facsimile edition by Rosamond Harding (Cambridge: Cambridge University Press, 1933).

piano, which was to enjoy enormous popularity in America for well over a hundred years, was first constructed in 1758 by Christian Friederici of Saxony. More or less fortunate experiments aided in transforming and fixing the specifications for the piano. There had been, for example, a vertical harpsichord, the *clavicytherium*. When the clavicytherium was provided with an appropriate set of hammers (*ca.* 1740), it emerged as the upright piano.

Piano manufacturing houses in England and Germany almost simultaneously produced distinguished yet different models. French harpsichord builders, however, resisted the new instrument, resulting in only a few pianos being built in France prior to 1770. Voltaire, a staunch defender of the harpsichord, called the new pianos "tinkers' instruments."[20] In spite of French opposition, piano virtuosos like Clementi and Mozart, who were traveling about to concertize at this time, finally made the new instrument a necessity in the French capital.

In due course, Paris had its own piano factory, the house of Erard (Ehrhard). The first Erard piano dates from 1777. It was built by Sébastien Erard (1752–1831) at the residence of the Duchesse de Villeroi, who also provided the funds. This initial attempt was so successful that in 1779 Sébastien and his brother Jean-Baptiste established a factory, which became one of the first famous piano houses. The Erard was the first Parisian piano equipped with foot pedals. Ignace Pleyel (1757–1831), a German who owned a music publishing house in Paris, also began to manufacture pianos there in 1809, thereby starting a lively competition with Erard that still continues today.

By the last quarter of the eighteenth century, piano manufacture extended beyond these few cities. England had its Zumpe, Broadwood, and Shudi, as well as a branch of Erard; Germany its Stein and Silbermann; and Pleyel and Erard still competed in Paris (Ill. 14–17). In America, manufacturing houses capable of competing with the European makers also opened up at this time (Ill. 18). The first American piano was made in 1775 by John Behrent in Philadelphia; Benjamin Crehore of Milton, Mass., also began building pianos about this time. Henry Steinway, who was born in Germany in 1797, became one of the great United States builders. Transporting to America the house he had begun in Brunswick, Steinway turned out American pianos that seriously challenged the European instruments. Builders and composers collaborated to solve technical problems. Mozart gave his "performer's" advice to Stein. When Stein's daughter Nanette inherited the business, she in her turn had Beethoven's friendship and counsel.

[20] Letter to Madame la Marquise du Deffand, December 8, 1774. In Voltaire, *Oeuvres Complètes* (Paris: Garnier Frères, 1882), Vol. 49 (Correspondance XVII), 151.

During the early nineteenth century, experiments were made with pianos of diverse shapes and construction. In England, France, and elsewhere, the small upright piano became popular because of its practicality and low price. In America, Alpheus Babcock invented the metal framework (1825) that was to become standard for all later pianos (Ill. 19–20). And a few fantastic inventions appeared in the early nineteenth century, some only briefly. For instance, there were the vertical obelisk piano, the "Giraffe" piano, the lyre piano, and the "piano-secretary" (a piano disguised as a secretary and designed by Henri Pape, at one time director of the house of Pleyel). Pape, to his credit, also created the felt hammer in 1826. The "Turkish stop" (consisting of drums, little bells, and metallic rods suitable for executing the "Bacchanals" of Daniel Steibelt) was another addition to these piano novelties, most of which soon passed into oblivion (Ill. 21).

Fortunately, serious research continued with worthwhile results. In 1821 Pierre Erard secured a patent for a double-escapement mechanism, which had been perfected by his uncle Sébastien, founder of the firm. This mechanism made possible quicker, subtler note repetitions, thus facilitating the spread of virtuosity by such agile performers as Sigismund Thalberg and Franz Liszt. No doubt this invention encouraged Liszt to compose and perform his *Douze Études Transcendantes* (Twelve Transcendental Études, 1838). The Erard invention transformed finger technique and opened up unheard-of possibilities of execution. At first reserved for concert grand pianos, the double-escapement mechanism was finally applied to upright pianos in 1842; this invention has provided the basis for all escapement mechanisms used since then (Ill. 22).

The "modern piano" developed during the years 1830–1850. Piano manufacturers mass-produced the two basic models, upright and grand. In this century, one may choose from a number of fine pianos, depending on the specific qualities required in a keyboard instrument. In Germany, the Blüthner and Bechstein pianos have usurped the spotlight; in France, Pleyel and Erard are still very highly esteemed, but Gaveau is offering some strong competition; in Austria, the Bösendorfer piano is recognized for its lyrical tone quality and because it is so well suited to the music of Beethoven and the Romantic composers. Steinway and Baldwin are the foremost American piano manufacturers.

In this century, too, the harpsichord and clavichord have again come into favor. Due in great measure to the late Wanda Landowska (1877–1959), the harpsichord and clavichord are no longer considered antiquated instruments. On the contrary, they are being produced in increasing numbers by both European and American builders; Challis, Dolmetsch, Mendler-Schramm, Merzdorf, Neupert, Pleyel, Sperrhake, and Wittmayer are among the more prominent.

Contemporary composers at home and abroad are devoting a considerable amount of their time and talent to writing especially for the keyboard. The twentieth century can look forward to ever increasing interest and activity in the performing and composing of keyboard music.

BIBLIOGRAPHY

Baines, Anthony, ed. *Musical Instruments through the Ages.* London: Penguin Books, 1961.

Bie, Oscar. *Das Klavier.* Berlin: Paul Cassirer, 1921.

Closson, Ernest. *History of the Piano* (translated by Delano Ames). London: Paul Elek, 1947.

Dale, William. *Tschudi, the Harpsichord Maker.* London: Constable & Co., Ltd., 1913.

Dolge, Alfred. *Pianos and Their Makers.* Covina, Calif.: Covina Publishing Co., 1911. Dover reprint

Flood, W. H. Grattan. "The Eschiquier Virginal." *Music and Letters,* Vol. VI, No. 2, 1925.

Galpin, Francis W. *A Textbook of European Musical Instruments.* New York: E. P. Dutton & Co., Inc., 1937.

Geiringer, Karl. *Musical Instruments.* New York: Oxford University Press, 1945.

Harding, Rosamond E. M. *The Pianoforte: Its History Traced to the Great Exhibition of 1851.* Cambridge: Cambridge University Press, 1933.

Harich-Schneider, Eta. *The Harpsichord. An Introduction to Technique, Style and the Historical Sources.* St. Louis: Concordia Publishing House, 1954.

Le Cerf, G. and E. R. Labande, eds. *Les Instruments de Musique du XVe Siècle. Les Traités d'Henri Arnault de Zwolle et de divers Anonymes.* Paris: Editions Picard, 1932.

Locard, Paul. *Le Piano.* Paris: Presses Universitaires de France, 1954. Collection "*Que Sais-Je?*"

Michel, N. E. *Michel's Piano Atlas.* Rivera, Calif.: 9123 Terradell Ave., 1957.

Russell, Raymond. *The Harpsichord and Clavichord.* London: Faber & Faber, 1959.

Sachs, Curt. *Das Klavier.* Berlin: Julius Bard, 1923.

Sachs, Curt. *The History of Musical Instruments.* New York: W. W. Norton & Co., Inc., 1940.

Shortridge, John D. *Italian Harpsichord-Building in the 16th and 17th Centuries.* Washington, D.C.: Smithsonian Institution, 1960. United States National Museum Bulletin 225.

Winternitz, Emanuel. *Keyboard Instruments.* New York: Metropolitan Museum of Art, 1961.

2

EARLY
KEYBOARD
MUSIC

The pipe organ is the oldest of all keyboard instruments. By natural sequence the music written for the later stringed keyboard instruments—harpsichord and clavichord—includes certain stylistic elements traceable to early organ music. During the Middle Ages, most churches had organs, but they were used merely in a supporting role. The organ served to sustain the vocal polyphony of the choir and at times alternated with the choir in the different sections of the divine service. A true keyboard style did not evolve until the latter half of the fifteenth century.

THE BEGINNINGS

The first music known to have been written with a keyboard instrument in mind, rather than being transcribed from other sources, dates from the early part of the fourteenth century. The *Robertsbridge Codex* (*ca.* 1320)[1] contains the first notated organ music, in two and three voices. It would be too soon to speak of a real organ style because these compositions are limited mainly to parallel movements in fourths, fifths, and octaves. Early vocal polyphony undoubtedly served as a model for these instrumental works.

There are six pieces in the *Robertsbridge Codex.* Three are in the general form of the *estampie,* and although a definite keyboard style is not yet visible, these works are instrumentally conceived. Example 1[2] illustrates

[1] *Robertsbridge Codex* (British Museum, add. 28550).

[2] This *estampie* may be found in: (a) Davison and Apel, *Historical Anthology of Music* (Cambridge: Harvard University Press, 1946); (b) Curt Sachs, *The Evolution of Piano Music* (New York: E. B. Marks Music Corp., 1944); (c) Willi Apel, *Musik aus früher Zeit* (Mainz: Edition Schott, 1932). These anthologies contain fine examples of early keyboard music as do the following: Arnold Schering, *Geschichte der Musik in Beispielen* (Leipzig: Breitkopf & Härtel, 1931), reprint by Broude Brothers in 1950; Johannes Wolf, *Music of Earlier Times* (New York: Broude Brothers, n.d.); John Klein, *The First Four Centuries of Music for the Organ* (New York: Associated Music Publishers, Inc., 1948).

the structure and style of the *estampie*. It has a series of *puncta* (sections), each supplied with an *ouvert* ending (half cadence) and a *clos* ending (final cadence). The movement is almost entirely in parallel fifths. There are traces of vocal style, such as the *hoquetus* in the second measure, and there is direct repetition evident in the *ouvert* ending.

Ex. 1. *Robertsbridge Codex: estampie*

Several small collections have been found, which indicate that by the early fifteenth century there was an increase in music written for the keyboard. These early collections—known as the *Sagan, Winsem,* and *Breslau* manuscripts[3]—contain mostly instrumental settings for sections of the Mass. The general pattern is rather stereotyped, usually a liturgical melody supplied with florid counterpoint. Considerably advanced beyond these

[3] For a discussion of these manuscripts see Gerald Bedbrook, *Keyboard Music from the Middle Ages to the Beginnings of the Baroque* (London: Macmillan & Co., 1949), pp. 21–24.

collections is the *Ileborgh Tablature* (1448),[4] in which there is a definite
attempt to establish a tonal center and to indicate clearly parts for the pedal
in some pieces. Here are hints of a genuine keyboard style, for the compositions do not have continuous parallel movement. Instead, they take on the
characteristics of the prelude, in which a free melodic line plays such an
important role. The *Ileborgh* manuscript has five short preludes and three
mensurae. The composer or the compiler (the manuscript is not clear on
this point) designates them as being written in the modern manner, which
probably refers to the fact that some are in duple time.

In the *Praeambulum bonum super C* (Good Prelude on C) it is interesting to see how frequently the intervals of the sixth and third occur and
also the full chord at the end, all unusual for their day (Ex. 2).[5] The augmented fourth D–G♯ is curious, especially since it occupies such a prominent
place.

Ex. 2. *Ileborgh Tablature: Praeambulum bonum super C*

The mensura *Frowe al myn hoffen an dyr lyed* (Lady, all my hope
depends on you)[6] is consonant in its use of thirds and triads, and it ends

⁴ *Ileborgh Tablature* (Curtis Institute of Music, Philadelphia, Pa.) (LC) Mll, 127 pp.
⁵ Bedbrook, *op. cit.*, p. 25. By permission of Macmillan & Co., Ltd.
⁶ *Ibid.*, p. 26.

on a major third. Also worth noting is the melodic line that descends gradually by phrases, spanning the range of a twelfth (Ex. 3).

Ex. 3. *Ileborgh Tablature: mensura*

Conrad Paumann (1410–1473), the Nuremberg organist, eventually formulated the rules for instrumental handling of counterpoint in his *Fundamentum Organisandi* (Principles of Composition).[7] But it must be kept in mind that this development of a keyboard style was the outgrowth of theories and experiments covering several centuries. The manner in which Paumann put his theories into operation changed the entire concept of keyboard composition. In his *Mit ganczem Willen* (With all my heart) Paumann places the popular melody in the bass line and employs a florid soprano line above it. Here also begin the germs of the prelude and the toccata. As yet there is no definite line drawn between compositions for organ and compositions for other keyboard instruments, but in Paumann's *Mit ganczem Willen* (Ex. 4) the instrumental style becomes evident in the disregard for strict part writing; one finds writing in five and three voices. Although this composition has principally a melodic soprano line with accompaniment, measures fourteen and fifteen have a series of first-inversion triads that break the monotony. There is great rhythmic variety in the melodic line, well illustrated in measures three to six; and in the entire piece there are not two identical figurations.

The *Buxheim Organ Book*,[8] written or collected about 1475, shows

[7] *Fundamentum Organisandi* (Codex Zb. 14, Prince Stolberg Library, Wernigerode). Modern reprint by Konrad Ameln, *Lochemer Liederbuch und Fundamentum Organisandi* (Kassel: Bärenreiter Verlag, 1925).

[8] *Buxheimer Orgelbuch* (Munich: Bayerischen Staatsbibliothek, MS. 3725). A facsimile was edited by B. A. Wallner for Bärenreiter in 1955. The modern transcription (B. A. Wallner) appears in Vols. 37–39 of *Das Erbe Deutsche Musik* (Bärenreiter, 1958–1959). A selection of pieces (transcribed by A. Booth) appears in two volumes published by Hinrichsen.

Ex. 4. Paumann: *Mit ganczem Willen*

further progress in the extension of melodic inventiveness. There are some 220 keyboard arrangements of songs in this collection, most of them by composers in the Burgundian school,[9] with other compositions attributed to Dunstable, Paumann, and Legrant. More significant are the thirty instrumental preludes included in the *Buxheim Organ Book*. In these preludes, improvisatory passages are alternated with chordal sections. In addition,

[9] The Burgundian school actually consisted of composers from Belgium, Holland, Burgundy, and a sizable portion of France.

the earlier practice of *fauxbourdon*—this had played a chief role in vocal music during the late Middle Ages (1300–1450) and had been revived by Paumann—is here again applied to the keyboard, with a distinct flavor of modality maintained through the arrangement of the accidentals.

The *Praeambulum super* G (Prelude on G) has a single melodic line without accompaniment, alternating with root-position triads. Another point to observe is the distinct feeling of modern tonality in the final cadence (Ex. 5).

Ex. 5. *Buxheim Organ Book: Praeambulum super G*

The third section of the *Praeambulum super* C suggests a true virtuoso style, although a formally organized pattern is as yet lacking (Ex. 6, p. 22). The final cadence has almost a subdominant-dominant-tonic relationship.

KEYBOARD COMPOSERS
OF THE RENAISSANCE

Germany and Austria

The first great figure in early Renaissance instrumental music is **Arnolt Schlick** (1460–1517). A Heidelberg organist, Schlick was also a leading

Ex. 6. *Buxheim Organ Book: Praeambulum super C*

composer in the school of organ composition that eventually led to Bach. The architectonic nobility in Schlick's compositions links him to the late Middle Ages while the lyric flow of his melodies announces the coming Renaissance. His first publication was a treatise on organ building entitled *Spiegel der Orgelmacher und Organisten* (Mirror of Organ Builders and Organists).[10] His collection of music *Tabulaturen Etlicher Lobgesang und lidlein uff die orgeln und lauten* (Tablature of Several Hymns and Songs for Organ and Lute)[11] contains fourteen pieces for organ, twelve for lute and voice, and three for lute solo.

Most of Schlick's keyboard works are in the style of the organ chorale. The example reproduced here (Ex. 7) from his *Maria zart* (Tender Mary)[12] has the melody stated in the soprano with a countermelody in the tenor. The work is in strict three-part construction, but the individual voices move with grace and maintain considerable variety. The harmonic concept is skillfully conceived, the first and third beats of almost every measure containing at least the root and third of a triad. Note how the tenor enters in

[10] Modern reprint by Ernest Flade (Mainz: Druck und Verlag von Paul Smets, 1932, second edition, 1951).

[11] Modern reprint by G. Harms (Klecken, 1924).

[12] John Klein, *The First Four Centuries*, *op. cit.*, I, 50; this is one of several collections containing Schlick's *Maria zart*.

imitation and how the initial sixteenth-note figure in the soprano is echoed in the other parts from time to time.

Ex. 7. Schlick: *Maria zart*

Paul Hofhaimer (1459–1537) was a contemporary of Arnolt Schlick, but he composed in a different fashion. Hofhaimer, an Austrian, gave a warm harmonic texture to his music. His works adhere closely to early Renaissance practice, while Schlick's organ works contain basic elements of later medieval technique as well as those of the early Renaissance.

Example 8[13] illustrates skillful handling of the three voices. The lower voice acts as a support for the two top voices, yet it has a graceful line all its own. The tenor moves in weaving sixteenth notes, but the moment the soprano line takes on similar note values, the tenor values are augmented to eighth notes. In contrast to the open, hollow harmonies of previous schools, Hofhaimer's work, as seen here, tends to use full, sonorous chords complete with thirds; observe beats two and three in the first bar and beats one, two, and three in the third bar. Hofhaimer and Schlick probably intended their compositions for an organ having a minimum of two manuals and a pedal keyboard. These early trios need contrasting keyboard colors to be effective.

[13] Bedbrook, *op. cit.*, p. 42.

Ex. 8. Hofhaimer: *O Dulcis Maria* (O Sweet Mary)

Paul Hofhaimer founded what has been called the Viennese school, despite the fact that many of his pupils came from northern Germany, Switzerland, and other regions. Three composers in this group contributed materially to the advancement of keyboard style: Johann Buchner, Hans Kotter, and Leonhard Kleber.

Johann Buchner (1483–*ca.* 1538) wrote music somewhat similar to Hofhaimer's. A manuscript collection of his works includes a section on notation and fingering. In this manuscript thirty-four sections are entirely devoted to liturgical-chant settings in the style of the organ chorale. Example 9[14] shows the liturgical melody appearing in two voices—first in the bass, then in the soprano. Especially interesting are the many successions of thirds and sixths. Buchner offers less variety than either Hofhaimer or Schlick. The parallel movement indicates an adherence to earlier keyboard writings, but the constant use of thirds and sixths shows at least an attempt toward more mature harmonic practices.

Ex. 9. Buchner: *Quem terra, pontus*

---

[14] Johann Buchner, *Fundamentbuch* (Universitätsbibliothek Basel Ms. F. I. 8). Reprint in Volume V of *Vierteljahrschrift für Musikwissenschaft* (Leipzig, 1885–1894).

Hans Kotter (1485–1541) composed organ-chorale types of compositions, preludes, arrangements of songs, and some early dances. These last compositions could indicate that Kotter's work, at least in part, was written for the harpsichord or clavichord. The *Praeambulum in fa* (Prelude in F) is a striking departure from contemporary writing in its time (Ex. 10).[15] Schlick, Hofhaimer, and Buchner clearly intended their works for organ with pedal register, but this prelude of Kotter's could just as well have been written for the harpsichord or clavichord. There are only three voices, very closely spaced. The melodic line covers a range of two octaves, and the whole work is very tonal.

Ex. 10. Kotter: *Praeambulum in fa*

With the appearance of **Leonhard Kleber** (1490–1556), a marked change in composing becomes apparent. His music shows a more "modern" tendency that anticipates the age of the Gabrielis and gives a glimpse of even later masters. Kleber is lavish with ornamentation, especially trills and fioriture around one note. Because of this ornamentation Kleber sometimes is called the first composer in the German Colorist school. He also creates manifold contrasts within a single piece. The composition reproduced here

[15] Hans Kotter, *Orgeltabulatur* (Universitätsbibliothek Basel Ms. F. IX. 22, fol. 84v.).

in part (Ex. 11)[16] is plainly divided into three sections. The first section is chordal with a prominent soprano melody; the second uses only two voices in which imitation plays an important role; and the third returns to chordal style. Although the harmonies are simple, the handling of the individual voices brings forth considerable diversity, particularly at cadence points.

Ex. 11. Kleber: *Finale in re seu preambalon* (Finale in D in Prelude Style)

France

During the years 1530–1531 the Parisian music publisher Pierre Attaignant printed seven collections of keyboard works, as listed:

---

[16] Leonhard Kleber, *Orgeltabulaturbuch* (Staatsbibliothek Berlin Ms. Z 26). Seventeen preludes are reprinted in *Monatshefte für Musikgeschichte* (1888).

1. *Dix neuf chansons musicales reduictes en la tabulature des Orgues Espinettes Manichordions et telz semblables instruments. . . . Jdibus Januarii, 1530.*

2. *Vingt et cinq chansons musicales reduictes en la tabulature des Orgues Espinettes Manichordions et telz semblables instruments musicaulx. Kal'. Februarii 1530.*

3. *Vingt et six chansons musicales reduictes en la tabulature des Orgues Espinettes Manichordions et telz semblables instrumentz musicaulx . . . 1530.*

4. *Magnificat sur les huit tons avec Te Deum laudamus et deux Preludes, le tout mys en tabulature des Orgues Espinettes et Manichordions . . . Kal'. Martii 1530.*

5. *Quatorze Gaillardes neuf Pavannes, sept Branles et deux Basses Dances le tout reduict de musique en la tabulature du jeu Dorgues Espinettes Manichordions et telz semblables instrumentz musicaulx, 1530.*

6. *Tabulature pour le jeu Dorges Espinetes et Manichordions sur le plain chant de Cuncti potens et Kyrie fons. Avec leurs Et in terra. Patrem. Sanctus et Agnus Dei, 1530.*

7. *Treze Motetz musicaulx avec ung Prelude le tout reduict en la Tabulature des Orgues Espinettes et Manichordions et telz semblables instruments. . . . Kal'. Avril 1531.*

The pieces in these collections are mostly arrangements of sacred and secular vocal works from the Franco-Flemish school and are of comparatively little interest in keyboard history. To judge by the title of each collection, the compositions may be played on the organ, harpsichord (*espinette*), clavichord (*manichordion*), and other similar instruments. However, the dances in the fifth collection are definitely secular in character and are obviously meant for either the harpsichord or clavichord.

The *gaillarde* (galliard) appears for the first time in print in the Attaignant collections. It exhibits the gay characteristics that later popularized the form in other countries. The *gaillarde* partially reproduced here (Ex. 12)[17] has three sections: A B A. The harmony is clear and tonal. Each series of eight measures contains two almost identical phrases. The ornamentation is kept to a minimum, and sometimes is omitted altogether. And as yet there is no explicit harpsichord style. The strict chordal style

[17] *Musik aus früher Zeit, op. cit.,* II, 21.

and the melodic line with chordal accompaniment could just as easily be organ technique.

Ex. 12. *Quatorze Gaillardes* (Attaignant): *Gaillarde*

England

Another important reference for early keyboard music is the *Royal Appendix 58,*[18] a manuscript now in the British Museum. This manuscript contains ten instrumental pieces dating from approximately 1520 to 1540; although most of these are dances that can be played by various instrumental combinations, at least three pieces are intended for the keyboard. One of these, *A Hornepype* by the Englishman **Hugh Aston** (*ca.* 1480–1520), is first of all remarkable for its length—a keyboard piece with 153 measures is most unusual for this early period. In addition, the entire piece is constructed, with few exceptions, on a bass pattern derived from a triad on F alternating with its dominant on C. Interest is sustained by diverse and fanciful figurations constructed above this basic pattern. Effects of syncopation occur frequently, combined with other examples of rhythmic diversity. Bear in mind that this is music written for the virginal, and some of the skips and leaps seem truly remarkable (Ex. 13).

The other two pieces in the *Royal Appendix*—*My Lady Careys Dompe* and *The Short Mesure of My Lady Wynkfylds Rownde*—are anonymous (perhaps also by Aston), but they are constructed like *A Hornepype,* using an ostinato-type bass.

From the latter part of Henry VIII's reign (1509–1547) to about 1575,

---

[18] Pieces from this manuscript are reprinted in *Anthology of Early Keyboard Music* (London: Schott & Co., Ltd., 1951), I, "Ten Pieces by Hugh Aston and Others."

Ex. 13. Aston: *A Hornepype*

England had a brief flowering of organ composition. Samples from the period have been saved in several manuscripts, particularly the *Mulliner Book*. This manuscript was partly compiled sometime around 1550 with works by John Taverner, Richard Farrant, and John Redford, well-known composers in that day. Another more recent addition lists compositions dated as late as 1575, including pieces by John Munday, Christopher Tye, and William Blitheman. In his introduction to the modern edition, the English musicologist Denis Stevens writes: "The Mulliner Book alone runs the whole gamut of sixteenth-century music: Latin motets, English anthems, arrangements of part-songs, transcriptions of consort music, plainsong fantasias for organ, dance-music for clavichord or virginals, music for cittern and gittern."[19]

Since more than half the pieces in the *Mulliner Book* are built on plainsong, it can be assumed that they are primarily intended for organ. The few secular works are significant, historically speaking—though most are transcriptions of vocal works—in that they provide the only discernible link between the earlier virginal pieces by Hugh Aston and the magnificent music bequeathed to us by the virginal school that flourished in England during the last third of the sixteenth century.

Italy

During the Renaissance in Italy, keyboard composition flourished remarkably; it was an activity unmatched by any other country. Italian reper-

[19] *The Mulliner Book*, ed. Denis Stevens. In Vol. I of *Musica Britannica* (London: Stainer & Bell, Ltd., 1954). Quotation from the introduction by permission of the publishers.

toire was for the most part limited to the *ricercar* and *fantasia*, forms governed by highly developed contrapuntal rules. Examples from earlier music schools show that composers in the different countries were satisfied to use a liturgical melody around which they embroidered a florid counterpoint. But the Italians in the sixteenth century worked chiefly with basic motives that appeared in all voices, either in their original form or subjected to transformation—such as diminution, augmentation, variation. The *ricercar* is more disciplined than the *fantasia* and represents one of the highest forms of contrapuntal art. The *Recerchari Motetti Canzoni* (1523)[20] by **Marco Antonio Cavazzoni** (1480–1559)—also known as Marc'Antonio da Bologna—is one of the earliest Italian collections. It has only eight pieces: four transcriptions of French songs, two *ricercari*, and two transcriptions of motets.

Girolamo Cavazzoni (*ca.* 1500–*ca.* 1560), son of Marco Antonio, is known as one of the first important contributors to the development of scope and style in keyboard technique. In 1543 he published a collection of *ricercari, canzoni,* hymns, and Magnificats.[21] Cavazzoni expanded his themes at length, sacrificing detail to the ensemble. His work is characterized by flowing melodic periods, a real sense of polyphony and architecture, and beautiful cadences, with much use of the subdominant.

Finally, Renaissance Italy produced three great masters: **Andrea Gabrieli** (*ca.* 1510–1586), his nephew **Giovanni Gabrieli** (1557–1612), and **Claudio Merulo** (1533–1604).

Andrea Gabrieli, in his *ricercari*, follows the practices of his predecessors, but in his toccatas and preludes he displays hitherto unknown concepts of florid style. Although some of his works are designated for either organ or harpsichord, the basic style of most of Andrea's music—particularly the use of sustained sonorities—seems to suggest organ performance. Most noteworthy is the fact that in his preludes and toccatas he brought forth an original idea of idiomatic scalar passages, a new procedure that was used henceforth in moderation by all schools of composition. The following excerpt (Ex. 14)[22] illustrates what variety Andrea Gabrieli obtained by means of a scalar melodic line, despite simplicity of harmony. Imitation, sequence—in fact, all of the less rigid techniques of contrapuntal style—are used here, but with a new concept.

Claudio Merulo was among the best organists of his day. He attracted

---

[20] Marc'Antonio da Bologna (Marco Antonio Cavazzoni), *Recerchari Motetti Canzoni* (Venezia: Bernard, 1523). A modern transcription may be found in Knud Jeppesen, *Die Italienische Orgelmusik am Anfang des Cinquecento* (Copenhagen: Einar Munksgaard, 1943).

[21] G. Cavazzoni, *Intavolatura cioe recercari canzoni himni magnificati* (Venezia: Scotto, 1543). See also Jeppesen, *op. cit.*

[22] *Intonazioni d'organo di Andrea Gabrieli et di Giovanni suo nepote* (Venezia: Gardano, 1593).

Ex. 14. A. Gabrieli: *Intonazione settimo tono* (Intonation in the seventh mode)

many pupils, not only because of his skill in performance but also for his ability in composition. His organ compositions seem far ahead of their time. Even in his toccatas Merulo uses the technique of developing germ motives; but he does this in such a free, graceful manner that the effect is entirely different from that of earlier works using the same method. With Merulo there is more fluidity and continuity. In addition, he divides his toccatas into a number of sections, alternating chordal passages with florid sections. This basic idea was seized upon by some of his contemporaries and became standard procedure for later composers. Johann Sebastian Bach used the same principle of contrast in his keyboard toccatas.

In Example 15[23] notice the development of the sixteenth-note figure of four notes. Merulo later expands this into a motive of five notes, then seven, and finally eight notes. He achieves wide contrast in rhythm and melodic movement although the harmonic design remains rather simple.

Giovanni Gabrieli, Andrea Gabrieli's nephew and the third member in this trio of Italian Renaissance music masters, composed primarily for the organ, although some of the techniques he developed were later applied to the harpsichord. Giovanni's talent is most fully displayed in his *ricercari* and *canzoni,* forms which he received from his predecessors and which he perfected. An outstanding characteristic of Giovanni Gabrieli's music was its use of an extremely personalized principal theme. Some of his themes equal those used by J. S. Bach a hundred years later. Apart from his skill in matters of form and structure, Gabrieli infused into his works a spontaneity and freshness that mirror the vivacity of the Venetian spirit.

[23] *Toccate d'Intauolatura d'organo di Claudio Merulo* (Roma: Sim. Verovio, 1604).

Ex. 15. C. Merulo: *Toccata*

Spain

The greatest keyboard-music composer in Spain during the later Renaissance was **Antonio de Cabezón** (1510–1566), who through his playing and his compositions not only enriched keyboard literature but produced a salutary effect on the music of other composers as well. Cabezón designated his music for keyboard (*tecla*), harp (*arpa*), and guitar (*vihuela*), and he gave no indication as to which instrument was most appropriate. However, it is logical to assume that the liturgical pieces were intended for the organ, while the variations on popular songs have a secular character indicating that they were intended for harpsichord or clavichord.

Only recently has Cabezón's music won proper recognition. He was a man dedicated to preserving the highest standards for musical composition. There is a mild austerity present in his writings and always a seriousness behind each work. The austerity, fortunately, is tempered with compassion and spiritual warmth, two important factors that contribute to the classic contours distinguishing every type of musical composition Cabezón created.

For the harpsichord and clavichord, Cabezón revealed unimagined possibilities for keyboard figuration with his *diferencias* or variations. Here the Spanish composer strikes a note that is far from casual. His compositions in this field are finely organized, skillfully conceived works of art. They are true variations in every sense of the word, not merely the ornamenting or embellishing of a theme. In these transformations of well-known songs and tunes, Cabezón followed a precedent established by the *vihuelistas*, notably Luis de Narváez.

When Felipe II of Spain married Mary I of England in 1554 and traveled to England for his wedding, one prominent member of the royal entourage was Antonio de Cabezón, whose talents as performer and composer were quickly recognized by the English people. He must have exchanged ideas with English keyboard-music composers, for the concept of variation employed by the English virginal or harpsichord school is often akin to that of the Spaniard. There is also a similarity between his cadential phrase endings and those in many English compositions of the time. The same is true of certain melodic formulas consistently used by Cabezón.

Antonio de Cabezón treated variation form as one continuous unit by joining the several variations in unbroken sequence. In the *Diferencias sobre el canto llano del caballero* (Variations on the Song of the Cavalier), the melody of the popular song is stated simply, supported by transparent counterpoint. In the first variation,[24] the theme remains in the soprano but is expanded and embellished. In the following three variations, this *caballero* melody is transferred to the alto and tenor voices, enveloped in weaving lines of graceful counterpoint. Other variations by Cabezón—on *La Pavana italiana, La Gallarda milanesa, Guárdame las Vacas*—make lasting contributions to the Renaissance keyboard repertoire (Ex. 16).[25]

POSTLUDE

During the late sixteenth century and the seventeenth century, musical composition underwent a significant transformation. In the early sixteenth century very little distinction had been made between works for harpsichord and works for organ. For example, the works published by Pierre Attaignant were for either organ, clavichord, or harpsichord. Antonio de Cabezón's *Obras de Música* were for harp, *vihuela*, or "keyboard instruments." In other words, the stringed keyboard instruments had not de-

[24] Since many European composers of the Renaissance and early Baroque assumed that everyone was familiar with the theme itself, it is often difficult to ascertain if the opening measures of a composition present the actual theme or a variation of the theme.

[25] A short representative collection of the instrumental music of Cabezón will be found in Antonio de Cabezón, *Claviermusik*, ed. M. S. Kastner (Mainz: Schott, 1951); the *Obras de Música* are found in Volumes 3, 4, 7, 8 of *Hispaniae Schola Musica Sacra*, ed. Felipe Pedrell (1895–1898).

Ex. 16. A. de Cabezón: *Diferencias sobre el canto llano del caballero*. Examples of variation technique.

veloped enough of a basic style to warrant independent compositions of their own.

However, just before the end of the sixteenth century the harpsichord began to assert its independence. One of the obvious reasons for this lies in its improved construction. Another reason is that the harpsichordists themselves were determined to usurp the position long occupied by the lutenists. Up to the late sixteenth century, the lute was the most popular secular instrument in most European countries. It not only was used for song accompaniment but possessed its own literature as well. Lutenists were sought after for social gatherings and concerts. During the early and mid-sixteenth century, the harpsichord had no independent literature and was used merely as an accompanying medium, either for court dances or as a chordal framework in music for several instruments. When the actual possibilities of the harpsichord were realized, composers set about to create a literature that first equaled the lute repertoire and eventually relegated it into obscurity.

An independent literature for harpsichord and clavichord, then, emerged as a synthesis of two elements—evolving lute and organ style. The lutenists prior to the seventeenth century had developed their own literature. At first confined to transcriptions of vocal works, this lute repertoire soon expanded to include dances and pieces in improvisatory style. Early harpsichordists then took these lute pieces and arranged them for the keyboard. The final step in development came when composers appropriated stylistic elements from both lute and organ to create an independent style for harpsichord and clavichord.

BIBLIOGRAPHY

Bedbrook, Gerald Stares. *Keyboard Music from the Middle Ages to the Beginnings of the Baroque.* London: Macmillan & Co., Ltd., 1949.

Bie, Oscar. *Das Klavier.* Berlin: Paul Cassirer, 1921.

Cellier, A. and H. Bachelin. *L'Orgue.* Paris: Librairie Delagrave, 1933.

Dart, Thurston. "Cavazzoni and Cabezón." *Music and Letters,* Vol. XXXVI, No. 1, 1955.

Jeppesen, Knud. *Die Italienische Orgelmusik am Anfang des Cinquecento.* Copenhagen: Einar Munksgaard, 1943.

Kinkeldey, Otto. *Orgel und Klavier in der Musik des 16. Jahrhunderts.* Leipzig: Breitkopf & Härtel, 1910.

Reese, Gustave. *Music in the Renaissance.* New York: W. W. Norton & Co., Inc., 1959.

Seiffert, Max. *Geschichte der Klaviermusik.* Vol. 1. Leipzig: Breitkopf & Härtel, 1899.

PART

II

3

HARPSICHORD MUSIC:
ITS FORMS AND
CHARACTERISTICS

In most respects, the late Renaissance and Baroque ages in music history proved to be advantageous for keyboard composition. Beginning about 1550 and extending to 1750, this era is notable for its recognition of the harpsichord. During this time the harpsichord assumed a place in virtually every musical ensemble. Beyond its use as a supporting instrument, the harpsichord soon achieved a repertoire of its own. Indeed, most composers after 1650 singled out at least some part of their writing for the keyboard—either harpsichord or organ, or both.

In contrast to the sophisticated linear style of the Renaissance, Baroque music is bolder, more realistic in expression. Although Baroque keyboard music shows certain regional differences, it nevertheless takes on over-all characteristics that distinguish it from the preceding Renaissance period and the subsequent Pre-Classic period.

To begin with, the old church modes slowly yielded to concepts of major and minor tonality. During the last half of the seventeenth century, these new ideas crystallized and made possible the science of harmony (chords and their relationships). Modulation was another outgrowth of this tonal stabilization. Dissonance, usually treated with great respect and some temerity by Renaissance composers, became part of the expressive language of Baroque writers.

Melodically, the basically vocal lines of Renaissance music were transformed into instrumental themes. In using larger intervals—melodic leaps in either direction—Baroque composers oriented their compositions toward the specialities of keyboard instruments. Repeated motives and phrases became particularly popular (these were most effective on instruments with two keyboards). Since *crescendo* and *diminuendo* are impossible on the harpsichord because of the method of tone production, the composers partially compensated for this deficiency by the "echo" effect. A phrase could be played on one keyboard with a strong dynamic level, then "echoed" or repeated softly on the second keyboard. These echoings sometimes are called *terrace dynamics*.

Baroque rhythm as applied to harpsichord music is spirited and vital. Since accent per se is impossible on this instrument, rhythm is greatly dependent upon phrasing, note values, harmony, and ornamentation. And ornamentation plays a significant role in Baroque keyboard music. The assorted embellishments—trills, mordents, to mention but two—were used differently by each composer. These ornaments, for example, were effective in maintaining a rhythmic accent; they were necessary to delineate a slow, lyrical phrase line; and they were suitable for introducing dissonances. Lastly, the ornamentation served to create an elegant style.

The texture of keyboard music changed substantially in the Baroque period. During the early seventeenth century, composers concentrated on a purely homophonic style, basically a melody with chordal accompaniment. Gradually, beginning about mid-seventeenth century, this homophonic approach was judiciously combined with elements of polyphonic texture, creating what might be called a harmono-polyphonic style. This synthesis achieved its most perfect expression in the music of Johann Sebastian Bach.

The term Rococo is applied to certain composers and compositions written during the late Baroque and Pre-Classic eras. Rococo music is characterized by profuse ornamentation, light texture, and occasional superficiality. It was used primarily by French and Italian composers of the day and is known also as the *style galant.*

KEYBOARD FORMS

Before examining harpsichord music in individual countries, one should keep in mind the several compositional forms favored by Baroque composers. Although these forms did not necessarily originate in either the seventeenth or eighteenth century, they did in most instances reach perfection sometime during the first half of the latter century. There are three important compositional forms: the *suite* (and closely related *sonata*); the *variation;* and the *fugue,* which was frequently preceded by a *prelude, toccata,* or *fantasia* (fantasy).

The Suite

Partie, Partita, Ouverture, Suite: German
Partita, Sonata da camera: Italian
Ordre, Suite: French
Lessons: English

The suite usually denotes a cycle (or series) of dance pieces changing in tempo and meter yet preserving key unity throughout. Each suite section —excluding the optional introductory movement (prelude, overture, etc.) —was constructed in bipartite form. This structure was used by the Baroque composers not only in suite movements but elsewhere—for example, in a theme that was to be submitted to variation technique. Bipartite form means that the musical structure is separated roughly into two sections, each section marked for repetition, if the performer so desires. The first section has one theme—sometimes fragments of a second—and toward the end of this first section there occurs a modulation to the dominant or relative major key of the initial tonality. The second section has some brief development or variation of the theme, then a modulation back to the original key.

The suite can be traced back to the paired dances written for the lute —beginning about the fourteenth century in France, Germany, and Italy. (All dances discussed in this chapter are described in the Glossary.) Lute composers in these countries preferred a set of two dances, with the second dance treated as a kind of variation of the first.

One fourteenth-century dance called *Lamento di Tristan*[1] has a section in triple time followed immediately by a section in duple meter. The *Glogauer Liederbuch* (1460)[2] contains many dances in quadruple meter, each followed by a dance in triple meter. A little later, Hans Neusidler resorts to the same practice of dance-coupling in *Der Juden Tanz*[3] for lute.

As early as 1455, music history comments on the slow and stately character of the *bassadanza* (or *basse danse*), a dance probably descended from the *estampie* and ordinarily in duple time. The *saltarello*, a leaping dance in triple meter, often served as an after-dance or coupling-dance with the *bassadanza*.

The courtly *pavane* replaced the *bassadanza* in the early sixteenth century. About this same time, the *passamezzo* appeared—like the pavane, yet faster and lighter. The *galliard*, a dance in triple meter, came to be coupled with the *pavane*. The galliard first appeared in Lombardy at the end of the fifteenth century. In 1529 the French publisher Attaignant published a series of galliards; the English composers appropriated this dance form about 1541. The pavane and galliard were a popular combination after 1550.

The *allemande* probably had its beginnings in France or the Netherlands. About 1600, it ceased to be used for dancing and became a stylized dance type. Sébastien de Brossard, an early-eighteenth-century writer, de-

---

[1] *Lamento di Tristan* (British Museum, Add. 29987, fol. 63r–63v).
[2] *Das Glogauer Liederbuch*, new edition by H. Ringmann, 1936.
[3] Reprint in *Denkmäler der Tonkunst in Oesterreich* XVIII, ii.

fined the allemande as a "grave symphony, usually in duple time, often in quadruple: it has two sections, each of which is played twice."[4]

During the sixteenth century the *minuet* form gradually evolved in France. It was popular as an instrumental ensemble piece during the reign of Louis XIV and consisted of three sections: Minuet I, Minuet II or Minuet *en trio* (written for three instruments only), and Minuet I. Later the term Minuet II was dropped and *Trio* was used—even though the entire minuet might be played by only one keyboard instrument.

The *courante*, of French origin, was very much in vogue from 1660 to 1700. After 1700 it no longer was danced but continued to be a favorite form of the harpsichord schools. As a keyboard piece, it existed in two stylized types. The *courante*, or French type, was a dance of moderate tempo in ternary meter, usually based on a 3/2 scheme, which could be accented several ways (1 2 3 4 5 6 or 1 2 3 4 5 6). The Italian *corrente* is much less restrained in character and shows more rhythmic stability. The latter type utilizes a running melodic line supported by a chordal accompaniment.

The *sarabande* was a popular dance in Spain before 1600. By 1650 it had spread throughout the Continent and later received independent instrumental treatment. The sarabande was a dance of noble character usually written with notes of long value, although considerable ornamentation is in evidence. It is written in ternary measure, begins on a strong beat, and often presents a prolongation of the second beat. Typically, there are two sections of eight measures each.

England apparently introduced the *gigue* or *jig*, a piece in ternary meter. It first appeared in virginal music about 1603 and some forty years later traveled to the Continent where it was cultivated with great delight. The gigue is "an air ordinarily for instruments, almost always in triple time, which is full of dotted syncopated notes, which make the melody gay and, in a manner of speaking, sparkling."[5] The continental type is characterized by a fugal entry for each of its two sections.

A gay, rapid dance in duple meter, the *bourrée* was discovered in Auvergne at the end of the sixteenth century; it was assimilated into the suite group about the time of Lully.

Dating more or less from the beginning of the seventeenth century in France, the *unmeasured prelude* probably goes back to the stylistic processes of the early-sixteenth-century Italian school. (The measured prelude was also used, but was found most often in Germany.) As the initial though optional member of the French Baroque suite for the lute, the unmeasured

[4] Sébastien de Brossard, *Dictionnaire de Musique* (Paris: Ballard, 1703), p. 5. English translation by the author.
[5] Brossard, *op. cit.*, p. 30.

prelude was improvisatory, made up of chords alternating with passage work. Manfred Bukofzer described it thus: "This dignified introduction was composed in a most peculiar manner without fixed note values like a rhapsodic toccata. The lute player was supposed to bring the freely hovering lines into a rhythmical order according to his own conceit so that no two performances of the same prelude were identical."[6]

The unmeasured prelude seemed to serve a dual purpose. First, it provided the lutenist with an opportunity to test his instrument for exact pitch; and second, it allowed him to warm up, so to speak, before proceeding to the allemandes, courantes, and gigues. This same explanation applied to the prelude as used by the French harpsichordists, for equal temperament was not yet a common practice; and even if it were, the harpsichord required frequent tuning then as it does today.

Just prior to the seventeenth century, other dances and short pieces were included in the suite collections. Such types as the *chaconne, passacaglia, canaris, gigue d'Angleterre*, etc., did not become integral parts of the suite but were interpolated from time to time at the discretion of the composer.

This abundant fund of dance forms and occasional pieces—gradually evolved over a long time—was drawn upon by the Baroque harpsichord composers. In England the early virginal composers had been contented with individual dances wherein variations of the several sections took on an important role. The later English harpsichord composers grouped dances into suites, or *lessons*, although they paid little heed to the sequence of the dances.

During the late seventeenth century and through the eighteenth, many Italian and Spanish keyboard composers produced individual pieces in bipartite form (see page 40), which they called "*sonatas*." However, the Italians also freely used the term sonata to designate *groups* of pieces, but these groups were really suites. The term sonata is an abbreviation of two forms common to Italy: the *sonata da camera* or "chamber sonata" (a series of dance movements using a common or nearly related tonality), and the *sonata da chiesa* or "church sonata" (a group of pieces contrasting in texture and tempo, each piece retaining the bipartite structure).

Early French *clavecin* composers grouped their *Pièces de Clavecin* into suites; however, they concentrated more on each separate piece than on group arrangement. Therefore, one suite might contain several allemandes, courantes, and gigues. Later on, when the descriptive piece became popular in France, the idea of the suite became even more ephemeral.

What is known as the classic suite finally emerged with Johann Froberger, who blended continental dance forms with the stylistic processes of

---

[6] Manfred Bukofzer, *Music in the Baroque Era* (New York: W. W. Norton, 1947), p. 168.

the French Baroque. In his earlier suites, Froberger used only three dances: *allemande, courante, sarabande*. Soon four basic dances became the standard for the suite. Froberger did not, however, place the gigue at the end. His movement sequences for the suite dances were:

allemande		*allemande*
gigue		*courante*
courante	or	*gigue*
sarabande		*sarabande*

By the eighteenth century—due in great part to Johann Sebastian Bach—the German suite had become more or less standardized as follows:

1. Introductory optional movement: *prelude* (measured), *overture, fantasia,* etc.

2. *allemande*

3. *courante*

4. *sarabande*

5. Optional dances: *gavotte, bourrée, passepied,* etc.

6. *gigue*

Composers in other countries took up this form from time to time, but on the whole it remained a German creation.

The Variation

The principle of variation is based on simultaneous contrast of repetition and change. An idea is presented, then reiterated, and accompanied by or enveloped in alterations or diversions of various sorts.

There are several types of variation procedures, which may be used singly or in combination.[7] In the *recurring bass line,* a melodic phrase of four or eight measures is designed, frequently in triple meter and minor tonality. This bass melody remains constant; anything else may change. Compositions utilizing this method bear various names such as *ground, basso ostinato, chaconne,* and *passacaglia.*

In the Baroque era, the terms chaconne and passacaglia were used interchangeably. Therefore, they also apply to variation based on a *recurring harmonic pattern.* Here the basic harmony is the constant factor. The composer may use great imagination in rhythmic, melodic, and motivic metamorphosis, but he must preserve the harmonic outline.

---

[7] See William S. Newman, *Understanding Music* (New York: Harper & Brothers, 1953), chapter XI, for a fuller discussion of variation.

In the *recurring binary melody,* a theme sixteen to thirty-two measures long is presented in binary or bipartite form and is usually sustained by a comparatively simple accompaniment. This accompaniment undergoes no radical change, but the melodic line is ornamented, changed rhythmically, and otherwise paraphrased. One further comment: if the theme happened to be a well-known dance tune or song, the composer frequently refrained from stating it at all. Instead, he started his composition with the first variation.

Sixteenth-century Spanish music supplies some early examples of keyboard variation. What these amount to are polyphonic settings of a theme (usually a popular song or dance) presented in different contrapuntal voices.

The English virginal composers applied variation treatment to individual dances, such as the *pavane,* but in addition they created independent sets of variations that display superior skill and imagination.

The Baroque "theme and variations" found its greatest success in Germany and Austria. Some composers, such as Froberger, combined variation technique with the suite, producing a hybrid form called the *variation suite.* In this event, the *courante, sarabande,* and *gigue* became variations on the initial material presented in the *allemande.* In Germany, the theme and variations attained its most distinguished development with Johann Sebastian Bach's *Goldberg Variations.*

The Fugue

The *fugue* form was in its prime during the Baroque age. Of course, there are later instances when the fugue made brief appearances; Beethoven and Mendelssohn wrote fugues, and in our own time composers such as Paul Hindemith and Samuel Barber have used fugal form for keyboard pieces.

The fugue developed from the Renaissance *ricercar* and organ *canzona.* The ricercar (derived from the *motet*) was made up of several sections, each section being a fugal exposition—the presentation of a basic theme or subject in each polyphonic voice. In some ricercars each section had its own theme. In others, a single theme served in different guises for the several sections. The organ canzona is a contrapuntal form similar to the ricercar but less rigid and more lively. To picture these types, as well as the emerging fugue form, imagine that the keyboard is treated like a vocal ensemble: a certain portion of the keyboard is reserved for the soprano line, a lower section for the alto, another for the tenor, and so forth.

\

When the theme is presented, therefore, it is "sung" by the different voices on the keyboard.

A fugue is a contrapuntal composition worked out according to pre-scribed rules and tenets of keyboard counterpoint. It habitually employs three or four voices, occasionally five. The subject—a fairly short melodic phrase—is stated in one voice, unaccompanied. Then the second voice or answer enters with the same melody—this time transposed a fifth—while the first voice begins the countersubject, a new melody. When the second voice has completed the subject, it begins the countersubject, and so on. The so-called exposition of a fugue takes place when the subject has been stated in all voices.

After this, the fugue proceeds to alternate "episodes" and "entries." An episode occurs when there is a section of a fugue without a voice part stating the subject in full. On the other hand, an entry occurs when there is a return of the complete subject in one of the voice parts. Toward the end, at the climax of the fugue, all voice parts may enter with the subject in close succession (*stretto*). Here the original theme may be presented in one voice and simultaneously offered in stretched or contracted form in another voice. The fugue, generally speaking, consists of an exposition followed by alternating episodes and entries; it terminates with a closing section containing statements of the subject.

A piece in contrasting style usually preceded the fugue, and for this the Baroque composer could select from several quasi-improvisatory types, such as the *prelude, toccata,* etc. The prelude (in measured rhythms) had a principal motive that was expanded by repetition and modulation. The toccata, fundamentally a work in rapid tempo, had alternating passages of different textures. And the *fantasy* included elements from both the prelude and toccata. Actually, the three types had many characteristics in com-mon, especially in relation to harpsichord composition. The desired ob-jective was music in free style, or noncontrapuntal style, to contrast with the fugue's polyphonic character. Other forms, such as the *overture*, also were used in combination with the fugue.

EPILOGUE

The suite, variation, and fugue were the forms used most universally by Baroque keyboard composers. There were others, but they were rather exclusively confined to individual countries or sporadically used by in-dividual composers. These other forms will be discussed as they are en-countered in later chapters.

After the Baroque period, the scene changed apropos these forms. The variation, restricted to a basically homophonic texture, continued into the Classic era. The suite gradually disappeared although one of its members, the minuet, was incorporated into Classic sonata form. The fugue as a keyboard form lost its prominence until the early nineteenth century.

BIBLIOGRAPHY

Clercx, Susanne. *Le Baroque et la Musique*. Brussels: Éditions de la Librairie encyclopédique, 1948.

Gress, Richard. *Die Entwicklung der Klaviervariation von Andrea Gabrieli bis zu Johann Sebastian Bach*. Stuttgart: L. Zechnell, 1929.

Nelson, Robert. *The Technique of Variation*. Los Angeles and Berkeley: University of California Press, 1948.

Newman, Wm. S. *The Sonata in the Baroque Era*. Chapel Hill: The University of North Carolina Press, 1959.

Newman, Wm. S. *Understanding Music*. New York: Harper & Brothers, 1953.

Schmitz, Hans-Peter. *Die Kunst der Verzierung im 18. Jahrhundert*. Kassel: Bärenreiter Verlag, 1955.

Tovey, Donald Francis. *The Forms of Music*. Cleveland: World Publishing Co., 1963. A Meridian Book.

Walther, Johann Gottfried. *Musikalisches Lexikon (1732)*. Put in facsimile and edited by Richard Schaal. Kassel: Bärenreiter Verlag, 1953.

4

ENGLISH
KEYBOARD MUSIC
THROUGH PURCELL

England was the first country to liberate harpsichord music from organ music and to form a distinct harpsichord style independent of organ technique. For fifty years, approximately the latter half of the sixteenth century, English composers avidly produced secular pieces for keyboard instruments. There are various but not always verifiable reasons for the popularity of virginal music at this time. One theory suggests that the imposed Protestantism in England stifled church-music composition, with the result that the English composers turned to a secular instrument—the virginal. Then, too, the physical shift from organ to virginal composition came about naturally. English organists usually had at their disposal an organ with one or two manuals and no pedals. The registers were soft, though clear, in contrast to those of the pompous instruments in some European countries. Low passages in thirds, which would have sounded muddy on larger instruments, issued forth bright and transparent on these English organs. This comparative similarity between the two instruments, organ and virginal, is perhaps another factor that contributed to the brilliant flowering of secular keyboard music in England.

However, there is little material available today to help in tracing the origins of the patterned scalar technique so idiomatic of virginal music. Hugh Aston's *Hornepype* and several other sixteenth-century pieces in the *Royal Appendix* 58 show definite signs of these techniques; but such compositions are isolated examples, and as yet no other manuscripts have been found which might clarify the incomplete picture. One opinion is that later composers, using the *Hornepype* as a model, were quick to recognize a style naturally suited to the virginal and then proceeded to exploit this idiom with infinite variety.

The virginal was a great favorite of the English monarchs. Elizabeth of York, wife of King Henry VII (reigned 1485–1509), and Catherine of Aragon, first wife of King Henry VIII (reigned 1509–1547), both played this instrument. Henry VIII himself was numbered among the virginal performers, a company that also included Mary Tudor and Queen Elizabeth. And it was said of Mary Stuart that she played "reasonably for a queen." Following the royal fashion, English society took up the virginal; William Shakespeare immortalized the instrument in his "Sonnet to a Lady Playing the Virginal." (Sonnet CXXVIII).

> *How oft, when thou, my music, music play'st*
>   *Upon that blessed wood whose motion sounds*
> *With thy sweet fingers, when thou gently sway'st*
>   *The wiry concord that mine ear confounds,*
> *Do I envy those jacks, that nimble leap*
>   *To kiss the tender inward of thy hand,*
> *Whilst my poor lips, which should that harvest reap,*
>   *At the wood's boldness by thee blushing stand!*
> *To be so tickled, they would change their state*
>   *And situation with those dancing chips,*
> *O'er whom thy fingers walk with gentle gait,*
>   *Making dead wood more bless'd than living lips.*
>   *Since saucy jacks so happy are in this,*
>   *Give them thy fingers, me thy lips to kiss.*

VIRGINAL MUSIC COLLECTIONS

The most important manuscripts and collections of English virginal music known to date are listed below.

1. *My Lady Nevells Booke.*[1] Housed in the library of the Marquess of Abergavenny, this manuscript was copied out by one John Baldwyne and is dated 1591. It has forty-three compositions by William Byrd, who was probably Lady Nevell's music teacher.

2. *Parthenia or the Maydenhead of the first musicke that ever was printed for the Virginalls* (London: G. Lowe, 1611).[2] This published collection contains twenty-one pieces by John Bull, William Byrd, and Orlando Gibbons.

3. *Fitzwilliam Virginal Book.*[3] All the important composers of

[1] Modern edition by Hilda Andrews (London, 1926). Reissued by Broude Brothers, New York, n.d.
[2] Modern reprint by Kurt Stone (New York: Broude Brothers, 1951).
[3] Modern edition by Fuller-Maitland and Barclay Squire (New York: Broude Brothers), two volumes. A paperback edition is published by Dover Publications (1964). A small collection of pieces from the *Fitzwilliam Virginal Book* is published by the British and Continental Music Agencies, Ltd., two volumes.

the period contributed to this manuscript, dating from about 1621 and kept now in the Fitzwilliam Museum at Cambridge. The modern edition of this manuscript is referred to as FVB in the notes to this chapter.

4. *Benjamin Cosyn's Virginal Book*.[4] This manuscript (*ca.* 1605–1622) is in the Royal Library of the British Museum and is made up of ninety-eight works by Benjamin Cosyn, Orlando Gibbons, John Bull, Thomas Tallis, William Byrd, and others.

5. *Will Forster's Virginal Book*.[5] Also in the Royal Library of the British Museum, this manuscript (1624) has works mostly by William Byrd, Thomas Morley, and John Ward.

6. *Parthenia In-Violata* or *Mayden-Musicke for the Virginalls and Bass-Viol*.[6] The single extant copy of this publication is in the New York Public Library. It was probably published in 1625. It contains seventeen pieces by Bull, Edmund Hooper, John Coprario, and others.

7. The *Dublin Virginal Book*[7] is found in the library of Trinity College, Dublin. The manuscript is dated 1583 and contains thirty pieces, all untitled and nearly all anonymous.

VIRGINAL MUSIC COMPOSERS

William Byrd (1542–1623) dominated the first-generation English keyboard composers. He was not only organist at the Chapel Royal, but also a lyric poet expert at writing descriptive music, such as *The Bells*. Byrd's talents as a musician had many facets, one of which, his ability to compose superb choral music, earned him the title of the "English Palestrina." **Thomas Tallis** (*ca.* 1505–1585), co-organist at the Chapel Royal, and **William Blitheman** (*d.* 1591) belong to Byrd's generation.

Perhaps the most famous names in the English virginal school are counted among the second-generation composers: Peter Philips, John Bull, and Giles Farnaby.

[4] A modern edition of twenty-five pieces from this collection was made in 1918 by Fuller-Maitland and Barclay Squire. The keyboard music of Orlando Gibbons is published in Vol. XX of *Musica Britannica* (ed. Gerald Hendrie).

[5] Modern editions of pieces by Byrd have been made by Fellowes (London, 1950) and Tuttle (Paris, n.d.).

[6] A practical edition of *Parthenia In-Violata* has been published by Peters. The New York Public Library has published (1961) a facsimile of the original copy.

[7] A modern edition of the *Dublin Virginal Book* is yet to appear. Thurston Dart describes its contents in an article "New Sources of Virginal Music" in *Music and Letters*, XXV, 1954.

Peter Philips (*ca.* 1555–1628)—a Roman Catholic seeking refuge from the persecutions under Elizabeth I—went to Rome and later to Antwerp, where he became organist to the Archduke Albert. Philips' own compositions are a synthesis of the severity of the *ricercar*, the chromaticism of the madrigal school, and the ornamental line typical of Italian music.

John Bull (1562–1628), onetime organist at the Chapel Royal, likewise left England for religious reasons. He lived in Brussels, then Antwerp. A master of contrapuntal devices, yet endowed with innate musical sensitivity, Bull exercised the full range of his skill and talent to create virginal music. He excelled in the variation, and his reputation in this field is well substantiated by the thirty variations on the theme of *Walsingham*,[8] in which he subjects the melody and its framework to most keyboard devices known at the time.

Giles Farnaby (*ca.* 1560–1640), a more spontaneous composer than either Philips or Bull, endowed his music with a grace and verve that make it seem to the twentieth-century ear more "modern" than the music of his contemporaries.

The outstanding spokesman for the third-generation composers was **Orlando Gibbons** (1583–1625), court virginalist and a musician sincerely respected by his colleagues. Gibbons possessed a competent technical apparatus, but his keyboard works often appear somewhat rigid and artificial.

THE *FITZWILLIAM* *VIRGINAL BOOK*

The *Fitzwilliam Virginal Book*, with its nearly three hundred compositions by representative composers of the English keyboard school, provides an excellent means for studying the devices and techniques used by these composers as well as the musical forms they employed. The *Fitzwilliam Virginal Book* embraces many forms: dances, fantasies, motets, preludes, airs (varied or amplified), contrapuntal inventions, masquerades, and liturgical plainsong. Apart from the music written by the above-mentioned composers, the collection includes works by Richard Farnaby, Robert Johnson, Thomas Morley, John Munday, Martin Peerson, Ferdinando Richardson, William Tisdall, Thomas Tomkins, Francis Tregian, and many others. The writing techniques appear to be a blend of the old with the new, a harking back to previous centuries coupled with a looking ahead for new modes of expression. Here and there examples of *fauxbourdon*

[8] *FVB*, I, 1.

appear which, despite the frequent feeling of modern tonality, have their true origins in the fourteenth and fifteenth centuries (Ex. 1).[9]

Ex. 1. John Bull: *In Nomine*

Imitative treatment, an integral part of Renaissance vocal music, is found in some of the more strictly contrapuntal virginal pieces (Ex. 2).[10] With these English composers, however, imitation is only a means to an end and as such is used with great freedom.

Ex. 2. William Byrd: *Fantasia*

A most striking device favored by virginal composers was their method of embellishing melodic segments and phrases by the addition of notes. This may be described as a type of instrumental variation wherein the original motive becomes at times so encumbered with extraneous notes as to be completely transformed (Ex. 3).[11]

Sequential treatment, an important technical device in Hugh Aston's *Hornepype,* was appropriated by the virginal composers as part of their

[9] *Ibid.*, II, 34.   [10] *Ibid.*, I, 37.   [11] *Ibid.*, II, 148.

Ex. 3. Giles Farnaby: *Rosasolis* (Sundew)

becomes

figurative apparatus. It appears in various guises but almost always is in-serted with skill and imagination (Ex. 4).[12]

Ex. 4. Giles Farnaby: *His Humor*

From a purely technical point of view, many virginal pieces are ex-ceedingly difficult to play. One frequently encounters such devices as note repetition (Ex. 5).[13]

Ex. 5. John Bull: *Pavana*

Rhythmic patterns of all kinds, used either singly or combined with

[12] *Ibid.*, II, 262.   [13] *Ibid.*, I, 62.

other rhythmic patterns, are exploited in this music. In many instances there seems to be a genuine attempt at experimentation in matters of rhythm. Doubtlessly the ideas are based upon rhythms in the vocal music of the day (Ex. 6).[14]

Ex. 6. John Bull: *Walsingham*

On the whole, the English composers placed much emphasis on motives used as accompaniment figures. These patterned figurations have wide variety and originality, and their influence can be seen projected throughout the entire history of secular keyboard music. The following examples (Ex. 7) are taken from pieces in the *Fitzwilliam Virginal Book*.

The harmonies in the majority of these English virginal compositions are quite simple. The sometimes disarming expressions of modality result from the alternately raised and lowered leading tone and the shifting of major and minor triads. Frequent passages of repeated notes, low-spaced thirds, a free concept of texture (both contrapuntally and harmonically), and florid passages in the bass line all point to a definite harpsichord idiom —a style that is established completely independent of organ style.

Only two types of ornaments are illustrated in the *Fitzwilliam Virginal Book*. According to the modern-edition editors, the sign (♪) may indicate a slide of a third upward, or a double appoggiatura, or possibly a mordent. The second sign (♪) may stand for a short or long trill, a *Pralltriller*, or a mordent.[15] There are other music scholars who give a different interpretation to these signs. Faced with this seeming confusion and uncertainty about the interpretation of these ornaments—or graces, as they are called in England—one is inclined to agree with Charles van den Borren.

> From the multiplicity and the comparative confusion of these interpretations, we may come to the conclusion that the question of deciding how the virginalistic graces ought to be exe-

---

[14] *Ibid.*, I, 1.
[15] See Edward Dannreuther, *Musical Ornamentation* (London: Novello & Co., Ltd.), I, 17–32. This work, originally in two volumes, has recently been reissued in one volume (Kalmus).

Ex. 7. Accompaniment figures from the *Fitzwilliam Virginal Book*

cuted is still far from being settled. Moreover, the problem is of
no very great importance; we have, in fact, a conviction that the
graces are purely superficial ornaments only, the presence of
which has no determining influence on the stylistic physiognomy
of virginal compositions. In that particular the latter differ entirely from the French pieces for the harpsichord of the epoch of
Couperin, in which the graces have generally a decorative duty
or an expressive meaning which confers on them a true and
actual value. It suffices to read (them) just as they are—that is
to say, deprived of their ornaments—...to come to the conclusion that these compositions are wholly sufficient in themselves,
and that the mordents and shakes add nothing to their beauty.[16]

Variation technique used in harpsichord music is basically English in
origin. However, it is worth recalling that when Antonio de Cabezón, the
Spanish organist and harpsichordist, went to England in 1554 for a com-

[16] Charles van den Borren, *The Sources of Keyboard Music in England* (London: Novello
& Co., Ltd., 1913), p. 148.

paratively brief sojourn, he was able to show English composers the techniques of a well-ordered, systematized variation form which, in Spain at
least, was then being used by composers of *vihuela* and organ music.
Cabezón was able to offer the models for variation technique, models
which the English virginalists in turn were to adopt and to infuse with a
sparkling gaiety, with an effervescence and a wit that are amazing, considering that stringed keyboard music was in an early stage at the time.

From a qualitative point of view, the variations on secular songs in
the *Fitzwilliam Virginal Book* are significant in keyboard history. The
virginalists—although not as prolific in producing variations on songs as
in writing variations on dance themes—nevertheless display their own
originality and powerful expression. These variations on secular songs differ
in style; some use quasi-polyphonic texture, while others vary a melodic
line supported by chords. The former is illustrated in William Byrd's fourteen variations on *The Wood's So Wild*[17] and in the more virtuoso variations by Orlando Gibbons on the same theme. Byrd's variations on *Walsingham*[18] and his setting of *The Mayden's Song*[19] are also polyphonic in
texture.

Melodic sets of variations are rather rare with the virginalists—at
least they are rarely used by the composers who contributed to the Cambridge manuscript. The most famous, however, and perhaps the best known
of all virginal compositions, is Byrd's *The Carmans Whistle*.[20] Based on
a popular song of the day, the theme is supplied with eight variations,
each one preserving the original melody's bouncy rhythm. The theme is
present in the final variation, though buried under a series of ponderous
chords.

John Bull composed thirty variations on the theme of *Walsingham*,[21]
thereby providing one of the longer, more involved works in the *Fitzwilliam Virginal Book*. The initial theme is in *a* minor, the theme itself
being divided into two sections; but near the end of each section there is
a wavering toward a final cadence in *A* major. Bull skillfully utilizes this
shifting tonality in his variations. He employs virtually every conceivable
virginal figuration known at the time: imitations of all sorts, passages with
note repetitions, broken intervals and chords, rhythmic complexity. In
every case, however, the original melody remains as the top or soprano line.

The harmonic variation, wherein the variations themselves are constructed upon a fixed bass pattern, is identical to the *ground*, a form used
again and again in English instrumental music. Very few harmonic varia-

[17] *FVB*, I, 263.   [20] *Ibid.*, I, 214.
[18] *Ibid.*, I, 267.   [21] *Ibid.*, I, 1.
[19] *Ibid.*, II, 67.

tions occur in the *Fitzwilliam Virginal Book*; Byrd's settings of *Tregians Ground*[22] and *Malt's come downe*[23] are the most outstanding.

As might be expected during an early formative period, many variations composed by the virginalists do not fall into any one well-defined category or type. Instead, the composers tried the procedures described above in different combinations to create more diversified interest and more flexible expression. And, indeed, they succeeded. The well-rounded form of Byrd's *Fortune*,[24] as well as his variations on *Sellinger's Round*[25] and his charming *O Mistris Myne*,[26] are proof enough of this. Most of the well-known virginal composers of the day wrote variations using this fusion of techniques—such composers as Munday in his *Goe from My Window*[27] and Farnaby in *Bony Sweet Robin*,[28] *Daphne*,[29] *Pawles Wharfe*,[30] and *Rosasolis*.[31]

The variations on dance tunes, although more popular with the composers, are in a way less distinguished than those based on songs. Although the composers utilize techniques similar to those used in the secular song variations, working with the dance themes they created less complicated and less solidly constructed works, though not necessarily less charming nor less interesting. The pavanes and galliards were most frequently subjected to variation technique. Sometimes the pavane appears coupled to the galliard, sometimes each dance appears by itself, but both are constructed along similar lines. Most pavanes and galliards are divided into three sections. After each section is stated, there follows immediately a variation of that section; the schematic pattern for such a treatment would be AA' BB' CC'.

Often the title of the dance gives a clue to its origin or the idea behind its composition. For example, some are named in honor of individuals, such as *Pavana of My Lord Lumley*[32] by Bull, and *Lady Montegle's Paven*[33] by Byrd. Occasionally the pavane title will refer to the expressive content therein, such as Philips' *Pauana Doloroso*;[34] or the title may at times describe the style to be encountered, such as Tisdall's *Pavana Chromatica*.[35] Fanciful titles such as these were consistently used during this period, a custom that carried over into the Baroque age and was adopted by the French clavecin composers in particular.

Although variation technique is perhaps the most basic among those used by the virginal composers, not all dances necessarily received this treatment. The allemandes (almans) and courantes (corantos)—not quite so prominent in the virginalists' repertoire—are treated in a much less

22 *Ibid.*, I, 226.   27 *Ibid.*, I, 153.   32 *Ibid.*, I, 149.
23 *Ibid.*, II, 166.   28 *Ibid.*, II, 77.   33 *Ibid.*, II, 483.
24 *Ibid.*, I, 254.   29 *Ibid.*, II, 12.   34 *Ibid.*, I, 321.
25 *Ibid.*, I, 248.   30 *Ibid.*, II, 17.   35 *Ibid.*, II, 278.
26 *Ibid.*, I, 258.   31 *Ibid.*, II, 34.

sophisticated manner than the pavanes and galliards. Harmonically solid in their construction, they nevertheless are conceived in a folk-art spirit, uncomplicated by any scholarly restrictions or rules. Most of these dances are bisectional, sometimes followed by variations. As for the gigue (gigg), the *Fitzwilliam Virginal Book* has only five examples. Among these, the *Gigg*[36] by Byrd and *The King's Hunt*[37] by Bull seem to represent best the buoyant, fresh spirit associated with the gigue.

Apart from these more common types, several unusual dances find their place in this great collection. A *Toye*[38] by Farnaby is one of five pieces with this title. It is not actually the name for any special dance pattern, but rather an indication of the playful, capricious spirit in the music itself. Other dances, such as the *Volta* and *Spagnioletta*, are also in the Cambridge manuscript.

The attempts at descriptive music in the *Fitzwilliam Virginal Book* are largely naïve. John Munday offers a *Fantasia*[39] in which he tries to describe various states of weather: *Faire Wether, Lightening, Thunder; Calme Wether, Lightening, Thunder; Faire Wether, Lightening, Thunder; Faire Wether, Lightening, Thunder;* and finally, *A Cleare Day.* By far the most successful descriptive piece is Byrd's *The Bells.*[40] From an initial rhythmic motive using two notes, Byrd constructs a rather lengthy fantasy with unusual effects throughout, capped by a fine climax.

This has been but a brief perusal of the *Fitzwilliam Virginal Book.* It includes many other types of compositions than those presented here. There are some pieces constructed on plainsong fragments and some which are quite frankly scholastic exercises, interesting though they may be from a structural standpoint. But for a glimpse into the vital, charming works created by this first great school of harpsichord composers, it is the variations and dances that are at once the most representative of the time and the most delightful to listen to.

Catholic persecution in England did, as we know, drive many of these early composers into exile, voluntarily or by force. Thomas Morley settled in Rome, then in Antwerp. Peter Philips went to the Continent in 1591, John Bull in 1613, both eventually living in the Low Countries. Thus, it became possible for these English composers to exchange ideas with composers in other countries, notably the Dutchman **J. P. Sweelinck** (1562–1621). This Dutch composer was the *homme du monde* in the true sense of the word. He was familiar with all schools and proceeded to adopt for his own purposes whatever pleased him. As Norbert Dufourcq has so aptly put it, "In his fantasies and toccatas, he preaches an Italian doctrine, while

---

[36] *Ibid.*, II, 237.   [39] *Ibid.*, I, 23.
[37] *Ibid.*, II, 116.   [40] *Ibid.*, I, 274.
[38] *Ibid.*, II, 421.

employing an English vocabulary."[41] Four compositions by Sweelinck appear in the *Fitzwilliam Virginal Book,* and John Bull wrote a *fantasia* on one of Sweelinck's themes. Unlike his English contemporaries, however, Sweelinck never made any distinction between his works for organ and those for harpsichord.

The English virginal school proper came to a close with **Thomas Tomkins** (1572–1656), organist at Worcester Cathedral. Tomkins apparently was composing right to the very end of his life; one virginal piece is dated 1654. His keyboard music includes organ pieces and virginal or harpsichord compositions written in a quasi-polyphonic style derived from some of his predecessors.[42]

THE ENGLISH
HARPSICHORD SCHOOL

Less and less virginal music appeared in the latter half of the century, for the larger, more colorful harpsichord (also called the harpsicon) began to receive popular attention. For about a hundred years (*ca.* 1650–1750) there were numerous composers who wrote some music for the harpsichord.

England's conspicuous musical figure from the seventeenth century is **Henry Purcell** (*ca.* 1658–1695). Although better remembered for his vocal and orchestral works, Purcell designed his keyboard music with great charm and simplicity. He borrowed from the French their ornaments and their suite form. He borrowed from the Italians their melodic powers. Purcell's harpsichord music consists essentially of suites and lessons.[43] His eight suites are unequal in quality. The opening prelude, if present at all, usually is followed by an allemande and courante. Apart from this sequence, there is really no consistency in the suites. The preludes are improvisatory and quite short, just as all Purcell's keyboard compositions are short. Sometimes he adds an English dance to the suite, such as the *hornpipe.* Sometimes he puts in an Italian air, a minuet, or fantasies called *voluntaries.* And at other times he includes a *trumpet tune,* or movements borrowed from the French repertoire, such as *gavotte, bourrée,* or *rigaudon.* Each piece in the Purcell suites is usually in two or three voices and is characterized by an extremely simple texture. The harmonies are standard;

[41] Norbert Dufourcq, *Le Clavecin* (Paris: Presses Universitaires de France, 1949), p. 41.
[42] *Thomas Tomkins Keyboard Music,* ed. Stephen Tuttle, in Vol. V of *Musica Britannica* (London: Stainer & Bell, Ltd., 1955). A small collection of Tomkins' music is found in Schott's *Anthology of Early Keyboard Music, op. cit.,* IV, ed. Frank Dawes.
[43] The complete harpsichord works in four volumes are edited by Wm. Barclay Squire (London: J. & W. Chester, Ltd., 1918). Another source for music of this period is found in *Purcell and His Contemporaries,* issued by Hinrichsen.

although the earlier school used only two types of ornaments in great abundance, Purcell's works employ seven types, all used with discrimination and care.

The lessons, which perhaps best exhibit his style, include minuets, marches, Scottish and Irish airs, preludes, allemandes, variations on a ground, and descriptive pages, such as *The Queen's Dolour*. In the ground, the ostinato always remains as the bottom line while simple configurations create interest, both melodically and rhythmically, above the bass.

One of Henry Purcell's best-known harpsichord works, his *Trumpet Tune* in D major (Ex. 8), is only one page long and is based entirely on two chords—D major and A major. The piece is in three voices, freely treated. There are never more than two ornaments in one measure and no ornamentation at all in many measures. Yet with these sparse means Purcell has created an endearing miniature of quality.

Ex. 8. Purcell: *Trumpet Tune*

Another keyboard composer of this period is **John Blow** (1649–1708), onetime organist at Westminster Abbey. Blow wrote a good deal of harpsichord music.[44] The early pavane and galliard, often found in pairs, are replaced in Dr. Blow's works by the allemande and courante, to which he added a sarabande. Usually a ground (similar to the chaconne or passacaglia) appears at the beginning or at the end of this trio or suite of pieces.

William Croft (1678–1727), a pupil of Dr. Blow, is best remembered as the man who wrote the fine hymn tune *St. Anne*. Some of his keyboard pieces[45] are lovely in their graceful handling of pure harpsichord style, yet they are overshadowed by his solo songs, which reveal a genuine talent for this type of writing.

Jeremiah Clarke (*ca.* 1673–1707), one of Croft's contemporaries, must have enjoyed a fine reputation in his day, if one can depend upon the title

[44] A collection of Blow's keyboard music is found in *The Contemporaries of Purcell,* ed. Fuller-Maitland (London: J. & W. Chester, Ltd., 1921), I, II.
[45] *Ibid.,* V.

affixed to a collection dated 1711: *Choice Lessons for the Harpsichord or Spinett Being the Works of the Late Famous Mr. Jeremiah Clarke.*[46]

Until the opening of the eighteenth century, keyboard writing in England was limited to English composers. However, with the arrival of Dieupart, Smith, and Handel (see Chapter 10), the scene becomes a bit more cosmopolitan. **Charles Dieupart,** a talented Frenchman, was active in London as violinist, clavecinist, and composer from about 1700 to 1740, the year of his death. His only published work, *Six Suites de Clavessin, Divisées en Ouvertures, Allemandes, Courantes, Sarabandes, Gavottes, Menuets, Rondeaux, et Gigues,*[47] was brought out by the editor Étienne Roger in Amsterdam. J. S. Bach was acquainted with Dieupart's music; he must have admired it, for he based the *Prelude* of his *English Suite in A Major* on the *Gigue* from Dieupart's *Suite in A Major.*

Another intruder on the predominantly British scene was **Johann Christoph Schmid** (1712–1795). He was born in Germany but later moved to London, where he became John Christopher Smith. The Smith suites, which appeared in London,[48] have the mark of his teacher Handel, and it is sad that they are so neglected today. These works indicate a real knowledge of the keyboard idiom and display scrupulous workmanship. The delightful *Siciliana* from the *Suite in C Minor* is particularly attractive.

The final member in this list of English keyboard composers (or those writing in England) is **Thomas Arne** (1710–1778). His *VIII Sonatas or Lessons for the Harpsichord*[49] are actually short suites, each containing from two to four pieces varying in quality. Considering his prodigious output in other areas—operas, masques, pantomimes, and incidental music—Arne's comparatively few keyboard works cannot be conceived as important except for the intrinsic value in each isolated piece.

Apart from Henry Purcell's keyboard works (and perhaps those of Smith), English harpsichord music during the period *ca.* 1650–1750 seems rather anticlimactic when it is compared to the music bequeathed by the virginal school that preceded it. By the mid-eighteenth century, there no longer was any actual school of English keyboard composers. And it was not until the late nineteenth century that British composers revived their interest in keyboard music.[50]

---

[46] *Ibid.,* III, IV.

[47] Dieupart's *Suite in F Minor* appears in *The Art of the Suite,* ed. Y. Pessl (New York: E. B. Marks Music Corp., 1947). The entire set of six was edited by P. Brunold for Editions de l'Oiseau-Lyre in 1934.

[48] Nine suites by Smith are published in *Le Trésor des Pianistes* (Leduc).

[49] These are found in Arne, *Popular Pieces,* ed. Pauer (London: Augener, Ltd.).

[50] The study of Scottish harpsichord music during the seventeenth and eighteenth centuries is in its infancy and very little material is available on this subject. For a short collection see *Early Scottish Keyboard Music,* ed. Kenneth Elliott (London: Stainer & Bell, Ltd.).

BIBLIOGRAPHY

Adams, Robert Lee. *The Development of a Keyboard Idiom in England during the English Renaissance.* Dissertation. Washington University, 1960. 3 Vols.

Borren, Charles van den. *The Sources of Keyboard Music in England* (translated by James Matthew). London: Novello & Co., Ltd., 1913.

Dart, Thurston. "New Sources of Virginal Music." *Music and Letters*, Vol. XXXV, No. 2, 1954.

Tuttle, Stephen Davidson. *William Byrd: A Study of the History of English Keyboard Music to 1623.* Dissertation. Harvard University, 1941. 2 Vols.

Whittaker, W. Gillies. "Byrd and Bull's 'Walsingham' Variations." *Music Review,* Vol. 3, No. 4, 1942.

5

ITALIAN

CEMBALO

MUSIC

Incentive for Italian *cembalo* (harpsichord) composition came principally from the native lutenists in the fifteenth and sixteenth centuries. The ability of one of these illustrious lute composers, Francesco da Milano (1497–*ca.* 1573), has been described in this fashion: "The essential mark of Francesco's talent consists in the inexhaustible variety which he imposed on all his pieces, a variety which borders on the prodigious."[1] Eventually, dances and songs in lute tablature were transcribed for keyboard instruments. Then, when the technique acquired in the process of transcribing lute pieces blended with Girolamo Frescobaldi's remarkable contribution— a new stylistic approach to keyboard composition—the beginnings of a *cembalo* tradition were firmly established. The independent harpsichord music appearing in Italy about the mid-sixteenth century shows very clearly its background in lute repertoire. *Le Forze d'Hercole* (The Strength of Hercules), a *pavane*-like dance with square rhythm, chordal structure, and harmonic poverty, is most likely a lute piece transcribed for keyboard (Ex. 1).[2] The works of Francesco Bendusi (*d.* after 1553)[3] fall into the same category.

The earliest printed volume devoted entirely to the harpsichord— *Il Primo Libro d'Intavolatura di Balli d'Arpicordo* (The First Book of Harpsichord Dances)[4] by Giovanni Maria Radino—came out in 1592. It contains a *Pass'e Mezo* (*passamezzo*) with four variations, a galliard derived from the *Pass'e Mezo*, two pavanes, and four galliards. The writing is still modal with scattered imitative passages. Basically, the style is that of an undulating melodic line supported by block chords.

---

[1] Lionel De La Laurencie, *Les Luthistes* (Paris: Laurens, 1928), p. 27.
[2] Willi Apel, *Musik aus früher Zeit* (Mainz: Schott, 1934), I, 23.
[3] *Ibid.*, I, 23–24. One of the two pieces found in the Apel collection, *Desiderata*, may also be found in Curt Sachs, *The Evolution of Piano Music* (New York: E. B. Marks Music Corp., 1944), p. 13.
[4] *Il Primo Libro d'Intavolatura di Balli d'Arpicordo di Gio. Maria Radino*. Modern transcription by Rosamond E. M. Harding (New York: Broude Bros., 1949).

Ex. 1. *Le Forze d'Hercole*

Giovanni Picchi, organist at the Casa Grande (this probably refers to the cathedral) in Venice, may have enjoyed an international reputation in his time, for one of his toccatas, an exuberant piece, appears in the *Fitzwilliam Virginal Book*. Picchi's talent was in the variation. At the beginning of his *Intavolatura di Balli d'Arpicordo* (Score of Harpsichord Dances)[5] of 1621 there is a *passamezzo* in six sections, each one constructed on the same bass pattern. Here is great diversity: imitations, chordal accompaniments, syncopation, etc.

Early Italian harpsichord repertoire is composed of dances—more than likely the dances used at court balls. One of these dances, the *Ballo alla Polacha* (Polish Dance), is by Picchi. In it the violin's influence can be detected in the melodic motives, and the entire piece resounds with rhythmic energy.

Giovanni Maria Trabaci (*ca.* 1575–1647) was organist and chapelmaster at the court of Naples from 1603 to 1616. Although his collection *Ricercate, Canzone francese, Capricci, Canti fermi, Gagliardi, Partite diverse, Toccate, Durezze* (1603) contains much that is obviously for organ, the partitas (see Chapter 3) and eight galliards belong to the harpsichord repertoire and reveal some progress in keyboard music. The galliards are solidly constructed and show a force and liberty of expression unusual for their time (Ex. 2).[6]

One partita in the Trabaci collection consists of fifteen variations on the then well-known *Aria di Ruggiero*, variations rich in invention and imagination. Some of his other partitas—the *Partite sopra Fedele*, for instance—offer various points of interest, such as an unusual chromatic concept. In a second book, appearing in 1615, Trabaci says that the *"cembalo è signor"* to all other instruments.

Much less substantial is the music written by the Neapolitan **Antonio Valente** (known as *Il Cieco*), who was organist at the church of Sant'-

[5] Giovanni Picchi, *Intavolatura di Balli d'Arpicordo,* facsimile reprint (Milano: Bollettino Bibliografico Musicale, 1934).

[6] See *L'Arte musicale in Italia,* ed. Torchi, III, 367. See also Sachs, *op. cit.,* p. 14.

Ex. 2. Trabaci: *Gagliarda*

Angelo de Nido. His collection *Intavolatura di Cimbalo: Recercate, Fantasie et Canzone francese* appeared in 1576.[7]

GIROLAMO FRESCOBALDI

Girolamo Frescobaldi (1583–1643) is the true successor to Italy's Renaissance masters, Andrea and Giovanni Gabrieli and Claudio Merulo. Frescobaldi, organist at the Basilica of Saint Peter in Rome from 1608 until his death in 1643 (excepting the years 1628–1634), left a musical testament rich in texture and remarkable for its diversity. He does not usually dwell for long on one musical subject but creates various themes within a single framework. When he does resort to repetition of thematic ideas, the repetitions are always varied, there is always a thematic transformation. In fact, Frescobaldi pushed the art of variation to new horizons. Rhythmic figures modify, expand, and contract his themes, yet these themes always remain recognizable.

In other rhythmic matters, Frescobaldi used an approach that contrasted with those of his more conventional contemporaries. Coupled with his *chiaroscuro* harmonies was an idea for relaxation of rhythmic squareness, which is reechoed some two hundred years later in the *tempo rubato* beloved by the Romantics. Listen to him as he directs the performance of his *toccatas*:

> Firstly, that kind of style must not be subject to time. We
> see the same thing done in modern madrigals, which, notwith-

---

[7] A *ballo lombardo* by Valente has been edited by Caravaglios in the *Revista musicale italiana*, 1916, p. 505.

standing their difficulties, are rendered easier to sing, thanks to the variations of the time, which is beaten now slowly, now quickly, and even held in the air, according to the expression of the music, or the sense of the words.[8]

Frescobaldi ushered in a new stylistic era in Italian composition for keyboard instruments. His basic approach was to continue the traditions established by Giovanni Gabrieli and Claudio Merulo and in addition to bestow upon them his own vivid concepts of tonal drama. His harmony is colorful, yet remains mostly within the bounds of modality. However, the new harmonic experiments made by Monteverdi in his operas were often repeated by Frescobaldi in solo keyboard literature. Other elements of Frescobaldi's style are a frequent, almost systematic use of chromaticism plus a most skillful exploitation of imitative and fugal devices.

Frescobaldi did not always differentiate between works for organ and those for harpsichord. Many collections bear the indication *Intavolatura di Cembalo et Organo* (Score for Harpsichord and Organ). His compositions appropriate to the harpsichord may be divided into four general categories: *ricercari, canzoni, caprices; partitas*—that is, variations on popular airs; *toccatas;* and dances.[9]

Frescobaldi's first volume of harpsichord music, entitled *Toccate e Partite d'Intavolatura di Cimbalo*, appeared in 1614; it reveals the lyric aspect of his style: twelve *toccate, balletti, correnti, capricci, ciacone*, and *partite* (variations) based on well-known themes such as *Ruggiero, La Monica, Romanesca*, and *La Follia*. The *Recercari et Canzoni franzese fatte sopra diversi oblighi* (1615) discloses a Venetian influence: fragmentation, equal exploitation of each episode. In 1624 Frescobaldi returned to a more polyphonic style with a new collection called *Il Primo Libro di Capricci Fatti Sopra Diversi Soggetti*. In it are *capriccios* on the song of the cuckoo (*sopra il Cucho*), the themes of *La Spagnoletta*, and the *Aria di Ruggiero*.

One of his most beloved keyboard pieces—*Aria detta Frescobalda*—appeared in another volume dated 1624, *Il Secondo Libro di Toccate, Canzoni, Versi d'Hinni, Magnificat, Gagliarde, Correnti et altre Partite d'Intavolatura di Cembalo et Organo*. The variations on the *Aria detta Frescobalda*[10] form a type of *variation suite*. The first section is a theme, which

---

[8] Preface to the first volume of toccatas, quoted from Arnold Dolmetsch, *The Interpretation of the Music of the XVII and XVIII Centuries* (London: Oxford University Press, 1946), p. 5.

[9] Most of the keyboard music of Frescobaldi has been republished by Bärenreiter Music Publishers and by Peters Edition. Volume III of the *Orgel und Klavier Werke* (Bärenreiter) is of particular interest.

[10] An accessible reprint is found in *Early Keyboard Music*, ed. Oesterle (New York: G. Schirmer, 1932), I, 52. Another source is *Clavicembalisti Italiani* (Ricordi), I.

is divided into two parts, followed by several variations. Of the four variations on the theme, the second is a galliard, the third an allemande, and
the fourth a courante (Ex. 3). Girolamo Frescobaldi's keyboard masterpiece—the *Fiori Musicale* (1635)—is definitely intended for the organ,

Ex. 3. Frescobaldi: *Aria detta Frescobalda*

containing as it does liturgical settings for three Masses. With the *Fiori Musicale,* Italian organ music reaches its highest peak of artistic perfection.

OTHER EARLY COMPOSERS

For thirty years after the death of the great Frescobaldi, the violin dominated Italy's musical landscape, with only sporadic appearances of keyboard music to keep the tradition alive. **Michel Angelo Rossi** (*ca.* 1600–1660), a pupil of Frescobaldi, was in a small way an innovator with his toccatas and courantes for organ or harpsichord.[11] An unusual mixture of chromatic alterations, as well as scalar figurations similar to those of the virginalists, impart to his works a blend of the old and new.

Bernardo Pasquini (1637–1710), the only Italian harpsichord composer of superior talent to be found in the latter half of the seventeenth century, was highly esteemed by his contemporaries. During his lifetime he was reckoned the greatest performing organist in Italy. He took part in concerts sponsored by Christina of Sweden and performances organized by the famous violinist Archangelo Corelli. Pasquini was at one time in Prince Giovanni-Battista Borghese's retinue and was also supposed to have played for Louis XIV. Considered an excellent teacher, he was instrumental in developing such composers as Francesco Durante and others.

Between 1697 and 1708, Pasquini composed four volumes containing various types of isolated pieces and some sonatas. Frescobaldi's *canzoni* and *caprices* seem to be the point of departure for Pasquini's emerging style. And yet it is apparent that Pasquini sought—successfully—to abandon the earlier master's strict, more rigid style. He acquired a technique more suitable to the cembalo and in doing so he laid the groundwork in this field for future composers.

Pasquini's toccatas—no longer governed by traditional tenets of contrapuntal rules—are based on fancy and imagination. Sweeping arpeggios, prolonged trills, fugato passages, testify to the Tuscan composer's intuitive grasp of the cembalo idiom. Pasquini's *Toccata sul Canto del Cuculo*[12] is an effective fantasy on the song of the cuckoo, laden with some rather outlandish keyboard figurations and virtuoso trills. As one of the first genre pieces of this type it is unusual, yet it seems heavy and stolid when compared with similar pieces by the French clavecinists.

Pasquini was one of the first Italians to cultivate the keyboard suite consisting of allemande, courante, and gigue. Instead of using the term suite, he called this ensemble of dances a *sonata.* Some of the movements

---

[11] Four toccatas by Rossi are found in *Antichi Maestri Italiani. Toccate per Clavicembalo o Pianoforte,* ed. Boghen (Milano: G. Ricordi).

[12] Reprinted in *Italian Masters XVII–XVIII Centuries,* ed. Philipp (New York: International Music Co.), p. 32.

in Pasquini's sonatas contain two themes and in this respect he is a precursor of later similar works by Domenico Scarlatti.

Dr. Charles Burney, English music historian, composer, and performer, made a tour of the Italian provinces in the year 1770. Upon his return to England, he published a book describing his experiences and impressions while traveling through the peninsula. In this book Burney makes a somewhat dogmatic statement to the effect that to his knowledge there were neither outstanding harpsichordists nor first-rate composers of harpsichord music in Italy. Although the good doctor was often prone to exaggerate in order to prove a point, there is some truth in his statement. To begin with, the best Italian harpsichord composer, Domenico Scarlatti, had worked primarily in Spain, not Italy. As to that part of Burney's statement concerning the lack of good harpsichordists, this was perhaps bound to be true, since the instrument itself was not commonly used as a solo medium.

In eighteenth-century Italy, opera was a fully developed art form cultivated by the people with an unbelievable fervor and enthusiasm. Opera influenced all music, both secular and sacred. In the field of pure instrumental music, the violin reigned supreme. In the concerto, in chamber music, in symphonic ensembles, it was the violin that molded and shaped the style and forms of the music.

The harpsichord was always visible during this era but primarily as a medium for accompanying and for sustaining other instruments. It was present in the opera pit, and it held together the harmonic framework in the Baroque *trio sonata* and the *concerto grosso*. As a solo instrument, the harpsichord found a place merely as a means for private entertainment, and in this capacity it was confined to the upper social strata. Princes and dukes in the various small principalities that comprised Italy amused themselves during their leisure with melodious pieces on the harpsichord. Worldly prelates played for relaxation before going to the opera.

Alessandro Scarlatti (1660–1725), a famous opera composer in early-eighteenth-century Italy, devoted most of his time and talents to operatic scores—about sixty-five of them—and to other forms of vocal music. At the same time, however, he did write a small amount of keyboard music which is, when compared with the miniature masterpieces by his celebrated son Domenico, somewhat pallid. Frequent sequential passages and unimaginative series of left-hand accompaniment chords detract from the effectiveness. Alessandro wrote, among other things, a series of toccatas for the cembalo. His *Toccata in G Minor*[13] is rather difficult, endowed with harmonic solidarity and consistency of texture.

---

[13] This toccata and another one by A. Scarlatti are found in *Antichi Maestri Italiani, op. cit.* See also Alessandro Scarlatti, *Primo e Secondo Libro di Toccate,* ed. R. Gerlin (Milano: I Classici Musicali Italiani, 1943).

DOMENICO SCARLATTI

These early composers, then, are the ones whose works and techniques were available to the great **Domenico Scarlatti** (1685–1757) had he chosen to use them. But it is quite apparent that the Neapolitan went far beyond these models. What is so remarkable is the fact that Domenico Scarlatti created from his own imagination and innate technical skill the multitude of exquisite miniatures for which keyboard literature shall forever be grateful.

More than any of his contemporaries, Scarlatti prepared the way for a future school of piano composition. Although he was born in Naples, his harpsichord works were largely composed in Madrid or other Spanish cities where the royal court stayed, for during the latter part of his life Scarlatti lived in Spain under the patronage of Queen María Bárbara. Thus it happened that the more than five hundred Scarlatti pieces destined for the harpsichord[14] were created in Spain, not his native Italy.

Although Domenico Scarlatti did not avail himself of the framework of the suite as such, he did adopt for his own purposes the individual dances of the suite, each with its own unique characteristics. He himself published only thirty works of this type, a portfolio modestly called *Essercizi per Gravicembalo* (Exercises for Harpsichord, 1738). However, each of the little one-movement pieces thus fashioned bears the title of sonata. Scarlatti conceived his sonatas not as mere technical exercises but as *études* similar in purpose and intent to those later ones by Chopin—short, concise essays wherein one particular technical device or figuration is exploited.

Most editions of Scarlatti present each sonata as an independent piece, yet some writers believe that the composer intended a performance in pairs. This would be in line with the practice of other Italian composers of the period. The paired sonatas would be related by contrast or complement. One may be in a major key and the other in a minor tonality, but both have the same tonic.

Today, many Scarlatti sonatas appear as piano solos, and although they are extremely delightful for both pianist and listener, it should be borne in mind that Scarlatti wrote them for the harpsichord. The coloristic effects, the choice of tonalities, the harmony, and the audacious modulations find their perfect fulfillment in the different registers of the harpsichord, a fact that has been well demonstrated by contemporary harpsichordists.

[14] Domenico Scarlatti, *Opere Complete per Clavicembalo*, ed. A. Longo (Milano: G. Ricordi), 11 Vols. The finest contemporary study of Scarlatti is that of Ralph Kirkpatrick (Princeton: Princeton University Press, 1953). Kirkpatrick has revised the Longo catalogue—therefore in the musical examples the Kirkpatrick catalogue numbers are included with those of Longo. Kirkpatrick also presents the theory (pp. 141–143) that the sonatas were originally meant to be performed in pairs.

Generally speaking, each Scarlatti sonata is in one movement with two sections, each marked to be repeated if the performer so desires. The sonatas often are based on a single theme, but sometimes two or even three themes are involved. Although there are other factors, these artistic inventions are in essence the embryo for the coming *sonata-allegro* form, which was to find its fulfillment in C. P. E. Bach, Joseph Haydn, and Wolfgang Mozart. Scarlatti's themes are rather brief, with striking and original contours. In whatever form the themes emerge, they are invariably clear and simple. He combined his themes with harmonic color that never wavers Elegance is the result—an elegance Scarlatti alone created—and it bears his unmistakable stamp.

Dr. Charles Burney, while on one of his famous musical tours through Europe in 1770, met in Vienna a M. l'Augier who had been a close acquaintance of Scarlatti. Burney's account of his conversation with l'Augier is both interesting and informative:

He (l'Augier) has been in France, Spain, Portugal, Italy, and Constantinople, and is, in short, a living history of modern music. In Spain, he was intimately acquainted with Domenico Scarlatti, who, at seventy-three, composed for him a great number of harpsichord lessons which he now possesses, and of which he favoured me with copies. The book in which they are transcribed, contains forty-two pieces, among which are several slow movements; and of all these, I, who have been a collector of Scarlatti's compositions all my life, had never seen more than three or four. They were composed in 1756, when Scarlatti was too fat to cross his hands as he used to do, so that these are not so difficult, as his more juvenile works, which were made for his scholar and patroness, the late Queen of Spain, when Princess of Asturias.

Scarlatti frequently told M. l'Augier that he was sensible he had broke through all the rules of composition in his lessons; but asked if his deviations from these rules offended the ear? and upon being answered in the negative, he said, that he thought there was scarce any other rule, worth the attention of a man of genius, than that of not displeasing the only sense of which music is the object.

There are many pages in Scarlatti's pieces, in which he imitated the melody of tunes sung by carriers, muleteers, and common people. He used to say, that the music of Alberti, and of several other modern composers, did not in the execution, want a harpsichord, as it might be equally well, or perhaps, better expressed by any other instrument; but, as nature had given him ten fingers, and as his instrument had employment for them all, he saw no reason why he should not use them.[15]

Many Scarlatti sonatas betray the above-mentioned Spanish influence. He frequently infuses into his music a spirit recalling Spanish popular dance forms, such as the *zapateado* or *polo*. In fact, a good portion of his more effective pieces have a fairly rapid tempo, variants of *allegro*, so to speak. One of his most frequently played works, the *Sonata in C Major, L. 104* (Ex. 4),[16] reminds one of a typical Spanish *jota*. Other sonatas in dance style which show a Spanish influence are those in *F Major, L. 279; G Major, L. 290;* and *D Major, L. 14.*

Ex. 4. D. Scarlatti: *Sonata in C Major, L. 104* (Kirkp. 159)

Beyond the lively dance spirit, Scarlatti gave additional Spanish flavor to his music by using note repetition (Ex. 5).[17] The repetition of one note is characteristic in Spanish guitar music, particularly music for *flamenco* singing and dancing. Of course, note repetition also occurs earlier in the virginal works by English composers, but Domenico Scarlatti took his cue from Spain.

Ex. 5. D. Scarlatti: *Sonata in D Major, L. 465* (Kirkp. 96)

[15] *Dr. Burney's Musical Tours in Europe*, ed. Percy Scholes (London: Oxford University Press, 1959), II, 86–87.
[16] Domenico Scarlatti, *op. cit.*, III, 12.   [17] *Ibid.*, X, 72.

Scarlatti often uses the *acciaccatura* or "crush" to give an impression of strumming on a guitar. Other eighteenth-century composers used these dissonant chords but never with such telling effect (Ex. 6).[18]

Ex. 6. D. Scarlatti: *Sonata in B-flat Major, L. 39* (Kirkp. 249)

Scarlatti sets his melodic theme against a basic rhythmic figure and re-echoes the theme throughout the full keyboard range. Many times the theme is stated in the right hand and then is taken up by the left hand in imitation, as though a kind of *fughetta* were to take place (Ex. 7).[19]

Ex. 7. D. Scarlatti: *Sonata in C Major, L. 305* (Kirkp. 251)

But several measures later this imitative treatment ceases, to make way for a plastic, often chromatic subject, which has a profile contrasting to the preceding theme and is accompanied by warm characteristic chords. Scarlatti must have been overwhelmed with creative themes. Every aesthetic idea seemed to flower into a group of combinations. Divided, broken, reconstituted in all or in part, these themes nourish a series of concise developments.

Certain artifices seem deliberately designed to overcome the tonal drawbacks of the harpsichord—for example, such Scarlatti devices as the crossing of hands, the echoing back and forth from the extreme reaches of the keyboard, the successions of thirds that make for such brilliancy, the bass figures of arpeggiated or broken elements, and the embroideries thrown around a note to highlight it.

Scarlatti uses comparatively few ornaments. He makes a single exception, the trill, for which he exhibits a special preference. With the trill

18 *Ibid.*, I, 140.   19 *Ibid.*, VII, 21.

Scarlatti uses the *appoggiatura* and above all the *acciaccatura,* that orna-ment whereby a nonharmonic tone is struck simultaneously with the chord that follows it, in order to give the chord a less determined sound, as though meant to obliterate the sonority.

If Scarlatti's music does not strive for profundity, it forever has its elegance. A relentless searcher for brilliant and unusual effects, Scarlatti avoids triviality and aims for an expressive, sometimes dramatic line. He is, in effect, a harbinger of Romanticism, fifty years ahead of his time.

LATER CEMBALO COMPOSERS

Although no one equaled Domenico Scarlatti in craftsmanship and individuality, his contemporary **Francesco Durante** (1684–1755) was not far behind. The toccatas (*studii*) in his *Sonate per cembalo divisi in studii e divertimenti* (1732)[20] reveal traits and inflections associated with the violin sonata. Durante's use of parallel octaves, sixths, and thirds indicates that he was no slave to rules, yet he held his technique within the bounds of good taste. Of the studies or toccatas, the third and fifth are fugues treated with flexibility and imagination; the others are freely composed in quasi-contrapuntal imitative style. The *divertimenti* form a unity with the *studii,* not only through use of identical key but also in subtle technical and motivic similarities. The individual divertimenti vary in stylistic approach. Num-ber three is a canon at the octave while number six is a typically Italianate gigue.

Despite the attractive workmanship of Durante's music, neither he nor any composer who immediately followed him could quite measure up to Scarlatti. **Domenico Zipoli** (1688–1726), an organist at the Jesuit church in Rome, at times reminds one of Handel. Zipoli called his sets of pieces sonatas, but they really are suites and are often melodious, sometimes quite substantial. His *Suite (Sonata) in B Minor*[21] opens with a *Lento* movement displaying a good feeling for keyboard counterpoint. The succeeding *Cou-rante* is based on a running succession of sixteenth notes founded on a solid harmonic bass. The short and florid *Aria* sounds better when played on the piano, while the concluding *Gavotte* is appealing with its sequential figures tossed about from right to left hand.

In 1727, **Azzolino della Ciaia** (1671–1755) presented six sonatas to the musical world. Each has four movements: a toccata in improvisatory style,

[20] Francesco Durante, *Sei Studii e Sei Divertimenti per Cembalo,* ed. Paumgartner (Kas-sel: Bärenreiter, 1949).
[21] Reprint in *Italian Masters, op. cit.,* p. 42. For a more extensive collection, see Domenico Zipoli, *Orgel und Cembalowerke,* ed. Tagliavini (Heidelberg: Willy Mueller, Suddeutsche Musikverlag), II.

a fugal canzone, and two concluding pieces called *Tempo I* and *Tempo II* respectively.[22] This composer was an experimentalist, for he submits the sonata to arduous, complicated treatment. There are attractive technical features: expansive leaps; passages in parallel thirds, sixths, and octaves; an effective if profuse ornamentation; and an early example of an upward *glissando*. But the total picture is not entirely positive. Della Ciaia, in moments of self-imposed grandeur, attempts to create extravagant music from simple motives. His use—or misuse—of false relations and his treatment of dissonances are usually not successful.

Benedetto Marcello (1686–1739), lawyer, poet, and composer, is known for his vocal works, but he did make an attractive contribution to keyboard repertoire with some thirteen cembalo sonatas. These works date from around 1710–1720 and contain from three to five movements in the general pattern of the *church sonata:* slow-fast-slow-fast. William Newman writes: "The outstanding traits of Marcello's sonatas are . . . contrapuntal and harmonic interest, clear-cut themes, and a remarkably developed sense of phrase balance."[23] Most Marcello sonatas are today unknown to either keyboard performers or to their audiences. Instead, separate movements have occasionally been detached from the original framework and appear as single pieces in early music collections. This is regrettable, for the complete sonatas are worth hearing.

The Marcello *Sonata in B-flat Major,* reprinted by Pauer in *Alte Meister,*[24] is a magnificent keyboard composition from every point of view —harmony, melodic line, rhythmic imagination. Here an *Adagio* and *Poco maestoso* in dotted rhythms contrast with two ebullient show pieces, a toccata-like *Vivace* and a surprisingly orchestral *Presto.*

The Venetian **Domenico Alberti** (*ca.* 1710–1740) wrote about thirty-six sonatas. Alberti's name has been linked with a procedure—the broken-triad accompaniment figure (Ex. 8)[25]—which was used throughout the Classic period, sometimes with skill, often with resultant tedium. The so-called Alberti bass was used by this musician, although he probably did not "invent" it. Alberti's contributions to the panorama of keyboard composition are decidedly on the positive side. Two movements in fast tempo are standard in some Alberti sonatas. In others the composer replaces one of the rapid movements with one in moderate tempo. A step toward actual

[22] A toccata by della Ciaia is found in *Antichi Maestri Italiani, op. cit.,* p. 114. Béla Bartók has "arranged" a *Sonata in G Major* for piano (C. Fischer). A much more satisfactory edition of the same sonata was made by Buonamici for Edizioni R. Maurri of Florence.

[23] William Newman, *The Sonata in the Baroque Era* (Chapel Hill: University of North Carolina Press, 1959), p. 177. Short pieces by Marcello are published by Lemoine, Ricordi, and International Music Co.

[24] Pauer, *Alte Meister* (Leipzig: Breitkopf & Härtel), V.

[25] A sonata by Alberti is found in *Thirteen Keyboard Sonatas of the 18th and 19th Centuries,* ed. Wm. Newman (Chapel Hill: University of North Carolina Press, 1947), p. 42.

sonata-allegro form (see Chapter 11) was achieved by Alberti when he conceived his individual sonata movements as ternary structures rather than the traditional binary forms favored by his predecessors. Those who came after him did not always carry the inherent implications in ternary design further but at least Alberti had indicated the possibilities. These contributions to sonata form plus his skillful handling of rhythms and harmony within a predominately homophonic style proclaim Alberti a musician of talent and of import to future generations.[26]

Ex. 8. D. Alberti: *Sonata in G Major (Allegro)*

Giovanni Battista Pescetti (*ca.* 1704–1766) was another Venetian. A great traveler, he stayed for a time in London (*ca.* 1738–?) and there published his collection of keyboard music, nine *Sonate per Gravicembalo.*[27] By 1762 he was again in Venice as second organist at the great cathedral of St. Mark.

In his sonatas Pescetti blended the typical bipartite sonata form of the Italians with the spirit of the dance suite. Stylistically he stands as a bridge between Alberti and Domenico Scarlatti. There are also moments when he oddly resembles a fellow musician residing in England—George F. Handel.

Pescetti's *Sonata in C Minor*[28] is divided into three brief movements. The first opens in lightly textured fugato style but soon settles down to a series of suspensions and modulations. The second movement, *Moderato,* makes elaborate use of the Alberti bass, above which floats a highly ornamented melodic line. The final *Presto* is a gigue-like piece, which is perhaps the most effective of the three due to its simple texture and rhythmic vivacity.

A more lyrical and more elegant composer was **Baldassare Galuppi** (1706–1785), called *Il Buranello* (he was born on Burano island, near Venice). Galuppi achieved his reputation as an opera composer, and the

---

[26] See *Thirteen Keyboard Sonatas, op. cit.,* for a biographical study of Alberti. This study is in turn based on a book by Fausto Torrefranca, *Le Origini Italiane del Romanticismo Musicale, I Primitivi della Sonata Moderna* (Turin, 1930).

[27] Isolated pieces by Pescetti are found in *Clavicembalisti Italiani, op. cit.,* I, and *Clavecinistes Italiens* (Heugel).

[28] *Alte Meister, op. cit.,* VI.

comparatively few keyboard pieces that he wrote betray this occupation with melody and titillating rhythmic designs. His sonatas defy any generalized descriptions. Some are in one movement; these have a superficial resemblance to those of Domenico Scarlatti without, however, the Neapolitan's pinch of genius. Other sonatas go to the opposite extreme and gather together four movements that have little in common except tonal unity.

Among Galuppi's keyboard sonatas, the *Sonata in D Major*[29] most often appears in harpsichord music collections. This sonata has four movements: an aria-like *Adagio*, an exuberant *Allegro*, a somber *Largo*, and a rollicking concluding *Gigue*. Although Galuppi's music is harmonious for the listener, it is not always suited to the keyboard performer. The composer uses full chords in awkward progressions that are almost impossible to play smoothly on the harpsichord.

Domenico Paradisi (1710–1792)—a pupil of Nicolo Porpora, the opera composer—lived for many years in London, where he gave harpsichord and singing lessons. The articulate Dr. Charles Burney knew him and described him as one of the most popular teachers in London. Performers such as Cramer and Clementi studied his compositions with apparent seriousness.

Paradisi is known for his twelve *Sonate di Gravicembalo* (1754).[30] These sonatas display variety in form and spirit, and it is a pity they are not performed more frequently. Each of the sonatas contains two movements of contrasting character and tempo. Paradisi uses the framework of the Scarlatti prototype. Sometimes he sketches one theme, elsewhere two. In the second section of this binary structure there is usually some fragmentary development followed by a thematic restatement, which not infrequently contains unexpected melodic and harmonic surprises.

Only recently has the importance of **Giovanni Marco Rutini** (1723–1797) been recognized and placed in perspective. This Florentine composer probably wrote close to twenty sonatas.[31] These fine, solidly constructed works are advanced in both detail and length. Three sections usually feature a *minuet* or *andante* flanked by two exuberant rhythmic movements. These proclaim Rutini as an important forerunner to Wolfgang Mozart, a feeling strengthened by the fact that Mozart actually knew Rutini's music.[32]

In Naples, **Domenico Cimarosa** (1749–1801) achieved an international

---

[29] Reprint in *Italian Masters, op. cit.,* p. 4. Other sonatas are in B. Galuppi, *Quatro Sonate per Pianoforte o Clavicembalo,* ed. Piccioli (Milano: Edizioni Suvini Zerboni, 1952).

[30] Ten sonatas by Paradisi (Paradies) are found in *Le Trésor des Pianistes* (A. Leduc). Isolated pieces in *Clavicembalisti Italiani, op. cit.,* II, and *Old Masters of the 17th and 18th Centuries* (Peters), I.

[31] Isolated pieces by Rutini in *Clavicembalisti Italiani, op. cit.,* II, and *Clavecinistes Italiens, op. cit.* A complete sonata is in *Alte Meister, op. cit.,* V.

[32] Letter from Leopold Mozart to his wife, August 18, 1771.

reputation with his more than sixty operas. He was far less successful at composing instrumental music. Cimarosa's one-movement sonatas for cembalo[33] are rather pale exercises deriving to some extent from Mozart but totally lacking that composer's sophistication and melodic plasticity.

Among the outstanding contrapuntists and teachers in eighteenth-century Italy is the highly respected **Padre Giambattista Martini** (1706–1784). He was a devoted friend of Wolfgang Mozart, and the two maintained a substantial correspondence. Martini was the author of two scholarly works: the *Storia della Musica* (History of Music, 1781) and the *Esemplare . . . di contrapunto* (Contrapuntal Source Book, 1775). In his keyboard sonatas, which he designated for organ or harpsichord, Martini used a variety of dances and pieces in the style of the church sonata. These sonatas appeared in 1742 (twelve) and in 1747 (six). One movement from the sonatas of 1742, a little *Gavotte*,[34] is a splendid example of contrapuntal technique applied to a dance form (Ex. 9).

Ex. 9.   G. B. Martini: *Gavotte*

Ferdinando Gasparo Turini (1748–1812) qualifies as the Liszt of the eighteenth century. He was born in Brescia. In 1772 he became blind, but nevertheless maintained his post as organist at the monastery of Santa Giustina in Padua. At least two collections of sonatas by Turini are extant: a set of six in 1784 and twelve in 1804. When one finds an example of Turini's writing today, it turns out to be the brilliant, effective *Presto* from a *Sonata in G Minor*. This is a delightful piece, but to give the composer a just appraisal one should study a complete sonata, not just one movement.

Turini's *Sonata in D-flat Major*[35] is a work whose virtuoso propensities are just as attractive now as in the eighteenth century. To begin with, the key is unusual for the period. Second, the style of writing is highly imagina-

[33] Domenico Cimarosa, *32 Sonates*, ed. F. Boghen (Paris: Editions Max Eschig, 1928).
[34] Reprint in *Old Masters*, *op. cit.* See also Padre G. Martini, *Sechs Sonaten für Cembalo oder Klavier*, ed. Hoffmann-Erbrecht (Leipzig: Breitkopf & Härtel, 1954). A *Prelude, Fugue and Allegro* are in *Alte Meister*, *op. cit.*, I.
[35] A complete sonata by Turini is in *Les Maîtres du Clavecin*, ed. Köhler (Braunschweig: Henry Litolff's Verlag), II.

tive. The first movement, *Allegro assai*, is a joy to hear and to play. Scale passages, wide leaps in the right hand, melodic material in the left hand, parallel sixths and thirds, all combine in merry felicity. An *Andante* in 9/8 meter slows the pace for a moment; however, the final *Prestissimo* fashions a gigue whose initial measures almost sound like a call to the hounds!

One of the last harpsichord composers in Italy, **Giovanni Battista Grazioli** (*ca.* 1746–1820) was successively second organist (1782), then first organist (1785) at St. Mark's Cathedral in Venice. Grazioli published two sets of cembalo sonatas, six in each.[36] Pleasing and fascinating with their modest, unassuming proportions and sophisticated grace, these three-movement sonatas have certain characteristics reminiscent of Baldassare Galuppi.

With the advent (exact dates unknown) of Grazioli's late-Rococo miniatures, the age of the harpsichord in Italy for all intents and purposes came to an end. Toward the close of the eighteenth century, as the mature Classic period approached, the Italians produced fewer and fewer keyboard compositions. During the latter part of that century, when most keyboard composers were writing music for the increasingly popular piano, young **Luigi Cherubini** (1760–1842) wrote six harpsichord sonatas (*ca.* 1780).[37] The style in these interesting little works is Classic but they lack the pure expression achieved by Haydn and Mozart. Each sonata has two movements: an initial bipartite movement in sonata-allegro form and a concluding rondo. Excessive use of Alberti bass occasionally makes for monotony in the rhythm. The so-called rondos are for the most part written in A B A form with a middle section in quasi-improvisatory style. Apart from Cherubini's cembalo sonatas there are only isolated instances of music composed especially for the keyboard during this period. Enthusiasm for opera swept over the country and Italy abandoned keyboard-music composition for well over a hundred years.

BIBLIOGRAPHY

Benton, Rita. "Form in the Sonatas of Domenico Scarlatti." *Music Review*, Vol. 13, No. 4, 1952.

Boghen, Felice. "Sonates de Cimarosa pour le Fortepiano." *Revue Musicale*, Vol. V (July 1, 1924) and supplement.

[36] G. B. Grazioli, *Dodici Sonate per Cembalo*, ed. R. Gerlin (Milano: I Classici Musicali Italiani, 1943).
[37] Luigi Cherubini, *Sei Sonate per Cembalo* (Milano: Carisch S. P. A., 1958).

Borren, Charles van den. "Contribution au Catalogue Thématique des Sonates de Galuppi." *Revista Musicale Italiana*, 1923 (XXX).

Brofsky, Howard. *The Instrumental Music of Padre Martini*. Dissertation (in progress). New York University.

Burns, Joseph Albert. *Neapolitan Keyboard Music from Valente to Frescobaldi*. Dissertation. Harvard University, 1953. 2 Vols.

Gerstenberg, Walter. *Die Klavierkompositionen Domenico Scarlattis*. Regensburg: G. Bosse, 1933.

Haynes, Maurice Brooks. *The Keyboard Works of Bernardo Pasquini*. Dissertation. Indiana University, 1960. 4 Vols.

Keller, Hermann. *Domenico Scarlatti*. Leipzig: Edition Peters, 1957.

Kirkpatrick, Ralph. *Domenico Scarlatti*. Princeton: Princeton University Press, 1953.

Machabey, Armand. *Girolamo Frescobaldi*. Paris: Éditions du vieux Colombier, 1952.

Monroe, James Frank. *Italian Keyboard Music in the Interim between Frescobaldi and Pasquini*. Dissertation. University of North Carolina, 1959.

Newman, Wm. S. "The Keyboard Sonatas of Benedetto Marcello." *Acta Musicologica*, XXIX, 1957.

Redlich, Hans. "Girolamo Frescobaldi." *Music Review*, Vol. 14, No. 4, 1953.

Stone, David Leon. *The Italian Sonata for Harpsichord and Pianoforte in the Eighteenth Century*. Dissertation. Harvard University, 1952. 3 Vols.

Torrefranca, Fausto. "Le Sonate per Cembalo del Buranello." *Revista Musicale Italiana*, 1911 (XVIII).

6

THE

FRENCH

CLAVECINISTS

The French clavecinists (harpsichordists) flourished amid the luxurious atmosphere of the royal court and the aristocratic salons. Although history pays great attention to the excellent literature and art produced in late-seventeenth-century and eighteenth-century France, many contemporary accounts of that period remind us of the favored position held by music, particularly in court circles.

Louis XIV was a musician as his father had been. He played the lute and harpsichord well and the guitar even better. He had a good ear and sang well. He composed little pieces, among them "a very beautiful courante." He apparently loved his musicians better than his sculptors and his painters. He ennobled Lully, he assisted at the marriage of Lalande. He followed their works. The subject of each of Lully's operas was presented for his approval. He examined the poem, even going so far as hearing it sung before anyone else. He kept Lalande near him, had him write numerous little works and went to examine them several times a day. His preferences were for a decorative style, powerful and pompous. He delighted in operatic prologues where the events of his life were presented in allegory and his glory celebrated . . . But he was interested in all styles of music. He enjoyed the concerts given in 1682 by the German violinist Westhoff, and the works of the Italian school when, at the end of his reign, Italian music was again in vogue.

One might almost say that Louis XIV lived in music. At meals, in the chapel, at games, at promenades, at the hunt, in the country, he listened to his violins; in the evenings in his apartments, acts of operas; other evenings, little concerts where he sometimes sang. Apart from this, the court, the city, and the kingdom had a passion for music. The airs of Lully were sung by persons of distinction and by "all the cooks of France." They were sung at street corners and at the Pont-Neuf. The opera "in spite of the misery common to all estates" was established at Lyons in 1668. A troup played alternately at Marseilles, Lyons, Montpellier. Provincial academies of music—there were quite a few—gave operatic concerts, under the supervision of Lully. The great but severe Arnauld deplored in 1694 the fact that "the poison of the songs of Quinault and of Lully had spread throughout France."[1]

Numerous concerts were played for the king, but many private concerts were sponsored by the lesser nobility, the wealthy bourgeois patrons, or the musicians themselves. In a letter dated 1655, the Dutch scientist Christian Huygens writes:

> Yesterday we were entertained by Monsieur de Chambonnières whom we had seen several days previously. He came to fetch us in his carriage and first took us to the assembly of the honestly curious which he had initiated himself, as I have told you before. From there we went to his house where he played the harpsichord admirably well ... I don't have the time to go into detail about the festivities or even to impart to you the qualities which constitute Monsieur de Chambonnières' beautiful playing.[2]

About the same time Michel de Marolles, in his discourse on "the excellence of the city of Paris," lists the musicians whom he has known in that city:

> As for the lute, I have heard it played admirably by some of those and again by the messieurs Mésangeau, le Bret, Gaultier, Marandé, Blancrochet and des Forges. The spinet [small harpsichord] and the organ were ravishing under the hands of the messieurs de la Barre, Chantelouse, Chambonnière, Henry du Mont and Monar.[3]

INFLUENCE OF
THE FRENCH LUTENISTS

The German musicologist Max Seiffert held the opinion that the French clavecin school received its impetus from the English virginal school

[1] Ernest Lavisse, *Histoire de France* (Paris: Hachette, 1911), VII, 137. English translation by the author.

[2] *Oeuvres de Christian Huygens* (La Haye: M. Nijhoff, 1888), correspondence, I, letter number 239 to Constantyn, père, à Paris, 15 Oct., 1655. English translation by the author.

[3] *Mémoires de Michel de Marolles* (Paris: Antoine de Sommaville, 2nd ed., 1656–1657), II, 261. English translation by the author.

through French lutenists.[4] It is true that the French lutenists used the English type of florid variation, and furthermore the use of evocative titles and symbols for ornaments (see Chapter 4) can also be traced to English origins. However, the clavecin composers were not constrained by the technical handicaps of the lute. They therefore appropriated the style but adapted it to the more flexible capabilities of their keyboard instrument.

Manfred Bukofzer supported the same view as Seiffert.[5] Indeed it does seem impossible that the well-constructed pieces of Chambonnières or Louis Couperin could have sprung from the French basse danse a hundred years earlier. In the old basse danse, contrary motion in the quasi-polyphonic texture seems almost forbidden; instead, parallel sixths and thirds apparently represent the acme of good taste. The *Bauyn Manuscript*,[6] now in the *Bibliothèque Nationale de Paris*, helps in part to confirm the Bukofzer and Seiffert theory. This manuscript contains original keyboard works by early clavecin composers, but in addition it includes keyboard "transcriptions" or arrangements of lute pieces by such well-known composers as René Mézangeau.

The lute had enjoyed great popularity in France even before the beginning of the seventeenth century. Employed as an accompanying instrument to the *air de cour* (court air), it gradually assumed a solo repertoire of its own. Originally this repertoire consisted of transcriptions of vocal works, but gradually a unique collection of compositions evolved (predominantly dances), guided by three generations of lutenists.

Briefly, the first generation of French lutenists included Antoine Francisque (1570–1605), author of the *Trésor d'Orphée* (Orpheus' Treasure), and J. B. Bésard (1567–1625), who published a series of volumes called collectively *Thesaurus Harmonicus* (Harmonic Thesaurus), in which each individual book is devoted to one dance form—that is, a book of allemandes, a book of courantes, etc. The second generation of French lute composers is dominated by Nicolas Vallet (1583–1626), René Mézangeau (*d.* 1639), François Richard (*d.* 1650), and Ennemond Gaultier (1575–1651). At this time the dances were not grouped by form but were arranged in order of key.

The prominent figure in the third generation is **Denis Gaultier** (*ca.* 1600–1672), whose lute works date from 1640. Gaultier's collection entitled *Rhétorique des Dieux* (Rhetoric of the Gods) marks the apogee in lute repertoire. His unmeasured prelude (see pages 41–42) is fully developed and

---

[4] Max Seiffert, *Geschichte der Klaviermusik* (Leipzig: Breitkopf & Härtel, 1899), pp. 155–156.
[5] Manfred Bukofzer, *Music in the Baroque Era* (New York: W. W. Norton, 1947), p. 169.
[6] *Bauyn Manuscript*, Bibliothèque Nationale, Res. Vm[7] 674.

his music abounds with ornaments, melodic fragmentation, and other characteristics pertaining to the classic lute style. Other lutenists followed
Gaultier—composers like François Pinel, Perrine, Jacques Gallot, and
Charles Mouton—but sometime around 1680 the lute was forced to relinquish to the harpsichord its position as the favorite secular instrument.

Thus, the high point in lute composition coincided with the first actual
clavecin music in France. Early-seventeenth-century lutenists took the
quasi-polyphonic models of the English virginal school and modified them
even further, for the lute strings were not kindly disposed toward polyphony. This modification tended to strengthen the harmonic texture. Then
the lutenists also increased the varieties of ornaments so that by the time
Chambonnières, the first important French clavecin composer, came upon
the scene there were already eight types of ornamentation in common use.
From these Chambonnières chose seven.

To their credit, the French lutenists brought in other dances to add to
the pavane and galliard derived from the English. The allemande, courante,
sarabande, gigue, bourrée, menuet, etc., though not as yet presented in
orderly sequence, still enhanced the music by being different compositions
in different tempos. In the later lute school, at least, there was unity of key
or mode in the dances comprising each group of pieces. Throughout the
lute period and into that of the early clavecin composers, first importance
was placed upon the individual dance rather than on a series of dances that
might comprise a suite.

French clavecin compositions fall into three general categories:
dances, the rondeau, and the variation. The *rondeau* was exceedingly popular and often masqueraded under other names. Examples of variation form
are numerous: Rameau's simple *Gavotte,* for instance, is followed by a
series of mixed harmonic and melodic variations; another approach can be
observed in his *Les Niais de Sologne* (The Simpletons of Sologne) where a
composition in ample ternary form is itself subjected to two variations.

JACQUES CHAMPION
DE CHAMBONNIÈRES

Although doubtlessly there were talented clavecinists before **Jacques
Champion de Chambonnières** (1601–1672), their works have either disappeared or remain anonymous. G. Jean-Aubry has stated, "It may be said
that Chambonnières is the founder of that school of French harpsichordists
which was only to come to its end in the last years of the eighteenth century, at the moment when the Italianism of the virtuoso began to influence
in an unfortunate way the ancient purity of style which the French school

had up to then never ceased to display."[7] So it was Chambonnières who established the technical firmness and broad character that were to have such influence upon the compositions of later keyboard composers. If to the modern ear his music does not "sound" like later music, this in no way detracts from the fact that Chambonnières furnished the models for future generations of composers.

Authors differ in their evaluation of Chambonnières:

> He [Chambonnières] left only two collections of *Pièces de Clavessin*, both printed in the year of his death and recently [1925] republished in one volume. But these few pieces, generally shorter dance forms, have a dash, delicacy, and melodic breadth that give them an incontestable place next to the greatest masters of the harpsichord.[8]

> A specially beautiful trait, to be found particularly in the allemandes, is the extended flow of the musical phrase.[9]

> Interesting, his music nevertheless deceives by a kind of aristocratic negligence, a disdain for all development; perhaps he adapted himself to the taste of his public; truthfully, the salon audiences "don't listen long," and the pieces are executed in the midst of the noise of conversations; it suffices that they be rhythmic and they must be short.[10]

To examine Chambonnières' music is to discover that he was barely acquainted with the possibilities of the major and minor modes as we know them today. The arbitrary shifting of accidentals and the impression of continual modulation in his music suggest an experimental stage in keyboard composition. Just shortly before Chambonnières began to compose, the French lutenists were still placing the proper church-mode name at the head of each composition. Yet the idea of major and minor tonalities was emerging, for the lutenist Denis Gaultier, a contemporary of Chambonnières, takes pride in introducing compositions in entirely new keys, such as *a* minor.

The cadences occurring within Chambonnières' phrases are noteworthy in that the composer—in a strikingly modern conception of harmony—frequently uses a deceptive cadence that creates continuity within the phrase (Ex. 1).

[7] G. Jean-Aubry, *An Introduction to French Music* (London: Palmer and Hayward, 1917), p. 21.

[8] Curt Sachs, *Our Musical Heritage: A Short History of Music, 2nd Edition* (Englewood Cliffs, N.J.: Prentice-Hall, Inc., 1955), p. 194. © 1955 by permission of the publisher.

[9] Willi Apel, *Masters of the Keyboard* (Cambridge: Harvard University Press, 1947), p. 92.

[10] Gaudefroy-Demombynes, *Histoire de la Musique Française* (Paris: Payot, 1946), p. 56. English translation by the author.

Ex. 1. Chambonnières: *Allemande*

The final cadences are usually terminated with a broken chord or a slow arpeggio, which not only presents each chord member separately but also emphasizes the force of the cadence. English virginal composers favored the broken-chord ending, and the French lutenists gave it importance as an integral part of their *style brisé* or broken style (Ex. 2).

Ex. 2. Chambonnières: *Examples of cadence endings*

In the period immediately preceding the French harpsichord school, vocal music with an emphasis on counterpoint prevailed; yet most French keyboard composers made sparing use of strict counterpoint. With Chambonnières, one finds voice leading that is sound and logical (Ex. 3).[11]

When one examines Chambonnières' *Pièces de Clavessin* (Harpsichord Pieces), it becomes evident that the primary use of ornaments in his time was to create elegant style; in other words, the ornament was used flamboyantly, with little regard for its individual effect. The second func-

[11] *Oeuvres Complètes de Chambonnières*, eds. Brunold and Tessier (Paris: Senart, 1925). Three pieces may be found in *Les Clavecinistes Français* (Durand), IV, and in *The Art of the Suite*, ed. Pessl (New York: E. B. Marks Music Corp.). Most of the ornaments are omitted from the eight pieces found in *Early Keyboard Music*, ed. Oesterle (New York: G. Schirmer), I.

Ex. 3. Chambonnières: *Courante and Sarabande*

tion of the ornaments was to create flowing continuity in both the melodic line and inner parts.

A CLAVECIN
TRADITION DEVELOPS

One day, about 1655, some young people in the neighborhood of Chaumes-en-Brie (the location of Chambonnières' estate) presented a little concert to honor the composer. Three brothers named Couperin took part in the concert and when Chambonnières, enchanted with the *bonne symphonie,* asked who had composed it, he was told it was by young Louis Couperin. After this introduction, so the story goes, Chambonnières more or less sponsored the young man, took him to Paris, and presented him at court. Louis Couperin became organist at the church of Saint-Gervais in Paris as well as one of the organists at the King's Chapel. This **Louis Couperin** (1626–1661) was an uncle of the famous François Couperin, called *le Grand* (the Great).

Couperin's music is distinguished by a great manifestation of major and minor tonality, an interest in and command of contrapuntal keyboard technique, and an attitude of restraint in ornamentation and chord selection.[12] Among Couperin's sarabandes is one in perfect canonic imitation, the imitation starting on the third beat. The voice leading throughout is excellent (Ex. 4).

[12] *Pièces de Clavecin de Louis Couperin,* ed. Brunold-Dart (Monaco: Editions de l'Oiseau-Lyre, 1959).

Ex. 4. L. Couperin: *Sarabande*

In ornamentation Louis Couperin exhibits extreme caution. Generally speaking, only especially long note values receive ornaments, and their function is to sustain the sound (Ex. 5).

Ex. 5. L. Couperin: *Chaconne*

Couperin repeats ideas and phrases for emphasis. On a harpsichord with two keyboards, the initial phrase may be played on the lower keyboard, then repeated on the soft clavier. (This echo effect was a favorite device among Baroque composers.) In the general movement of parts, it is rare to find any note value smaller than an eighth note—the most frequent exceptions being little melodic figures that are repeated over and over. The omission of all superfluous movement adds immeasurably to the dignity of Couperin's music (Ex. 6).

Ex. 6. L. Couperin: *Chaconne*

Max Seiffert presents an excellent evaluation of Louis Couperin:

> Louis Couperin follows his master (Chambonnières) to the
> extreme end; his suites cover the whole circle of keys: *c* minor,

C major, d minor, D major, e minor, F major, f-sharp minor, g minor, G major, A major, a minor, b minor—that is, an almost complete major and minor system, extended to all possible to-nalities which could be used in accordance with the contemporary temperament. Marpurg tells once: "The reduction of the twelve church modes (to major and minor) takes place in the middle of the past century, and in fact we must give the honor to a musician in France, a musician whose name I read long ago in a book whose title I can no longer remember. At the time I paid little attention to this remarkable change, which laid the foundation for a new kind of melodic structure. Perhaps some-one else will discover the name of this skillful musician. He de-serves an outstanding place in the history of music." For this honor, Louis Couperin should be nominated.[13]

Whether Seiffert is right or wrong in his assumption is difficult to say. At any rate, it is certain that Louis Couperin exhibits remarkable facility in handling major and minor tonalities.

The clavecin school in its several generations produced some notable composers as well as some rather commonplace ones. The few keyboard pieces left by **Henri Dumont** (1610–1684) provide a scant basis for an ac-curate analysis of his contribution. Although born in Belgium, Dumont spent his mature life (from 1638) in France. He was a musician of fair talent; from 1660 he served as *intendant de la musique* to Marie-Thérèse, wife of Louis XIV, and in 1663 he was named master of the King's Chapel. Dumont did not publish any keyboard music. Found in manuscript are some seventeen pieces, among them eleven allemandes.[14] Though he did not specify any particular keyboard instrument, he must have thought of the harpsichord when writing his allemandes and single courante. His ap-proach is similar to that of Chambonnières, including the style brisé ap-propriated from the French lutenists.

Jean-Henry d'Anglebert (1628–1691), at one time organist to the Duke d'Orleans, succeeded his teacher Chambonnières in the post of *Epinette de la Chambre* (Chamber Harpsichordist). In 1664 he was named *Ordinaire de la Chambre du Roy pour le Clavecin* (Ordinary of the King's Chamber for the Harpsichord). Anglebert published his book *Pièces de Clavecin*[15] in 1689 and a second edition was made by the Parisian publisher Ballard in

---

[13] Seiffert, *op. cit.*, p. 164. Seiffert is quoting from Friedrich W. Marpurg, *Kritische Ein-leitung in die Geschichte und Lehrsätze der alten und neuen Musik* (Berlin: August Lange, 1759), p. 138. English translation by the author.

[14] Henri Dumont, *L'Oeuvre pour Clavier* (Paris: Editions musicales de la Schola Can-torum, 1956).

[15] J. Henry d'Anglebert, *Pièces de Clavecin*, ed. Roesgen-Champion (Paris: Librairie E. Droz, 1934).

1703. This book has pieces grouped in suites containing the standard dance forms. Here and there among the suites, however, are several transcriptions of Jean-Baptiste Lully's operatic works. Anglebert also wrote twenty-two variations on the famous theme *Folies d'Espagne*. His music, delightful though some of it may be, represents no great advancement beyond the accomplishments of his predecessors. In fact, when matched against the workmanship of Chambonnières and Louis Couperin, much of his music seems stilted, lacking scope and sureness. His writing is literally covered with ornaments. A table at the beginning of his collection lists twenty-nine ornaments with their explanations.

Nicolas Le Bègue (1630–1702), a contemporary of Anglebert, was a noted organist, composer, and clavecinist. A serious musician, he conscientiously fulfilled the tasks imposed upon him by his position and was highly respected in his day. The first volume of his *Pièces de Clavessin*[16] appeared in 1677 with a preface by the composer attempting to explain his manner of presenting the unmeasured prelude, which he included in all but two of the suites:

> I have tried to present these preludes with as much facility as possible as much for conformity as to the way of playing them, for which the manner is to separate and immediately restrike the chords rather than to hold them together as in playing the organ. If things are found to be obscure, I beg my intelligent performers to excuse me by considering the great difficulty in making this method of playing preludes intelligible to everyone. [English translation by the author.]

Ten years later in the *Mercure Galant* (a literary and musical gazette) for October, 1687, appeared the following announcement:

> Mr. Le Bègue, organist to the king, has composed a book of the most beautiful harpsichord pieces that have yet appeared, containing *allemandes, gavottes, menuets, bourrées* as well as *chaconnes, sarabandes* and others. Those of your friends who enjoy the harpsichord will find this book at the shop of Mr. Noel, rue Simon Le Franc, between the Swan and the Golden Lion. [English translation by the author.]

This announcement suggests that the second volume (which bears no date) of Le Bègue's *Pièces de Clavecin* appeared in 1687. It is amusing to note that the articles in the *Mercure Galant* are written in feminine gender (*celles, amies*), as though this music was primarily intended for the ladies.

---

[16] Nicolas Le Bègue, *Oeuvres de Clavecin*, ed. N. Dufourcq (Monaco: Editions de l'Oiseau-Lyre, 1956).

For a frank appraisal of Le Bègue, one is inclined to agree with the present-day musicologist Norbert Dufourcq who writes "the man had little genius, but a great knowledge and talent."[17] Le Bègue's works reflect the spirit of his era as well as reveal the aesthetic concept of music in his day. In keyboard history they help to bridge the gap between the first attempts at an original repertoire for the harpsichord and the finely constructed compositions of the eighteenth century. In Nicolas Le Bègue's two books of harpsichord pieces, one discovers characteristic devices used so consistently that they form an integral part of his style: the *harpègement* or breaking up of triads and chords; modulation by common tone, chromatic alteration, and assumption of key; use of the deceptive cadence to extend the phrase line; and use of similar rhythmic figures within an individual work. Le Bègue was also the first French composer to regulate the suite outline to a framework of allemande, courante, sarabande, and gigue, plus any other additional or optional dances.

Jean-Baptiste Lully (1632–1687) is one of the greatest opera composers France has produced. An Italian by birth, he went to France at an early age, and by means of intrigue, subterfuge, and talent succeeded in establishing himself as musical dictator in his adopted country. The few pieces he composed for the harpsichord obviously do not class him as a true clavecin composer. An *Air tendre*, a lilting, graceful piece, is followed by an extremely fine *Courante* and a sparkling *Gigue*.[18] These three pieces are more Italian than French in spirit, but they are remarkable for their harmonic stability and solid cadences.

A second generation of composers took up the suite with its dances— so typically French in elegance, ornamentation, and grace. **Louis Marchand** (1669–1732), **Elizabeth Jacquet de La Guerre** (*ca.* 1664–1729), **Louis-Nicolas Clérambault** (1675–1749), and **Gaspard Le Roux** (*d.* after 1705) are members of this group. In their compositions the individual dances become more supple, the movement more flexible. Marchand, a well-known organist in his day, left two suites for harpsichord.[19] In style these refer back to Chambonnières rather than ahead to François Couperin. Earnestness and seriousness of purpose rather than grace and charm characterize Marchand's work.

Elizabeth Jacquet de La Guerre, wife of the organist at the Sainte-Chapelle and a royal favorite, has contributed a book of a dozen pieces, the *Pièces de Clavecin* (1707),[20] which adds a new element to the traditional

---

[17] Norbert Dufourcq, *La Musique d'Orgue Française* (Paris: Librairie Floury, 1949), p. 70.
[18] *Les Clavecinistes Français,* ed. Diémer (Paris: Durand & Cie.), II.
[19] Louis Marchand, *Pièces de Clavecin,* ed. T. Dart (Monaco: Editions de l'Oiseau-Lyre, 1960).
[20] Elizabeth Jacquet de La Guerre, *Pièces de Clavecin,* ed. P. Brunold (Paris: Editions de l'Oiseau-Lyre, 1938).

style of her day. The pieces are subtle, delicate adaptations of current Italianisms and a few of them presage things to come. Her *Sarabande in G Major*, for instance, sounds like the later sarabandes by Handel.

L. N. Clérambault is well known for his organ pieces and *cantatas,* but his *Livre de Clavecin* (1704)[21] has been ignored by the musical world. Clérambault was organist at Saint-Sulpice in Paris and *surintendant de la musique* for the celebrated Madame de Maintenon. His melodies are expressive, his ornamentation sensitive and in good taste.

There is very little material available about Gaspard Le Roux. He seems to have been born in Paris around 1660, but his death date is unknown because he disappeared from sight after his *Pièces de Clavecin*[22] were published in 1705. From what facts are known, M. Le Roux was a very successful teacher; according to a 1695 list of organists and clavecinists established for taxation, he paid as much income tax as did François Couperin, Marchand, Le Bègue, and others in the same professional category. His *Pièces de Clavecin* is one of the most amazing clavecin collections from the early eighteenth century. The pieces not only are in advance of their time in harmony and stylistic treatment; they are also some of the most beautiful compositions written prior to François Couperin. Le Roux's collection appeared just one year before Jean-Philippe Rameau's first clavecin pieces and eight years ahead of François Couperin's first publication. Of course, some years had passed since Chambonnières and Louis Couperin began the clavecin tradition and a gradual change was to be expected. Le Roux's works show many changes, principally the establishment of a secure harmonic foundation. His essential harmonic treatment was carried on through the eighteenth century by other composers. On page two of the collection, Le Roux explains in a preface his reasons for publishing the compositions and clarifies the content of his collection:

> Although I have spared neither my cares nor my pains in seeing that my compositions left my hands in the best possible condition, I have never entertained the idea of exposing them to the eyes of the public. But, encouraged by those who have knowledge of these things and disturbed by the gross faults that I have noticed in copies of my *Pièces de Clavessin* which have circulated in spite of me, I have finally decided to have them engraved and to sound out the taste of the public who alone may decide the merit of the works. If these are unfortunately not acceptable, I then ask pardon for having made a bad gift to

[21] Louis-Nicolas Clérambault, *Pièces de Clavecin*, ed. Brunold (Paris: Editions de l'Oiseau-Lyre, 1938).

[22] Gaspard Le Roux, *Complete Works for Clavecin*, ed. Fuller (New York: Alpeg, *ca.* 1959).

the public. If, on the contrary, this attempt at composition does not displease, the public will be glad to know that I wish to offer other compositions which will be of a higher order and more worthy of its approbation. Finally, to facilitate the execution of these pieces for those who wish to learn them, I have notated the ornaments and the manner of execution in a·special table, besides those whose execution has already been absorbed into the notation. [English translation by the author.]

The pieces in this collection may be played in several ways: first as clavier solos, second with two clavecins (at the end of the collection are several parts for a second harpsichord), and finally as an instrumental trio. For the last version, Le Roux supplies two string parts and a figured bass.

The numerous seventh and ninth chords occurring in the collection must have been intentional. Only occasionally do they seem the result of a suspension. Otherwise, they are stated boldly and often on strongly accented beats (Ex. 7).

Ex. 7. Le Roux: *Chaconne*

In his book *L'Esthétique de Jean Sébastien Bach,* André Pirro points out the fact that the principal theme in the *Prelude* from J. S. Bach's *English Suite in A Major* is almost identical with that in Le Roux's *Gigue in A Major.*[23] Since Bach's *English Suites* were not completed until at least 1717, Le Roux's collection would therefore be first chronologically. However, the fact that Bach may have copied a few bars from Le Roux is minor. What should be borne in mind is that Bach evidently knew the works of this French composer (as well as other French composers). Le Roux's *Allemande La Vauvert* and *Allemande grave* are so similar to Bach's compositions in the same genre that mere coincidence is impossible. But the masterful Bach adds a depth to the French *esprit,* a depth that cannot be said to lie within the scope of Le Roux's talent.

[23] André Pirro, *L'Esthétique de Jean Sébastien Bach* (Paris: Librairie Fischbacher, 1907), p. 431. As a matter of fact, Le Roux was well enough known in Germany to be included in J. G. Walther's *Musikalisches Lexicon* of 1732.

FRANÇOIS COUPERIN

The French clavecin tradition, firmly established by Chambonnières and Louis Couperin, reached its peak both in style and technique with the magnificent creations of François Couperin, surnamed the Great.

From mid-seventeenth century to 1826 seven Couperins successively filled the organ post at the church of Saint-Gervais in Paris. This was indeed a musical dynasty. Several Couperins were extremely talented, but **François Couperin** (1668–1733) was the genius. He published four harpsichord collections in Paris, the first volume in 1713, the second in 1717, the third book in 1722, and the fourth and final collection in 1730.[24] In addition, his famous *L'Art de Toucher le Clavecin* (The Art of Playing the Harpsichord) appeared in 1717.[25] Instead of gathering his pieces into suites, as was the common practice, Couperin put his pieces into larger groups called *ordres* or *orders,* in which the first and last piece of each order are in the same tonality. The other pieces are either in the same tonality or in closely related keys. The *ordre* was Couperin's personalized version of the keyboard suite. An ordre often began with several pieces in the style of an allemande, courante and sarabande, but mostly contained descriptive pieces with fanciful titles.

Couperin's art was objective; his aim was to describe exactly what he saw in nature or the picturesque rather than to express his own inner sentiments. And Couperin was a master at whatever he attempted. Every facet of his technique and inspiration—melodic contour, ornaments, harmonic color, rhythms—was focused toward this end. This objective art of François Couperin is expressed in many characteristic traits. His use of what one might call arpeggiated harmony, his preciseness in matters of phrase balance, his frequent use of dotted rhythms coupled with his fantasy and imagination, all make for a style that is both unique and sensitive. His style is the outgrowth of a formidable personal technique based on a framework already established by his compatriots but revitalized by his constant use of the rondeau. The Italian elements in Couperin's style show up in the symmetrical developments and in the subtle, sensitive melodies adorned with myriad ornaments. The correct performance of these ornaments was strictly enjoined by the composer.[26]

The twenty-seven *ordres* of clavecin pieces are the result of painstak-

[24] François Couperin, *Pièces de Clavecin*, eds. J. Brahms and F. Chrysander (London: Augener, Ltd.), 4 vols. Durand also publishes the complete solo pieces. In the complete works (11 Vols.) edited by Maurice Cauchie (Paris: Editions de l'Oiseau-Lyre, 1932) the *clavecin* pieces occupy Vols. 2–5.

[25] François Couperin, *L'Art de Toucher le Clavecin* (Wiesbaden: Breitkopf & Härtel, 1933). The text of this reprint is in French, German, and English.

[26] If one reads through Couperin's *L'Art de Toucher le Clavecin*, it becomes obvious that he was constantly concerned with ornaments and the problems involved in their execution.

ing labor. The order itself contained from four to twenty-three pieces. In the first sets there are vestiges of an earlier style, remnants of the old tradition. Yet little by little Couperin eliminates allemandes and courantes and replaces them with dozens of miniature evocative or descriptive pieces. Couperin delights in recalling the world of nature: *Les Abeilles* (Bees), *Les Papillons* (Butterflies), *Les Moucherons* (Flies), *Le Rossignol en Amour* (The Nightingale in Love), *Les Bergeries* (Pastoral Scenes). Sometimes his portraits are objects more or less animated by sound or movement: *Le Reveille-matin* (The Alarm Clock), *Le Bavolet flottant* (The Floating Bonnet), *Le Tic-toc-choc* (The Ticking Clock), *Les Petits Moulins à vent* (The Little Windmills). He also attempts more complicated subjects: the picturesque actuality, anecdotes of the time, as for example *Les Plaisirs de Saint-Germain-en-Laye* (The Pleasures of Saint-Germain); naïve allegories such as *Le Carillon de Cythère* (The Carillon of Cythera), *Les Barricades mystérieuses* (The Mysterious Barricades); or even satirical caricatures such as *Les Fastes de la grande et ancienne Ménéstrandise*, wherein Couperin ridicules the minstrels who would force the clavecin teachers to join their corporate society.

He further extends his horizons to include the psychological. His "character" portrayals give a good idea of the milieu in which Couperin lived and worked. First of all, the family portraits: *La Couperin* (his wife); *La Couperinette* and *La Crouilly* (his daughter). Then there are the references to his musical colleagues: *La Forqueray* (Antoine Forqueray, viola da gamba player); *La Garnier* (Gabriel Garnier, organist at the Chapelle Royale); *La Morinète* (daughter of the composer Jean Baptiste Morin). A final addition to this gallery of portraits is a group of what one might call "people of quality": *La Princesse de Chabeuil* (daughter of the prince of Monaco); *La Princesse Marie* (Marie Leczinska, queen consort of France); *La Mènetou* (Mlle. de Mennetoud, daughter of the Duchesse de la Ferté). All this is ingenious, subtle, and as the French would say *précieux* and withal delightful. This pertains as well to a suite called *Les Dominos ou les Folies françaises,* a kind of psychological ballet with curious titles: *L'Ardeur* under the pink domino, *L'Esperance* under the green domino, *La Fidelité* under the blue domino, *Les Vieux Galants* and *Les Trésorières Surannées* under the purple and dead-leaf dominos, *La Coquetterie* under different dominos. These clever titles would be quite annoying if the music were slight. The music, however, is magnificent. For example, if one looks beyond the titles of *Les Folies françaises,* what emerges is a series of variations on a ground, a large *chaconne* which explores a series of moods through the various pieces, each of which is, of course, a variation.

In the *Bavolet flottant,* Couperin describes a trailing ribbon fastened to a headdress of the period as it waves to the caprice of a light rhythm. Delicate ornaments add to the portrait's elegance (Ex. 8).

Ex. 8. F. Couperin: *Le Bavolet flottant*

Couperin is poetic when the occasion demands, as in the charming *Rossignol en Amour,* a piece outstanding for the tender charm in its melody and the refined taste evident in the ornaments chosen to give the stylized transposition of a bird's song (Ex. 9).

Ex. 9. F. Couperin: *Le Rossignol en Amour*

Thus, François Couperin not only has a firm command of harpsichord style—he composed for his instrument as no one before had done—but he reveals a truly creative talent. His melodic imagination displays admirable freshness. He possesses a delicate harmonic sense. His themes show the inspirations of an impassioned musician: perfectly created, firm in line, vivid and enduring in color. His art never wavers; it consistently exhibits a magnificent technique.

Couperin's music is not always characterized by grace and wit alone. Many pages in his *Pièces de Clavecin* prove that he knew how to express tenderness, a certain melancholy languor. Here is what he writes in favor of expressive execution: "Custom has made me recognize that the hands vigorous and capable of executing that which is the most rapid and most light are not always those that succeed the most in tender and sentimental pieces, and I confess in good faith that I prefer that which touches me to

that which surprises me."[27] There are surprising moments of deep profundity that expose his most serious countenance. This is the case with the
Pasacaille (actually not a passacaglia but a rondeau!), which has an implied note of tragedy. It is perhaps his noblest piece.

Couperin's work represents one stage of perfection in *clavecin* development in eighteenth-century France. He succeeded in what he wished to do
—that is, to fuse French elegance and clarity with contemporary Italian
expressive power and richness, qualities he admired above all in Corelli.
The French musicologist Jean-Aubry summed up the art of Couperin:
"Everything Couperin writes is inspired by discretion and by grace; he
does not like to *insist,* he writes for the elect, for cultivated people, and
especially he writes for his own pleasure and to satisfy that taste for seeing,
for living, for seizing the charm or the absurdity of things and of people—
a taste very French, and one to be found again today in the composers now
around us."[28]

JEAN-PHILIPPE RAMEAU

The music of **Jean-Philippe Rameau** (1683–1764), organist, clavecinist, composer, and theorist, represents the ultimate purity of the classical
style achieved by the French clavecin school. Quoting again from Jean-
Aubry: "Rameau is French rationalism in all its regularity and orderliness,
in all its comprehensiveness of preparation, and, paradoxically, in all its
freedom and even audacity of expression."[29]

Rameau and Couperin were equally gifted, but their music attracts for
different reasons. Since Rameau was a theorist, one would expect to find
in his works a sure technique and a firm musical substance, all handled
under the disciplined imagination of the composer. His music is perhaps
less spontaneous than that of François Couperin, for he writes in a style
that presupposes a profound knowledge of harmonic theory. He searches
for truth and perfection and, having approached his goals, attains a power
and an extraordinary majesty of expression. In matters of pure technique,
his main concern was to use the keyboard as a sustaining instrument.
Rameau's pieces—many of which sound very effective on the piano—are
examples of the highest artistic standard set by the French clavecin composers. There were fine composers who followed Rameau and some contemporary with him, to be sure, but there were very few equal to him.

Rameau left three harpsichord collections.[30] The first volume, published when he was twenty-three, contains only ten pieces. Its style recalls

---

[27] Preface to the first book of *Pièces de Clavecin.* Translation by the author.
[28] Jean-Aubry, *op. cit.,* p. 23.　　　[29] *Ibid.,* p. 26.
[30] Jean-Philippe Rameau, *Pièces de Clavecin,* ed. Saint-Saëns (Paris: Durand & Cie.).
A more recent edition has been made by E. R. Jacobi (Kassel: Bärenreiter, 1958).

Louis Marchand, a musician admired by the young Rameau. However, this collection already shows traces of Jean-Philippe's personality and the equilibrium of his later style. Here is found the unmeasured prelude serving as an introduction to a spritely gigue. The second book of *Pièces de Clavecin* (1724) confirms Rameau's own personal style. Although this style derives in part from Couperin (arpeggiated harmony), it is mostly pure Rameau. He revels in chromatic dissonance and reveals his predilection for the highly developed rondeau spiced with unusual modulations. Rameau, despite his theoretical background, is not at all timid in composing imitative pieces like *Le Rappel des Oiseaux* (The Recall of the Birds) and *Les Tourbillons*. He himself described the latter as "*tourbillons de poussière excités par de grands vents*" (clouds of dust stirred up by gusts of wind).[31] The music is often lyrically tender, with finesse and flexibility; elsewhere it is lively, with an astonishing rhythmic invention. In each individual piece the *agréments* (ornaments) help to create an expression whose impact is at once profound and beautiful. A few of the classic dance forms—allemande, courante, and two gigues—are included in the second collection. But for the most part, character pieces and works with provocative and descriptive titles make up the sets. In *Les Niais de Sologne* (The Simpletons of Sologne), a section in A B A form with an ample melodic line set against a bass of frolicking eighth notes is submitted to two *doubles* or variations, the second of which has virtuoso scope. *Les Cyclopes* (The Cyclops), a work in three generally outlined sections, presages future sonata-allegro form—at least in spirit—with its two themes, which are slightly varied and then recapitulated.

In 1731 Rameau published his *Nouvelles Suites de Pièces de Clavecin*. This collection remains a monumental landmark in harpsichord history. Aesthetically, Rameau further develops what he began in his second book. Here appear germs of sonata construction, with two themes or two facets of one idea being developed and then restated. He had a genuine talent for allotting the anecdotal or realistic element its rightful place in music. To judge by the *co-co-dai* of the hen in *La Poule*, he was an early admirer of genuinely imitative music, maintaining a tradition that was to continue into the nineteenth century (Ex. 10).

In a piece called *Les Trois Mains* (The Three Hands), Rameau gives the illusion of three hands at the keyboard. A *Gavotte* with variations offers six charming variations on a graceful dance. *Les Sauvages* (The Savages) is a delightful sketch that Rameau later inserted into his opera-ballet *Les Indes Galantes* (The Gallant Indies, 1735). And in *L'Enharmonique*, he modulates with a rapidity quite unusual for the mid-eighteenth century. Rameau well deserves a lasting place in the annals of music history. He is

[31] Letter to Houdar de la Motte, October 25, 1727.

Ex. 10. Rameau: *La Poule*

co co co co co   co co dai   etc.

a true classic musician of the French school, and the last of the great clavecin composers.

OTHER CLAVECINISTS

Contemporary with Rameau and extending even further into the late eighteenth century were several clavecinists who, although well recognized in their own era, are in the majority now almost forgotten. **Jean-François Dandrieu** (1682–1738) wrote three books of *clavecin* pieces (1718, 1728, 1732)[32] that are pleasing enough, though not at all profound and at times harmonically dull. He expresses preference for the rondeau, a form admirably suiting his temperament. *Les Tourbillons,* with its cascades of figurations, is veritably a whirlwind of sound. *Les Fifres* (The Fifers), a miniature march with a particularly sparse *écriture,* is effective. In *Caquet* (Chatter) one can literally hear the tongue-wagging, which is the subject of this bit of spoofing.

The prolific composer **Joseph Bodin de Boismortier** (1682–1765) composed a collection of *Quatre Suites de Pièces de Clavecin* (1736),[33] his only work in this field. Despite his use of the usual flamboyant titles—*La Caverneuse, La Décharnée, La Belliqueuse*—his writing is unusually sober and restrained for this period.

Louis Claude Daquin (1694–1772), composer of popular *Noëls* for organ, has left portraits and imitative pieces of inimitable grace.[34] His preference for the Italian style is amply displayed in miniature sketches like *Le Coucou* (The Cuckoo) and *L'Hirondelle* (The Swallow).

And there are other French clavecin composers—**Nicolas Siret** (1663–1754), **François Dagincourt** (1684–1758), **Antoine Dornel** (1685–1765), **Joseph Royer** (*ca.* 1700–1755), **Jacques DuPhly** (1715–1789)[35]—but their music only repeats what greater composers had already better expressed.

---

[32] Twelve pieces by Dandrieu are found in *Les Clavecinistes Français, op. cit.,* II.

[33] Joseph Bodin de Boismortier, *Quatre Suites de Pièces de Clavecin,* ed. Erwin R. Jacobi (Munich: F. E. C. Leuckart, 1960).

[34] Four pieces by Daquin are included in *The Art of the Suite, op. cit.*

[35] Representative compositions by these composers may be seen in the four volumes comprising *Les Clavecinistes Français, op. cit.* An interesting one-volume anthology, *Französische Klaviermusik des 18. Jahrhunderts* was edited by Walter Georgii for Arno Volk Verlag.

BIBLIOGRAPHY

Berthier, Paul. *Réflections sur l'Art et la Vie de Jean-Philippe Rameau*. Paris: Editions A. & J. Picard, 1957.

Bouvet, Charles. *Les Couperin*. Paris: Librairie Delagrave, 1919.

Daval, Pierre. *La Musique en France au XVIIIe Siècle*. Paris: Payot, 1961.

Gillespie, John. *The Music for Harpsichord of Nicholas Le Bègue*. Dissertation. University of Southern California, 1951.

Girdlestone, Cuthbert. *Jean-Philippe Rameau*. London: Cassell & Co., Ltd., 1957.

Hofman, Shlomo. *L'Oeuvre de Clavecin de François Couperin Le Grand*. Paris: A. & J. Picard, 1961.

Klitenic, Zelik. *The Clavecin Works of Jean-Philippe Rameau*. Dissertation. University of Pennsylvania, 1955.

Mellers, Wilfrid. *François Couperin and the French Classical Tradition*. London: Dennis Dobson, Ltd., 1950. Dover reprint

Migot, Georges. *Jean-Philippe Rameau*. Paris: Librairie Delagrave, 1930.

7

KEYBOARD MUSIC
IN BELGIUM
AND HOLLAND

In the Low Countries—Belgium and Holland—serious harpsichord composition made a somewhat belated appearance. Germany, France, and Italy date their respective harpsichord traditions from the latter part of the seventeenth century, but Belgium and Holland did not begin to assemble much substantial harpsichord repertoire until the following century. To be sure, numerous examples of harpsichord music written there prior to the eighteenth century have been preserved, but these are mainly brief, light-textured dances and pieces based on popular tunes of the day—tunes deriving not only from the Low Countries but from France and England as well.

The British Museum now has a modest collection of thirty-three pieces called the *Susanne van Soldt Manuscript*[1] in honor of its original owner. Susanne van Soldt was the English-born daughter of an Antwerp merchant. The manuscript has several divisions, and the portion containing the Netherlands compositions dates from around 1599. Apart from some settings for psalms, these Netherlands pieces are mostly arrangements of dance tunes then popular on the Continent. The music is not very interesting, but it does provide the only source (as yet) of sixteenth-century Dutch harpsichord music.

The *Leningrad Manuscript*[2] takes its name from the fact that it is located now in the library of the Academy of Sciences at Leningrad. Although the manuscript bears the date 1646, the Dutch music probably was added shortly after 1650; and this Dutch segment—except for three pieces by J. P. Sweelinck—is limited chiefly to settings of popular tunes. The music is conservative, somewhat resembling the style of the English virginal school forty years earlier.

A third collection is called the *Gresse Manuscript*[3] because two alle-

---

[1] A modern edition may be found in Volume III of *Monumenta Musica Neerlandica,* ed. Alan Curtis (Amsterdam: Vereniging Voor Nederlandse Muziekgeschiedenis, 1961).
[2] *Ibid.*   [3] *Ibid.*

mandes and a pair of three-movement suites in it are attributed to Jb. (Jacob?) Gresse. His suites are obviously based on current French models, although a certain northern influence—predominantly that of Buxtehude —can be identified. Except for the Gresse music, the manuscript has little to offer.

The final item in this survey of early Netherlands keyboard manuscripts is a collection originally written out for a certain Anna Maria van Eyl and dated 1671.[4] This manuscript was compiled by Gisbert Steenwick (d. 1679), organist and carilloneur of the Groote Kerk (Great Church) in Arnhem from 1665 to 1674. Nine pieces in the collection are signed by Steenwick. His music is pleasant and reveals some skill in harmonic-variation devices. Perhaps the best pieces in this manuscript are Steenwick's two allemandes and *La Grévelinde*—a theme with two variations.

These sixteenth-century and early-seventeenth-century collections of Netherlands harpsichord music were assembled for the purpose of giving enjoyment to their respective owners, and perhaps also to assist them with their keyboard lessons. In general, the pieces in the volumes are unpretentious and uncomplicated. They cannot be credited with laying foundations for a future school of composition nor with expanding musical horizons in either Belgium or Holland. Their purpose was simply to provide entertainment, and this they could have accomplished admirably.

JAN PIETERSZOON SWEELINCK

Dutch keyboard history does have one prominent seventeenth-century composer, **Jan Pieterszoon Sweelinck** (1562–1621), who for more than forty years presided daily at the organ of the Oude Kerk (Old Church) in Amsterdam. Sweelinck's fine reputation stems not only from his excellent playing and composing but from his teaching as well. Some of his students later became famous, among them Samuel Scheidt. Even Bach and Handel ultimately benefited from a tradition in organ technique and composition that had various basic roots in Sweelinck's music. Some early historians believed that he studied in Italy with the famous theorist Giuseppe Zarlino. This is not true, despite the fact that the Dutchman obviously was well versed in contemporary Italian musical practice. His music presents a synthesis of techniques: some derived from the English virginal school and others are commonly associated with the Italian composers. Today Sweelinck is better known for his instrumental works than for

---

[4] A modern edition may be found in Volume II of *Monumenta Musica Neerlandica*, ed. Frits Noske (Amsterdam: Vereniging Voor Nederlandse Musiekgeschiedenis, 1959).

the numerous vocal compositions he produced. He gives no indication in the keyboard pieces as to which are intended for organ and which for harpsichord. His keyboard repertoire includes thirteen fantasias, six echo-fantasias, thirteen toccatas, and twenty-four chorale variations, seven variations on popular tunes, and five variations on popular dances.[5] The variations, written in a florid style, were very likely intended for the harpsichord. To the variation technique which he borrowed from the English, Sweelinck added his personal concept of counterpoint and harmonic cadential treatment. He habitually omits the theme and begins with the first variation, since everyone in his day supposedly was acquainted with the theme. Four attractive sets of variations stand out in his repertoire: those on the sacred song *Mein junges Leben hat ein End* (My Young Life Is Ended—Ex. 1); on the popular French song *Est-ce Mars?* (Is It Mars?); on the English song *Onder een linde groene* (Under a Green Lime); and on *Ick Voer al over de Rhyn* (I Crossed the Rhine).

Ex. 1.   J. P. Sweelinck: *Mein junges Leben hat ein End*

BELGIUM

Nearly one hundred years intervenes between those keyboard works by J. P. Sweelinck and the next distinguished harpsichord music composed in the Netherlands. Then it becomes quite clear that eighteenth-century composers in Belgium and Holland were little influenced by Sweelinck. Instead, they were inspired by French, German, and Italian models. And curiously enough, there actually were few Dutch composers to continue the Sweelinck tradition, for in the eighteenth century it was the Belgian composers—not the Dutch—who produced most of the "Netherlands" harpsichord repertoire.

John Loeillet

The most celebrated of these Belgian keyboard composers is **Jean-Baptiste Loeillet** (1680–1730), also known as John Loeillet. He was born in Ghent but for many years lived in London, where he died.[6] Loeillet made a name for himself in London musical circles both as a composer and as the organizer of an extremely popular weekly concert series. He wrote two books of harpsichord pieces. The music is appealing and eclectic with traces of English, French, and Italian styles.[7] Well balanced in form and embellished with interesting detail, these harpsichord pieces constitute an excellent repertoire; indeed, Loeillet proves himself to be master of his talent, developing his inspiration with a natural freedom and grace. Sometimes he adheres to traditional suite patterns: allemande, courante, sarabande, gigue. On other occasions he prefers a more flexible sequence as, for example, in the trilogy suggesting an English influence: *Aire, Hornpipe, Cibel*. But whatever the form may be, Loeillet consistently displays personal skill in his fluent handling of the distinctive rhythms proper to each stylized dance.

Most Belgian harpsichord composers in Loeillet's time had little opportunity to absorb any British influence, except perhaps indirectly through Handel, whose music was known to some of them. A more direct influ-

[5] Jan Pieterszoon Sweelinck, *Werken voor Orgel en Clavecimbel*. In Vol. 1 of his *Werken*, ed. M. Seiffert (Amsterdam: G. Alsbach, 1943). Three series of variations are found in Sweelinck, *Liedvariationen für Klavier* (Mainz: B. Schott's Söhne, 1935).

[6] See the article by Brian Priestman, "The Keyboard Works of John Loeillet" in the *Music Review* (Vol. 16, No. 2, 1955).

[7] The complete keyboard works of Loeillet, published in Belgium, are unfortunately out of print. They may perhaps be found in various music libraries. Isolated pieces and suites are available in several collections of old music: *Alte Meister* (Breitkopf & Härtel), III, and *Clavicembalisti Belgi* (Ricordi).

ence came from the French clavecinists—François Couperin, Jean-Philippe Rameau, Jean François Dandrieu, François Dagincourt, and Louis Claude Daquin—during the Regency and the early years of the reign of Louis XV. In addition, there was a period from about 1720 to 1745 when contemporary Italian school practices penetrated into the Low Countries.

Joseph-Hector Fiocco

The Italian influence comes through in the music of **Joseph-Hector Fiocco** (1703–1741), a native of Brussels. His harpsichord music under the title *Opus I* appeared sometime between 1731 and 1737.[8] This collection consists of two suites modeled after the *ordres* of François Couperin; each suite contains a series of twelve dances or characteristic pieces designed to exhibit as much variety as possible. The first suite displays features of both the French and the Italian schools. Certain basic Italian elements are discernible: a hesitation in the use of broken chords, a tendency toward homophonic texture, and an attempt at a lyric melodic line. Judging from the individual titles of the last portion—*Adagio, Allegro, Andante,* and *Vivace*—this first suite is like the Italian sonata rather than the typically French series of miniature tone pictures. The latter, however, are used very effectively in the second suite, written in the French manner. The fine workmanship in these two suites recommends the Belgian Joseph-Hector Fiocco for the *petit maître* class beside France's Dandrieu and Dagincourt. Fiocco's music is graceful and picturesque, the melodies refined and delicate. At the same time, it must be admitted that he occasionally pushes ingenuity to the extreme in his search for something different.

Dieudonné Raick

The effort to create an international style is also apparent in the music of **Dieudonné Raick** (1702–1764). An ordained canon, Raick served as organist at Antwerp, Louvain, and Ghent. His several suites and sonatas for harpsichord[9] reveal qualities taken from French, Italian, and German models, yet he manages to create quite an attractive style. Raick must have been especially well acquainted with French and Italian repertoires, for his music is basically Latin inspired. There is fine sensitivity in the well-balanced phrases and the fluid melodic line. In striving for originality, he produces fresh new details free from conventional formulas. Latin verve

[8] Joseph-Hector Fiocco, *Werken voor Clavecimbel.* In *Monumenta Musicae Belgicae* (Berchem-Antwerpen: "De Ring," 1936). An *Allegro* from the first suite is published by Edition Heuwekemeijer.
[9] The keyboard works of Raick are published by "De Ring" in Belgium. This volume was out of print in 1964. An *Allemande* may be found in *Clavicembalisti Belgi* (Ricordi).

overwhelms the more lively dances—gavotte, minuet, gigue—with sustained flexibility and rhythmic sweep.

Josse Boutmy

Josse Boutmy (1697–1779), who was highly regarded by his Belgian contemporaries, is almost unknown beyond his own country. He was born in Ghent but spent the latter decades of his life in Brussels as first organist at the Royal Chapel. Between 1738 and about 1750, Boutmy composed three harpsichord collections.[10] Here again, as with Dieudonné Raick, Italian and French stylistic elements mingle harmoniously. Boutmy's tendency toward rich harmonic color and decorative ornamentation brings to mind Jean-Philippe Rameau. The quality of Boutmy's clavecin collections is uneven. Some pieces are short-winded and artificial in their developmental devices; nevertheless the over-all effect is still good. There are moments of solemnity and even grandeur in the *Overtures* prefacing some of the suites. Boutmy can be humorous and gay—traits disclosed in the delightful Bach-like *Allegro* from the fifth suite in Book III (Ex. 2). His talent for musical description is manifested in the *Bruit de guerre* (Din of War) that opens the second suite in Book I. Basically his music is sturdy and given to realism; and his craftsmanship—second only to that of Jean-Baptiste Loeillet among the Netherlands composers—exhibits a superb sense of style.

Ex. 2. J. Boutmy: *Suite No. 5: Allegro*

---

[10] Josse Boutmy, *Werken Voor Klavicimbel.* In *Monumenta Musicae Belgicae* (Antwerpen: "De Ring," 1943).

Charles-Joseph van Helmont

The modern edition of several works by **Charles-Joseph van Helmont** (1715–1790)[11] shows a French influence tempered by unavoidable provincialisms. Van Helmont, choirmaster at the collegiate church in Brussels, seems to have had small knowledge of foreign music apart from the works of François Couperin. Couperin's influence is unmistakable in such miniatures as *La Françoise* and *La Sauteuse*, although lack of refinement in details precludes any comparison between the workmanship in these miniatures and that of their French counterparts. Nonetheless, a quaint personal accent, an elegance born of maturity, distinguishes van Helmont's music.

HOLLAND

While Belgium produced several keyboard composers during the eighteenth century, Holland had only one prominent harpsichord composer: **Gerhardus Havingha** (1696–1753). He was born in Groningen and spent most of his life as organist at the reformed church (Grote Kerk) in Alkmaar. Havingha's single surviving published work is a collection of eight suites[12] engraved in 1725 in Amsterdam. At that time this music was subject to much discussion. Some critics thought the suites too personal in style, too modern. Today these same suites may be appreciated for just these qualities. Havingha was indeed an original musician and his ideas of ornamentation are unique. For example, here is one ornament he uses preceded by the original sign (Ex. 3).

Ex. 3. G. Havingha: *Example from Table of Ornaments*

Havingha's choice of tonalities is also curious. One suite is written in the key of *b-flat* minor and another suite in *A-sharp* major. Each suite begins with an *Overture* made up of several sections in contrasting textures. The traditional allemande, courante, and sarabande are always present; the gigue is often missing. Other types of short pieces—marches,

---

[11] The modern edition of van Helmont's keyboard music, published in Antwerp by "De Ring" was out of print in 1964.

[12] Gerhardus Havingha, *Werken Voor Clavicimbel.* In *Monumenta Musicae Belgicae* (Berchem-Antwerpen: "De Ring," 1951).

minuets, airs, fantasias, entrées (similar to a two-part invention)—are prominent in the collection. It has been suggested that Havingha was influenced to some extent by the *Lessons for Harpsichord,* which George Handel published in 1720. This is plausible; however the basic inspiration still came from the composer himself. In spite of an unorthodox approach, the music is worthwhile and places Havingha among the noteworthy Flemish keyboard composers.

In addition to the fine compositions in Havingha's repertoire, there are in existence other attractive keyboard pieces written by minor Dutch composers. An entry dated 1686 in the registers of Leyden University concerns a *Musicus Academiae* named Rittmeister **Henricus Albicastro.** The gentleman referred to is probably Henrico del Biswang, also known as Hainz Weissenburg. (Latinization of names was in vogue at that time.) Albicastro was born a Swiss, took part in the war of Spanish Succession, and finally settled in Holland. His keyboard works include canzonas, canons, fantasias, and toccatas. A *Suite in G Minor*[13] shows Italian influence. Its opening *Allegro molto* is interesting because of the repeated phrase endings, indicating an echo effect on the harpsichord. The following *Bourrée* and *Minuetto* are effective examples of two-part writing. The concluding *Giga,* although it has some awkward voice leading, still offers artful imitative writing.

Little is known about **Rynoldus Popma van Oevering.** His compositions date from the first half of the eighteenth century, when he served as organist at several churches in Leeuwarden. His only known keyboard work, *Opus I,* is titled *VI Suittes voor't Clavier* and is dedicated to the Princess Maria Louisa, wife of William IV of the house of Orange. Oevering's *Suite No. 4 in C Major*[14] is classic in its approach, consisting of a *Capriccio, Allemande, Corrente* (in French style), *Sarabande, Gavotta, Minuetto,* and *Giga.* The entire suite shows two-part writing reduced to its barest essentials without becoming stereotyped.

Elias Brönnemuller, a music master in Amsterdam, was not Dutch by birth. He lived first in Hamburg, then in 1709 established himself in the Low Countries. Very little is known about his music. Selections from a *Suite I*[15] include a somewhat commonplace *Toccatina* followed by a piece called *Fuga* that is really not a fugue but two short sections in contrasting tempos, each with a theme treated in imitation.

Christian Friedrich Ruppe was born in 1752 or 1753 in Salzungen (Meiningen). In 1787 he was at Leyden University as *Musicus,* and around 1790 he secured the organist post at the Lutheran Church in Leyden.

---

[13] *Le Più Belle Pagine dei Clavicembalisti Olandesi* (Milano: Ricordi, 1960).
[14] *Ibid.* The complete suites are published by Breitkopf & Härtel.
[15] *Ibid.*

Most of his keyboard music is for harpsichord or piano in company with other instruments: *sonatas, divertissements, overtures,* and *sonatinas.* His *Rondo in D*[16] is a charming piece probably written for the piano. It shows the influence of the Classic school and compares favorably with similar works by Joseph Haydn.

Harpsichord music from Holland and Belgium—more than that of any other European country—has been ignored by both publishers and performers until recently. Since 1950 a considerable amount of music has appeared in modern editions. Though limited, the repertoire of the Netherlands should be recognized along with the French, Italian, and German repertoires. Some of it is certainly mediocre, but a great deal of it is good and should be brought to the attention of students interested in keyboard music.

BIBLIOGRAPHY

Borren, Charles van den. *Geschiedenis van de Musiek in de Nederlanden.* Amsterdam: Wereldbibliotheek, 1949. 2 Vols.

Closson, E. and Ch. van den Borren, eds. *La Musique en Belgique du Moyen Age à Nos Jours.* Bruxelles: La Renaissance du Livre, 1950.

Curtis, Alan. *Sweelinck's Keyboard Works: English Elements in Dutch Music of the 'Gouden Eeuw.'* Dissertation. University of Illinois, 1963.

Priestman, Brian. "The Keyboard Works of John Loeillet." *Music Review,* Vol. 16, No. 2, 1955.

Tusler, Robert L. *The Organ Music of Jan Pieterszoon Sweelinck.* Bilthoven: A. B. Creyghton, 1958. 2 Vols.

[16] *Ibid.*

8

KEYBOARD MUSIC
IN SPAIN AND PORTUGAL
IN THE EIGHTEENTH CENTURY

SPAIN

Spanish keyboard music offers very little to compare with the originality of the English virginal school, the elegance of the French clavecin
school, or the sparkling vitality of the Italian cembalo school. In eighteenth-century Spain, composing for the harpsichord was apparently only
a diversion for musicians who worked seriously in other fields of music.
Moreover, the Spanish court, unlike French royalty, treated its native
musicians indifferently, sometimes rewarding them, sometimes ignoring
them. As a result, Spanish keyboard music—particularly harpsichord music
—is not based upon a steadily progressive tradition.

There is no evidence that any harpsichord music was printed in Spain
during the first part of the eighteenth century. The secular keyboard repertoire for that period has been preserved in a manuscript of music for
harpsichord now in the *Biblioteca Nacional de Madrid*. The manuscript
collection is titled *Libro de música de clavicímbalo del S^r. D^n. Francisco
de Tejada 1721* (Book of Harpsichord Music ... 1721).[1] It was discovered
in Seville in 1872, and most of the compositions are anonymous.

Among the eighty-eight pieces in the Tejada collection are forty-five
exceedingly simple minuets. In fact, these minuets suggest the thought
that they must have been intended for dancing. Many appear to have a
theatrical or popular origin, bearing such titles as *Dueña hermosa* (Beautiful Mistress), *Triste memoria* (Sad Recollection), *Triumfe el amor* (Love
Triumphs).

Other dance forms in this manuscript—*alemanda, pas pie* (*passepied*),
gallardus (*galliard*)—are also uncomplicated in their construction, especially when compared with music written by composers in other countries
at that same time: Louis Couperin and Jean-Henry d'Anglebert in France,

---

[1] Biblioteca Nacional de Madrid, *Libro de música de clavicímbalo del S^r. D^n. Francisco
de Tejada 1721*. M.815 (= G. = 6^a · = 16). Procedencia: Fondo Barbieri.

for instance; Johann Kuhnau in Germany; and Bernardo Pasquini in Italy. The Spanish music has almost no ornamentation and involves only the plainest harmonies. However, some pieces in the collection are more serious in intent than the minuets. One of these, a theme entitled *Faborita,* has three variations. In addition, there are several transcriptions of works by Coreli (*sic.* Corelli) and two *Tonadillas de Navidad,* which may be keyboard arrangements of popular Spanish Christmas songs of that era.

Another manuscript in the *Biblioteca Nacional de Madrid* is dated more than forty years after the Tejada collection. Its title page reads *Joan Roig y Posas, Comercian en Barcelona 1764.*[2] Again, the greater part is anonymous, but during the forty-year span the style of writing has changed considerably. This music reveals a Pre-Classic influence in the contour and expressiveness of melodic line and the obvious attempts at development sections, although each separate work is so brief as to appear fragmentary.

Four pieces in the 1764 manuscript are collectively titled *Sonatas para Clave y Organo, muy faciles y de buen gusto* (Sonatas for Keyboard and Organ, very easy and in good taste). They are short and easy and indeed in good taste. The following example (Ex. 1) from a *Sonata in A Minor* shows the contours of Classic style in an early formative stage.

Ex. 1. Anonymous: *Sonata in A Minor*

Halfway through the manuscript appears this title: *Síguese 12 Minuetes para Clave y Piano Fuerte, compuestos por D. Joaquín Montero* (Following are 12 Minuets for Keyboard and Piano, Composed by D. Joaquín Montero). Joaquín Montero was organist at the parochial church of San Pedro el Real in Seville during the second half of the eighteenth century. There are only ten minuets in this group—not twelve as the title states—and they are true miniatures. They do not have a contrasting trio, and their average length is only sixteen measures. Concise as they are, these minuets have an appealing charm.

The Spanish harpsichord school, if such it may be called, received its impetus from three sources: first, the influence of Domenico Scarlatti—the

---

[2] Biblioteca Nacional de Madrid, *Joan Roig y Posas Comercian en Barcelona 1764.* M. 2810. Procedencia: Fondo Barbieri.

Italian composer who spent virtually his entire career in Spain; second, the technical devices of the guitar. Needless to say, the third is that ardent nationalism that pervades almost all Spanish secular music.

Scarlatti's influence was most profound. From 1721, the Neapolitan composer had been in Portugal as music teacher to the royal princesses. When one of them, María Bárbara de Braganza, went to Madrid to marry the future Ferdinand VI, Scarlatti accompanied her. There has been much speculation about where the composer spent his last years, but recent investigation seems to indicate that he remained in Spain until his death. He brought to the Iberian peninsula techniques and formulas for a pure harpsichord style, and it was he who provided the framework of the one-movement, bisectional sonata. For inspiration while in Spain, Scarlatti drew extensively upon the folk songs and dances, the urban popular music, and all the exuberant Spanish rhythms surrounding him during those his most productive years.

Guitar techniques are prominent in Spanish harpsichord and piano works of the eighteenth and nineteenth centuries: repeated bass figures, broken or arpeggiated figures, short melodic motives and phrases, and incessant repetitions of one note. The folkloric or nationalistic element in these same compositions comes out clearly in the use of dance idioms, such as the *zapateado* and *polo*.

Antonio Soler

Padre Antonio Soler (1729–1783) was the most distinguished eighteenth-century Spanish composer, especially in keyboard music. It is now certain that he was a pupil of Scarlatti. Soler composed scores of harpsichord sonatas[3] whose form adheres rather consistently to the Scarlattian mold: a one-movement, two-sectional structure, sometimes monothematic and sometimes having secondary motives. The music modulates in the first section and returns to the original tonality in the second, with some fragmentary development also in the second section. In the Soler sonatas one finds the same technical devices as those employed by Scarlatti—for example, frequent use of repeated notes. Compare Soler's use of repeated notes with that of Scarlatti (Ex. 2).

This device, of course, originated with the guitar. It is still heard today in *flamenco* music. And for another comparison, Soler, like Scarlatti, occa-

[3] Padre Antonio Soler, *Sonatas,* ed. Padre Samuel Rubio (Madrid: Union Musical Española, 1957–1962). Six volumes containing ninety-nine sonatas have been published to date. In the musical examples, the letter R is used to identify the sonata in Padre Rubio's edition. Frederick Marvin has also edited several volumes of Soler sonatas for Mills Music, Inc. Excerpts from the Soler *Sonatas* reprinted by permission of Union Musical Española, Editores, Madrid, Spain.

Ex. 2. Scarlatti: *Sonata in D Major, L. 465* (Kirkp. 96)

Soler: *Sonata in D Major, R. 84*

sionally devotes the major portion of a work to the exploitation of one dominant procedure, such as crossing of hands (Ex. 3).

Ex. 3. Scarlatti: *Sonata in F-sharp Minor, L. 481* (Kirkp. 35)

Soler: *Sonata in D-flat Major, R. 88*

Other Scarlatti devices—trills, passages in thirds, large skips in the bass, and repeated phrases—are amply displayed in the music of Padre Soler.

This comparison between the two composers is not drawn to imply that Soler servilely followed the idioms and stylistic tendencies of Scarlatti. As Joaquín Nin so aptly has stated: "When the Padre Soler appropriated certain modes, certain turns, certain popular Spanish expressions which Scarlatti had dignified and consecrated with that marvelous skill which the whole world admires today, Soler, I repeat, far from committing the sin of imitation, merely reclaimed his own property and reintroduced into his vocabulary the Spanish idioms borrowed by the Neapolitan."[4]

Soler's use of a four-note embellishment around a principal melody note is characteristic of many Spanish folk melodies (Ex. 4).

Ex. 4. Soler: *Sonata in D Major, R. 86*

His use of the arpeggiated bass figure recalls the technique indigenous to the guitar, Spain's beloved instrument (Ex. 5).

Ex. 5. Soler: *Sonata in D Major, R. 86*

The lilting rhythms in many of the Soler compositions—in 3/8, 6/8, and 12/8 meter—also reveal his Spanish heritage.

Other Spanish Composers

When Padre Soler died in 1783, the Classic movement in music was growing rapidly throughout most of Europe. The sonata, with either three or four movements, was all-prevailing. It would seem logical to find this same evolution in Spain, but not at all! The Spanish composers—most of them priests and most of them independent, nationalistic Catalonians as well—kept on writing their miniature one-movement, bisectional sonatas until about the middle of the nineteenth century.

One notable exception is **Manuel Blasco de Nebra** (*ca.* 1750–1784).

[4] Joaquín Nin, "The Bi-Centenary of Antonio Soler," *The Chesterian* (Jan.–Feb., 1930).

While he was organist at Seville Cathedral, Señor Blasco published in Madrid a set of six keyboard sonatas of high musical value.[5] Each sonata has two movements—an adagio followed by an allegro or presto. These are definitely works of Classic breadth, influenced by the music of Joseph Haydn and Luigi Boccherini. Each movement in the Nebra sonatas usually has a clear statement of two themes, a brief development section, and recapitulation of the themes. The allegro and presto movements are the most characteristic, containing a genuine Spanish flavor (Ex. 6).

Ex. 6. Blasco de Nebra: *Sonata I: Allegro*

Blasco de Nebra: *Sonata V: Presto*

From the late eighteenth century into the early nineteenth century, Spanish composers apparently found less inspiration in Scarlatti and turned instead to Haydn or Boccherini. Still, more than a trace of Scarlatti remains in the preference for the one-movement sonata.

Félix Máximo López was born in Madrid about 1742. The *Biblioteca Nacional de Madrid* has a manuscript containing twenty of his compositions.[6] Most of these are sonatas reminiscent of the Scarlatti period, but the naïve simplicity of some and the lilting Spanish rhythm of others make

[5] Manuel Blasco de Nebra, *Seis Sonatas para Clave y Fuerte Piano Compuestas por D. Manuel Blasco de Nebra, Organista de la S. Yglesia Cathedral de Sevilla. Obra Primera.* Original edition in Library of Congress, Washington, D.C. (M23.B6 Op.1 Caso). Modern reprint of *Presto* to Sonata V in Davison and Apel, *Historical Anthology of Music* (Cambridge: Harvard University Press, 1950), II. *Sonata I* is reprinted in Wm. S. Newman, *Thirteen Keyboard Sonatas of the 18th and 19th Centuries* (Chapel Hill: University of North Carolina Press, 1947).

[6] Biblioteca Nacional de Madrid, *Música de Clave de Dⁿ. Félix Máximo López, Organista D.L.R.C.D.S.M.C.* M.1234 (= G. = 5ᵃ · = 17). Procedencia: Fondo Barbieri.

them interesting, worthwhile contributions to Spanish keyboard literature (Ex. 7).

Ex. 7. Máximo López: *Pieza de Clave* (Keyboard Piece)

Other composers active into the nineteenth century are **Padre Rafael Anglés** (*ca.* 1731–1816), **Padre Felipe Rodríguez** (1759–1814), **Mateo Albéniz** (*ca.* 1760–1831), and **Padre José Gallés** (1761–1836).[7] The majority of Anglés' works, which have been reprinted by Joaquín Nin, take Haydn as a starting point, albeit an Italianized Haydn. And the Haydn influence shows up again in the music of Rodríguez, music also possessing a tinge of romanticism. Albéniz makes use of forms like the *zapateado*, giving a Spanish character to his music. A manuscript collection of sonatas by Gallés is now in Barcelona. Although still adhering to the one-movement form, these sonatas indicate that Gallés had a good training as well as a refined taste for keyboard music.

This, then, is a brief account of Spanish keyboard music written during the period, approximately, from 1720 until 1820. With the exception of Padre Antonio Soler, it is doubtful whether these various Spanish composers took their keyboard works seriously. Most of them spent their lives in the service of the Church, writing sacred choral music and organ music, and it is easy to imagine that their keyboard compositions might have been composed for diversion. If this is true, they admirably fulfilled their purpose.

PORTUGAL

Very little is known about keyboard music in Portugal during the seventeenth and eighteenth centuries. History merely records that the royal court heard and sponsored many concerts, often importing foreign musicians, especially Italians, who influenced the native composers.

[7] The most representative collections of Spanish keyboard music are those edited by Joaquín Nin: *Seize Sonates Anciennes d'Auteurs Espagnols* (Paris: Max Eschig, 1925) and *Dix-sept Sonates et Pièces Anciennes d'Auteurs Espagnols* (Paris: Max Eschig, 1929). Ricordi publishes a small volume of Spanish keyboard music as does Summy-Birchard.

The keyboard music turned out during the seventeenth century was limited mainly to organ works and there were many composers contributing to the repertoire. The most noteworthy in the group was a priest, **Manuel Rodrigues Coelho,** born in 1583 in Elvas near the Spanish border. He was church organist in his hometown before becoming organist at Lisbon Cathedral in 1603, and he went on from there to the Royal Chapel. Coelho wrote the earliest known published work of Portuguese instrumental music, the *Flores de Musica* (Musical Flowers). This is a collection of *tentos* (ricercari or preludes) for organ, clavichord, or harp; it was printed by Craesbeeck in Lisbon in 1620. Such an admirable collection places Coelho among the notable group of predecessors to Bach, beside such men as Frescobaldi in Italy, Sweelinck in Holland, and Scheidt in Germany.[8]

In the eighteenth century, Portugal produced a fine harpsichord composer, **José Antonio Carlos de Seixas** (1704–1742), who was born in Coimbra. At an early age he went to Lisbon, where he became a friend and pupil of Domenico Scarlatti. Although his works took the same form as Scarlatti's, Seixas used the terms *toccata* and *sonata* interchangeably. Naturally, these toccatas, or sonatas, show a Scarlatti influence, but in addition they suggest that Seixas was also impressed by contemporary Italian and Spanish composers. Nonetheless, his music has its own particular and personal characteristics. Some of the pieces are unusual in that they recall elements of the suite as it developed in France and Germany; in such cases the toccatas are followed by minuets, gigues, etc.

The toccatas usually have one or two themes, which are developed and slightly expanded. Repetition of motives tends to create a certain monotony, but harmonically the toccatas are conspicuous for Seixas uses some harmonic procedures evidently unknown to Scarlatti, or at least not used by him.

Another eighteenth-century keyboard composer, **Joao de Sousa Carvalho** (*d.* 1798), is sometimes called the Portuguese Mozart because of his operatic style. Much of his keyboard music reveals that it was written during the period of transition from harpsichord to piano. His works, also called *toccatas,* are brilliantly conceived. He makes extensive use of chordal accompaniment in the left hand, as might be expected in this transition period. Carvalho studied in Italy for several years, and doubtlessly all the clavier music he heard there influenced his own compositions.

Frei Jacinto was contemporary with Seixas, but little is known about

[8] Two compositions of Coelho are found in *Cravistas Portuguezes,* ed. M. S. Kastner (Mainz: Schott, 1935), 2 vols. See also *Flores de Musica,* ed. Kastner (Kassel: Bärenreiter Verlag, 1959, 1961), 2 vols.

his life and dates. The only available works by this composer are two sonatas published by S. Kastner.[9]

BIBLIOGRAPHY

Chase, Gilbert. *The Music of Spain,* second revised edition. New York: Dover Publications, 1959.

Nin, Joaquín. "The Bi-Centenary of Antonio Soler." *The Chesterian,* Jan.–Feb., 1930.

Salazar, Adolfo. *La Música de España.* Buenos Aires: Espasa-Calpe Argentina, S. A., 1953.

Subirá, José. *Historia de la Música Española e Hispanoamericana.* Barcelona: Salvat Editores, S. A., 1953.

[9] *Cravistas Portuguezes, op. cit.*

9

KEYBOARD MUSIC
IN GERMANY AND AUSTRIA
IN THE SEVENTEENTH
AND EIGHTEENTH CENTURIES

Throughout the sixteenth and early seventeenth centuries, German and Austrian composers had neither the inspiration nor the inclination to write for any keyboard instrument except the organ. Religious conflicts resulting from the Reformation—both Protestant and Catholic—and the ultimate rise of two distinct theologies and philosophies created an atmosphere unsympathetic to the mood of gay sonatas and dances that might enhance a stringed keyboard repertoire. As a result, most composers devoted their talents and efforts to writing music suitable for the divine services.

Of course, there were exceptions. The illustrious **Samuel Scheidt** (1587–1654) occasionally wrote secular music. Born in Halle in northern Germany, he had studied with the cosmopolitan Dutch composer Jan Sweelinck. This association enabled Scheidt to introduce into his own country the essence of Sweelinck's basic style—a fusion of the warm-textured, suavely melodic language from Italy with the delightful patterned-variation technique taken from the English virginal composers. Several sets of variations are included in Scheidt's superb collection entitled *Tabulatura Nova* or *New Tablature* (1624).[1] For example, there are variations on the Netherlands song *Ei, du feiner Reiter* (Ho, Thou Splendid Rider); twenty variations on a classic tune called *Bergamasca*, featuring much note repetition and rhythmic changes; and seven effective variations on a French song *Est-ce Mars?* previously set in a similar manner by Sweelinck. Scheidt's acquaintance with the English school is evident in his nine variations on a galliard by John Dowland. Among the most difficult of the secular variation sets in this collection is one that subjects the folk song *Wehe, Windgen, Wehe* (Blow, Wind, Blow) to twelve masterful variations displaying great imagination and skill.

---

[1] Samuel Scheidt, *Ausgewählte Werke für Orgel und Klavier* (New York: Peters Edition). This collection includes the dance variations and variations on secular songs.

In the mid-seventeenth century, the German and Austrian composers began to look beyond the organ keyboard for additional media of expression. They had two other keyboard instruments at hand, since both the clavichord and the harpsichord were popular in Germany, but the titles in the resultant eighteenth-century repertoire rarely indicate which instrument is to be used. Some composers, such as Christian Gottlob Neefe and Johann Nikolaus Forkel, clearly specify the use of the clavichord. Daniel Gottlieb Türk and Johann Wilhelm Hässler use the indication *Bebung*, or tremolo, referring to the clavichord.

Careful examination of the individual compositions often discloses a clue as to which instrument (harpsichord or clavichord) is intended. Certain indications such as *cantabile* or *grazioso*—terms suggesting the mood or spirit of a piece—are typically indicative of clavichord literature. And long note values may indicate *Bebung*. On the other hand, contrasting phrases suggest typical harpsichord music, particularly for a harpsichord with two keyboards. The music designed for a two-keyboard harpsichord has longer phrases and themes and frequently less modulation. Rapid passages, arpeggiated chords, wide leaps, crossing of hands, repeated notes—any or all of these suggest harpsichord performance. However, since the purpose of this chapter is to provide a general survey, the term harpsichord is used even though performance on a clavichord might be just as feasible.

JOHANN JACOB FROBERGER

The harpsichord suite in Germany achieved its classic form around 1650 under the guidance of **Johann Jacob Froberger** (1616–1667), a pupil of Girolamo Frescobaldi. Froberger, born in Stuttgart, acquired a fine reputation during his lifetime as both clavierist and composer. As court organist in Vienna for many years, he had ample opportunity to assimilate the musical culture of that city. An international traveler, he visited Rome —where he studied with Frescobaldi—and Paris, Brussels, and London. Consequently, he was able to design music having great variety. Seen in retrospect, Froberger's works comprise a preamble to the superb German keyboard music of the eighteenth century. His music is robust, profoundly expressive, and lyric, yet withal harmonically poor.

Froberger was famous as both composer and performer of organ and harpsichord music. His organ compositions include *toccatas, fantasies, ricercari, canzone,* and *capriccios*. In these he follows the general precepts of his master Frescobaldi. Specifically, the fugal episodes of his toccatas can be traced to Claudio Merulo; the influence of the Gabrielis is seen in his thematic elaborations.

In his harpsichord compositions, Froberger blended organ technique with some variation patterns in the manner of Sweelinck and the early English virginal school. This pioneer of German harpsichord music established the framework of the suite in Germany. His mature keyboard suites use the four standard dance types: allemande, courante, sarabande, and gigue (see Chapter 3).

One of Johann Froberger's best-known keyboard works is his suite or partita based on the theme *Auff die Mayerin*.[2] The simple theme is followed by seven variations using different dance forms (Ex. 1). The second variation is a gigue; the fifth is called *Partita cromatica* and is based on alternating ascending and descending chromatic progressions; the sixth variation is a courante; and the last one is a sarabande. Typical of Froberger's music, the entire suite is without ornaments. Obviously the performer is to supply them.

Froberger was one of the first German composers to attempt expressive music. He portrays personal sentiments in such works as the *Lamento sur la mort douloureuse de Ferdinand VI Roi des Romains* (Lament on the Grievous Death of Ferdinand VI, King of the Romans) and the *Allemande faite en passant le Rhin dans une barque en péril* (Allemande Made while Crossing the Rhine in a Boat in Distress). The first movement to his *Suite in A Minor* is entitled *Plainte faite à Londres pour passer la mélancholie, laquelle se joue lentement avec discretion* (Dirge made in London to while away melancholy, which is played slowly with discretion). This movement is actually a slow allemande, if played according to Froberger's suggestion.

For the most part, late-seventeenth-century German and Austrian composers drew upon two foreign sources in formulating their own keyboard style: Italy and the Low Countries. The Italians had the weightiest impact on this German-Austrian group, of which the Austrians and Bavarians produced more than did the composers in northern Germany.

COURT COMPOSERS OF AUSTRIA

Alessandro Poglietti (*d.* 1683) was organist at the Imperial Court Chapel in Vienna from 1661 until his death at the hands of the Turks during the siege of Vienna. Contemporary accounts describe him as a prominent court figure. Most Poglietti compositions are for organ or harpsichord. He was one of the first Austrian composers to write purely descrip-

---

[2] *Old Masters of the 16th, 17th and 18th Centuries*, ed. Niemann (New York: Kalmus). The complete harpsichord works of Froberger may be found in Volumes 8, 13, and 21 of the *Denkmäler der Tonkunst in Österreich*.

Ex. 1. J. J. Froberger: *Auff die Mayerin.* Examples of variation technique

Partita Cromatica

Courante

tive music, and his most elaborate composition from this point of view is a gargantuan suite entitled *Rossignolo*.[3]

Rossignolo (Nightingale) includes the following pieces in order of appearance: *Toccata; Canzona; Allemande* with two variations; *Courante* with one variation; *Sarabande* with one variation; *Gigue* with one variation; then an *Aria allemagna con alcuni Variazioni sopra l'Età della Maestà Vostra* (German Aria with Several Variations on the Birthday of the Empress Eleanor Magdalena Theresa); *Ricercar per lo Rossignolo; Capriccio per lo Rossignolo sopra il Ricercar;* and *Aria bizzara del Rossignolo.* The most unusual item in the suite is the set of variations to the German Aria. A work

[3] *Denkmäler der Tonkunst in Österreich* (Graz: Akademische Druck- U. Verlagsanstalt), Vol. 27. This volume contains works by Poglietti, F. T. Richter, and G. Reutter.

of fantasy, these variations burst with imitations: Bohemian Bagpipe (*Bömisch. Dudlsackh.*), a Dutch flute (*Hollandisch: Flagolett*), Bavarian chalumeau (*Bayrische Schalmay*), Hungarian violins, scenes from Poland and France, imitations of hens, sounds of bells, scenes of war. Certainly Poglietti demanded and expected too much from the harpsichord; however, some of these musical descriptions are quite clever, and the variations as a whole are good examples of early keyboard music in Austria.

Sopra la Ribellione di Ungheria (The Hungarian Rebellion) is another descriptive suite by Poglietti, but less ambitious than *Rossignolo* and more orthodox in format. A short *Toccatina* is followed by the standard dances, each of which is supplied with a descriptive title: *Allemande "La Prisonnie"* (The Prison), *Courante "Le Proces"* (The Trial), *Sarabande "La Sentence,"* and *Gigue "La Lige"* (The prisoner's hands and feet are tied). After the dances, Poglietti adds the final tragicomic touch with a section marked *"La Decapitation"* (The Beheading) to be played *avec discretion* (with discretion)! Following that is a *Passacaglia* and a concluding eight measures called *"Les Kloches"* (The Bells).

After Poglietti's untimely death, the organist post at the Viennese court was filled by **Ferdinand Tobias Richter** (1649–1711), who enjoyed a fine reputation as both organist and composer. His harpsichord suites display none of the Poglietti penchant for the descriptive, imitative keyboard piece, nor do they adhere to the standard sequence of dances established by Froberger. Instead, the contents of three Richter suites[4] indicate that his personal preference stood somewhere between these two categories.

Toccatina   Capriccio   Allemande   Courante   Minuet
Toccatina   Allemande   Bourrée   Sarabande   Minuet   Gigue
Toccatina   Adagio   Allemande   Courante   Passacaglia

Georg Reutter (1656–1738) succeeded Richter as court organist in Vienna in 1700; like Richter, he had the reputation of being a good composer, though most of his compositions seem to be oriented toward the organ rather than the harpsichord. Reutter's keyboard repertoire includes *capriccios, fugues, canzonas,* and *ricercars,*[5] works which prove that he had a sound technique and a scholarly command of keyboard counterpoint.

Saxony-born **Johann Caspar Kerll** (1627–1693), a disciple of Giacomo Carissimi at Rome, was more respectful of Italian tradition than Poglietti. It is quite possible that Kerll studied with Frescobaldi about the same time as did Froberger, and he betrays his debt to Frescobaldi in his capriccios, toccatas, and canzonas. Kerll's personal style is at times unusual in that he resolves discords in new, unexpected ways. In spite of his devotion to Fres-

---

[4] *Ibid.*   [5] *Ibid.*

cobaldi, he took into consideration the Viennese fondness for descriptive music when he composed *Battaglias* (Battle Scenes) and the capriccio *Der Kuckuck* (The Cuckoo).[6] Based on the familiar two-note figure also used by Bernardo Pasquini and Louis Claude Daquin, *Der Kuckuck*—because of the incessant repetition of this figure and poor harmonic construction—is somewhat dull. But Kerll must have liked the composition, for he wrote three different versions of it.

THE FRENCH INFLUENCE

Not all German and Austrian keyboard music produced during this period was influenced by Italian or Flemish-English models. There were at least two composers who looked to the French for inspiration. The first, **Georg Muffat** (1653–1704), was an Alsatian who had been organist at Strasbourg, Salzburg, and Passau. Muffat studied under both Lully and Pasquini, trying to merge their styles into a primarily French framework. In 1690 at Augsburg he published his famous organ collection *Apparatus musico-organisticus*, dedicated to Leopold I, emperor of the Holy Roman Empire. This work includes twelve *toccatas*, a *chaconne*, and a *passacaglia*.[7]

The second French-inspired composer was the celebrated organist **Johann Pachelbel** (1653–1706), who lived in Nürnberg. Written in true French tradition, his suites are arranged according to a logical plan; i.e., the first in *c* minor, the next in *C* major, then *d* minor, *D* major, etc.[8] However, these little keyboard collections are comparatively unimportant in relation to Pachelbel's organ works; it is the organ compositions that proclaim him an important predecessor of Johann Sebastian Bach.

DIETRICH BUXTEHUDE

Another composer who achieved his greatest success with organ works is the Danish-born **Dietrich Buxtehude** (1637–1707), who worked mostly in Germany. His harpsichord music in itself supplies little indication of his great ability in musical composition. Buxtehude's harpsichord collection contains nineteen suites and six sets of variations of uneven quality and substance.[9] These works very likely date from the 1680's or earlier. Despite their variable quality—some unevenness in the musical quality and com-

---

[6] *Old Masters, op. cit.*

[7] The twelve toccatas may be found in Volume 58 of the *Denkmäler der Tonkunst in Österreich.*

[8] Pachelbel, *Selected Keyboard Works* (New York: Peters Edition).

[9] Dietrich Buxtehude, *Klaver Vaerker* (Copenhagen: Wilhelm Hansen).

positional technique—these harpsichord pieces are characteristic of Buxtehude's general musical style: imaginative, vigorous, and expressive.

The themes of the variations are partly Buxtehude's own invention; otherwise, they are derived from other composers or from well-known folk songs. For example, *More Palatino* is a Latin students' song; *Rofilis* is taken from a ballet by Lully; and *La Capricciosa* appears in the last variation of J. S. Bach's *Goldberg Variations* as a folk song *Kraut und Rüben*. The connection with Bach goes even deeper, for Buxtehude's mature writings and his organ playing were greatly admired by Bach.

JOHANN CASPAR FERDINAND FISCHER

Considered one of the best keyboard performers of his day, **Johann Caspar Ferdinand Fischer** (*ca.* 1665–1746) is known to music-history students for his *Ariadne musica Neo-organoedum* (1715).[10] Consisting of twenty preludes and fugues in as many different keys, the *Ariadne* was intended as a guide to lead young organists through the maze of the then modern keys, both major and minor. As such, the work is an immediate forerunner to Bach's *Well-Tempered Clavier*. Fischer also composed two interesting harpsichord collections. The first, *Les Pièces de Clavecin,* was published at Schlakenwerth in 1696 and then republished in Augsburg in 1698 under a different title, *Musicalisches Blumenbüschlein* (Little Musical Flower Bushes). Although this collection has eight little suites for keyboard, each introduced by a prelude, they do not adhere to the order of dances established by Froberger. The fifth suite has only a *Prelude* and a set of variations, the eighth suite a *Prelude* and *Chaconne*. The *Prelude* to the second suite, with numerous repetitions of full chords, suggests that the suites were written with the clavichord in mind (Ex. 2).[11]

Ex. 2. Fischer: *Prelude* (*Musicalisches Blumenbüschlein*)

[10] J. C. F. Fischer, *Ausgewählte Klavierwerke* (London: Schott). Another publication is *Musikalisches Blumenbüschlein: eine Auswahl aus dem Klavierwerk,* ed. L. J. Beer (Magdeburg: Heinrichshofen's Verlag, 1943).

[11] *Old Masters, op. cit.*

A *Rondeau* from the same suite is typically French, particularly in its orna-mentation and cadential treatment.

Fischer's second collection, *Musikalischer Parnassus*, has no publication date. It has nine suites, each one named for a Muse, and here Fischer makes fewer concessions to French taste, especially in the ornamentation. The *Suite in A Minor*, titled *Melpomene*,[12] is dedicated to the Muse of tragedy. The movements still do not agree with the accepted order of the keyboard dance suite. A series of suspensions is the basic treatment given the *Praeludium*. The *Allemande* is somewhat like those in the *French Suites* of J. S. Bach, except that the voice leading and chord spacing are at times rather poor. A *Passepied* and *Rondeau* follow, then give way to a *Chaconne* with a typical descending bass pattern. A light-textured *Gigue* comes next, and the suite concludes with a *Bourrée* and two *Minuets*.

GEORG BÖHM

When Johann Sebastian Bach was in the choir at the *Michaeliskirche* in Luneberg, the organist of the *Johanniskirche* in that same city was **Georg Böhm** (1661–1733). Probably young Bach heard this man and knew his music. Böhm composed numerous vocal and organ pieces and eleven harp-sichord suites showing several influences.[13] In an excellent study of the life and works of J. S. Bach, Philipp Spitta analyzed several of Böhm's works in an attempt to show that Böhm was an early influence on Bach.[14]

In Germany, the keyboard suite reached its first high point with the music of Georg Böhm. He maintained excellent musical quality in his compositions, which may have played a role later on in the formation of certain masterworks by Bach. In addition, Böhm made use of all existing types of keyboard suite, thus illustrating the inherent versatility of this par-ticular form. Some of his suites appear to be inspired directly from French sources. For example, *Suite No. 2 in D Major* contains an *Ouverture* in the French manner followed by an *Air, Rigaudon, Rondo, Menuet*, and *Cha-conne*. The variation suite used by Frescobaldi and Froberger is also repre-sented in the Böhm collection: the *Courante, Sarabande*, and *Gigue* in his *Suite No. 3 in D Minor* are variants of the initial *Allemande*.

---

[12] *The Art of the Suite*, ed. Pessl (New York: E. B. Marks Music Corp.).

[13] Georg Böhm, *Sämtliche Werke, Klavier-und Orgelwerke* (Wiesbaden: Breitkopf & Härtel), I.

[14] Philipp Spitta, *Johann Sebastian Bach* (New York: Dover Publications, 1951), I, 210–217, 241.

JOHANN KUHNAU

Johann Kuhnau (1660–1722) was cantor of St. Thomas' Church in Leipzig just before Johann Sebastian Bach accepted that position. Kuhnau was one of the first composers in Germany to adapt the title and form of the church sonata to the harpsichord. "His musical skills went a good deal farther than those normally deemed sufficient for an organist and choir-master—even if one takes into consideration that the ability to compose was, in his time, a requirement essential to anyone holding a church position of some consequence. Among his literary works the most extensive was his satirical novel *Der musikalische Quacksalber* (1700), in which he criticized and ridiculed the musical scene of his day."[15]

Kuhnau's keyboard music—four sets of compositions—appeared between 1689 and 1700. The *Neue Clavier Übung* (New Keyboard Exercise)[16] is divided into two parts. The first part (1689) contains seven suites (*Parteien*) in as many major keys—*C-D-E-F-G-A-B♭*—and the second part (1692) presents seven suites divided among seven minor keys. These early works are inconsistent in quality and craftsmanship. A frequent lack of tonal direction and unimaginative chord sequences are defects that are only partially compensated for by Kuhnau's competent keyboard style.

The *Clavier Übung* was followed by the *Frische Clavier-Früchte* (New Keyboard Harvest, 1696),[17] a set of seven church sonatas, each containing a series of four or five movements in contrasting textures. Here the pieces lose some of the suite characteristics and begin to approach the form that eventually became the Classic sonata. A typical sonata from this collection has four movements broken up by short adagios. A good sense of rhythm and solid counterpoint is present in the preludes. By contrast, the dance movements seem rather pallid.

The most interesting of all Kuhnau's keyboard works is the set of six *Biblischer Historien* (Biblical Sonatas, 1700),[18] which he designated for organ, harpsichord, and other similar instruments. These so-called sonatas are programmatic works built upon scenes drawn from the Old Testament: *The Fight between David and Goliath; Saul Cured through Music by David; Jacob's Wedding; The Mortally Ill and Then Restored Hezekiah; The 'Saviour of Israel/Gideon; Jacob's Death and Burial.* These sonatas were tremendously successful, a fact due as much to the purported program or events they described as to their musical value. To express his mental images, Kuhnau uses manifold forms ranging from various dance forms to

---

[15] Johann Kuhnau, *Six Biblical Sonatas for Keyboard*, ed. Kurt Stone (New York: Broude Brothers), Introduction, iv.

[16] Johann Kuhnau, *Klavierwerke*, in *Denkmäler Deutscher Tonkunst* (Wiesbaden: Breitkopf & Härtel), Vol. 4.

[17] *Ibid.*   [18] *Ibid.*

the chorale-prelude. And to help his listeners follow the exact meaning of the sonatas, Kuhnau prefaces each one with a rather lengthy dissertation about the textual content of the story.

The *Biblical Sonatas* are no longer frequently performed, although *The Fight between David and Goliath* is still found in several collections of old music. The naïvely dramatic work begins with a *Prelude*—in pompous dotted rhythms—proclaiming the bravado of Goliath. A prayer of the Israelites follows, a chorale-prelude setting of the sixteenth-century German hymn melody *Aus tiefer Noth* (In My Despair). David gains courage and puts his confidence in God in the third movement, a dance in triple meter. Then comes the battle: the stone is hurled to the flourish of a rapid scale passage, and the giant falls to the ground with a series of short descending chromatic figures. The Philistines flee to an accompaniment of rapid thirds and sixths. The Israelites express their happiness and the ladies give a concert for David amid great jubilation. This sonata, as well as the others (not all equally effective) is now available in attractive reprints.[19]

OTHER HARPSICHORD COMPOSERS

After Kuhnau's death, the post of cantor at St. Thomas' Church in Leipzig was offered to **Johann Christoph Graupner** (1683–1760), one of Kuhnau's pupils. When Graupner refused the position, it went to the second choice—Johann Sebastian Bach. Yet today few even know about Graupner, who at the time apparently ranked equal to Bach as a musician. Graupner's most active years (1712–1760) were spent as *Kapellmeister* (chapelmaster) to the Landgrave Ernst Ludwig of Hesse-Darmstadt. As a keyboard composer, he wrote at least forty-three suites,[20] some of which were published during his lifetime (1718, 1722, 1733). In matters of style, Graupner adhered to the idioms and practices of his own generation. His writing is not uniform, however, passing from the simplest form to a heavy, complicated texture, all within the same suite. But there are many passages testifying to a fertile imagination, and the suites as a whole are attractive enough.

Gottlieb Muffat (1690–1770) was influenced by the fact that his father Georg had for many years studied in Paris. But Gottlieb's suites for harpsichord, framed by *overtures, fantasies,* and *preludes,* are sturdier and more vigorous than their contemporary counterparts in France. Using J. C. F. Fischer and François Couperin as models, Muffat produced music in the

---

[19] *Ibid.* See also footnote 15.
[20] Johann Christoph Graupner, *Acht Partiten,* ed. Hoffmann-Erbrecht (Leipzig: Breitkopf & Härtel).

faithful French manner, even using such French titles as *La Coquette* and *Menuet en Cornes de Chasse* (Minuet in Imitation of Hunting Horns). His splendid work, the *Componimenti Musicali per il Cembalo* (Musical Compositions for Harpsichord)[21]—dedicated to Charles VI and published at that monarch's expense—is a collection of six suites and a chaconne, each one illustrating his extraordinary talent. The overtures, preludes, or fantasies that preface each suite are exceptionally fine. Occasionally this introductory movement is an overture in the French style—slow, stately first and final sections and a central section in quick fugal style. At times the first movement is almost a miniature suite in itself. The *Prelude* from the second suite contains a *Tempo Giusto, Allegretto,* and *Adagio.* In the fourth suite, the *Fantasie* opens with a virtuoso toccata-like passage followed by a short *Adagio,* and then concludes with a real four-voice *Fugue.* In general, the other sections of the suite conform to the classic norm in Germany: allemande, courante, sarabande, optional dances, gigue. In style it is oriented to the light-textured fabric found in the *French Suites* of J. S. Bach.

An author and critic, **Johann Mattheson** (1681–1764) wrote much that remains worthwhile. As a composer, he was only moderately successful. Mattheson published a sarcastic commentary about Johann Kuhnau's *Biblical Sonatas,* a criticism that had little effect on their popularity. Mattheson's only early music, dating from about 1713–1714, consists of sonatas similar to Kuhnau's in form. Mattheson mixes *fantasies, airs,* and *preludes* with French dances. One sonata for solo harpsichord (1713) was dedicated "to the one who can play it best." On the whole, Mattheson's sonatas are virtuoso pieces, often having but a single movement. His are not progressive works in any respect, although some are impressive in their technical competency. The collection *Die wohlklingende Fingersprache* (Harmonious Finger Talk, 1735)[22] is dedicated to Mattheson's friend, George Frederick Handel. It has twelve very effective fugues in two and three voices. A second edition appeared in 1749 in Nürnberg under the title *Les Doits parlans* (Expressive Fingers).

Georg Philipp Telemann (1681–1767) was one of the most prolific writers in all music history, but unfortunately, his gigantic output is all but ignored today. Telemann searched France for ideas with which he hoped to reform music in Germany. He was inspired by Couperin, Lully, and Rameau, and he favored eclecticism more than any of his German colleagues.

Much of the Telemann repertoire is worth reviving: perhaps some of the *sonatas* and *fugues,* which blend French *galanterie* with Italian vigor;

---

[21] This collection is found complete in Vol. 7 of the *Denkmäler der Tonkunst in Österreich.*
[22] Johann Mattheson, *Die wohlklingende Fingersprache,* ed. Hoffmann-Erbrecht (Leipzig: Breitkopf & Härtel).

the imitative pieces (like *La Porte*); the *fantasies;* and the Pasquini-like *sonatas.* One of the most delightful facets of his particular talent is seen in the *Fantasies,* available in modern editions.[23] These Rococo miniatures have a lively opening section with light and clear-textured writing, a brief slow section in homophonic style, and then a return to the initial section.

In the group of seventeenth- and eighteenth-century German and Austrian composers, several are outstanding for their serious intentions and an appreciable skill in presenting musical ideas developed with some talent and imagination.[24] But no one composer seemed able to assimilate the best features of the progress of keyboard idioms up to this point; the great talent was missing that could create masterpieces from that accumulated knowledge and experience. That talent belonged to Johann Sebastian Bach.

BIBLIOGRAPHY

Ambros, August Wilhelm. *Geschichte der Musik,* revised by H. Leichtentritt. Leipzig: F. E. C. Leuckart, 1909. Vol. IV.

Bukofzer, Manfred. *Music in the Baroque Era.* New York: W. W. Norton & Co., Inc., 1947.

Haas, Dr. Robert. *Die Musik des Barocks.* Wildpark-Potsdam: Akademische Verlagsgesellschaft Athenaion, 1929.

Lorenz, H. *Die Klaviermusik Dietrich Buxtehudes.* Dissertation. Kiel, Germany, 1952.

Nolte, E. V. *The Instrumental Works of Johann Pachelbel.* Dissertation. Northwestern University, 1954.

---

[23] G. P. Telemann, *Fantaisies pour le Clavessin* (New York: Broude Brothers). *Six Overtures* in two volumes are available in Volumes IV and V of *Deutsche Klaviermusik des 17. und 18. Jahrhunderts* (Vieweg Musikverlag).

[24] A good representation of the composers of this period is found in Volumes II and III of *Deutsche Klaviermusik des 17. und 18. Jahrhunderts,* eds. Fischer and Oberdoerffer (Berlin: Vieweg Musikverlag). Another source is *Keyboard Music of the Baroque and Rococo,* ed. W. Georgii (Köln: Arno Volk, 1960), 3 Vols.

10

BACH

AND

HANDEL

JOHANN SEBASTIAN BACH

At the present time there are numerous volumes dealing with the life and works of **Johann Sebastian Bach** (1685–1750). Albert Schweitzer[1] and Philipp Spitta[2] have long since set high standards of superb scholarship with their books about Bach. In fact, enough has been written in this field to warrant a book about the books; that is, a book dealing with the research alone.[3] In view of all this literature, little can be added to what already has been said pertinent to the essential aspects of Bach's music.

It is generally conceded that Bach was not a great innovator; even his sons said that their father looked back rather than ahead. He did, however, take the existing forms of keyboard music, strip them of all superfluity, and polish them to a high peak of perfection, as if to say to future composers: "Here is the essence of what can be done or said through these forms; study them and assimilate them; then forge ahead to new horizons." Coming on the scene at a crucial time in music history—that period when contrapuntal style began to merge with a predominantly harmonic style—Bach and his art reflect the image of that moment. In addition, his writings form a crossroad at which the influences from the north (Sweelinck, Buxtehude), the south (Pachelbel, Froberger, Vivaldi, Corelli), and the west (Couperin, Grigny) were gathered. His masterful assimilation of these historical and geographical influences is total. Nevertheless, his own originality is ever present, even in his youthful works. Almost everything Bach wrote during

---

[1] Albert Schweitzer, *J. S. Bach*, trans. E. Newman (London: Adam & Charles Black, 1949), 2 Vols.

[2] Philipp Spitta, *Johann Sebastian Bach*, trans. Bell & Fuller-Maitland (New York: Dover Publications, 1951), 3 Vols. in 2.

[3] Friedrich Blume, *Two Centuries of Bach*, trans. S. Godman (London: Oxford University Press, 1950).

his lifetime displays his talent for melodic and rhythmic invention and harmonic audacity.[4]

With few exceptions, every piece that Bach wrote reveals an earnest objective aided by a formidable technical apparatus. This technical apparatus, however, never obtrudes; it serves as a cleverly concealed scaffold upon which Bach builds his magnificent tonal edifices.

Only once did Bach yield to program music in his keyboard writings. Johann Kuhnau had just published his six *Biblical Sonatas* (1700) based on scenes from the Old Testament, and despite the critic Mattheson's protestations and sarcasm, these sonatas enjoyed a great success. Then in 1704 Bach wrote his *Capriccio sopra la lontananza del suo fratello dilettissimo* (Capriccio on the Departure of His Beloved Brother) in honor of his brother Johann Jacob, who was going to Sweden as oboist in the army of King Charles XII. The *Capriccio* is divided into six sections, each supplied with a description of the musical content. It is clear that while the young Bach allowed himself this taste of program music, his attitude was not serious; a humorous touch pervades more than one section. Johann Jacob's friends attempt to persuade him to renounce his Swedish post; they describe the possible dangers; when he refuses, the friends cry out in lamentation— *allgemeines lamento* (the term itself is tragicomic); the posthorn signals departure; and the *Capriccio* concludes with a double fugue. In this last section, the posthorn motive becomes the theme and undergoes various contrapuntal combinations as it accompanies the inflexible voyager. Here, of course, Bach is within his artistic rights because the signal of the posthorn is a musical motive. But in the other sections it would be impossible without the titles to divine the exact thought of the young master.

While Bach was at Cöthen (1717–1723) as music director for a Calvinist prince, he had neither a choir nor an adequate organ at his immediate disposal. With astonishing ease he turned from choral and organ writing to harpsichord, orchestral, and chamber music. What is even more astonishing, Bach created masterpiece upon masterpiece in these new fields.

The Well-Tempered Clavier

Precisely at this time the tempered scale began to be generally applied to keyboard instruments. Yet, for this scale to be used and recommended

---

[4] There are several fine editions of Bach's keyboard music. Edwin Kalmus publishes the complete works in a fine authoritative edition. The Peters Edition is also quite good. G. Henle Verlag in Munich has superior editions of many Bach keyboard works. One may of course consult the complete edition, *Johann Sebastian Bach's Werke*, originally published by Breitkopf & Härtel for the Bach-Gesellschaft, and reprinted by J. W. Edwards of Ann Arbor, Michigan, in 1949 (46 volumes). The *Neue Ausgabe Sämtliche Werke*, published by Bärenreiter from 1955, is still in progress.

by artists like Bach, it had to guarantee important advantages over the older systems. Previous to tempered tuning, the performer who wished to play in all keys on instruments with fixed sounds (organ, clavichord, harpsichord) would have required so many notes on his instrument that the playing would have been impossible. Also, under the old system the presence of half tones of different sizes meant that keys employing many sharps or flats could not be used without retuning the instrument. Consequently, the composers had limited themselves to certain keys. A contemporary of Bach said that they wrote only rarely in *B* major and *A-flat* major, never in *F-sharp* major or in *C-sharp* major. Equal temperament noticeably reduced these difficulties and made enharmonic transitions easier. In view of the importance modulation assumed in later composition, one can realize the influence exerted by tempered tuning, not only on the piano but on the development of music in general.

The practicability of a tempered scale had been recognized as early as 1691. Andreas Werckmeister wrote a treatise titled "Musical Temperament or ... mathematical instruction on how to produce ... well-tempered intonation on the clavier." And the advantages of the system were demonstrated in miniature by Johann Caspar Ferdinand Fischer in his *Ariadne Musica* (*ca.* 1710). Then in 1719 Johann Mattheson offered a further demonstration in his *Organistenprobe* (Essay for Organists), "twenty-four easy and as many somewhat more difficult examples in all the keys."

It was now Bach's turn to demonstrate the possibilities introduced by the new scale system. The result was the *Wohltemperiertes Klavier* (Well-Tempered Clavier). This celebrated work is a collection of two sets (twenty-four in each) of *preludes and fugues* in all the major and minor keys; the first volume dates from 1722 and the second was finished in Leipzig between 1740 and 1744. The lengthy title of the first volume emphasizes that its primary purpose is to instruct: *The Well-Tempered Clavier or Preludes and Fugues through all the tones and semitones, both as regards the "tertia major" or "Ut Re Mi," and as concerns the "tertia minor" or "Re Mi Fa." For the Use and Profit of the Musical Youth Desirous of Learning, as well as for the Pastime of those Already Skilled in this Study, drawn up and written by Johann Sebastian Bach, Capellmeister to His Serene Highness the Prince of Anhalt-Cöthen, etc. and Director of His Chamber Music. Anno 1722.*[5]

Never before had any work written for instructional purposes achieved such high artistic value. With the *Well-Tempered Clavier*, Bach raised the harpsichord (and clavichord) to the same lofty heights that he attained for the organ fugue. A word of explanation about the title: *Clavier* in Ger-

---

[5] Hans David and Arthur Mendel, *The Bach Reader* (New York: W. W. Norton, 1945), p. 85.

man means a keyboard instrument—no specific keyboard; therefore, this collection is for keyboard instruments in general. However, some preludes and fugues do seem clearly meant for a specific instrument. For example, in the first book the *Prelude and Fugue in C-sharp Minor* and the *Prelude and Fugue in E-flat Minor,* with their lyrical and sustained quality, are most effective on the clavichord; on the other hand, the *Fugue in A Minor* from the same book has its best effect when played on an organ with pedals.

Whatever the instrument called for, Bach always expresses his own eloquent personality. Each of the ninety-six pieces has its individual complete form, each has its own physiognomy; yet the *Well-Tempered Clavier* as a whole reflects the spirit of the master. Nevertheless, his music is not overtly emotional. As a musical craftsman, he has too much aristocratic reserve to make common display of his joy and sadness. He does not insistently impose his emotions on the music, and in his discourse he avoids speaking too freely of his sentiments.

The relationship between the preludes and the fugues in the *Well-Tempered Clavier* varies infinitely. Frequently the prelude sparkles rapidly, giving the impression of an étude. Sometimes it is related to the fugue. At other times it is in complete opposition to the fugue, the only similarity being the common key in which the two are written.

Who can forget the first *Prelude* (Book I) with its undulating harmonies in lute style, or the fantasy-like *Prelude in C Minor* with its contrasting passages? The virtuoso *Prelude and Fugue in C-sharp Major* from the first book constitutes a real workout in this unusual key. The exuberant lilt of the *Prelude in D Major* is in striking contrast to the *Fugue in D Major,* whose dotted rhythms are reminiscent of the *French Overture.* One of the most beautiful fugues in the first book is the last one (in *b* minor), which has a chromatic subject treated in sequence (Ex. 1) and then subjected to a marvelous and skillful development. An obvious style difference occurs in the two volumes; the preludes in aria style and in binary form contained in the second collection do not often appear in the first collection.

Ex. 1. J. S. Bach: *Well-Tempered Clavier Book I: Fugue in B Minor*

When Bach wrote in fugal form, he always created a theme with some identifiable characteristic. This might be a subtle emotional quality or a rhythmic principle, either of which could then provide the basic mood or motion for the whole movement. Consequently, his fugues portray every sentiment, from profound melancholy to spontaneous gaiety.

Inventions and Sinfonias

Bach was considering his pupils again when he wrote his *Inventions*. These two- and three-part inventions were originally written for Wilhelm Friedemann's *Clavierbüchlein* (Little Keyboard Book) and were called *Preambles* and *Fantasias* respectively. Bach revised them in 1723 with the title *Inventionen und Sinfonien* and an explanatory title: *Upright Instruction wherein the lovers of the clavier, and especially those desirous of learning, are shown a clear way not alone (1) to learn to play clearly in two voices, but also, after further progress, (2) to deal correctly and well with three "obbligato" parts; furthermore, at the same time not alone to have good "inventiones," but to develop the same well, and above all to arrive at a singing style in playing and at the same time to acquire a strong foretaste of composition.*[6]

The German musicologist Philipp Spitta maintained that "the sovereign independence with which all the forms of music are applied—the canon, the fugue, free imitation, double and triple counterpoint, episodic working-out, inversions of the theme—all combining and following each other in pieces of very moderate extent, without anywhere obtruding themselves on our notice; these are what render the Inventionen und Sinfonian unique in the whole body of clavier music."[7]

The collection contains fifteen *Inventions* in two voices and fifteen *Sinfonias* in three voices. The term inventions applies, properly speaking, only to the first half, but it has become customary to extend it to include the entire collection. The outward form of the two-part inventions is similar to song form in three parts: A B A. The only exception is *No. 6 in E Major*, which is in bipartite form. Certain preludes by Kuhnau and Fischer probably served as a point of departure for the two-part inventions. The sequence of keys used for them in the collection is orderly, and only unusual tonalities such as *C-sharp* major, *c-sharp* minor, *e-flat* minor, and *F-sharp* major are omitted. The three-part inventions are similar in form to the two-part inventions.

Suites

Bach's six *French Suites* date from this same period, several of them

    [6] *Ibid.*, p. 86.
    [7] From *Johann Sebastian Bach* (Vol. II) by Philipp Spitta. Copyright 1951 by Dover Publications, Inc. Published by Dover Publications, Inc., New York 14, N.Y., at $12.50, and reprinted through permission of the publisher.

having been included in the *Notenbüchlein* he assembled in 1722. *French Suites* is not Bach's title (he wrote only *Suites pour le Clavecin*). Did it originate because the suite movements have French titles? Was it applied because the music has that incomparable grace so often associated with the French, or because of the consistency of its fabric? Certainly these suites, or rather the dances contained therein, are most elegant. The melodic and rhythmic contrasts reveal a prodigious invention. Indeed, there is something in these masterworks that brings Versailles to mind: distinction without affectation, lightness without frivolity. The *French Suites* are written in impeccable taste, and in many ways they are Bach's best examples of the suite form.

In these suites the prelude is missing but the standard dances are present: the allemande, grave and serious; the courante, amiable and lively (four are written in the Italian florid style); the slow sarabande, lyrical and full of ornaments; and the gigue, where the resources of the keyboard are used with ingenuity.

Bach probably began the *English Suites* before the *French Suites,* although they were not completed until after the latter. Once more the title is a matter of conjecture; Bach may have been at least partially inspired by the suites of Charles Dieupart, a reputable French composer who worked mostly in England (see Chapter 4). Bach is known to have copied out several movements from Dieupart's suites to use as models for his own compositions.

The first movement in all the *English Suites* is a prelude. With Bach, this prelude emerges clothed in various musical trappings: in one, the spirit of the fugue is evoked and highlighted; in another, features of the concerto form are delineated; the *da capo* aria is outlined in a third. The basic components of the dance suite do, of course, dominate the *English Suites*. The courantes in general are not as convincing as those in the *French Suites*. The sarabandes, on the contrary, show an admirable breadth of movement and a fine command of this classic form. Each suite contains only a pair of galanteries, or extra dances. In some instances, there are two dances of the same type, the second serving as a kind of trio or contrasting section.

As a group, Bach's *English Suites* are less impressive than either his *French Suites* or *Partitas*. Although there are many beautiful dances in the *English Suites*, the collection as a whole displays neither the elegance and sophisticated simplicity of the *French Suites* nor the imagination and ingenuity found in the *Partitas*.

The six *Partitas* and the *Overture in B Minor* are part of a four-volume series called *Clavierübung* (Keyboard Exercise), which Bach himself published between 1731 and 1742. The six *Partitas* are more adventurous than anything else he wrote. For instance, he does not always use the basic dances: the final movement in *Partita No. 2* is a *Capriccio* in 2/4 meter. In addition, the movements are not always in customary sequence: *Partitas No. 4* and *6* have galanteries between the courante and sarabande. Yet despite these deviations, or perhaps because of them, the *Partitas* present a panorama of highly original dance stylizations, interesting for both performer and listener.

The prelude used in the *English Suites* becomes transformed in the *Partitas*. It is the free *Praeludium* in the first *Partita*. Then it is a *Sinfonia* in the second, which is almost orchestral. In *Partitas* three and four it appears as a Baroque fantasy and appears again as the improvisatory *Praeambulum* for the fifth *Partita*. In the last *Partita* it becomes a grandiose, severe *Toccata*.

In *Partita No. 4* there is an *Allemande* that overshadows all other allemandes. Yet, generally speaking, the basic dances used in the *Partitas* do not always demonstrate their customary traits. The courantes differ in style: four are French-type courantes and four are Italian. The most delightful French example is the *Courante* in the fourth *Partita*, but the second also contains a striking French *Courante*. Among the Italian-model courantes, which abound with florid running passages, the one most ideally representative of its prototype is found in the last *Partita*.

The sarabandes of the *Partitas* are not particularly conspicuous. Some are so ornate that their basic framework is obscured. Others entirely discard their usual stately character and do not even begin on the first beat of the measure. This is true of the sarabandes in *Partitas No. 3, 5,* and *6*. The character of the gigue also varies. The essentially homophonic gigue of *Partita No. 1* was transformed by Gluck into an aria *"J'implore et je tremble"* for his opera *Iphigénie en Tauride*. The gigue in *No. 2* is missing altogether and in its place stands a *Capriccio*. Four of the *Partitas* contain gigues in fugal texture.

Bach inserts only one or two galanteries in each *Partita,* and he avoids the traditional names and dance types. To enrich his galanteries—*aria, passepied, burlesca, scherzo, rondo, caprice*—he has reshaped the contours of bipartite form; the writing is never too heavy, its complexity never a complication.

Bach's magnificent single suite, the *Partita in B Minor*—or more correctly the *Overture in B Minor*—is important to consider. The opening movement is a *French Overture* with a solemn introduction, a gigue-like middle section, and a return to the first section. The allemande is missing from this architectural masterpiece; the movements in sequence are: *Courante, Gavotte I, Gavotte II, Passepied I, Passepied II, Sarabande, Bourrée I, Bourrée II, Gigue,* and *Echo*.

The *Goldberg Variations*

Bach's masterpiece for the harpsichord, the crowning achievement of Baroque keyboard music, is the *Aria with Thirty Variations*, better known as the *Goldberg Variations (Klavierübung IV)*.[8] This great work sums up, as it were, all that the Baroque period could offer in variation technique. Bach's biographer Johann Forkel gives an interesting account of its composition:

> For this model, according to which all variations should be made, though, for reasons easily understood, not a single one has been made after it, we are indebted to Count Kaiserling, formerly Russian Ambassador at the Court of the Elector of Saxony, who frequently resided in Leipzig, and brought with him Goldberg, who has been mentioned above, to have him instructed by Bach in music. The Count was often sickly, and then had sleepless nights. At these times Goldberg, who lived in the house with him, had to pass the night in an adjoining room to play something to him when he could not sleep. The Count once said to Bach that he should like to have some clavier pieces for his Goldberg, which should be of such a soft and somewhat lively character that he might be a little cheered up by them in his sleepless nights. Bach thought he could best fulfill this wish by variations, which, on account of the constant sameness of the fundamental harmony, he had hitherto considered as an ungrateful task. But as at this time all his works were models of art, these variations also became such under his hand. This is, indeed, the only model of the kind that he has left us. The Count thereafter called them nothing but his variations. He was never weary of hearing them; and for a long time, when the sleepless nights came, he used to say: "Dear Goldberg, do play me one of my variations." Bach was, perhaps, never so well rewarded for any work as for this; the Count made him a present of a golden goblet, filled with a hundred Louis d'ors. But their worth as a work of art would not have been paid if the present had been a thousand times as great.[9]

The theme for the *Goldberg Variations* came from a notebook which Bach compiled and presented to his second wife, Anna Magdalena Bach, in

---

[8] The finest edition of the *Goldberg Variations* is that made by Ralph Kirkpatrick (G. Schirmer).

[9] Hans David and Arthur Mendel, *The Bach Reader* (New York: W. W. Norton & Co., Inc., 1945), pp. 338–339.

1725.[10] It is a two-part lyrical theme (*Aria*), richly ornate, but with a solid harmonic support (Ex. 2). This support forms the framework on which the variations are based; the only change in harmony is from major to minor.

Ex. 2. J. S. Bach: *Goldberg Variations: Aria*

The formal plan consists of ten series of three variations each—two characteristic variations plus a *canon*. The canons start at the unison and progress through the ninth. These magnificent contrapuntal works are so skillfully conceived that one is seldom aware of their technical intricacies. Many times the two canonic parts are accompanied by an active bass obbligato, thus making a three-voice instead of a two-voice variation. It is not surprising that Bach chose the comparatively technical form of the canon; with his impressive technical ability, writing in this style was as natural as verse writing for a poet.

The variations framing the canons are all the more remarkable for their immense variety when one considers that they are all within the same harmonic framework: the fifth variation exploits crossing of hands in a light and gay spirit; the seventh variation is a kind of *siciliana;* the tenth is a *fughetta.* Variations thirteen and twenty-five are embellished arias, beautifully devised and presented with great breadth of expression. The sixteenth variation is a *French Overture.* The last variation is unusual: it is a *quodlibet* or potpourri in which Bach has adroitly fused two popular German folk songs.

A work Bach definitely specified for a harpsichord with two keyboards, the *Goldberg Variations* stands as one of the great keyboard works of all times; it is the result of profound inspiration and displays a superb talent for idiomatic keyboard writing. One must agree with the English writer Sir Donald Tovey that "until Beethoven wrote the 'Waldstein' Sonata, the 'Goldberg' Variations were the most brilliant piece of sheer instrumental display extant. No other work by Bach himself, or by Domenico Scarlatti,

---

[10] Anna Magdalena's Notebook contains not only her husband's music but that of other composers. In fact, it is not at all certain that Bach composed the sarabande-type aria used as a basis for the *Goldberg Variations.*

not even any concerto by Mozart or any earlier work of Beethoven could compare with it for instrumental brilliance."[11]

Other Works

Although the suites and the *Goldberg Variations* constitute the prime examples of Bach's harpsichord music, many other works in his repertoire are almost as fine. There are the *Toccatas,* for example, in which Bach— continuing a tradition begun by Claudio Merulo in the sixteenth century— varies the sections within each composition by means of changing texture, improvisatory passages, chordal sections, fugal techniques, and dance-like movements. Another collection, the eighteen *Preludes for Beginners,* was written at Cöthen in 1723. And finally, there are Bach's keyboard transcriptions of numerous concerti written by some of his eighteenth-century contemporaries.

The *Chromatic Fantasy and Fugue* and the *Italian Concerto* are the best of Bach's single pieces. The former was probably finished in Leipzig in 1730. This *Fantasy* shows extreme contrasts, with its abandon and yet almost dramatic logic in development. The toccata-like flourishes of the first part somehow maintain a miraculous equilibrium. They stand in contrast to the second section, which is brought in by the arpeggiated chords of the transition. A similar dramatic treatment occurs in the three-voice fugue that follows; the chromaticism of the fugal exposition gradually gives way to a freer treatment of the polyphonic voices. The expansive coda delineates the theme in homophonic texture supported by chordal accompaniment.

The *Concerto in the Italian Manner,* commonly called the *Italian Concerto* (included in *Clavierübung II*), was published in 1735. Written expressly for solo harpsichord with two keyboards, this masterpiece reveals Bach the organist, Bach the symphonist, and Bach the master of concerto form. Why is this masterpiece called Italian and why a concerto? First, the three movements comprising the concerto—*Allegro, Andante, Presto*—conform to the general plan of the concerto in Italy. Second, "this 'Concerto' represents the clavier arrangement of an orchestral work with a single soloist, the exact model of which exists in the composer's imagination only."[12] In its opening measures the *Allegro* recalls the robust orchestral tutti (Ex. 3), against which are opposed the linear motives of the solo voice. These solo passages are played on one keyboard while the other keyboard

[11] Donald Francis Tovey, *Essays in Musical Analysis. Chamber Music* (London: Oxford University Press, 1949), p. 35.
[12] Karl Geiringer, *The Bach Family* (London: George Allen and Unwin, Ltd., 1954), p. 276.

Ex. 3.   J. S. Bach: *Italian Concerto: Allegro*

sustains batteries of chords, as in the Italian style. The *Andante* is lyrical and almost dramatic with its recitatives and syncopation, but it also has ample melodic contours. The *concertato* style comes again in the final *Presto* where Bach has created deliberate and skillful opposition between the tutti and soloist. This finale evokes that jubilant sentiment so characteristic of Bach.

GEORGE FREDERICK HANDEL

Bach and Handel are generally considered the musical giants of the Baroque age, but Handel could not qualify if only his harpsichord music were evaluated. Even a cursory glance at the list of his works (excluding, of course, his magnificent organ concerti) shows that keyboard composition was of no great interest to him. Handel's genius simply does not manifest itself in his harpsichord music as it does in his operas and oratorios.

Born in Saxony, **George Frederick Handel** (1685–1759) became an international musician par excellence. He traveled extensively and wherever he went—Paris, Naples, Venice, London—he turned a keen ear to the music being produced around him. Although he spent the greater part of his life in England composing for an English public, he remained true to his Germanic heritage. Two musical luminaries of his time influenced his style: the German Reinhard Keiser (1674–1739), a popular composer of German opera, and Dietrich Buxtehude (1637–1707), the famous Danish-German organist.

Handel was not a lyric composer. He wrote neither to enlighten the soul nor to lay bare his innermost feelings, but rather to move his audience. His music belongs to the category of arts intended for the masses: architecture, decorative painting, tragedy. It is robust, energetic music.

Handel's harpsichord works consist of three collections and a kind of appendix formed by six fugues.[13] The first collection, the only one published

---

[13] The Handel suites (in two volumes) as well as the fugues are available in Peters Edition. Bärenreiter also publishes the suites in a fine edition.

(1720) by Handel himself, is by far the most remarkable. It contains eight beautiful suites, rich in musical substance and strong in technique. The succeeding collections are uneven in quality. The second, published unbeknown to Handel, includes many of his youthful works: little suites, less developed than those in the first collection, but often charming; and many variations definitely instrumental, such as the *Gavotte in G* or the *Chaconne in G* with its sixty-two variations. The third collection is a hodgepodge: some suites, a *Fantasy*, a *Caprice*, little *Sonatas*, and even *Lessons* for his pupils, the daughters of the Prince of Galles.

Six large fugues complete the corpus of Handel's keyboard music. This indeed is the work of a splendid improvisor. Moreover, these fugues have an enormous attraction because of Handel's unique ability to express "vocality." It is a tribute to these qualities that two of the fugues, one in *g* minor and one in *a* minor, became choruses for his oratorio *Israel in Egypt*.

Handel's keyboard music has complete clarity, usually resulting from a precise design monumentally conceived; but it is far less substantial than Bach's music. Handel's keyboard music is decorative rather than profound, and meant to be enjoyed for its vitality and the frankness of its rhythm. Symmetrical formulas—clichés, if one were to be unkind—are prominent. However, Handel was full of inspirations that he developed not only with vigor but often with grace and tenderness.

Another of Handel's characteristics is his universality. He did not confine himself to being strictly a German musician—though with his genius this could have had its own greatness—but instead he became a European musician. His master Friedrich Zachau (1663–1712) had prepared him well. According to Handel's friend Mattheson, Zachau "showed Handel the different ways of writing and composing of different nations." Handel's personal curiosity and his travels expanded this knowledge. His greatest strength lies in a Saxon robustness singularly enriched and modified by foreign influences. The Italian element seems to predominate, for Handel was a true Italian by adoption; he not only borrowed Italian writing procedures; he also appropriated the fashion of the lofty, noble approach—the style of the Italians. He enjoyed and absorbed French music: the *clavecin* music, the *chansons*. Finally, the great English composer Henry Purcell exerted a very positive influence on him.

This international flavor is very apparent in Handel's suites. Some are the German type with four dances: allemande, courante, sarabande (often omitted), and gigue, the whole preceded by a prelude. Other suites belong to the *sonata da chiesa* type of the Italians, in which allegros and prestos alternate with adagios and lentos. Many of the individual pieces also exhibit these foreign influences: a German national style in allemandes and courantes in the serious manner of Kuhnau, Froberger, and Krieger; several lentos in the ornate style *à l'Italienne;* some prestos and capriccios imitating the virtuosity of Scarlatti and Pasquini. Finally, the entire eighth suite in the second collection has the elegance and refinement, the *esprit* of the French clavecinists.

Among the eight suites comprising Handel's 1720 collection, only *No. 4* contains the standard dance forms in their classic order. The other suites consist of dance combinations, pieces in fugal style, and movements of various tempos in bipartite form. A typical example of his suites is *No. 5 in E Major.* In it a lightly contrapuntal *Prelude* leads to a brief but effective *Allemande* and *Courante;* the sarabande is missing; and the suite terminates with a charming air and five variations. This last movement sometimes bears the title "Harmonious Blacksmith." According to one writer,[14] this title came from an English publisher named Lintern who wanted to link the great composer's name with that of his own father—a musical blacksmith and admirer of Handel. A second source states that the music publisher himself was a former blacksmith.[15] Another well-known suite is *No. 7 in G Minor* with its *Overture* in French style; *Andante; Allegro;* elegant *Sarabande;* miniature *Gigue;* and grandiose *Passacaille.*

One must not deduce that these elements appear haphazardly. The collections are not mosaics made of patched pieces. An original touch, more easy to feel than to define, runs through the pages, supplying unity and life to the different elements. Handel's harpsichord works well deserved the success they received.

BIBLIOGRAPHY

Blume, Friedrich. *Two Centuries of Bach* (translated by S. Godman). London: Oxford University Press, 1950.

Bodky, Erwin. *The Interpretation of Bach's Keyboard Works.* Cambridge: Harvard University Press, 1960.

Cart, William. *J.-S. Bach.* Lausanne: F. Rouge & Cie., 1946.

David, Hans and Arthur Mendel, eds. *The Bach Reader.* New York: W. W. Norton & Co., Inc., 1945.

[14] Herbert Westerby, *The History of Pianoforte Music* (London: Kegan, Paul, Trench, Trubner & Co., Ltd., 1924), p. 49.
[15] See item 10 under "Nicknamed Compositions" in *The Oxford Companion to Music* (9th edition, edited by Percy A. Scholes).

Emery, Walter. *Bach's Ornaments*. London: Novello & Co., Ltd., 1953.

Geiringer, Karl. *The Bach Family*. New York: Oxford University Press, 1954.

Hauptfuehrer, George. *The Harpsichord Suites of Handel in Relation to Keyboard Suites of Some of His Predecessors and Contemporaries*. Dissertation (in progress). Indiana University.

Keller, Hermann. *Die Klavierwerke Bachs*. Leipzig: Edition Peters, 1950.

Pirro, André. *L'Esthétique de Jean Sébastien Bach*. Paris: Librairie Fischbacher, 1907.

Roethlisberger, Edmond. *Le Clavecin dans l'Oeuvre de J-S Bach*. Genève: Edition Henn, 1920.

Schweitzer, Albert. *J. S. Bach* (translated by Ernest Newman). London: A. & C. Black, 1923. 2 Vols. Dover reprint

Spitta, Philipp. *Johann Sebastian Bach* (translated by Bell and Fuller-Maitland). New York: Dover Publications, 1951. 3 Vols. in 2.

Weinstock, Herbert. *Handel*. New York: Alfred A. Knopf, 1946.

Williams, C. F. Abdy. *Bach*. London: J. M. Dent & Sons, Ltd., 1934.

PART
III

11

EIGHTEENTH-CENTURY

CLASSICISM

During the second half of the eighteenth century a momentous stylistic change took place in all the arts. This period is frequently called the Age of Reason. The work that first inspired and then symbolized the era was Diderot's *Encyclopedia,* a vast compendium of logic that viewed all fields of human endeavor in a quasi-mathematical framework.

In the arts this propensity for the exercise of reason found its fulfillment in Classicism. The visual arts turned to the objectivity and restraint discernible in models from ancient Greece and Rome. The painter Jacques David not only chose subject matter from Roman history (*Oath of the Horatii*); he even clothed his figures in the appropriate flowing, draped garments.

In music there was no model to imitate. An entirely new aesthetic developed, based on *abstract* ideals of symmetry, balance, and clarity. Musical Classicism was not a completely new product; elements of rococo style—profuse ornamentation, facile harmonies—were fused with a sentimentality that the Germans called *Empfindsamkeit,* particularly during the Pre-Classic period.

The Pre-Classic period is the description commonly given to the years between the era of Johann Sebastian Bach and the mature stages of Joseph Haydn and Wolfgang Mozart. The most characteristic Pre-Classic composers came from Germany and Austria. This period was devoted to experimentation; new techniques and ideas were tested, some old methods were discarded. During this time the Baroque contrapunto-harmonic style gave way to the almost purely harmonic, homophonic style, which became a feature of the succeeding Classic period. The lengthy melodic lines favored by Baroque composers were replaced by concise, expressive themes. A new idea also emerged—that of thematic contrast. The suite gradually disappeared; the toccata was lost for some time to come; and the fugue was employed only sporadically. The variation, however, has kept its place in the repertoire of musical forms to this day.

The finished, refined musical result of Classicism was a style in which objectivity and emotional restraint were fitted into an elegant and original formal structure: the sonata. In the Baroque period, the term sonata had been rather indiscriminately applied to several musical types. The bipartite, one-movement piece of the Scarlatti school was called a sonata. Series of dances were called sonatas, although they were actually suites. And the so-called church sonata—a series of movements in which sections were contrasted by different textures and tempos—also was common in the Baroque era.

During the Pre-Classic and Classic periods, the sonata crystallized into a specific musical form, and as such it became the favorite vehicle of expression for Pre-Classic and Classic composers. The term "sonata" indicated a composition with three or four movements written according to certain predetermined rules for either one instrument or a combination of instruments. Its exact origins are uncertain because the final form is the result of ideas borrowed from many sources. Most likely the idea of three movements in a fast-slow-fast sequence can be traced to the Italian overture. Both Scarlatti and Rameau—in whose one-movement works several themes and their development can be detected in embryo—contributed to the idea of developing several themes within a single composition.

Each sonata movement is constructed on formal principles. From the composer's point of view, the first movement of the sonata is the most important. For purposes of analysis, the form for the first movement is now called *sonata-allegro* (the *allegro* here has nothing to do with tempo); that is, in most sonatas, the first movement is constructed in *sonata-allegro* form. The initial movement may be preceded by a slow introduction, but this happens more frequently in chamber music and symphonies than in keyboard music. The first movement proper is divided into three sections: (1) exposition, (2) development, and (3) recapitulation.

The *exposition section* "exposes" or states the themes; there are at least two themes—one vigorous, the other a contrasting lyrical one. If the first theme is in a major key, a modulation to the dominant ushers in the second theme; but if the first theme is in a minor key, then the second theme appears in the relative major key. After these themes have been stated, the exposition section terminates with a *codetta*, a little ending usually based on the first theme. The *development section* allows the composer to exercise his imagination and ingenuity by manipulating the two themes. In the Pre-Classic and Classic eras, the old contrapuntal devices that stretched or shortened the themes were sometimes employed. For the keyboard, the themes often were echoed and tossed about in different registers. Syncopation was commonly used. In fact, the composer engaged every device at his disposal (and discretion) to display the inherent flexibility of his themes. After this development there is a modulation back to the original key. Finally, the *recapitulation section* restates the themes (this time the second theme remains in the original key), and the first movement closes with a coda or ending.

The second movement—the slow movement—may be constructed in any one of several forms. Once again the composer may choose sonata-allegro; or maybe simple song form A B A; or he may prefer a theme and variations; or possibly a type of rondo. It is most essential to have the spirit of the slow movement established and maintained, to have lyricism in the music, and to create melodies with sustained, expressive outlines.

The third and last movement of the sonata may also be written in sonata-allegro form, but customarily the Pre-Classic and Classic composers chose a rondo derived from the French rondeau used by François Couperin and his contemporaries. The rondo offered a basic theme, which alternated with new material (couplets); but there was always a final return to the main theme.

If the sonata has four movements (this is rarely encountered in the eighteenth century), an extra movement is inserted immediately after the slow movement. During the late eighteenth century the "extra" was usually a minuet, the only dance form preserved from the old suite. Like the Baroque minuet, it had three parts: the minuet proper, a trio or contrasting section, and a repeat of the initial minuet.

This is a very general outline of the sonata as it appeared during the Classic period after undergoing its transformation throughout the Pre-Classic era and the early works by Haydn. It must be stressed that this is a loose framework to build upon, since almost every sonata has some deviation from the typical pattern.

BIBLIOGRAPHY

Barford, Philip. "The Sonata-Principle: A Study of Musical Thought in the Eighteenth Century." *Music Review*, 1952 (XIII).

Newman, Wm. S. *The Sonata in the Classic Era*. Chapel Hill: The University of North Carolina Press, 1963.

Selva, Blanche. *Quelques Mots sur la Sonate*. Paris: Librairie Paul Delaplane, 1914.

Shedlock, John S. *The Pianoforte Sonata*. London: Methuen & Co., 1895. Reprint by Da Capo Press, N.Y., 1964.

Tovey, Donald Francis. *The Forms of Music*. Cleveland: World Publishing Co., 1963. A Meridian Book.

12

THE SONS

OF BACH

AND THEIR CONTEMPORARIES

Pre-Classic keyboard music received its most important contributions from the several sons of Johann Sebastian Bach. The most talented and best known are **Wilhelm Friedemann** (1710–1784), **Carl Philipp Emanuel** (1714–1788), and **Johann Christian** (1735–1782). These three composers ranked among the best musicians of the day, particularly Carl Philipp Emanuel.

WILHELM FRIEDEMANN BACH

Friedemann was the second child but the first son born to Johann Sebastian and his first wife, Maria Barbara. He had no consistent musical training until he was ten, when his father wrote out for him what is called the *Clavierbüchlein vor Wilhelm Friedemann Bach* (Little Keyboard Book for Wilhelm Friedemann Bach).[1] The senior Bach's little preludes and fugues for beginners also were written for Friedemann's instruction. Friedemann himself produced assorted keyboard works, among them nine sonatas,[2] two sonatas for two claviers, twelve polonaises,[3] ten fantasias, and other pieces. Like his father, he was a fine performer and expert improvisor. Although he lived at the time the sonata form and Classic style were taking shape, Friedemann wrote more like his father than either of his brothers.

Friedemann's sonatas are written in a standard three-movement cycle. He frequently adheres to his father's basic stylistic idioms—for example, keyboard counterpoint in fugato passages. At other times, it is obvious that Friedemann had an open mind for new ideas: contrasting themes, experimentation in figuration, contrast in tempos within a single movement.

The first movement—*Allegro ma non troppo*—of Wilhelm Friedemann

---

[1] The complete *Clavierbüchlein* is available in Kalmus edition.
[2] Friedemann's clavier sonatas are published by Nagel's Music Archive.
[3] The twelve *Polonaises* may be found in Peters Edition.

Bach's *Sonata in E-flat Major*[4] has an initial theme five measures long, a theme which avoids the square rhythm of a four-measure phrase (Ex. 1). When the second theme appears it turns out to be not a real theme but a scalar configuration; however, the idea does contrast with the lyric cut of the first theme. Then the first theme undergoes a short, rather unimaginative development before the recapitulation. Both themes are presented in the recapitulation. The second movement recalls an earlier era. Fundamentally, it is a contrapuntally conceived piece with a kind of obbligato bass line running throughout, somewhat reminiscent of the canons in J. S. Bach's *Goldberg Variations*. The third movement, *Presto*, is outstanding for its rhythmic drive.

Ex. 1. W. F. Bach: *Sonata in E-flat Major: Allegro*

The *Sonata in E-flat Major* indicates by its style and structure that at the time it was written the Classic sonata was still in a formative stage. Any idea of a homophonic texture—a melody with accompaniment—seems possible for just a brief time before the thought is broken up by scale passages, arpeggios, and all sorts of extraneous and unorganized devices.

CARL PHILIPP EMANUEL BACH

The second surviving son of Johann Sebastian and his first wife Maria Barbara was Carl Philipp Emanuel Bach (1714–1788). Like his father and brother, he was an expert keyboard performer, and he served as private accompanist to Frederick the Great in Berlin from 1740 to 1767. Later he moved to Hamburg where he became general music director of that city's five main churches. Because of these positions, he is sometimes known as the Berlin Bach or the Hamburg Bach. Emanuel wrote numerous sonatas and other pieces for the keyboard (his favorite instrument was supposedly the clavichord). The following list is representative of his keyboard works.

[4] See the collection *Sons of Bach*, ed. Wm. Newman (New York: Music Press, Inc., 1947). Excerpts in this chapter used by permission of the copyright owner, Mercury Music Corp., N.Y.

1. Six "Prussian" sonatas (1742) dedicated to Frederick II.

2. Six "Württemberg" sonatas (1744) dedicated to Carl Eugene, Duke of Württemberg.

3. Six sonatas "with varied reprises" (1760) dedicated to the Princess Amelia of Prussia.

4. Six sonatas "*à l'usage des Dames*" (for ladies), 1770.

5. *Clavier—Sonaten für Kenner und Liebhaber* (1779, 1780, 1781, 1783, 1785, 1787).[5]

In addition, Emanuel authored a book entitled *Versuch über die wahre Art das Clavier zu spielen* (Essay on the True Art of Playing Keyboard Instruments),[6] a comprehensive treatise that proved to be invaluable to later musicians who were concerned with technique, fingering, and ornamentation.

Emanuel played an important role in the creation of the keyboard sonata.[7] Most of his own sonatas have three movements in the expected sequence of fast-slow-fast tempos. He seems to tread a middle path, occasionally glancing back to the Baroque and yet also looking to the future. Some of his sonata movements are in clear binary form like those of his predecessors. Other movements, hinting of things to come, show a definite development of two themes (previously expressed in correct tonal relationship) and then a recapitulation of these themes.

Contributing to the sonata's structural framework was not Emanuel's primary achievement. He made important contributions to the molding of an idiomatic piano style by his personal knowledge of and experience with the art of playing and expressing details on the clavier. These stylistic elements influenced the composers of the Classic period, even the later Beethoven. Emanuel built his sonata movements to emphasize expressive detail—a tendency sometimes exaggerated, especially in the slow movements.

Emanuel was an untiring innovator. He created fantasy-like movements unlike any of the conventional sonata-movement forms. In his *Sonata in G Minor* (Ex. 2)[8] the opening *Allegro* movement is a good example of this. A type of scalar flourish, reminding one of the *Chromatic Fantasy*

[5] The Prussian sonatas are published by Nagel's Music Archive as are the Württemberg sonatas. Breitkopf & Härtel has six volumes *Die sechs Sammlungen von Sonaten, freien Fantasien und Rondos für Kenner und Liebhaber*. Peters and International Music Co. also publish collections of Emanuel's sonatas. Emanuel's compositions are identified by means of numbers from a catalogue made by A. Wotquenne (see Bibliography at the end of the chapter).

[6] C. P. E. Bach, *Essay on the True Art of Playing Keyboard Instruments*, translated and edited by Wm. Mitchell (New York: W. W. Norton & Co., Inc., 1949).

[7] See Karl Geiringer, *The Bach Family* (London: George Allen & Unwin, Ltd., 1954), pp. 354–360.

[8] *Sons of Bach, op. cit.*

of J. S. Bach, alternates with bravura runs in octaves very much like the last movement of the later *Sonata in B-flat Minor* by Chopin.

Ex. 2. C. P. E. Bach: *Sonata in G Minor: Allegro* (Wot. 65/17)

(quasi cadenza)

Emanuel also indulged in unorthodox tonal relationships. In one sonata movement in *d* minor, the second theme is in *B-flat* major instead of the anticipated *F* major. This freedom is also apparent in the tonal sequence of movements. A *Sonata in G Minor* has only its first movement in minor; the other movements are in major. Occasionally he indulges in cadenzas and long passages with no bar lines, an idea taken from the concerto and adapted to the solo keyboard. Mozart used this device several times in his clavier sonatas—for example, the *Sonata in B-flat Major, K.333.*

Unusual modulations and changes of key now and then account for the erratic nature of Emanuel's music. The first movement of the *Sonata in G Major*—from the collection of sonatas with varied reprises—contains no bar line between the exposition and development, and the movement ends on the dominant, in *D* major. Changes of time within a given movement mark another innovation that greatly influenced composers of a much later period.

Emanuel Bach paid careful attention to the expressiveness of his music, a quality especially apparent in his slow movements, which so often are moving and lyrical (Ex. 3). Emanuel's music sometimes becomes cluttered with nonessential notes, becoming complex in a situation that calls for simplicity and clarity.

C. P. E. Bach's clavier music is seldom heard today. Much of it, although it offers exciting new examples for those who directly followed

Ex. 3. C. P. E. Bach: *Sonata in G Major: Adagio e sostenuto* (Wot. 65/48)

him, now appears stilted, its themes fashioned with *too much* care and method. Still, there are individual works of great beauty among the vast output of this particular Bach, and these pieces deserve a hearing.

Stylistically Emanuel's niche in the eighteenth-century musical scene is as the foremost exponent of the *Empfindsamer Stil* (sensitive style), a term used to describe the North-German style of the second half of the eighteenth century. This style attempted to express true and natural feelings through a subjective and emotional use of the musical vocabulary. "Emanuel adopted for his instrumental works elements from the *opera seria* of his time, such as recitatives, ariosos, and certain forms of aria accompaniments; sometimes his sonatas appear like keyboard transcriptions of dramatic compositions. He had learned from his father that transplanting musical idioms from one medium to another could produce outstanding results. Nevertheless, his technique of transferring elements of the dramatic vocal style into keyboard music had never before been used to such an extent and with equal success."[9]

JOHANN CHRISTIAN BACH

Johann Christian (1735–1782), youngest of J. S. Bach's sons, received his early training from his half-brother Emanuel after the death of their father. The strongest influences on him came as a result of his years in Italy (during part of this period he was a pupil of the renowned Padre Martini). He spent the last two decades of his life in England where, as the spiritual heir of Handel, he continued the tradition of writing facile, melodious Italian operas.

Christian wrote about seventy sonatas for keyboard (about two-thirds of these are accompanied by other instruments). Some were definitely destined for the piano, since he was the first person in England to play a concert (1768) on the new pianoforte. He stands much nearer the Classic

[9] *The Bach Family, op. cit.,* pp. 352–353.

period than either of his two brothers; yet structurally he frequently clings to the past. For example, in the first movement of *Sonata in B-flat Major* (T.342/6),[10] a long section in the principal key is followed by another section in the dominant key, *F* major. After the double bar and a repeat of the first part, the principal idea of the first section is stated, developed, and expanded. Then the second section is literally repeated *in toto* with a slightly exasperating insistence. The themes of the two sections, however, are broadly contrasting: the first is very lyrical, bringing to mind Christian's Italian training; the second is constructed as a series of broken-chord figurations. The accompaniment to the lyrical theme is in Classic style, although the bare, broken thirds breathe monotony. The *Andante* has an elegant, refined shape rather than that of sustained, lyrical design (Ex. 4). A series of thirds in the right hand and repeated notes and octaves in the left hand betray a feeling for virtuosity despite the basic stylistic requisites for the slow movement. The third movement, *Prestissimo,* is actually a gigue with a definite Italianate touch, a striking reminder of Baldassare Galuppi.

Ex. 4. J. C. Bach: *Sonata in B-flat Major: Andante* (T.342/6)

CONTEMPORARIES OF BACH'S SONS

Several musicians contemporary with Bach's sons had the good fortune to study with the old cantor of Leipzig, but not all of these pupils achieved recognition.

Christoph Nichelmann (1717–1762), one of J. S. Bach's pupils, worked in company with Emanuel Bach for twelve years as second chamber cembalist to Frederick the Great. Nichelmann's works, from their titles, were intended for the ladies. His collections are *Sei Brevi Sonate all'uso delle Dame* (Six Short Sonatas for Ladies, 1745) and *Brevi Sonate da Cembalo all'uso di chi ama il Cembalo, massime delle Dame* (Short Harpsichord

---

[10] *Sons of Bach, op. cit.* Christian's compositions are identified by means of numbers from a catalogue made by C. S. Terry (see Bibliography at the end of the chapter).

Sonatas for Harpsichord Lovers, Chiefly the Ladies). Few of his works appear in reprint apart from several little harpsichord pieces in the French style which, though charming, offer nothing different from many other pieces of similar quality.[11]

J. S. Bach thought very highly of another of his pupils, **Johann Ludwig Krebs** (1713–1780). This organist is best known for his *Clavier Übung*, which may be played "just as easily on the harpsichord as on the organ." Krebs wrote several *Partitas*[12] in which the preludes are skillfully conceived fantasy forms with the melodic idea extended in a characteristic Baroque manner. The fugues in the *Partitas* are worked out meticulously and expertly, and the dance movements are a credit to an accomplished pupil.

Johann Philipp Kirnberger (1721–1783), also a student of the senior Bach, composed fugues for keyboard or organ following the old polyphonic style, but his most delightful inspirations are in the collection *Diverses Pièces pour le Clavecin* (1780),[13] which revived dances that had practically fallen into disuse, like the *Forlane* and the *Loure*. Among the effective sets of variations in this collection, there is one on a minuet bearing the strange title *Cossack Dance*.

Johann Gottfried Müthel (1718–1788) has been generally overlooked until recently. He went to Leipzig to study with J. S. Bach in 1750, the year the master died. Bach not only accepted the young man as a pupil but took him into his own house for the few remaining months of his life. Müthel later became a close friend of Emanuel Bach and developed into one of the best clavier players and composers of his time. From 1753 to 1788 he was organist at the Lutheran church in Riga.

Müthel's published compositions include three sonatas and two ariosos (each with twelve variations), which appeared in Nürnberg in 1756.[14] The title of the collection specifies *clavecin*, that is, harpsichord; but the style as well as the profusion of dynamic markings—*F, p, pp*—strongly suggest piano performance.

Müthel must have been successful in his own day, for Dr. Charles Burney classes him with the finest composers of the time. Burney's account of Müthel's music is worth reproducing here:

> M. Johann Gottfried Müthel, of Riga, being by birth and
> education a German, deserves a place here, though he is at pres-

---

[11] Several short pieces of Nichelmann are found in *Old Masters of the 16th, 17th and 18th Centuries*, ed. Niemann (New York: Kalmus).

[12] Two *Partitas* by Krebs are found in I and II of *Alte Meister*, ed. Pauer (Leipzig: Breitkopf & Härtel).

[13] See *Old Masters, op. cit.*

[14] Both the *Sonatas* and *Ariosi* of Müthel are published (in two volumes) by Breitkopf & Härtel.

ent established in a city which appertains to Russia. When a student upon keyed instruments has vanquished all the difficulties to be found in the lessons of Handel, Scarlatti, Schobert, Eckard, and C. P. E. Bach; and, like Alexander, laments that nothing more remains to conquer, I would recommend to him, as an exercise for patience and perseverance, the compositions of Müthel; which are so full of novelty, taste, and contrivance, that I should not hesitate to rank them among the greatest productions of the present age. Extraordinary as are the genius and performance of this musician, he is but little known in Germany, and all I could gather there concerning him is, that he received instructions from Sebastian Bach, and lived some time at Schwerin, before he settled in Riga.

The style of this composer more resembles that of Emanuel Bach, than any other. But the passages are entirely his own, and reflect as much honour upon his head as his hand. Indeed his writings abound with difficulties, which to common hearers, as well as common players, must appear too elaborate; for even his accompaniments are so charged as to require performers, for each instrument, of equal abilities to his own, which is expecting too much, in musicians of this nether world.[15]

As Burney states, Müthel's music does resemble that of Emanuel Bach. Each sonata contains three movements, and each individual movement is extraordinarily long for this period. Furthermore, he employs certain experimental procedures in his keyboard music—pauses, profuse ornaments, dynamic and tempo contrasts—which classify him as an early exponent of *Sturm und Drang* (Storm and Stress).[16] He appears unconcerned with formal problems but concentrates on technique and on style in relation to expression and emotion.

Johann Peter Kellner (1705–1772), also contemporary with Bach's sons, had a fair reputation, but his music is almost forgotten today. He spent nearly his whole life as cantor at Gräfenroda in Thuringia, his birthplace. He became acquainted with J. S. Bach's music at an early age, and even as a mature musician he steadfastly displayed great admiration for both Bach and Handel. Logically, then, Kellner's own music could be expected to show attractive features reminiscent of these two composers. But since very little Kellner music has been reprinted,[17] it is difficult either

---

[15] *Dr. Burney's Musical Tours in Europe*, ed. P. Scholes (London: Oxford University Press, 1959), II, 240–241.

[16] The term "Storm and Stress" (*Sturm und Drang*) is often used to describe a romantic crisis, a breaking away from strictures of rules. This term was first applied to a German literary movement of the latter half of the eighteenth century, a movement which led to Romanticism.

[17] The only examples of Kellner's writings available in modern edition are found in *Deutsche Klaviermusik des 17. und 18. Jahrhunderts*, III, edited by Fischer and Oberdoerffer for Vieweg.

to agree or disagree with Seiffert,[18] who ranks Kellner's suites among the best produced after the generation of J. S. Bach and Gottlieb Muffat. Johann Kellner's outstanding keyboard publication *Certamen musicum bestehend aus Präludien, Fugen, Allemanden* (Musical Contest Consisting of Preludes, Fugues, Allemandes) is a collection of six suites (1739–1749). Another edition of eight suites appeared shortly thereafter (1749–1756).

The name of **Giovanni Benedetto Platti** (*ca.* 1690–1763) is more prominent in Germany than in his native Italy, for he appeared in Mainz as early as 1720. A Venice-trained composer, Platti seems to have spent most of his mature life at Würzburg in various musical capacities. Two sets of keyboard sonatas (six in each) appeared around 1742 and 1746 as *Opus 1* and *Opus 4* respectively.[19] Each sonata in the first collection is modeled after the *sonata da chiesa* (church sonata), with four movements according to the general plan: slow-fast-slow-fast. Here the bipartite form of the Baroque period is favored. In the second portfolio a three-movement sequence is encountered three times. In this and in other structural details the collection approaches similar works by J. S. Bach's sons and other Pre-Classic composers.

Seen through his keyboard works, Platti's innate musical talent is very evident. Sparkling harmonic texture and a sensible use of chromaticism and ornamentation impart a delightful color to his music. The melodies are lyric and expressive, and the composer expands and develops these themes with obvious relish and sensitivity.

In one instance the Bach tradition was carried as far east as Russia. **Johann Wilhelm Hässler** (1747–1822) was born in Erfurt and studied there with his uncle Johann Christian Kittel, a pupil of J. S. Bach. Hässler at first combined two professions—business and music; but, in 1780, he relinquished his business career, and became a successful pianist and composer. In 1794 he settled in Moscow where he remained until his death.

An examination of several Hässler compositions shows his admiration for and imitation of Emanuel Bach. This is especially true in his many sonatas for two, three, and four hands, which appeared (without opus numbers) from 1776 to 1793.[20] After his move to Moscow, he began to number his compositions. All forty-nine opuses written there are for piano, some in ensemble with various obbligato instruments.

All the native-born Pre-Classic composers discussed in this chapter

---

[18] Max Seiffert, *Geschichte der Klaviermusik* (Leipzig: Breitkopf & Härtel, 1899), pp. 361–367.

[19] G. B. Platti, *Zwölf Sonaten*, ed. L. Hoffmann-Erbrecht (Leipzig: Breitkopf & Härtel), 2 Vols.

[20] Many Hässler compositions were included in *Le Trésor des Pianistes*. Schott edition publishes a few pieces and Peters edits *Six Easy Sonatas*. The best account of Hässler's career in Russia is found in Robert Aloys Mooser, *Annales de la Musique et des Musiciens en Russie au XVIIIe Siècle* (Genève: Mont-Blanc, 1948–1951), II, 659–661.
for Vieweg.

have come from north Germany or middle Germany; one exception is
Johann Ernst Eberlin (1702–1762), who was born in Upper Swabia. Eberlin was cathedral organist and court chapelmaster at Salzburg. His *IX
Toccate e Fugue* (Augsburg, 1747) for organ pay scant attention to the
pedal, and some of them can be played most effectively on other keyboard
instruments.

Only one notable keyboard composer appeared in Austria between
the time of Muffat and that of Haydn. He was **Georg Christoph Wagenseil**
(1715–1777), a pupil of the famous theorist J. J. Fux and a music teacher
at the court of Maria Theresa. Uneven structure and texture in Wagenseil's
early sonatas indicate an insecure technique, but his *Divertimenti publicati
per commodo dei Principianti* (Divertimentos Published for the Use of
Beginners)[21] are gratifying, inspired keyboard pieces. Each *Divertimento*
has two movements in fast tempo and a minuet. Some of the fast movements
—in fact most of them—are in sonata form with only one theme. Wagenseil's
compositions reveal that he had a good command of harmony. Several of his
procedures serve as a bridge from one period in music history to another.
For example, it is not clear whether his *Divertimento in F* should be linked
with some of the preludes by J. S. Bach or with the as yet unthought-of
Impromptus by Schubert (particularly the *Impromptu in G-flat Major*).

During the Pre-Classic period, then, the basic outlines of the sonata
took shape—perhaps subconsciously but at any rate very realistically. Experiments in structural form, expressive qualities, developmental procedures, and tonal design all helped in the formation of the sonata. Johann
Sebastian Bach's sons and pupils and their contemporaries contributed to
this musical revolution. The ultimate formula of the sonata was passed on
to the Classic composers—namely Haydn and Mozart—who perfected it
and gave it more elegant proportions.

BIBLIOGRAPHY

Bach, Carl Philipp Emanuel. *Essay on the True Art of Playing Keyboard Instruments* (translated by Wm. Mitchell). New York: W. W. Norton &
Co., Inc., 1949.

---

[21] The *Divertimenti* of Wagenseil were published by Nagel's Archive, but in 1964 were
out of print. A *Divertimento in F Minor* is found in *Keyboard Music of the Baroque and
Rococo*, ed. W. Georgii (Cologne: Arno Volk Verlag), III.

Campbell, Robert G. *The Works of Johann Gottfried Müthel.* Dissertation (in progress). Indiana University.

Canave, Paz Corazon. *A Re-Evaluation of the Role Played by Carl Philipp Emmanuel Bach in the Development of the Clavier Sonata.* Washington, D.C.: Catholic University of America Press, 1956.

Geiringer, Karl. *The Bach Family.* London: George Allen & Unwin, Ltd., 1954. (Published in the United States by Oxford University Press).

Horstman, Jean. *The Instrumental Music of Johann Ludwig Krebs.* Dissertation. Boston University, 1959.

Mekota, Beth. *The Keyboard Music of John Christian Bach.* Dissertation (in progress). University of Michigan.

Newman, Wm. S. "The Keyboard Sonatas of Bach's Sons and Their Relation to the Classic Sonata Concept." Proceedings for the *Music Teachers National Association,* 1949.

Reeser, Eduard. *The Sons of Bach.* Stockholm: Continental Book Co., 1946.

Terry, Charles Sanford. *John Christian Bach.* London: Oxford University Press, 1929.

Wotquenne, Alfred. *Thematisches Verzeichnis der Werke von Carl Philipp Emanuel Bach.* Leipzig: Breitkopf & Härtel, 1905.

13

HAYDN

AND

MOZART

Like most historical eras, the Classic period has no exact dates. The years fixing "period" boundaries for the arts differ according to the subject of discussion—music, literature, or the graphic arts. It is particularly difficult to establish definite years for each period in music history. So far we have seen that elements of the Classic style appeared in the Baroque era —early harbingers, so to speak, of a new age. And in the midst of the Classic period there came into being some of the principles associated with the subsequent early Romantic school.

Generally speaking, Classicism in music covers the period dating from the more mature compositions of Haydn through the early works of Beethoven (from about 1775 to 1815). The special characteristics identified with Classicism—clarity, balance, and restraint—were achieved by experimentation with sonata form as handed down from the Pre-Classic period. The Classicists added and discarded until the sonata form attained the mature framework perceived in the later masterworks of Mozart and Haydn.

The piano itself was a great help to early Classic composers. Haydn and Mozart both wrote most of their keyboard works for piano, not harpsichord. Although the piano tone at the time had a light quality, its sustaining pedal, improved key action, and possibilities for nuance were indispensable factors in the evolution of the Classic style.

FRANZ JOSEPH HAYDN

Joseph Haydn (1732–1809) was one composer fortunate enough to have his talents acknowledged while he was still alive. His creative years were largely patronized by the Esterhazy family; his chief duty was to supply music for this family of *melomanes*. Haydn, almost entirely self-taught, enjoyed a tremendous success, and his music was performed all over Europe.

Attempts have been made to show that Haydn was influenced by Croatian folk melodies, that he fashioned his melodic designs from Italian models, and that he admired and imitated French clarity and elegance. There may be partial truth in all this but the unalterable fact is that Haydn remained Haydn: a simple, rather imperturbable individual who possessed an inner serenity and an optimistic outlook.

Haydn had before him the models of two basic sonata types. One originated in the north and reached fulfillment with C. P. E. Bach and W. F. Bach. This sonata type had a framework of three movements—fast-slow-fast. Two themes were presented, elaborated, and restated in the first movement. The second sonata type centered around Vienna in the south. Although usually limited to three movements, this sonata structure gave the minuet equal stature with other movements and generally preserved the same tonality throughout. The *Divertimenti* of Christoph Wagenseil[1] are typical of this Austrian characteristic. Some of Haydn's early sonatas may be considered *Divertimenti*, since they follow the Wagenseil prototypes.

Any attempt to discover an authoritative, definitive edition of Haydn's works leads to a certain confusion. One edition lists thirty sonatas, another twenty-four, and a third adds opus numbers to the sonatas. There seems to be no reason for the arbitrary grouping of his keyboard music. In 1918 Karl Päsler made a catalogue for a projected Collected Edition, which was initiated by Breitkopf and Härtel. This catalogue was later adopted and included in Group XVI of Anthony van Hoboken's thematic catalogue (see Bibliography). This chronological catalogue (correct for the most part) lists fifty-two sonatas, several of which are of doubtful authenticity. One of the best editions of Haydn sonatas is that of C. F. Peters.[2] For this chapter, the sonatas have the Päsler (Hoboken) numbers included in their titles and the corresponding Peters number placed in parentheses. The number of any sonata will be in arabic numerals, the number of any sonata movement in roman numerals.

It is curious that Haydn, who was not a pianist, should have composed more than fifty piano sonatas and several short piano pieces. What seems more logical is the discovery that he progressively lost interest in keyboard composition and concentrated instead on the string quartet and symphony. Haydn wrote only three piano sonatas during the last twenty years of his life.

Haydn experimented a good deal with the piano sonata, much more

[1] See discussion of these works in Chapter 12.

[2] The sonatas of the Peters Edition are in five volumes. An extra volume includes the various short compositions (This is based on the Päsler text, but edited by Martienssen). Breitkopf & Härtel publishes forty-two sonatas in four volumes and Universal Edition also has a four-volume set. Kalmus publishes thirty-four sonatas.

so than Mozart. With only three exceptions, Mozart's sonatas adhere to this three-movement structure: a fast opening movement in sonata-allegro form, a slow movement in song form or rondo form, and a finale in rondo or sonata-allegro form. Haydn also followed this pattern in many of his works, but in addition he composed nine sonatas with just two movements and two with four movements. Haydn's first movement is sometimes a theme and variations, and frequently the final movement is cast in minuet form.

There are other interesting points of comparison between Haydn and Mozart. Haydn seldom used a virtuoso or dynamic approach to the sonata. In contrast to Mozart's *allegro* markings, Haydn chose *allegro moderato* or even *moderato*. But in choice of tonality, the two composers show an affinity. It is quite remarkable that only five of Haydn's fifty-two sonatas are in a minor key (in some sonatas all the movements remain in the same key), and only two of Mozart's seventeen sonatas are in a minor key.

After 1772 Mozart and Haydn began to exchange ideas. From Haydn, Mozart learned about thematic development and ingenious methods of modulation. Haydn (in the 1780's) observed how Mozart stressed the importance of the second theme and how he contrasted it with the first theme. Haydn's development sections had been little more than short passages in which the tonal center was flexible. After hearing Mozart's music, he expanded his development sections, thereby providing an opportunity to work out and manipulate the subject matter he had presented in the exposition. Haydn usually chose to modify the recapitulation section more than Mozart.

For the first movement of his more mature sonatas, Haydn frequently used two themes, which, however, are not always markedly contrasting. Many Haydn themes are built in irregular periods of three, five, or seven measures, and he shows a tendency to suppress the importance of the second subject or theme. As a matter of fact, in passages where Mozart automatically introduces a new (second) theme, Haydn often seeks some fresh guise in which to present his first theme, thus reserving any new material for a less obvious occasion. With his personal predilection for clarity, Haydn often neatly separates the three sections of his first movement by a retard, a silence, a measure or two of chordal passages, or an organ point. One favorite Haydn device occurs in the development section; he builds the first part of the development section around the second theme and then goes on to develop the first theme, leading to the recapitulation. His development section is usually short, although at times it may contain the emotional climax of the entire movement.

For his middle movements Haydn ran the gamut from two-part song form to full-fledged sonata-allegro form. He was one of the first to introduce variation form in the slow movement. Sometimes his second movement slides imperceptibly into the finale. And once he tried to link all three movements together in the *Sonata No. 30 in A Major* (36). If he selects a minuet for the middle movement, then the trio section, instead of being another minuet in the manner of his predecessors', often becomes a real contrast to the minuet. Haydn was a master of the minuet. He gave it his own personal contours. In his later sonatas, however, the true minuet flavor has disappeared and all that remains is the indication *tempo di minuetto*. Those central movements marked *andante* and *adagio* are the least personal parts of his sonatas. His simple, robust personality was not lyrically inclined. The andantes are often exceptionally dry, sounding like the harpsichord style of long ago. On the other hand, he displayed great ingenuity in his sparkling finales, usually written in rondo form. Here he uses the indications *presto* and even *prestissimo*, setting into motion an indescribable verve and dash, an inherent optimistic spirit.

For Haydn the sonata form became a framework in which melodic structure went hand in hand with contrast of key. To the tonal design of sonata form inherited from earlier composers Haydn added a clear thematic structure. This basic structure of the future Classic sonata had been appropriated from the north German school. Haydn's indebtedness went beyond matters of form. Many other features of his music resemble certain Pre-Classic procedures: the use of repeated notes (9/I), syncopation effects (25/II), heavy chords contrasting with lyric melody (39/I), the use of triplet figures (17/I).

From the outset of his creative career to the year 1766, Haydn wrote sixteen sonatas for the pianoforte. Each of these early works shows the influence of the Viennese school: a minuet is present in each; a tonal unity is usually preserved. Elements of sonata-allegro form are discernible in some movements but in an embryonic state: for example, a series of motives, framed in unequal phrases, following one upon the other with little concern over their development (22/I). As he progressed through this period, he gradually clarified his ideas, reducing the number of themes to two and occasionally creating the second theme from the first (43/I).

Typical of Haydn's early divertimento-like sonatas is *No. 11 in G Major* (11). Only four pages long, this little work has three movements, two of which are in miniature. The opening *Presto* (Ex. 1) presents a rhythmic motive that is expanded a little, then repeated. Another section (in g minor) with contrasting texture offers a bit of variety and is followed by a *da capo* of the initial section. The central *Andante* is the most progressive (and most extensive) of the three movements. Two brief themes are stated, developed in an uncomplicated manner, and finally recapitulated. In typical divertimento fashion, the final movement of this sonata

Ex. 1. J. Haydn: *Sonata No. 11 in G Major* (11): *Presto*

is a gracious *Menuet* with a contrasting *Trio* based on a triplet motive.

Between 1767 and 1771, Haydn's music underwent further crystallization. During those years he composed eight sonatas in which the structure surpasses the level of the divertimento. One of the most attractive sonatas from this period is *No. 20 in C Minor* (25), a work written at a time of personal crisis. Unusually dramatic and laced with wide contrasts between poetry and violence, this sonata seems to discard all past procedures and searches for new paths. The other seven sonatas have a more restrained spirit yet their structure has become increasingly pliable.

From 1774 to 1784, Haydn wrote about ten sonatas that emphasize lyricism and ornamentation and show a preference for the theme and variation. The early works in this group are inconsistent; for instance, a well-rounded movement is often succeeded by an inferior one. But after 1780 Haydn had sonata-allegro form under control, and he began to handle it with imagination: the development is ample, the recapitulation more diversified in character. One example of this improved structure—*Sonata No. 36 in C-sharp Minor* (6)—has a second subject derived from the first, as well as a surprising, interesting recapitulation. The movements in *Sonata No. 30 in A Major* (36) are linked together in an attempt at unification, and *Sonata No. 32 in B Minor* (39) has a strong rhythmic drive.

One of the most popular sonatas from this group is *No. 37 in D Major* (7). Here Haydn assumes full command of his scintillating, effervescent style. This fine example of the Classic sonata has exuberant first and last movements. The virtuosity in the initial movement becomes apparent from its title, *Allegro con brio*. The first theme (in *D* major) is stated (Ex. 2), extended, and separated from the second theme by a rest. There is a real codetta, which is later expanded into the concluding coda. The development section is artful though short. The second movement, *Largo e sostenuto*, is little more than an interlude of four lines. It ends on an *A*-major chord, presupposing an *attacca* into the *Finale*. In the *Finale* a lively theme is stated three times, each statement separated by two highly contrasting interludes—a fitting climax for this diverting and artistically invigorating sonata.

Ex. 2. J. Haydn: *Sonata No. 37 in D Major* (7): *Allegro con brio*

The last few years of Haydn's keyboard writing were productive. There are first of all several rather short works. The *Fantasia in C* (Hob. XVII:4—1789) is really a rondo and the most effective one that he ever wrote. The delightful *Variations in F Minor* (Hob. XVII:6—1793) were originally titled *Sonata* by Haydn. This piece has one of the longest themes ever conceived for variations: a bisectional *Andante* (plus repetitions) and a *Trio* in two sections, all forming part of the theme, or rather comprising a double theme. For the *Andante,* Haydn wrote only two variations and a *Finale.* The work is outstanding and must be classed with his finest sonatas.

The five sonatas from these last years (1789–1794) represent the culmination of Haydn's keyboard style. *No. 48 in C Major* (24) was written as a contribution to a musical potpourri published by Breitkopf and Härtel in 1789; *No. 49 in E-flat Major* (3) was dedicated to Marianne von Genziger; and the last three were written in London for Thérèse Jansen (Mme. Bartolozzi). All these sonatas have an expressive freedom quite unusual for their time. Each sonata has its distinctly personal characteristics, and each reveals the extraordinary fantasy of the composer. In these five highly diversified sonatas, Haydn employs all the forms he had encountered: sonata-allegro, double variation, slow movements in song form, rondo, and rondo-sonata.

Although a composer's last works are not necessarily his best, in Haydn's case all the experience and skill acquired through the years culminate in his later keyboard compositions. One of his last piano sonatas, *Sonata No. 52 in E-flat Major* (1), is a masterwork that displays his lifetime efforts at keyboard composing.[3]

The massive impression of the first movement, *Allegro,* of this sonata is established right from the opening bars (Ex. 3). He stresses the significance of this theme, even extends it, as though trying to delay the ap-

---

[3] Oliver Strunk believes that *Sonata No. 52 in E-flat Major* was written first, followed by *No. 51 in D Major* and finally *No. 50 in C Major* (See his 1934 article "Notes on a Haydn Autograph," in the *Musical Quarterly*).

Ex. 3. J. Haydn: *Sonata No. 52 in E-flat Major* (1): *Allegro*

pearance of the second idea. This second theme (in *B-flat*) lightens the prevailing mood and leads to the bare, mysterious octaves of the codetta. Wonderful modulations take place in the development: there are passages in *C* major, in *A-flat* major, and in *E* major. The recapitulation is abbreviated.

The *Adagio* is more effective than usual for Haydn, though it is still not as convincing as similar examples by Mozart. It is written in ample song form (A B A). Yet despite the external techniques, the entire movement is dominated by the initial rhythmic motive. This strong rhythmic pattern, the little cadenza figures, the light ornamentation, all contribute to the luster of this movement.

The finale *Presto* uses a form borrowing elements from both sonata-allegro and rondo—a hybrid, really, but it has its own logic and forceful expression. The rest and the pause are used here with great effectiveness.

With this masterpiece—in which virtuosity, harmonic audacity, lyric suavity, and technical maturity marvelously intermingle—and with the two other sonatas of 1794–1795, Joseph Haydn takes leave of the piano sonata. The Viennese master benefited from the lessons of the Pre-Classic composers, but his own intuitive musical skill created these delightful sonatas that shine so brightly in their eighteenth-century setting.

WOLFGANG AMADEUS MOZART

For **Wolfgang Amadeus Mozart** (1756–1791) the term genius is the only appellation that seems appropriate. One has merely to compare a minuet written by the six-year-old Wolfgang with one composed by his father Leopold[4] to understand that the son had a God-given gift for music. Following the Salzburg-born Mozart throughout his brief life—into France, Italy, and Austria—one realizes his enormous capacity for assimilation. Everything that impressed him was stored in his mind. Mozart's Italian

[4] Wyzewa et Saint-Foix, *W.-A. Mozart* (Paris: Desclée de Brouwer et Cie., 1936), I, 14.

style became more Italianate than the Italians. The same holds true of his French style. Some of his most charming piano sonatas were written during sojourns in France.

Mozart was a performing pianist and gave numerous concerts, especially in his youth. He composed his own music for these performances, much of it while actually on tour. He also improvised some of his works on the spot, then later wrote them down. Obviously his musical apparatus was prodigious.

Mozart's music for solo clavier consists mostly of variations, sonatas, and a few *fantasias*.[5] He was a great symphonist and opera composer and did not always find the best expression for his genius in his keyboard works, particularly the early ones. Many were written in haste and on demand: a sonata for a wealthy pupil, something to fill in a concert program, another work on commission. And yet, in the fairly substantial amount of solo keyboard music there are several genuine masterpieces.

Mozart wrote seventeen independent sets of variations for solo clavier distributed throughout *K.24* to *K.613*.[6] After the Baroque period and the variations of J. S. Bach, variation form had undergone considerable changes. Pre-Classic composers had been content to repeat a theme five or six times without introducing any other modification apart from embroidering it with new accompaniment figures, or with alterations in phrasing details. The variation at that time also emphasized the Alberti bass, the crossing of hands, and all the artifices of modern virtuosity that were then being substituted for the firm musical structures inherited from the old school.

The theme and variations that reached Mozart's hands was primarily a product of Paris, where it was very popular. If the theme was in duple time, there was usually one variation in triple meter. There was also one adagio variation and, if the theme was in a major key, one variation in minor mode. Many Mozart variations sound like those of his contemporaries or immediate predecessors. He is rather timid in his approach to the variation—quite the opposite of his concept of sonata form—and it is apparent that he did not take his variations too seriously. That they are charming is undeniable, but to say that they represent Mozart's best clavier writing would be an exaggeration.

[5] Kalmus publishes both the *Sonatas* (*Urtext*) and the complete *Variations* in splendid editions. Especially fine is the edition made by Nathan Broder (*Sonatas* and *Fantasias* only) for Theodore Presser Company. Mozart's complete works were published by Breitkopf & Härtel, reprinted in forty volumes by J. W. Edwards in 1951. The *Neue Ausgabe*, begun by Bärenreiter in 1959, is still in progress.

[6] The letter *K.* refers to a chronological catalogue of Mozart's works made by Ludwig Köchel. He was sometimes incorrect in his assumptions and Alfred Einstein issued a revised catalogue in 1937 (new edition. 1964). However, the Köchel numbers are still used as a means of identification.

Twelve variations that he wrote on the old French nursery rhyme, "*Ah, vous dirai-je maman,*" *K.265,* merely present a lovely series of configurations about this naïve folk song. The same can be said about other Mozart variations, such as those on a *Minuet of Duport, K.573,* an aria from the opera *The Pilgrims of Mecca* by Gluck, *K.455, Lison dormais, K.264,* and *La Belle Françoise, K.353.*

The seventeen sonatas for solo clavier present an entirely different Mozart, for in these he follows the path established by Joseph Haydn and C. P. E. Bach. However, Mozart explores the expressive qualities of the piano more than Haydn had done. And as Mozart matured he began to give more importance to developmental procedure, to so-called bridge passages linking one theme to another.

In the first movements, which are usually in sonata-allegro form, the themes are nicely contrasted. Some of these clavier themes consist solely of a series of different motives, but in the entire framework—thanks to Mozart's wonderful command of accompaniment technique—these themes are very striking and lend themselves admirably to development.

In contrast to the short, often cursory middle movements composed by Haydn, Mozart's *andantes* and *adagios* equal the finest of any age. In curtailing his slow movements, Haydn was bowing to the contemporary taste of a rather frivolous public that reveled in virtuosity. "On the other hand, the most wonderful fact about Mozart was that he directed his art toward success without any sacrifice of himself. He made no concessions that he need blush for; he deceived the public, but he guided it well. He gave people the illusion that they understood his ideas; while, as a matter of fact, the applause that greeted his works was excited only by passages which were solely composed for applause. And what matter? So long as there was applause, the work was successful, and the composer was free to create new works."[7]

Mozart felt the need to express himself amply in his slow movements; and he did just that. His central movements, usually adagio or andante, represent some of the first successful attempts at using the piano's expressive qualities. The slow movements are sometimes in simple song form (A B A), at other times in rondo form. In their simplicity lies their difficulty. The sparseness of writing, the long melodic lines, the subtle phrasing all call for utmost skill and good taste on the part of the performer.

Mozart always retained his enthusiasm for the adagio or andante. In fact, his piano sonatas from beginning to end, from *K.279* through *K.576,* consistently exhibit excellent writing in these middle movements, even though some weaknesses appear in the allegros and prestos. For example,

[7] Romain Rolland, *Essays on Music* (New York: Allen, Towne & Heath, Inc., 1948), p. 250.

the slightly contrapuntal opening of the *Adagio* in *Sonata K.280* has a lovely meditative character. Another introspective adagio is found in *K.457*, a type of rondo in which the beautifully lyric original theme is varied by means of two additional statements. The andantes have a more down-to-earth quality than the adagios, although in general they maintain the same flowing lines, the same expressive lyricism.

Mozart's rondo finales are what one would expect from this vibrant individual who kept his buoyant spirit despite personal problems. His finales are lively and joyous. Occasionally, as in *K.311* and *K.333*, he inserts a cadenza, an odd procedure for a Classic sonata movement, but, of course, it is derived from C. P. E. Bach.

Mozart's first efforts at sonata writing for the clavier were entitled *Sonatas for the harpsichord, which may be played with the accompaniment of a violin, dedicated to Madame Victoire of France, by J. G. Wolfgang Mozart of Salzburg, aged seven, first work* (*K.6–7*). In these elementary works, in which the violin has practically no function, Mozart had not yet chosen between the Italian sonata in binary form à la Scarlatti and the German sonata in ternary form cultivated by J. S. Bach's sons. Needless to say, these childish efforts are never performed.

In 1774–1775 six sonatas appeared: *K. 279* through *K. 284*. They are not typical of the mature, polished Mozart, but they do reveal a gradual progression to the later works. The first theme in the opening *Allegro* in *K. 279* is somewhat awkward, and the second theme does not display the decided contrast so prominent in later sonatas. Constant sequential passages in this movement (as well as in others) and a somewhat excessive use of the Alberti bass suggest that Mozart was still feeling his way. This sonata somehow gives the feeling of an improvisation.

In the first movement of the second sonata (*K. 280*) Mozart's early habit of repeating rather tedious figurations is still evident. The second movement has a noble, simple texture that supplies expressive warmth. The third movement, *Presto*, begins to show Mozart's finest sonata writing: witty (with unexpected turns, such as an unusual use of rests) and restless (pressing brilliantly on to the climax).

Haydn's influence—and indirectly the influence of C. P. E. Bach—is still evident in the first two movements of the *Sonata in B-flat Major, K. 281*. However, the fact that Mozart was a pianist and Haydn was not stands out vividly in Mozart's superb piano compositions. Mozart changed his pace in his *Sonata in E-flat Major, K.282;* an *Adagio* appears as the first movement, an adagio providing a glimpse of the later Mozart. Two contrasting *minuets* occupy the space usually reserved for the slow movement. With the *Sonata K.283* Mozart indicates that he is freeing himself from the influence of his predecessors, at least in some technical matters. A Haydn influence remains, particularly in the development sections, where entirely new ideas are introduced.

The *Sonata in D Major, K.284,* sixth and last in this series, was composed at the request of Baron Dürnitz, whom Mozart met while visiting Munich. It was very important in the development of Mozart's style. For his previous sonatas the young composer had been satisfied to follow the ideals of the *style galant,* although he remained undecided as to what technical means he could best employ. This sonata shows not the least hesitation and marks the triumph of *galanterie* in Mozart's work.

The first movement, *Allegro,* of *Sonata, K. 284* is admittedly similar in spirit to its antecedents, but neither the *Andante* nor the finale have anything in common with previous corresponding movements. The *Andante* is entitled *Rondeau en Polonaise,* and in the finale Mozart has substituted a theme and variations for the usual rondo. He doubtlessly borrowed this new sonata concept from the French along with the title of the second movement, a title which more correctly should have been *Polonaise en Rondeau.* It is a simple rondeau whose theme has a polonaise rhythm. The entire movement has a brilliant, ornate cast, strangely different from the lyricism of the preceding sonatas; the lyricism is replaced by an exterior decoration incessantly renewed by a series of octaves in both hands, constantly modulating Alberti basses, and trills. For the first time, a theme and variations appears as the finale in a Mozart piano sonata. These are virtuoso variations, rich in sonority, uniformly constructed, and are a far cry from the simple variations composed as independent sets.

For two years Mozart played his first six sonatas in concert, and then he proceeded to write seven new ones. Two were written or completed in Mannheim, the other five took shape in Paris. Alfred Einstein had this to say about the two Mannheim sonatas—*C Major, K. 309* and *D Major, K. 311:*

> We are particularly well informed about the circumstances attending the composition of the first one. Mozart had improvised it in his last concert in Augsburg, on 22 October; or, to be more accurate, he had improvised the first and last movements, with a different slow movement. "I then played . . . all of a sudden a magnificent sonata in C major, out of my head, with a rondo at the end—full of din and sound," he wrote in a letter of 24 October, 1777. The characterization applies to both the first and last movements, particularly the passages in the rondo that have the thirty-second-note tremoli; but Mozart forgot to mention the subtlety with which he had brought this movement, "full of din and sound," to a pianissimo ending. Both movements are full of pianistic brilliance, the first being like the

transcription of a C major Salzburg symphony for a Stein piano. But the middle movement, an *Andante un poco adagio,* was not simply written down from memory in Mannheim, but rather freshly composed, for in it Mozart sought to paint the character of Mlle. Cannabich, daughter of his new friend, the Kapellmeister Cannabich. Since we know nothing of this young lady's character, we cannot judge whether the portrait is a faithful one or not. The movement is a "tender" and "sensitive" andante, containing ever more richly ornamented repetitions of the theme. How little Mozart was concerned with realism may be inferred from the fact that the slow movement of the other Mannheim sonata—an *Andante con espressione,* very childlike, very innocent—has also been taken to be the portrait of the young Rose Cannabich. The whole sonata is in a way a companion-piece to the sonata in C. Just as in the first movement of that work, the repetition of the initial motive is here avoided in the recapitulation and appears only as a surprise in the coda. In both sonatas the middle register of the instrument is cultivated in a new way; in both, the left hand no longer furnishes a mere accompaniment, but becomes a real partner in the dialogue; both works are showy. Mozart counted them among his more difficult piano sonatas—and rightly so, although even the apparently simplest clavier pieces by Mozart are difficult.[8]

It is rare to find in the works of any musician a stylistic transformation like that which is so prominent in the Paris sonatas. In Paris Mozart may have been influenced by Johann Schobert's sonatas; he not only purchased them but recommended them to his students. In the first movement of *K. 310* Mozart, instead of delineating a sharply defined second theme, resorts to a series of sixteenth notes, first in the right hand, then in the left, thus excluding the possibility of any theme capable of organic growth. New ideas come into play here, recalling the spirit of the concerto with its alternation of solo and tutti. Some techniques anticipate future periods of Romanticism, such as melodies placed in the bass and accompanied by a series of continuous modulations. The vigorous treatment, the rich harmonic language, and the expansive, expressive development given to these new ideas, supply ample proof that this sonata is written by a new Mozart. Its inner core—sometimes introspective, sometimes almost impassioned— challenges that school of thought which finds in Mozart only lightness and grace. An intimation of romantic individualism (romantic before the letter)

[8] Alfred Einstein, *Mozart,* trans. Mendel & Broder (New York: Oxford University Press, 1945), pp. 243–244. Hanns Dennerlein in his *Der Unbekannte Mozart* (Leipzig: Breitkopf & Härtel, 1951), p. 65, believes that the improvised sonata was *K. 330* rather than *K. 309.*

is evident in the central part of the *Andante* with its Schubertian trills and rhythmic patterns.

The second Paris sonata *K. 330 in C Major* has more restrained dimensions than the others in this set. Although its technical structure is more transparent, the *Sonata in C* has a full-bodied expression and a delightful choice of musical ideas. The first movement, *Allegro moderato,* presents three distinct though closely knit subjects. The development, though not extensive, is a fusion of melancholy and reflection, and it does not involve the more vital elements of the exposition. However, these initial themes are reintroduced in the recapitulation in such a way that the unconventional procedure is hardly noticeable. With an unexpected twist, Mozart uses material from the beginning of the development to conclude this outstanding movement. The *Allegretto* finale is also unusual in the folk quality of its initial theme.

The perennial Mozart favorite—the *Sonata in A Major, K. 331*—has helped to create an image that many people consider to be the typical Mozart. But this sonata is not typical. To begin with, the movement sequence is irregular: first a theme and variations, then a minuet followed by the celebrated *Rondo alla Turca.* Mozart could have conceived a sonata like this only in Paris, where the sonata form ordinarily included an andante with variations in place of an initial allegro and a minuet instead of the slow movement. The final rondo is a perfect example of a French rondo, with its minor and major sections followed by a *da capo.*

The theme and variations of the *Sonata in A Major, K. 331* has pure line and texture. Mozart wrote many variations and there are others perhaps more grandly conceived than these, but seldom did he produce variations with more suppleness or more clarity. He rarely departs from his original thematic line, except perhaps in the minor variation. The result is a continual and highly expressive melodic line. The beautiful *Menuetto* has a broad content not often encountered. The *Trio,* obviously written to imitate some by Schobert, flows with such grandeur that the usual adagio is hardly missed. From a formal viewpoint, the celebrated finale, *Alla Turca,* is another delightful example of a contemporary French rondo (Ex. 4). Its theme in *a* minor has a refrain in *A* major. The first interlude (in *f-sharp* minor) consists of a simple variation (in sixteenth notes) using the same accompaniment as the rondo theme itself; at the third appearance of the refrain, the accompaniment is in arpeggiated octaves.

The *Sonata in F Major, K. 332* was published by Mozart in 1784 along with *K. 330* and *K. 331.* Most likely it was written in Paris as part of the "six difficult sonatas" Mozart mentions in a letter dated September 11, 1778. He now seems to have discovered new means of expression, possibly the result of his Paris experiences. He expands his expressive ideas in matters

Ex. 4. W. A. Mozart: *Sonata in A Major, K.331: Alla Turca*

of detail as well as in the general ensemble. The initial *Allegro* uses ternary rhythm, a procedure rather rare in piano sonatas. The second subject brings to mind certain idiomatic features common to Viennese dances. The overall compactness of ideas and the straightforward approach impart to this sonata a classic quality that Mozart must have acquired in France. However, the magnificent finale—so powerful and rich in its texture, so imaginative and varied in its fantasy—announces the coming Romanticism.

The final sonata in this series—*K. 333 in B-flat Major*—is more lyric than any of the others and was finished either in Paris or when Mozart arrived in Salzburg. The first movement is tinged with the influence of Johann Christian Bach, who had come to Paris in 1778 and doubtlessly showed his latest sonatas to his friend Wolfgang. But by this time Mozart possessed such control of his style and such a masterful technique that any external influences were merely consumed to reappear later in Mozartean character. The *Andante cantabile*—judging by its profound character as well as the unusual harmonic progressions—belongs to the period of fully matured masterworks. Although the finale is not actually called a rondo, it offers a perfect model of this form enriched, enlarged, and varied in every conceivable way.

Mozart didn't compose another sonata until six years after the five Paris and the two Mannheim sonatas. That next sonata belongs in what Saint-Foix calls "*La Grande Période de Virtuosité*," the period from 1784 to 1788 during which the opera "The Marriage of Figaro" and some of Mozart's finest concerti for piano and orchestra were written. The *Sonata in C Minor, K. 457* was dedicated to Mozart's pupil Thérèse von Trattner, but unfortunately all correspondence about it has disappeared.

Even a brief glance at this sonata shows that no other music composed before Beethoven contains so many Beethovenian elements; the contrast of themes and the sense of ceaseless struggle are present in this astonishing and unexpected sonata. Under its brilliant format lies a somber and passionate tableau not found in any other Mozart sonata: strife among the elements of dominant forces. There is not only thematic contrast, but dynamic contrast; these occur in the first movement. The succeeding *Adagio* presents three expositions of one subject (Ex. 5)—a phrase molded of tender and noble sentiments, which usually concludes on the tonic. Two different themes, one grave, the other almost religious, insert themselves between the statements of the first subject to create a moving, subjective piece of music. The finale is equally somber although not as strongly proportioned. A kind of question-and-answer dialogue punctured by prophetic silences or rests gives this movement a feeling of despair quite unlike the usual Mozart.

Ex. 5.   W. A. Mozart: *Sonata in C Minor, K. 457: Adagio*

Mozart evidently felt that a sonata of such grand proportions, passionate outbursts, and noble allure needed an introduction, or prefatory movement. When he published the sonata, he prefaced it with the equally fine *Fantasy, K. 475,* the title for the two being *Fantaisie et Sonate pour le fortepiano composées pour Madame Thérèse de Trattner par le Maître de chapelle W. A. Mozart, oeuvre XI.* Mozart displays his great powers of improvisation in the *Fantasy,* but it is improvisation tempered by firm discipline. The work has five sections, each completely different, plus a return of the initial idea. The amazing thing is that these five sections, some virtuoso and some lyric, are fashioned with so much skill and artistry that they fit together into one splendid musical experience.

Some of the works written during this virtuoso period were intended to serve as instruction pieces. The *Sonata in C Major, K. 545* offers in essence the rudiments of what Mozart demanded from a student just embarking on a study of the piano. Unfortunately this sonata has been played more than any other Mozart piano work and is offered as a fine example of a typical Mozart sonata. It does present a true picture of Mozart but only in miniature; indeed, it contains just the barest hints of the characteristics of the mature composer. The constant use of the Alberti bass in the *Andante* is certainly not a procedure Mozart would have chosen had he written this sonata for himself to play. The *Rondo* sparkles, but it too is a miniature compared with the more brilliant Mozart rondos.

The *Sonata in B-flat Major, K. 570* is also simply constructed and probably was also an instruction piece. Still, although this little work is comparatively easy to execute, it has various characteristics of the mature Mozart.

One of the most difficult works Mozart ever wrote was his last sonata, the *Sonata in D Major, K. 576*. Conspicuous in its superior craftsmanship and skilled contrapuntal treatment, this sonata in some ways slips back into the past and in other ways foretells the future piano sonata. Its *Adagio*—elaborate, but with a transparent design and fluid movement—stood as a model for Beethoven. The finale is as remarkable for its structure as for its expressive and harmonic subtlety. This sonata occupies a unique place in the Mozart repertoire.

Mozart's keyboard sonatas may not invite favorable comparison with his operas and symphonies. They may not have the spontaneous charm of the chamber works. Nonetheless many are worthy examples of his talent, and some of them can hold their own with the finest keyboard creations of the Classic era.

BIBLIOGRAPHY

Abert, Hermann. "Joseph Haydns Klavierwerke." *Zeitschrift für Musikwissenschaft*, II (1919–1920) and III (1920–1921).

Badura-Skoda, Eva and Paul. *Interpreting Mozart on the Keyboard* (translated by L. Black). New York: St. Martin's Press, 1962.

Broder, Nathan. "Mozart and the Clavier." *Musical Quarterly*, October 1941.

Brunner, Hans. *Das Klavierklangsideal Mozarts und die Klaviere seiner Zeit*. Augsburg: Dr. B. Filser Verlag, 1933.

Burk, John N. *Mozart and His Music*. New York: Random House, 1959.

Dennerlein, Hanns. *Der Unbekannte Mozart*. Leipzig: Breitkopf & Härtel, 1951.

Dent, Edward J. "Haydn's Pianoforte Works." *Monthly Music Record*, 1932 (LXII).

Einstein, Alfred. *Mozart*. New York: Oxford University Press, 1945.

Geiringer, Karl. *Haydn*. Second edition. New York: Doubleday & Co., Inc., 1963. An Anchor book.

Hoboken, Anthony van. *Joseph Haydn. Thematisch-bibliographisches Werkverzeichnis.* Mainz: B. Schott's Söhne, 1957.

King, A. Hyatt. "Mozart's Piano Music." *Music Review,* Vol. 5, 1944.

Köchel, Ludwig Ritter von. *Chronologisch-thematisches Verzeichnis sämtlicher Tonwerke Wolfgang Amade Mozarts,* sixth edition, supplemental material by A. Einstein. Wiesbaden: Breitkopf & Härtel, 1963.

Landon, H. C. Robbins and D. Mitchell, eds. *The Mozart Companion.* New York: Oxford University Press, 1956.

Mitchell, Wm. J. "The Haydn Sonatas." *Piano Quarterly,* No. 7, 1954.

Radcliffe, Philip. "The Piano Sonatas of Joseph Haydn." *Music Review,* Vol. 7, No. 3, 1946.

Richner, Thomas. *Orientation for Interpreting Mozart's Piano Sonatas.* New York: Teachers College, Columbia University, 1953.

Russell, John. "Mozart and the Pianoforte." *Music Review,* Vol. 1, No. 3, 1940.

Vignal, Marc. "L'Oeuvre pour Piano seul de Joseph Haydn." *La Revue Musicale,* 1961. *Carnet Critique No. 249.*

Wyzewa, T. de and G. de Saint-Foix. *W.-A. Mozart.* Paris: Desclée de Brouwer et Cie., 1936–1946. 5 Vols.

14

BEETHOVEN

Ludwig van Beethoven (1770–1827) is one composer whose greatness has gone beyond the limits of musical sound. This incredible, talented man constructed magnificent tonal edifices and by the impact of his personal nature touched deep into the inner core of his fellow man. He possessed an indomitable will tempered by a rare capacity for love and tenderness, and he had the gift to translate all his strong emotions into music that continually enriches mankind's spiritual treasures. His music reaches us today as passionate and powerful; for the master of Bonn it was painfully personal.

In the eighteenth century, music was designed to assist at ceremonial and social functions: at religious services, at royal diversion, or simply as public entertainment. If a composer had an emotional temperament, this had some effect on his music, but intimate feelings were suppressed and appeared only discreetly or not at all. Before Beethoven, music's primary purpose was to please the audience, which meant nothing could be too serious, nothing too difficult. Such an attitude resulted in an impersonal kind of music. Beethoven changed this approach to music. The more free rein he allowed his genius, the more personal his art became. The public could enjoy his music, too, but in addition to the listening pleasure, they could partake of the composer's intense emotions.

The salient facts about Beethoven are well known: his somewhat haphazard studies with Albrechtsberger, Salieri, and Haydn; the beginnings of his hearing difficulties; his friendship with the Brunswick family and Giulietta Guicciardi; the composition of the Heiligenstadt Testament, in which he contemplates suicide; his meeting with Bettina Brentano and Goethe; his complete deafness; and the long agony that ended March 26, 1827, during a clap of thunder. All these affected the substance of his music.

One facet of his creative genius finds expression as vital energy in his music while another reveals itself in his rhythms. Beethoven's themes are clothed in rhythms that pulsate through an entire work. His skill in development, another aspect of his genius, is always closely related to his unique concept of rhythm. He arrived at a simple theme after numerous preliminary sketches, but from this unadorned theme he created a world of experience. His developments are never mechanical or coldly scholastic; they seem alive, spontaneous, and emotional. His thoughts, never vapid, never mediocre, are translated into music that shows this intensity. Consequently, Beethoven's melodies possess a transcendent individuality. In them all human experience—love, heroism, sadness, ecstasy, joy—are lyrically delineated.

In matters of musical aesthetics and style, Ludwig van Beethoven is one of history's most remarkable innovators. Beethoven's keyboard works clearly display the outstanding characteristics of his gift for innovation. By following these works, we can penetrate to the beginnings of his genius and watch it unfold on the artistic as well as the human plane, for with Beethoven the work and the man are one. A high point in music history occurs in his piano music: his contribution to the sonata.

The Beethoven sonatas reveal that the composer was engrossed with form. In his early years he seemed to prefer a four-movement structure, which may have been an attempt to lift the piano sonata to trio or quartet status. However, a three-movement sonata soon proved to be the most satisfactory vehicle for his prodigious creative powers: an agitated first movement in which opposing elements are played against each other; an introspective, lyric second movement; and a frequently dramatic finale wherein the conflicts of the first movement become firmly resolved. Whenever Beethoven expanded the slow movement, it assumed the center of the stage, interrupting the continuity between the first and last movements. At times he reduced the slow movement to a brief episode, but in *Opus 109* and *Opus 111* he placed it at the end to climax the entire sonata.

In a book called *Beethoven and His Three Styles* (1855)[1] Wilhelm von Lenz divides the works of the Bonn master into three consecutive periods, each having special stylistic features. In some ways this classification, which was adopted by Fétis, d'Indy, and others, is not entirely acceptable. Beethoven's cumulative technique and progress—traceable in his handling of form and counterpoint—cannot be arbitrarily fragmented and classified. On the other hand, artificial as they may seem, these categories do partially correspond to reality; for an artist expresses himself differently during youth, maturity, and old age. It is unwise to follow this categorization rigidly. Wilhelm von Lenz's three periods are better used as a practical outline for examining the principal characteristics of the various compositions.

---

[1] Wilhelm von Lenz, *Beethoven et ses trois Styles* (Paris: Lavinée, 1855), 2 Vols. in 1.

The three commonly adopted categories are: the period of imitation or assimilation, youthful works up to 1802; the period of realization, from 1802 to about 1816; the period of contemplation, from 1816 to 1827. Beethoven composed fifteen piano sonatas within the first period, twelve in the second period, and five in the third.[2]

When Beethoven arrived on the music scene, the piano sonata had only recently been brought to Classic perfection by C. P. E. Bach, Haydn, and Mozart. Besides his contact with their music, Beethoven in the early years must have been influenced by other composers. It has been claimed that F. Wilhelm Rust (1739–1796) from Dessau probably played a role in formulating Beethoven's style, and it is true that Rust had a fair reputation in his own day and that he composed attractive piano sonatas.[3] Still, there is no concrete proof that Beethoven was even acquainted with the Rust sonatas. More positive influences can be found in the sonatas of Muzio Clementi (1752–1832), which Beethoven played and admired as a young man. Beethoven perhaps borrowed some of Clementi's writing procedures for his first sonatas. After that, all came from the master's phenomenal creative facility.

FIRST PERIOD

The piano sonatas that Beethoven wrote before he reached thirty-one usually conform to the Classic shape bequeathed by Haydn and Mozart. Yet little by little the originality of his growing genius indulges in liberties that foretell the coming metamorphosis. During this first period he gradually discarded the *minuet,* the last surviving member of the suite. Even when he did insert a minuet in a four-movement sonata, it was a far cry from the elegant, sophisticated Mozartean type. More frequently Beethoven replaced the minuet with a *scherzo*—a lively, capricious movement. (His preference for the scherzo goes back as early as *Sonata Opus 2, No. 2* [1795], dedicated to Joseph Haydn). Then sometimes both minuet and scherzo are missing. The result is a sonata in three movements, seen in *Opus 10, Nos. 1* and *2,* in *Opus 14, No. 1,* and in the sonatas *Opus 13* (*Pathétique*) and *Opus 27, No. 2.*

In many instances Beethoven rearranges the movements. In *Opus 26* a funeral march becomes the third movement and the scherzo is moved to second position.

[2] Beethoven's solo piano music is available in several attractive editions. The most recent is that from G. Henle Verlag. Most major publishers handle Beethoven's sonatas, but the most reliable (in addition to Henle) are those of Kalmus and Universal. Beethoven's complete works were published by Breitkopf & Härtel, reprinted by J. W. Edwards in 1949 (24 Vols.).

[3] Salabert in Paris published a selection of Rust sonatas (edited by Vincent d'Indy).

Sonata Opus 13 has an initial *Allegro molto* preceded by an extended slow introduction. In the *Sonata Opus 26* the customary *allegro* is replaced by a *Tema con variazioni*. Beethoven continued to initiate changes. An *Allegro* serves as the second movement in *Sonata Opus 27, No. 1*, and the first movement of *Opus 27, No. 2* is a lyric *Adagio sostenuto*.

Apart from these technical transformations, the purpose and spirit of the sonata began to alter under Beethoven's guidance. Where this form had been no more than a divertissement, in a master's hands it quickly took on serious intentions surpassing mere grace and sophistication. Each Beethoven sonata uncovers a personal emotion for the listener—heroic, joyous, or tragic—according to the musical dictates of the composer. Thematic contrasts dominating the sonata—especially in the first movements—assume the role of dramatic protagonists and forcefully interpret the feelings Beethoven seemed compelled to inject into his music. The change that he eventually made in the underlying meaning of the sonata was shaping up even in his first published sonatas, in which he gives new meaning to the traditional formulas used by Haydn and Mozart.

Opus 2 includes three sonatas written in 1795, published in 1796, and dedicated to Joseph Haydn. Each sonata shows a different face: the first is dramatic, the second projects a lyric strain, and the third is strictly a virtuoso piece. The minuet retains its classic niche in *Opus 2, No. 1, in F Minor*, but in the two succeeding works it is displaced by a *scherzo*. The arpeggiated, ascending first theme of the initial *Allegro* in the first sonata is an echo from the past; Mozart made use of it and so did other composers. The *Adagio* from that same sonata is decidedly Haydnesque. In *Sonata No. 2, in A Major*, the *Largo appassionato* is an early example of many lovely slow movements to come, while the concluding *Rondo* always remained one of Beethoven's favorite compositions in this form.

Karl Czerny maintained that Beethoven wrote his *Sonata Opus 7 in E-flat Major* (1796) while in a passionate state of mind. The work is a masterpiece, complete and perfect to the smallest detail, the first sonata to substantiate his genius. Its first movement is grander than any up to this point, with the development section more completely worked out. A sudden passage in *C* major is an unexpected surprise. The fourth movement, *Rondo*, is a landmark in perfection for this form. It has seldom been equaled, never surpassed.

Beethoven's *Opus 10*, published in 1798, contains three sonatas wholly indicative of his first period; they show a respect for established rules modified by the composer's progressive outlook. At the time, however, these sonatas were considered perplexing and too experimental by some critics. A contemporary music periodical (*Allgemeine Musikalische Zeitung*) stated: "The abundance of the themes leads Beethoven to accumulate thoughts without order and in bizarre grouping of such kind that his art appears artificial and remains obscure." This critical "abundance of themes" arose from misunderstanding. Beethoven's tendency to present a single theme in many guises baffled his contemporaries, but he continued the practice to the end of his life. What was then taken for chaos was actually precise organization.

Apropos the three sonatas of *Opus 10,* the third (in D major) is the most interesting, displaying a highly creative mind resolving thematic problems within the traditional four-movement framework. In the very first measures of the initial *Presto,* one senses Beethoven's new approach. This *Presto* is constructed in the standard sonata-allegro mold, but the hitherto restrained form bursts forth here as an impassioned, fiery outburst quite typical of the young genius.

The second movement, the most remarkable of the four movements, is marked *Largo e mesto.* This movement not only unveils the future Beethoven, but its spiritual expression forms the apex of the entire work. It is the first of his many magnificent slow movements, a *largo* whose personal intensity testifies to the composer's passionate nature (Ex. 1).

Ex. 1. Beethoven: *Sonata Opus 10, No. 3, in D Major: Largo e mesto*

The third movement of *Opus 10, No. 3* is a delightful Classic *Menuetto.* It is one of Beethoven's last keyboard minuets written for a sonata; thereafter he used the *scherzo.* The finale is a *Rondo* with four statements of the rondo theme plus three interludes and a coda, all treated somewhat like variations of the theme. This *Rondo* is straightforward and bright, but even here echoes of the *Largo e mesto* impose themselves dexterously.

Sonata Opus 13 in C Minor appeared in 1799 with a dedication to a patron, Prince Karl von Lichnowsky. This sonata, bearing the subtitle *Pathétique,* is one of Beethoven's most popular compositions. His editors supplied the descriptive title, doubtlessly with his permission. The word *Pathétique*—a French adjective meaning "touching" or "moving"—adequately sums up the mood of this sonata composed when Beethoven experienced the first signs of the deafness that blighted his mature life. "In order to give you some idea of this strange deafness," he wrote to a friend several years later, "let me tell you that in the theatre I have to place myself quite close to the orchestra in order to understand what the actor is saying, and that at a distance I cannot hear the high notes of instruments or voices. . . . Already I have often cursed my Creator and my existence. Plutarch has shown me the path of resignation. If it is at all possible, I will bid defiance to my fate, though I feel that as long as I live there will be moments when I shall be God's most unhappy creature."[4]

Sonata Pathétique has three movements. An initial *Allegro molto e con brio* is preceded by a dramatic slow introduction that sets the tone of the whole sonata, stamping the work with tragic overtones. The first movement, *Allegro,* dominated by sadness and futility, is so connected to the introduction that the latter must be repeated in part before the development section begins. Then the second theme, in *e-flat* minor, increases the agitation in this movement. The *Adagio cantabile,* set in rondo form, is full of grandeur and is decidedly lyrical. And the final movement has a classic *Rondo* with four refrains and three interludes, followed by a brilliant coda.

The next two sonatas—*Opus 14* (*E Major* and *G Major*)—are quite different, although both were published in 1799, the same year as the *Pathétique. Opus 14* presents a character markedly different from *Opus 13;* the former contains two sonatas which are pastoral. The first, in *E* major, has three movements, with a scherzo-like *Allegretto* substituting for the usual central *adagio.*

Beethoven displays his firm command of technique in the *Sonata Opus 22 in B-flat Major.* He showed a special fondness for this sonata, a natural preference since he resolved many musical problems while composing it

The *Sonata Opus 26 in A-flat Major* (1801) is extraordinary in that it has not a single movement written in sonata-allegro form. The external framework is refreshing because it breaks completely with tradition in sequence of movements: *Tema con variazioni, Scherzo, Marcia funebre sulla morte d'un eroe,* and *Allegro.* Beethoven almost succeeds in removing eighteenth-century influences, notably from Haydn and Mozart. His inspiration, too, seems to be on a higher plane and more securely handled, with further evidence of his progressive emancipation in form and spirit.

The first-movement theme, *Andante,* is in song form (A B A) and is followed by five characteristic variations. *Scherzo*—the second movement —seems to prolong intentionally the prevailing atmosphere of the last of the preceding variations. A *Funeral march on the death of a hero* substitutes for a slow movement. (Beethoven supposedly wrote this funeral

[4] Emily Anderson, ed., *The Letters of Beethoven* (New York: St. Martin's Press Inc., 1961), I, 60. Reprinted by permission of Macmillan & Company, Ltd.

march after hearing one like it by Ferdinando Paer [1771–1839]; he later orchestrated the march for use in the play *Eleonore Prohaska* by Johann Duncker.) The *Allegro* finale is a delightful rondo with three statements of the principal theme. Beethoven may have received inspiration for this *Allegro* from hearing the pianist-composer Johann Baptist Cramer and from studying Cramer's sonatas.

Beethoven again avoided sonata-allegro form in the first movements of his two sonatas in *Opus 27*. To accentuate the omission, he adds "*quasi una Fantasia*" to each sonata title, proving once more that he was not overly concerned with the sonata's traditional structure. The musical content of the second sonata in *Opus 27* justifies the term "Fantasia." Its subtitle "Moonlight" does not come from Beethoven, however, but from a publisher who borrowed it from an article by the writer Heinrich Rellstab. Rellstab claimed that the title had been prompted by the vision "of a boat on Lake Lucerne [where Beethoven had never been] by a luminous night."

Beethoven wrote his "*Moonlight Sonata*" (*Opus 27, No. 2*) in 1802. Contrary to all tradition, it begins with a quasi-improvisatory slow movement, *Adagio sostenuto*, a delightful piece wherein lyric expressiveness and rich harmonic color happily consort. It is constructed in triplets of eighth notes, triplets whose melodic design is echoed in the finale. The second movement—Liszt called it "a flower between abysses"—is titled *Allegretto*, but it is really a *scherzo* with a classic trio full of invigorating spontaneity. The *Presto agitato* finale—more extended than in any previous sonata—reverts to the drama of the first movement; but although the latter was characterized by calm sadness, the finale is tumultuous, animated, and tragic. It is based on sonata-allegro form with two themes.

The final sonata included in the first period of this arbitrary classification is *Opus 28 in D Major*, published in 1802 and known also as the "Pastoral Sonata" because of its idyllic character. Here Beethoven strives for closer unity between the various sections of the first movement, *Allegro;* the second movement, *Andante,* was one of his favorites.

SECOND PERIOD

This period extends from Beethoven's thirty-second to his forty-seventh year, a period during which he worked resolutely to effect the metamorphosis of sonata form, to create a sonata of vaster dimensions. He no longer felt compelled to retain the restricting details of Classic form. He began to treat this form's basic outlines with complete liberty, making them subservient to the demands of his imagination. He used only those Classic elements that would not interfere with the ever expanding horizons of his inspiration.

Beethoven's change of attitude began in 1802, the year of the Testament of Heiligenstadt, his last will and testament. After a time of mental depression, he had made up his mind to struggle on forcefully and intensely. This second period shows his full physical and spiritual maturity. During this same era, notable mechanical improvements were developed for the piano and Beethoven hastened to exploit them.

The first keyboard works in the second period—three sonatas comprising *Opus 31*—are quasi-experimental, permitting Beethoven to take stock of his new forces. He then proceeded to write masterworks, such as *Opus 53 in C Major (Waldstein)* and *Opus 57 (Appassionata)*, in which his writing style becomes stabilized and consistently and creatively personal. Throughout this second period, Beethoven was busy with a new stylistic detail: similarity between the themes or rhythmic patterns of different movements in a given sonata. *Sonata Opus 31, No. 3* is an obvious example of this; a basic rhythmic formula dominates the principal themes yet does not essentially disturb the inherent character of each.

Beethoven allowed himself great freedom of form during this period. Of the twelve sonatas in this classification, five have only two movements, one is a four-movement work (*Opus 31, No. 3*), and six have three movements. Also, the slow movement is either omitted altogether—*Opus 31, No. 3, Opus 49, Nos. 1 and 2, Opus 54*—or it is minimized. For the other individual movements, sonata-allegro form predominates in this new Beethoven framework. The traditions of the *rondo* remain insofar as they do not restrain his creative processes.

Several curious features appear for the first time in the three sonatas comprising *Opus 31* (1802). In the initial *Allegro vivace* of the *Sonata No. 1 in G Major*, the secondary theme is in the key of *B* major instead of the anticipated *D* major. The first movement of the *Sonata No. 2 in D Minor* is even more unorthodox. Its brief *Largo* introduction and the *Allegro* complementary phrase are in the dominant key; when they are completed, the whole procedure is immediately repeated, this time beginning in C major! Not until the twenty-first measure is there a completely satisfying passage in the key of *d* minor. In the recapitulation section, Beethoven carries this unusual formula to even further unorthodox treatment.

Certain writing techniques in the *Sonata Opus 31, No. 3, in E-flat Major* point toward exploitation of mechanical improvements made on the piano; for example, the staccato and trills in both the first movement and the scherzo. This is the only four-movement sonata from the second period, but still the traditional slow movement is absent. Instead one finds a *Scherzo* and a *Menuetto* framed by an initial *Allegro* and a final *Presto con fuoco*. Each individual movement is subjected to an expansive working-out, additional proof of Beethoven's efforts to give vaster dimensions to his sonatas.

The two "easy" sonatas of *Opus 49* (*G Minor* and *G Major*) seem incongruous, situated as they are between the highly progressive works of *Opus 31* and the virtuoso *Sonata Opus 53 in C Major*. Although published in 1805, the two "easy" sonatas possibly were written nine years earlier and set aside by the composer. It is believed that Beethoven's brother Karl found the works and sent them to a publisher. That Beethoven did not intend to publish the sonatas (or rather sonatinas) seems clear from the fact that he used a *menuetto* section from the second one in his *Septet Opus 20*. Although they may appear anachronistic, these little sonatas have moments of charm and are useful in introducing young pianists to Beethoven sonatas.

Sonata Opus 53 in C Major (1804) is known as the "*Waldstein Sonata*" because of its dedication to Count von Waldstein, one of Beethoven's benefactors in Bonn. It was composed during a relatively happy and untroubled moment in Beethoven's life, and he tells of this rare carefree attitude in a letter to his pupil Ries: "For the life of me I should never have thought that I could be so lazy as I am here. If an outbreak of really hard work is going to follow, then indeed something fine may be the result."[5] The result is this bright, gracious sonata that stresses both technical and virtuoso aspects with masterful taste. It is extremely difficult to play and in a sense announces the sonatas of the third period.

The *Waldstein Sonata* has just two movements: an *Allegro con brio*, then a final *Rondo* marked *Allegretto moderato*. The rondo, however, is prefaced by a brief *Introduzione: Adagio molto* that assumes the position of a central slow movement even though it is only an introduction. The slow movement originally written for this sonata proved to be too long, so Beethoven published it separately (it is sometimes called *Andante Favori*). In the *Allegro con brio*, the exposition section presents the first theme twice, the second time with a rhythmic variant. The second theme is not in the key of the dominant but in the major tonality of the mediant (*E* major). The final *Rondo*—in traditional form—contains transformed statements of the basic theme and an early statement of one procedure which Beethoven later employed in the extended variation: the use of prolonged trills. This radiant rondo serves as a welcome foil to the violent first movement.

Between the dazzling *Sonata Opus 53* and the tempestuous *Appassionata Opus 57*, Beethoven composed a miniature sonata in two movements, *Opus 54 in F Major*. The spirit of the first movement indicates a minuet and, indeed, this is called for in the tempo marking *In tempo d'un*

---

[5] *Ibid.*, I, 114.

Menuetto. A delicate theme in triple meter is enlarged upon and alternated with passages in staccato octaves and sixths. The second movement, *Allegretto,* is a kind of graceful perpetual motion using a single theme.

In the interval 1804–1805, Beethoven isolated himself; he felt friendless and badly treated by a public that had received his *Eroica* symphony coldly; and he felt his deafness increasing rapidly, which heightened his solitude. Nonetheless, he wrote his *Sonata Opus 57 in F Minor.* Begun in 1804 and completed about 1806, this work—known as the *Appassionata*—is the one that Beethoven considered his greatest sonata up to that date. His editor Cranz in Hamburg applied the name *Appassionata,* perhaps with Beethoven's permission, for he did not publicly protest the title. The *Appassionata* represents a climax in Beethoven's keyboard writing. With this sonata he approaches perfect unity, a unity in which form and idea fuse to achieve equilibrium between content and expression, between structure and feeling.

Formally speaking, the sonata has three movements: *Allegro assai, Andante con moto,* and *Allegro non troppo.* Both allegros are in sonata-allegro form, but for the first time Beethoven omits repeat marks in the first-movement exposition. This is part of the work's logic since the predominant mood demands that the performer and the listener go forward—to repeat would disturb the aesthetic effect. The central movement is very short. A sixteen-measure theme is developed and amplified in the course of three successive variations rising progressively to the upper part of the keyboard. A reference to the original theme follows the last variation and proceeds without pause into the final *Allegro non troppo,* in which Beethoven introduces a new theme in the development section and places repeat signs for both development and recapitulation. The three movements preserve unity through thematic relationships. In the initial *Allegro assai* the principal theme consists of two complementary elements (Ex. 2). The first of these elements engenders the second theme (measures 36–37) and bears a strong resemblance to the principal theme in the finale (measures 20–21). The second element is similar to the theme of the *Andante* (measures 1–4) and has some rhythmic and melodic features in common with the finale's second theme.

If the *Appassionata* can be acclaimed as a dramatic work, a superb blending of virtuosity and craftsmanship, then the next sonatas represent a definite change of approach. Gone is the frank virtuosity, supplanted by lyricism and disarming simplicity. *Sonata Opus 78 in F-sharp Major,* a miniature masterpiece, was written in 1809. Two short movements—preceded by a four-measure introduction—contain all that Beethoven has to say in this particular work, but his music has an inner beauty, an irrepressible candor, and a naïve spirit. Conceived on an equally contracted frame-

Ex. 2. Beethoven: *Sonata Opus 57 in F Minor: Allegro assai*

work, the *Sonatine Opus 79 in G Major* (*Sonate facile*) was also written in 1809. It has three small movements: *Presto alla tedesca, Andante,* and *Vivace.* Each movement is worked out briefly with only a suggestion of any formal procedures. There is no pretense at grandeur—just simple, basic sentiments honestly stated and depicted with sound musicianship.

The only Beethoven piano sonata to suggest extramusical ideas is *Opus 81a* (1809), dedicated to the Archduke Rudolph of Austria, a student and friend of Beethoven. On May 4, 1809, the French armies marched on Vienna, and the court, including the young archduke, was obliged to leave the city and take refuge at Breda. Beethoven, greatly affected by all this, conceived this sonata on the occasion of the exodus. It has three movements: *Das Lebewohl* (*Les Adieux*), *Abwesenheit* (*L'Absence*), and *Das Wiedersehen* (*Le Retour*); it revolves around a single theme from which all other themes emanate. A brief *Adagio,* a slow introduction to introduce the basic theme, precedes the first movement, *Allegro,* which is in sonata-allegro form and has its first section repeated. The second movement, *Andante espressivo,* is built on two ideas derived from the initial motive, yet each idea has a distinctly separate character. The sonata continues without a break; the final movement establishes a mood of triumph and exultation.

After the appearance of *Sonata Opus 81a,* five years elapsed before Beethoven composed another—the *Sonata Opus 90 in E Minor,* dedicated in honor of the engagement of his patron, Count Moritz Lichnowsky. There are only two movements and they stand in sharp contrast to each other. The first movement is in *e* minor and the finale is a rondo in *E* major. Instead of the customary Italian tempo markings, Beethoven provides German descriptions of each movement's character. Thus the first movement is *Mit Lebhaftigkeit und durchaus mit Empfindung und Ausdruck* (With movement and with feeling and expression throughout) and the second movement is *Nicht zu geschwind und sehr singbar vorzutragen* (Not too fast and with a singing melody). The first movement remains mostly in *e* minor except for the *b* minor second theme. Motivic construction is clearly evident throughout this movement; the outward melodic cast never obliterates the inherent dramatic content. A clear-cut rondo based on a simple sixteen-bar theme serves as the second movement. Its reiterated refrain and repeated phrases would be monotonous without the small details that Beethoven infuses to create variety.

In addition to the sonatas of the second period, a word should be said about Beethoven's *Thirty-Two Variations in C Minor*. Composed in the years 1806–1807, they constitute an attractive chaconne wherein are displayed a good sampling of variation techniques. Beethoven professed little admiration for this work, but nevertheless the *Thirty-Two Variations* have steadily held their popularity through the years.

THIRD PERIOD

The five sonatas belonging to the so-called third period uphold Beethoven's later creative genius. He died at the age of fifty-seven, but his last piano sonata was composed when he was fifty-two. His confident spirit and artistic integrity, which made possible the tumultuous, passionate works of the second period, stayed with him to the end of his life. When his everyday existence turned into disorder, when he shunned his friends, when his health failed, still inner power and conviction sustained him. This enabled him to rise above the daily vicissitudes, and he went on to create nobler keyboard sonatas than ever before.

During this final period he subjected sonata form to the extraordinary fantasy of his mature musicianship. Of the five sonatas, one has two movements, three contain three movements, and one has four movements; but they all show an exceptional interest in developmental techniques. Individual movements are sometimes interrupted by foreign episodes, resulting in a totally new manner of expression; he often uses the *fugue* and *dramatic recitative* for these passages. Polyphonic writing becomes more frequent and more complex, harmonic concepts more daring. Several of these final sonatas challenge the performer with tremendous difficulties, the consequence of a creative style that sometimes seems to transcend the piano's limitations. At the same time, Beethoven's preoccupation with relationship of themes persisted, affirming itself with subtle force.

Sonata Opus 101 in A Major, written in 1816, was dedicated to Baroness Dorothea Ertmann, one of Beethoven's pupils and a distinguished pianist. While the preceding *Opus 90* in many ways deferred to the past, this *A Major* sonata so completely disregards standard form that it almost seems a work of fantasy—fantasy in the best sense of the word. The first movement is probably the shortest of its kind ever written by Beethoven; it is just over two pages. Basic sections of typical first-movement form are present in essence, although the second theme is missing. The usual scherzo gives way to a structure, *Vivace alla marcia,* in 4/4 meter with rhythmic details like those of the later Robert Schumann. Beethoven introduces a *canon* in the trio or middle section of this movement. And he uses a fugue in the development section of the final movement, creating a hybrid type, the first of its kind: a sonata-allegro movement preceded by a slow introduction and containing a fugue in its development section. This sonata is the creative product of a magnificent inspiration aided by a liberal approach to structure and content.

Sonata Opus 106 in B-flat Major (Hammer-Klavier), dedicated to the Archduke Rudolph, is the most powerful keyboard monument in Beethoven's monumental repertoire (he used the German term *Hammer-Klavier* instead of the more common *Pianoforte*). It also confronts the performer with formidable technical problems. Beethoven wrote thus about the conditions under which he composed it: "My situation is now so difficult that I have to resort to every means merely to enable me to preserve this dreary life."[6] Misery, sickness, suspicion of persecution, an obsession with death—all the composer's unhappiness saturates his masterpiece.

The general plan is: *Allegro, Scherzo, Adagio sostenuto,* and *Largo-Allegro risoluto (Fuga a tre voci, con alcune licenze).* At the very beginning the listener feels the impact of this music, and realizes he is confronting a musical colossus. The initial grandiose *Allegro*—in traditional sonata-allegro form—has two contrasting themes dominating its exposition section, which is repeated *da capo;* and the contrapuntal development section advances to breathtaking dimensions.

Next, a *Scherzo—Assai vivace—*has more or less Classic form: scherzo-trio-scherzo. However, a *Presto* and a short *Prestissimo* section intervene before the repeat of the *Scherzo.* The spirit in this movement is nothing like that originally associated with the scherzo. Beethoven makes it strange, with brusque contrasts.

The atmosphere surrounding the third movement, *Adagio,* is well defined by Beethoven—*Appassionato e con molto sentimento*—as well as by indications throughout, such as *espressivo, molto espressivo, con grand'espressione.* This is the longest adagio he wrote for a piano sonata; it takes some twenty minutes to play. The music represents meditation of the highest order. There are moments of somber melancholy, then contrasting colors of brightness and calm. A brief *Largo* prefacing the fugue is really an improvisatory introduction. After the preceding passionate meditation (*Adagio*), Beethoven indulges in a recitative type only slightly resembling the traditional formula of classic recitative. These ten musical lines lead into the *Fugue.* From early youth Beethoven had been intrigued by con-

---

[6] *Ibid.,* II, 763.

trapuntal writing. This is seen, for example, in the first movement of *Opus 14, No. 1*. In the present fugue, however, he surpasses himself and perhaps overextends himself; the work is extremely difficult. He also allows himself many deviations in this fugue, creating a fugue within a fugue (*sempre dolce cantabile*). The new fugue subject eventually combines with that of the old, enriching it before permitting it to conclude with the grand flourish that marks the end of this sonata.

The last three Beethoven sonatas—*Opus 109 in E Major, Opus 110 in A-flat Major,* and *Opus 111 in C Minor*—stand as his most intimate and movingly introspective keyboard works. He gives full vent to his artistic dictates on subjectivism, with no apparent concern about explicit formal matters. The *Sonata Opus 109 in E Major* (1820) begins with a *Vivace ma non troppo*. As this section progresses, it reveals an attempt to reconcile two basically disparate ideas: a *vivace* theme that alternates with an *adagio* passage. The *Prestissimo* is an interlude connecting the two outer movements; the finale is a theme and variations. This is the first time Beethoven used a theme and variations as a piano-sonata finale, and this lyrical theme, *Andante molto cantabile, ed espressivo*, with its six rich variations, is certainly his finest contribution to the form, a permanent tribute to the man and his spirit.

Sonata Opus 110 in A-flat Major (1821) is one of Beethoven's most astonishingly expressive works. It contains the ultimate essentials of his mature characteristics: expansive developments; liberty in form; a transformation of the Classic sonata framework by the introduction of the dramatic recitative and the fugue; and finally, a thematic similarity, or rather a genesis of themes from an initial theme.

From a structural point of view *Sonata Opus 110* contains three movements: a *Moderato cantabile, molto espressivo* in sonata-allegro form but treated with considerable liberty; an *Allegro molto*, which has a scherzo character (one theme was supposedly derived from a Silesian folk song); and a finale divided into four sections which, under Beethoven's control, form one harmonious whole. These sections are:

1. *Adagio, Recitative,* and *Arioso:* a brief introduction of a lyric *Adagio;* a dramatic *Recitative;* then the *Arioso dolente,* accompanied by heavy, thick chords in the bass.

2. An initial *Fugue* of tragic overtones.

3. An *Arioso* symmetric with the first one.

4. Finally, a second *Fuga* whose subject comes from the inversion of the first. Beethoven has noted this *poi a poi di nuevo vivente* as though to emphasize the triumphal note on which the sonata achieves its superb conclusion.

Opus 111 in C Minor (1822) is the last of the thirty-two Beethoven sonatas, and it is a perfect argument for the two-movement sonata. The two movements are unrelated, yet they augment and complement each other in the manner that only Beethoven's genius could project. A brief introduction (*Maestoso*) to the first movement leads by means of a series of modulations to the *Allegro con brio ed appassionato*. This allegro is remarkable for the skillful way in which Beethoven evolves the *A-flat* theme from the initial one in *c* minor. The theme of the second movement, *Arietta*, replies to the dramatic message of the *Allegro*, thereby imparting a strong internal unity to the whole work. This theme, to be played *Adagio molto semplice e cantabile*, is simple in itself but underlined with manifest implications (Ex. 3). Five variations follow; more appropriately, they might

Ex. 3. Beethoven: *Sonata Opus 111 in C Minor: Arietta*

be called progressions or extensions. Unlike most variations these great patterned amplifications of the initial subject have no opposition, no attempt at diversity. The theme's original spirit is prolonged, preserving the unity and at the same time transporting the listener to unimagined realms of sound.

Other keyboard works apart from the sonatas fall within the third period: the two sets of *Bagatelles Opus 119* and *Opus 126;* the *Rondo a Capriccio in G Major Opus 129;* and the so-called "Diabelli" *Variations Opus 120.* The delightful *Rondo a Capriccio,* posthumously discovered, was published in 1828 without an opus number. Later the *Opus 129* was given to it, although the exact date of composition is unknown. The original manuscript bears the inscription *Die Wüth über den verlornen Groschen, ausgetobt in einer Caprice* (Rage over the Lost Penny, Abated in a Caprice). Here is the jovial Beethoven. The *Rondo* fumes and frets, rants and rages—a true tempest in a teapot.

The *Variations Opus 120* consists of thirty-three variations on a waltz composed by the Viennese music publisher Anton Diabelli. The publisher had written to fifty-one composers requesting one waltz variation from each of them for publication as a single collection. Instead of one variation Beethoven turned in thirty-three. The waltz theme itself is inconsequential (Beethoven called it a *Schusterfleck*—a cobbler's patch), yet the master succeeded in creating from it a magnificent set of paraphrases. Many musicians consider that in this case Beethoven accomplished for the piano what Bach did for the harpsichord with his *Goldberg Variations*.

Beethoven's genius lives in his sonatas, particularly several from the second period and all from the third period. The panorama of his keyboard works from *Opus 2* through *Opus 111* shows a profound and unique transformation of style and musical vocabulary. With the sumptuous works of his third period Beethoven inaugurated a new era and opened the door for Schumann, Liszt, and a host of others.

If Romanticism were to be defined as an imaginative power, as a lyricism stirred up by vehement passions, then Beethoven could be considered the first, indeed the greatest Romantic. However, the word Romanticism denotes a certain break with tradition, and Beethoven was reared in an atmosphere of tradition. One must envisage him, therefore, as a Classic composer with broad scope, one who not only endowed the old forms with greater plasticity but who in his mature years offered a glimpse of future horizons to the coming Romantics.

BIBLIOGRAPHY

Anderson, Emily, ed., *The Letters of Beethoven*. New York: St. Martin's Press, Inc., 1961. 3 Vols.

Barford, Philip. "Beethoven's Last Sonata." *Music and Letters*, 1954 (XXXV).

Bekker, Paul. *Beethoven* (translated by M. Bozman). London: J. M. Dent & Sons, Ltd., 1932.

Burk, John N. *The Life and Works of Beethoven*. New York: The Modern Library, 1946.

Cockshoot, John. *The Fugue in Beethoven's Piano Music*. London: Routledge and Kegan Paul, 1959.

Fischer, Edwin. *Ludwig van Beethovens Klaviersonaten*. Wiesbaden: Insel-Verlag, 1956.

Lenz, Wilhelm von. *Beethoven et ses trois Styles*. Paris: Lavinée, 1855. 2 Vols. in 1.

Nettl, Paul. *Beethoven Encyclopedia*. New York: Philosophical Library, 1956.

Prod'homme, J. G. *Les Sonates pour Piano de Beethoven 1782–1823*. Paris: Delagrave, 1937.

Riemann, Hugo. *Ludwig van Beethovens sämtliche Klavier-Solosonaten*. Berlin: M. Hesse, 1919–1920.

Tovey, Donald Francis. *A Companion to Beethoven's Pianoforte Sonatas*. London: Associated Board of the Royal Schools of Music, 1948.

Tovey, Donald Francis. *Beethoven*. New York: Oxford University Press, 1945.

PART
IV

15

ROMANTICISM

Romanticism and all that it brings to mind is not confined to any one period. Supremacy of heart over intellect, of emotion over reason—this credo has its advocates in every age. No one who has heard a Gregorian chant, a Palestrina Mass, or even a Mozart sonata can deny that while other factors may predominate, elements of Romanticism are vitally present.

At one time, namely the period succeeding the Viennese Classical school, Romanticism became a cult in a progressive sense. Following the usual pattern, a Romantic literary movement came first—in several stages. During the *Sturm und Drang* (Storm and Stress) movement[1] that engulfed Germany and moved into other countries, Goethe's novel *Die Leiden des Jungen Werthers* (The Sorrows of Young Werther) became the prototype for a melancholy, depressive kind of Romanticism that stimulated artistic creation; but its end product always portrayed pessimistic sentiments. When this attitude was later modified, the Romantic movement swept onward. In France fictitious poems signed by the third-century poet Ossian gave impetus to one of the greatest periods in French literature.

There have been numerous definitions of literary Romanticism. Mme. de Stael in her *Littérature* (1800) indicates that for her Romanticism was a return to Christian and national inspiration. And Stendhal (Henri Beyle) in *Racine et Shakespeare* (1823) writes, "Romanticism is the art of presenting to the nations those literary works which . . . are capable of giving them the most pleasure. Classicism, on the contrary, presents to them the literature which gave the greatest pleasure to their great-grandfathers." And in the Romantic school of painters, artists like Delacroix (1798–1863) strove for brightness, color, and freshness in their paintings to oppose the cold classic style of artists like Ingres (1780–1867).

Alice Gabeaud, a contemporary French writer, has some interesting comments on the general subject of Romanticism:

[1] See Chapter 12, footnote 16.

> This movement is a kind of artistic revolution which consists in rejecting all which recalls the servitude of art to the amusement of an aristocracy: it ... presents the following characteristics: 1. Abolution of all that appears conventional; 2. Cult of the ego; the artist ... always assumes the role of the hero; 3. Love of nature, accompanied by the more and more scrupulous care in the description of the picturesque; 4. Exaggeration of the sentiments resulting in violent and sometimes extravagant passion; 5. Taste for the fantastic: imagination plays the greatest role and searches to impress the reader, the listener or the watcher, in such a way as to move them as much as possible.[2]

Romanticism provided a splendid environment for music. A distinguished writer on music has this to say: "Musical Romanticism may be characterized as an art which emphasizes the subjective and the emotional possibilities of music and neglects the formal and structural point of view."[3]

This is a good beginning. We already know that inspiration was essential to the Romantics. To find inspiration they searched into nature's beauties and explored her phenomena; they delved into history's stirring events and pageantry. However, the statement that Romanticism in music "neglects the formal and structural point of view" must be somewhat qualified because the best and the most representative Romantic composers conscientiously observed formal and structural principles.

Compare, for example, Berlioz with Schumann. The French may seriously contend that music's three great B's are Bach, Beethoven, and Berlioz (Bach, Beethoven, and Brahms is more common), but Berlioz' vehement, intentional plunge into undisciplined excesses with little formal support left him with less to offer than Schumann. The two composers had equally strong sentiments, no doubt, but Robert Schumann handled his material more judiciously.

Every age has its distinguishing manner or mood, but it is always accompanied by elements from other styles. Composers in the nineteenth century emphasized the subjective and the personal, the natural and the fantastic, but their inspiration was meant to be governed by universal rules of form and structure. Composers who chose their materials wisely have survived; the others dwindle down through mediocrity to oblivion.

The Romantics favored the piano. Equally at home in the salon or on the concert stage, the piano was able to convey the composer's innermost feelings as well as his vivid, sometimes theatrical emotions. Innumer-

---

[2] Alice Gabeaud, *Histoire de la Musique* (Paris: Librairie Larousse, 1930), p. 120. English translation by the author.

[3] Willi Apel, *Harvard Dictionary of Music* (Cambridge: Harvard University Press, 1944), p. 650.

able short, distinctive pieces were written especially for the piano: idiomatic, musical epigrams, which in some ways correspond instrumentally to the lied and art song vocally.

The characteristic piano piece, therefore, was the favorite means of keyboard expression during the nineteenth century. It was most often in ternary form (A B A) whether two pages or twelve pages long. Beyond this basic formal outline, the composer could release his imagination and inspiration to embellish the framework. Sonata form was used sparingly and, apart from the Weber and Schubert sonatas, does not represent typical Romantic keyboard style.

In one way or another the conspicuous traits of Romanticism in general can be applied to piano literature. For example, the Romantics' obsession with the dramatic and the mysterious—so prominent in the flamboyant operas of the period—influenced the piano music of Weber and Liszt. That the Romantic composers felt a close bond with literature is evident in the numerous descriptive titles—*Kreisleriana, Mephisto Waltz*, etc.— given to Romantic piano music. Evidence that the Romantics wanted to break their ties with the Classic period lies in their greater concern with expressive rather than structural qualities in music.

BIBLIOGRAPHY

Einstein, Alfred. *Music in the Romantic Era.* New York: W. W. Norton & Co., Inc., 1947.

McKinney, H. D. and W. R. Anderson. *Music in History.* New York: American Book Co., 1940.

Sachs, Curt. *The Commonwealth of Art.* New York: W. W. Norton & Co., Inc., 1946.

Stites, Raymond. *The Arts and Man.* New York: McGraw-Hill Book Co., Inc., 1940.

Sypher, Wylie. *Rococo to Cubism in Art and Literature.* New York: Random House, 1960.

Thimme, D. and W. W. Heist, eds. *An Introduction to Literature and the Fine Arts.* East Lansing: Michigan State College Press, 1950.

Walbank, T. W. and A. M. Taylor. *Civilization Past and Present.* Chicago: Scott, Foresman & Co., 1949. 2 Vols.

Wold, M. and E. Cykler. *An Introduction to Music and Art in the Western World.* Dubuque: Wm. C. Brown Co., 1958.

16

THE ROMANTIC COMPOSERS:
WEBER, SCHUBERT, MENDELSSOHN,
AND SCHUMANN

Beethoven's positive influence lasted through the whole nineteenth century: his ideas of tonal drama and his concept of motivic construction had revealed myriad developmental possibilities. Some early Romantic composers were directly influenced by him. Others drew upon their own resources. Thus the piano music written during the first forty years or so of the nineteenth century has great variety, a matchless diversity created almost within the shadow of the Classic restraint.

CARL MARIA VON WEBER

The piano music of **Carl Maria von Weber** (1786–1826) has long been derided as old-fashioned, bombastic, and trite; and for these reasons, Weber has been denied importance in every area of composition except opera. This is an unfair appraisal of a man who helped to formulate various factors in musical Romanticism. Weber had a fine reputation as composer in his own day and was also one of the best pianists of the time. To be sure, there are defects in his music. When compared to the sonatas of Beethoven, Weber's works lack cohesion. In his melodies he often misses that certain turn of phrase necessary for vitality so they frequently appear lifeless—for instance, the theme reprinted here from the *Rondo of Sonata Opus 49 in D Minor* is merely a series of ascending and descending scales (Ex. 1).

On the positive side Weber must be credited with two extremely important elements of nineteenth-century composition. First, as one of that century's pioneer composers, he introduced dramatic effects—keyboard tremolos, powerful crescendos, impassioned outbursts, etc.—that influenced music for nearly one hundred years. Consider, for example, the opening bars to the *Sonata Opus 39 in A-flat Major* (Ex. 2). The effect—achieved with tremolo, arpeggiated chords, ascending and descending melodic line—is no

Ex. 1. Weber: *Sonata Opus 49: Rondo*

Ex. 2. Weber: *Sonata Opus 39: Allegro moderato*

doubt a by-product of his penchant for opera; his approach here is very appropriate for establishing the dominant mood of this sonata.

Second, Weber introduced keyboard techniques that were developed more fully by later composers: large stretches for the hand; wide leaps from one keyboard register to another; rapid passages in thirds, sixths, and octaves; and dramatic crescendos; all these abound in his keyboard writings.

Weber's finest keyboard works are the four piano sonatas described by Philipp Spitta as fantasies in sonata form:[1] *Opus 24 in C Major* (1812); *Opus 39 in A-flat Major* (1816); *Opus 49 in D Minor* (1816); and *Opus 70 in E Minor* (1822).[2] The *Rondo* from the first sonata, under the title *Perpetual Motion,* has been performed endlessly as a solo concert piece and, though not a masterwork, it is an excellent illustration of melodious qualities manipulated at great speed.

Opus 39 in A-flat Major is the only one of the four sonatas played today in its entirety. The melodies, after an introductory theme (Ex. 2), are exciting and expansive, even though they are supported by a rather monotonous accompaniment (Ex. 3).

Ex. 3. Weber: *Sonata Opus 39: Allegro moderato*

These themes fit into a severely contrasting framework in which tremolos, arpeggiated chords, and series of octave passages all contribute to create a noble, though sometimes flamboyant, movement.

The *Andante* from this same sonata contains one of those melodic-harmonic figurations for which Weber is famous (Ex. 4). Even this movement, which is lyric at first, builds to a powerful middle section before returning to the serene lines of the beginning.

Although the third movement is titled *Minuetto capriccioso,* it is a scherzo with a vivacious first section and a veritable *pathétique* trio. On

---

[1] See the article on Weber in Grove's *Dictionary of Music and Musicians* (Fifth edition, 1954), Vol. IX, pp. 195–222.

[2] Weber's complete keyboard works (in three volumes) are available in Peters Edition. Durand of Paris publishes the sonatas. These as well as *Opuses 62, 65,* and *72* are also found in Augener Edition.

Ex. 4. Weber: *Sonata Opus 39: Andante*

the whole, Weber's minuets (or scherzos) are quite successful, and they disclose the composer's attractive flair for fantasy.

The rondos terminating each sonata sparkle with joy and verve despite some rather trite thematic material. *Perpetual Motion* (the rondo from the first sonata) and the rondo in the *Sonata Opus 49 in D Minor* are both successful, but neither one equals the rondo of the second *Sonata Opus 39 in A-flat Major* for consistently fine quality and dramatic impact.

More popular by far than any individual sonata is the *Invitation to the Dance Opus 65* (1819), which Berlioz orchestrated for the celebrated ballet *Le Spectre de la Rose*. When Weber finished the composition, he played it for his wife Caroline, accompanying the performance with the following commentary: " 'First approach of the dancer (measures 1–5); the lady's evasive reply (5–9); his pressing invitation (9–13); her consent (13–16); they enter into conversation—he begins (17–19), she replies (19–21), he speaks with greater warmth (21–23), she sympathetically agrees (23–25). Now for the dance! He addresses her with regard to it (25–27), her answer (27–29), they draw together (29–31), take their places, are waiting for the commencement of the dance (31–35).—The dance.—Conclusion: his thanks, her reply, their retirement. Silence.' The commentary leaves us in the lurch as to the main part of the composition, the dance."[3] This description is doubtlessly too much of a good thing for a simply constructed waltz of moderate length; still, this was true Romantic tradition and must be evaluated as such.

Weber's sonatas and the *Invitation to the Dance* are indicative of the path taken by early-nineteenth-century composers, but he had displayed the Romantic impulse even sooner in *Momento Capriccioso Opus 12* (1808). This rapid-fire piece with its changing pianissimo chords is like a glimpse into elfin land. Weber used this fantasy style again later in the *Rondo Brillante Opus 62* (1819) and the *Polacca Brillante Opus 72* (1819).

There are passages of excellent pianistic writing in other Weber piano

---

[3] Frederick Niecks, *Programme Music in the Last Four Centuries* (London: Novello & Ltd., *ca.* 1906), pp. 138–139.

works, including ten sets of variations, all of which are rarely heard now. Carl Maria von Weber's reputation as a composer for piano stands or falls on his sonatas and a small body of single compositions.

FRANZ SCHUBERT

Franz Schubert (1797–1828), justly famous as creator of the nineteenth-century *lied,* also wrote many piano works that illustrate both his strength and his weakness as a composer. In his estimation the piano was designed for intimate expression, and he envisioned at least part of his own inspiration in terms of the epigrammatic character piece—quasi-improvisatory in feeling, as though born of spontaneous ideas.

Some of Schubert's most engaging thoughts are presented in his six *Moments Musicals Opus 94*[4] published in July, 1828. The title is appropriate, for in these little pieces in song form Schubert was content to express his mental images without expounding upon them.

There are moments of reverie (*Number 1 in C Major*) when Schubert speaks like Schumann. The third *Moment Musical*—originally a separate composition called *Air russe*—is the most popular of the six. This miniature march in *f* minor is typically Schubert in its gradual moving toward the key of *F* major for the ending. The fourth piece, written in clear ternary form, contains two well-constructed themes: one built upon constantly reiterated sixteenth notes, the second concentrating on a characteristic rhythmic motive. Suspensions in the opening section of the sixth piece give the effect of sighing, a sharp contrast to the direct approach in the trio or middle section.

Franz Schubert wrote two sets of *Impromptus* (*Opus 90* and *Opus 142*) in 1828, the year of his death; at that time such a title was a recent invention. The model for them had appeared in 1822 in the *Impromptus Opus 7*[5] by Jan Worzischek (1791–1825), a Bohemian pianist and composer. As a musical type, Schubert's *Impromptus* also had antecedents in the *Eclogues, Rhapsodies,* and *Dithyrambs*[6] by another Bohemian, Jan Tomaschek (1774–1850).

Schubert's *Impromptus*[7] have excellent musical qualities: they are short, the ideas are succinct and lucid, and the texture is free of any superabundance of notes. Above all, they show the composer's melodic genius. The very title *Impromptu* suggests spontaneous improvisation, and Schubert

---

[4] Breitkopf & Härtel publishes Schubert's complete piano music in seven volumes. The *Moments Musicals* are also available in Schirmer, Peters and Henle editions.

[5] Jan Worzischek, *Impromptus Opus 7* (Prague: Artia).

[6] Jan Tomaschek, *Tre Ditirambi Opus 65* (Prague: Artia). Augener publishes ten *Eclogues.*

[7] Henle and Peters publish the *Impromptus.* Most of these are also published by Schott (edited by W. Georgii).

gives this impression in these pieces; yet the *Impromptus* are polished art forms. Only the first two of *Opus 90* (there are four altogether) were published during his lifetime; the others did not appear until 1857.

Impromptu Opus 90, No. 2, in E-flat Major is like a study piece. Rippling cascades of triplets in the right hand are interrupted by an incisive, dogmatic middle section. *Impromptu No. 4* is fashioned along similar lines except that the first section has a lovely cello-like melody to offset the exuberant character of the whole composition. By contrast, the third *Impromptu* is an introspective, lyrical poem. Originally written in the key of *G-flat* major (six flats), it was transposed to the key of *G* major when published in 1857.

In 1838 the publisher Diabelli brought out Schubert's other set of *Impromptus* (four), assigning them opus number *142*. The second in this group, in *A-flat* major, is similar to a sarabande in its initial theme and rhythmic motive; the trio seems somewhat extended for such a small-scale piece. Schubert dispenses with traditional ternary form in *Impromptu No. 3 in B-flat Major,* which is a theme with five variations. This theme— one of Schubert's favorites—was extracted from his ill-fated stage work *Rosamunde.*

Ludwig van Beethoven had bequeathed to the nineteenth century the grand prototype of the sonata, showing how much freedom could be achieved within the confines of a comparatively rigid structure. The Romantic composers who came after Beethoven also professed a desire, sometimes halfheartedly, to write sonatas. Weber, Schubert, Schumann, Liszt, Chopin, and Brahms all used sonata form at times, but (excluding Weber and Schubert) their sonatas represent their least effective keyboard writings.

Schubert was always interested in the piano sonata. Many that he wrote are incomplete; that is, they are fragmentary or have movements missing. Including both the complete and incomplete works, there are twenty-one sonatas. Ten or eleven of the completed works usually appear in the published editions,[8] but the random opus numbers are disconcerting since they give no clue at all to the chronological order of the sonatas.

Schubert would have had a pattern to follow in the Beethoven sonatas had he chosen to use it; but Schubert's compositions do not have the motivic construction of the Beethoven works, nor did he try experiments with form as Beethoven had done. Schubert thought almost entirely in melodic terms, particularly the kind of melodies that lend a happy expression to his songs. It is obvious that most of these melodies were not susceptible to prolonged development.

---

[8] Apart from the Breitkopf complete edition, the Schubert sonatas may be obtained in Peters Edition. Henle is also preparing the sonatas. The *"Wanderer"* Fantasy is published by Schott.

Schubert's sonatas are not virtuoso works. In the first movements he seldom strives for a straightforward development section; he prefers highly effective modulations and lightly disguised restatements, and he relies heavily on melodic lines supported by accompaniment chords. The tempo indication in the slow movements is more often *andante* than *adagio;* in the two outer movements the qualitative *moderato* is frequently encountered.

Sonata Opus 42 in A Minor was written in 1825 and published in 1826. An ominous initial theme controls the first movement; then this forceful theme, transposed to the key of *c* minor, serves in lieu of a second theme. The theme of the second movement *Andante* (in *C* major) is lyrical although the spirit is restless. A series of free transformations or variations— in *C* major, *c* minor, and *A-flat*—complement this theme. The *Scherzo*— the third movement—includes syncopation to heighten its agitated mien, and the generally fatalistic atmosphere of the sonata is rounded out in the finale, an elegant *Rondo*.

Also written in 1825, *Sonata Opus 53 in D Major* is a little more decidedly virtuoso. Tempo changes within the first movement announce new forces at work, and the whole movement seems to be dominated by triplets. Both the second movement and the *Scherzo* are extra long and appear to go beyond the limits of their original material, but the rondo finale, containing echoes of Classicism, provides a delightful end and climax.

Sonata Opus 120 in A Major is a pure joy in its lyric effusion. Written in 1819, it is one of Schubert's shorter sonatas; there are only three movements and they have modest dimensions. The middle *Andante*, a song, is controlled throughout by its initial rhythm.

Four years later, in 1823, Schubert composed the *Sonata Opus 143 in A Minor.* It is a curious work, punctuated with explosive outbursts and shimmering with hints of orchestral coloring, and yet somehow intimate in feeling. Its *Andante* is an exquisite evocation of tonal atmosphere.

Schubert's last three sonatas—in *c* minor, *A* major, and *B-flat* major— date from 1828 but are without opus numbers. All three are skilled essays in expressive directness and intimate detail. The third—*Sonata in B-flat Major*—is the one heard most frequently now. Its first movement, *Moderato,* presents one melodic idea after another, and the thematic lyricism becomes intensified only in the development. The *Andante* is a marvel of introspection with its strains of pathos and resignation, while the *Scherzo* is pleasingly compact. Schubert used that curious hybrid structure, the rondo-sonata form, for the finale and then filled it with surprises—unexpected rests and passionate explosions—a sharp contrast to the otherwise calm tone of the sonata.

Of all the Schubert ventures into sonata form, *Opus 78 in C Major* emerges as one of the most gratifying. When it was written in 1826 it was considered a collection of four pieces: *Fantasia, Andante, Menuetto,* and *Allegretto.* Nevertheless, this series comprises a sonata and, as a matter of fact, one of Schubert's very best. The *Fantasia* in sonata-allegro form unveils its climax in the development section. Mood contrasts mold the basic character of the *Andante,* and the *Menuetto* is in Schubert's finest waltz style. Typically Viennese is the final movement, *Allegretto,* which brings to mind the *Gemütlichkeit* of Schubert's surroundings.

Schubert's piano sonatas are lyrical, personal works, and as such they mirror the composer's sensitive nature. He made few concessions to virtuosity; only once did he create a large piano work blatantly exploiting technical elements, and then he placed them as highlights rather than as means to an end. This was the *Fantasy Opus 15,* written in 1822 and published the next year. It has four movements—*Allegro con fuoco, Adagio, Presto, Allegro*—all unified through their relationship with the second movement, *Adagio,* which contains variations on a theme taken from one of Schubert's better-known songs, *Der Wanderer.* (The entire work is often called the "Wanderer" Fantasy.) Rhythmic patterns in this *Adagio* determine the basic rhythmic components of the other movements. The first movement, *Allegro con fuoco,* has a relentless drive relieved only slightly by the second theme, which is still dominated by the same rhythmic impulse. The *Presto* movement, a scherzo, has thematic material derived from the first movement. Similar themes are used in the finale, *Allegro,* but here they are presented in fugal exposition.

Fantasy, Opus 15 appears in another version, a piano-and-orchestra arrangement by Liszt. In either version, this is not one of Schubert's best works. It is neverthless interesting because its virtuoso components present a different side of this lyric composer whose melodic inventiveness was unequaled by any other nineteenth-century composer.

FELIX MENDELSSOHN

The piano music of **Felix Mendelssohn-Bartholdy** (1809–1847), so popular during the nineteenth century, is rarely heard today. Although his compositions frequently display more than enough examples of one widespread weakness in early Romantic music—exaggerated sentimentalism—they also reveal a well-trained musician. Mendelssohn's compositions are soundly constructed; furthermore, he possessed an innate sense of musical style that makes his music charming, if not enduring.

Mendelssohn looked upon the piano as an important medium; thus, he wrote a quantity of keyboard music.[9] His *Lieder ohne Worte* (Songs

[9] Mendelssohn's complete piano music is published by Peters (five volumes). Hansen of Copenhagen offers the *Songs without Words,* also *Opus 14* and *Opus 16.*

without Words) continue the Schubert tradition—short, lyrical genre pieces —that lasted through the Romantic period. The *Songs without Words* (the title seems to have originated with Mendelssohn) represent a new field in piano music in which lyric or melodic style combines with harmonic, instrumental style.

The *Songs without Words* (forty-eight in all) were published in sets of six. *Opus 19,* the first book, was composed from the end of 1830 to the beginning of 1832. Mendelssohn made trips to Switzerland and Italy during that time, and his travels indirectly influenced this early collection. The first edition, published in London, bore the title *Original Melodies for the Pianoforte;* the second edition carried the title *Songs without Words.*

Six Romances, Opus 30 was the title given to the second book, published in 1835. Four other collections later appeared from the publisher Simrock: *Opus 38* (1837); *Opus 53* (1841); *Opus 62* (1844); and *Opus 67* (1845). Simrock also published two posthumous sets, *Opus 85* and *Opus 102.* The rapid succession of these publications testifies to their success with musicians, professional and amateur alike.

Most pieces bear characteristic titles which, except for three selected by Mendelssohn—*barcarolle, duo,* and *chanson populaire*—were added by editors and pianists. Many titles were assigned during Mendelssohn's lifetime; and although he did not publicly protest this practice, his letters indicate that he disapproved of the poetic appendages.

Mendelssohn follows Schubert in spirit, yet he appears not to have been measurably influenced by him. In fact, it is doubtful that Mendelssohn knew much about Schubert's piano music. Mendelssohn's dependence upon his immediate circle is more obvious: his teacher, L. Berger; a fellow student, W. Taubert; and finally his good friend, I. Moscheles. One of Berger's *Études*[10] could have been a model for the *Songs without Words* (Ex. 5).

Ex. 5. L. Berger: *Étude Opus 12, No. 11*

Allegro moderato e cantabile

---

[10] See Walter Georgii, *Klaviermusik* (Zurich: Atlantis-Verlag, 1950), p. 290. Berger's *Étude Opus 12, No. 11* is published in the series *Anthology of Music,* "*Romanticism in Music,*" ed. K. Stephenson (Cologne: Arno Volk Verlag).

Mendelssohn himself speaks of being profoundly impressed by an early (1831) Taubert work, *An die Geliebte, Acht Minnelieder für das Pianoforte* (To the Beloved, Eight Love Songs for the Piano—Ex. 6).[11]

Ex. 6. W. Taubert: *Minnelied Opus 16, No. 2*

The standard procedures for the *Lieder ohne Worte* derive from three types of vocal music: accompanied solo song, accompanied duet, and unaccompanied choral music. Throughout the sets the first type is preponderant, and the general formal plan is classic A B A design. The third section is never a mere repetition of the first but rather an enriched reexposition. In every piece in all the collections the third section ends with a little coda, recalling a similar usage frequently found in the lied or solo song itself.

Melodically the *Lieder ohne Worte* are products of a quite original musical language, a style unlike any other composer's. The melodic line does not always have vocal contours and at times extends beyond a normal vocal *tessitura*, but there is a lyric quality in this singing melodic line that comes from Mendelssohn's personal and novel inspiration.

Mendelssohn develops accompaniment figures in three ways. Occasionally he chooses a chordal accompaniment in the Schubert manner. More often he uses either broken chords in syncopation or else widely arpeggiated figures in the left hand and tonal-density enrichment in the right hand.

Before Mendelssohn sent the first set of *Lieder ohne Worte* to the publisher, he had already composed a quantity of other piano music, including three piano sonatas, an idiom he never again attempted. *Sonata Opus 105 in G Minor* was probably written as early as 1821; it overflows with youthful high spirits and discrepancies. *Sonata Opus 6 in E Major* (1826) is Beethovenesque in conception; the third, *Sonata Opus 106 in B-flat Major*, is more mature. *Opus 105* and *Opus 106* were not published until 1868.

Other piano works composed by Mendelssohn before he was twenty

[11] *Ibid.*, p. 291.

include the *Capriccio Opus 5, Characterstücke Opus 7, Rondo Capriccioso Opus 14, Irish Fantasy Opus 15,* and *Trois Fantaisies ou Caprices Opus 16.* *Opus 7* and *Opus 14* are the best. In *Opus 7* numbers one and six are grave and noble andantes in Mendelssohn's somewhat oversentimentalized style. Two and four belong in the *Perpetual Motion* category, and number seven is a typical Mendelssohnian scherzo. The third and fifth *Characterstücke* show what excellent musical equipment Mendelssohn had at his disposal: three is a free fugue and five is a classic fugue with a Bach-like subject.

No apologies are necessary for *Opus 14,* the ever famous and popular *Rondo Capriccioso,* which was published in 1833 though probably written much earlier. The introductory *Andante* is not outstanding, but the *Rondo* in scherzo style—with continuous staccato treatment in 6/8 meter—is an excellent example of Mendelssohn's clear, characteristic keyboard style. The succeeding *Opus 15,* a *Fantasy* on an Irish song (The Last Rose of Summer), is pleasant.

Among Mendelssohn's later piano works the most noteworthy are *Fantasy in F-sharp Minor Opus 28,* the *Six Preludes and Fugues Opus 35,* and the *Variations Sèrieuses Opus 54.* Like Schubert and Schumann with their piano fantasies in C major, Mendelssohn thought it wise to call his three-movement work *Opus 28* (1833) a *Fantasy.* Beethoven had provided an outline for Mendelssohn—*Sonata Opus 27, No. 2, in C-sharp Minor,* "*Sonata quasi una fantasia*"—by putting the actual fantasia at the beginning, a characteristic movement in the middle, and a sonata-allegro movement at the end. The first movement, *Andante,* of Mendelssohn's *Fantasy* has a moderately lyrical principal theme at the beginning, middle, and end, alternating with passionate outbursts. A fine contrast is supplied by the quietly flowing second movement, despite its length. And the brilliant finale *Presto* is in 6/8 meter with eighth-note passages in the right hand opposing sixteenth-note left-hand figurations.

Six Preludes and Fugues appeared in 1837 and perhaps took five years to write. The *Preludes* might really be described as études, for each exploits a particular technical device. The *Fugues* are true fugues, though clearly Romantic, and are for the most part dramatically conceived, with good climaxes. The first, *Prelude and Fugue in E Minor,* is the best known as well as the finest. Its fugue subject, in Bach style, adheres to classic methods for exposition, inversion, entries, etc. The work terminates with a powerful chorale and a quiet coda derived from the fugue subject.

Of all Mendelssohn's piano works, the *Variations Sérieuses* (1841) are heard the most frequently. The work is extremely pianistic and is an excellent example of variation form. Although it never exploits virtuosity for its own sake, numerous characteristic keyboard figurations are used with skill: staccato technique, syncopation, melody in inner voices, broken-octave and chordal passages. The composition concludes with a brilliantly conceived finale.

ROBERT SCHUMANN

For some, **Robert Schumann** (1810–1856) personifies the Romantic artist of the early nineteenth century. His stormy love affair and ultimate marriage with Clara Wieck and his progressive mental illness and final breakdown have been stressed too much—often more than his actual contributions as a composer. In addition to composing, Schumann was chief contributor to the musical gazette *Neue Zeitschrift für Musik,* which he founded to promote promising talent and to chastise composers whom he felt were inferior.

As one of the most representative composers of the Romantic period, Schumann's real ability shone in the art song and the short piano piece. His best keyboard works are finely wrought miniatures—tone paintings, mood pictures, psychological delineations—and these are the pieces that preserve his name. Although he ventured into larger keyboard forms, he was more at home with short piano pieces or lieder.[12] He wrote beautiful examples in both idioms, and thus helped in transmitting both traditions to future composers.

Schumann customarily grouped his piano pieces in series. Sometimes the series is a narration, with each separate piece bearing a descriptive title. However, such narratives are usually disjointed so that the order of the pieces is unimportant. This is well illustrated by such suites as the *Albumblätter* (Album Leaves), *Album for the Young,* and the *Fantasy Pieces.* In other instances the series of pieces has a logical succession of psychological portraits, such as the collections *Carnaval, Kinderscenen,* and *Waldscenen.* And finally, some series of piano pieces bear only a general title—*Kreisleriana, Papillons, Davidsbündlertänze, Noveletten,* and *Humoresquen*—but each individual piece illustrates or comments upon the main title. Some piano collections were supposedly influenced by literary sources; the *Papillons* (Butterflies) were purported to be inspired by Jean Paul's *Flegeljahre* (Years of Indiscretion), and the *Kreisleriana* drawn from E. T. A. Hoffmann's *Phantasiestücke in Callot's Manier* (Fantasy Pieces in Callot's Style, 1815). On the other hand, the literary association can be misleading, for as

---

[12] Two good editions of Schumann's complete piano music are available: Kalmus (ed. Clara Schumann); Peters (ed. Sauer).

Schumann himself confessed, "The titles of all my compositions never occur to me until I have finished composing."[13]

An overall look at Schumann's pianoforte works helps to reveal typical characteristics of his keyboard compositions. First, unlike Beethoven, Schumann did not markedly change his style. Apart from the *Gesänge der Frühe Opus 133* (Morning Songs) and the *Concert Allegro Opus 134*, both of which betray his advancing insanity, the late works differ little from his youthful writings except in technical matters.

Second, Schumann's piano works—most of them written between 1829 and 1839—breathe intimacy, sentimentality, and subjectivity. Extremely acute to everything around him, he was sentimental in a positive sense. A dreamer and idealist whose inner life became his real life, Schumann in his music exalts passion to a degree seldom surpassed in the nineteenth century.

Schumann's compositions are not exclusively derived from musical or literary sources; he was also involved with psychological matters. This preoccupation—which is evidenced by musical complexities, enigmas, and obscure descriptive titles—lends a spirit of fantasy to his music.

A feeling of improvisation permeates many of the piano pieces—for example, the opening of *Aufschwung* (Soaring—Ex. 7):

Ex. 7.   R. Schumann: *Aufschwung Opus 12, No. 2*

This is not a careful, scholarly introduction. It is a passionate outburst that demands attention. Schumann does this over and over again, using diverse means to induce an improvisatory effect. He creates a feeling of reticence by using suspensions and an atmosphere of restless agitation by using varied figures.

Schumann admired Bach and doubtlessly studied examples from the Leipzig cantor's vast contrapuntal catalogue. On several occasions in his own career Schumann conscientiously tried to revive the spirit of the contrapuntists: *Four Fugues Opus 72; Seven Pieces in Fughetta Form Opus 126*. These attempts are only moderately successful. Schumann's best contra-

[13] Letter to Simonin de Sire, March 15, 1839. In Robert Schumann, *On Music and Musicians* (New York: Pantheon Books, 1946), p. 259.

puntal writing appears sporadically in different keyboard works. The canon found in the third piece of the *Papillons,* the second movement of the *Fantasy in C Major,* and the seventh variation in the *Études Symphoniques* all show that Schumann could produce not only learned fugues but contrapuntal texture with vitality, a quality often lacking in keyboard polyphony. His music has been criticized for this uneven use of counterpoint.

Schumann has been criticized also for creating an impression of improvisation without formal structural support. But Schumann was a product of the Romantic period, and form was not one of his foremost concerns. In fact, he criticized contemporary music that leaned too heavily on structural elements. His own form grew out of his musical material, and this form— or lack of it—served him best in the short piano piece. The themes in these short compositions are brief, rarely over four measures in length, and usually each piece concentrates on repetition of one given idea. The melodies are often constructed in an ascending line, which gives them an interrogatory character (Ex. 8).

Ex. 8. R. Schumann: *Vogel als Prophet* (Bird as Prophet) *Opus 82, No. 7*

Schumann knew the piano well; he was acquainted with its strengths and its weaknesses and he was aware of the textural possibilities it offered. He often exploited the dark colors of the keyboard palette, as Brahms did later.

It seems natural that Schumann, with his ideas of progressive form, was inordinately fond of the variation. With this favorite form he approached serious keyboard composition—the *Abegg Variations Opus 1* (1830). (Meta Abegg and Schumann met at a dance.) Each note of the theme represents a musical letter contained in her name Abegg—according to the German letters A-B♭-E-G-G. Eventually this theme is inverted to appear as G-G-E-B♭-A. The work consists of a statement of the theme, three variations, and a *Finale alla Fantasia* preceded by a large *Cantabile* section.

The second Schumann opus appeared in 1832; this is a charming series of twelve kaleidescopic miniatures called *Papillons.* As a title *Papillons* is baffling. One Viennese critic called this work a mirror of the nature of butterflies, but this the composer denied. In order to tie in a literary connection with Jean Paul Richter's novel *Flegeljahre*,[14] Schumann deliberately related certain passages of his music to the corresponding prose. (He never published these explanations.) In the story two very different brothers are courting a girl named Wina. In the final chapter they all attend a masked ball. Vult, the intellectual brother, hopes to win the girl by exchanging masks. In an explanatory letter to his friend Henriette Voigt, Schumann wrote, "When you have a minute to spare, I beg of you to read the last chapter of the *Flegeljahre*, where all is to be found in black and white. . . . I may also mention that I set the words to the music and not the music to the words—the opposite seems to me a foolish proceeding." And to the famous Berlin critic Heinrich Rellstab he wrote, "You remember the last scene in the *Flegeljahre*,—the masked ball, Walt, Vult, masks, confessions, anger, revelations, hasty departure, concluding scene, and then the departing brother. Often I turned over the last page: for the end seemed to me a new beginning—almost unconsciously I was at the pianoforte, and thus came into existence one papillon after another."[15] The *Papillons* is such a delightful, transparent collection of miniatures that the literary connotation seems somewhat superfluous. Its introduction, reminiscent of Weber's *Invitation to the Dance*, contains one of Schumann's characteristic interrogative phrases. The finale is quite original, containing an old German dance tune—the *Grossvater Tanz* (Grandfather Dance)—and a technique first tried in the *Abegg Variations*: a sustained chord whose various notes disappear one by one.

Some early Schumann opuses are studies based on *Caprices* of Paganini, *Intermezzi, Impromptus* on a theme of Clara Wieck, and a *Toccata in C Major*. The *Paganini Studies* (*Opus 3* and *Opus 10*) are decidedly less effective than Liszt's similar compositions, for when it came to problems involving sheer technique, Schumann ran a poor second to Liszt the piano wizard. *Toccata Opus 7* is a fine study in right-hand passage work, but it cannot be included among Schumann's best compositions.

As self-appointed leader of the legendary *League of David*, the stronghold of progressive composers, Schumann expressed his sentiments in the *Dances of the League of David Opus 6* (1837). "The *Davidsbündlertänze* are one of Schumann's most subjective works. He had already published compositions under his duple pseudonym, 'Florestan und Eusebius,' and now, in addition to printing the two names on the title-page, he appended to

---

[14] Johann Paul Friedrich Richter (1763–1825) was known in literary circles as Jean Paul. His literary works were in vogue during the first half of the nineteenth century. They shed much light on the essence of Romanticism in Germany.

[15] Niecks, *op. cit.*, p. 193.

each of the separate pieces the initial of one or the other—or both—of these fictitious personalities, according to whether the musical content was the expression of the passionate or the dreamy side of his nature. The music thus conceived is so intimate in its delineation of personal moods that possibly it can be enjoyed and appreciated to the full only by players or listeners who have been initiated into the ways of thought of the imaginary *Davidsbund* which was so lively a reality to Schumann himself. No one who has ever heard the traditional interpretation of this work by a Clara Schumann pupil can have failed to perceive that the performer regards the *Davidsbündlertänze* as the quintessence of Schumann's pianistic art."[16]

Schumann's happiness at the time weaves through his music; his cheerful spirits are proclaimed in the directions for the performer: lively, with humor, very fast, wild and full of life. These dances were meant to be played as a group; some of them end with Schumann's characteristic interrogatory turn of phrase, leaving one in suspense.

Among the first ten opuses, the best—both in musicianship and structure—is *Carnaval Opus 9* (1835). This collection of twenty-one pieces also has a subtitle: *Scènes mignonnes sur quatre notes* (Little scenes on four notes). Schumann took the four notes from Asch, the small town in which Ernestine von Fricken lived. (At one time he thought of marrying Ernestine.) He freely manipulates these four notes in a kind of variation; however, unlike a regular theme and variations, his four-note theme is not presented as such in the beginning but makes its entrance, unadorned, in the ninth piece. (This composition has the mysterious title *Sphinxes* and, incidentally, is omitted in performance.) According to German notation, the musical letters derived from ASCH have two results in *Carnaval:* A-S-C-H; As-C-H —in English notation A-Eb-C-B; Ab-C-B.

Carnaval reflects its composer. Its colorful characters are outwardly gay and inwardly melancholy. The *Préambule*, a joyous prelude, sets the stage for the parade of characters who appear to be drawn from the old Italian *Commedia dell'Arte*. First come two clowns—*Pierrot* and *Arlequin*—one reflective, the other exultant. Then a *Valse Noble* uses A-Eb-C-B for its initial motive. Now two more revelers arrive—*Eusebius* the introvert, *Florestan* the extrovert. The spirit of *Coquette* is everything the name implies and is answered in the following *Réplique*. *Papillons* (which is not related melodically to Schumann's suite *Opus 2* of the same name) and *Dancing Letters* move along in vivid procession. The impassioned *Chiarina* (Schumann's name for Clara) passes into a nocturne—*Chopin*—inspired by similar works by that composer, whom Schumann admired.

Other sections, *Estrella* (Ernestine von Fricken), *Reconnaissance* (a

---

[16] Gerald Abraham, ed., *A Schumann Symposium* (London: Oxford University Press, 1952), p. 51.

recognition scene?), and *Pantalon and Colombine* (more clowns), continue the array of kaleidoscopic miniatures. *Valse Allemande* (German Waltz) is interrupted by a virtuoso section, *Paganini,* in tribute to the great violinist. A brief, nostalgic *Aveu* (Confession) and a *Promenade* lead to a *Pause* (which is not a pause at all). *Carnaval* concludes dramatically with the brilliant *Marche des Davidsbündler contre les Philistins* (March of the League of David against the Philistines). This last piece was a tribute to those composers who advocated a progressive and refined musical culture —not the old conservative traditions and yet not the capricious, superficial music so frequently produced in the Romantic period.

Schumann's three piano sonatas—he dedicated the first to his wife Clara—date from approximately 1835–1836. As examples of pianistic writing, they unfortunately point out what difficulties he faced in attempting to project large-scale ideas in extended form. As examples of the piano sonata, they sometimes negate the innumerable possibilities of thematic development so amply illustrated in the Beethoven sonatas. Yet there are some compensating factors: a wealth of musical ideas and some splendid examples of typically Romantic tonal poetry.

Sonata Opus 11 in F-sharp Minor is the finest of the three. Its slow movement, *Aria,* is a delightful lyric effusion, and the *Scherzo* sparkles with energy. *Sonata Opus 14 in F Minor,* weakest of the three sonatas, was originally called *Concert sans Orchestre* (Concerto without Orchestra). Schumann revised much of it at a time when his mental powers were deteriorating; as a result the work is repetitious and does not hang together. *Sonata Opus 22 in G Minor,* his shortest sonata, is very satisfying. Good musical ideas are logically developed in the initial movement, which has a wonderful drive, and the *Andantino* is carefully fashioned so that the whole sonata has an enduring beauty.

One of his most successful large works is the *Études Symphoniques Opus 13* (1834) based on a theme borrowed from Ernestine von Fricken's father. What Schumann creates here are massive variations built around a rather simple theme—architectural variations which, unlike most of his writings, are difficult to execute. The theme is used melodically, or else only as a bass line for support. Also, some études are free and not visibly based on the theme. He uses the variation techniques skillfully and diversely; his *Études* contrast vividly with each other yet together they present a unified work. They require neither titles nor any of his extramusical descriptions; the music itself speaks with authority and power.

Franz Liszt, always eager to perform music by composers he liked, never performed the *Fantasy Opus 17 in C Major* (1836), which Schumann dedicated to him. It may be that this composition did not sufficiently challenge the Hungarian pianist's technical abilities; for despite its considerable length it is lyrical, filled with the passionate outpourings that Schumann uniquely created.

At the beginning of the *Fantasy*—a sonata-type work in three movements—four lines from the poet Schlegel are quoted as a motto:

> *Durch alle Tone tönet*
> *Im bunten Erdentraum*
> *Ein leiser Ton gezogen*
> *Für den, der heimlich lauschet.*
>
> (Through all the tones that vibrate
> About earth's mingled dream
> One whispered note is sounding
> For ears intent to hear.)[17]

This would be puzzling were it not for the fact that the first movement contains fragments of the final song from Beethoven's song-cycle *An die ferne Geliebte*.[18] The main theme of the *Fantasy's* first section—*Durchaus fantastisch und leidenschaftlich vorzutragen* (To be played in a fantastic and impassioned manner throughout)—dominates the first movement. This superlyrical theme tinged with longing is later contrasted with a more studied theme—*Im Legenden-Ton* (In the Tone of a Legend)—that takes the place of a development section. The second movement—marked *Durchaus energisch* (Energetic throughout)—is the most powerful, an efficient blending of chordal and contrapuntal writing. *Langsam getragen* (Played slowly), the final movement, is a tender reverie, more optimistic than the first movement.

Combining as it does important sonata and variation elements, the *Fantasy* is perhaps more typical of Schumann's musical concepts than most of his compositions. Its strength lies in its single-minded purpose: the expression of poetical sentiments and lyricism tinged with melancholy.

Schumann borrowed the term *Phantasiestück* (Fantasy Piece) from E. T. A. Hoffmann,[19] using it as a general title to cover miscellaneous little pieces that portrayed his flights of fancy, his epigrammatic flashes of inspiration. *Opus 12* is a suite containing eight contrasting pieces, mood impressions that display typical Schumannesque techniques such as rhythmic motives and all types of figurations. A characteristic piece from this collection is the ever popular *Aufschwung* (Soaring). It has two contrasting motives, the first questioning and the second more positive.

[17] Percy M. Young, *Tragic Muse. The Life and Works of Robert Schumann* (London: Hutchinson, 1957), p. 110. Reprinted by permission of Dr. Young and Hutchinson & Co., Ltd.

[18] Schumann originally intended the *Fantasy* as a tribute to Beethoven. He even remarked that a theme from the *Eroica Symphony* was to be used in one of the movements.

[19] Ernst Theodor Amadeus Hoffmann (1776–1822) was a writer-musician who exerted considerable influence on Schumann. Particularly important is the collection of tales *Phantasiestücke in Callots Manier* (4 Vols., 1814). Hoffmann himself wrote articles of music criticism which he signed Johannes Kreisler, Kapellmeister.

In 1838 Schumann wrote to Clara, ". . . since my last letter I again have a whole book of new things ready. *Kreisleriana* I am going to call them, in which you and a thought of you play the chief part, and I will dedicate it to you—yes, to you and to no one else. You will smile so sweetly when you recognize yourself. My music now seems to me so wonderfully complex for all its simplicity, so eloquent from the heart, and it has the same effect on all to whom I play it, which I now do gladly and often."[20]

From a musical point of view the *Kreisleriana* is one of Schumann's finest works; from the listener's point of view, it is one of the hardest to assimilate. Composed of eight extended pieces, the set is dominated as much by the memory of Kreisler—a fictional conductor who was immortalized in the stories of E. T. A. Hoffmann—as by any thought of Clara. Incidentally, the suite is not dedicated to Clara but to Chopin. What is interesting about this collection is not the construction procedures but the great variety of moods depicted.

Faschingsschwank aus Wien Opus 26 (Viennese Carnival) was written in 1839 after a visit to Vienna. It had been a wonderful trip for Schumann, as he was able to forage through some forgotten Schubert manuscripts. *Faschingsschwank* has five pieces and Schumann called it a romantic sonata. The first movement, with its waltz tunes, contains a hint of the *Marseillaise,* a song prohibited in the Austrian capital; the other movements are *Romanza, Scherzino, Intermezzo,* and *Finale.* Vienna must have left Schumann with gay memories. The capricious, joyous, passionate, and impertinent *Faschingsschwank* is one of his most extrovert works.

Schumann's solo piano works total thirty-six opus numbers, but individual discussion is out of place here. One should mention, however, the light, transparent sketches called *Novelletten Opus 21;* the *Nachtstücke Opus 23* (Night Pieces), with their disquieting evocation of the Hoffmann-esque grotesque; the *Kinderscenen Opus 15* (Scenes from Childhood), conceived by Schumann as "Souvenirs for those who have grown up" and again as "for little children by a big child"; and finally, those rather innocuous, uncomplicated sketches that comprise the *Album für die Jugend Opus 68* (Album for the Young).

EPILOGUE

Each of these early-nineteenth-century composers—Weber, Schubert, Mendelssohn, Schumann—made important contributions toward the establishment of a stable Romantic tradition. Their combined influence was last-

---

[20] Letter to Clara Wieck, April 13, 1838. In Frederick Niecks, *Robert Schumann* (London: J. M. Dent & Sons, Ltd., 1925), p. 187.

ing, for elements of their tradition also are discernible in twentieth-century music.

Weber's dramatic approach widened the keyboard's expressionistic vistas, while his preoccupation with technique provided a groundwork for Liszt and later generations. Schubert repeatedly stressed the effective impact of simplicity in his music, and his versatility with melody has been the admiration of many who would, if they could, learn his lyric secrets.

Mendelssohn proved an effective bridge leading to the height of the Romantic period. He showed that techniques from the Baroque and Classic periods could be successfully merged with the new ideals, giving them an element of soundness and solidity.

Finally, Schumann, with his extramusical preoccupations and his sometimes obscure experiments in musical description, is perhaps the most typical Romantic composer. His successful transfer of pure emotion into pure sound was unique in his time and remains so today.

BIBLIOGRAPHY

Abraham, Gerald, ed. *Schumann. A Symposium.* London: Oxford University Press, 1952.

Basch, Victor. *Schumann* (translated by C. A. Phillips). New York: Tudor Publishing Co., 1936.

Brown, Maurice. "An Introduction to Schubert's Sonatas of 1817." *Music Review,* Vol. 12, No. 1, 1951.

Brown, Maurice. *Schubert.* London: Macmillan & Co., Ltd., 1958.

Deutsch, Otto Erich. *The Schubert Reader* (translated by E. Blom). New York: W. W. Norton & Co., Inc., 1947.

Einstein, Alfred. *Schubert.* New York: Oxford University Press, 1951.

Flower, Newman. *Franz Schubert. The Man and His Circle.* New York: Frederick A. Stokes Co., 1928.

Gertler, Wolfgang. *Robert Schumann in seiner frühen Klavierwerken.* Leipzig: Druck von Radelli und Hille, 1931.

Jacob, Heinrich Eduard. *Felix Mendelssohn and His Times* (translated by R. & C. Winston). Englewood Cliffs, N.J.: Prentice-Hall, Inc., 1963.

Radcliffe, Philip. *Mendelssohn.* London: J. M. Dent & Sons, Ltd., 1954.

Schumann, Robert. *On Music and Musicians* (translated by Paul Rosenfeld). New York: Pantheon, 1946.

Young, Percy M. *Tragic Muse. The Life and Works of Robert Schumann.* London: Hutchinson, 1957.

17

THE

ROMANTIC COMPOSERS:

CHOPIN

Of all the composers who have created piano music, **Frédéric François Chopin** (1810–1849), universally idolized in his own century and in ours, holds the enviable position of being the one whose music is most frequently performed. His contemporaries, perhaps from jealousy, were sometimes slighting. "A sick room talent," said John Field. "He was dying all his life," remarked Hector Berlioz. Even in distant Russia, Mily Balakirev compared him to "a nervous society lady." Despite these disparaging epithets, the fact remains that Chopin invented a keyboard style that fits ideally into nineteenth-century Romanticism. His music is subjective and tinged with melancholy; it suggests a never ending search for the unattainable, yet invariably the mood is clothed in an impeccable technical apparatus.

Born in Poland in 1810 of a Polish mother and a French father, Chopin gave his first public performance at nine and began concertizing at an early age. In 1829 he performed in Austria and Bohemia, where he became successful both as a pianist and as the composer of extremely original piano music; but he found his musical home in Paris. Poland was torn by revolution, and Paris—at that time Europe's liveliest music center—befriended many exiled Polish aristocrats. While there, Chopin formed congenial friendships with Franz Liszt, Vincenzo Bellini, Honoré de Balzac, and Heinrich Heine. The most publicized period of his life was spent with the French writer George Sand (Mme. Aurore Dudevant). What began as maternal affection turned into a *grande affaire*, and for seven years Chopin remained under her influence—in Paris, at her country home in Nohant, and in Majorca for one season. He broke off this relationship toward the end of his life. Ill with consumption and weakened from a concert tour through England and Scotland, he returned to Paris, where he died in 1849.

Chopin's musical style is exceptionally individualistic, so distinct and personal that some elements are instantly recognizable as belonging to him. His music is as readily identifiable as an El Greco painting or a Baudelaire poem; one reason for the easy access to his works is their ready charm. "The charm of this music has a double essence; it is the emanation of a poetic sensitivity which is singularly profound, ardent and subtle, rich in meditation, caprice, and passion—and it is also the expression of a race, this Polish race so nervous and so naturally refined, chivalric, feminine in its supple grace, with its élans of heroism and of sudden violence, and of access of wild melancholy, which can lead to despair. Thus Chopin is in turn—and very often simultaneously—a personal poet and the singer of his race."[1]

A prominent and very engaging feature of his music is its melodic structure. His melodies are basically vocal rather than instrumental and his music may therefore be said to derive more from Schubert than anyone else. Unlike Beethoven he never uses the symphonic-type melodies that lend themselves to ample development and to motivic construction. Chopin's melodies are capable of elaboration, but it is a kind of self-development relying on harmonic change, modulation, rhythmic transformation and, above all, ornamentation.

The source of most Chopin melodies can be traced to the dance or to song. Those pieces that are dance inspired are the melodies for the *Mazurkas, Polonaises,* and *Waltzes;* there are also disguised dances in other types, such as the *Étude Opus 25, No. 9.* From vocal models come almost all of his slow themes, like that in the *Étude Opus 10, No. 3.* Chopin was fond of Italian opera, particularly Bellini operas, and many of his melodies reveal a touch of Bellinian bel canto—always, however, molded into his own manner of expression.

Often these melodies seem deliberately designed for the voice, because they are lyric (usually diatonic) and fashioned into regular eight-bar periods. There are numerous examples of a melodic idea being repeated several times, such as the *Nocturne Opus 9, No. 2; Prélude Opus 28, No. 6;* and *Polonaise Opus 53.* With Chopin this repetition serves to intensify the original idea and can give rise to thrilling consequences.

An important factor in Chopin's melody is chromaticism, which he employs as a device to vary or to develop themes. Compare the three different statements of one melody in the *Nocturne Opus 27, No. 2, in D-flat Major.* How changed the entire melodic spirit becomes through the chromatic variances! Sometimes this procedure produces a favorite Chopin device: the melodic line is interrupted by a cadenza-like chromatic figure, which eventually comes to repose, allowing the melody to continue.

Another outstanding characteristic of Chopin is his concept of harmony. His writing shows no inclination toward strict polyphony and counterpoint, but his unique harmonic practices were so ahead of his time that they puzzled even Schumann. Chopin's ideas about harmony were extraor-

---

[1] Louis Aguettant, *La Musique de Piano des Origines à Ravel* (Paris: Editions Albin Michel, 1954), pp. 184–185. English translation by the author.

dinary for the early nineteenth century, and they influenced many later composers. His harmonic idiom is complicated. Here are a few salient points: (1) The modulation—remarkably free for the period—is accomplished in various ways: enharmonically and by assumption of key, to mention only two. (2) Dissonance is also liberally treated. Sometimes there are so many passing and nonharmonic tones that the harmony is veiled, as though the composer were trying to disguise it. The boldness in some series of dissonances completely perplexed Chopin's contemporaries, but these dissonances create harmonic color not encountered again until Debussy. (3) Frequently the harmony itself engenders the melody. In the *Étude Opus 25, No. 1, in A-flat Major*, for example, the melody emerges as the result of shimmering arpeggios. Chopin's melody preserves its vitality only when considered in its harmonic framework.

Chopin had a dramatic command of rhythm regardless of the prevailing spirit or mood, a command well displayed in the *Prélude Opus 28, No. 24, in D Minor* and the opening movement of the *Sonata Opus 35*. By the same token, the lyric effect in pieces like the *Étude Opus 10, No. 6* depends in large measure on the inherent rhythmic concept. But it is the *Mazurkas* (see page 229) that best illustrate Chopin's adeptness in rhythm because there the basic impression actually depends on the rhythm—the rhythm *is* the mazurka. Although both are written in triple meter and have a similar texture, the *Waltzes* and the *Mazurkas* are rarely confused, thanks to the characteristic rhythm each one possesses.

A prominent element of Chopin's pianistic style—and one that is the most abused—is his use of *tempo rubato* (literally, stolen time), which calls for a loosening of strict tempo. Without *rubato* his music loses much of its charm and emotional impact. On the other hand, undisciplined use of this expressionistic device results in sugary sentimentality, a complete distortion of his original intent. He gave the clue to correct usage when he said the hand supplying the accompaniment should keep a strict rhythm while the melodic line is played in *tempo rubato*.

Another conspicuous feature of Chopin's music stems from his preoccupation with the sostenuto (damper) pedal, which either curtails sounds or permits them to vibrate through the air. Chopin's genius lies primarily in lyrical music (a cantabile art), and he uses the sostenuto pedal to achieve his sustained melodic lines and to coordinate his characteristic widely spaced accompaniment figures.

Before discussing any of the works, it might be interesting to recall yet another aspect of Chopin's music, brought to attention by the late Alfred Cortot, one of the great interpreters of Chopin's compositions. "Everything in Chopin points to the existence of a secret link between the radiance of nature and the internal blossoming of his musical ideas; the unconscious reaction of the creative mind to the seasons, coinciding with the period of the year when his cough eased and his fits of suffocation became less frequent. We can see how, with a symbolism completely in tune with Chopin's genius, his inspiration adjusted itself to the rebirth of the year, the harvesting of the earth's abundance, to the time when the flowers open and nightingales sob out their songs into the night. One pays even closer attention to that natural instinct which bound the frail musician to physical phenomena, which seem to bear no relation to his art, but which he suffered to enter into him in the way that a still pool holds the heat of the sun's rays."[2]

PRÉLUDES

The twenty-four *Préludes*[3] were published in 1839 and have been subjected to a disheartening amount of Romantic exaggeration. One may read that Chopin wrote his preludes while vacationing in Majorca with George Sand, yet more reliable sources say that he had written or sketched most of the preludes before leaving for Majorca. There are also vivid descriptions about the circumstances surrounding several individual preludes. The *Préludes* do not require flowery romanticization; they stand on their beauty and artistic merit. Schumann found them amazing, a pure enchantment; Liszt felt that although they were brief they had magnificent spiritual proportions.

There are two singular points about the *Préludes*. First, they are very much like Bach's preludes, not in technical style but in attitude and basic concept. Like Bach, Chopin wrote twenty-four preludes (plus a later single one), one in each major and minor key. Often the prelude is based on a single idea, sometimes only a motive. The first *Prélude* is built upon a series of simple modulating figures (Ex. 1). The *Préludes* are fragmentary and may seem like sketches, but they faithfully reflect the soul of the Romantic musician: brief portrayals, some melancholy and even desperate (*No. 24*), others light and gay (*No. 3*).

Second, Chopin's *Préludes* are independent preludes. Before his time, the prelude had been coupled with the fugue or had served as an introduction to a suite of dances. Chopin's works are preludes to nothing in particular except perhaps a mood or a fleeting impression. Played as a set,

[2] Reprinted from *In Search of Chopin* by Alfred Cortot, trans. C. & R. Clarke (New York: Abelard Press, 1952), p. 71. By permission of Abelard-Schumann Ltd. All rights reserved. Copyright 1952.

[3] The best available edition of Chopin's piano music, only slightly edited by Paderewski, is published by the Frédéric Chopin Institute, available through E. B. Marks Music Corp. Other acceptable editions are Kalmus (basically a revision by Liszt) and Augener (ed. Klindworth-Scharwenka). Salabert of Paris has an attractive publication edited by Alfred Cortot.

Ex. 1. F. Chopin: *Prélude Opus 28, No. 1*

they provide a tonal mosaic, a prism of different hues. Heard singly, each emerges as a delectable inspiration born of concentrated emotion.

ÉTUDES

The *Études* contain the essence of Chopin's distinctive traits: the harmonic fluidity, melodic voluptuousness, and inner vitality that characterize his whole pianistic repertoire. All the more remarkable is that they were written when Chopin was a young man. The twelve *Études Opus 10* were composed between his nineteenth and twenty-fourth years—a masterpiece for so early a work! Although they were published later, the twelve *Études Opus 25* are almost contemporary with the first set.

The golden age of the étude or study piece was initiated in 1817 with the *Gradus ad Parnassum* of Muzio Clementi. Successively came the études by Clementi's disciple J. B. Cramer and the prodigious collections of Karl Czerny, some of which appeared at the time Chopin began composing his own works. These early études were usually based on classical late-eighteenth-century techniques—exploitation of scalar techniques, arpeggios—so they do not explore numerous problems perceivable in the final Beethoven sonatas. Excellent as they are, they remain studies in technique. Chopin's *Études* go beyond this. They include not only the expected studies in various matters of technique but also studies dealing with musicianship.

Each étude is devoted to the exploitation of one particular pianistic problem: *Opus 10, No. 1* consists of a series of brilliant right-hand arpeggios; *No. 5*, the so-called "Black Key Étude," calls for execution chiefly on black notes; and *Opus 10, No. 11* is based on a series of widely spaced harplike chords. The last étude of *Opus 10*, the "Revolutionary Étude," develops a spectacular succession of left-hand scalar passages. *Opus 25, No. 6* concentrates on parallel thirds, particularly hard for pianists.

However, technique alone is but one side of piano music and piano playing, in some ways merely a means to an end. Chopin realized this, and many of his *Études* are designed to call attention to subtler problems of musicianship. Sometimes this approach is combined with virtuosity, as in *Opus 10, No. 3;* the lyric melodic line in the first and last sections of this work opposes the dramatic middle section, where sets of augmented and diminished intervals, in both hands, brilliantly compete.

At other times technique is pushed to the background and other keyboard problems have priority. *Opus 10, No. 6* is a long songlike elegy demanding the utmost lyricism in the delineation of its melodic line; *sempre legatissimo,* orders Chopin—that is, maintain evenness so that the single notes of the melody are bound together into an organic entity. *Opus 25, No. 7,* sometimes called the "Cello Étude," contains a diminutive tonal drama: a short recitative in the left hand expands into a broad melody, another melody enters in the right hand; the ensuing interplay between these two lyric lines is unusually beautiful.

Opus 25, No. 11 is a whirlwind of sound, emanating from a torrent of notes in the right hand set against the square chordal structure of the left hand. *No. 12,* fundamentally only a series of parallel arpeggios, builds to a mighty climax. Joy permeates *Opus 25, No. 9,* the so-called "Butterfly Étude," with an almost flippant touch that belies its difficulty. *Opus 25, No. 1* is strictly impressionistic. Shimmering broken figurations appear from nowhere, evoking an indescribable atmosphere quite as effective as that in some of Debussy's preludes.

NOCTURNES

Of all Chopin's works, the *Nocturnes* are the most introspective, the most genuinely subjective. The title and content of the nocturne were not original with Chopin. The Irishman **John Field** (1782–1837)[4] first used this form. Field, a favorite pupil of Clementi, lived for thirty years in Moscow, where he taught Michael Glinka. Field's music is understandably all but forgotten. Three of his four mediocre sonatas make up his *Opus 1.* More convincing are his graceful rondos, evidently written with greater enthusiasm. He continues to be remembered in the twentieth century not for his music but because he originated the form that Chopin used: a short elegy of great lyric intensity. Field's classic model is a simple melody with harmonic accompaniment.

It is easy to pick out the details in Field's nocturnes that appealed to Chopin: the idea of the nocturne itself—atmospheric, usually nostalgic; and the coloratura passages occasionally interrupting the melodic line (Ex. 2).

---

[4] John Field's *Opus 1* (three sonatas) and four *Nocturnes* are published by Augener. The complete *Nocturnes* are published by Ricordi, Peters, and G. Schirmer. Schirmer also issues one *Rondo.*

Ex. 2.   J. Field: *Nocturne in E Major*

Chopin's own genius filled in the rest of the framework. Today Field's *Nocturnes* sound empty and lifeless, his accompaniment figures seem monotonous, and many pieces lack cohesion and wander aimlessly. These *Nocturnes* stay alive only because of their historical interest; they represent the embryonic stage of a musical type that reached its ultimate perfection in the music of Frédéric Chopin.

By refining the contours and enriching the harmonic texture of the nocturne, Chopin made it a desirable art form. In it he released his innermost thoughts, disclosing his sadness and nostalgia. His *Nocturnes* are like musical readings of nineteenth-century French poetry, recalling Alfred de Musset's line, "*Les plus désespérés sont les chants les plus beaux.*" (The most beautiful songs are the saddest songs.)

The nineteen *Nocturnes*—scattered from *Opus 9* through *Opus 72*—were composed at different periods. Most of them are in basic ternary form A B A; however, the original theme's restatement is varied through Chopin's unique ornamentation. Melancholy pervades most of them. Many melodies have an initial downward sweep, increasing this pensive atmosphere: *Opus 9, No. 1; Opus 27, No. 2; Opus 37, No. 1; Opus 72, No. 1* (Ex. 3).

The texture in the *Nocturnes* generally comes from an elaborate melody supported by undulating broken figures in the bass. At times extremely florid, these melodies often show instances of Chopin's little cadenza-like fioriture. In the less effective early *Nocturnes* (*Opus 9* and *Opus 15*) the writing is not as disciplined as in later compositions. The middle section of *Opus 9, No. 1*, for example, has simply a series of parallel octaves for a melody. But by the time Chopin reached *Opus 27*, he was using the nocturne form to give his innermost thoughts their most beautiful expression.

Ex. 3. F. Chopin: *Nocturne Opus 37, No. 1*

Opus 27, No. 2, in D-flat Major is one of the loveliest; the melody dips downward, then rises successively higher while parallel thirds clearly heighten the emotional effect. Such progressions in thirds, in company with sixths and other intervals, also have wonderful results in *Opus 37, No. 2*.

For the most part the *Nocturnes* are not dramatic. *Opus 48, No. 1, in C Minor* is an exception. Like the other *Nocturnes,* its first section is meditative, but the middle section grows to a lavish climax—massive harplike chords are interrupted by octave passages in both hands. Then the third section, instead of returning to the calm spirit of the initial section, continues the turbulence and is marked *doppio movimento.*

As a collection Chopin's *Nocturnes* are definitely unequal in quality; yet separately they present some marvelous strains of pure lyricism, and several achieve perfection in mood painting. Moreover, they disclose the emotions of their creator.

IMPROMPTUS

The four *Impromptus,* written when Chopin was about thirty, are refined diversions generally having two themes, one very pianistic and the other lyric. The graceful melodies are supplied with delightful chromaticism, but still the *Impromptus* do not present Chopin at his best. They constitute good salon music, charming divertissements, yet their substance cannot match that of the *Études* or the *Préludes. Impromptu Opus 29 in A-flat* is typical, *Impromptu Opus 51 in G-flat* is more subtle, and *Fantasy-Impromptu Opus 66* is more passionate. The least effective of the four, *Opus 36 in F-sharp,* is more like a nocturne.

POLONAISES

The title *Polonaise* had been used by J. S. Bach, J. Christian Bach, Weber, and others. The classic polonaise is a dance of noble allure and moderately fast tempo. Liszt remarked that Chopin's *Polonaises,* "characterized by an energetic rhythm, galvanize and electrify the torpor of indifference. The most noble traditional feelings of ancient Poland are embodied in them. . . . They bring vividly before the imagination, the ancient Poles, as we find them described in their chronicles; gifted with powerful organizations, subtle intellects, indomitable courage and earnest piety, mingled with high-born courtesy and a gallantry which never deserted them, whether on the eve of battle, during its exciting course, in the triumph of victory, or amidst the gloom of defeat."[5] These *Polonaises* or dances should, therefore, be played with a certain majesty—often emphasized by Chopin through the tempo marking *Allegro maestoso.*

Formally, Chopin's polonaise is tripartite, somewhat resembling a scherzo, with contrasting textures in the center section. The rhythm is ternary with a frequent anacrusis of two sixteenths before the second beat.

Chopin revitalized the spirit of the polonaise. He kept the title and the basic ideas to use as a foundation upon which he designed a keyboard poem praising his native land—its struggles, its eternal hope, its sorrows. His early polonaises are not wholly conceived in this frame of mind, and by the same token they are less impressive than the others.

The temperament of Chopin's polonaise as he ultimately conceived it began with *Opus 26, No. 1, in C-sharp Minor.* In this particular case, however, the initial verve is not carried to its fullest expansion, so that this rather short polonaise seems abbreviated. Chopin reached his full measure of expression in this form somewhat later. *Opus 26, No. 2, in E-flat Minor* arouses feelings of foreboding. Sometimes subtitled "Revolt," this troubled work suggests a struggle against relentless fate. The "Military Polonaise," *Opus 40, No. 1, in A Major,* is much brighter, a brisk, crisp march in triple meter, expansively melodic in the middle section. Number two of the same opus (in *c* minor) admirably fits its sometime title "*Pathétique.*" A broad left-hand melody in octaves is supported by solemn full chords in the right hand; and the middle section, largely chromatic, uses motivic repetition for emphasis.

Opus 44 in F-sharp Minor is the first of the *Grandes Polonaises,* and it resembles in spirit the more profound *Scherzos.* Chopin generously uses his mature technical devices for this stately work. Melodic lines are variously created: singly, in thirds and sixths, and in octaves. Frequent trills accentuate the dramatic content. In the center a *Mazurka, doppio movimento* provides an unexpected contrast.

Opus 53 in A-flat Major remains the grand example of all polonaises,

[5] Franz Liszt, *Life of Chopin,* trans. M. Cook (Boston: Oliver Ditson & Co., n.d.), p. 31. A new translation by E. N. Waters has recently appeared (New York: Free Press, 1963).

a superb epic still, even though it has been played nearly to death, often very badly. The primary theme, with its surprisingly bare accompaniment, is an aristocratic march without any obvious pretention. In the trio—after a fanfare of arpeggiated chords—an equally rhythmic melodic motive is set up accompanied by formidable series of descending octaves. Then, after a more lyric passage, the initial noble theme is reintroduced.

Chopin's last work in this form, the *Polonaise-Fantaisie Opus 61*, appeared in 1846 (the polonaises of *Opus 71* are early works published posthumously), and it is a proper climax to the imposing compositions he wrote in this particular style. Its poetic qualities approach those in the *Ballades*, while its rhythmic drive and lofty disposition make it a true *Polonaise*.

MAZURKAS

"If the mighty autocrat of the North [Czar of Russia] knew what a dangerous enemy threatened him in Chopin's works, in the simple melodies of his mazurkas, he would forbid this music. Chopin's works are guns buried in flowers."[6] So wrote Robert Schumann.

Chopin's *Mazurkas* (there are more than fifty of them) clearly show the composer as an harmonic innovator. These pieces have been and continue to be neglected in favor of his more dramatic or more lyric compositions. This is a grave error. In some of the mazurkas Chopin reveals himself as a truly unique composer.

Originally a Polish dance of heroic cast, the mazurka has a basic rhythm in triple meter with the principal accent on the second or third beat rather than on the first. Chopin elevated this folk dance to an art form yet saved the mazurka's native charm and uniqueness. In these pieces—abbreviated polonaises, perhaps—Chopin has put the best of himself; they are little poems reflecting on all emotions, from sheer happiness through sarcasm to utter despair.

It is extremely difficult to generalize about the *Mazurkas* because each one is different from all others. Chopin seldom borrows directly from Polish folk repertoire for his melodies, but he draws inspiration from it. His *Mazurkas* are often constructed on modal scales rather than major or minor; and his rhythms are so diversified that they defy any general classification.

Some of the *Mazurkas*, especially the earlier ones, are real dances that could be danced to. At the beginning of his active career, he apparently felt close to the dance in a more or less primitive form. As time passed he amplified and stylized his original concepts. A typical primitive example is

[6] Robert Schumann, *On Music and Musicians*, trans. Paul Rosenfeld (New York: Pantheon, 1946), p. 132.

the *Mazurka Opus 6, No. 3*, a kind of rustic dance with a drone bass. The first *Mazurka* of this same opus (in *f-sharp* minor) is more elegant. Other mazurkas that are more decidedly dance types are *Opus 7, No. 1* and *Opus 30, No. 3*. Some of them have less dance quality, preserving a basic rhythm, but concentrating on a more elegiac quality: *Opus 50, No. 3, in C-sharp Minor; Opus 17, Nos. 2 and 4;* and *Opus 24, No. 1.*

WALTZES

Chopin stylized the *Polonaise* and the *Mazurka* and produced master-pieces in these two forms. He also stylized the *Waltz* but not quite so suc-cessfully, and it is unfortunate that his waltzes are heard so much instead of his more musically substantial works. The waltzes are not negligible by any means. They are meant to charm and charm they do, nothing more. They mirror the humors and caprices of the composer but in a diminished and often superficial way.

Eight of the fourteen *Waltzes* were published with Chopin's consent during his lifetime; the others appeared posthumously. They are in song form like most of his works, but it is reduced song form compared to that used for the *Polonaises*. A look at the waltz portfolios shows the same evo-lution in the waltzes as in the other two dance forms. The first waltzes are dances for dancing, the later ones are solely for listening. In the early waltzes, titled *Valses Brillantes,* Chopin reminisces about souvenirs of a ball: resplendent costumes, sparkling illumination, and graceful dancers. Not long after, however, Chopin stylized his waltz form to the "salon" waltz, his special creation.

Some of the most beautiful *Waltzes* have a slow tempo not in keeping with the usual waltz spirit. The nostalgic left-hand melody in *Opus 34, No. 2* and the graceful lyric curve of *Opus 69, No. 1* are lovely when placed in harmonic context. More animated waltzes, such as *Opus 64, No. 1* (the "Minute Waltz") and *Opus 42,* are well written; but altogether the waltzes do not exemplify Chopin's finest writing.

SONATAS

Two of Chopin's three piano sonatas merit serious consideration. *Sonata Opus 4 in C Minor* is definitely a student attempt, awkwardly constructed and lacking inspiration. Passages here and there hint of the remarkable things to come, but there are not enough of these passages to warrant a place for this sonata in standard piano repertoire. There are structural weaknesses in the other two sonatas as well; Chopin was not at home in sonata form. His musical imaginings did not adapt themselves easily to the architectural requirements laid out for exposition, development, and recapitulation. However, if these two sonatas are interpreted as collections of dramatic poems, their expressive content is overwhelming and it becomes only too evident that this is magnificent music.

Sonata Opus 35 in B-flat Minor was finished while Chopin was with George Sand in Majorca. He once wrote to his friend Fontana, "I am composing here a sonata in B-flat minor, in which will be included the funeral march which you already have. There is an Allegro, then a Scherzo in E-flat minor, the March, and a short Finale of about three pages. After the march, the left hand discourses in unison with the right hand."[7] Robert Schumann, in reviewing the work, was not at all convinced of the appropriateness of the title. "The idea of calling it a sonata is a caprice, if not a jest, for he has simply bound together four of his most reckless children; thus under his name smuggling them into a place into which they could not else have penetrated."[8] Yet Schumann was wrong; the work does have unity—a unity more to be experienced than analyzed. The first movement is as dramatic as Chopin was capable of making it. A four-bar introduction, *Grave*, begins with an initial skip of a diminished seventh. The opening movement proper, *Doppio movimento,* has two themes, the first of which is an agitated motive built on a characteristic figure (Ex. 4).

Ex. 4. F. Chopin: *Sonata Opus 35: Doppio movimento*

The second theme is more lyrical and stable. These two opposing elements vie with each other in the development; the lyric theme wins, for it alone appears in the recapitulation. Chopin must have decided that the incessant repetitions of the first theme-motive in the exposition, plus its various guises in the development, would only be weakened by any further restatements.

The *Scherzo* in this sonata, unruly and full of abrupt leaps, is some-

[7] Henri Bidou, *Chopin*, trans. C. Phillips (New York: Tudor Publishing Co., 1927), pp. 185–186.
[8] Schumann, *op. cit.*, p. 140.

what like a Beethoven scherzo. Placing a premium on melody, the *Trio* contrasts nicely with the lively character of this *Scherzo*. Familiar to everyone, the *Marche Funèbre* is constructed on a succession of deceivingly simple chords; the middle section in *D-flat* major relieves the prevailing somber shades. In some ways the *Finale* is the finest movement as well as a magnificent climax to this beautiful sonata. Cumulative harmonies, produced by tumultuous chromatic progressions played with both hands an octave apart, create an overpowering effect accentuated by a consistent rhythm in triplets.

Sonata Opus 58 in B Minor, written a few years before Chopin's death, more strictly adheres to tenets of classic sonata form. This sonata is neither as fantastic nor as histrionic as *Opus 35;* thus, it is more intimate and profound in its sadness. The opening *Allegro maestoso* forms around contrasting themes, one predominantly rhythmic, the other melodic. A nostalgic *Trio* is set within the brilliant *Scherzo*. One of the really inspired sections—the *Largo*—is in song form; and the vigorous, rhythmic *Finale* is well written in rondo form with three statements.

BALLADES

Chopin wrote four single-movement works of large proportions, which he called *Ballades*. *Ballade Opus 23 in G Minor* was published in 1836; number two, *Opus 38 in F Major*, in 1840; number three, *Opus 47 in A-flat*, appeared in 1841; and the final *Ballade, Opus 52 in F Minor*, came out in 1843. Seldom is Chopin's mighty imagination so well displayed. His pieces have nothing in common with the old poetical ballad made up of three strophes followed by a refrain. They are closer to the Romantic ballads of Friedrich Schiller and Johann Wolfgang von Goethe and have an even greater affinity with those of the Polish poets Adam Mickiewicz and Yulius Slovatski, whose narrative poems deal with legendary or fantastic subjects. The *Ballades* do have an aura of romantic legend, but Chopin never thought out his inspiration in specifically detailed relationships. If it is true that the Mickiewicz ballads inspired him, as he reportedly told Schumann, it can only have been in a hazy sense. *Ballade in G Minor* is fashioned more like a narrative than the others.

The third *Ballade* has elegance, but the other three possess a grandeur that at times becomes epic. Each musical poem exposes impassioned emotions in lyric effusion ending on a tragic note. Of the four *Ballades*, the second and the spectacular fourth give the best portrayals of these stark emotions.

The first, *Ballade Opus 23*, elicited praise from both Schumann and

Liszt, who singled out its savage feeling. According to some writers, there is a connection (this seems extremely tenuous) between this *Ballade* and Mickiewicz's poem *Konrad Valenrod*, which describes battles between Lithuanian pagans and Christian knights. Chopin dedicated the second *Ballade* to Schumann, and this too was supposedly inspired by a Mickiewicz poem titled *Switez* (a lake in Lithuania that engulfed a medieval city). If Chopin really was inspired by this legend, it must have been in a general sense, perhaps shown in the contrast between the exquisite beauty of the first theme and the violence of the second theme. This alternation, repeated several times with thematic variations, ends with violence triumphant.

Liszt reported that the third *Ballade* was improvised on the spot for Heinrich Heine, the German poet for whom Chopin wished to comment musically on the *Willi* (another Mickiewicz poem recounting the adventures of *Ondine*, sister of the *Lorelei*). And the fourth *Ballade* is supposed to have been inspired by the Lithuanian ballad of the *Budrys*, concerning heroism and love during the war of the Lettons against the Russians, Teutons, and Poles.

It is difficult to ascertain what, if any, was the predetermined plan for the *Ballades*. The only set principle is that each is constructed on two primary melodic ideas. Here and there are techniques related to the sonata, rondo, and variation. Otherwise, Chopin gave free rein to his inspiration, and his genius chose not to accommodate the constraint of traditional rules.

SCHERZOS

The Italian word *scherzo* refers to a witty character or a joke. Although it had been used in music even before the time of Bach, the scherzo form came into its own when Beethoven endowed it with greater amplitude and musical substance and used it in place of the gay minuet. Under Chopin the *scherzo* again became a new creation. A far cry from anything witty or capricious, his *Scherzos* are towering tragic poems revealing their composer's conflicts and tribulations.

Structurally, Chopin's *Scherzos* derive from both the minuet and the rondo, yet neither form is ever perceptibly present. One exception—*Scherzo Opus 39*—is constructed like sonata-allegro form (two ideas, the second of which is amplified). Usually the main body of the *Scherzo* has two contrasting themes, each developed or varied, then stated and restated before the entrance of the *Trio*. This latter is a contrasting section, decidedly lyrical, like that in the feminine and meditative theme of the first *Scherzo Opus 20*, a Polish *Noel* taken directly from folk song. The first section of this *Opus 20* has a restless nature recalling the first movement of the *Sonata in B-flat Minor.*

Perhaps the best known of the four *Scherzos* is *No. 2, in B-flat Minor,* in which a kind of interrogative figure (measures 1–3) is answered by full-textured chords. After several repetitions of this idea, another motive with enlarged contours intrudes, leading to the first encounter with a melody. The entire section is repeated, leading to the *Trio* or middle section, an astonishing bit of sparse writing. This initial simplicity, however, soon gives way to a lengthy dramatic passage that eventually turns back to the initial ideas.

Scherzo Opus 39 surpasses the other three in sheer beauty and skillful structural handling. The opening figure—four quarter notes within a bar of triple meter—is a novel venture. Then follows a series of octave passages in both hands, leading to a passage in which liberally used staccato notes add a Mendelssohnian touch. A new section in *D-flat* major contains the most delectable music of the entire *Scherzo:* a brief block of bare chords followed by shimmering impressionistic descending figurations. These two ideas are repeated over and over with ever changing variation, and the effect is unutterably beautiful.

Often published with the *Scherzos* and bearing a spiritual tie with them, the *Fantasy Opus 49 in F Minor* is a showcase for Chopin's talent of pure melodic inventiveness and his achievement of unity through apparently unrelated ideas and techniques.

Études, Nocturnes, Polonaises, Mazurkas, Impromptus, Préludes, Scherzos, and *Ballades*—these have made Chopin the most beloved of all keyboard composers. He wrote other works, too—such as the *Rondos,* a form for which he had little affinity, the *Bolero Opus 19,* and the *Tarentelle Opus 43*—but none of these enhance his reputation.

Apart from the collections there are two fine separate works, *Berceuse Opus 57* and *Barcarolle Opus 60.* The *Berceuse* was written in 1843 and published in 1845. Here the harmony maintains, with few exceptions, the simple tonic and dominant pattern of the initial left-hand design (Ex. 5). "The piece is made continuous and continually interesting by means of a strict pianistic manipulation of the melody, a treatment making use of grace notes, roulades, fioriture, trills, chromatically ascending and descending arabesques."[9]

In both the *Barcarolle* and the *Berceuse* Chopin was able to create a beautiful composition with imaginative depth out of rather meager materials. A barcarolle is meant to be in 6/8 meter and played in fairly leisurely tempo. But Chopin uses a rhythmic framework of 12/8 meter, with a strong

⁹ Herbert Weinstock, *Chopin* (New York: Alfred A. Knopf, 1949), p. 274.

Ex. 5. F. Chopin: *Berceuse*

accent on the first and seventh beat and a secondary accent on the fourth and tenth beat. The piece is dominated by this constant twelve beats per measure, though at times the rhythmic accent changes.

Composed in 1847, the *Barcarolle* begins with a preliminary introduction terminating with six beats of rest. The basic rhythmic pattern is then established in the left hand. After two measures of this pattern, the principal theme begins, expressed mostly in thirds and sixths. Trills are abundant, intensified by the use of double trills in the right hand. The middle section (or what appears to be) is in *A* major (the first section was in *F-sharp* major), and after several measures a subtheme appears, a theme later dominating the section. The return of the first section is achieved with octaves in the accompaniment, and a novel effect is provided when the subtheme of the second section again controls the scene.

Pianistically the *Barcarolle* and the *Berceuse* are among the most attractive of Chopin's works. They are well formed, exceedingly gratifying to play, and provide an outlet for the most characteristic keyboard figurations employed by the composer.

Chopin is a true poet of the piano. Unfortunately, he has often been placed in the category of talented composers of salon music, a habit even of some of his biographers. Chopin himself knew that his talents were best disposed toward piano music. He remained almost exclusively a keyboard composer, and in that field he was a genius. Many of his works rank as living masterpieces of tonal art. "Chopin is and remains the most audacious, the proudest poetical genius of the time," said Robert Schumann.

BIBLIOGRAPHY

Bidou, Henri. *Chopin* (translated by C. A. Phillips). New York: Tudor Publishing Co., 1927.

Cortot, Alfred. *In Search of Chopin* (translated by C. & R. Clarke). N   ork: Abelard Press, 1952.

Gide, André. *Notes sur Chopin*. Paris: L'Arche, 1948.

Liszt, Franz. *Life of Chopin* (translated by M. W. Cook). Boston: Oliver Ditson & Co., n.d.

Pourtalès, Guy de. *Polonaise. The Life of Chopin* (translated by Chas. Bayly, Jr.). New York: Henry Holt & Co., 1927.

Weinstock, Herbert. *Chopin*. New York: Alfred A. Knopf, 1949.

18

THE

ROMANTIC COMPOSERS:

LISZT

The Hungarian **Franz Liszt** (1811–1886) remains an enigmatic musical celebrity. Was he a genius, a composer of daring originality who created new musical forms and eloquence? Or was he a charlatan, a facile performer who designed his compositions to pamper the artificial taste of the public? To be accurate, one must concede that there is some truth in both propositions.

Liszt was a true son of the nineteenth century, a typical product of the Romantic age. His music can prompt the listener to scorn as well as to admiration, but no one can ignore the extraordinary personality of this "Mephistopheles disguised as an abbé," as he was once described. In the fashion of the inconsistent Romantics, he was spiritual yet worldly, religious yet skeptical. He produced more than seven hundred works, including many that are either uneven in quality, superficially constructed, or downright dull. Nevertheless, Franz Liszt has had a strong influence on late-nineteenth-century and twentieth-century composers.

Liszt's personal life affected his music. In his youth (until about 1838) he was the wizard of the piano, a flamboyant Romantic who already had defied convention by his liaison with the Comtesse Marie d'Agoult, who bore him three illegitimate children. Virtuoso pieces predominate in his works from these years: the first version of the *Transcendental Études;* the *Études* based on Paganini violin pieces; the bravura *Grand Galop Chromatique;* and numerous fantasias and transcriptions. Still, all was not fire and brilliance. At the same time, Liszt wrote the first two books of the *Années de Pélerinage* (Years of Pilgrimage), in which he often attains moments of sheer lyrical beauty.

For eight years (1839–1847) before the so-called Weimar period, Liszt concertized extensively in England, Poland, Russia, and Portugal. Considering the unsettled and difficult life facing the traveling concert artist, it is surprising that he composed as much as he did then. These works are mainly fantasias based on operas (*Sonnambula, Norma, Lucrezia Borgia, Don*

Giovanni), most of which have been forgotten. The *Hungarian Rhapsodies,* although not actually completed in these years, were sketched and worked over as he became increasingly interested in Hungarian popular music.

Liszt's most fruitful writing years occurred between 1848 and 1861; he lived at Weimar when not conducting or playing elsewhere. Many of his mature masterworks took shape at Weimar, and at the same time Liszt was extremely generous in propagandizing music by other composers. He also began a new love affair, this time with the Princess Sayn-Wittgenstein.

In 1861 Liszt—who had waited vainly in Rome to see if the Princess might obtain a divorce so that they could be married—took minor orders and became the Abbé Liszt. Thereafter, until his death in 1886, he divided his time between Rome, Budapest, and Weimar, composing some of his most convincing religious works.

Liszt did more to develop piano technique than any of his predecessors or contemporaries, with the possible exception of his teacher Karl Czerny. Liszt's compositions abound in the more obvious technical devices, such as octave passages. Sometimes his devices are used to reinforce a melodic line, sometimes as accompaniment figures, and sometimes simply to add bravura. Chromatic progressions by octaves (occasionally tenths!) and massive chords figure prominently along with trills, double trills, and all kinds of ornamentation.

The recitative-cadenza, used with restraint and caution by Chopin, received lavish treatment by Liszt. He might insert just a short fragment or at other times lengthy, glittering, and often diffuse scalar designs; or again, showy sequential passages.

Liszt's piano transcriptions of orchestral works, such as Berlioz' *Symphonie Fantastique* or Beethoven's *Symphonies,* prove that he had an uncanny ability for recreating orchestral fabric at the keyboard. On the other hand, technical aspects far outshine the musical substance in much of his music. Liszt, king of pianists in his day, wrote to display his own phenomenal technique and he was very successful, but the music produced for that purpose falls short in musical value and in many cases exhibits what is today called bad taste.

Frequently the fault was not with Liszt. In his transcriptions of certain operas, he could do little to improve upon the stilted quality and artificial content of the original vehicle. This is especially true in his transcriptions of *Niobe* by Pacini, Raff's *King Alfred,* and *La Fiancée* by Auber.

Beyond technical considerations there is a great deal in his music that is fine and worth studying. Although he was born a Hungarian and resided for many years in Germany, Liszt was at heart a French Romantic. His music shows this and so does his temperament, which was typical of the *mal du siècle.* Early in life he became aware of his cultural deficiencies. He

read avidly to improve himself, becoming especially fond of the French
literati of his day. As a result, the majority of his compositions have French
titles. Lamartine and Victor Hugo exerted extramusical influences, which
were significant to him as a composer. And following the precedent set by
Berlioz, Liszt's music is preponderantly programmatic or, at the least, dependent on ideas and concepts outside of the music field.

In some respects Liszt anticipated Impressionism much more than any
of his contemporaries. He was not so interested in actual successions of
sounds as in the simultaneous blending of sounds or tone clusters—that is,
in music for the sake of sound. As a marvelous showman and exhibitionist,
he delighted in sounding together as much of the keyboard as physically
possible.

In his large-scale works Liszt used a procedure which he called *transformation of theme*. A series of themes or motives is stated and then each
one is submitted to various alterations or transformations. In other words,
development in itself became a form for Liszt. Such an approach was, of
course, more suitable for works of broad scope; yet his works, pianistic and
otherwise, indicate that he avoided direct repetition of sections and even
phrases. He preferred his own type of developmental method, using constant
variation and transformation of thematic material. However, his ideas of
variation or transformation are sometimes amusing—for instance, when he
takes one section and repeats it verbatim in a different key.

Liszt's piano works run to well over four hundred[1] if all arrangements
and transcriptions are included. Naturally, the quality is irregular and it is
unnecessary to describe each work here. We can discuss the more representative works, those which preserve the name of Franz Liszt as a skilled
craftsman in pianistic writing as well as a musicianly artist.

ORIGINAL WORKS

Liszt wrote several sets of études, of which the *Études d'Execution
Transcendante* (Transcendental Études) demand the most of the pianist.
These were first published in 1827, expanded and reworked in 1839, and
again revised and published in 1852. There are twelve études in all; ten are
supplied with titles. *Preludio* contains within its brief two pages chromatic
sequences, massive chords, series of trills, and right-hand broken arpeggios.
The untitled second étude in *a* minor seems designed as a bravura study,
nothing else. *Paysage* (Landscape), number three in the set, is a calm elegy

[1] The most complete collection of Liszt's piano music is published by Peters Edition (The
Breitkopf complete edition was out of print in 1964). Most of the better-known works are
found here. Salabert, G. Schirmer, and Ricordi issue a large quantity of Liszt's music.

with an alternation of theme between hands. *Mazeppa* appears in two versions—as a piano piece and as a symphonic poem—but the vibrant piano composition is much more effective than the orchestral presentation. This poetical music explores awesome problems in technique yet retains musical coherence.

Feux follets (Will-o'-the-Wisp) is a lesson in light touch and dexterity, while *Vision* shows how a series of arpeggiated figures may be used to best advantage. "*Eroica* and *Wilde Jagd* have their character sufficiently outlined in their titles, and each is the progenitor of numerous other works. To the first of these Liszt returned again and again, particularly in the third and tenth *Hungarian Rhapsodies.* This peculiar rhapsodical mood, this 'vibrating of the heroic string,' to quote a phrase used by Liszt in discussing Chopin's Polonaises, was more essentially of his own invention, and it is actually in Liszt that it appears for the first time in history. As for the *Wilde Jagd* [Wild Hunt], its inspiration was more fruitful in other composers, and its theme does not appear again with Liszt. For some reason, it chiefly affected his French disciples; César Franck, in *Le Chasseur Maudit*, was indebted to the *Wilde Jagd*. Yet the subject was essentially German in origin, owing some of its possibilities to Weber and the *Freischütz*."[2]

Ricordanza (Remembrance) is deceiving because its grace and beauty mask the fact that it is technically a hardship, particularly if the performer wishes to achieve the desired effortless effect. Somehow Liszt's abundant ornamental arabesques are never superfluous. The other untitled étude, number ten in *f* minor, relies solely on technical drive and is one of the least successful of the set. *Harmonies du Soir* (Evening Harmonies) creates a peaceful evening atmosphere. It has a violent contrasting section, then a return to a *tempo tranquillo,* and terminates with widely spaced harplike chords. A fitting conclusion to the set of études comes with *Chasse-neige* (Snow Plough), a veritable tornado of fleeting sounds.

Liszt's études do not measure up musically to Chopin's. However, the two composers experimented with entirely different problems in their études; since Liszt's creative talents were best suited to technical matters, his études stand as solid examples of his personal art.

His most consistently well-written piano compositions appear in three volumes entitled *Années de Pélerinage* (the last book came out several years after the composer's death). On the whole, the pieces are brief, but they are uncommonly compact in texture and formal structure. Some titles seem old-fashioned and sentimental; after all, they were written more than a hundred years ago when such titles were not only acceptable but desirable.

The first volume—inspired by visits to Switzerland—took its final form

---

[2] Sacheverell Sitwell, *Liszt* (Boston: Houghton Mifflin Company, 1934), pp. 63–64.

in 1855, but the works were based on previous pieces in the *Album d'un Voyageur* (1842). In their ultimate form the *Années de Pélerinage: Première Année: Suisse* consist of nine individual pieces. The *Chapelle de Guillaume Tell* (Chapel of William Tell) begins with a simplicity unusual for Liszt. Horn calls appear, grow louder, then fade away—an effective if short evocation of the Swiss national hero. Written for the Comtesse d'Agoult, *Au Lac de Wallenstadt* (By the Lake of Wallenstadt) creates an illusion of waves through an undulating bass figure, while the serene melody soars above. *Pastorale,* which follows, is a gemlike miniature with much rhythmic variety to add to the general effect. *Au Bord d'une Source* (On the Edge of a Spring) is one of the finest pieces in the collection. There is an air of mystery in the hypnotic rhythmic reiterations, and an acute sensation of rippling waters.

The next two compositions are more ambitious. *Orage* (Storm) is a tempestuous description of a mountain storm. The *Vallée d'Obermann* (Valley of Obermann) is prefaced with two quotations, one from the novel *Obermann* by Étienne Pivert de Sénancour and one from Lord Byron's *Childe Harold.* Filled with stormy and gloomy contrasts, the atmosphere in this long piece is relieved at the end with bright vivacity. *Églogue* (Pastoral Poem) evokes a peaceful countryside and *Le Mal du Pays* (Nostalgia) does the same, adding a pungent, wistful flavor. The final work, a nocturne called *Les Cloches de Genève* (The Bells of Geneva), is attractive enough but does not reach the musical stature of its companions.

The *Années de Pélerinage: Seconde Année: Italie* (published in 1858) is superior to the first. Most of its pieces maintain a tighter framework, the musical ideas are broader and clearly expressed. Each was inspired by a work of art: a painting, sculpture, poem, or song.

Sposalizio (Wedding), first in this series, was inspired by a Raphael painting at the Milan Brera Gallery; *Il Penseroso* (The Thoughtful One) recalls Michelangelo's imposing statue of Lorenzo de Medici in the New Sacristy at Florence. These two dignified, noble tonal portraits are drawn carefully and imaginatively. The latter, with its bold chromatic progressions, anticipates what later proved to be a powerful tool in the hands of Richard Wagner (Ex. 1).

Canzonetta del Salvator Rosa seems to be a keyboard setting of a text by that almost legendary painter-poet-musician. A straightforward harmonic design and simple melodic line are absorbed by Liszt in a charming setting.

Liszt wrote three songs in 1838–1839, using the Petrarch sonnets numbers 47, 104, and 123 as texts. Later on he changed these songs into piano compositions for this Italian album. Though not superior examples of the Romantic keyboard miniature, they are competent and pleasing, both as song transcriptions and as piano pieces. The final portrait provides the single

Ex. 1.   F. Liszt: *Il Penseroso*

exception to an otherwise excellent collection. The title *Après une Lecture du Dante* (After Reading Dante) is from a Victor Hugo poem—Liszt added the subtitle *Fantasia quasi sonata.* Bristling with technical difficulties, the music nevertheless is completely ineffectual. The repeated strident, hollow octaves seem to demand more than the piano can absorb.

An appendix to the Italian collection appeared in an edition of 1861 under the general title *Venezia e Napoli.* Its three pieces, *Gondoliera, Canzone,* and *Tarantella,* are built around themes by other composers and they are not distinguished.

The third set of the *Années de Pélerinage,* published posthumously, consists of seven pieces composed between 1867 and 1877. The first and last, *Angelus* and *Sursum corda* (Lift up Your Hearts), are acceptable enough but are not good examples of Liszt's mature period. The *Marche funèbre* (Funeral March), in memory of the Emperor Maximilian of Mexico, and *Sunt lacrymae rerum,* written in quasi-Hungarian modal style, are both rather ordinary. Three compositions inspired by Villa d'Este are excellent, fashioned with skill and fantasy. Liszt spent part of each year at the Villa d'Este. He knew it well and his impressions of that showplace are deftly pointed up in these sparkling pieces. *Les Jeux d'eaux à la Villa d'Este* (The Fountains at the Villa d'Este) is an important forerunner to Maurice Ravel's *Jeux d'eaux,* and as such it is a precursor of the Impressionist school. The other two pieces, each titled *Cyprès de la Villa d'Este* (The Cypresses at the Villa d'Este), are equally fine musical paintings.

In 1854 Liszt published the *Sonata in B Minor,* acclaimed as a unique masterpiece on one hand, and on the other rejected as an awkward attempt at expanded pianistic writing. However, between Beethoven's late works and the appearance of Brahms's *Sonata Opus 5 in F Minor* few really fine sonatas appeared, and certainly none as original as this one by Liszt. For a work written "*en plein Romanticisme,*" it is incredibly disciplined, molded with meticulous attention to detail. Some critics find the melodic ideas insipid and the various bridge passages careless and inconsistent, but it is safe to assume that these critics do not care for Liszt in any form. The *Sonata* follows the same principles used in the symphonic poems. Liszt's basic construction principle—transformation of theme—is adhered to steadily and creatively.

Three sections divide the sonata: *Lento assai-Allegro energico; Andante sostenuto;* and *Allegro energico.* The first opens with the immediate statement of three motives (Ex. 2).

Ex. 2. F. Liszt: *Sonata in B Minor*

These are followed some four pages later by the passage shown in Ex. 3. Each of these motives or themes is subjected to different transformations or guises. For example, the second motive appears in Ex. 4. The original third motive, a vigorous one, becomes lyrical (Ex. 5).

Example 5 illustrates the unique manner in which Liszt manipulated his theme-motives. The final *Allegro energico* begins with a *fugato* section, its subject being derived from motives two and three. Recapitulation of a great deal of material from the first movement leads to a jubilant *stretto* passage based on motive number two; then the *Sonata* ends as quietly as it began, truly a dramatic poem of heroic proportions.

Liszt's *Concert Études* are uneven. Of the three he wrote in 1838—

Ex. 3.   F. Liszt: *Sonata in B Minor*

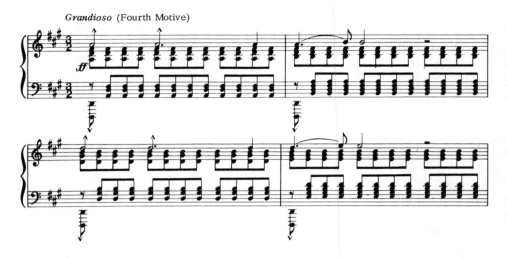

Ex. 4.   F. Liszt: *Sonata in B Minor*

Ex. 5.   F. Liszt: *Sonata in B Minor*

Il Lamento (Lament), *La Leggierezza* (Frivolity), and *Un Sospiro* (A Sigh)—the last is the loveliest and the most original. Other concert études, such as *Waldesrauschen* (Forest Murmurs) and *Gnomenreigen* (Dance of the Gnomes), are fine technical studies although not of great musical value.

There are also several religiously inspired works: first, the two *Lé-gendes: St. François d'Assise prédicant aux Oiseaux* (St. Francis of Assisi Preaching to the Birds) and *St. François de Paule marchant sur les Flots* (St. Francis of Paola Walking on the Waves). "There is nothing more original in the whole piano-repertory than these two pieces. The second of them, especially, is a truly extraordinary production. They seem to belong, both of them, to the art of the Jesuits, to the painting and architecture of the Seicento. We are reminded of Padre Pozzo and of Longhena. The second of these pieces, taken from the life of the Calabrian saint, founder of the Mendicant Order of Minims, was a frequent subject with that wild and fantastic painter, Alessandro Magnasco, who seems to hover between El Greco and Salvator Rosa. The mention of his name will, perhaps, give an indication of the strange atmosphere of *St. François de Paule marchant sur les Flots*. As pictorial suggestion, as direct interpretation of the story into music, as creation of immediate visual effect by that means, this piece of music is without precedent."[3]

Finally, there are the *Harmonies Poétiques et Religieuses* (Poetic and Religious Harmonies). The original publication (1835) included four pieces; six more were added for a future edition (1853). Any virtuosity in these compositions exists only to create atmosphere. The third piece *Béné-diction de Dieu dans la Solitude* (Benediction of God in Solitude) is the most noteworthy.

TRANSCRIPTIONS AND OPERATIC FANTASIAS

Liszt arranged countless orchestral, vocal, and instrumental composi-tions for the piano, but as might be expected, very few have survived. In his own day he accomplished two purposes with this sort of music. For one thing, he provided a means for hearing music not always available for performance in the original version. In so doing he rendered a service (per-haps a dubious one) to many lesser-known composers. The second reason for these transcriptions and fantasias was strictly personal, for in playing his often overly flamboyant compositions, Liszt could display fully his phenom-enal pianistic powers.

In the works classed as transcriptions, the best by far are the *Six Grandes Etudes d'après les Caprices de Paganini*. In 1832 Liszt had written a large fantasia on a theme from Paganini's *Concerto Opus 7 in B Minor*. For the ultimate collection (1851) he united an abbreviated version of this

---

[3] *Ibid.*, pp. 267–268.

—called *La Campanella* (The Bell)—with transcriptions of five violin caprices by Paganini to form this excellent series of *Études*.

Liszt was impressed with Paganini's already legendary wizardry in
violin playing, and he was more than successful in transplanting the Paganini studies to the keyboard. As studies they are very difficult; on the other
hand, they have wonderful musical quality. In the second *Étude* the scalar
violin figures are molded into a genuine keyboard idiom. The third, *La
Campanella,* has remained a favorite to the present day, an astonishing
display of right-hand brilliance. The final *Étude* is a theme and variations;
this theme was later used by Brahms and Rachmaninov.

Liszt transcribed many instrumental works for solo piano: Beethoven's
nine *Symphonies;* the major works of Berlioz; overtures by Weber; the organ
works of Bach. In another vein entirely, he made keyboard arrangements of
almost sixty songs by Schubert and also songs by Rossini, Schumann, and
others. From this huge mass of transcriptions, it is safe to say that almost
none are performed today, except several from Bach. There is no point in
playing Schubert's *Erlking* or Beethoven's *Fourth Symphony* as piano solos
when they can be heard in their original form.

Liszt's operatic fantasias have suffered a similar fate. A glance at a
catalogue of his piano music will show a considerable number of fantasias
based on operas: *I Puritani, Sonnambula,* and *Norma* by Bellini; *Robert Le
Diable* and *Les Huguenots* by Meyerbeer; *Ernani* and *Simone Boccanegra*
by Verdi; *Don Giovanni* and *Figaro* by Mozart. There are several reasons
why these have vanished from piano repertoire, but first and foremost,
pianists feel that the extremely difficult technical problems encountered do
not compensate for the sometimes poor and often superficial musical substance. One exception is the *Réminiscences de Don Juan* (1843). Although
staggering with problems of virtuosity, this fantasy on Mozart's opera is a
superior piece of music.

The *Hungarian Rhapsodies* partake of both transcription and fantasy.
They have been more widely played—and overplayed—than anything else
he wrote, especially the second *Rhapsody*. It has been subjected to every
conceivable transcription from harmonica to jazz band. Liszt composed
twenty *Rhapsodies,* but the first fifteen are heard the most. These fifteen
were published in final form between 1851 and 1854; he later added five
more to the series. Although not equal to his finest works, the *Rhapsodies*
are convincing in their coloristic effects. In many passages Liszt successfully
recreates impressions of instruments like the violin and cimbalom.

There is little support for the theory that the *Rhapsodies* are in any way
epics of Hungarian nationalism. Too often Liszt is primarily interested in
matters of technique; otherwise, they emerge as an unrelated mixture of
gypsy music and obvious Italianisms. Still, some—like the atmospheric

third or the quasi-nationalistic ninth (*Carnaval de Pesth*)—are interesting and worth an occasional hearing. Number ten has a rather majestic cast, and fifteen is a free setting of the famous *Rakoczy March*.

It is true that one must search diligently through Liszt's total keyboard pieces to find the works of quality and substance. He composed many for himself for particular occasions or circumstances, and they were perhaps played only by him. But the *Sonata,* the *Années de Pélerinage,* and the *Études* prove his talent. They bear the mark of a dedicated and original composer and of a pianist who endowed his instrument with moments of nobility, beauty, and daring expressionistic power.

BIBLIOGRAPHY

Friedheim, Arthur. *Life and Liszt,* ed. Theodore L. Bullock. New York: Taplinger Publishing Co., Inc., 1961.

Huneker, James. *Franz Liszt.* New York: Charles Scribner's Sons, 1924.

Kókai, Rudolf. *Franz Liszt in seinen frühen Klavierwerken.* Leipzig: F. Wagner, 1933.

Pourtalès, Guy de. *Franz Liszt* (translated by E. S. Brooks). New York: Henry Holt & Co., 1926.

Searle, Humphrey. *The Music of Franz Liszt.* London: Williams & Norgate, Ltd., 1954.

Sitwell, Sacheverell. *Liszt.* New York: Houghton Mifflin Co., 1934.

19

TECHNIQUE

AND

TECHNICIANS

Franz Liszt is one of a small group of nineteenth-century musicians who won lasting fame as both pianists and composers. Even today Liszt is included among history's great keyboard performers, and at the same time a goodly number of his compositions are still regularly presented in concert. However, many other composer-pianists in the nineteenth century flourished happily, if not quite as glamorously as Franz Liszt. From the early 1800's— the piano by then had progressed to its basically modern form—to our own era, the keyboard technician has been a significant figure in the musical life of the western world. But inevitably the question must arise as to what has happened to the music written by those composer-pianists so admired in their own day.

Most of these piano virtuosos wrote a quantity of keyboard music, nearly always brilliant but, alas, superficial. They were excellent pianists and naturally extremely interested in techniques pertaining to the physical problems of piano playing. Thus it is the technical studies—the "teaching" études and exercises—which, by serving future pianists, have preserved the reputations of these composer-pianists.

Writing instructional material for the keyboard began many years before the Romantic period. François Couperin *le Grand* was one of the first to provide such assistance. In his splendidly written and sometimes naïve *L'Art de Toucher le Clavecin,* Couperin does not restrict himself to matters of technique in harpsichord playing; he even discusses such topics as the facial expression deemed proper for the performer. Couperin also provides several musical *Préludes* as practical examples to accompany his general text. Another "method" book for keyboard instruction—Carl Philipp Emanuel Bach's *Versuch über die wahre Art das Clavier zu spielen*—is more detailed than Couperin's slender volume. Emanuel treats many aspects of keyboard playing, and his book is a superb introduction to performance practice in the eighteenth century. These two instructional works were written by well-known keyboard performers, but Couperin and Emanuel Bach in addition have always been highly regarded as composers of skillfully wrought keyboard sonatas, variations, and dances.

This combination—the extraordinary keyboard artist who was also a composer of mature and finely constructed keyboard works—occurred only rarely in the nineteenth century, and Liszt was the prime example. At the same time, however, there were other nineteenth-century virtuoso pianists who wrote acceptable, sometimes excellent, études and exercises to develop technique and improve digital facility.

MUZIO CLEMENTI

In the estimation of some musicologists, **Muzio Clementi** (1752–1832) —that *bête noir* of aspiring young pianists—is the father of piano technique. Clementi was born in Rome and received a good foundation in music from various Italian teachers. At fourteen he was taken to Great Britain under the patronage of Peter Beckford, an English gentleman who remained his benefactor for seven years while he studied in preparation for his successful presentation to London society as pianist and composer.

In 1781, during a tour of European musical centers, Clementi met Haydn in Vienna and also Mozart, with whom he contested in a piano performance resulting in a draw. Back again in England from 1782 until 1802, he taught, gave piano concerts, conducted, and engaged in piano manufacture and music publishing. Then in 1802 he and his pupil John Field toured Europe, stopping at Paris and Vienna en route to Russia, where Field eventually settled. By 1810 Clementi was permanently established in London, having relinquished the concert stage in order to devote all his attention to making pianos.

It would be a fine tribute if one could say that he is remembered for his sixty-four piano sonatas,[1] but unfortunately they are seldom heard—a regrettable omission for several are more than historically interesting. Clementi must be recognized as the *first* composer to achieve the fully matured piano sonata of the late Classic period. His works were admired by Beethoven, who studied them carefully. Because he was an accomplished keyboard artist, Clementi quickly understood the peculiarities of the piano as distinguished from the characteristics indigenous to the harpsichord. His piano sonatas supply sonorous evidence of this; *Sonata Opus 40, No. 2, in B Minor* and the three sonatas of *Opus 50*, for instance, display admirably precise form, concise thematic presentation, and a classically pure style. In

---

[1] Although the complete sonatas are not available any more, many publishers offer a judicious selection: Augener (20); Ricordi (14); Peters (24); Schirmer (12). Henle Verlag has an excellent edition of *Sonata Opus 50, No. 3, in G Minor*.

addition, an unusual depth of expression and dramatic power pervade Clementi's last sonata, written in 1821, the *Sonata Opus 50, No. 3, in G Minor* (subtitled *Didone abbandonata*).

Even though Clementi's sonatas are now infrequently heard, his fame as a pioneer in piano technique will forever be secure. His *opus magnum* in that field is the *Gradus Ad Parnassum* (Steps to Parnassus),[2] a collection of one hundred studies in pianistic dexterity that became the models for dozens of similar works later in the nineteenth century.

DANIEL STEIBELT

The standards set by Clementi had no reinforcement from his German contemporary **Daniel Steibelt** (1765–1823), who in some ways was a musical mountebank. He lived in many places, including London, St. Petersburg, and Paris, and his compositions were seldom original (except in very unrefined ways). Several times accused of musical plagiarism, he once had to leave Paris on this account. On a piano tour through Germany and Austria, he was particularly unsuccessful in Vienna, where he competed and lost in a musical contest with Beethoven. After he married an English tambourine player, he composed pieces for piano and tambourine, which he and his virtuoso wife performed on tour.

As composers, Steibelt and others of his type (i.e. Jan Vanhal [1739–1813], who composed battle pieces) are responsible for giving impetus to the hundreds of insipid, shallow salon pieces that flooded the nineteenth century. In a minor way, Steibelt contributed to the piano-instruction repertoire; in *Méthode*,[3] published in three languages, he claimed that he invented the pedal signs adopted by Clementi, Cramer, and others. His *Études* consist of fifty studies in a two-volume set.

JOHANN HUMMEL

Mozart seldom became keenly enthusiastic about a piano student, but the Hungarian **Johann Nepomuk Hummel** (1778–1837) was such a rare exception that Mozart took him into his home, taught him, and presented him in a concert. As Hummel progressed from student to pianist-composer,

---

[2] Selections from *Gradus Ad Parnassum* are easily obtainable at Durand, Schirmer, Ricordi, and other publishers. Augener publishes the complete work in 3 Vols.

[3] Both Augener and Ricordi publish the *Études* or *Studies Opus 78*. *Six Sonatinas Opus 49* also appear in Ricordi's catalogue. Several works are listed by Durand: *Le berger et son troupeau, L'Orage, Rondo turc, Sonatine Opus 41*. Salabert (Senart) also publishes the last two works.

he had more good fortune in receiving lessons and advice from such masters as Haydn, Salieri, Clementi, and Albrechtsberger. In turn, he helped guide Czerny, Hiller, and Henselt.

Hummel was a marvelous success on the concert stage. His natural gift for improvisation and his sensitive interpretations of works by other composers as well as his own won him hearty applause. In view of so many creditable factors, it does seem that he should have created worthwhile, long-lasting sonatas and variations, but such is not the case; he composed sixty-nine works for solo piano, including seven sonatas, and every one has disappeared from piano repertoire. It requires just a small sampling of these compositions to appreciate their disappearance, for Hummel's basic musical ideas are devoid of any deep feeling. Even though they are clothed in skillful and often very tasteful dress, this cannot hide their shallow nature, and the listener senses that Hummel was far more concerned with decoration than essential musical structure.

Hummel's *Klavierschule* (Keyboard School, 1828)[4] has more value than any of his compositions. In it he described new ideas of fingering and ornamentation which, in modified form, influenced the later writers, who wrote countless books of exercises and études designed to develop good keyboard technique.

JOHANN CRAMER

One of Muzio Clementi's more illustrious pupils, **Johann Baptist Cramer** (1771–1858) was, like his teacher, a pianist, composer, and publisher. German by birth, Cramer moved to London with his family when he was a year old and spent most of his life in the British capital. He studied two years with Clementi, using the works of Handel, Bach, Scarlatti, Haydn, and Mozart to test and formulate his own keyboard facility. After 1788 he undertook several European concert tours, and in 1824 he established the J. B. Cramer and Co. publishing house.

Cramer maintained an enviable, respected position in early-nineteenth-century musical society. As a keyboard performer he was applauded for his expressive, sensitive touch and for his unsurpassable ability to sight-read. In his own piano compositions he directed his talents toward cultivating a refined musical style rather than exploiting keyboard dexterity. Like Clementi, however, Cramer's one-hundred-plus sonatas and other works have been forgotten. His contribution to music history is the *Grosse praktische*

---

[4] The *Klavierschule* and *Sonatas* are not immediately available. Several short works may be found: Augener publishes a collection of *16 Characteristic Pieces*, Peters a *Rondo Opus 11*, C. Fischer a *Rondo in C* and *Variations on a Theme from "Armide."*

Pianoforte Schule (Great Practical Piano School),[5] a multivolumed collection of instructional pieces and exercises. The fifth and best part of this set consists of eighty-four studies divided into two equal parts. After several editions, he revised this fifth part, adding sixteen more études to make a total of one hundred in this *Opus 81*. The second part of this piano-method set—a hundred daily studies called *Schule der Geläufigkeit Opus 100* (School of Dexterity)—is also excellent.

FRIEDRICH KALKBRENNER

When Chopin arrived in Paris in 1831, one of the first musicians he met was **Friedrich Kalkbrenner** (1785–1849), a German who migrated to Paris as a youth and won first prize in piano at the Paris Conservatory. From 1814 to 1823 Kalkbrenner was nicely established in London as a performer and teacher, with a clientele drawn from British high society. Nonetheless, in 1824 he returned to Paris where, in addition to composing and performing, he became a member of the Pleyel & Cie. piano firm.

Kalkbrenner's reputation was at its highest peak when he and Chopin met; he was then writing prolifically—brilliant but musically poor works—for an enthusiastic public. Chopin played for Kalkbrenner hoping to receive a good introduction to Parisian musical circles, but Kalkbrenner proposed that Chopin study with him for three years before attempting any concerts in Paris. Chopin declined the honor and managed exceedingly well without the benefit of Herr Kalkbrenner's tutelage. The two men remained on good terms, and Chopin even dedicated his *Piano Concerto in E Minor* to the German. The fantasias and the potpourris that sustained Kalkbrenner's reputation during the mid-nineteenth century have understandably fallen into limbo. Only one work, his collection of études accompanying the *Méthode pour Apprendre le Pianoforte Opus 108* (Method for Learning to Play the Piano),[6] has proved to have permanent qualities.

KARL CZERNY

One of the nineteenth century's fruitful composers was **Karl Czerny** (1791–1857), a Viennese pianist who as a youth prepared for three years under the watchful, almost paternal eye of Beethoven. His later friendship

---

[5] Augener publishes sixty-three studies from *Opus 100* and G. Schirmer offers two sets of fifty and eighty-four selected studies. Durand also lists several volumes of studies.

[6] At present writing, almost nothing of Kalkbrenner is available. Only C. Fischer lists a single work: *Introduction and Rondo Opus 52*.

with Hummel perhaps influenced his own compositions, but a more beneficial acquaintance was Clementi, whose teaching method he studied.
Czerny retired comparatively soon from the concert stage, becoming somewhat of a recluse, although he continued to compose and teach. He accepted
only gifted students, of whom Franz Liszt achieved the greatest reputation.

A Czerny catalogue lists almost eight hundred opus numbers. Like
Kalkbrenner, this Viennese composer-pianist conceded to the superficial
taste of at least one segment of society—turning out numerous operatic
fantasias for piano. And again like Kalkbrenner, Czerny's best keyboard
works are scholastic, particularly the *Theoretical and Practical Pianoforte
School* in three volumes.[7] Of this huge aggregation of technical studies,
Opuses 299, 300, 335, 399, 400, and *450* are still used today; their approach
to all types of keyboard problems is still appropriate and serviceable.

IGNAZ MOSCHELES

Today the name of **Ignaz Moscheles** (1794–1870) usually draws a complete blank, but during his lifetime this German-Bohemian pianist-composer
enjoyed a tremendous reputation. Reared on a musical fare of Mozart and
Clementi, Moscheles quickly attained success as a pianist in Vienna. After
his marriage he lived for ten years in London, where he became acquainted
with Clementi and Cramer; but he left London when Mendelssohn invited
him to teach piano at the newly formed Leipzig Conservatory and stayed
in Leipzig from 1844 to 1866.

Moscheles stands as the foremost pianist in the gap between the active
concert careers of Hummel and Chopin. His clean, incisive touch and
superb technique were respected by all the musical world. As a composer,
however, he wrote mostly ephemera; for example, the *Variations on the
Alexander March.* His most carefully written works are the three *Allegri
di bravura Opus 51, Twenty-four Études Opus 70,* and *Characterische
Studien Opus 95,*[8] but even these are infrequently used in the twentieth
century.

SIGISMUND THALBERG

Sigismund Thalberg (1812–1871), an Austrian musician who perfected

---

[7] Most of the publishers in Europe and America publish a large selection of Czerny
studies. For example, G. Schirmer prints *Opuses 139, 261, 299, 335, 337, 636, 740, 755, 802,
821, 849* plus a *Toccata Opus 92.* As an example of Czerny's concert works, International
Music Co. lists the *Variations "La Ricordanza."*

[8] A surprising amount of Moscheles music is still printed: *Three Concert Études Opus 51*
(Peters); *Twenty-Four Studies Opus 70* (Schirmer); *Twelve Characteristic Études Opus 95*
(Ricordi).

his keyboard playing under Hummel and Kalkbrenner, was considered almost a serious rival to Liszt. After numerous European concert tours, he retired to Brazil as a vintner.

Thalberg's compositions have not passed the test of time.[9] Almost thirty of his many piano works are operatic fantasias, a type long since fallen into oblivion. A familiar characteristic in much of his music presents the illusion of three hands at the keyboard; the melody is divided between the first and second fingers of each hand while the other fingers supply a bass line and accompaniment figures.

HENRI HERZ

In 1818 the *Conservatoire de Paris* awarded a first prize in piano to **Henri (Heinrich) Herz** (1803–1888), a young Viennese pianist who, although never equaling Moscheles or Hummel, managed a lucrative career in the same profession. He taught at the Paris Conservatory after graduation, and the compositions he turned out with apparent ease were in demand by the Parisian publishers. While still a young man he went into business with a piano manufacturer, later establishing his own factory. From 1845 to 1851 he made extensive concert tours in the United States, Mexico, and the West Indies, but thereafter devoted himself exclusively to the business of piano manufacture.

Herz wrote more than two hundred works for piano, all of them typical of his role as pianist: showy and superficial. Like most concert artists of that time, he wrote a series of instructional materials in *Méthode Complète de Piano Opus 100*.[10]

ALKAN

One forgotten composer whose works, at least in part, deserve revivification is **Alkan** (1813–1888). Alkan was the pen name of Charles Henri Valentin Morhange, who even as a youth was a well-known virtuoso and much in demand as a teacher. As a member of the artistic circle surrounding Victor Hugo and George Sand, he was friendly with Chopin.

Sometimes called the "Berlioz of the piano," he possessed a remarkable sense of tonal color and a talent for pictorial description. His titles—*Scherzo*

---

[9] The following Thalberg works are currently available: *Études Opus 25* (Universal); *Twelve Studies Opus 26* (Augener); *Home, Sweet Home Air Varié Opus 72* (C. Fischer).
[10] Herz's collection of scales and exercises is published by Augener, C. Fischer, Ricordi, Hansen. In addition, Ricordi lists a solo work entitled *Le petit démon*.

diabolico, Morte, Marche funèbre—suggest that he leaned toward the lugubrious, and sometimes the obscure. He wrote seventy-eight numbered opuses and many pieces without opus numbers, including compositions for organ, pedal piano, and many transcriptions. His greatest pianistic contributions are *Opus 35* and *Opus 39:* two sets of extended études in all the major and minor keys. The latter opus contains, among other things, a symphony in four movements and a three-movement concerto for piano solo. One of the finest études is the last in *Opus 39,* a set of variations called *Le Festin d'Ésope* (Aesop's Feast).[11]

OTHER PIANIST-COMPOSERS

Carl Reinecke (1824–1910) is perhaps better known than some of his contemporaries. Successful as pianist, composer, and teacher, he remained active to the age of seventy-eight. Reinecke wrote operas, incidental music, a lot of chamber music, oratorios, and cantatas, but it is his piano compositions—solo pieces, exercises, educational works—that preserve his name.[12]

Among the last of the nineteenth-century pianist-composers, the Danish **Ludwig Schytte** (1848–1909) took his advanced studies with Taubert in Berlin and Liszt in Weimar, eventually settling in Vienna as performer, teacher, and composer. He is remembered today as the originator of countless light, gracious pieces, such as *Naturstimmen Opus 22* (Voices of Nature) and *Pantomimen Opus 30* (Pantomimes).[13]

With the coming of the twentieth century, the era of the composer virtuoso came to an end. Composers like Debussy and Ravel were competent pianists, but they were too immersed in their creative work to be concerned with publicizing their performing abilities. There have been, of course, some few instances of this composer-performer combination in the past fifty years: **Walter Gieseking** (1895–1956) dabbled occasionally but not too seriously in composition; **Ignacy Paderewski** (1860–1941) had a more serious penchant for composing, yet he never achieved any real success in that field.[14] Finally, there is in **Sergei Rachmaninov** (1873–1943), an isolated example of a superb keyboard artist who managed to acquire an equally fine reputation as composer (see Chapter 21). For the most part,

---

[11] Alkan's complete piano works used to be published, but only the following pieces are now generally available: *The Wind. Étude Opus 15, No. 2* (Schirmer); *Allegro Barbaro* (Leeds); *Two Preludes from Opus 31* (Augener); *Études Opus 39* and *Opus 76* (Costellat).

[12] Many little teaching pieces are listed by C. Fischer. Augener also has several collections.

[13] *Special Studies Opus 75* (Hansen); *25 Short and Melodious Studies Opus 108* (G. Schirmer); short pieces from *Opus 22* and *Opus 15* (C. Fischer).

[14] Both G. Schirmer and C. Fischer supply ample lists of Paderewski's light piano pieces.

however, twentieth-century composers leave to other musicians the task of interpreting and performing their works.

BIBLIOGRAPHY

Allorto, Riccardo. *Le Sonate per Pianoforte di Muzio Clementi.* Firenze: Leo S. Olschki, 1959.

Barford, Philip. "Formalism in Clementi's Pianoforte Sonatas." *Monthly Music Record,* 1952 (LXXXII).

Bellamann, H. H. "The Piano Works of C. V. Alkan." *Musical Quarterly,* April, 1924.

Dale, Kathleen. "Hours with Muzio Clementi." *Music and Letters,* 1943 (XXIV).

Ganz, Peter Felix. *The Development of the Étude for Pianoforte.* Dissertation. Northwestern University, 1960.

Tighe, Sister Alice Eugene. *The Piano Sonatas of Muzio Clementi.* Dissertation (in progress). University of Michigan.

Türk, Daniel Gottlob. *Klavierschule* (facsimile ed. Erwin R. Jacobi). Kassel: Bärenreiter Verlag, 1962.

20

BRAHMS

AND

THE LATE NINETEENTH CENTURY

IN GERMANY

The invaluable legacy of piano music bequeathed by Weber, Schubert, and Schumann established a fine tradition in Germany and Austria that continued into the late nineteenth century. This tradition was preserved despite the fact that the composer who came next chronologically, **Joachim Raff** (1822–1882), did very little to uphold it. Although the Swiss-German Raff was closely associated with both Liszt and Mendelssohn, their respective—and respectable—talents seemed to make little imprint on his own music. His compositions have a decidedly uneven quality, and it is safe to say that of the more than one hundred opuses for piano solo[1] almost none are heard today. The kindest comment that may be made about these forgotten works is that they are "agreeable."

JOHANNES BRAHMS

Johannes Brahms (1833–1897), born in Hamburg, is Schumann's rightful artistic and spiritual successor. This "Romantic Classicist" was a skilled artisan of musical fabric who fortunately was born in the "Romantic" nineteenth century; hence, under his able touch seemingly contradictory attributes of Romantic and Classic merge successfully in his music—a happy fusion of poetry and sound workmanship, a delightful mixture of Classical form clothed in the multicolored hues of German Romanticism.

In his piano music Brahms shunned bravura and brilliance for their own sake, seeking instead to create durable basic matter from which to fashion tonal compositions stamped with sound craftsmanship, vitality, and above all an innate musical coherence. His music is difficult to play, but the difficulty arises because of his musical language. In fact, much of the keyboard music may be considered unpianistic from a conventional point of view; but

[1] A good idea of the type of music written by Raff may be obtained by consulting the catalogues of C. Fischer and Augener.

again this is the outcome of his universal concept. For Johannes Brahms, this concept and craftsmanship resulted in music that at times transcends any confining performance medium.

Brahms, like Chopin and Schumann, wrote highly personalized music. His piano works, with passages in thirds, sixths, and octaves, plus doublings of these intervals, often convey a feeling of density yet stability. Many piano compositions have an orchestral quality, but it is hard to say whether or not this is deliberate. In addition, Brahms was blessed with a superior rhythmic sense; his music abounds in syncopations, polyrhythms, and other similar devices of rhythmic transformation. Finally, one prominent feature of the piano music is its contrapuntal character, which is expected when one recalls that Brahms enjoyed transposing at sight J. S. Bach's fugues from one key to another. Frequently he employs two melodic lines simultaneously (Ex. 1).

Ex. 1.   Brahms: *Intermezzo, Opus 116, No. 2*

The compositions for solo piano[2] span forty years. Brahms began in 1853 with the *Sonata Opus 1 in C Major* and continued intermittently until 1893, when he completed his final work for the piano, the *Klavierstücke Opus 119* (Piano Pieces).

Some interesting observations can be gleaned from a catalogue of his piano music. To begin with, among the first five works he published there are three sonatas—*Opuses 1, 2,* and *5*—but after that he never again at-

[2] Kalmus, Peters, and Breitkopf & Härtel offer almost complete editions of Brahms's piano music. Many compositions are published by G. Henle Verlag. The Gluck-Brahms *Gavotte* is available through C. Fischer. Brahms's complete works were published by Breitkopf & Härtel, reprinted in twenty-six volumes by J. W. Edwards (1949).

tempted a piano sonata. To continue, the catalogue reveals that the piano works as a whole fall chronologically into three rather distinct groups. The first group includes the three above-mentioned sonatas and the *Scherzo Opus 4* which, structurally at least, qualifies as a sonata movement. Then a second group comprising four opus numbers (*Opus 9, Opus 21, Nos. 1* and *2, Opus 24,* and *Opus 35*) consists of variations on themes by Schumann, Paganini, Handel, Brahms himself, and one based on a Hungarian song. A third group, covering works scattered from *Opus 76* through *Opus 119*, lists mostly short character pieces clustered into collections under such titles as *Phantasien* or *Klavierstücke.*

Thus Brahms, in the course of his creative career passed from the complexity of sonata form to the flexibility of the variation, finally arriving at a point where his inner feelings could find expression only in the epigrammatic piano piece of introspective nature.

Sonata Opus 1 in C Major—a vast Nordic poem like the two sonatas that follow it—is dedicated to Brahms's friend, the great violinist Joseph Joachim. The first theme of the opening *Allegro,* with its series of bare chords and parallel octaves, reminds one of certain passages in Grieg's music. Basic elements of Brahms's mature style are already in evidence here: parallel sixths, profuse passages in thirds, and contrapuntal devices such as imitation and canon.

The *Andante* of this first sonata presents a simple folk-song melody (Ex. 2), the text of which is used as a motto.

Ex. 2.   Brahms: *Sonata Opus 1: Andante*

Ver - stoh - len geht der Mond auf, blau, blau, Blü - me - lein,

This melody is then varied four times; however, in these fundamentally plain variations, the melodic line always preserves the outlines of the original theme, and this is accompanied by a consistently used triplet figuration. *Scherzo,* the third movement, begins in *e* minor with a driving, vital 6/8 rhythm. The trio section in *C* major becomes even more agitated, subsides briefly, then plunges directly into a repeat of the scherzo's first section. A rhythmic transformation of the first movement provides the basic substance for the *Finale,* a most effective conclusion. On the whole, this early Brahms sonata is remarkable for its solid structure and logical thematic treatment.

Sonata Opus 2 in F-sharp Minor has the same kind of rhythmic vitality as *Opus 1*. Dramatic tension dominates the first movement, in which a progression of climaxes and denouements engage in an heroically proportioned conflict. The second movement, *Andante con espressione*, is in variation form like its corresponding sister in *Opus 1* but is without textual adornment. According to Brahms's friend Albert Dietrich, the composer had in mind the words of an old German love song when he wrote this movement. A rhythmic transformation of this theme supplies the initial idea of the *Scherzo*, which with its question-and-answer treatment has a clearly Schumannesque effect. The *Finale* of this the most romantic of Brahms's piano sonatas begins with a brief introduction that serves as inspiration for the principal subject. This whole movement, with its harplike sections, lyrically effusive trills, and coloristic shadings, is a credit to Brahms's talent. Furthermore, it is a genuine tribute to his artistic finesse that he can speak in the language of the nineteenth century and still respect the disciplines of an earlier epoch.

Sonata Opus 5 in F Minor, which proved to be Brahms's premature farewell to the piano sonata, has five movements, the first of which—*Allegro maestoso*—maintains a steady contrast between a rhythmical *forte* motive and an evenly paced lyrical section. The second movement, *Andante,* is an extended elegy in *f* minor dwelling upon diverse lyrical thoughts that are ultimately capped by a tender coda in *D-flat* major. A kind of musical commentary is laid out in the fourth movement, an *Intermezzo* whose somber theme in *b-flat* minor is closely related to that of the *Andante* (the subtitle to this fourth movement is *Rückblick*, i.e. retrospect). These two lyrical movements are separated by an almost athletic *Scherzo* that starts off with a sweeping arpeggiated figure. The *Finale* is one of Brahms's most difficult piano pieces, successful not only in its rhythmic and melodic contrasts but in its textural contrasts as well. This noble movement and the lovely, introspective *Andante* are two good reasons why this third sonata is the most frequently heard.

Brahms favored the variation over all classic forms. He evidently felt that variation framework was the best vehicle for expressing his musical thoughts; and he was right, for only the theme and variations allows great freedom within a limited harmonic and melodic framework, permitting the composer to indicate several moods and emotions within one self-contained composition. Brahms had used this general framework in two of his sonatas. He continued with five independent sets of variations for piano solo, one for piano duet, and another, *Variations on a Theme of Haydn,* for two pianos.

Variations on a Theme of Robert Schumann Opus 9 could be interpreted as a grateful gesture in memory of Brahms's late friend, since Schumann had given him much encouragement. The sonorous, languid theme comes from Schumann's *Bunte Blätter Opus 99, No. 1* (*Albumblatt No. 1*), and Brahms's variations are primarily melodic variants of that theme, usually appearing in the soprano line. A Schumannesque strain clings to the variations because Brahms not only preserves the initial melody throughout but often employs the original harmonic scheme with its typically Schumann "sigh" (a note lowered chromatically and then returned to its unaltered form). In the ninth variation a reference to Schumann's *Opus 99, No. 2* reaffirms the idea that Brahms intended this as a memorial to his friend. The following variation has a bass line that is an exact inversion of the soprano melody it accompanies—evidence of Brahms's interest in contrapuntal devices. Taken as a whole, the Schumann variations are the product of a youthful master craftsman, remarkable for their utter musicality.

Opus 21 includes *Variations on an Original Theme* and *Variations on a Hungarian Song*. Even pianists who draw heavily from Brahms for concert numbers avoid these two sets of variations, perhaps because they are essentially musicians' variations. Their strongest feature is superb workmanship. An intellectual logic controls them and, while this logic is fine for craftsmanship, it cannot compete with the appealing emotional content of other Brahms compositions—the Handel variations, or even many of the little character pieces.

The theme for *Opus 21, No. 1* contains two balanced periods of nine measures each. Only Brahms could have conceived such a theme to work with: widely spaced bass chords, the melody presented in block chords. These variations are not easily determined; that is, only various elements inherent to the theme are incorporated into the variation structure. Sometimes the harmony is merely commented upon, at other times broad outlines of the original melody are visible. Variation five exhibits exceptional contrapuntal technique with a canon *in moto contrario*.

The *Variations on a Hungarian Song*—based on a song whose contours fit alternate measures of 3/4 and 4/4 meter—are excellent examples of variation technique, a technique Brahms later expanded into a more pliable, less exacting working medium. Variations ten through thirteen are planned progressions in diminution: from eighth notes to sixteenth notes, then sixteenth notes in triplet rhythm, and finally thirty-second notes. This exercise in diminution leads into a long, brilliant finale, concluding with a straightforward statement of the original theme.

Brahms's variation-form masterpiece is *Opus 24*, the *Variations and Fugue on a Theme of Handel*. The theme is derived from the last section of Handel's *Suite in B-flat Major* for harpsichord. In its original setting, Handel surrounded the theme with five variations; the Brahms version has twenty-five variations and a fugue. Handel's original theme adapts well to variation treatment: the harmonic outline is precise, the melodic design is diatonic, and the structure, two sections of four measures each, is even.

Tonal color is not often related to piano discussion, but in *Opus 24* the unusual textures of the variations overstep keyboard limitations. In certain passages it is easy to hear orchestral sounds; for example, the closely spaced harmonies in the seventh variation bring to mind a choir of French horns, while the biting staccato of number eight suggests pungent woodwinds. The legato tenth variation is like a string orchestra with its swiftly moving harmonies, and Brahms himself titled variation twenty-two *Alla Musette*.

One clear-cut characteristic of all these variations is the skillful way in which Brahms manipulates harmonic and contrapuntal elements—either combining them or else concentrating on the development of a single texture. Variation six is a strict canon at the octave; then again, canonic treatment is used unconstrainedly in variation sixteen. In the concluding fugue —a magnificent climax—Brahms blends his two techniques, counterpoint and harmony, so beautifully that the intensive power and dramatic impact in this work stand up well in comparison with Bach's finest fugues. Strictly harmonic variations also have their place in *Opus 24;* for instance, in variation fourteen Brahms gives a free hand to his fondness for passages of parallel sixths.

Only the hearing—or better, the playing—of this masterwork in variation form can adequately convey Brahms's superb mastery of this type of music—music that must within its own boundaries transmit a series of brief emotional experiences.

Brahms's final venture in solo keyboard variation form is the two-volume *Variations on a Theme by Paganini Opus 35*, each volume supplied with a finale. In concert they are often played as a continuous work by omitting the last section (finale) of the first set. The *Paganini Variations* (or *Studies*) illustrate one of the infrequent exceptions to Brahms's habit of avoiding technique for its own sake. The work is fiendishly difficult, abounding in complicated passages of sixths and thirds, glissando octaves, prolonged trills, prodigious leaps, and rhythmic complexities; yet in spite of the frankly bravura cast of the variations in general, there is still at hand sound musicality and logical construction.

The Paganini theme is the same one Liszt used in the last of his *Grandes Études de Paganini*, a rhythmically interesting melody enveloped in a series of extremely simple harmonies. Brahms takes advantage of every possibility this theme offers, at one time accentuating the harmonic outline and at another time borrowing motives and rhythm from the melody. His variations are not comparable to *Opus 24* in matters of innate musical quality; but under the touch of an eloquent keyboard artist, they become animated and surprisingly dramatic. Because their emotional elements have a secure musical background, Brahms's variations have escaped the category of pretentious studies.

Excluding comparatively large-scale works, the majority of Brahms's piano music comprises seven opus numbers: *Ballades Opus 10*, inspired by the Scotch ballad *Edward*, ranks among his less representative music; three books of *Klavierstücke Opuses 76, 118, 119;* one book of *Phantasien Opus 116;* three *Intermezzi Opus 117;* and the two *Rhapsodies Opus 79* (another rhapsody is included in *Opus 119*).

These works (excepting the *Ballades*) practically all date from the last twenty years of the composer's life. They are the artistic creations of a mature mind aided by a musical finesse that strips away all external trappings and rejects any display of superficial strength. Instead of being flashy, many are brief, introspective pieces in which lyricism, conciseness, and emotional experience merge for short, even fleeting, moments. Here speaks the Brahms of the *Lied*, for these keyboard compositions are truly songs—immensely varied, picturing wonderful contrasts in imagery and imagination.

The same techniques and modes of expression that evolved in the larger keyboard works are here applied by Brahms in abbreviated, concentrated form. For structure he prefers song form (A B A), but the harmonic details stem from his ever evolving musical style. He approaches the primary melodic interest diversely; sometimes the melody is concealed in an inner voice (*Opus 119, No. 3*), or the opening melodic idea may be based on a chord outline (*Opus 116, No. 3*). Individual titles only hint at a composition's content. Most are entitled either *Capriccio* or *Intermezzo*—three *Rhapsodies*, a *Romance*, and a *Ballade* are exceptions—with the *Capriccios* typically being more outgoing, direct, and vigorous than the *Intermezzi*. Naturally the three *Rhapsodies*, broader in scope and content, fall into a different category. They are "rhapsodic" even though restricted to a rather severe framework. Fervent, impetuous flashes accompany the textural flexibility of the first two *Rhapsodies Opus 79*, while the final *Rhapsody Opus 119, No. 4* is stately and heroic.

In addition to their compact presentation and mature musical substance, the *Capriccios* and *Intermezzi* make an even sharper impact by conveying genuine emotions. Space prohibits mention of these individual pieces now, but we can highlight some of their representative characteristics: the sometimes naïve folklike quality in *Intermezzo Opus 117, No. 1;* a restless agitation in *Opus 119, No. 2;* dramatic pathos in *Opus 118, No. 6;* the revery of *Opus 118, No. 2;* the quizzical Schumannesque elements of *Opus 116, No. 4.*

Thus far we have accounted for the major portion of Brahms's solo keyboard works. Besides the five studies based on pieces by other composers—Chopin, Weber, and Bach (including an arrangement for left hand alone of the famous violin *Chaconne*)—Brahms wrote an arrangement of a charming *Gavotte* from Gluck's opera *Iphigenia in Aulis* and also composed sixteen *Waltzes* (*Opus 39*), which are delightful examples of the master in his lighter moments.

Brahms was the perfect poet when composing for the piano. His inborn North German earnestness joined with his sensitivity to all nature, resulting in an enormous variety of tonal experiences, rich in quality and rewarding in their ideals.

MAX REGER

After Brahms's death, the musical torch was passed to **Max Reger** (1873–1916), the logical composer to continue the glorious tradition in German music so faithfully preserved throughout the nineteenth century. But whereas Schumann, Schubert, and Brahms were international artists, Reger's reputation never really extended beyond Germany. At the present time only a small group of professional musicians recognize his name, and it is difficult to discover why. Reger had a fine musical training that centered around a serious study of Bach and Brahms. He first attracted attention as a highly expressive and musical pianist. As soloist, accompanist, and chamber music performer, he brought his own works before the public; and although success came hard, it did arrive and Reger achieved a good reputation in his own land.

Reger's solo piano music is distributed among twenty-one opus numbers scattered from *Opus 11* through *Opus 143*, many of which are collections with numerous pieces (there are also fifteen works without opus numbers). Several large extended works are included: the *Variations and Fugue on a Theme of J. S. Bach Opus 81*, and a set of *Variations on a Theme of Telemann Opus 134*. And there are numerous other works, frequently grouped under headings similar to some used by Brahms: *Piano Pieces Opus 44*, *Improvisations Opus 18*, *Waltzes Opus 11*, *Fantasy Pieces Opus 26*, *Humoresques Opus 20*, *Intermezzi Opus 45*, and *Silhouettes Opus 53*.[3]

The answer to how many of these pieces are played outside of Germany would be, from all appearances, none. After the naïveté in so much of Schubert's music and the comparative simplicity of Brahms's *Intermezzi*,

---

[3] Even though Reger's music is not widely played, it is still available. The following is a sampling: *Variations and Fugue on a Theme of Telemann Opus 134*, *Dreams at the Fireside Opus 143* (Peters); *Variations and Fugue on a Theme of J. S. Bach Opus 81*, *From My Diary Opus 82*, *Four Sonatinas Opus 89*, *Six Preludes and Fugues Opus 99*, *Episodes Opus 115* (Bote & Bock); *Waltzes Opus 11*, *Improvisations Opus 18* (Schott).

Reger's piano music seems singularly obtuse and cluttered. As a classicist and Bach devotee, he loaded his keyboard works with an overdose of counterpoint, adding to it chromaticism used to the saturation point. The music appears so burdened as to be no longer piano music. It is unfortunate, for Reger was a conscientious, earnest musician who lived only for his art.

MINOR COMPOSERS

Brahms and Reger were not isolated piano composers in late-nineteenth-century Germany. There were a host of others, but these were inferior talents. One of Hummel's pupils, the Bavarian **Adolph von Henselt** (1814–1899), spent most of his years in St. Petersburg, Russia, where he was in great demand as a piano teacher. He is one of the few respected composers of his period who wrote comparatively little music. The frankly sentimental aura of his *Concert Variations on a Theme of Donizetti Opus 1* shows Hummel's influence. Henselt's personal style comes through in the *Études characteristiques de Concert Opus 2* and the *Douze Études de Salon Opus 5*.[4] His particular specialty was extended chords accompanying a lyric melody. The concert études are skillfully conceived, necessitating large hands for satisfactory execution.

The graceful piano compositions of the German **Adolf Jensen** (1837–1879) were obviously influenced by Chopin and Schumann. **Theodor Kirchner** (1823–1903), a friend of both Mendelssohn and Schumann, achieved moderate success with the small characteristic study. His prolific *Opus 65* includes sixty preludes, and *Opus 71* has one hundred little studies. **Stephen Heller** (1813–1888) was born in Pesth and, like Chopin and Henselt, he wrote almost exclusively for piano. His best works are *Twenty-Four Preludes Opus 81*; the first part of the *Spaziergänge eines Einsamen Opus 78* (Promenades of a Lonely One); *Kinderszenen Opus 124* (Scenes from Childhood); and books three and four of the *Notebooks for Young and Old Opus 138*.[5]

In the early twentieth century almost every drawing room and parlor boasted at least one volume of Moszkowski's *Spanish Dances* on its pianoforte. **Moritz Moszkowski** (1854–1925), a German pianist-composer of Polish descent, won fame as a young writer of light salon music. His *Spanish*

---

[4] G. Schirmer publishes Henselt's *Twelve Characteristic Concert Studies Opus 2*. Pieces from *Opuses 5, 13, 15,* and *25* are in the Augener catalogue.

[5] A few of Jensen's compositions are still available: *Twenty-Five Études Opus 32, Waltzes Opus 33, Nos. 7* and *8* (G. Schirmer); *Little Songs and Dances Opus 35* (C. Fischer); pieces from *Opuses 12, 17, 33, 44* (Augener). Of Kirchner's prolific output, about the only available piece is an *Album Leaf Opus 7, No. 2* (C. Fischer). On the other hand, a voluminous quantity of Heller's music is still obtainable (G. Schirmer, C. Fischer, Augener, and other publishers).

Dances[6] were so popular that he tried to equal that success by writing synthetic music of other lands; however, he is still known chiefly for the former.

The music of **Eugen d'Albert** (1864–1932) might be described as the last gasp of pure German Romanticism. The cosmopolitan d'Albert was born in Great Britain of French parents but preferred to be considered a German. His early studies in England—with Stainer, Prout, Sullivan, and Pauer—were later confirmed with Liszt. Once established as a concert pianist, d'Albert associated himself with Germany. As a composer he is now rated only moderately successful. His keyboard works are comparatively early. A *Suite Opus 1 in D Minor* contains six pieces in the classic Baroque sequence—*Allemande, Courante, Sarabande, Gavotte, Musette,* and *Gigue.* The leisurely counterpoint and clear texture point to an open imitation of Bach. *Sonata Opus 10 in F-sharp Minor* is never heard anymore, but the four *Clavierstücke Opus 16* are worthwhile and interesting: *Waltz, Scherzo, Intermezzo,* and *Ballade.*[7]

Brahms dominated late-nineteenth-century German keyboard music. No other composer could even remotely match his superb craftsmanship and sublime invention. And the twentieth century has not yet produced another German composer so dedicated to keyboard composition.

BIBLIOGRAPHY

Evans, Edwin. *Handbook to the Pianoforte Works of Johannes Brahms.* London: Wm. Reeves, n.d.

Geiringer, Karl. *Brahms. His Life and Work,* Second Edition, revised and enlarged. New York: Doubleday & Co., 1961. An Anchor Book.

Litzmann, Dr. Berthold, ed. *Letters of Clara Schumann and Johannes Brahms 1853–1896.* New York: Longmans, Green & Co., 1927. 2 Vols.

Niemann, Walter. *Brahms* (translated by C. A. Phillips). New York: Grosset & Dunlap, 1946.

Tovey, Donald Francis. *Essays in Musical Analysis. Chamber Music.* London: Oxford University Press, 1949. pp. 167–185.

---

[6] Peters, Augener, and G. Schirmer all list a great quantity of Moszkowski's pieces.
[7] D'Albert's *Suite Opus 1* is published by Bote & Bock.

21

THE

SLAVIC COUNTRIES

IN THE ROMANTIC ERA

RUSSIA

The Russians are latecomers on the scene of serious musical composition, and comparatively little information exists about their musical activities during the Baroque and Classic eras. Music for their concerts and operas was largely provided by non-Russians residing in their country—composers such as Galuppi, who for years provided the Russian aristocracy with the Latin-inspired music later scorned by many native Russian composers.

Michael Glinka (1804–1857), considered the father of Russian art music, was at least Russia's busiest native-born composer during the first half of the nineteenth century. But Glinka and his contemporary **Alexander Dargomijsky** (1813–1869), apart from some innocuous salon pieces, best voiced their thoughts in the dramatic vehicle of opera. Serious piano composition made little progress in Russia until the so-called *Russian Five* came along.

The Five

The *Russian Five*—Balakirev, Mussorgsky, Borodin, Cui, and Rimsky-Korsakov—were all passionate standard-bearers of native Russian music; they were all cognizant of the originality and richness flowing through Slavic folklore. There are various types of Russian folk songs, some of which are very ancient; the epics retell time-honored Russian legends, the others narrate happenings in daily family life—songs of marriage, love, death, work, etc. The rhythms in this vast corpus of musical folk art are quite free, and the melodies are modal rather than tonal. And from this plentiful source the *Russian Five*—the first notable group of Slavic composers—gathered their prime inspirational material.

Around 1857, the twenty-year-old Balakirev was presented to Mussorgsky by Cui, whom he had met shortly before. In 1862 Mussorgsky introduced to Balakirev a new devotee of Russian art, Borodin. Rimsky-Korsakov came into the group last. These musicians, nearly all of them at one time or other dependent upon another profession for a livelihood, nevertheless shared a common dream: to write music inspired by Russian folk elements. But since Russian art music offered scant technical models, these composers were forced to turn to the west, to the works of Beethoven, Schumann, Liszt, and Berlioz. Then, equipped with the semblance of a technique (in some cases quite inadequate), they sought inspiration from their native folk music in an attempt to create a national Russian music school.

Despite their high-sounding ideals, it must be admitted that pianistically speaking the *Five* turned out a meager amount of works with sound workmanship and genuine inspiration. **César Cui** (1835–1918) wrote a few saccharine pieces that can only be described as salon music and not very good salon music at that. **Nicolas Rimsky-Korsakov** (1844–1908) scarcely improved upon this, although his piano concerto is of higher caliber than his solo piano music.[1]

The remaining three composers fared somewhat better. **Mily Balakirev** (1837–1910) headed the group, and it was he who persuaded some of the other musicians to attempt musical composition. Besides his own music, oriental at its source, Balakirev must be credited for his help in compiling into accessible form some of the immense treasures contained in Russian folk song and dance. In 1897 he was appointed a member of a commission of the Imperial Russian Geographical Society for the publication of Russian folk songs in performing editions. Balakirev had already, in 1866, arranged forty Russian folk songs for voice and piano. One year after his new appointment, he contributed *Thirty Songs of the Russian People.*

Balakirev composed during two comparatively short creative periods, oddly separated by a twenty-five-year silence. From the first writing stage comes the oriental fantasy *Islamey* (1869), based on themes from Armenia and the Caucasus region. *Islamey* is terribly difficult to play—the technical apparatus is borrowed from Liszt—and is constructed principally of variations on two oriental-type themes, one of which is a violent rhythmical one initially exposed without accompaniment (Ex. 1). The second theme is more lyrical. These two themes alternate, reappearing each time clothed in fresh, colorful garments.

During his second writing interval he preferred classic forms, and the *Sonata in B-flat Minor* (1905) is a substantial work typical of that time.

---

[1] Boston Music Co. publishes a *Prelude in A-flat* by Cui. Two salon pieces (*Berceuse* and *Marionettes Espagnoles*) are available through Augener. Rimsky-Korsakov's *Novelette Opus 11, No. 2* is published by Boosey & Hawkes.

Ex. 1.   Balakirev: *Islamey*

The first movement, *Andantino,* is a singular yet rather successful endeavor to accommodate essentially fugal subject matter to sonata-allegro framework. The other three movements—a highly developed *Mazurka,* a nocturne-like *Intermezzo,* and agitated *Finale*—combine echoes of Chopin and Liszt with snatches from Russian folk song.[2]

Alexander Borodin (1833–1887), by vocation a professor of organic chemistry, was also a cellist, pianist, and skilled composer. In this last capacity he is best represented by his symphonic music and the remarkable opera *Prince Igor.* However, he did create one miniature gem for piano: the *Petite Suite* (1878–1885),[3] a collection of seven short pieces—*Au Couvent, Intermezzo,* two *Mazurkas, Sérénade, Nocturne,* and *Rêverie*—followed by an extended *Scherzo.* The unrelated essays in this tiny masterpiece are concise, characteristic studies, but upon each one the composer has bestowed an individual touch. A monastic serenity enhanced by tolling bells; a transparent *Intermezzo;* two contrasting *Mazurkas,* where melodies glide from one hand to the other; a guitar-like accompaniment in *Sérénade;* the lyrically beautiful *Nocturne;* the succinctness of the *Rêverie*—all these attractive accents make the *Petite Suite* charming. The *Scherzo* is a challenge to play—with its insistent pedal points—but the performer will admire its concentrated energy and original ideas.

Finally, **Modest Mussorgsky** (1839–1881), the last of the *Russian Five,* wrote a first-rate piano work equal to the finest pages of Schumann or Liszt. Again here is a Russian composer with just one serious work (he also wrote some light, unimportant salon music) to represent him in piano music. This is the collection called *Pictures at an Exhibition,* a suite occasioned by the

---

[2] There are several editions of *Islamey.* That of C. Fischer is readily available and is as good as any. The piano *Sonata* is published by W. Zimmerman.
[3] The *Petite Suite* is published by Alphonse Leduc in Paris.

tragic death in 1873 of Mussorgsky's close friend Victor Hartmann, an artist as well as a noted architect. At a memorial exhibition of Hartmann's works in 1874, Mussorgsky, strolling among the watercolors and drawings hung on the walls, hit upon the idea of composing short pieces to describe Hartmann's various scenes. He became so engrossed in his project that the actual writing took only a few weeks.

The *Pictures*—ten tonal portraits joined together by an interlude (*Promenade*) that is varied four times—could well have been modeled after any of Schumann's cyclic suites, such as *Carnaval*. Mussorgsky's typical works clearly indicate that he needed an extramusical impulse to serve as guide or stimulus; in this instance his inspiration came from Hartmann's pictures, many of which have long since disappeared. The only clue to their pictorial content is found in a few notes made by Mussorgsky's friend Vladimir Stasov for the first edition of the piano score.[4]

Serving both as a link between pictures and as a musical accompaniment for the observer as he wanders from picture to picture, the opening *Promenade*, in alternating measures of 5/4 and 6/4 meter, is reduced and altered in subsequent appearances. Picture number one—"a little *Gnome* walking awkwardly on deformed legs"—comes pathetically to life in the musical portrait. *The Old Castle* with a minstrel singing beneath its ancient walls is too long-winded and is thus one of the least impressive musical portrayals. But things brighten up with the next sketch, *Tuileries: Children at Play*, based on Hartmann's scene of children with their nurses in the Tuileries gardens in Paris. This happy picture prompted Mussorgsky to write a gay, noisy piece, echoing the children's cries at play.

In the musical version of *Bydlo* (a Polish oxcart), the cart rumbles up on two immense wheels from afar, passes by, and fades into the distance. A costume designed by Hartmann for the ballet of *Trilby* (based on the tale by Charles Nodier) furnished inspiration for *The Ballet of Unhatched Chicks*, an entrancing scherzino. A really effective bit of program music appears in *Samuel Goldenberg and Schmuyle*, an amusing caricature of a rich merchant and a poor merchant wrangling. Mussorgsky's bold, pompous rich man has his say, the poor merchant answers in high-pitched tones, and then they argue simultaneously in a clever sequence of polymelody.

A clattering, bustling market square can be plainly heard in the music of *The Market Place at Limoges*, a toccata-like piece that proceeds without interruption to *The Catacombs*. In the picture, Hartmann drew himself and friends as they explored the Roman catacombs in Paris. In the music, the atmospheric introduction is intensified by two notations: the Latin

---

[4] The best edition of the *Pictures at an Exhibition* is that published by International Music Co. It contains reproductions of several Hartmann drawings and paintings and a foreword by Alfred Frankenstein.

"Con mortuis in lingua mortua" (With the dead in a dead language) and then (in Russian) "Hartmann's creative departed spirit leads me to the place of skulls, and calls to them—a light glows faintly from the interior of the skulls." *The Hut on Chicken Feet* depicts the mythical hut of Russia's famous witch Baba Yaga. Mussorgsky describes the witch and her weird dwelling with a wild dance that leads directly into the exciting finale called *The Great Gate at Kiev;* and with the sounds of monks chanting against a background of great, glad bells, the *Pictures at an Exhibition* comes to a close.

Although the composer was pleased with his creation, the public paid it little attention, and the work was not published until five years after Mussorgsky's death. In 1923 Maurice Ravel arranged it for orchestra, a magnificent version heard more than the original piano score.

Thus *The Five*—Balakirev, Mussorgsky, Borodin, Cui, Rimsky-Korsakov—searched their native culture for inspiration. Other Russian composers preferred to work from predominantly German models and some French models. Anton Rubinstein and Peter Tchaikovsky belong to this category.

Anton Rubinstein

There is no denying that **Anton Rubinstein** (1829–1894) was a spectacular pianist. During his prime he was one of a small coterie that could successfully challenge Franz Liszt's legendary piano sorcery, and the seven "Historical Piano Recitals" that he presented on a grand farewell concert tour firmly established him as the foremost pianist of his day. But even with such fame, Rubinstein yearned for recognition as a composer and worked prodigiously to realize that goal. His gigantic output of one hundred and twenty-one opuses includes about fifty written for piano, totaling well over two hundred individual piano pieces. It was a sad blow to Rubinstein when he discovered that audiences paid to hear him play the music of other composers, not his own.

What compositional talent he had lay in his ability to create attractive melodies clothed in rather novel technical figuration. The following represent his most competently written keyboard works: *Tarantelle Opus 82; Kamennoi Ostrow Opus 10* (twenty-four pieces); and *Valse-Caprice.*[5] In general, however, his piano works show little freshness, and too often slickness and sentimentality prevent the music from taking on substance. Apart from the concertos, there is small chance for a revival of Rubinstein's

---

[5] Some of Rubinstein's voluminous output is still available: *Valse-Caprice, Barcarolles, Études Opus 23* (G. Schirmer); *Soirées musicales Opus 109* (Durand). Peters Edition has an album containing eleven pieces.

music; but this "Free Artist," to quote from Catherine Drinker Bowen,[6] nevertheless has earned a permanent place in Russian musical history, for he exercised an incalculable influence on music in his country. He attempted to share his own love for music by educating the masses to good piano repertoire from all periods. More than that, he founded St. Petersburg Conservatory. And his piano mastery was incredible!

Peter Tchaikovsky

One of Rubinstein's pupils in music composition achieved the ambition cherished by his master. **Peter Tchaikovsky** (1840–1893), although not as prolific a composer as his teacher, wrote a quantity of piano music. Tchaikovsky's compositions contain some of the qualities missing from Rubinstein's music. Even so, Tchaikovsky's piano music seldom rises above the level of fairly adequate salon music—he was not deft at keyboard composition. Because his melodic accompaniments are unimaginative and tedious and his musical texture is as unpianistic as Chopin's is highly pianistic, almost all the Tchaikovsky solo keyboard music remains in obscurity.[7] His fame rests in the realm of orchestra—symphonies and ballet music.

Alexander Scriabin

In the light of comparison with his predecessors and contemporaries, **Alexander Scriabin** (1872–1915) emerges as a composer with a unique approach. Except for six symphonic works, his output is exclusively for piano. Scriabin was the least Russian of all the native composers and his music takes nothing from Slavic folk elements; instead, Liszt and Chopin were his youthful models and later on Richard Wagner, whose harmonic patterns he particularly admired. Scriabin, who considered himself to be a philosopher as much as a musician, impregnated his writings with the spirit of Nietzsche and oriental philosophy. His personal belief in a free, all-powerful personality that identified itself with the cosmos (I am God, I am the world, I am the center of the universe) contributed toward the creation of his nervous, excited pianistic works.

At first Scriabin composed short salon pieces in the style of that time. The Chopinesque *Études Opus 8* and the *Twenty-Four Preludes Opus 11* are agreeably romantic products of the composer's youth. As he gradually realized what his personal artistic goal should be, he produced increasing

---

[6] Catherine Drinker Bowen, *"Free Artist." The Story of Anton and Nicholas Rubinstein* (New York: Random House, 1939).
[7] Peters publishes a large selection of Tchaikovsky, including three volumes of *Selected Piano Works*. Augener and G. Schirmer also have large catalogues of Tchaikovsky.

numbers of consistently fine—and daringly unorthodox—works, noteworthy because they opened up entirely new harmonic concepts to Russian and non-Russian alike.

Scriabin arrived at his mature convictions around 1910 when he evolved an harmonic system based on a series of fourths instead of conventional thirds. He built entire compositions on chords, the so-called "mystic" chords, of which Example 2 is a classic example.

Ex. 2.   A. Scriabin: *"Mystic" chord*

This mystic, ecstatic nature is emphasized by the performing stipulations: *"avec une joie exaltée"; "avec une celeste volupté."* The pedal is important in his piano music; he insists on its use to bind together the widely spread sonorities. His unusual rhythmic groupings and profuse trills to provide color make this music extremely difficult to play.

Scriabin applied his pseudo-philosophical mysticism to the composition of a series of "poems," which show the harmonic richness and rhythmic complexities characteristic of his later style. The "poems" for piano bear unusual titles: *Poème tragique Opus 34; Poème satanique Opus 36; Poème fantasque Opus 45, No. 2; Poème ailé Opus 51, No. 3; Poème-Nocturne Opus 61.* These poems typify Scriabin's characteristic expression of his personal brand of art, and they contain the finest examples of his strange inspiration.

The piano sonata found fulfillment in Russia with Scriabin's ten creations, in which the musical substance progressively breaks up into a transparent, ethereal framework of sound.[8] The first four sonatas (1892–1903) still betray the spell of Liszt and Chopin, but with *Sonata No. 5 Opus 53* a new world of sensation and sound is brought into play. The sonata bears as a motto a quatrain emphasizing the composer's ecstatic mood.

> *Je vous appelle à la vie, ô forces mystérieuses!*
> *Noyée dans les obscures profondeurs*
> *De l'esprit créateur, craintives*
> *Ébauches de vie, à vous j'apporte l'audace.*

---

[8] The ten *Sonatas* are available through Leeds Music Corp. Several of the poems are published by Boosey & Hawkes.

(I call you to life, oh mysterious forces!
Bathed in the obscure depths
Of the Creator-Spirit, fearful
Schemes of life, to you I bring audacity.)
[Translation by the author]

The ecstasy of this brief one-movement work is accentuated in the expressive indications for the different sections: *Impetuoso; Languido; Presto con allegrezza; Allegro fantastico; Presto tumultuoso esalto*. The work is fragmentary, yet by this very fact Scriabin creates his desired atmosphere of nervous tension, fervent exaltation, and at times a certain diabolic sarcasm.

In contrast, the sixth sonata is more subdued. It begins in a somewhat mysterious, hushed atmosphere, which eventually succumbs to a certain rhythmic intensity. The most technically difficult sonata of all is *Sonata No. 7 Opus 64* (1912), a fiendish extravaganza of technical and rhythmic devices. The composer himself gave it the subtitle *"The White Mass."* He appended *"The Black Mass"* to his *Sonata No. 9 Opus 68* (1913), a work of brevity and apparent simplicity. This is one of the finest of the sonatas, displaying with great precision the subtleties of mood and rhythm so characteristic of Scriabin.

Sonata No. 8 Opus 66 (1913) is too long and perhaps difficult to comprehend—if one can truly comprehend Scriabin at all. The final sonata, *No. 10 Opus 70* (1913), is even more remote; nevertheless the synthesis of harmonic richness with unexpected metrical designs distills an unusual experience.

Minor Keyboard Composers

Succeeding generations produced quantities of musicians but only a slight supply of good music. The late-nineteenth-century Russian composers were not genuinely creative; they worked with formulas derived either from western techniques or their Russian predecessors, but the arrangements of these formulas are not very imaginative. The available Russian piano collections by late-nineteenth and early-twentieth-century composers offer chiefly this same saccharine, insipid music.[9] Romantic influences lingered on in Russia; in fact, the first twenty-five years or so of the twentieth cen-

---

[9] Most general collections of Russian piano music have little that is interesting. Composers such as Karganoff, Kopylov, etc., are still often included, although the music has no intrinsic value. E. B. Marks Music Corp. issues a collection of so-called *Favorite Russian Composers* in Volume 22 of their Radio City Piano Albums series. Augener also publishes a two-volume set. A more recent collection is *Slavische Klaviermusik*, ed. W. Frickert and published by W. Zimmermann.

tury produced, with the exception of Scriabin, merely a conscious prolongation of that aesthetic—Romanticism—which by then was almost a memory in other countries.

Anatol Liadov (1855–1914), one of Rimsky-Korsakov's pupils, wrote several pieces, including seven preludes reminiscent of Chopin. Only his charming little piece called *Musical Snuff Box, Opus 32*[10] (which cleverly imitates a mechanical music box) is heard today and very rarely at that.

Anton Arensky (1861–1906) is known outside Russia because of his music for two pianos. A Tchaikovsky influence runs throughout the nearly one hundred piano pieces Arensky composed, but altogether his music is suavely lyric and tends to be eclectic rather than nationalistic. His more attractive keyboard repertoire includes *Logaoedics Opus 28* (Essays with Forgotten Rhythms) in which he attempts musical translations of some old Greek poetical rhythms.[11]

Other Russian composers were active into the early twentieth century, but they are not well known since their keyboard works are neither as extensive nor as provocative as Scriabin's. The name of **Sergei Liapunov** (1859–1924), professor of composition at St. Petersburg Conservatory, is retained in Russian music history only by virtue of his twelve *Transcendental Études*[12] (modeled after Liszt), a collection more interesting for technical points than musical value. Liapunov, a member of the Balakirev clique, may be considered a nationalist composer, though not an especially creative one.

More expert workmanship exists in the music of **Alexander Glazunov** (1865–1936), who studied with Rimsky-Korsakov while still in his teens and wrote his first symphony at sixteen. Most of his characteristic works are early for he stopped writing at forty. In his serious attempts at keyboard music—*Three Études Opus 31, Theme and Variations Opus 72, Sonatas Opus 74* and *Opus 75*—a pallid nationalism envelops eighteenth-century Classic elements and certain procedures traceable to Liszt.[13]

Alexander Gretchaninov (1864–1956), who wrote prolifically during his long life, seems to be stylistically—as a successful sacred-music composer—a direct successor to the Russian Five, but his compositions for piano are uninspired and unimportant. A few isolated works (he wrote numerous *morceaux de salon*) like the two *Sonatines Opus 110* and the *Sonata Opus 129 in G Minor* hold some interest.[14]

There are two other Russians to be considered in this chapter: Rach-

---

[10] The *Musical Snuff Box*, as well as several other pieces of Liadov, is published by C. Fischer.

[11] *Paeons*, number two of the *Logaoedics Opus 28*, is published by C. Fischer, as well as several other compositions.

[12] The *Transcendental Études* by Liapunov are published in four volumes by Zimmermann.

[13] The large-scale works of Glazunov are published by Boosey & Hawkes.

[14] Schott publishes most of Gretchaninov's piano music. A few pieces appear in the catalogue of Max Eschig.

maninov and Medtner. Both are important composers who theoretically belong to the twentieth century, yet their works are so tinged with nineteenth-century Romanticism that they fall logically into the latter frame of reference.

Sergei Rachmaninov

Sergei Rachmaninov (1873–1943) was a spectacular pianist equal to any of the leading twentieth-century virtuosos. In addition, he ranks high on the list of composers in his day, not for any effects he may have impressed upon younger artists but for the inherent beauty in his own music.

"Rachmaninov's piano style stemmed directly from the romantic masters of the West, especially Chopin and Liszt, with occasional passing reference to Schumann, and even Brahms. It is interesting to note that the Russian composer must have observed, but almost totally disregarded, Debussy's revolutionary treatment of the piano. Instead he concentrated on the Chopin-Liszt framework of singing melodies and rich sonorities, decorated by elaborate technical embellishments. Though the formula was old he yet contrived to use it with individuality."[15]

Unlike some of his contemporaries, Rachmaninov knew his way about the actual physical keyboard. As a result, his compositions are pianistically secure; they reflect a convincing keyboard idiom: sonorous textures that often require incredible stretches of the hand; florid decoration, with arabesques that almost blend the romantic with the rococo. Rachmaninov had a special skill as a melodist. His songs contain some of the most hauntingly beautiful passages to be found in vocal literature. In transferring this talent to the keyboard, the composer managed to create a characteristically limpid, nostalgic melodic line. This has played an important role in the success achieved by several piano works, especially the concertos. Good examples of his melodic skill can be found in the middle section of *Polichinelle Opus 3, No. 4* and various other pieces in *Opus 3* and *Opus 10*.

Rachmaninov's finest music for solo piano are the *Preludes Opus 23* and *Opus 32*. Like Chopin and J. S. Bach before him, he wrote altogether twenty-four preludes, one in each major and minor key. First came the famous and exquisitely fashioned *Prelude in C-sharp Minor Opus 3, No. 2*. Then in 1904 he wrote the ten preludes of *Opus 23*, and in 1910 the thirteen *Preludes Opus 32* appeared. Each prelude—whether introspective, impassioned, or outwardly virtuoso—is a treasure of pianism, an expertly designed, enchanting tonal picture. The preludes of *Opus 32* represent the peak of his master command of keyboard style. The fifteen *Études-Tableaux*

---

[15] Richard Anthony Leonard, *A History of Russian Music* (New York: The Macmillan Company, 1957), p. 238.

comprising *Opus 33* and *Opus 39* were supposedly inspired by as many pictures (by Arnold Böcklin?), but the composer never clarified the reference. Although they are attractive they cannot match the splendid achievements of the *Preludes*.

Rachmaninov ventured only twice into the realm of the piano sonata and with debatable success. His first *Sonata in D Minor Opus 28* appeared in 1907 and had few performances—except by Rachmaninov himself. The second work, *Sonata in B-flat Minor Opus 36*, is of fine quality. It was published in 1913 but Rachmaninov later became dissatisfied with it, for he complained about its inordinate length and busywork. In 1931 he brought out a revised version vastly superior to the original. It is exceptionally difficult, yet a pianist endowed with the necessary large hands will find a serious study of it worthwhile. One finds here almost a musical compendium of the Russian composer's technical devices (and some expressive ones, too).

Two sets of variations mark the composer's other ventures into larger keyboard forms. *Opus 22* consists of *Variations on a Theme of Chopin* (1903). The theme is Chopin's *Prelude Opus 28, No. 20*. Certain individual variations are attractive enough, but as a whole the work cannot in any way compare to Rachmaninov's last keyboard work, *Variations on a Theme by Corelli Opus 42* (1932). The theme was taken from the Italian composer's *Violin Sonata No. 12*, to which the Russian supplied twenty rather short variations. In this his final tribute to the piano, Rachmaninov proves himself a resourceful and imaginative composer, creating a series of mood sketches with rare beauty and individuality.[16]

Nicolas Medtner

Nicolas Medtner (1880–1951), a Russian of German ancestry, toured as a concert pianist and also taught briefly at the Moscow Conservatory. When he settled down to composing, Medtner apparently looked in two directions for inspiration. As a composer with a talent for writing in restricted forms like the sonata, he was a neo-classicist; but as a devotee of cross relations, shifting rhythms, and syncopation, and as a continuator of latter-day romanticism, Medtner follows the path of Johannes Brahms.

Medtner's music is almost exclusively for piano, both solo instrument and piano in chamber ensemble. These piano works betray his fondness for the sonata, and he employed Classic sonata form with fine abandon. Thirteen of his large-scale keyboard compositions are titled *Sonata. Opus 11*

---

[16] Both the *Preludes* and *Études-Tableaux* are published by International Music Co. and Boosey & Hawkes. IMC also has available the *Sonata Opus 28*, *Sonata Opus 36*, and the Chopin *Variations*.

perhaps started as an ordinary sonata, but as each movement grew it took on expanded dimensions; as a result the *Sonata-Triad* emerged with each of its three movements fashioned with first-movement importance. *Opus 25, No. 1* may have been intended as a *Fairy Tale;* it ended up as a sonata, and so did *Opus 27.*

The Romantic era's beloved epigrammatic character piece was also lovingly cultivated by Medtner. He used the term *Fairy Tale* to describe some of his characteristic, decidedly individual pieces. Thirty-three *Fairy Tales* are scattered among eleven opus numbers. The conservatism laying over these little works is tempered by unusual rhythmic combinations and the composer's inborn musicality.[17]

Among this group of Russian composers who were writing into the twentieth century, only one—Alexander Scriabin—has proved a focal point for future developments. He was a controversial figure in his own era; his chromatic harmony and mystical enigmas puzzled his contemporaries. On the other hand, Scriabin's unorthodox approach pointed the way to unexplored regions; therefore, he must be recognized as an early proponent of some basic contemporary techniques.

BOHEMIA

Bohemia (now a part of Czechoslovakia) has been musically active since the sixteenth century. During the sixteenth and the seventeenth centuries, however, most professional musicians working there were foreigners. Composers such as Jacob Handl (Austria), Hans Leo Hassler (Germany), and Philippe de Monte (Netherlands) all encouraged music education in Bohemia and helped to raise native musical standards.

Georg Benda

In the eighteenth century native Bohemian musicians—both performers and composers—began to emerge. **Georg Benda** (1722–1795), contemporary with the Pre-Classic period, was for some seven years a member of the court orchestra in Berlin; then for twenty-eight years he was *Kapellmeister* at the Thuringian court of Gotha. Many eighteenth-century musicians valued Benda's music; Mozart was especially fond of it. Benda's personal style merges German (he doubtlessly knew Carl Philipp Emanuel Bach) and Italian elements into his innate Bohemian temperament. In

---

[17] Simrock publishes the *Sonata-Triad.* Most of the other piano music of Medtner is published by Zimmermann.

addition to six harpsichord sonatas published in Berlin in 1757, he wrote other keyboard works, including a concerto for harpsichord and strings.[18] The slow movements in Benda's keyboard compositions rank among the most expressive of his time.

Jan Vanhal

Keyboard composition continued in Bohemia—though not with such high-quality products—in the works of **Jan Vanhal** (1739–1813), whose advanced musical studies with Karl Ditters von Dittersdorf led him to Vienna. After some time spent in Italy and Hungary, Vanhal settled in the Austrian capital. As a composer he was strongly influenced by Haydn. His better works show a skillful approach to compositional techniques, and his melodies are frequently quite eloquent.

Vanhal wrote a great deal—more than a hundred symphonies, a hundred string quartets, and many works in other media. He wrote numerous descriptive piano pieces, of which the battle scenes were the favorites in his own day. Such works as *Die Schlacht bei Würzburg* (The Battle at Würzburg) and *Le Combat naval de Trafalgar et la mort de Nelson* (The Trafalgar Naval Battle and the Death of Nelson) doubtlessly elicited enthusiastic applause from Vanhal's contemporaries, but today they are forgotten.[19]

Jan Dussek

One of the early piano virtuosos, **Jan Ladislav Dussek** (1760–1812) lived in a state of perpetual movement. He studied principally in Germany, where Emanuel Bach encouraged him to become a concert pianist. As a youth, he traveled extensively over Europe and England, made his first real success in Amsterdam, and from Holland went to Hamburg, Berlin, St. Petersburg, Paris, Italy, and London. He spent his last years as music director to the Prince de Talleyrand in Paris.

Dussek unfortunately is not remembered for his compositions. Although many of them, such as the *Rondo on the Quickstep*, are quite frankly "potboilers," compositions that he himself probably never played, still there are some fifty important piano sonatas.[20] These sonatas contain traces of stylistic elements that later found complete fulfillment in Beethoven, Weber,

---

[18] Benda's harpsichord sonatas, as well as the concerto, are published by Artia of Czechoslovakia. Two pieces are in *Alte Meister* (Breitkopf & Härtel), Volume II.

[19] Two *Sonatinas* by Vanhal appear in Vol. 17 of *Musica Antiqua Bohemica* issued by Artia. This volume also contains sonatinas by Benda, Dussek, and Worzischek.

[20] Peters publishes Dussek's *Sonata Opus 61. Sonata Opus 9, No. 1* is in the G. Schirmer catalogue and Artia of Czechoslovakia publishes the complete Dussek sonatas.

Schumann, Liszt, and even Brahms. In his earlier works, like *Sonata Opus 10 in G Minor,* the monotonous left-hand accompaniment figures obscure the rather effective melodic inventiveness. His mature sonatas, while structurally weak at times, possess a rich texture most unusual for his period. The lyricism and sustained elegance of the slow movements may be the outgrowth of Dussek's early training in organ, the instrument he abandoned for the piano.

His best piano works date from around 1810 to his death in 1812. Within this period he wrote his finest work, *Sonata Opus 70 in A-flat Major (Le Retour à Paris).* Since his first-quality works predate Weber, he may well be construed as a forerunner of that composer. *Opus 70* in four movements is remarkable for several things: the first movement, *Allegro,* is extraordinarily lengthy for this period; the second movement is a *Molto adagio* in the key of *E* major; the *Tempo di Menuetto* is again in *A-flat* but begins in *f-sharp* minor; and the finale is a *Scherzo* whose harmonic scheme tends to be static.

All these key changes suggest that Dussek enjoyed modulation. In the first movement alone the key signature changes seven times. Sometimes the modulations are so well concealed as to be almost imperceptible, but at other times the startling key changes are deliberately bold. The second movement, *Molto adagio con anima ed espressione,* reveals Dussek's real talent. This is an early attempt to exploit the piano's poetic possibilities, and moreover it is successful. Nothing is left to chance, all expression indications are clearly marked—*mezza voce, dolcissimo, ppp,* etc. Coloratura passages in the right hand are later echoed in Weber's compositions.

This sonata also has its weaknesses: the harmonic and rhythmic poverty of the last movement; a tendency to go to extremes in handling sequences. But on the whole *Opus 70* is a charming example of very early nineteenth-century writing by an accomplished composer.

Jan Tomaschek

Another genuine talent in pianistic writing, **Jan Tomaschek** (1774–1850) had a well-rounded education that included studies in mathematics, aesthetics, history, anatomy, and surgery. He was largely a self-taught musician; however, having once mastered the basic rules of composition, he became a respectable composer. He was on friendly terms with Goethe, Beethoven, and Haydn, but among composers he preferred Mozart. An industrious writer, Tomaschek left one hundred and fourteen numbered works and many others without opus numbers. For piano there are seven volumes of *Eclogues* (1807), three volumes of *Rhapsodies* (1810), three *Dithyrambs* (1818), and other compositions.[21]

21 Ten *Eclogues* by Tomaschek are published by Augener and the *Dithyrambs Opus 65* by Artia.

His personal style is sharpest in the piano music and songs—a romantic, lyrical style that influenced John Field and Franz Schubert and paved the way for Smetana. The light, melodious *Eclogues,* vigorous *Rhapsodies,* and dramatic *Dithyrambs* are important ancestors of the typical character piece popular in the Romantic age.

Jan Worzischek

Tomaschek's inroads upon lyricism were advanced by his devoted pupil **Jan Worzischek** (1791–1825), whose promising career ended prematurely. In Vienna in 1813, Worzischek cultivated Beethoven's friendship; Moscheles, Hummel, and Meyerbeer were also in his intimate circle. A conductor and organist, Worzischek was one of the first out-and-out Romanticists to work in Vienna. His *Impromptus Opus 7*[22] affected similar works by Schubert. Worzischek's *Impromptus* (and most of Schubert's) are in ternary form and contrive to evoke both mood and acute, intimate feeling —all within a few pages.

Bedrich Smetana

The name of **Bedrich Smetana** (1824–1884) automatically brings to mind colorful, nationalistic orchestral tone poems, such as *The Moldau.* Yet Smetana has some importance as a keyboard composer. He was a competent pianist, who looked to Liszt in matters of technique, and an ardent nationalist, who searched Chopin's music to find ways to exploit his own country's cultural heritage. Smetana's first purely personal expressions in music are the *Bagatelles* and *Impromptus* of 1844. Later he accomplished for the polka what Chopin achieved for the mazurka.[23]

Antonin Dvořák

Whereas Smetana is most often associated with the tone poem, **Antonin Dvořák** (1841–1904) is considered by many critics to be among the outstanding nineteenth-century symphonists. Encouraged by Johannes Brahms, who saw unique creativity in Dvořák's talent, the Bohemian musician eventually spent three years in New York as head of the National Conservatory.

---

[22] Artia issues the *Impromptus Opus 7* and two *Rhapsodies* by Worzischek.
[23] Smetana's *Polkas, Bagatelles,* and *Impromptus* are all published by Artia.

Dvořák's most original piano works are based on stylized dance forms: waltz, impromptu, mazurka, and furiant. His characteristic harmony, which at times points the way to twentieth-century "modernity," is well in evidence in such works as the *Poetic Pictures Opus 85* and the eight *Humoresques Opus 101* (No. 7 in *G-flat* major from the last set has become one of the most popular salon pieces of all times).[24]

BIBLIOGRAPHY

Bertensson, Sergei and Jay Leyda. *Sergei Rachmaninoff. A Lifetime in Music.* New York: New York University Press, 1956.

Bowen, Catherine Drinker. *"Free Artist." The Story of Anton and Nicholas Rubinstein.* New York: Random House, 1939.

Calvocoressi, M. D. and Gerald Abraham. *Masters of Russian Music.* New York: Alfred A. Knopf, 1936.

Gerstlé, Henry S. "Piano Music of Nicolas Medtner." *Musical Quarterly,* October, 1924.

Montagu-Nathan, M. *Contemporary Russian Composers.* London: Cecil Palmer & Hayward, 1917.

Riesemann, Oskar von. *Moussorgsky* (translated by P. England). New York: Tudor Publishing Co., 1935. Dover reprint

Thompson, Verne. *Wenzel Johann Tomaschek: His Predecessors, His Life, His Piano Works.* Dissertation. Eastman School of Music, 1955.

Weinstock, Herbert. *Tchaikovsky.* New York: Alfred A. Knopf, 1946.

[24] Most of Dvořák's piano music appears in the Artia catalogue.

22

THE

NORTH

COUNTRIES

During the nineteenth century, Scandinavia and Finland, like Russia, were slow in producing serious music. Scandinavian composers were educated mostly in Germany—usually at the Leipzig Conservatory—so their musical development in some ways parallels that of the German composers; and there the similarity ends. In sharp contrast with Germany, the Scandinavian countries have produced only a small amount of good piano music. One must search diligently through the idyls, the character pieces, etc., to find the occasional composition with sure workmanship and sincere inspiration.

NORWAY

One name immediately comes to mind when the subject of piano music arises: **Edvard Grieg** (1843–1907), who was born in Bergen and reached maturity along with Norway's renowned literary figures Björnson and Ibsen. Following the custom of the times, he was educated in Germany, but he knew early in life that he wanted to write music that would reproduce the vigorous spirit of his native land. His good friend Richard Nordraak—a promising composer who died at twenty-two—encouraged him in this desire. Nordraak, a fervent nationalist, collected Norwegian folk songs and had composed a few compositions inspired by folk matter.[1] To him must go the credit for arousing Grieg's interest in folk material. Spurred on by Nordraak's infectious enthusiasm, Grieg probed into the inspirational resources lying so close at hand.

His preoccupation with nationalistic music research led him to write several works which are actually arrangements of native folk songs and dances; they are exceptionally fine arrangements, imaginatively conceived

---

[1] C. Fischer publishes a *Valse Caprice* of Nordraak.

yet faithful to the spirit of the original melodies. *Opus 17* presents piano
arrangements of Norwegian folk songs and dances, *Opus 29* includes improvisations on two Norwegian songs, and *Opus 35* consists of Norwegian
dances for piano. There is also an orchestral version of the last group.

Grieg's creative style is just as unique as Chopin's though not so profound. Frequently Grieg's melodies break up into short phrases and motives
only two measures in length—a procedure derived from folk song—and then
the melodic fragments are restated either with variations or in sequence
(Ex. 1).

Ex. 1.   Grieg: *Arietta Opus 12, No. 1*

His music has a plentiful share of bare triads and open fifths used either as
a kind of drone bass, to set a scene, or as a preliminary introductory accompaniment (Ex. 2).

Ex. 2.   Grieg: *Mountain Dance Opus 19, No. 1*

Grieg had the gift of endowing rather ordinary devices with fresh meaning;
for instance, alternation of major and minor tonalities was in itself nothing
new, but this procedure took on new values in the light of his approach
(Ex. 3). Although at times his harmonic structure is ultraconventional, there
are other occasions when he uses distantly related chords with dash and
style. Chromaticism plays a significant role in Grieg's music; although it
may be merely ornamental, more often it is an integral part of the basic
structure. Note the descending chromatic harmony at the beginning of the

Ex. 3.   Grieg: *Waltz Opus 12, No. 2*

Ballade Opus 21 (Ex. 4). This is a most effective treatment of the folk

Ex. 4.   Grieg: *Ballade Opus 21*

melody. Other characteristics—his sudden rhythmic changes, his use of old
modes, his skillful concept of ornamentation—classify Grieg as a composer whose nationalist traits rival those of Mussorgsky and Borodin.

Opinions differ about Grieg's real value as a composer: some critics
dismiss him as mediocre; others consider him a master craftsman. The truth
lies somewhere between these two extremes. He might be called a *"petit
maître"*—that is, a composer excelling in miniature compositions (the song
and the short piano piece). But even in this respect he cannot be compared
with Schubert and Schumann, for he was an entirely different type of composer. Grieg, a realist, found inspiration in nature: the fjords, mountain
streams, and Norway's magnificent landscapes. As Norway's balladeer, Grieg
sang well.

Grieg had a stormy career, difficult from the start because in Norway
composers won prestige only if they were foreigners or else Norwegians acclaimed by foreigners. The Norwegian composer working at home was
looked upon disdainfully. Grieg so completely overcame these prejudices
that in his lifetime his own country, emulating the rest of the musical world,
acknowledged him as one of the finest of the nationalist composers.

In the long list of Grieg piano works[2] some are so poor that they rest in
oblivion, particularly the transcriptions he made of his own songs. On the

[2] Peters Edition publishes almost the complete piano music of Grieg.

other hand, there are some piano works that faithfully and skillfully present Grieg's personal musical vocabulary.

Only twice did he endeavor to create solo piano works in extended form; neither attempt was completely successful. His works of real substance begin with *Opus 6; Opus 7, Sonata in E Minor* (1865), is the only piano sonata he ever wrote. Usually he chose to ignore classic forms, but this does not mean he was incapable of handling them. The first movement of his sonata has rather straightforward sonata-allegro form combined with certain features reminiscent of Liszt's transformation of theme. In the development section, the principal subject is transformed and appears in its new guise in the recapitulation.

The *Andante* is a good example of his attitude toward form. It is a movement based on mood contrasts, surprising digressions, a series of antitheses, all held together in an amazingly unified framework. The third movement, *Minuet,* decidedly Germanic in spirit, is more abstract, with a trio that holds interest by its chords of the eleventh and thirteenth. In the straightforward modality of the finale—similar in character to the first movement—Grieg has once again assumed his Norwegian disposition.

Ballade Opus 24 emerges as an expansive tone poem created from variation treatment of a Norwegian folk song called "The Northern Folk." Even the initial harmonic setting of the folk melody, controlled by Grieg's adroit chromatic procedures, reveals what an imaginative composer he was. The actual theme occurs only now and again during the first several variations. Instead, accent falls on the harmonic outline and the descending chromatic line of the original setting. Variation three, an adagio, reintroduces the theme—a melody in thirds against a moving pattern of sixteenth notes. Then in succession follows a recitative passage; a *scherzando* based exclusively on the initial harmonic pattern; a rapid staccato passage in quasi-canonic treatment; and a broad, bold statement of the theme in chords. Further thematic manipulations bring about meter changes. As the variations advance to a conclusion, the theme outline becomes stronger, less concealed by artifice. The *Ballade* terminates with a simple statement of the theme as presented at the beginning.

Although the *Sonata* and *Ballade* represent Grieg's major keyboard contributions, they are rarely performed. His fame holds today for the charming miniatures, the little tonal portraits that proclaim him as Norway's musical poet.

In 1870–1871 Grieg composed *Pictures from Folk Life Opus 19,* a suite of three humoresques, all of them very impressive although not consistently pianistic. *Mountain Dance* employs the simplest procedures to depict the scene; a melody stated in octaves is then given an accompaniment in arpeggiated chords. The middle section involves some canonic treatment, builds to a tremendous climax, and falls back to a restatement of the first section. *Norwegian Bridal Procession*, one of Grieg's loveliest pieces, displays his talent for creating new sounds and new rhythmic combinations. An introduction of bare chord outlines precedes the ornamented melody, and open fifths inserted from time to time preserve the initial simplicity. Grieg uses chords of the ninth, eleventh, and thirteenth lavishly. This music, with its coloristic texture, alerts the listener to the impression Grieg made on the early composers of the twentieth century, particularly the Impressionists. The last piece, *From the Carnival,* is the poorest of the three. Although the middle section has delightful moments, the beginning section deals with banal ideas indifferently expressed. In an attempt to unify the suite, the coda includes references to the first two pieces.

Grieg found his ideal vehicle in the so-called *Lyric Pieces.* During his career he composed ten sets of these little mood pictures or epigrammatic poems. Demonstrating multiple textures and techniques and covering a wide emotional range, the *Lyric Pieces* were tremendously popular. The first set—*Opus 12*, composed in 1867—is a collection of eight contrasting pieces, a few of which suggest foreign influences. *Arietta* is flecked with Schumannisms and *Album Leaf* bears traces of Chopin, but the rest are completely Grieg at his lyrical best. *Watchman's Song*, inspired by a performance of Shakespeare's *Macbeth*, is an especially concise little work; even so, the watchman's call and the ghostly voices are piercingly clear—a tribute to Grieg's power to call up sights and sounds through plain, succinct means. Equally effective, fanciful, and inventive are *Dance of the Elves* and *Song of the Fatherland.* The remaining three pieces are only fair.

Berceuse opens the second set, *Opus 38* (1883), and is one of his most perfectly fashioned works. The prevailing serenity is upset when sadness enters in the middle section, and one cannot help remembering that the composer's only child Alexandra had died shortly after her first birthday. Two other excellent pieces in this set, *Halling* (Fling Dance) and *Springdans* (Spring Dance), are faithful representations of Norwegian folk life.

The third set of *Lyric Pieces Opus 43* (1884) contains several short pieces often heard today: *Butterfly*, with brief, nervous chromaticisms; *Lonely Wanderer*, a guileless sketch; *Erotik*, a tender love song; and finally, *To Spring*, full of hope and nostalgic yearnings.

Opus 47, published at Christmastime in 1888, contains easy, rather interesting pieces; they neither add to nor detract from the composer's reputation. The still-popular *Notturno* comes from book five, *Opus 54* (1891). Two pieces from the sixth set, *Opus 57* (1893), involve deep emotions: *Vanished Days* awakens melancholy, and the little piece *Gade* is a sad memorial to the composer Niels Gade. The others in this set are mostly pleasing but trivial salon pieces.

Opus 62 (1895) is ordinary. The best of the pieces are the expertly delineated *The Brook* and *Homeward Bound,* filled with excited anticipation. *Opus 65* and *Opus 68* were composed in 1896 and 1898 respectively. *In Ballad Style* is doubtlessly the finest piece in *Opus 65,* both structurally and stylistically; yet the one most frequently played is *Wedding Day at Troldhaugen,* a perennial favorite that rings out joyously in manifold blendings of tone colors. *Evening in the Mountains* from *Opus 68* is an enchanting descriptive piece clearly indicating the silent majesty of mountain scenery. The last set of *Lyric Pieces Opus 71* (1901) has little to recommend it.

If one checks over the music in this the major portion of Grieg's representative keyboard works, he must become aware of one fact about the composer. Normally, as an artist matures personally so his style matures and his techniques become assured. Not so with Grieg. After his youthful enthusiasm had subsided and the excitement of his early successes—particularly with the piano concerto—had also waned, he found it increasingly difficult to compose. Inspiration came haltingly and the actual writing became tedious. This state of affairs is painfully obvious in the rather commonplace techniques and devices, the pallid ideas of many later works. But despite this, Edvard Grieg must be remembered as the composer who has preserved the spirit of his beloved Norway, faithfully molded into variegated tonal fabrics of dignity and great warmth.

Norwegian art music began and ended with Grieg. The few composers who preceded him and those who succeeded him never reached his artistic integrity. **Agathe Backer-Gröndahl** (1847–1907), a well-known concert pianist who often played Grieg's music, was also a composer. Her numerous works—isolated pieces, concert études, etc.—are written in an agreeable, easy style, but they cannot be considered anything more than good examples of salon music: for example, *Fantasiestykker Opus 45.*[3]

Christian Sinding (1856–1941) was more purposeful. His music is inherently nationalistic like Grieg's but on a very reduced scale. Although pleasant and often stimulating, it never becomes profound. Sinding's *Marche Grotesque* and *Rustle of Spring,*[4] hardly known today, were popular for many years. His larger works, *Suite Opus 3* and *Sonata Opus 91,* never reach today's concert stage.

SWEDEN

The strongly individual accent that marks Norwegian folk music is missing in Swedish folk music. Most native Swedish composers turned to

---

[3] Backer-Gröndahl's works are not readily available. C. Fischer lists two pieces: *Serenade Opus 15, No. 1* and *Waltz Opus 36, No. 3.*
[4] Both C. Fischer and G. Schirmer offer a fair sampling of Sinding's piano music.

Germany for models, but unfortunately they had considerably less to say than their Germanic prototypes.

Emil Sjögren (1853–1918) studied at Stockholm Conservatory and later in Berlin. His travels placed him in contact with the music of César Franck and Camille Saint-Saëns, both of whom influenced his later works. His approach to music is fundamentally Scandinavian; he shows a vague resemblance to Grieg, but he lacks the Norwegian's nationalism. From 1883 to 1915 he devoted eleven opuses to keyboard music, of which the collection *Erotikon Opus 10* won first prize in a contest open to all Scandinavian composers in 1883. Of the five pieces in this suite, four are lyrical and the other, *No. 3 in A-flat,* is lively. These works make their point and are appealing, but they are seldom performed.[5]

DENMARK

The acknowledged father of Danish art music is **J. P. E. Hartmann** (1805–1900); Denmark's most famous composer is Hartmann's son-in-law **Niels Gade** (1817–1890). Violinist, conductor, and organist, Gade wrote in almost all compositional media. Some early-twentieth-century biographers contend that he was a skillful composer who wrote works highly tinged with Scandinavian folk-song elements. This may be so, but still there must be a reason for the current indifference to Gade's music.

Gade wrote a piano sonata (dedicated to Franz Liszt) and several groups of short piano pieces, including two opuses (*19* and *57*) of *Aquarellen* (Water Colors), none of which ever appear in recital. The pieces still available in print[6] have a modicum of local color. Gade's style is all too reminiscent of Mendelssohn, his ideas too facile, his expression too shallow. What he had to say was far better expressed by others.

Two of Gade's pupils, **August Winding** (1825–1900) and **Ludwig Schytte** (1848–1909), copied their teacher by writing small lyric pieces; in their day each attained considerable renown. Winding was especially successful with his *Piano Pieces in the Form of Études Opus 18.*[7]

The most significant Danish composer to date has been **Carl Nielsen** (1865–1931). Although his early works, like the pieces in *Opus 3* and *Opus 11,* are unimportant, *Chaconne Opus 32* (1916) suggests the mature style that blossomed in the finely developed *Variations Opus 40,* which prove his keen sense of musical style and pianistic know-how. Nielsen's keyboard

---

[5] Sjögren's *Erotikon Opus 10* is published by Boston Music Co.
[6] *Aquarellen Opus 19* and several other collections by Gade are published by W. Hansen.
[7] Winding's compositions are not readily available, but a generous number of works by Schytte are published by Hansen, G. Schirmer, C. Fischer, and Boston Music Co.

career reached its peak with the *Suite Opus 45* (1919) that he originally intended to call "Lucifer." His entire tonal palette participates in this suite to create a work not only of excellent quality but one that is extremely gratifying for the pianist.[8]

FINLAND

Finnish folk music, like Norwegian folk music, has rich substance and an individualistic style; Finland's greatest composer, **Jean Sibelius** (1865–1958), drew upon these folk-song treasures. As a Romantic symphonist, Sibelius has few peers, and as a song writer he can be strikingly original and shrewdly perceptive; but his piano music is consistently inferior. Fifteen opus numbers are devoted to the piano, and it is well that he stopped there. Mainly salon pieces, they seem to be without purpose. His *Piano Sonata Opus 12* has only a slightly higher quality. Commonplace harmonies and painfully monotonous accompaniment figures overshadow the first movement, *Allegro molto. Andantino,* the second movement, has two themes evidently inspired by folklore: the first a kind of somber folk song, the second a sprightly peasant dance. The last movement, *Vivacissimo,* is rhythmically interesting, but the ideas, repeated ad infinitum, are dull.[9]

If Sibelius' genius lay in orchestral writing, then by the same token the talents of **Selim Palmgren** (1878–1951) thrived in miniature forms, songs and short piano pieces. Palmgren can be as warmly nationalistic as Grieg; at the same time some of his music seems to be derived solely from his own innate musicality. His pianistic writings demonstrate his technical proficiency and a wonderful facility for conjuring up a brief mood or an ephemeral impression.

A good deal of Palmgren's music bears an obviously Impressionistic veneer in its use of parallel dissonant chords and the whole-tone scale (Ex. 5).

Ex. 5. Palmgren: *May Night*

pp misterioso

---

[8] Peters Edition publishes Nielsen's *Suite Opus 45* and Hansen the *Variations Opus 40*.

[9] Sibelius' salon music is available in many different editions. The *Sonata,* originally published by Breitkopf & Härtel, has been discontinued from their catalogue.

He knew how to clothe his musical thoughts in pianistic fabric. His best-known pieces are the exquisite miniatures *May Night, Bird Song,* and *The Sea*—all distinctly individual and stylistically consistent.[10]

BIBLIOGRAPHY

Abraham, Gerald, ed. *Grieg. A Symposium.* London: Oxford University Press, 1952.

Dale, Kathleen. *Nineteenth-Century Piano Music.* London: Oxford University Press, 1954.

Monrad-Johansen, David. *Edvard Grieg* (translated by M. Robertson). Princeton: Princeton University Press, 1938.

Petersen, F. S. *Carl Nielsen the Danish Composer.* Copenhagen: Det Berlingske Bogtrykkeri, n.d.

[10] A quantity of Palmgren's music is generally available. J. & W. Chester, C. Fischer, Augener, and Boston Music Co., among others, publish his compositions.

23

FRENCH

PIANO MUSIC

IN THE NINETEENTH CENTURY

By the mid-nineteenth century France had not produced one keyboard composer equal to Schubert, Mendelssohn, or Schumann. This strange situation in the land of Couperin and Rameau can be explained to a certain extent by the fact that French music at the time was largely dominated by foreigners. For the last few decades of the eighteenth century and about forty years of the nineteenth, Frenchmen preferred opera above all else, an idiom devoutly cultivated in their country by a succession of foreigners— Rossini, Meyerbeer, Cherubini—who were by nature unequipped to further native French musical culture.

In eighteenth-century France (until about 1770) amateurs and professionals alike were satisfied to adapt harpsichord music for piano performance. But between 1770 and about 1785 a new style gradually formed when composers attempted to utilize the piano's latent possibilities. During this transitional period they concentrated on writing and publishing sonatas in collections of three or six; of course there were also the inevitable *airs variés, potpourris,* and transcriptions. Naturally, most of these intermediate works retain certain traits characteristic of harpsichord music—numerous ornaments, trills, repeated notes.

EARLY FRENCH PIANO MUSIC

The first two composers discussed here are of Alsatian and German origin respectively. In Dr. Burney's evaluation of J. G. Müthel (see Chapter 12, page 155), he classes Handel, C. P. E. Bach, Scarlatti, Schobert, and Eckard together, perhaps as representing the best and most famous composers of his time. This is fine for Handel, Bach, and Scarlatti, but what of Schobert and Eckard? These last two have not kept their place in that eminent group.

Little is known about the life of **Johann Schobert** (*d.* 1767) beyond the fact that he was born in Alsace and later moved to Paris, where he and his entire family died from eating poisonous mushrooms. Among his compositions are numerous keyboard works. Up to this point, the keyboard instrument was usually assumed to be the accompanying instrument in group performances; but Schobert has the stringed instruments accompanying the harpsichord or piano, for the title pages announce them as pieces *"qui peuvent se jouer avec l'accompagnement du Violon"* (which may be played with the accompaniment of a violin). Mozart as a young man also wrote sonatas in this style but these works, as well as similar ones by Schobert, are seldom performed. Schobert's music is not readily available in modern playing editions except for occasional pieces.[1] An *Allegro molto* from a *Sonata in E-flat Major* shows the elements of sonata form but has only one theme. This theme is important both melodically and rhythmically, and each aspect receives close attention in each section.

Johann Gottfried Eckard (1735–1809) was a German musician who moved to Paris at an early age (*ca.* 1758). There he quickly acquired a reputation as clavierist and teacher, to which he later added that of composer. During Eckard's lifetime only three of his collections appeared in print: *Six Sonates pour le Clavecin oeuvre I* (1763), *Deux Sonates pour le Clavecin ou le Piano Forte oeuvre II* (1764), and *Menuet d'Exaudet avec des Variations pour le Clavecin* (1764).[2]

Eckard was among the first composers in France to prepare the way for the piano and piano composition. Although his first collection is titled *pour le Clavecin,* he explains in the preface that he has tried to make the music equally suitable for harpsichord, clavichord, or pianoforte. In his *Opus II* he adds "pianoforte" to the title. The music of *Opus II* shows a preoccupation with the new possibilities deriving from the piano. Besides that, he uses the abbreviation *cresc.* and a succession of *f*, *p*, and *pp* markings that indicate a *decrescendo*. All types of dynamic markings are present as well as interpretive indications.

Eckard's style seems to be a blend taken from his German contemporaries and the Italian keyboard composers of the last half of the eighteenth century. His sonata form is very flexible. Three of his eight sonatas have three movements, two have only two movements, and three have but a single movement. Within each sonata the character of the initial movement depends upon the composer's caprice: one of the initial movements is marked *Andante,* one *Cantabile,* another *Con Discretione;* and two three-

---

[1] Two short pieces are in *Alte Meister,* ed. Pauer (Leipzig: Breitkopf & Härtel), IV. A complete *Sonata in E-flat Major* appears in *Keyboard Music of the Baroque and Rococo,* ed. W. Georgii (Cologne: Arno Volk Verlag), III. The *Denkmäler deutscher Tonkunst* devotes Vol. 39 to selected works by Schobert.

[2] Johann Gottfried Eckard, *Oeuvres Complètes pour le Clavecin ou le Pianoforte* (Amsterdam: Edition Heuwekemeijer, 1956).

movement sonatas begin with an *Allegro* movement. The one-movement sonatas are titled *Andantino, Allegro,* and *Andante,* respectively. Each movement also varies in form. As he matured, Eckard preferred a kind of *sonata-allegro* form to his earlier *quasi-fantasia* form.

The best musicians of the time appreciated his music. In a letter dated 1772, Wolfgang Mozart requested his sister to send him the *Menuet d'Exaudet* by Eckard. This minuet originally came from a collection called *Six Sonates en Trio à deux Violons et Basse Continue* (1752) written by André-Joseph Exaudet. Eckard simplified the minuet and added six charming variations.

As a composer, **Jean-François Tapray** (1738–*ca.* 1819) was an improvisor whose sonatas for harpsichord or piano have not a glimmer of originality. But there is a definite qualitative improvement in the sonatas and numerous short pieces of **Nicolas Séjan** (1745–1819),[3] a keyboard virtuoso as well as composer. His musical ideas are carefully fashioned, though harpsichord techniques still predominate in his music.

Further contributions to French keyboard literature in this period were made by a pair of Alsatians born in Strasburg but residing in Paris. **Nicolas-Joseph Hüllmandel** (*ca.* 1751–1823), the darling of aristocratic society in his time, was a pupil of Emanuel Bach. He wrote ingenious but insensitive music; the eight sets of sonatas show classic contours usually associated with Mozart. On the other hand, **Jean-Frédéric Edelmann** (1749–1794), the second Alsatian, combined imagination with sensitivity in his keyboard works, chiefly intended for harpsichord. Other composers writing keyboard music during this changeover from harpsichord to piano were **Claude Balbastre** (1727–1799) and **Charles Broche** (1752–1803), the latter a pupil of Padre Martini.

Etienne Nicolas Méhul (1763–1817) introduced a new era with his first piano sonatas (1783). By the time this talented musician began writing, the harpsichord was already on its way out and piano virtuosos held the musical spotlight. He published two sonata collections (1783 and 1788) that prove his skill in development procedures[4] and his capacity for clear presentation of ideas.

More composers, variously talented, hastened to exploit the piano. **Jean-Louis Adam** (1758–1848), another Alsatian, adopted the virtuoso tactics of Steibelt and Dussek for his long manneristic sonatas. **Louis Jadin** (1768–1853), a Versailles musician with a gift for vibrant rhythms and

[3] The only collection of early French piano music which is readily available is *L'Ecole Française de Piano* (*1784–1845*), ed. Maurice Cauchie (Monaco: Editions de l'Oiseau-Lyre, 1957). This collection contains works by N. Séjan, Charles Bonjour, H. Jadin, Alexandre Boëly, and others.

[4] Méhul's *Sonata Opus 1, No. 3, in A Major* is published by both C. Fischer and Wilhelm Hansen.

clever modulation, composed several very acceptable sonatas. **Hyacinthe Jadin** (1769–1800), his brother, was less creative, though his music introduces a little early Romantic sentiment. **François Adrien Boieldieu** (1775–1834) wrote his piano compositions while still in his twenties.[5] Although his collections date from the last years of the eighteenth century, they really belong to the nineteenth. If at times they rely on Mozartean formulas, still there is a sentimentality and fantasy about them that leans toward the coming Romantic age.

France's best keyboard composer in the early nineteenth century was **Alexandre-Pierre-François Boëly** (1785–1858), who saturated himself with the music of Bach and Haydn and then wisely blended German stylistic elements with his native French traits, thus greatly enhancing his musical language. Beethoven's early sonatas were known in France before Boëly composed his *Opus 1* (*ca.* 1810) and they apparently had an influence on him. In turn, Boëly's countless keyboard works, for both piano and organ,[6] had a beneficial effect upon later composers like Saint-Saëns and Franck.

From 1840 to 1860 the French became more and more interested in French music written by French composers. By 1860 the stage was set, and for approximately fifty years French music production became as intense as it was creative—so outstanding that Norbert Dufourcq records this era as a golden age in French musical history.[7] The Franco-Prussian war (1871) added impetus to the movement when France turned to nationalism in an attempt to recoup her spiritual and moral forces; there was a sweeping upsurge of works by French composers, and instrumental music—symphonies and chamber works—assumed its rightful place beside opera.

CAMILLE SAINT-SAËNS

Rarely has one individual been so generously endowed as **Camille Saint-Saëns** (1835–1921), one of the first composers to promote French music. An exceptionally gifted pianist, he was admired by his contemporaries for his keyboard agility and his grand style, disciplined by a certain dryness in touch. Highly intelligent, his interests ranged beyond music; he could converse authoritatively on many subjects and at one time he edited the works of Jean-Philippe Rameau. A true Neo-Classicist, he not only was reared in Bach-Mozart traditions but he himself created works praised for their logical construction and pure style. Finally, as a progenitor of French

[5] The piano sonatas of Boieldieu were republished in 1944 by the *Société Française de Musicologie,* ed. Georges Favre. They are now out of print, available only in libraries.

[6] A large selection of works by Boëly is published by Salabert (collection Maurice Senart).

[7] See Norbert Dufourcq, *La Musique Française* (Paris: Librairie Larousse, 1949).

nationalism, Saint-Saëns founded—with Romain Bussine—the *Société Nationale de Musique* for the explicit purpose of propagating and exploiting French music.

With so many positive attributes to his credit, why is this composer not honored with Beethoven or even Liszt? What is missing from his music? Saint-Saëns himself has unwittingly supplied an answer that is well documented in his music. To him, emotion and sensitivity were synonymous with sentimentality, and he believed these elements were not requisite to good composition; even more than that, he felt they could lead to decadence in musical art. He wrote to his friend Camille Bellaigue, "The search for expression, truthful and legitimate though it may be, is the germ of decadence, which begins the moment the search for expression precedes that of formal perfection. . . . Art is made to express beauty and character; sensitivity only comes afterward and art can perfectly well do without it. It is even better for it when it does without it. . . . I have said and I will never cease to repeat, because it is the truth, that music like painting and sculpture exists by itself outside of all emotion. . . . The more that sensitivity develops, the more music and the other arts are estranged from pure art."[8]

This regrettable attitude helps to explain why so often Saint-Saëns' music is not convincing. His attitude especially affected his melodies which, although very correct in detail and constructed upon perfectly acceptable tenets of tension and climax, seem lifeless and unsatisfying. Just how wrong he was in his basic attitude—it detracts so much from the good musical qualities—is clearly demonstrated in the fact that nowhere in his keyboard music can one find a cantabile melody to compare with any of the "classic" slow movements of Mozart's sonatas. In general his harmony offers nothing new, no innovations of any kind. On the positive side are the original, imaginative rhythms that stem from his acquaintance with French music traditions.

Saint-Saëns wrote a considerable amount of piano music, nearly all ignored now.[9] The most attractive are the works adhering to his ideals of pure style and correct detail: the *Études* and the *Preludes and Fugues*. One exception is *Caprice sur des Airs de Ballet d'Alceste*, where Saint-Saëns treats the themes from Gluck's opera with respect and some ingenuity.

His best *Études* are in *Opus 52* (six études) and *Opus 111* (six études). They have neither the musical superiority of Chopin nor the extensive technical exploitations of Liszt; but viewed in the light of Saint-Saëns' aesthetic ideals, they are fine examples of his personal art. Among the twelve

---

[8] Camille Bellaigue, *Paroles et Musique* (Paris: Perrin et Cie., 1925), p. 152. English translation by the author.

[9] Durand of Paris publishes practically the complete piano compositions of Saint-Saëns, plus many piano transcriptions of orchestral works.

studies, two are enduring: the étude in chromatic thirds, *Prélude en fa mineur à Mains alternées*, and the often played *Étude en Forme de Valse*. More than anything else the *Preludes and Fugues* prove his mastery of strict contrapuntal techniques. Yet these are not merely exercises, for their transparent, suave expression deserves comparison with similar works by Mendelssohn.

EMMANUEL CHABRIER

Emmanuel Chabrier (1841–1894), unlike Saint-Saëns, wrote only a modest amount of piano music, but his music is important because it contains the germs of Impressionism. An Auvergnat turned Parisian, Chabrier at first had the reputation of being a musical dilettante; however, successful performances of his works in Germany led to recognition at home, where the newly formed *Société Nationale de Musique* presented his music.

Chabrier and Saint-Saëns have one point in common: each composer divulges his personality in his writing. In Chabrier's case the music all has a sparkling vitality and fantasy, with rhythmic energy especially prominent in his piano music. In addition, his fertile imagination created strange harmonic color effects. Structurally speaking, he usually adheres to the A B A plan of the minuet or scherzo.

Pièces pittoresques (1880), *Bourrée fantasque* (1891), and five posthumously published pieces almost account for his whole keyboard repertoire, and it is this small pianistic output that shows his real talent. After the premiere of *Pièces pittoresques* at a *Société Nationale* concert, César Franck wrote, "We have just heard something extraordinary. This music links our era with that of Couperin and Rameau." Quite apart from Franck's tribute, Chabrier's first keyboard offering is meritorious in that it holds the seeds of Impressionism that later bloomed so profusely. The title is a little misleading. These ten pieces are not picturesque in the sense of program or descriptive music; instead they present and sustain a mood, evoke an idea, or create an "impression." Evidently his object was to make the pieces contrasting; for instance, the sensitive, delicate *Mélancolie* contrasts with *Tourbillon*, which is said to be a musical portrait of the composer's own whirlwind personality. The finest piece *Idylle* is a lyrical gathering of spiritual thoughts, and it is opposed by a boisterous, brilliant *Scherzo-Valse*.

Eleven years later came his *Bourrée fantasque*, which preserves the duple meter of the classic bourrée, if not the true rhythm; and it has a style similar to several of his earlier piano pieces. Written in a completely pianistic musical idiom, this animated keyboard piece is an attractive venture into a virtuoso, colorful sound experience.

Probably written at about the same time as the *Bourrée fantasque,* the five posthumous pieces are *Aubade, Ballabile, Caprice, Feuillet d'album,* and *Ronde champêtre,* all as charming as Chabrier's other piano works although not as well known.[10]

CÉSAR FRANCK

César Franck (1822–1890), one of France's grand musicians, was Belgian by birth and German by blood, but he chose to live as a Frenchman and became naturalized in 1870. His musical life centered about the organ, and he was organist at various Parisian churches: Notre Dame de Lorette, St.-Jean-St.-François, and finally Ste.-Clotilde. In 1872 he was appointed to teach organ at the Paris Conservatory, but the class soon developed into a composition study group that produced many distinguished composers.

Franck has been compared musically to Bach, spiritually to Fra Angelico. There is, to be sure, some similarity between the cantor of Leipzig and the organist of Ste.-Clotilde: both spent their lives in rather lowly positions, both preferred contrapuntal forms, and both conceived music as a means to an end—the glorification of God. The comparison with Fra Angelico is another matter. It might be said that each man's art reflects an essentially pure soul. No doubt Franck's splendid musical works and Fra Angelico's lofty frescos at the monastery of St. Mark were inspired by the same spiritual source, but there the likeness ends. Techniques separate the two artists, the musician's approach being more complex, more scholarly.

César Franck's German roots enabled him to nourish French music with a sorely needed solidity and technical firmness that later bore fruit not only in his own compositions but in those of his disciples. In the first place, his music shows an architect at work erecting solid tonal structures capable of flexibility and mutation. Secondly, he is a contrapuntist; it is evident in his writing that he preferred the canon and fugue forms and, of course, their respective substructures. If sometimes they are excessive, this may be excused, for these two elements are always complemented by the composer's unceasing attempts at unity, a unity he often achieves by using a cyclic structure with several dominant themes reappearing in different sections of the same work.

Franck was more than a craftsman. Besides his sound background, he was further blessed with emotional capacities. His intensely expressive melodies, often diatonic, are quite dependent on the harmonic framework

---

[10] The *Bourrée fantasque* is published by E. B. Marks and the *Pièces pittoresques* by Enoch and International Music Co.

and this is where he reveals great originality: unexpected resolutions, series of seventh and ninth chords, parallel fifths, much chromaticism. This entirely new harmonic concept and the eloquent melodic lines—almost all with a downward sweep—are clothed in a superb framework. Franck's music marks a major contribution to music literature.

Franck's reputation centers around comparatively few works, all written after 1870 and affected by two different influences: the psychological aftermath of the Franco-Prussian war and the composer's stimulating experience as teacher at the *Conservatoire de Paris*. The only two solo piano works[11] in this group—*Prelude, Choral and Fugue* and *Prelude, Aria and Final*—are both masterpieces. The more often played *Prelude, Choral and Fugue* in a certain sense recalls Bach's great organ work *Toccata and Fugue in C Major*. Bach has an expansive adagio separating the fugue from the toccata. Franck's design places a choral between his two elements, and the melodic pattern of this choral dominates the entire composition.

With a striking bit of originality, the *Prelude's* initial theme—really an offshoot of the tonal design—appears as a syncopation and the restless, questioning mood of this theme runs throughout the work. Fragmentary sections (*a capriccioso*) interspersed between the statements of the initial theme contain seeds of the subject that later appears in the fugue. By means of a suspension and assumption of key, the *Prelude* merges into the *Choral*, initially in *E-flat* but soon moving to *c* minor. The beginning of this *Choral* shows how closely melody and harmony are interwoven in Franck's music (Ex. 1).

Ex. 1. Franck: *Choral*

This opening theme (Ex. 1) is calm yet inquisitive; a reply appears with the second theme—the choral, properly speaking—in a melody consisting of the top notes of a series of widely spaced arpeggiated chords. A

---

[11] Schott, Hansen, and Peters all publish both large piano works of César Franck.

chain of these questions and answers, each growing more intense, leads to a *poco allegro* section, a transitional passage to the *Fugue*. The fugue subject in *b* minor enters piecemeal several times before it is finally stated completely. The fugal theme itself is very chromatic, in a descending direction. Exposition of the fugue in four voices is exactly what one would expect from Franck's classic approach.

A short digression follows, then three successive statements in major and a short episode in which the theme is inverted. From here a triplet motive in *f-sharp* minor becomes important, an undulating motive above which rises the theme—sometimes only its beginning measures, at other times in motivic shape, and sometimes complete. A great crescendo occurs when the theme returns in octaves. From nowhere come a series of modulating arpeggios, recalling the *Prelude,* and then the *Choral* theme appears once again. Finally the music swells to a climax. The *Fugue* subject is heard underneath and simultaneous with the *Choral* theme; it makes one last entrance; and the work closes in a carillon-like burst of jubilation.

Franck's *Prelude, Aria and Final* has never been as popular as his *Prelude, Choral and Fugue.* Although both are constructed on a monumental scale, the *Prelude, Aria and Final* falls short in genuinely inspired emotions. This expansive triptych displays the composer more as a classicist, an exponent of sound workmanship and musicianly logic, and it somewhat resembles the sonatas Beethoven wrote during his last and most expressive period.

Franck's *Prelude,* in a free ternary form, sets forth a unique scheme of modulations that lends an attractive tonal instability to this first movement. Its basic theme is a magnificent phrase of forty-two measures, a melodic line both religious and majestic. The *Aria,* the center movement, is actually a theme subjected to variation treatment. Different thematic elements reechoing in the bass line surround the resulting variations with a mystical air. The concluding coda helps to resolve some of the tumultuous sentiments in this movement, then assumes further significance in the *Final,* written in sonata-allegro form. Two themes, one mournful and the other heroically triumphant, contend with each other in this last movement, ultimately giving way to the closing serene atmosphere.

When Franck began teaching at the Paris Conservatory, his ostensible duty was to conduct a course in organ; however, his organ class soon developed into a composition course from which he produced a number of extremely talented students. His original student group included Arthur Coquard, Henri Duparc, and Alexis de Castillon; among the later students who came to benefit from his vast experience were Vincent d'Indy, Augusta Holmès, Ernest Chausson, Guy Ropartz, and Charles Bordes.

VINCENT D'INDY

Franck's most celebrated and talented student, **Vincent d'Indy** (1851–1931), was born in Paris of a *cévenole* family. One of the highly respected professors and music scholars of his day, in 1896 he established—with Bordes and Alexandre Guilmant—the *Schola Cantorum*, an institution dedicated to the broad principles expounded by Franck, whose teaching in turn had been based upon the tradition established by the German composers, principally Bach and Beethoven. Franck derived his own musical doctrine from studying the Germans; he taught the art of thematic development and the large variation, and he advocated a preconceived tonal plan accompanied by an attempt to unify the various sections within one composition.

As chief defender of Franck's artistic standards, d'Indy was deeply serious about musical composition as well as being sensitively aware of the dignity in tonal art. He preserved Franck's ideals, incorporating them into his own works, but his music cannot compete with that of his master. This may be caused by the different attitudes the two men had in respect to form. For Franck the idea of form, particularly cyclic form, existed as a means to an end; that is, as a framework into which he fitted his original, imaginative tonal creations. For d'Indy all ideas of form, particularly those derived from Franck, became a creed. Such preoccupation with form and formalistic procedure accounts for d'Indy's severe, sometimes dogmatic writing. Still, his piano works are not in the Saint-Saëns category—d'Indy was capable of moments of great beauty, dramatically sweeping melodies, and unusual harmonic passages.

D'Indy wrote quite a lot of piano music: *Poème des Montagnes Opus 15; Helvetia Opus 17; Schumanniana Opus 30; Tableaux de Voyage Opus 33; Sonata Opus 63; Thème varié, Fugue et Chanson Opus 85; Fantasie sur un Vieil Air de Ronde Française Opus 99*, among others.[12] Space permits only a brief discussion of his representative works.

The composer himself described his first large work, *Poème des Montagnes* (Poem of the Mountains, 1881), as a symphonic poem for piano. Inspired by d'Indy's betrothal and subsequent marriage, the *Poème* is a subjective suite of quasi-programmatic impressions. Its three large sections are each subdivided so that the ensemble really totals ten pieces or *tableaux*, all unified by the "theme of the beloved" that dominates throughout. This work, constructed upon Franckian principles, deftly portrays the musical

---

[12] The compositions of d'Indy are scattered among several French publishers. A. Leduc publishes the *Tableaux de Voyage*, the *Sonata* is issued by Durand, the *Thème varié, Fugue et Chanson* by Salabert.

impressions of a talented composer: *Chant des Bruyères* (Song of the Heath) brings to mind the tranquillity in solitude and nature; *Brouillard* (Fog) contains a clever reference to Weber's *Freischütz;* and *Amour* (Love) is an ample, lyrical outpouring of nostalgia.

A voyage to Switzerland provided the impulse for writing *Helvetia* (1882), a set of three waltzes with the subtitles *Aarau, Schinznach,* and *Laufenburg.* Although they are constructed on rather conventional lines, these waltzes possess a grace and elegance inspired by nature and created by a sensitive, skillful musician.

Prompted by d'Indy's visit to Bayreuth and the Black Forest in Germany, the *Tableaux de Voyage* (Travel Pictures, 1889) show dexterity with formal matters more than those concerning sensitivity, emotion, and subjective inspiration. The descriptive pieces in this collection are uneven: some are just uninteresting, like the *Rêve* (Dream) with its obvious artificiality; others are impressively ingenious, such as the *Abbaye de Beuron,* which contains an echo of the musical notes formed by the letters BACH (Bb-A-C-Bb); finally, several are genuine mood pictures—*Lac vert* (Green Lake), *Pâturage* (Pasture), and *Halte au Soir* (Evening Rest). Performed as a whole, *Tableaux de Voyage* tends to be monotonous. There simply is not sufficient variety of texture and color to sustain interest throughout this rather lengthy work.

D'Indy amplified his concept of cyclic treatment until it reached its finest development in two later works: *Sonata* and *Thème varié, Fugue et Chanson.* Of course, the effectiveness of cyclic construction is contingent on the composer handling it. César Franck unified his *Prelude, Choral and Fugue* by means of sound melodic and harmonic frameworks that are also wonderfully expressive and beautiful. D'Indy's *Sonata,* contrarily, gives the impression of strained tonal architecture seeking unity for its own sake. Yet this sonata is a rewarding experience for those who will take the trouble to assimilate its complexities. Such a prodigious, noble poem could come only from a highly intellectual mind. D'Indy himself stated in his *Traité de Composition* (Essay on Composition) that the sonata is based on three generator themes, the first one dominating the whole work. An imposing introduction exposing the three themes is followed by four expanded variations of the first choral-like theme. The second movement, *Scherzo,* is based on the second theme of the introduction, and it is the sonata's most spontaneous section, abounding in unique rhythmic combinations. The third movement, written in sonata-allegro form, unites the three themes in a finale that is overburdened with complexities.

There is little opportunity today to hear the *Thème varié, Fugue et Chanson,* one of d'Indy's last piano works. This is unfortunate; although it is not a dazzling virtuoso piece, it has an attractive display of variation

form. The fugue and chanson succeeding the variations are only further
extensions of the initial theme which had already been varied.

DÉODAT DE SÉVÉRAC

Many other French composers of this period wrote piano music, but
on the whole they did not devote a great deal of time to keyboard composition. **Déodat de Sévérac** (1873–1921), one of Vincent d'Indy's pupils, was
greatly influenced by his early environment in his native Languedoc. Many
of his pages reflect the colorful image of this area in southern France, as
well as his own spontaneous original nature. He wrote several suites or
collections of short piano pieces: *Le Chant de la Terre* (Song of the Earth,
1900) includes seven pieces in the spirit of d'Indy's *Poème des Montagnes;*
a poetical freshness hangs over the collection titled *En Languedoc* (1904),
an effective, pianistic series of colorful miniatures; and the suite *Cerdaña*
(1910) merges French and Spanish elements in a blend of mysticism,
rhythm, and Gallic realism and clarity.[13]

GABRIEL FAURÉ

One of France's most beloved composers—and one very much misunder-
stood outside of France—is **Gabriel Fauré** (1845–1924). To his countrymen
Fauré is a classicist, a Frenchman whose music maintains the ideals of
Rameau. He cared little about creating new expressive modes or technical
devices; he was content to accept contemporary aesthetics, to regard himself as the logical product of a long-established tradition.

In a strictly French setting Fauré was indeed a classicist if the criterion
is balance of content and form, for his music maintains polarity between
melody and bass with surprising consistency. His classic roots grew from
his early student years at the *École Niedermeyer* where he received strong
doses of Bach, a treatment he accepted with apparent relish. Under Saint-
Saëns' teaching at the *École,* he learned the essentially French precepts of
clarity and unity, using them to build his own works and augmenting them
with his predominantly Romantic spirit.

In his piano music the harmony is often conceived in a linear manner,
with chords spread out in arpeggio fashion (Ex. 2). In other instances,
particularly in the later works, strict economy of notes results in a simple,
sometimes austere chordal structure (Ex. 3).

[13] Most of Sévérac's music is published by Salabert.

Ex. 2.   Fauré: *Impromptu No. 3, Op. 34*

Ex. 3.   Fauré: *Nocturne No. 5, Op. 37*

One outstanding feature in Fauré's piano works is the constant modulation that adds a volatile, fluid character to his music. Sometimes using modulation by common tones, sometimes by enharmonic means, he nevertheless always preserves tonal unity with skill and logic. Regardless of how it is presented, his harmony is immensely varied and usually contributes to the interest of any given work. He uses either standard major and minor tonalities or else bases his harmonies on modal scales.

There are other technicalities with Fauré—use of a series of seventh chords, suspensions, extreme keys, contrasting binary and ternary rhythms —but the first impression of his music is that it defies analysis. For lack of a better word, this inexplicable quality must be called charm. Swiftly moving modulations, subtle chromaticisms, and the easy flowing grace of the melodic line all contribute to this aristocratic music that is the essence of French *sensibilité*.

His works for piano solo include *Romances sans Paroles, Impromptus, Nocturnes, Barcarolles, Préludes, Variations,* and others.[14] The earlier works, like *Romances sans Paroles,* emanate from Chopin and are not very original. The five *Impromptus* give a better picture of his style in spite of the fact that they must be classed as refined salon pieces.

The *Barcarolles* and *Nocturnes* are his most important collections, and

[14] Hamelle and Durand, both of Paris, offer between them practically all of Fauré's piano music. Some of it also appears in other editions.

in these the later, mature compositions show his best pianistic art. When he decided upon the *Barcarolle*, Fauré chose a form or rather a type that had hitherto received scant attention: a music reflecting the rhythm of waves, of fugitive landscapes, of revery and of atmosphere. Of the thirteen *Barcarolles*, some are consistently lyrical, introspective, and calm; others are exuberant, frank, and outgoing. One of the finest examples is *Opus 66, No. 5, in F-sharp Minor*. The thirteen *Nocturnes* constitute his finest single group of piano pieces. His best writing went into the profound musical substance of this collection. Although earlier compositions dwell upon romantic ideas and tender nostalgia, the later *Nocturnes* are brooding, tragic poems dedicated to loneliness and despair.

All nine piano pieces in the *Préludes Opus 103* are difficult to comprehend. Their musical fabric is so personal, so bound up with intense meditation, that the content is revealed only after patient concentration on the part of both performer and listener.

A final word must be said concerning the *Thème et Variations Opus 73*, one of the most outstanding nineteenth-century works in variation form. The theme, in *c*-sharp minor, has the same nobility as Schumann's theme in *Études symphoniques*. Fauré treats his theme with increasing freedom as the variations progress; the first few variations use the thematic line as a basis, but the later variations depend only upon motives derived from the theme for their constructive elements. The composer utilized his whole pianistic palette in these variations, subtly demonstrating every aspect of his style with masterful technique.

PAUL DUKAS

Paul Dukas (1865–1935), one of the most influential musicians at the turn of the nineteenth century, was a music critic and distinguished teacher as well as a composer much admired by his contemporaries. As a composer he was partly self-taught. He used a logician's approach to music, building on a vast scale; but he softened this intellectualism with a disciplined sensitivity, a virile conception of rhythm, and a feeling for color. Dukas was instrumental in molding the styles of many twentieth-century composers.

The two keyboard works for which Dukas is remembered are the *Sonata in E-flat Minor* (1900) and the *Variations, Interlude and Finale on a Theme of Rameau* (1903).[15] The solid construction throughout the monumental sonata is unfortunately also the cause of its weakness, for the general impression is that the music is too heavy. There is obvious overdevelopment

---

[15] Durand publishes both large works of Dukas.

and, besides, this grandiose work borrows too much from Beethoven and Franck.

The first movement, *Modérément vif*, is in sonata-allegro form. It has two chief themes, one an agitated melody in minor mode and the other an appeasing theme in major mode. Also in sonata-allegro form, the second movement, *Calme, un peu lent*, has a contemplative, spiritual quality like that in certain Beethoven string quartets. The most personal movement, *Scherzo*, is a strident piece with a chromatic fughetta for the Trio. Dramatic recitative pervades the fourth movement, in which three principal themes are preceded by a chorale that reappears in the development section.

Dukas' second large work, written in 1903, is remarkable. The theme —based on the minuet *Le Lardon*—is extracted from Rameau's second book of harpsichord pieces; but in Dukas' eleven variations the theme is heard only in fragmentary form, as though it were a pretext for some rather effective writing. The *Interlude* gives the impression of an improvisation, while the *Finale* is really a twelfth variation ending with a transformed statement of the original minuet.

ALBERT ROUSSEL

One of Dukas' contemporaries, **Albert Roussel** (1869–1937) studied at the *Schola Cantorum* and later taught there. From his teacher Vincent d'Indy he learned the essentials for a good technique, which he then developed in a personal manner as he had very definite ideas concerning the aesthetics of composition. "What is by common consent called musical inspiration is, if I am not mistaken, the artist's faculty of conceiving the clearly expressed ideas that should be admirable both for quality and for copiousness. It presupposes the perfect function of a musically organized, sensitive, and imaginative brain, and the possession of a technique that enables the composer to solve the problems that will necessarily confront him."[16]

In point of time Roussel stands at the crossroads of the most diverse influences in French music: Franckism, Impressionism, and contemporary practices. As a tonal poet who felt close to all nature, he was attracted to Impressionism and the picturesque; but being a musical craftsman, his sense of logic and unity enabled him to mold these Impressionistic elements into a disciplined, solid framework. He sometimes indulges in long developments, but his themes have a distinctive freshness and he uses dissonance as his conscience dictates.

[16] "Inspiration," opinion of Albert Roussel, *The Chesterian*, January–February, 1928.

Roussel's first major piano work is a *Suite Opus 5* called *Rustiques* (1904–1906). Development and rhythm play the leading roles in this very personal music. In the first piece *La Danse au Bord de l'Eau* (Dance by the Water's Edge), a primary idea is expressed in 5/8 meter and accompaniment figures in triplets combine to fill the atmosphere with mystery and charm. His preoccupation with the picturesque comes forth in the second movement, *Promenade sentimentale en Forêt* (Sentimental Walk in the Forest); the music relates the noises in the forest, the cuckoo's song, and other sensations, all exquisitely delineated. In the dance movement *Retour de Fête* (Return from the Festival), terminating the suite, polytonality, intricate rhythms, and dissonance are used with imagination.

The *Suite in F-sharp Major Opus 14* was written during the years 1909–1910, and its four movements disclose a sense of form and construction. It is too bad that the whole work is seldom played for it is an excellent one of its kind. The somber spirit in the *Prélude* contrasts with the following *Sicilienne* with its graceful contours; the *Bourrée* adheres to the classic dance form, while the brusk, virile *Ronde* makes a perfect conclusion for the suite.

Roussel's last representative piano work is a two-movement (each movement subdivided) *Sonatine* from 1912. In the first movement's initial section *Modéré* he uses elements of sonata form; in the scherzo *Vif et très léger* he exposes a principal theme that could be interpreted as a sea chanty. The second movement *Modéré* is preceded by a section titled *Très lent*, in which Roussel the realist recreates an atmosphere recalling the Breton *pardons.*[17]

With Dukas and Roussel, French music almost imperceptibly reaches the path of contemporary music. These two men were extremely adroit in fusing the techniques of the past with the devices of their own time, thus creating a musical framework that pointed to the future with understanding and courage.

BIBLIOGRAPHY

Andriessen, Hendrik. *César Franck* (translated by Doyle-Davidson). Stockholm: The Continental Book Co., n.d.

[17] The *Suite Opus 14* and *Sonatine Opus 16* are published by Salabert. Durand lists the *Rustiques Opus 5.*

Cooper, Martin. *French Music from the Death of Berlioz to the Death of Fauré*. London: Oxford University Press, 1951.

Demuth, Norman. *Albert Roussel*. London: United Music Publishers, Ltd., n.d.

D'Indy, Vincent. *César Franck* (translated by R. Newmart). London: John Lane, The Bodley Head, 1910. Dover reprint

Favre, Georges. *La Musique Française de Piano avant 1830*. Paris: Didier, 1953.

Reeser, Eduard. *De Klaviersonate met Vioolbegeleiding in het parijsche Muziekleven ten Tijde van Mozart*. Rotterdam: W. L. & J. Brusse, 1939.

Saint-Saëns, Camille. *Musical Memories* (translated by E. G. Rich). Boston: Small, Maynard & Co., 1919.

Servières, Georges. *Gabriel Fauré*. Paris: Laurens, 1930.

24

EARLY AMERICAN
PIANO
MUSIC

One has only to read Gilbert Chase's excellent book[1] to become aware of America's colorful musical heritage, unique among all countries. However, it must be pointed out that vocal music predominated during the early period and that our forefathers, when they did turn to piano music, seemed perfectly content with imports from Europe. Therefore, actual keyboard composition in the United States has come at sporadic intervals, particularly before the twentieth century; and it must be admitted that as yet there has not been a great American composer of piano music. So far we have not produced a Chopin or Schumann, a Scriabin or Szymanowski.

EARLY KEYBOARD COMPOSERS

Musical circles flourished in eighteenth-century America, even though most of the music was supplied by foreign-born musicians. **Charles Theodore Pachelbel** (1690–1750), a composer-organist like his famous father Johann Pachelbel, played the organ at Trinity Church in Newport, Rhode Island, and gave many concerts.

Little is known about **James Bremner** (*d.* 1780), another composer of the colonial era. In 1763 he arrived in Philadelphia, opened a school and taught harpsichord, flute, and guitar. He is mentioned as being the organist at Christ Church in 1767. Bremner's chief claim to fame was as teacher of Francis Hopkinson, the American author who was one of the signers of the Declaration of Independence and also a skilled amateur musician. The little pieces from Bremner's pen—*Lady Coventry's Minuet, Lesson, March, Overture,* and *Trumpet Air*[2]—are slight essays in themselves. It is remarkable to find works of even this depth when one considers that American colonists had more vital things to do than write music.

---

[1] Gilbert Chase, *America's Music* (New York: McGraw-Hill Book Company, Inc., 1955).
[2] The works by Bremner mentioned in the text are found in a manuscript in the Hopkinson Collection, University of Pennsylvania Library.

A near contemporary of Bremner was **Valentino Nicolai,** a composer and pianist who probably spent his last years in London, where he died around 1798. Several sonatas for piano or harpsichord by Nicolai are extant.[3]

John Christopher Moller (*d.* 1803) was an all-around musician: composer, organist, pianist, publisher, and glass-harmonica virtuoso. After participating in a number of New York concerts, he came to Philadelphia as teacher and organist at Zion Church, and from 1792 he served as co-director of the city concerts. In 1795 he returned to New York City. Moller's existing works show a pleasing diversity: theme and variations, rondo, sonata—all are represented, and each shows a certain skill and talent.[4]

One of the really distinguished musicians of this early colonial period was **Alexander Reinagle** (1756–1809), who was born in Portsmouth, England. As a youth he fell under the spell (both musically and personally) of Johann Christian Bach and also became acquainted with Emanuel Bach in Hamburg. After 1786 he lived in America, making his home in Philadelphia; and we can assume that he won a solid reputation there, for George Washington engaged him as music teacher to his stepdaughter Nellie Custis. In 1793 Reinagle co-founded the New Theatre, which sponsored operatic productions.

Of the Reinagle piano music composed in the United States, four sonatas now exist in manuscript at the Library of Congress, Washington, D.C. Just one has been published and that only in a truncated version.[5] Three of the four sonatas have three movements in a fast-slow-fast sequence; the first sonata lacks a slow movement. All four, however, attest to Reinagle's respect for the music of Emanuel Bach; and they all show a trace of Joseph Haydn as well. "They reveal a fresh and lively invention, resourcefulness in development and figuration, a fine feeling for structure and proportion and a capacity for sustained lyrical expression in the Adagios."[6]

Another English-born Philadelphian was **Raynor Taylor** (1747–1825). Early in his career he was organist and teacher in Essex, also a director and composer to Sadler's Wells Theatre. In 1792 he was in Baltimore, Maryland, but soon moved to Philadelphia. Here, like Reinagle, he became one of the most prominent musicians in the early nineteenth century. He was organist at St. Peter's Church and was an important founder of the Musical Fund Society. Unfortunately his keyboard music is small in quan-

---

[3] The University of Pennsylvania Library possesses a copy of Nicolai's *Sonatas Op. XI;* the *Sonatas Op. III* are available at the Library of Congress, Washington, D.C.

[4] The Library of Congress has several of Moller's piano pieces: *Favorite La Chasse; Meddley with the most favorite Airs and Variations; Rondo.* A *Sonata VIII* is at the American Antiquarian Society, Worcester, Mass.

[5] *A Program of Early American Piano Music,* edited and arranged by John Tasker Howard, is published by J. Fischer. Contains music by Reinagle, Bremner, Taylor, Hewitt, Carr, and Moller.

[6] Gilbert Chase, *America's Music* (New York: McGraw-Hill Book Co., Inc., 1955), p. 116.

tity, though of a definite musicality. This latter is true of both his *Rondo* and *Sonata*.[7]

James Hewitt (1770–1827), member of a prominent English musical family, enjoyed a respectable reputation as violinist, composer, and publisher. He arrived in New York in 1792 and quickly achieved an excellent social standing as well as a musical reputation; he managed subscription concerts, performed as a violin virtuoso, and served as leader of the Old American Company orchestra. As a piano composer he was original, to say the least. One of his so-called sonatas is called *The 4th of July—A Grand Military Sonata for the Pianoforte* and ends with a paraphrase of "Hail Columbia." Another is titled *Battle of Trenton,* an intriguing attempt at describing the impossible. It contains the following subdivisions:

> Introduction—The Army in Motion—General Orders—Acclamation of the Americans—Drums Beat to Arms.
>
> Washington's March—The American Army Crossing the Delaware—Sound a Charge.
>
> Attack—Cannons—Bomb. Defeat of the Hessians—Flight of the Hessians—Begging Quarter—The Fight Renewed—General Confusion—The Hessians Surrender Themselves Prisoners of War—Articles of Capitulation Signed—Grief of Americans for the Loss of Their Comrades Killed in the Engagement.
>
> Yankee Doodle—Drums and Fifes—Quick Step for the Band—Trumpets of Victory—General Rejoicing.[8]

Such a seemingly unmusical conglomeration appears amusing and naïve in our twentieth century, but we must remember that other composers had also depicted battle scenes at the keyboard; for instance Kuhnau's *Battle between David and Goliath* and François Couperin's *La Triumphante.*

The final member of this early group is the English-born **Benjamin Carr** (*ca.* 1768–1831), who worked and died in Philadelphia. A musician thoroughly trained in the C. P. E. Bach school, Carr enjoyed a multifaceted career as pianist, organist, composer, publisher, and concert manager. Carr, along with Raynor Taylor, was a founder (1820) of the Musical Fund Society of Philadelphia. His musical compositions—to judge by the extant sonatas and divertimentos—show a better than average talent. The dominant trait of this talent is seen in the gracefully fashioned melodic lines and pleasant harmonic combinations.[9]

---

[7] A *Rondo for the Piano Forte* by Taylor may be found at the Library of Congress. The Sibley Music Library, Eastman School of Music, Rochester, N.Y., owns a *Sonata.*

[8] University of Pennsylvania Library has a copy of Hewitt's sonata.

[9] Copies of the six sonatas and three divertimentos are found at the Library of Congress.

LOUIS GOTTSCHALK

For the next keyboard composer of any stature we must skip almost half a century to **Louis Moreau Gottschalk** (1829–1869). Unfortunately for Mr. Gottschalk, until recently his only music in evidence was a sugary salon piece called *The Last Hope,* which for some unfathomable reason still lingers on; its principal theme appears as a hymn tune in some hymnals.

Gottschalk was born in New Orleans of English-Jewish and titled French-Creole parentage. In 1842 he began his advanced music studies in France, made a successful piano debut, and eventually concertized in France, Switzerland, and Spain. Then he spent several years giving recitals in the United States. His last seven years were consumed by restless trips throughout America, Canada, Central America, and South America, where he died in Rio de Janeiro.

Gottschalk wrote well over a hundred piano compositions in a highly eclectic, composite style, which seems natural in the light of his cosmopolitan existence. Although his European training doubtlessly bore fruit in his music, the exotic ambiance and excitement of New Orleans were directly responsible for the authenticity and success of pieces like *La Bamboula, Ojos criollos,* and *Le Banjo.* He was especially adept at fitting basically Creole and Caribbean music types into nineteenth-century virtuoso style. *La Bamboula,* one of his most popular piano pieces (at that time), introduces elements from the habanera and cakewalk, yet at the same time it has a certain finesse that can be traced only to France. From 1856 to 1862 Gottschalk traveled the Caribbean, gathering inspiration for some of his most effective music: *Souvenir de Puerto Rico, La Gallina (Danse cubaine),* and others.

To return to *The Last Hope Opus 16,* which Gottschalk in good faith subtitled *Méditation religieuse,* this was just one of countless salon pieces that he composed for a not overly discriminating public. A catalogue of his works lists titles like *The Water Sprite, Solitude, The Maiden's Blush, Love and Chivalry,* some of which are quite easy. Among his interesting and amusing virtuoso pieces, *L'Union* is a distinct paraphrase of three American patriotic airs: "The Star-Spangled Banner," "Hail Columbia," and "Yankee Doodle."[10]

EDWARD MACDOWELL

America's outstanding nineteenth-century musical figure is **Edward MacDowell** (1861–1908), the first American composer to gain international

---

[10] Theodore Presser publishes an attractive album of Gottschalk piano music and there is also a *Gottschalk Album* of three pieces issued by Augener. The *Souvenir de Puerto Rico* is listed by Music Press.

recognition. "When Edward MacDowell appeared on the scene, many Americans felt that here at last was 'the great American composer' awaited by the nation. But MacDowell was not a great composer. At his best he was a gifted miniaturist with an individual manner. Creatively, he looked toward the past, not toward the future. He does not mark the beginning of a new epoch in American music, but the closing of a fading era, the *fin de siècle* decline of the genteel tradition which had dominated American art since the days of Hopkinson and Hewitt."[11]

With this statement, Gilbert Chase accurately evaluates MacDowell, whose art was based on German Romanticism stemming from his long years in Germany. As a gifted miniaturist, it is precisely in the short, epigrammatic tone portraits that his creative talents are most fully expressed. His place in time, succinctly stated by Mr. Chase, accounts for his decreasing popularity; he does not belong with the great Romantics, Schumann and Brahms, but neither can he be regarded as a precursor of twentieth-century music. Few pianists indeed would presume to program a MacDowell sonata or suite.

MacDowell's piano music is rather substantial. First of all, a brief look at the suites: *Woodland Sketches* (1896), *New England Idyls* (1902), *Sea Pieces* (1898), and *Fireside Tales* (1902). As so often happens, the pieces within each collection vary in quality. In MacDowell's case it appears that his most popular set also has the best quality; the ten *Woodland Sketches* not only reveal his typical style, but some are also quite charming. If it were possible to go back to a first hearing of "To a Wild Rose," the listener might regain his joy in the simplicity and directness of this little sketch. Isolated pieces from his other suites are effective even now if one avoids the preconception that MacDowell "is an old-fashioned and outdated composer" —for example, *To the Sea* and *Song* (from the *Sea Pieces*) and *Brer Rabbit* (from the six *Fireside Tales*).

The *Twelve Études Opus 39* (1890)—short, characteristic pieces theoretically written for various technical purposes—not only accomplish their objective, but some in the set are as effective as the composer's solo pieces.

MacDowell's sonatas do not measure up to the shorter works. Quasi-programmatic, they include *No. 1, Opus 45 in G Minor* (*Tragica*); *No. 2, Opus 50 in G Minor* (*Eroica*); the "*Norse*" *Sonata Opus 57* and the "*Keltic*" *Sonata Opus 59*. The musical texture is too slight for sonata fabric and the continuity wavers although here and there are lovely moments.[12]

---

[11] Gilbert Chase, *America's Music* (McGraw-Hill Book Co., Inc., 1955), p. 364.
[12] MacDowell's music is easy to come by. Boston Music Co. puts out the *Woodland Sketches* and the *Études Opus 39*. *Sea Pieces* and three of the four sonatas, also *New England Idyls,* are published by Kalmus. Schmidt published the *Six Fireside Tales*. G. Schirmer now offers the *Sea Pieces, New England Idyls,* and *Woodland Sketches.*

Nothing further can be said about American piano music of the late nineteenth century and the early twentieth century. The only keyboard music from that time is purely salon music. It was the era of composers like **Arthur Foote** (1853–1937) and **Ethelbert Nevin** (1862–1901), author of such saccharine works as *Narcissus*. There were other keyboard composers, like **George Chadwick** (1854–1931), **Edgar Stillman Kelley** (1857–1944), **Horatio Parker** (1863–1919), and **Mrs. H. H. A. Beach** (1867–1944)—composers whose music enjoyed a certain initial popularity and then faded away. The United States was sadly in need of a musical renaissance; unfortunately, it made a belated appearance several decades after the beginning of the twentieth century (see Chapter 33).

BIBLIOGRAPHY

Chase, Gilbert. *America's Music.* New York: McGraw-Hill Book Co., Inc., 1955.

Doyle, John G. *The Piano Music of Louis Moreau Gottschalk.* Dissertation. New York University, 1960.

Howard, John Tasker. "The Hewitt Family in American Music." *Musical Quarterly,* January, 1931.

Howard, John Tasker. *Our American Music,* Third Edition. New York: Thomas Y. Crowell Co., 1946.

Porte, John F. *Edward MacDowell.* London: Kegan Paul, Trench, Trubner & Co., Ltd., 1922.

Sonneck, Oscar George Theodore. *A Bibliography of Early Secular American Music,* revised and enlarged by Wm. T. Upton. Washington, D.C.: The Library of Congress, 1945.

25

THE

GOLDEN AGE

OF SPANISH PIANO MUSIC

Spanish piano music of the early nineteenth century is not graced by the presence of keyboard masterworks, and in general all Spanish music of that period shows slight progress until late in the century. Italian music had invaded the Iberian peninsula, a factor that played a large part in stifling Spanish nationalism for many decades.

Evidently keyboard composers working in the first half of the century were still satisfied with the one-movement sonata, partially preserving that form inherited from Scarlatti and his Spanish contemporaries. One such composer, **Mateo Ferrer** (1788–1864), was organist at Barcelona cathedral. He was a skilled contrapuntist, but he clung to the old one-movement form; however, a sign of his moving with the times is the fact that his *Sonata in D Major*[1] is constructed in competent sonata-allegro form even though it has only one movement. Despite a deliberate use of a more advanced formalistic procedure, the sonata is anachronistic, for its style admits to the composer's admiration for Haydn and the young Beethoven.

Pedro Albéniz (1795–1855) helped to promote a better approach to piano composition; at least, he awakened interest in piano music. A son of Mateo Albéniz (see Chapter 8), Pedro studied piano in Paris with the then renowned pianists Kalkbrenner and Herz. Once back in Madrid, he received a professorial appointment at the Conservatory and later became organist at the Royal Chapel. His solo piano works, mostly operatic fantasias and potpourris, show no more originality than those of his keyboard teachers, except for one outstanding collection titled *Método de Piano* (1840), which was instrumental in inaugurating the Spanish school of piano playing.

One of the few first-rate composers at that time, **Juan Crisóstomo de Arriaga y Balzola** (1806–1826) very likely would have developed into a great composer if he had lived longer. His style, basically lined with Mozartean elements, often recalls early-Romantic German composers. His only

---

[1] In *Seize Sonates Anciennes d'Auteurs Espagnols*, ed. Joaquín Nin (Paris: Max Eschig).

published piano music consists of three *Estudios de Caracter* (Character-istic Studies),[2] of which the last two frequently bring Mendelssohn to mind, although the German composer was then too young to have had any influence on the Spaniard.

More prolific but decidedly less talented than Arriaga, **Nicolas Rod-ríguez Ledesma** (1791–1883) published a set of études similar to Czerny's, as well as six sonatas marked for either organ or piano but obviously written in a pianistic idiom.[3] Five of the six sonatas have three movements, con-forming to the general sequence of *Allegro, Andante, Theme and Variations.* All six sonatas are pleasing and unassuming, though at times they lack melodic inventiveness and sound structure. Completely un-Spanish, these sonatas are too often colored with the popular salon-music style of their day.

Juan Bautista Pujol (1835–1898) and **Joaquín Malats** (1872–1912), two minor composers of the late nineteenth century, were both excellent concert pianists and as such played an important role in advancing native Spanish music. Pujol's compositions—his fantasy *Rosas y Perlas* (Roses and Pearls)[4] is a typical example of nineteenth-century salon music—are com-pletely undistinguished. However, to his credit he instituted and main-tained the *Academia Pujol* in Barcelona, where many fine Spanish musicians received their training.

Malats' piano music has slipped into oblivion and doubtlessly will remain there. He is remembered mainly for his superb interpretation of the piano music of Isaac Albéniz (1860–1909). Malats' recitals featuring Isaac Albéniz' complete *Iberia,* a remarkable feat, stimulated public appre-ciation for Albéniz.

As we can see, very little piano music was produced in nineteenth-century Spain. During the last decades of that century and the early part of the twentieth, however, she came into her own with a keyboard renais-sance that resulted in a magnificent repertoire created by four distinguished composers: Isaac Albéniz, Enrique Granados, Manuel de Falla, and Joaquín Turina. Although many basic technical elements of this repertoire origi-nated in foreign lands, the spiritual and inspirational qualities definitely stem from the heart of the Iberian peninsula. These four composers form the nucleus of a Spanish nationalist school that took shape and developed, though at a slightly later date, along with those of Russia, Norway, France, and Bohemia.

The problem of how to free Spain from the influence of Italianism was resolved primarily by **Felipe Pedrell** (1841–1922) and **Federico Olmeda**

---

[2] The *Tres Estudios de Caracter* were published by Dotésio of Bilbao and are long out of print. A copy is preserved at the Bibliothèque Nationale de Paris.

[3] The Madrid Conservatory library possesses an original edition of these sonatas. They have not been reissued.

[4] *Rosas y Perlas* is published by the Union Musical Española.

(1865–1909). Much of the groundwork for Spanish nationalism was laid down by these two trailblazers. Their compositions are seldom played today, yet Spain owes them a great debt. By their efforts in collecting the vast, rich material in Spanish folk music and then by using this material in their own compositions, Pedrell and Olmeda demonstrated to other more gifted Spanish composers that there were tremendous creative possibilities to be found in their own native idiom.

ISAAC ALBÉNIZ

Isaac Albéniz (1860–1909) made the first significant contributions to this repertoire of dazzling, picturesque, and thoroughly refined piano music. As a child prodigy he gave his first concert at age four, followed later by the usual routine of concert tours and studies in Paris, Leipzig, and Madrid. He finally settled in Paris as professor of piano at the *Schola Cantorum*, remaining there until his death in 1909.

His finest and most representative music was composed toward the end of his short life while he lived in Paris in the atmosphere of Ernest Chausson, Gabriel Fauré, Vincent d'Indy, and Paul Dukas; but his association with this French force did not prevent his own music from reflecting the light of his innate Spanish culture. The masterworks of this most Spanish of Spanish composers include the piano compositions *La Vega, Azulejos, Navarra,* and *Iberia*.[5] They clearly reveal the basic characteristics of his art: objectivity and realism.

Albéniz was not a true Romantic in the sense that Chopin and Schumann were Romantics. The Spaniard described more of what he saw than of what he felt. Emotionally he was a more objective composer than his contemporaries in late-nineteenth-century Spain, but like them he received his creative inspirations from the natural beauties in his native country and from the vividly dramatic characteristics of his own people. It was the language and forms that he employed in his writing that set Albéniz apart from his fellow-composers in Spain, for in his music these elements came from a foreign culture, particularly the French music of his period.

La Vega—a step in the transition from early Albéniz works to the mature masterworks contained in *Iberia*—was the first composition in a projected but unfinished suite called *Alhambra*. The title, *La Vega*, refers to the gardens covering the flatlands in the environs of Granada while the music—chromatic and heavily dependent upon contrapuntal figurations— vaguely suggests César Franck. For its total effect and for the demands it

[5] *La Vega, Azulejos,* and *Navarra* are published by the Union Musical Española. The *Iberia* is available in a good edition by E. B. Marks.

makes of the pianist, *La Vega* has been compared with *Islamey*, the famous virtuoso piano piece by the Russian composer Mily Balakirev.

Azulejos (Glazed Tiles) was unfinished when Albéniz died, and Granados completed it. Lamentably, while the Albéniz music is a jewel of oriental coloring, Granados was unable to sustain this refinement in reworking the piece. *Navarra*, also incomplete when Albéniz died, was finished by Déodat de Sévérac. It has a *jota* rhythm but lacks the consistent exuberance ordinarily expected in a *jota*. In spite of this and some unfortunate traces of Sévérac's own style, *Navarra* emerges as a more convincing work than *Azulejos*.

Published in 1906–1909, the suite *Iberia* is Albéniz' masterpiece of pianistic writing. Its twelve pieces—distributed in four volumes—are all based on Spanish scenes and landscapes. Claude Debussy wrote one of the best testimonials to *Iberia*:

> Few works of music equal *El Albaicín* from the third volume of *Iberia*, where one recaptures the atmosphere of those evenings of Spain which exude the odors of flowers and brandy. . . . It is like the muffled sounds of a guitar sighing in the night, with abrupt awakenings, nervous starts. Without exactly using popular themes, this music comes from one who has drunk of them, heard them, up to the point of making them pass into his music so that it is impossible to perceive the line of demarcation.
>
> *Eritaña*, from the fourth volume of *Iberia*, describes the joy of mornings, the propitious encounter of an inn where the wine is cool. An incessantly changing crowd passes by amid gales of laughter punctuated by the tinkles of the tambourine. Never has music attained such diverse, such colored impressions; the eyes close as if dazzled by having seen too many images.
>
> There are many other things in these volumes of *Iberia*, where Albéniz has put the best of himself and carried his scruples of "writing" to exaggeration by this generous need which went to the point of "throwing the music out of the windows."[6]

Iberia exhibits in varying degrees all the characteristics of Albéniz' creative art and pianistic ability. As a result of his "generosity" this music has a richness and density that make it extremely difficult to play. Just the same, it must not be considered as pure transcendental virtuosity, but rather as a set of tone pictures, paintings that reproduce all colors in their just proportions regardless of the technique required. In many sections Albéniz uses formulas that appear to be closely related to those employed by Scarlatti, whose works Albéniz himself often had included on his own concert

---

[6] Claude Debussy, *"Les Concerts,"* in *Société Internationale de Musique* (December 1, 1913), p. 43. English translation by the author.

programs. In addition, Albéniz' personal concept of contrapuntal writing adds to the effect.

Evocación, the first piece in the *Iberia* collection, is one of the easiest from a technical standpoint. Its function is to set the scene, to suggest an atmosphere. *El Puerto,* title of the second piece, refers to the port of Cádiz; it creates a fleeting impression of a brief yet violent encounter. During the course of the music, Albéniz introduces several rhythmic dances indigenous to southern Spain. The first volume of *Iberia* concludes with *Corpus en Sevilla* (Corpus Christi in Seville), for which the Liszt rhapsodies were used as models. The city of Sevilla was for Albéniz synonymous with vitality and a brilliant, exciting happiness. *Corpus en Sevilla,* in turn, is one of the most vivid tonal descriptions achieved by any Spanish composer; and it is also one of the most challenging pieces in the suite.

Volume two begins with *Rondeña* which, as the title indicates, is constructed on the rhythm of the *rondeña*—that is, an alternation of bars of 6/8 and 3/4 meter. The attractiveness of the *Rondeña* lies in the almost hypnotic monotony of the rhythm that vies with the melodic contrasts of the upper registers. *Almería,* a marvel of construction, bears certain characteristics in common with *Rondeña:* both pieces have the alternation of 6/8 and 3/4 meters as a basic rhythm; both employ the same methods to obscure tonalities; and, in both, these tonalities are closely related. Sevilla's gypsy quarter—violent, passionate, and sparkling—is portrayed in *Triana,* the last piece in volume two. Written in free variation form, the work is built around two ideas: the principal element, that of the *paso-doble,* and the secondary one, the *marcha torera.* Albéniz has created fascinating music in this composition by alternating these two themes and progressively transforming and enriching them.

Volume three is the most perplexing. There are many interpretive problems and not all of them can be resolved. The composer recalls another gypsy quarter in *El Albaicín,* this time the gypsy section of Granada. Debussy praised *El Albaicín* for its mournful, quasi-guitar strains and its general atmosphere of "authenticity" achieved by the use of folklike themes. A dance song of Andalusian origin, *El Polo* proves weak when compared with other pieces in the *Iberia* collection. It has an abundance of rhythm but little else.

Lavapiés, the final piece in volume three, is a work of transcendent difficulties. The title is from one of Madrid's oldest sections, so called because of a church there where the foot-washing ritual was performed on Holy Thursday. Albéniz requests that his *Lavapiés* be played freely and joyously. Such happiness is what one would expect of Madrid, the city of the *majos* and *majas,* and Albéniz provides some buoyant, lavish motives to portray this gaiety.

If volume three is difficult and abstruse, then the last volume of the suite is clearly different. In this fourth volume Albéniz offers three varied settings of Andalusian sensitivity. The first piece, *Málaga*, is based on the rhythm of the *malagueña*, a rhythm dominating the piece but not in a pejorative sense. *Jerez*, which follows, is a name identified with the wines for which Spain is famous; this music contains some of the purest, most beautiful passages that Albéniz ever created for the piano. It is a masterpiece of sound, a blend of the most attractive elements of his personal style.

Eritaña makes a fitting climax to this collection of tone poems. It is named for an inn near Sevilla noted for dancing and gaiety, and the music to describe this is a mosaic of color laid on the foundation of a *sevillanas*. The emotional impact of *Eritaña* is beyond description, but it offers a wonderful challenge to the performer and is a fine example of Albéniz when he reached the point of "throwing the music out of the window."

Thus concludes the *opus magnum* of a faithful son of Spain. He recaptured the spirit of his homeland in this variegated collection of chiaroscuro pictures in music. The pieces are neither imitations of Spanish popular music nor are they romantic effusions on a given theme. In the truest sense of the word the *Iberia* of Isaac Albéniz *is* Spain.

ENRIQUE GRANADOS

When compared to Albéniz' turbulent existence, the life of **Enrique Granados** (1867–1916) seems calm, full of serious work and successful concert tours. Born in Catalonia to a Cuban father and a Galician mother, he completed his early studies in Spain, then went to Paris in 1887 as a private piano student with Charles Bériot. His first piano recital in Barcelona in 1890 was followed by others in Spain and France, both as soloist and accompanist, and in 1900 he returned to Barcelona where he founded the *Sociedad de Conciertos Clásicos*.

Henri Collet, the French musicologist who died in 1951, has recorded a penetrating, graphic description of the art of Granados:

> No musician less resembles Albéniz, Turina or Falla than Granados, who stands in contrast to his compatriots as does Rousseau to Balzac, as Delacroix to Goya, as Chopin to Mussorgsky, as romanticism to realism.
> Should one attribute the incurable romanticism of Granados to his heritage, Cuban by his father, Galician by his mother? To this curious mixture of Celtic nostalgia and voluptuous Creole unconcern? The truth is that in the Spanish musical renaissance of the twentieth century, Granados gives the appearance of a

belated nineteenth-century composer despite the new ideas in the *Goyescas*, to which he owes his fame.[7]

Granados has been criticized for being less "Spanish" in his music than Albéniz or Turina. Perhaps it is so that his works do not sound as "authentic" as those of his several contemporaries, but his subjective approach carried him beyond the limitations of actual Hispanicism. With Granados, Hispanicism served only as a basic outline, a means to an end; and along the road to his goal he composed some of the sublimest piano music ever written in the Spanish peninsula.

The technical problems found in Granados' works are not as complicated as those in Albéniz' music. Granados favored passages in thirds and contrapuntal figurations, and at times he ignored the traditional practices of keyboard notation; but all these must be recognized as offshoots of his tonal language, as necessary components of his stylistic dictates.

Four dance collections have added stature to Granados' reputation: the *Danzas Españolas* (Spanish Dances) published as a complete set in 1900. In these twelve dances the native atmosphere is far less Spanish than that revealed in similar pieces by Albéniz and Turina, but it must be emphasized that Granados wrote his *Danzas Españolas* to please the listener. They have pleased, and they still please. ·They exhibit refined elegance and noble character rather than imitate folk song.

In a letter to Joaquín Malats, Granados wrote: "I have composed a collection of 'goyescas' of great sweep and difficulty. They are the reward of my efforts to arrive. They say I have arrived. I fell in love with Goya's psychology, with his palette. With him and with the Duchess of Alba; with his lady *maja,* with his models, with his quarrels, his loves and his flirtations."

Granados worked for a long time on the *Goyescas,* jotting down ideas and sketches. Their definitive form began to take shape in his mind in 1909, and the six pieces, conceived as a suite, appeared in 1911. This suite is his own masterpiece and a masterpiece in the history of Spanish music. Its profound beauty can match anything written by Isaac Albéniz. One of his last works, its scenes—inspired by the paintings of Francisco Goya, the eighteenth-century Spanish artist whom Granados passionately admired —recapture in music the singularly dramatic atmosphere of Spain at the time of Carlos III and Carlos IV. Like the painter, the composer has brought to life the essence of both the aristocratic and the popular elements that distinguished the age of Goya.

The *Goyescas* has the subtitle *Los Majos Enamorados* from the Spanish

---

[7] Henri Collett, *L'Essor de la Musique Espagnole au XXe Siècle* (Paris: Max Eschig, 1929), pp. 82–83. Reprinted in 1950. English translation by the author.

words *enamorados* (in love) and *majos* (the name given to the gay members of Madrid's lower classes in Goya's time). With their female counterparts, the *majas*, the *majos* conducted themselves in a highly dramatic, swaggering, and exaggerated fashion.

This suite has been criticized for its lack of form, but if this is so, then by the same token Debussy's music lacks form. It must be admitted that the suite gives the impression of improvisations, but these are grand improvisations—coherent and unified. The music is typically nineteenth-century Romantic, vaguely reminiscent of Chopin, Liszt, and Schumann; but the essential spirit in this splendid work is completely and intensely Enrique Granados.

Los Requiebros (Gallant Compliments), first in the suite, is constructed on two fundamental motives adapted from an Andalusian song called *Tirana del Trípili*. In the love duet *Coloquio en la Reja* (Conversation through the Grilled Window) Granados calls for all the bass notes to imitate the guitar. There are two sections: the first stating the declaration of love; the second, the *copla* or song of the *maja*. The third piece, *El Fandango de Candil* (Fandango by Lamplight), is based on the *fandango*, a Spanish dance form strongly emphasizing rhythm. This particular *fandango* is fairly slow in tempo, but it sustains a driving rhythmic character throughout.

Quejas o la Maja y el Ruiseñor (The Maid and the Nightingale) is one of Granados' happiest inspirations, one of the loveliest pieces in piano literature (Ex. 1). It describes a dialogue between a maid, or *maja*, and a

Ex. 1.   E. Granados: *Goyescas: La Maja y el Ruiseñor*

nightingale, the latter appearing in the form of a cadenza at the end of the piece. Entitled *El Amor y la Muerte* (Love and Death), number five is a profoundly dramatic ballade. The theme of the love duet surges in the first slow passage; then toward the end there is a beautiful long soliloquy on the theme from the previous *maja* and nightingale piece; finally, the music portrays the death of the *majo*.

The concluding piece of the *Goyescas*, *Epílogo*—sometimes called

Serenade of the Specter—is reminiscent of several other dances of death; for example, Saint-Saëns' *Danse Macabre* and Liszt's *Todtentanz*. However, this dance of death comes from Spain so the specter, or death, must play a guitar instead of a fiddle, and all the music abounds in guitarlike imitations. The middle section contains a setting of the *Dies Irae*, a Gregorian chant used in the Roman Catholic burial service. Granados appropriates this theme but skillfully fashions his own musical fabric to accompany it (Ex. 2).

Ex. 2. E. Granados: *Goyescas: Epílogo*

In the concluding portions, the music hints at various themes from the several preceding compositions, the church bell tolls; then the specter, sounding each string of his guitar, disappears. Any further commentary is unnecessary. One must hear the *Goyescas* to appreciate the fact that this music equals many of the masterworks by Schumann, Chopin, or Brahms.[8]

MANUEL DE FALLA

Esteemed as one of the great Spanish composers of all times, **Manuel de Falla** (1876–1946) is the spiritual father of Spanish contemporary music. His mother, herself an excellent pianist, instilled in him his love for music. His family moved to Madrid when he was twenty, and there he studied piano under José Tragó and composition with Felipe Pedrell. In 1907 he realized his dream of a trip to Paris. Although he planned to spend just one week there listening to music and becoming acquainted with the works of his contemporaries, his seven-day visit stretched to a seven-year stay. He met and made friends with Debussy, Ravel, Dukas, and even Albéniz, who came to Paris for a time.

Falla's friendship with Debussy and Ravel could account for the Impressionistic feeling present in some of his compositions. Still, he is only

---

[8] Granados' *Spanish Dances* are published by G. Schirmer, Kalmus, and E. B. Marks. International Music Co. publishes the *Goyescas*.

partly an Impressionist; the weaker elements of Impressionism are missing from his music. Form and melodic line are sharply defined, while the rhythmic vitality is astonishing and attractive. If any one person influenced Falla's style, it was Paul Dukas, whose own music is distinguished by the same craftsmanship and refinement.

Falla took two completed piano pieces and one unfinished piano work with him to Paris. There he finished the incomplete score and wrote another. These four piano works, now known as the *Pièces Espagnoles* (Spanish Pieces), were played for his Parisian friends, who recommended them to the music publishing firm of Durand & Cie. Durand accepted the music and paid Falla three hundred francs, a considerable sum to pay for a musical work at that time.

Although the *Pièces Espagnoles* (1908) do not rank with Falla's most important works, they have the solid construction and meticulous workmanship that distinguish most of his compositions. *Aragonesa,* number one in the set, is a *jota. Cubana,* the second piece, has an unusual rhythmic accentuation produced by alternating passages in 3/4 and 6/8 meter. A kind of languid atmosphere persists throughout, with shifting modulations that add to the indeterminacy.

The third piece, *Montañesa,* subtitled *Landscape,* refers to a portion of Castile lying between Asturias and the Basque country. The music at the beginning is marked *quasi-campani* to imitate gently tinkling cattle bells that are softly echoed later on. By far the most popular of the set, the final *Andaluza* contains a synthesis of wild barbarianism and tender nostalgia. Its resounding initial chords set the scene effectively—Falla stipulates that the entire first section be "very rhythmic and with a savage feeling." By contrast the middle section, marked *doppio più lento,* is a song with typical Andalusian contour: diatonic, and embellished with ornamental flourishes at the phrase endings.

The only other composition that Falla originally intended for solo piano is *Fantasía Bética,* musically one of his most uncompromising works and also the last work that he wrote in a true "Spanish" idiom. It is not subtle nor is it likely to please the average devotee of piano music. The *Fantasía* is difficult, full of harsh dissonances and jarring contrasts, but it reveals a categorical authenticity of spirit and an undeniable image of all that is Andalusia.[9]

In addition to these works for solo piano, Falla made piano arrangements of some of his other compositions; but these arrangements—the *Danza Ritual del Fuego* (Ritual Fire Dance), for instance—are poorly done.

[9] Durand publishes Falla's *Pièces Espagnoles* and J. & W. Chester the *Fantasía Bética.*

JOAQUÍN TURINA

Joaquín Turina (1882–1949) was born in Sevilla, but as a youth he went to Madrid and concentrated on piano studies with José Tragó. Later he went to Paris and enrolled in the *Schola Cantorum,* where he was particularly attracted to the director Vincent d'Indy, a composer whose preference for cyclic treatment of large musical forms is mirrored in Turina's own *Sonata.*

Turina's compatriot Isaac Albéniz, also in Paris at that time, heard a concert devoted to works by the young man from Sevilla. Recognizing his musical potential, Albéniz persuaded Turina to channel his talents toward the enhancement of his Spanish heritage, with the result that many of Turina's compositions met with almost immediate acclaim.

Even though Turina soon abandoned the stylistic ideas he learned at the *Schola,* he always preserved fundamental traces of its technical doctrines. It is this technical sureness that often gives his works—where fantasy, color, and inspiration are less striking than with Albéniz—a solidarity and an equilibrium that Albéniz himself did not always achieve. Like Albéniz, Turina is a realistic, objective artist. To go still further with the Albéniz comparison, Turina—having in similar fashion undergone the influences of d'Indy, Fauré, Debussy, Ravel, and Dukas—writes in a Spanish idiom even though his technical equipment is foreign, predominantly French.

The suite *Sevilla,* composed and published in Paris in 1909, is a series of three extended pieces contributing largely, and with good reason, to their composer's fame. The first, *Sous Les Orangers* (Under the Orange Trees), combines *malagueña* and *habanera* rhythms. *Le Jeudi Saint à Minuit* (Holy Thursday at Midnight), the outstanding piece of the collection, somehow defies description, but more than anything else it is remarkable for its extraordinary imagery of nocturnal vagaries. *La Feria* (Holiday) vividly concludes the suite by means of two contrasting elements, one a frank and joyous *sevillanas,* the other a tango of exquisite grace.

The *Sonate Romantique* (1909), also a work of extended proportions, is based on a Spanish folk-song theme. Dedicated to Isaac Albéniz, this sonata is really a theme and variations.

Contes d'Espagne (Tales of Spain) consists of two collections (1918, 1928), each with seven evocations. They contain profound musical poetry although they are played less frequently than the *Sevilla.* In the first series of *Contes,* the realism that marks Turina's art is admirably applied. The first piece in the collection—created from the composer's visions—transports the listener *Devant la Tour du Clavero* (Before the Tower of Clavero) in Salamanca where a troop of archers is marching by. The next tableau portrays the *Vieille Eglise de Logroño* (Old Church of Logroño), where the spiritual vision of the composer is interrupted by the image of his beloved intruding on his mystical recollections. Other diversions are sought at *Miramar* at Valencia; the *Jardins de Murcie* (Gardens of Murcia) with their softly whispered murmurs; and the *Route de l'Alhambra*, recalling the Moorish cavalcades of the past. The *Contes d'Espagne* conclude with an amorous, lyrical scene at *La Caleta* (Small Bay) of Málaga and with the gentle seascape of *Rompeolas* (Breakwater) near Barcelona.[10]

When Joaquín Turina is compared with Albéniz, Granados, and Falla, he must be classed as a *petit maître;* nonetheless, his music discloses a firm mastery of form paired with the use of a regional Spanish idiom—that of his own Andalusia—at times truly inspired, at other times not quite convincing.

BIBLIOGRAPHY

Chase, Gilbert. *The Music of Spain*, second revised edition. New York: Dover Publications, 1959.

Collet, Henri. *Albéniz et Granados.* Paris: Editions Le Bon Plaisir, 1926. Reprinted in 1948.

Collet, Henri. *L'Essor de la Musique Espagnole au XXe Siècle.* Paris: Editions Max Eschig, 1929. Reprinted in 1950.

Fernández-Cid, Antonio. *Granados.* Madrid: Samarán Ediciones, 1956.

Laplane, Gabriel. *Albéniz, Su Vida y Su Obra.* Barcelona: Editorial Noguer, 1958.

Pahissa, Jaime. *Manuel de Falla* (translated by J. Wagstaff). London: Museum Press Limited, 1954.

Trend, J. B. *Manuel de Falla and Spanish Music.* New York: Alfred A. Knopf, 1929.

[10] Eschig publishes the *Sonate Romantique* and most of Turina's other works are listed in the Salabert catalogue.

PART
V

26

IMPRESSIONISM

As the nineteenth century drew to a close, the fine arts—both music and the visual arts—entered a new aesthetic era; this new phase, called Impressionism, lasted for only a few decades into the twentieth century (*ca.* 1870–1930). The term Impressionism was first applied to paintings by artists like Monet, Manet, and Renoir in France, where the Impressionist school flourished. Around 1870 a group of young artists abandoned the then accepted school of realism in favor of a new movement in painting, dedicated to ideals considered revolutionary by their contemporaries. Although the members of this early *avant-garde* school admitted that realistic presentations could be artistic, they maintained that for their purposes realism played no part in achieving an artistic result. They concentrated on the *manner* in which a picture was painted and were completely unconcerned with subject matter. Their chief aim was to reproduce the general impression of the moment made by the subject on the artist.

In literature, and especially in poetry, Impressionism was translated into a movement called Symbolism. The Symbolists wished to free verse techniques to achieve fluidity. Poetry's new function was to suggest, to evoke, but not to describe. The prophet for literary Impressionism was Charles Baudelaire, whose theories about sound and poetic music and the symbolic relations of scent and color are vividly displayed in his poem *Correspondances:*

> *La Nature est un temple où de vivants piliers*
> *Laissent parfois sortir de confuses paroles;*
> *L'homme y passe à travers des forêts de symboles*
> *Qui l'observent avec des regards familiers.*

> (Nature is a temple where living pillars
> Now and then emit confused words;
> Man passes through forests of symbols
> That regard him with familiar glances.)
> [English translation by the author]

The Symbolist movement attracted such gifted poets as Rimbaud, Verlaine, and Mallarmé. Rejecting realism, they chose to express their immediate reactions to a subject by means of symbolic words in lieu of prose. They advocated that syntax should be ignored and that words should be arranged for their emotional and aesthetic values. Verlaine illustrated this doctrine when he stated in one of his poems *"de la musique avant toute chose"* (music before everything), referring, of course, to the musicality of words and word combinations.

The basic theories of the Impressionists were most perfectly expressed in the sonorous art of music. Since music is essentially an abstract art, it was ideally suited to project Impressionism's vague images. The Impressionist composers had two favorite mediums: the orchestra because of its multi-hued tonal palette, and the piano because its damper pedal permitted vibrating harmonies to suspend in mid-air.

BIBLIOGRAPHY

Harvey, P. and J. E. Heseltine. *The Oxford Companion to French Literature.* London: Oxford University Press, 1959.

Rewald, John. *The History of Impressionism.* New York: The Museum of Modern Art, 1946.

Stites, Raymond. *The Arts and Man.* New York: McGraw-Hill Book Co., Inc., 1940.

Sypher, Wylie. *Rococo to Cubism in Art and Literature.* New York: Random House, 1960.

Wold, M. and E. Cykler. *An Introduction to Music and Art in the Western World.* Dubuque: Wm. C. Brown Co., 1958.

27

DEBUSSY

AND

RAVEL

CLAUDE DEBUSSY

The ideals and aims of the Impressionists and Symbolists were brought into the field of music principally by **Claude Achille Debussy** (1862–1918), one of the most important composers in the history of piano music. He refused—like Chopin and Liszt before him—to accept the keyboard restrictions set up by his predecessors and so proceeded to imagine different concepts of pianistic techniques and coloristic devices. He also introduced a new approach to musical composition, an approach influenced more by other arts than by any purely musical considerations. The music Debussy created through this unique approach has profoundly affected a fair share of later twentieth-century music.

Debussy showed little promise as a student at the Paris Conservatory. He bewildered his professors with his audacious chord progressions and unorthodox attitude toward musical composition. A summer tour through Russia as personal pianist for Mme. von Meck, patroness of Tchaikovsky, did much to broaden his musical horizons; he listened eagerly to the works of Russian nationalist composers and reveled in the colorful Slavic folk music. After winning the coveted *Prix de Rome,* he spent considerable time in that romantic Italian city, playing through Wagnerian opera scores and suffering from *mal du pays.* His admiration for Wagner waned when he became acquainted with Mussorgsky through *Boris Godonov;* and he found other musical delights in the Javanese music he heard at the Paris Exposition of 1889.

But no matter what musical influences touched Debussy, they can claim only secondary importance. (Where in his music does one find the stark realism of *Boris?*) Although he did use oriental scale types from time to time, his basic art is French. In truth the direct influences stimulating Debussy did not lie within musical bounds, for this original composer found his creative inspiration in Impressionist paintings and Symbolist literature.

The painters revealed to him the restless beauty of chiaroscuro, the contrasts between light and shadow, the vague expression of impressions, and the interplay of color. The Symbolist writers—perhaps the stronger force—showed him the art of suggestion through a word or the turn of a phrase, the drama of half tones, the beauty of sound for sound's sake. All this unquestionably had a major role in shaping the *génie* of *Claude de France,* but he expressed his personal interpretation of these ideas by means uniquely his own: the style was evolved, molded, and developed by Debussy alone.

Several aspects of the Debussy style are easily perceivable, at least in general outline, because they were so unique in his day. One noticeable feature is his use of harmony; in the light of standard nineteenth-century harmony, Debussy's method of harmony appears to have challenged all accepted writing practices. Rules meant nothing to him; he cared only about expressing his inner self.

What are these new harmonic concepts? First, Debussy freely used dissonance: sevenths, ninths, and elevenths appear on the dominant or other degrees of the scale, neither prepared nor resolved, often in series used consecutively. He also uses various altered chords or else a sustained chord with superimposed, foreign harmonies that lend a flavor of polytonality. In many instances he uses parallel series of perfect intervals: fifths, fourths, and octaves.

It is somewhat more difficult to sum up the melodic element in Debussy's music. One attractive feature arises from the diversity in his melodic procedure. Many times he preferred to construct melodies on modal scales. This blending of the old and new—fusing quasi-Gregorian chant with a highly original harmonic apparatus—results in an ultrasensitive tonal picture. However, modality was only one of several melodic possibilities available to Debussy. When he desired an oriental mood, he based his melodic ideas on the pentatonic scale: a five-note sequence (corresponding to the black notes on the piano keyboard) found in the music of many Eastern cultures. Elsewhere Debussy worked out a completely personalized scale, the whole-tone scale.

Debussy deftly and artistically handled other facets of composition. For instance, he depended heavily on modulation enhanced by the many passing and nonharmonic tones found in his music. His ideas on form and development were considered outlandish by his contemporaries. With Debussy the piano pieces develop somewhat organically: one idea is initiated and expanded; in the process, another idea blossoms in a seemingly logical fashion; and it in turn is subjected to the same treatment. Of course, Debussy often used a type of A B A ternary form for his short piano pieces, but even then he took great liberties with structure. Finally, he runs a full course in rhythms: from compositions almost intentionally static to sparkling pieces that contain the most modern animated rhythms.

As a practicing musician, Debussy was a pianist. He had no command of any other instrument and was only an indifferent conductor; therefore, in composing for the piano he took advantage of the one medium of expression responsive to his personal touch. The piano—an instrument of harmonic and tonal blending rather than one of simple melodic statement —was a natural experimental medium for a personal art based on these two attributes. He provided his piano music with scrupulous directions for performance, insisting that his music required no personal interpretation on the part of the pianist but that it should be played exactly as he stipulated.

Debussy's style in piano music changed very little. Once he knew what he wanted to say and once he could control the means of communicating his ideas, he composed exclusively in the "Debussy idiom." As he grew older, he worked to acquire a more intimate expressive method, but he rarely deviated from the basic techniques he had established by 1900.

The six pieces published in 1890—*Rêverie, Ballade, Valse Romantique, Mazurka, Nocturne,* and *Danse*—are youthful attempts. Written before he had formulated his style, they do not faithfully represent his aesthetic ideals. This is also true of the *Deux Arabesques* (Two Arabesques, 1888) although they do have a graceful charm: the first has duplets languidly played against triplets; the second has rhythmic vitality. These two pieces reflect the style of the romantic *morceaux de salon* rather than represent Debussy's mature talent.

The first indications of strong individualism come in the *Suite Bergamasque* (1890–1905). Although this suite contains four pieces, there is no attempt at tonal unity as in the classic French suite. On the whole, the collection barely hints at the masterpieces to follow: *Prélude* is clever in the Romantic vein; *Passepied* has the spirit of a pavane; the *Menuet* is classic, a style that Debussy soon discarded; and *Clair de Lune* is that portion of *Suite Bergamasque* anticipating the preludes that appeared twenty years later. The title *Clair de Lune* recalls the Paul Verlaine poem set to music by Fauré. It is a charming piano composition—with its volatile harmonies and diatonic melodic lines—but the attention given it could be far better spent on some of Debussy's finer works.

During the last decade of the nineteenth century Debussy wrote little piano music. In this period he discovered his true style and produced more mature works, such as the *String Quartet in G Minor* (1893), the orchestral *Nocturnes* (1893–1899), and the opera *Pelléas et Mélisande* (1892–1902). His second significant collection of piano pieces was his first keyboard masterpiece, the suite *Pour le Piano* (For the Piano, 1896–1901): *Prélude,*

Sarabande, and *Toccata.* The absence of Debussy's customary pictorial titles and the presence of some Baroque titles might suggest that he was looking to the past for inspiration. However, nothing could be further from the truth. The titles of the first and last pieces in this suite announce merely the use of free compositional forms, an aesthetic principle observed by Debussy throughout his career.

The musical elements of the *Prélude* are still somewhat unrefined, and the insistent use of the whole-tone scale becomes excessive. *Toccata* is a brilliant keyboard piece whose initial measures remind one of the tumultuous sonatas of Domenico Scarlatti. But the second idea is typically Debussy—nervous, excited, harmonically strange. The central *Sarabande* is the best part of the suite. Debussy holds to the implicit mood of this classic dance but his apparatus is strictly from his personal genius. Like a solemn, stately cortege, the tense atmosphere is produced by series of seventh chords, parallel fifths, and alternated groups of consonances and dissonances.

After *Pour le Piano* Debussy published a new piano collection every year or so. In 1903 he released the *Estampes* (*Pagodes, Soirée dans Grenade, Jardins sous la Pluie*). In the first two pieces he looks beyond French borders; number three is French. In *Pagodes* (Pagodas) Debussy engages the pentatonic scale to create an oriental milieu. Short melodic phrases and imitations of gongs and little bells add authentic elements to this atmospheric *Estampe* (Engraving).

No better critique of *Soirée dans Grenade* (Evening in Granada) could be found than the one by Manuel de Falla: "The force of imagination concentrated in the few pages of 'La Soirée dans Grenade' approaches the marvellous when it is borne in mind that they were written by a stranger guided almost exclusively by the visions of his genius . . . here it is Andalusia itself that we see; truth without authenticity, so to speak, since there is not a bar directly borrowed from Spanish folk-music and yet the whole piece to its smallest detail is redolent of Spain."[1]

Jardins sous la Pluie (Gardens in the Rain) is the favorite of the *Estampes.* In a delightful and rather amusing fashion, Debussy disperses two French folk songs among his fluid harmonies: *Nous n'irons plus au Bois* and *Do do, l'Enfant do.*

Two isolated pieces—*Masques* and *l'Isle joyeuse*—were composed in 1904. Both are highly developed, vivacious pieces written in a splendid pianistic idiom. *Masques* is a bit overextended and artificial; *l'Isle joyeuse* is bewitching. It captures in music the exact spirit of the *Embarquement pour Cythère*; it mirrors the ambiance of Verlaine and Watteau.

Two collections titled *Images* date from 1905–1907: volume one con-

---

[1] Manuel de Falla, "Claude Debussy and Spain," in *The Chesterian* (January, 1921), p. 355.

tains *Reflets dans l'Eau* (Reflections in the Water), *Hommage à Rameau, Mouvement;* and volume two has *Cloches à travers les Feuilles* (Bells through the Leaves), *Et la Lune descend sur le Temple qui fut* (And the Moon Descends on the Ruined Temple), and *Poissons d'or* (Goldfish). Among these various pieces are several excellent examples of what one may call Debussy's impressionism—an impressionism which only partly correlates with that of the other arts. While the French Impressionist painters wanted to set down the momentary impression of a given situation—i.e., the play of light on an object for a fleeting instant—Debussy desired more permanence in his music. Although he learned from the painters and Symbolists about sensitive language and delicate emotional expression, he nevertheless elected to make his music durable as well by instilling into it an underlying sense of unity.

Three of the *Images*—*Reflets dans l'Eau, Cloches à travers les Feuilles,* and *Poissons d'or*—reveal his ability to suggest the ephemeral and still preserve complete and masterful stylistic consistency. In *Reflets dans l'Eau,* for example, the listener feels that he can almost see the hundred and one flecks of sunlight mirrored in the reflections of a gently undulating pool. But, listening attentively, the listener finds a principal theme appearing three times, separated by contrasting episodes.

The rest of the *Images* are cut from different cloth. *Mouvement* is a kind of prelude based on insistent triplet rhythm. *Hommage à Rameau* is a lovely, solemn sarabande. The title *Et la Lune descend sur le Temple qui fut* suggests the extravagant Impressionist titles that Debussy used for some preludes, but this piece cannot match the later works; as a matter of fact, it is the weakest of the *Images*.

Not characteristic but thoroughly entrancing, the *Children's Corner* (1906–1908) is a volume dedicated to Debussy's little daughter: "to my dear Chou-Chou, with the tender apologies of her father for what is to follow." All the titles are in English, perhaps an innocently mischievous reference to the Anglomania prevalent at that time in France. (Chou-Chou's mother insisted that she be raised by an English nanny and surrounded her with English engravings of children's scenes.) In the first piece, *Doctor Gradus ad Parnassum,* one can easily imagine a child seated at a piano confronted with the ever-present exercises of Mr. Clementi. The ponderous rhythms in *Jimbo's Lullaby* make a wonderful cradlesong for a toy elephant. *Serenade for the Doll* is a tribute to a little girl's most cherished possession. *Snow Is Dancing* describes what the child sees as she looks out the window at falling ice crystals. Another toy is brought to mind with *The Little Shepherd,* while a mechanical wind-up toy is perhaps the object described in *Golliwog's Cake-Walk,* a grotesque dance concluding this visit into childhood scenes and reveries.

The essence of Debussy's talent rests in two volumes of *Préludes* (twelve pieces in each). The first book appeared in 1910, the second in 1913. Although the two prelude collections have similar intent and compositional plan, the second book is more *recherchée*, more concerned with creating a concise musical vocabulary. This is not important, for together these twenty-four *Préludes* reveal Debussy's genius guided by firm technique and a sincere expression that is both convincing and satisfying.

It seems unnecessary to consider each *Prélude* as it appears in the collections because there is no connection at all between consecutive works. One could invent an arbitrary classification of the basic ideas for the preludes. For instance, some are based quite openly on the dance or on elements taken from the dance.

Danseuses de Delphes (Delphic Dancers), with its dotted rhythms *lent et grave*, commemorates the postured movements of Greek dancers pictured on ancient pottery and friezes. Debussy indicates that *La Sérénade interrompue* (The Interrupted Serenade) be played *quasi-guitarra*, and his passages of repeated notes accentuate the Spanish flavor. Is the imp of Shakespeare's *Midsummer Night's Dream* the object of the humorous sketch *La Danse de Puck?* It would seem so from the capricious rhythms and rapidly changing harmonies. Another dance, a little ironical, is called *Minstrels;* here Debussy calls for an interpretation *nerveux et avec humour.*

One of the most delightful preludes in dance style is *La Puerta del Vino.* Debussy had received a postcard from Manuel de Falla showing that famous gate in Granada, but whether this is or is not an attempt at musical pictorialization is hardly important. The significant point is the distinct Spanish mood achieved by means of habanera rhythm, melodic embellishment, and guitar-like chord clusters (Ex. 1). One more prelude might be discussed in this dance-inspired group of pieces. Although not strictly in this category, *Hommage à S. Pickwick, Esq.* does depict the glitter and noise of the English music hall, a phenomenon that has no exact counterpart in any other country. This prelude begins *grave* with a quotation of the opening phrase of "God save the King." The movement becomes increasingly animated due to an interesting use of simultaneous rhythms in sixteenth notes, eighth notes, halves, and quarters (written on three staves).

Impressionist painters loved landscapes. As an Impressionist composer, Debussy composed several preludes dealing with natural phenomena. The first book of *Préludes* has two such scapes. *Le Vent dans la Plaine* (The Wind in the Plain) begins with a lightly textured rhythmic figure of six sixteenth notes, which weaves through the entire prelude. A melody rises, growing out of this basic figure and remaining wedded to it. Sharply contrasting chords occasionally interrupt the prevailing atmosphere without

Ex. 1.   Debussy: *La Puerta del Vino*

ever dissuading the insistency of the initial rhythm. A slightly different approach creates a buoyant, joyful mood in *Les Collines d'Anacapri* (The Hills of Anacapri). A brief motive stated at the beginning develops into the main idea. This theme is exposed with gaiety and abandon. Then a more expansive opposing theme (in octaves) intrudes to debate with the sprightly theme. Debussy marked the brilliant ending *lumineux,* a perfect clue to the prelude's character.

Several of the *Préludes* seem to be drawn from the unreal world of legend and the *féerique,* and one in this group is heard more than any other Debussy prelude: *La Cathédrale engloutie* (The Engulfed Cathedral), very likely inspired by the story of the legendary kingdom of Ys, a tale which Edouard Lalo expanded and transformed into an opera (*Le Roi d'Ys*). Debussy introduces a mystical feeling by means of a series of parallel fifths and octaves. Shortly, an undulating motive in the piano's lower register suggests swirling waters; with a mighty surge the cathedral comes up out of the sea. A bit of chantlike melody becomes audible before the cathedral, accompanied by more undulations, then slips back into its watery home. Such a graphic account may go beyond Debussy's original concept, but whatever the story this is indeed a richly descriptive piece of music.

The other preludes touching on fantasy do not conjure up such explicit pictures. *Ondine* is a radiantly hued composition in capricious rhythms; the famed sea sprite cavorts in her undersea kingdom. Another equally lively prelude is the restless, fluttering *Les Fées sont d'exquises Danseuses* (Fairies are Exquisite Dancers).

Most of the *Préludes* were designed simply to create atmosphere. This is true, for example, in *Les Sons et les Parfums tournent dans l'Air du soir* (Sounds and Perfumes Are Turning in the Evening Air), in which the line from Baudelaire's poem *Harmonie du Soir* is as vague and yet as suggestive as the prelude it accompanies. *Voiles* (Sails) is constructed almost entirely on the whole-tone scale; it is a superb example of Debussy's unique individuality. Titles like *Bruyères* (Heather), *Brouillards* (Mists), *Feuilles mortes* (Dead Leaves), and *Ce qu'a vu le Vent d'ouest* (What the West Wind Has Seen) substantiate the belief that Debussy hoped only to project a mood or a reaction. The very word *Canope* (Egyptian burial urn) sounds mysterious. One of the most positive examples of tightly knit musical construction is *Des Pas sur la Neige;* yet what is the significance of the title (Footsteps in the Snow)? Does the unobtrusive two-note motive suggest a figure plodding against a wintry night? It is hard to say.

The final prelude in the second book contains elements from all the earlier types in the two books. In *Feux d'artifice* (Fireworks) the atmosphere is obviously tense, but the fireworks explosions are surprisingly pictorial and realistic. A touch of patriotism—a reference to the *Marseillaise* —closes the final prelude.

Debussy's *Préludes*—or even just one—offer a profusion of new sounds. But more than that they supply convincing proof that music has acquired forceful expression, that it is capable of illustrating the inexpressible, and that it can suggest the unreal in a most realistic fashion.

Well aware that his music represented a novel departure from tradition, Debussy created two volumes—six studies in each—of imaginative études covering different aspects of his personalized language; these twelve études were published in 1915. As exercises in technique they fulfill a real purpose; as works of art they are—as were Chopin's *Études*—highly musical.[2]

MAURICE RAVEL

There has long been a tendency—either spoken or implied—to regard Claude Debussy and **Maurice Ravel** (1875–1937) as the two truly representative Impressionist composers; this is only partly correct. Although they were contemporaries and admired each other's works, they had substantially different ideas about musical composition. Many of Debussy's unorthodox harmonic techniques were incorporated in Ravel's music; and vice versa, Ravel's *Jeux d'eau* (1901) disclosed to Debussy a wealth of coloristic sound combinations. But the two composers did not approach musical composition in the same way. Ravel's background, musical education, and keen in-

---

[2] Durand of Paris is the publisher of Debussy's music; however, the suite *Pour le Piano* and the *Suite Bergamasque* have recently been issued by G. Schirmer.

tellect guided him in creating works equally as superb in craftsmanship as Debussy's are superior for freedom of form.

Ravel was born at Ciboure between Saint-Jean-de-Luz and the Spanish frontier. His father was a naturalized Swiss from Savoy, his mother was Basque. At the *Conservatoire de Paris* he studied with Bériot and Fauré, as well as others, and while in Paris he met Erik Satie, whose bold experiments in composition interested him. Ravel made several unsuccessful attempts to win the *Prix de Rome*. "Mr. Ravel may take us for country bumpkins; but he shouldn't consider us imbeciles." This remark summarized the opinion of the committee that barred Ravel from the prize in composition. The situation turned into a *cause célèbre* and Ravel found himself famous. The rest of his life is the history of his compositions.

Through his mother, Ravel had a sympathetic link to the Iberian peninsula, which may account for his preoccupation with Spanish motifs. He used Spanish titles, Spanish rhythms, and imitations of Spanish instruments consistently throughout his career, not during only one phase. In addition to this Spanish influence, Ravel loved the dance more than any other musical form. He drew upon both ancient and modern dances, infusing into them his personal manner of expression. Many of his compositions display humor—at times lugubrious, at times sarcastic.

When it comes to examining the texture of Ravel's music, comparison with Debussy is inevitable. Like Debussy, he worked out an original harmonic concept that was considered quite provocative at the time. Whereas Debussy prefers ninth and eleventh chords built on the dominant, Ravel likes major sevenths and supertonic ninths. Ravel's harmony is for the most part crisper and more outgoing than Debussy's; and his rhythms are more piquant and sharply punctuated. The two composers are also disparate in form; Ravel adhered more closely to classic rules. He was a musical architect who unfailingly fitted his tonal fabric into a logical, self-analytical framework. Sonata form was his first choice; however, when he chose dance forms he carefully observed the classic principles relevant to them.

During Ravel's lifetime some critics felt that his painstaking fastidiousness with form detracted from the lyric and emotional content of his music. Ravel once said that it was not necessary for the musician to possess the sensitivity he wished to communicate through his works—a statement not to be taken too seriously when we discover that Ravel's friends have claimed that he himself was very emotional and subjective. To confirm this claim, one has only to listen to Ravel's music—for example, the *Oiseaux tristes* from his *Miroirs* or the epilogue to *Valses nobles et sentimentales*. To communicate sensitivity in a manner so intimate, Ravel surely had to be aware of it himself.

Ravel's major works for solo piano are: *Pavane pour une Infante défunte* (1899), *Jeux d'eau* (1901), *Miroirs* (1905), *Sonatine* (1905), *Gaspard de la Nuit* (1908), *Valses nobles et sentimentales* (1911), and the *Tombeau de Couperin* (1917).[3]

Nowadays *Pavane pour une Infante défunte* (Pavane for a Dead Infanta) is usually heard in the orchestral transcription prepared by Ravel. It has become one of his most beloved works, but in later life he himself became dissatisfied with the *Pavane*. "It doesn't bother me to speak of it. It is so old that the composer has become its critic. In retrospect, I no longer see the qualities. But, alas, I easily discern the errors. The influence of Chabrier is too obtrusive and the form is rather poor."[4] Ravel's severe self-criticism is scarcely justified even though it must be admitted that *Pavane* is not equal to many of the later piano pieces. It is rather unpianistic, which is surprising because Ravel was a good pianist. Moreover, the melodic lines seem quite undistinguished when compared with his later linear concepts. Nonetheless, *Pavane* offers pleasant music, solemn and earnest; and the harmonic element is interestingly rearranged in the two successive restatements of the principal theme.

When Ravel presented *Jeux d'eau* (Fountains) in 1901 he opened up a new era of sound. The piece is dedicated to Gabriel Fauré and is prefaced by an epigraph from Henri de Régnier: "The river god laughing from the water which is tickling him." Ravel's intentional concentration upon form is already apparent in this music. He wrote of this work: "Inspired by the noise of water, cascades, springs, the *Jeux d'eau* is based on two motives, in the manner of first-movement sonata form without, however, conforming to the classic tonal scheme."[5]

Ravel's technical procedures in the difficult and dazzling *Jeux d'eau* are similar to those in Liszt's *Jeux d'Eau à la Villa d'Este*. But not at all like Liszt is the end effect achieved by Ravel: a delicacy emanating from his exploration of the half tones in the pianistic palette; and myriad fleeting sensations impelled by cascades of eleventh chords, dominant ninths, and major sevenths.

Five pieces comprise the *Miroirs: Noctuelles, Oiseaux tristes, Une Barque sur l'Océan, Alborada del gracioso*, and *La Vallée des cloches*. As the title implies, Ravel does not intend to draw out actual descriptions but merely to suggest, as reflections seen through a mirror. Each piece is a separate entity, each is a masterpiece of magical sound.

---

[3] Ravel's piano works are issued by several publishers: *Pavane, Sonatine* (E. B. Marks and Durand); *Jeux d'eau, Miroirs* (G. Schirmer); *Gaspard de la Nuit, Valses nobles et sentimentales, Tombeau de Couperin* (Durand).

[4] This self-critique by Ravel is found in the February, 1912, issue of the bulletin of the S.I.M. (*Société Internationale de Musique*).

[5] These remarks of Ravel are taken from an autobiographical sketch which first appeared in print in the *Revue Musicale* (December, 1920).

Fluttering night moths hovering about a light are vividly delineated in *Noctuelles*. The wavering, agitated atmosphere is maintained by variations of the initial motive (Ex. 2).

Ex. 2.   Ravel: *Noctuelles*

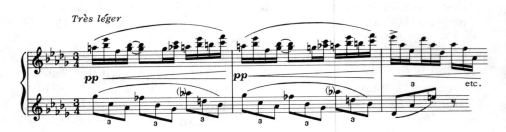

Oiseaux tristes (Sad Birds) is a melancholy portrait built on a repeated note figure and a little nostalgic flourish of melody. Its shining beauty makes it one of the best in the set. In the third number, *Une Barque sur l'Océan* (A Boat on the Ocean), Ravel uses techniques that he handled more convincingly elsewhere. A left-hand broken figure establishes an undulating rhythm against which broken melodic motives intrude from time to time. The most individualistic of the five pieces—and also the best representative of Ravel's mature style—is *Alborada del gracioso*. The gyrations of a Spanish clown are described with an accent as authentic as it is unique. A suggestion of hemiola rhythm at the beginning is broadened to an animated rhapsodic section. Repeated notes, guitar imitations, and recitative passages punctuated by rhythmic fragments all add to the luster of this sparkling, significant work. The last composition, *La Vallée des cloches*, is a picturesque sketch—similar to several in Liszt's *Années de Pélerinage*—in which a pastoral scene is dominated by a softly modulated, rhythmically vital bell motive.

Ravel's classicism is particularly evident in his *Sonatine*. The three movements are unified by themes stemming from similar origins. The first movement, *Modéré*, manipulates two themes in abbreviated sonata-allegro form: the first theme begins with a downward skip of a fourth; the secondary idea is fashioned from pairs of repeated motives. A short development section is abundant with classic elements blended with twentieth-century elements. Here Ravel uses the false start and countless open fifths and fourths. The latter is a familiar device in his personal musical vocabulary.

In contrast with the first movement, *Mouvement de Menuet* begins with a melodic *upward* skip of a fifth, and the initial four-measure phrase is repeated in a series of tasteful transformations. Only fourteen measures long, the middle section adapts the principal theme of the first movement to a ternary meter; then, with an insistent reiteration of the downward leap of a fourth, it returns to the *Menuet* proper. The third movement, *Animé*, is a synthesis of the material presented in the first two movements. It contains components of the rondo as well as of sonata-allegro form yet strictly speaking is neither. The main theme of the first movement appears more than once; leaps—upward and downward—of fourths and fifths give the impression of a summary, as it were, of all the aspects and ideas contributing to this delightful *Sonatine*.

The suite *Gaspard de la Nuit* is one of the most difficult compositions in solo-piano repertoire. It poses baffling problems to the pianist, which may be the reason why the work is rarely heard. And still *Gaspard de la Nuit* cannot be exactly classed as a virtuoso work because a lot of the problems involved are musical, not technical. Whatever difficulties do turn up result from Ravel's superb craftsmanship and innate "sensitivity"; they never obtrude on their own.

The three poems—as Ravel called them—of *Gaspard de la Nuit* were inspired by three poems by an obscure mid-eighteenth-century poet, Aloysius Bertrand. According to the esoteric Bertrand, his poems were vivid, vivacious water colors, poetic paintings like the graphic pictures of Jacques Callot.

In the first poem, *Ondine,* the sea sprite has left her lake to sing her song at the poet's window: "Listen! It is I, Ondine, flecking with drops of water the sonorous panes of your window illuminated by the pale rays of the moon." But her avowal of love is for naught because the poet loves a mortal. Hearing this, "she cried several tears, burst into laughter, and disappeared in droplets, which streamed down my blue window panes." A rhythmic-harmonic motive imitates a murmuring atmosphere while the melody emerges, rising upon itself in a melancholy nostalgic gesture. This initial melodic invention is heard again and again, but each time it is enveloped in variegated swirls of glistening arpeggiated arabesques.

"It is the bell which sounds from the walls of a town on the horizon and a corpse hanging from a gibbet, reddened as the setting sun." Thus Bertrand describes the subject matter of *Le Gibet*. Ravel maintains this lugubrious feeling by an almost hypnotic insistence on a repeated octave *B-flat*. Seventh and ninth chords, a mournful melody always bordering on despair, alternations of all kinds, make this brief piece (written entirely on three staves) a memorable venture into the macabre.

Scarbo, the final piece, evokes the image of a grotesque dwarf, an image that might have come straight from the *Tales of Hoffmann*. Musically speaking, *Scarbo* is a brilliant scherzo—a magnificent exploration into the fantastic—wherein two themes are subjected to super imagination. The first theme is powerfully rhythmic: "How often have I seen him descend from the ceiling, pirouette on one foot, and roll across the room like the bobbin from a witch's distaff." The second theme, gay and dancelike, describes the apparition of Scarbo dancing by the light of the moon. "Did I expect him to disappear? The dwarf grew tall between the moon and me like the tower of a Gothic cathedral." The singular scherzo, so glittering and virtuoso, fades away in a whisper of sound; and thus concludes this illustrious monument to the art of Ravel.

Ravel's admiration for the dance is evident in the *Valses nobles et sentimentales* written in 1911. The splendid collection of stylized dances was conceived as a chain of waltzes, following Schubert's classic examples. They are not difficult to play, the virtuosity of *Gaspard* having yielded to a subtler style notable for clarity and harmonic ingenuity. As a motto, Ravel placed in the score a quotation from Henri de Régnier, "the constantly new and delicious pleasure of a useless occupation." In these waltzes Ravel's mature musical language tells its own story with incisive rhythms, sharp outlines, direct expression, and a fresh approach to harmony. To be precise, there are seven waltzes and an epilogue quoting the previous material.

Finally, there is *Le Tombeau de Couperin* (1917), the ultimate salute made by Ravel the classicist to his admiration for structural logic. As the title announces, this is a musical homage to the memory of the great clavecinist François Couperin *le Grand,* and Ravel also intended it as a memorial to friends killed in World War I. Each of the six pieces is dedicated to one of these friends. Musically, *Le Tombeau de Couperin* is a monument to the name of its composer. It embodies his genius, presenting him as a master of his craft in complete control of his own unique tonal fabric.

This suite (for it is actually that) opens with a capricious *Prélude* in which suave counterpoint and liquid ornaments delight the ear. A somber *Fugue* follows, a true polyphonic piece whose melodic idea is punctuated by rests; Ravel's fugue revives old Baroque techniques but several modern procedures are introduced. The principal theme of the lovely *Forlane*—in 6/8 meter—has an old-fashioned pattern. Heard three times, this theme is accompanied by an episode in piquant harmonies. A more jubilant piece, *Rigaudon,* follows. It engages definite eighteenth-century methods, such as the crossing of hands *à la Scarlatti,* and its central section in ternary form has exquisite pastoral overtones. Typical of Ravel, the *Menuet* with its musette-like trio leads into the impressive *Toccata.* The rhythmic drive in this finale is tremendous: it never relaxes, but builds and builds to a mighty climax—virtuosity not common with Ravel.

The Impressionist movement was short-lived. There were other composers, of course—Respighi in Italy, Delius in England, Griffes in the United States—who appropriated certain Impressionist techniques; but pure Impressionism is essentially French, and Debussy and Ravel remain the finest authors of this unique musical language.

BIBLIOGRAPHY

Debussy, Claude. *Monsieur Croche, The Dilettante Hater* (translated by B. N. Langdon Davies). New York: Lear Publishers, 1928. Dover reprint

Lockspeiser, Edward. *Debussy*. New York: Collier, 1962. A paperback in the Great Composers Series.

Lockspeiser, Edward. *Debussy. His Life and Mind*. New York: The Macmillan Co., 1962. Vol. I (1862–1902).

Mersman, Dr. Hans. *Die Moderne Musik*. Wildpark-Potsdam: Akademische Verlagsgesellschaft Athenaion, 1929.

Myers, Rollo H. *Ravel*. New York: Thomas Yoseloff, 1960.

Schmitz, E. Robert. *The Piano Works of Claude Debussy*. New York: Duell, Sloan & Pearce, 1950. Dover reprint

Seroff, Victor. *Maurice Ravel*. New York: Henry Holt & Co., 1953.

Thompson, Oscar. *Debussy, Man and Artist*. New York: Dodd, Mead & Co., 1937.

Vallas, Léon. *Claude Debussy, His Life and Works* (translated by M. & G. O'Brien). London: Oxford University Press, 1933.

28

THE
TWENTIETH
CENTURY

It has been noted that certain stylistic similarities may be observed in the music of all Baroque composers. Each artist had his own expressive language, to be sure, but the manner of expression was disciplined by generally accepted rules and concepts. The same may be said of the composers in the Classic period and to a certain extent most composers in the first half of the nineteenth century. Later, Nationalism arose to temper and diffuse pure Romanticism; and Impressionism took musical composition far beyond the limits of tradition. In the twentieth century one may search in vain for one "contemporary" style, for today's music has many sounds and many styles.

After the turn of the century—Impressionism and a post-Romanticism were coexisting—many composers began to question their ultimate objectives and the latent possibilities of musical growth. An artist supposedly reflects the cultural progress and stature of his era, but the twentieth century is a mechanistic age, an atomic age, an age of doubt and questioning and reassessment. How can such ideas be mirrored in art? A composer is expected to assist in formulating contemporary musical trends, perhaps to prophesy future ones. But what can be done with the overused nineteenth-century materials and traditional scalar systems which have literally been expended? These are some of the problems facing twentieth-century composers, and the solutions are being discovered in different ways.

The approaches to these problems vary according to the spiritual and psychological makeup of each artist. He may be a sensationalist, a musical iconoclast who seeks quick fame by breaking down accepted concepts, or he may be a sincere experimentalist who patiently searches into the possibilities of opening up new tonal horizons. Some music written in this century clings to another age, which means that its composers are essentially Romantics, albeit displaced Romantics. Other composers prefer to synthesize the past with the present to preserve a semblance of stylistic evolution.

Two musical avenues have been and are open to twentieth-century composers. They could take existing scales, divide and subdivide their intervals, and thus produce microtonal music. Or they might seek new ways of restating and rearranging older traditions of harmony, melody, and rhythm. Most have chosen the second way: the results show infinite variety. Some writers have changed the traditional habit of chords in thirds to chords in fourths. Others superimpose one harmonic progression on top of another.

About 1909, **Arnold Schönberg** (1874–1951) made a startling impact on the music world with a new aesthetic—eventually expressed in terms of twelve-tone composition—and Schönberg's followers have generously endowed this century with works either derived directly from him or partially influenced by his techniques.

Composers ordinarily pass through several developmental stages before arriving at a mature style; and since this style more often than not is a mélange of several basic approaches, involving elements from the different stages, strict classification of a composer is not always possible or for that matter necessary.

Despite the seeming diversity of approaches and disparity of techniques involved, certain characteristics are typical of our century. Dissonance becomes an end unto itself—whether achieved by polytonality, quartal harmony, or atonality. Rhythm has attained great flexibility and an even greater complexity; counterpoint has become newly important. Paradoxically, however, most contemporary composers will assert that they eschew overabundant details and the beclouding of musical substance. Their alleged goal is to express musically their reaction to the twentieth century and to do so with clarity, objectivity, and realism.

BIBLIOGRAPHY

McKinney, H. D. and W. R. Anderson. *Music in History*. New York: American Book Co., 1940.

Meyers, Bernard S. *Understanding the Arts*, revised edition. New York: Holt, Rinehart and Winston, 1963.

Stites, Raymond. *The Arts and Man*. New York: McGraw-Hill Book Co., Inc., 1940.

Sypher, Wylie. *Rococo to Cubism in Art and Literature*. New York: Random House, 1960.

Thimme, D. and W. W. Heist, eds. *An Introduction to Literature and the Fine Arts*. East Lansing: Michigan State College Press, 1950.

Wold, M. and E. Cykler. *An Introduction to Music and Art in the Western World*. Dubuque: Wm. C. Brown Co., 1958.

29

TWENTIETH-CENTURY
KEYBOARD MUSIC:
GERMANY, AUSTRIA, ITALY,
AND THE SLAVIC COUNTRIES

GERMANY AND AUSTRIA

One of the outstanding musicians to appear in Germany toward the end of the nineteenth century was **Ferruccio Busoni** (1866–1924). Busoni, of Italian-German descent, was born in Italy but spent most of his mature, productive life in Germany. He wrote voluminous piano music as well as four operas, many songs, chamber music, etc. Little of it is heard now, fortunately, for it lacks creative imagination. Although such works as the *Sonatines* or the *Fantasia Contrapuntistica* definitely reveal the touch of a skillful, intellectual composer, they also disclose the sad need for emotional sensitivity. For example, the *Fantasia* (1910) contains three fugues, each supplied with a variation; the final coup comes when the three fugue subjects are not only combined with each other but are fitted to the principal subject of Bach's *Art of the Fugue!* Busoni considered the *Fantasia* the most important of his piano works and once wrote to his wife that it sounded like something between César Franck and the Beethoven *Hammerklavier Sonata*. The complete design of the *Fantasia* consists of:

Chorale-Variations on "Ehre sei Gott in der Höhe"
followed by a Quadruple Fugue
on a Bach Fragment

1. Chorale-Variations (Introduction, Chorale and Variations, Transition)
2. Fuga I, Fuga II, Fuga III
3. Intermezzo
4. Variatio I, Variatio II, Variatio III
5. Cadenza
6. Fuga IV
7. Coda

The work is a weighty collection of contrapuntal techniques and as such
has been studied and assimilated by many twentieth-century composers.
Its value lies in this rather than in its beauty or interest as a concert piece.

Although Busoni's original works are almost ignored by performing
pianists, his keyboard transcriptions of various works by J. S. Bach remain
of interest. Certain aspects of ornamentation are incorrect, but the transcriptions on the whole show proper respect for the originals. Particularly
outstanding are the *Chaconne* from the fourth violin *Partita* and several
organ chorale-preludes: *Wachet auf* (Sleepers, Wake); *Nun komm der
Heiden Heiland* (Come Thou, of Man the Saviour); and *Nun freuet euch,
lieben Christen* (Rejoice, Beloved Christians).[1]

Busoni was a powerful figure in European musical society, but his
influence on succeeding generations was confined to matters of basic technique. Thus this intellectual and skillful musician remains all but unknown
to the majority of those interested in the keyboard and its music.

Expressionism

One of the musically momentous events in this century occurred with
the birth of the Expressionist school pioneered by three composers—Arnold
Schönberg, Alban Berg, and Anton Webern. Its music was the German-
Austrian answer to French Impressionism. Like Impressionism, German
Expressionism (the term used to describe the atonal aesthetic) in music
derived principally from painting and literature—from artists like Paul
Klee and Wassily Kandinsky, from writers like Stefan George. In place of
the languid, misty chiaroscuro typical of the Impressionists, the Expres-
sionists accented the macabre, violence, hysteria, and irrationality. They
changed the concept of beauty to fit their own unique views of subconscious
reality.

The composers of this period developed a writing style commonly
called "atonal." The use of atonality did not necessarily comprise a musical
revolution; the foundation for it had been well prepared. In the nineteenth
century Richard Wagner had pushed chromaticism almost to the point of
tonal disintegration. In the early years of the twentieth century, Debussy
and the Impressionists staunchly repudiated traditional harmonic concepts
of consonance and dissonance. The final step was to reject all ideas of tonality and of key relationships. There was henceforth no difference between
the seven diatonic notes within a scale (i.e. C–D–E–F–G–A–B) and the
five auxiliary chromatic notes (C#–D#–F#–G#–A#): all twelve tones

---

[1] Most of Busoni's available original piano music is published by Breitkopf & Härtel. The
Fantasia Contrapuntistica has, however, been dropped from their catalogue. Breitkopf has also
edited Busoni's keyboard transcriptions of Bach.

comprising an octave were equal in every respect and were treated as such. In order to clarify his thinking, Arnold Schönberg formulated the twelve-tone (dodecaphonic) system of composition, which has remained the basic approach to the atonal style of writing.

The compositional idea is based on a tone row, a somewhat synthetic melody made up of all the tones comprising the chromatic scale (twelve-tone, i.e., the twelve chromatic notes contained within an octave). No note appears more than once within the set. The notes of the tone row are usually used to create both harmony and melody, to construct all contrapuntal materials. Transformations of the row through inversion, retrograde, and retrograde-inversion, make further expansion possible. Finally, the tone row or set—plus each of its transformations—is statable upon any degree of the semitonal scale.

Atonal music often has remarkable vitality, the result of imaginative rhythmic treatment, and it is amply supplied with expressive and interpretative markings. The following example by **Ernst Krenek** shows the basic approach to dodecaphony (Ex. 1).

Ex. 1.   Ernst Krenek: Example from *Twelve Short Piano Pieces Written in the Twelve-Tone Technique Op. 83*

Arnold Schönberg

The person most responsible for formulating and developing musical Expressionism was **Arnold Schönberg** (1874–1951). Piano music holds an important position throughout his creative development: almost every basic change in his evolving style is accompanied by a piano work or a group of piano pieces.

Three Piano Pieces Opus 11 (1908) are his first compositions in atonal style. In the very first piece (Ex. 2) it is obvious that distinctions between consonance and dissonance no longer exist. The essentially contrapuntal character of atonality emerges in these three pieces, where devices like canonic imitation are highlighted.

Ex. 2.   Arnold Schönberg: *Piano Piece Op. 11, No. 1*

By permission of Universal Edition, Vienna, copyright owner.

The first work from Schönberg's mature twelve-tone period is for keyboard—*Opus 23, Five Piano Pieces* (1923). The *Suite for Piano Opus 25* was written in 1925 and the last pieces for solo piano date from 1932—*Piano Pieces Opus 33a* and *Opus 33b*.[2]

Five Piano Pieces Opus 23 illustrate Schönberg's growing comprehension of the possibilities offered by his new system. In these pieces he handles the atonal technique of his earlier works with greater dexterity and freedom. The rhythms are more pungent and complex. In 1934 he wrote concerning these pieces, "Here I arrived at a technique which I called (for myself) 'composing with tones,' a very vague term, but it meant something to me. Namely: in contrast to the ordinary way of using a motive, I used it already almost in the manner of a 'basic set of twelve tones,' I built other motives and themes from it, and also accompaniments and other chords—but the theme did not consist of twelve tones."[3] The last piece of *Opus 23* shows that by this time the composer had actually formulated in his mind the basic rules of twelve-tone composition.

Suite Opus 25 illustrates that Schönberg had achieved even more flexibility in handling the dodecaphonic apparatus. Entitled *Praeludium, Gavotte with Minuet, Intermezzo, Minuet with Trio,* and *Gigue,* these pieces retain rhythmic reminders of their eighteenth- and nineteenth-cen-

---

[2] The *Opus 11* piano pieces are published by Universal Edition as are also the *Suite Opus 25* and the pieces *Opus 33*. The *Five Piano Pieces Opus 23* were issued by Wilhelm Hansen in 1923.

[3] Letter from Arnold Schönberg to Nicolas Slonimsky, June 3, 1937. In Nicolas Slonimsky, *Music Since 1900*, 3rd Edition, revised and enlarged (New York: Coleman-Ross Co., Inc., 1949), p. 681. Copyright 1949 by Coleman-Ross Company, Inc., New York. Used by permission.

tury prototypes even though structurally they speak a strikingly new language. The two *Piano Pieces Opus 33* elaborate still further on the unorthodox and uncompromising qualities of atonality, although texture and rhythm consort in a more restrained, transparent atmosphere.

Alban Berg

One of Schönberg's most gifted pupils, **Alban Berg** (1885–1935) accented a different aspect of Expressionism—emotionalism—and from its abstract patterns he shaped more lyric designs. Known chiefly for his opera *Wozzeck,* a violin concerto, and the *Lyric Suite* for string quartet, Berg also wrote one unique keyboard work, the *Sonata Opus 1* (1908).[4] This early one-movement sonata is in classic first movement form: exposition, expanded development, varied recapitulation, and coda. Although it is not constructed on actual twelve-tone technique, it closely simulates that approach: super dissonance, thick harmonic texture, concentrated musical expression, and strong formal elements. By pushing tonality to its limits, this work offers much that is interesting, but it is not one of Berg's representative compositions.

Anton Webern

Compared with Berg's style, the music of **Anton Webern** (1883–1945) tends to show lean texture, an extreme economy of means, and concentrated energy. He emphasizes contrapuntal devices and sweeping rhythmic and dynamic contrasts. Webern's single keyboard work—*Piano Variations Opus 27* (1936)[5]—sharply outlines his stark classic style: big skips, surprising rhythms, all combined with an exaggeration of every expressionistic detail. Also detectable here is the composer's admiration for procedures involving retrograde inversions, canons, and the like.

The *Avant-Garde*

These three Austrians—Schönberg, Berg, Webern—were the avowed proponents of dodecaphony, and today Germany and Austria still foster a young generation of atonalists and experimentalists. **Karlheinz Stockhausen** (*b.* 1928) is perhaps the leading figure in the German *avant-garde* group. His music is derived from Webern insofar as it strives for the utmost purity in abstract expression. Stockhausen's chief occupation is with strictly experimental music that eschews ordinary notions of unity, thematic develop-

---

[4] The Berg *Sonata Opus 1* is published by Universal Edition.
[5] Universal Edition publishes the Webern *Variations Opus 27.*

ment, and in fact most of the commonly accepted goals in musical composition. The element of chance—where the performer himself becomes a composer of sorts—is nowhere stressed more eloquently than in Stockhausen's *Klavierstück XI* (1956), which comes in several versions (*sic* packages!). One is a tube containing a long strip of paper with nineteen segments of music. The actual "doing" of the piece is complicated, but basically the pianist selects various segments *au hazard* and plays each according to directions contained in the preceding segment! It is difficult to be objective about such goings-on, yet the composer himself (the original composer) is undoubtedly serious in his superunorthodox approach.

Stockhausen's earlier *Klavierstück I–IV* (1952–1954) are not so astonishing, but they most certainly do not fit into the category of "conventional" piano music. At first glance the pieces seem unplayable, but the composer offers a note of explanation: "The tempo of each piece, determined by the smallest note-value, is 'as fast as possible.' When the player has found this tempo and determined it metronomically, all the more complicated time proportions . . . can be replaced by changes of tempo." Is this to be the music of the future? Time will tell.

Although Stockhausen's music has been the most publicized beyond the borders of his own country, other present-day German composers are also using techniques derived basically from Schönberg's principles. In his eight piano pieces called *Konfigurationen*, **Bernd Aloys Zimmermann** (*b.* 1918) seems occupied mainly with manipulating extreme dynamic controls within a few short measures. **Giselher Klebe** (*b.* 1925) handles the twelve-tone apparatus both strictly and freely in his *Vier Inventionen Opus 26*, while **Hans Werner Henze** (*b.* 1926) delights in series of rhythmic complexes in his three-movement *Sonata per Pianoforte*. Another atonalist, **Jürg Baur** has written an impressive *Capriccio: Studie nach einer Zwölftonreihe* (1957).[6]

Other German Composers

Despite the inroads made by Expressionism, other composers from Germany and Austria are writing music with more conventional outlines. The modern dean of German composers was undoubtedly **Paul Hindemith** (1895–1963). During his earlier years, Hindemith experimented with various stylistic formulas—polytonality, atonality, modality, chord systems of unusual intervals—and each experience contributed to his ultimate style.

---

[6] Stockhausen's piano works appear in Universal Edition; Schott publishes Henze and Zimmermann's music; Klebe's *Inventionen* are issued by Bote & Bock; Baur's *Capriccio* by Breitkopf & Härtel.

As a mature composer he adopted an advanced harmonic concept involving a free use of the twelve tones yet preserving the tradition of tonality. This master musician evolved a personalized, lucid writing style that places the linear element (dissonant counterpoint) in a most attractive light. However, there is a sameness of sound in his music that is likely to be monotonous for the listener who finds his pleasure in variety. As an exponent of at least one trend of contemporary music, Hindemith was a fine craftsman whose serious concern with music's formal elements has resulted in solid, durable tonal canvases.

One of Hindemith's most effective works is an early composition for piano solo, the *Suite "1922" Opus 26* in five movements: *Marsch, Schimmy, Nachtstück, Boston,* and *Ragtime,* in the mood of a parody on dance styles from the early twenties. Each movement demands a specific approach; nevertheless, the general atmosphere has the feeling of unrestrained freedom in expression and rhythmic design.

Hindemith's three piano sonatas were all written in 1936. *Sonata No. 1* was inspired by Friederich Hölderlin's poem *Der Main.* This large-scale work in five movements embodies Hindemith's typical writing style: concentrated, musicianly, classic. The somewhat cursory first movement serves as an introduction to the entire work. In A B A form, the second movement requests performance *Im Zeitmass eines sehr langsamen Marsches* (in the tempo of a slow march). The lyrical center section contrasts with the vibrant sheen of the ponderously rhythmic sections embracing it. The lengthy third movement is sectionalized, yet an innate unity leads one passage logically into the other. A similarity to Brahms's third piano sonata is evident in the fourth movement, a kind of *Rückblick* or retrospective passage closely related to the opening movement. The sonata closes in an energetic, rhythmic mood with the final movement marked *Lebhaft.*

The second *Sonata* has smaller dimensions, is technically easier, and is not so dramatic and serious. There are only three movements: the first in transparent sonata form, a middle movement like an exuberant scherzo, and the final *Rondo,* which is prefaced by a slow passage in dotted rhythms.

In contrast to the previous work, *Sonata No. 3* is extremely difficult to play. In some ways the choicest of the three sonatas, it is a good example of Hindemith's command of keyboard sonority and contrapuntal intricacies. The last of the four movements is a powerful double fugue.

Hindemith's *Ludus Tonalis* (1943) is a kind of contemporary *Well-Tempered Clavier* in that it consists of twelve fugues in twelve keys, joined by contrasting interludes. In either three or four voices, these fugues make a fine compendium of twentieth-century contrapuntal techniques.[7]

---

[7] The Schott catalogue lists Hindemith's important piano music: three *Sonatas, Suite Opus 26, Ludus Tonalis.*

Another well-known German, the fine concert pianist **Wilhelm Kempff** (*b.* 1895), is by no means an insignificant composer, judging by his conventional but imaginatively written *Sonata Opus 47*.[8]

Boris Blacher (*b.* 1903), a leading figure in German contemporary music, has become known outside his native country only since the Second World War; still his name is an important one. He has written in many idioms. Intent upon rhythmical problems, Blacher has incorporated some of his personal ideas in his keyboard music. *Ornamente Opus 37* (1950) contains seven studies in shifting meters. Each measure uses a different meter, the pattern being worked out according to preconceived plans. Blacher enlarges upon this theory and makes it more meaningful in *Sonata Opus 39*.[9] The texture is bare, the action sacrificed almost entirely to a display of rhythm.

ITALY

Italian keyboard composition remained at low ebb during the nineteenth century because Italy at that time was deeply engulfed in opera. After the *cembalo* composers passed from the scene, hardly any other writers came forward to continue the keyboard tradition—except for a conspicuous few near the end of the nineteenth century. What Italy needed was a dynamic talent to compete against the reigning opera mania. At the end of the century, when Italian *verismo* was shaping the lyric stage, several champions of instrumental music dedicated themselves almost exclusively to nonoperatic compositions. However, instead of looking to the magnificent Italian Baroque for models, they unfortunately chose to copy the German Romantics, chiefly Brahms. Two of these composers, Martucci and Sgambati, possessed enough skill in musical composition to give a little aid to their cause.

Giuseppe Martucci (1856–1909) began as a piano prodigy, then served as a professor of piano at Naples Conservatory before turning to conducting. A catalogue of his works lists many little character pieces for piano.[10]

Giovanni Sgambati (1841–1914) became celebrated as a pianist in Rome, where he also studied with Liszt and gave orchestral concerts featuring works by the great German masters. His twelve opuses devoted to piano music prove that he had a vast knowledge of the piano and its capa-

---

[8] Salabert offers the Kempff *Sonata Opus 47*, published in 1959.
[9] Blacher's keyboard music is published by Bote & Bock of Berlin-Wiesbaden.
[10] G. Ricordi publishes several pieces by Martucci.

bilities. There are, among others, a *Prelude and Fugue, Études,. Nocturnes,* and a romantically inspired *Suite.*[11]

Alfredo Casella

It was left to another generation to delve into Italy's glorious past and to produce a new classicism directed toward instrumental music, a feat neatly accomplished by **Alfredo Casella** (1883–1947), whose objectives were a clean break with Romanticism and a return to instrumental counterpoint. Casella lived away from Italy for almost twenty years—he resided in Paris from his thirteenth to thirty-second year—and this doubtlessly played a positive role in shaping his musical style. Among his co-students in Paris, he made friends with Maurice Ravel and Charles Koechlin. From 1906 to 1909 he toured Europe as harpsichordist with the *Société des Instruments Anciens;* his familiarity with the harpsichord is evident in his attitudes concerning keyboard texture.

Casella, who devoted considerable time to piano composition, always remained interested in harmony and dissonance; consequently, his keyboard works have a unique individual character. In attempting to form a new expressionistic language, he first concentrated on ancient dance forms and nationalism; then he became engrossed with chromaticism (*Piano Sonata* of 1916). Later (about 1923) he achieved wonderfully lucid form and content and consistent tonal purity. He described his objectives in his memoirs, "For us Italians, the so-called return to the golden age of our instrumental music was no more than a renunciation of the rigid Beethovenian form, of the easy seductions of the symphonic poem, and of the inconsistency of impressionism, restoring in the place of these doctrines our old polyphonic instrumental disciplines, which were not a goal in themselves but a means toward the rediscovery with present-day resources of the old, admirable, easy, free discursiveness of music."[12]

Casella had a mischievous humor, musically speaking, somewhat like Ravel. In a series of short keyboard pieces entiled *A la Manière de* (1911, 1913) he parodies larger works written by prominent musical personalities. Thus *Symphonia Molestica* brings to mind a noted work by Richard Strauss (*Symphonia Domestica*); *Almanazor ou le Mariage d'Adelaïde* recalls in clever turns of phrase Ravel's *Valses Nobles et Sentimentales.*

But Casella wrote more significant works too: the sonorous, polychordal

---

[11] Little pieces by Sgambati are found in the catalogues of G. Schirmer, Schott, and Ricordi.

[12] Alfredo Casella, *Music in My Time,* trans. and ed. S. Norton (Norman: University of Oklahoma Press, 1955), p. 226. Copyright by the University of Oklahoma Press.

tone poem *A Notte Alta* (To a Deep Night, 1917); *Due Ricercari Sul Nome B. A. C. H.* (Two Ricercars on the Name Bach, 1932), where a dexterous, polyphonic *Funèbre* (in memory of his mother) contrasts with the rhythmic, percussive *Ostinato*; and the large-scale *Sinfonia, Arioso and Toccata* (1936). Another pair of pieces is found in *Deux Contrastes* (1918): a melodic *Grazioso* (*Hommage à Chopin*) followed by a composition with the amusing title *Antigrazioso*.

As a practicing pianist Casella was intent upon problems involving technique, an absorption that led him to write his *Sei Studi Opus 70* (1944), obviously modeled on similar études by Chopin. In fact, study number two is subtitled *Omaggio a Chopin*.[13]

Gian Malipiero

The ideals set up by Casella were eagerly embraced by **Gian Francesco Malipiero** (*b.* 1882), who also searched into Italy's past for his inspiration, especially for works by Venetian composers. His music is related to sixteenth-century melodic types, and Gregorian chant seems to have influenced him. In structural concepts he is unique: melodic sections follow each other like series of episodes, indicating an aversion to formal thematic development. He also takes great liberties with rhythm. Malipiero wrote a large amount of keyboard music, of which the four impressionistic pieces comprising *Preludi Autunnali* (1914) are most effective. Four sketches in dissonance—*Risonanze* (1918)—effectively explore various aspects of polytonality.[14]

Ottorino Respighi

The rather consistent high standards maintained by Casella and Malipiero fell by the way with **Ottorino Respighi** (1879–1936). As a student of Max Bruch, he was not sympathetic with their dependence on Italian models, and in his own music he combined elements of French Impressionism with an overt German Romanticism. His piano pieces, such as *Study in A-Flat* and *Three Preludes on Gregorian Themes* (1921), are only fair; they are synthetic works without much character.[15]

---

[13] The Ricordi catalogue lists Casella's *A Notte Alta* and *Due Ricercari Sul Nome "Bach."* The *Deux Contrastes* are published by J. & W. Chester; Salabert puts out the *A la Manière de* in two volumes. *Sinfonia, Arioso and Toccata Opus 59* is available by Carisch, and Edizioni Curci lists the *Six Studies Opus 70*.

[14] Malipiero's piano pieces are scattered among several publishing houses. Salabert: *Poemetti Lunari, Preludi Autunnali;* and F. Bongiovanni: *Risonanze.*

[15] Universal Edition publishes the *Three Preludes on Gregorian Melodies* and Bongiovanni lists several short pieces—a *Nocturne* and an *Étude.*

Other Composers

There are of course many contemporary Italian musicians who have written effective keyboard music. **Mario Castelnuovo-Tedesco** (*b.* 1895) has created the deeply moving rhapsody *Le Danze del Re David* (Dances of King David, 1925), based on traditional Hebrew themes. A more recent work is his *English Suite* (published 1962) for piano or harpsichord: a *Preludio, quasi un improvvisazione, Andante,* and *Giga.* The *Tre Pezzi* (Three Pieces) of 1956 by **Giuseppe Barbera** are delightful little sketches. **Bonaventura Baratelli's** *Pagine Liriche* (Lyric Pages) offers nine poems inspired by paintings, literature, and music.

Pietro Montani (*b.* 1895) displays his musical skill in several ways: he is a pianist, an editor, and a composer. In the last capacity he has written, among other piano compositions, a delightful series of brief character pieces collectively titled *L'Arca di Noè* (Noah's Ark). The amusing *Capriccio del cucù* from this set is another addition to the long list of "cuckoo" pieces.

The year 1957 brought fourth a trio of superb piano works by two fine Italian musicians. **Sandro Fuga** (*b.* 1906) wrote two: a large-scale *Sonata* in four movements and *Variazioni Gioconde,* a theme with twelve elegantly fashioned variations. The second composer, **Franco Margola** (*b.* 1908), professor at the Conservatory of Rome, has written three sonatas. The clear-textured *Sonata No. 3* (1957) is a good example of his forthright style.[16]

Dodecaphony was introduced to Italian keyboard music by **Luigi Dallapiccola** (*b.* 1904). His early works are not atonal. For example, the *Sonatina Canonica in Mi Bemolle Maggiore Su "Capricci" di Niccolò Paganini* is written, as the title states, in the "key" of *B-flat* major. This *Sonatina* contains four short pieces in canonic style. Here Dallapiccola handles dissonance and counterpoint in a purely personal manner. The first movement, *Allegretto comodo,* has simple three-part form. In the first and last sections, an organ point on *E-flat* moves in steady pace. Above this organ point the composer unfolds his canon, the imitating voice entering in augmentation. The middle section, *Allegro,* features linear motives, which scurry busily over the different registers of the keyboard.

Even when Dallapiccola uses twelve-tone procedures, his approach is unlike Schönberg's. Atonality for the Italian is an experience, a vision rather than a technique. In 1952—on commission for the Pittsburgh International Contemporary Music Festival—he wrote the *Quaderno Musicale di An-*

---

[16] M. Castelnuovo-Tedesco: *Le Danze del Re David* (A. Forlivesi); *Six Canons Opus 142* (Leeds Music Corp.); *English Suite* (Mills Music). Giuseppe Barbera: *3 Pezzi* (Ricordi). Bonaventura Baratelli: *Pagine Liriche* (Proprietà dell'Autore). Pietro Montani: *L'Arca di Noè* (Ricordi). Sandro Fuga: *Sonata* (1957); *Variazioni Gioconde* (Ricordi). Franco Margola: *3ª Sonata* (Ricordi).

nalibera (Annalibera's Musical Exercise Book). This modest collection of eleven short pieces is one of the choicest keyboard works written by any European composer of this century. Here is a truly pure writing style: great rhythmic subtlety, cerebral canonic structures alternating with pieces of fantasy. The composer specifies that the pieces are to be played as a single work, a suite. A prelude called *Simbolo* (Symbol) opens the *Quaderno,* and a brief *Quartina* (Quatrain) serves as a coda. Of the other nine pieces, three are contrapuntal studies, of which the second one—*Canon Contrario Motu*—is unusually attractive (Ex. 3). The six other pieces are more freely contrived and bear titles such as *Linee* (Lines) and *Fregi* (Friezes).[17]

Ex. 3. Luigi Dallapiccola: *Quaderno Musicale di Annalibera*
No. 5—*Contrapunctus Secundus*

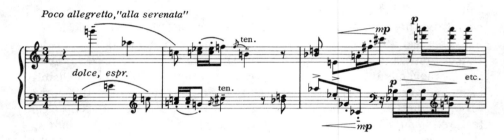

By permission of Edizioni Suvini Zerboni, Milan, Italy.

RUSSIA

Russian keyboard music has been uneven. The Romanticism of the late-nineteenth-century schools—one nationalist, the other more European-oriented—persisted until the 1917 Bolshevik Revolution. Alexander Scriabin exerted a new influence in the early twentieth century on the young composers looking for different, vital expressive methods. After the revolution, the Communist government instructed Russian composers to write music that would appeal to the masses; the Bolshevik party frowned upon experimental music.

In those years following the revolution, musicians formed various organizations. The "Russian Association of Proletarian Musicians" strove for art forms suitable to the working class; the "Association for Contemporary Music" tried to present advanced types of current European music; and in

[17] Suvini Zerboni publishes both the *Sonatina Canonica* and the *Quaderno Musicale.*

1932 the "Union of Soviet Composers" was organized in an effort to combine the aims and ideals of all the various groups into harmonious unity—both musically and politically.

Nicolas Miaskovsky

Nicolas Miaskovsky (1881–1950) was a fellow student of Prokofiev at St. Petersburg Conservatory, studying with Liadov and Rimsky-Korsakov, but Miaskovsky is hardly known beyond Russia. He gained national recognition through his twenty-seven symphonies, few of which are ever heard in Europe or America. All in all, there is nothing very original about his music, which remains basically within the Romantic tradition. It is frequently sentimental although occasionally peppered with dissonant harmony. He consistently uses the fourth and augmented fourth and applies counterpoint lavishly.

The sad mood surrounding Miaskovsky's music is perhaps its one characteristic—and redeeming—feature. The early *Sonata in F-sharp Minor* (1912), full of turbulent emotionalism and heightened by Scriabinesque chromaticisms, is not typical of his mature style. *Sonata Opus 27 in C Minor* (1924) exploits virtuosity in the grand manner; later a simpler writing style controls the three-movement *Sonata Opus 83 in D Minor*.[18]

Serge Prokofiev

One of the finest twentieth-century composers is **Serge Prokofiev** (1891–1953), who began his career as a concert pianist. In his autobiography he names five principal factors that have dominated his art in varying degrees at different periods. These elements are: (1) classicism—an affinity for forms indigenous to the Baroque and Classic periods; (2) innovation—a striving for a new harmonic language and the means for expressing stronger emotions; (3) the toccata or motor element, where rhythmic vitality plays an important role; (4) the lyric element; and (5) an element of either grotesqueness, jesting, or mockery, so typical of pieces like *Suggestion Diabolique* (1909).

Prokofiev sought freedom from typical nineteenth-century techniques. He uses the piano's full sonority, at the same time treating it as a basically percussive instrument. His music, which has become extremely popular, often suggests strange, psychological elements. He wrote more than one hundred short piano pieces of all types.

One of the most delightful collections is *Ten Little Piano Pieces Opus*

---

[18] Universal Edition lists some rather unimportant *Reminiscences Opus 29*. Otherwise, his music may be ordered through Leeds Music Corp.

12, written intermittently from 1908 through 1913. All the attractive features of Prokofiev's style are found here in miniature. Each of the ten pieces is attractive in its own way but only several of the more distinctive can be mentioned here. The *Marche* is a terse, pompous overture with two short, alternating themes; the popular *Gavotte* features a heavy-handed treatment of this graceful dance form; *Mazurka* is built entirely in quartal harmony, yet maintains the basic features of the dance. Strangely enough, Prokofiev specifies that the *Prélude* is for piano *or* harp. Here shimmering broken figurations in the right hand support an essentially modest melodic line. This set of ten highly stylized pieces is a convincing testimonial to Prokofiev's mastery of his craft.

Prokofiev's finest keyboard writing is exhibited in the nine piano sonatas. Their composition covers a span of over forty years (1907–1953). The three-movement *Sonata No. 1 in F Minor Opus 1* was originally written in 1907, but Prokofiev soon became dissatisfied with the second and third movements. In 1909 he published the first movement revised into a one-movement sonata. This eclectic piece contains many passing references to Schumann (*F-sharp Minor Sonata*), Rachmaninov, and Scriabin. Prokofiev's biting style is not yet apparent, the melodies are diatonic, and the harmonies romantic.

The emerging musical vocabulary of the Russian composer is more than evident in the second sonata, *Opus 14 in D Minor,* which was coolly received at its premiere in 1914. It developed from a one-movement sonatine, enlarged by a *Scherzo* (written earlier for a class in composition) and two additional movements. The harmonic palette is enriched with biting dissonance, the rhythmic framework is lively, and the melodies are vigorous and angular.

The third, *Sonata in A Minor Opus 28* (begun in 1907, completed in 1917), is a great favorite with pianists. Dramatic passion, clarity, unrestrained enthusiasm, all are packed into a one-movement sonata in classic form. It emphasizes melody, or rather melodies, which Prokofiev has submitted to motivic development.

After this energetic third sonata he wrote the restrained and somewhat melancholy *Sonata in C Minor Opus 29.* The next sonata has two versions: *Sonata No. 5 in C Major* originated in 1923 as *Opus 38;* the composer believed it to be too intricate, its texture too chromatic, so he extracted a simplified version, published in 1955 as *Opus 135.* This completely objective, formal work is less frequently played than the others.

One of Prokofiev's virtuoso keyboard works is his sixth, *Sonata in A Major Opus 82.* The diabolic pianistic gymnastics involved in this large-scale, four-movement creation limit its performance to a few fine pianists. In 1942 Prokofiev completed *Sonata in B-flat Major Opus 83* (the seventh); this piece is typical of the Russian composer in the way its brittle percussive style consorts with lyrical passages. The tightly knit first movement is followed by an *Andante doloroso* with a richly sonorous melodic line—Prokofiev here reverts to his youthful romantic style. The *Precipitato,* or third movement, becomes almost hypnotic in its rhythmic propulsion.

The last two sonatas—*B-flat Major Opus 84* and *C Major Opus 103*—present a more reserved aspect of the composer's style. The nervous tension and exuberant dissonances of earlier sonatas are replaced by a calm, introspective atmosphere, a most refreshing coda to this collection.[19]

Igor Stravinsky

Igor Stravinsky (*b.* 1882) should properly be included here even though for many years he has preferred to live in the United States. Stravinsky's biting, acid style and rhythmic fantasy have made him one of this century's most influential composers; there is scarcely a composer under fifty who does not owe some stylistic trait to this Russian musician.

Viewed in perspective, his keyboard music is not as important as his other works. His approach is orchestral and it is in that medium that he is most attractive. One exception is the *Trois Mouvements de Petrouchka* (1921), three vividly colorful (and extremely difficult) scenes extracted from his celebrated ballet and paraphrased for piano by the composer.

His other large-scale keyboard works are not convincing. In the three-movement *Sonata* of 1924 the term sonata applies only in its original meaning of "sounding piece." Even less effective is *Sérénade en La* (1925), written in eighteenth-century serenade style. The music is not pianistic, and the lean, gaunt texture does little to enhance the scant amount of imagination.[20]

Dmitri Kabalevsky

A critic and musicologist as well as imaginative composer, **Dmitri Kabalevsky** (*b.* 1904) was one of Miaskovsky's pupils at Moscow Conservatory. Although he looks to the past, Kabalevsky is an expert craftsman with an inherent gift for lyricism. Much of his music has been written for young people—*Sonatinas, Children's Pieces Opus 27, Variations Opus 40*—and

[19] Prokofiev's music is readily available: *Sonatas Opus 1* and *14, Piano Pieces Opus 12, Toccata Opus 11* (Forberg through Peters); *Sonatas Opuses 28, 29, 38, Visions Fugitives Opus 22, Two Sonatinas Opus 54* (Boosey & Hawkes); Complete *Sonatas* (Kalmus); *Four Pieces Opus 4, Four Pieces Opus 32, Sonatas, Three Pieces Opus 95, Sarcasms Opus 17, Visions Fugitives Opus 22* (Leeds).

[20] Most of Stravinsky's keyboard music is handled by Boosey & Hawkes: *Trois Mouvements de Petrouchka, Sonata, Sérénade en La.*

they are unusually appealing. His *Twenty-Four Preludes Opus 38* (*ca.* 1946) call for mature technique, and *Sonata No. 2, Opus 45 in E-flat* is even more difficult: its four large movements border on the virtuoso. *Sonata Opus 46 in F Major* is written in plainer language and is conventional in appearance.[21] There are three short movements (the entire sonata is only twenty-three pages long). The quizzical *Allegro con moto* is fashioned in clear, melodic sonata-allegro form. Rapid modulations and pleasant dissonances give the movement its character. Following are a brief *Andante cantabile* written in a rather dense harmonic texture and a boisterous *Allegro giocoso*.

Aram Khachaturian

Armenian-born **Aram Khachaturian** (*b.* 1903) has produced few piano compositions. His background accounts for the folk idiom dominating much of his music. Avoiding formal developmental procedures, Khachaturian surrounds his ornamented thematic material with multiple parallel-chord progressions. Two of his keyboard works are quite interesting: *Poem* (1927) is an effective purveyor of colorful atmosphere, while the famous *Toccata* is a brilliant showpiece with a contrasting lyric middle section.[22]

Dmitri Shostakovitch

The most widely acknowledged composer residing in Russia today is **Dmitri Shostakovitch** (*b.* 1906). His early works, written in his twenties, are strongly influenced by Prokofiev and Stravinsky—this is especially true of the one-movement *Piano Sonata No. 1, Opus 12* (1926). In general, Shostakovitch's keyboard music displays a spirit of new classicism marked by textural simplicity and structural clarity.

During 1932–1933 Shostakovitch wrote a series of twenty-four *Preludes Opus 34* (one in each major and minor key), each of which—in the manner of Bach and Chopin—develops and comments upon a single musical idea. In the process, he paraphrases other composers' styles, even offers parodies of salon music. And as a further comment on this sometimes tongue-in-cheek approach, the *Prelude in E Minor* is not a prelude but a fugue!

Opus 34 doubtlessly helped Shostakovitch to acquire more skill in this type of writing. What ultimately followed was a twentieth-century *Well-Tempered Clavier*, the *Twenty-Four Preludes and Fugues Opus 87*, completed in 1951. This mature and lengthy work (well over two hundred pages) must be considered a major contribution to twentieth-century

---

[21] A most complete listing of Kabalevsky's piano music is found in the catalogue of Leeds Music Corp.

[22] Leeds publishes the few piano pieces written by Khachaturian.

contrapuntal art. The only other similar work is Paul Hindemith's *Ludus Tonalis*. In *Opus 87* Shostakovitch proves his mastery of both counterpoint and the intricacies of fugal writing, and he shows that the utmost variety of mood and character is possible within the framework of the prelude and fugue; each of these twenty-four preludes and fugues is totally different from the others.

Some of the more distinctive preludes are worth noting. *Prelude in C Major* initiates an elegant sarabande rhythm and maintains this character throughout. The *Prelude in A Minor* and the *Prelude in B-flat Major* are obviously fashioned as études. The classic outlines of the passacaglia emerge in *Prelude in G-sharp Minor,* while *Prelude in E Major* (written on three staves) moves in cadence like a miniature march.

The fugues may lack the interesting variety found in the preludes, but they provide a good textbook of contemporary contrapuntal practice. They range from two to five voices. Some (*Fugue in G Major*) are treated like a gigue, others (*Fugue in E Minor*) are more serious. One of the most interesting is the *Fugue in D-flat Major*. The fugue subject is almost like a tone row: all the notes of the chromatic scale are used, except one. The subject is set into measures of two, three, and five time units. Needless to say, the development of this subject is equally startling, and it is almost a shock when this highly dissonant work concludes in the key of *D-flat.*[23]

The Russian composers—excluding Prokofiev and Shostakovitch—have not devoted their talents very generously to keyboard music, but in fairness it should be pointed out that the piano is not a typical Russian instrument; it is not equipped to exploit the multihued tonal colors so prevalent in native Russian music.

CZECHOSLOVAKIA AND POLAND

Dvořák and Smetana introduced a nationalism into Czechoslovakian music that extended into the twentieth century and is even now still apparent. One pioneer in contemporary music, however, was **Leoš Janáček** (1854–1928), who spent most of his life in his native Moravia. Janáček's musical development came slowly; his first really significant work appeared after he was forty, and he was sixty before he became generally recognized. His unique approach to composition—an unusual concept of harmony and modality, the use and reuse of similar melodic material, and a consistent use of extended variation—makes him a genuine contributor to twentieth-century music. He wrote only a small amount of piano music, including

[23] *Sonata Opus 64, Twenty-Four Preludes Opus 34,* and the two volumes comprising *Twenty-Four Preludes and Fugues Opus 87* are available at Leeds.

Sonata 1.x.1905 in two movements, some delightful miniatures and, of all things, *"Music for Indian Club Swinging"* (1895).

There are two other talented Czechoslovakian composers who should be noted. **Vitezslav Novak** (1870–1949) acquired a national style with his discovery of Moravian and Slovakian folk music. His *Sonata Eroica Opus 24* (1900) adheres to romantic emotionalism but a folk-song spirit is prominent in both rhythm and melody. A group of *Sonatinas* (1919) and *Variations on a Theme by Schumann* (1893) are equally fine examples of Novak's writing.[24]

Finally, one composer's fame has reached far beyond his native Czechoslovakia, possibly because of his background; **Bohuslav Martinu** (1890–1959) lived for long periods in France and America, and in France he studied under Albert Roussel. Judging by his more than one hundred and fifty compositions, he might be described as a Neo-Classicist, especially in matters of structure and rhythm, but his melodies are derived from Moravian folk song.

Martinu's keyboard music consists largely of little miniatures that might be considered salon music. There are also some successful settings of Czech dances and three books of *Études and Polkas* (1945). An unusual exception to this repertoire of miniatures is his three-movement *Sonata No. 1*, which highlights bitonal texture. The developmental procedure is cumulative in that one motive is fashioned from a preceding one.[25]

Early-twentieth-century Polish music is identified with conservatism. Elements and techniques from nineteenth-century western music had been absorbed by an older generation of Polish composers and since then nothing new had happened. To combat this static condition, some musicians in 1905 formed the "Association of Young Polish Composers," later known as "Young Poland in Music."

The new group's outstanding personality, **Karol Szymanowski** (1882–1937), had early developed a fondness for classical forms, but he tempered this inclination with a natural talent for harmonic subtlety and rhythmic elasticity. Szymanowski's youthful admiration for Max Reger's musical style is easily discernible in *Sonata No. 2, Opus 21* (1910); however, as he matured he turned away from conventional tonality and charged his music with chromatic elaboration in the manner of Scriabin. This change in style characterizes the *Métopes Opus 29* (1915), three florid tone pictures presented in improvisatory fashion. At the same time, he found himself as a composer so that thereafter his characteristic style became stabilized. *Twelve Études Opus 33* (1917) and the fine one-movement *Sonata No. 3*,

---

[24] The music of both Janáček and Novak is published by Artia of Czechoslovakia.
[25] Boosey & Hawkes handles most of Martinu's music: *Études and Polkas, Fables, Puppets.* M. Eschig publishes *Sonata No. 1.*

Opus 36 (1917) present an accurate picture of Szymanowski's contemporary idiom.[26]

BIBLIOGRAPHY

Busoni, Ferruccio. *Letters to His Wife* (translated by Rosamond Ley). London: Edward Arnold & Co., 1938.

Ewen, David. *European Composers Today.* New York: The H. W. Wilson Co., 1954.

Guerrini, Guido. *Ferruccio Busoni.* Firenze: Casa Editrice Monsalvato, 1944.

Hartog, Howard, ed. *European Music in the Twentieth Century.* New York: F. A. Praeger, 1957.

Hull, A. Eaglefield. *Scriabin.* London: Kegan Paul, Trench, Trubner & Co., Ltd., 1927.

Mersman, Dr. Hans. *Die Moderne Musik.* Wildpark-Potsdam: Akademische Verlagsgesellschaft Athenaion, 1929.

Nestyev, Israel V. *Prokofiev* (translated by F. Jonas). Stanford: Stanford University Press, 1960.

Olkhovsky, Andrey. *Music under the Soviets.* London: Routledge & Kegan Paul, Ltd., 1955.

Redlich, H. F. *Alban Berg.* New York: Abelard-Schuman Ltd., 1957.

Seroff, Victor. *Dmitri Shostakovich.* New York: Alfred A. Knopf, 1943.

Stuckenschmidt, H. H. *Arnold Schoenberg* (translated by Roberts and Searle). New York: Grove Press, 1959.

Tuttle, T. Temple. "Schönberg's Compositions for Piano Solo." *Music Review,* Vol. 18, No. 4, 1957.

[26] Universal Edition is the publishing house for Szymanowski's works: *Sonatas II* and *III, Métopes Opus 29, Twelve Études Opus 33,* and numerous others.

30

TWENTIETH-CENTURY
KEYBOARD MUSIC:
FRANCE, HUNGARY, HOLLAND,
SPAIN, AND ENGLAND

FRANCE

The music picture in twentieth-century France is filled with contra-dictions, with manifestos and counter-manifestos. Gabriel Fauré's pupils and disciples prolonged Romanticism far beyond its natural productive life. Debussy and Ravel—each in his own way—exerted far-reaching influences in both a positive and negative sense. And foreign influences, particularly Germanic, played their roles in directing the French music of this era along its tortuous path. As a result of these diverse circumstances and pressures, France has produced some superb, beautiful music and, alas, an impossible assortment of poor music.

Erik Satie

A very important and enigmatic figure during the early years was **Erik Satie** (1866–1925), whom some critics regard as a direct precursor of Im-pressionism while others brush him off as an eccentric dilettante. Both positions are valid. Many elements account for Satie's style or rather his styles, for there are several. His early friendships with Debussy, Jean Cocteau, and Pablo Picasso are understandably important influences. In addition, his belated—he was forty—contrapuntal studies with d'Indy and Roussel at the *Schola Cantorum* had a decided effect on his later writing.

There are detectable flaws in Satie's music, yet it is so intimate that from within its core there emerges a strikingly original personality. A vital segment of this personality grew (about 1887) out of his preoccupation with the mystic secrets of Rosicrucianism. In 1887 he wrote three *Sarabandes,* whose suave chromatic harmonies create a distinctly melancholy air. It must be admitted that certain stylistic traits in these works could be interpreted as forerunners of Impressionism. This also applies to his three *Gymnopédies* (1888) and the three *Gnossiennes* (1890), in which the harmonies become simpler and a feeling of modality prevails. (This trinitarian format remained with Satie throughout his life.) In contrast to Debussy's predominantly harmonic approach, Satie's series of parallel chords—sevenths, ninths, and elevenths—are habitually dependent on delicately designed melodic patterns.

Satie's passionate engrossment with the esoteric revelations of the Rosicrucian brotherhood (*Rose-Croix*) dominated his artistic production for several years. The *Sonneries de la Rose-Croix* (Fanfares of the Rosicrucians) of 1892 and *Prélude de la Porte Héroïque du Ciel* (Prelude of the Heroic Heavenly Gate) of 1894, which he dedicated to himself, give a faithful picture of Satie the mystic. Static chord groupings are treated in modal style, like plainsong accompaniments, and alternate with free melody in octaves. It is all purely decorative music, just one side of a versatile composer.

Toward the turn of the century, Satie entered a phase where apparent facetious humor disguises the music's really serious mien and originality. The often amusing verbal comments that he added to the scores are perhaps a self-protective apparatus which is, of course, unnecessary. Melody-types of popular timbre are merged with a linear approach, mostly in two parts, and severe contrapuntal workings also occur frequently. In the *Pièces Froides* (Cold Pieces, 1897) an elegant marriage of plainsong and symmetrical clarity results in a delightful series of pieces.

Satie's true worth, however, lies in the ten piano suites or collections, which appeared from 1912 to 1915. Diatonic harmony disciplined by strict note economy strengthens the assumption that with this series of miniatures (such as *Véritables Préludes Flasques*, *Embryons Desséchés*, and *Heures Séculaires et Instantanées*) and the unbelievably original *Sports et Divertissements* (Sports and Diversions), Satie approached an artistic expression both nonsentimental and nonrhetorical. One might say that the composer maintained an "attitude" of ingenuity and used *naïveté* as a method.

In later years Satie omitted the ironic elements from his works, creating a style in which continual rhythm and texture founded on fourths and fifths indicate that his maturity derived naturally from previous musical experiences. His final keyboard work is a collection of five well-designed *Nocturnes* (1919).[1]

Charles Koechlin

Charles Koechlin (1867–1951), one of Satie's contemporaries, is for the most part disregarded except in France. His precision, clarity, and masterful

---

[1] M. Eschig and Salabert between them publish most of Satie's music: *Embryons Desséchés, Heures Séculaires et Instantanées, Véritables Préludes Flasques, Vieux Sequins et Vieilles Cuirasses, Nocturnes 4* and *5* (Eschig); *Gymnopédies, Gnossiennes, Nocturnes 1–3, Pièces Froides, Prélude de la Porte Héroïque du Ciel, Sarabandes, Sonneries de la Rose-Croix* (Salabert).

use of instrumental counterpoint forcefully illustrate the fact that he continues along the path set down by Saint-Saëns and Fauré; yet he goes far beyond his teacher Fauré in harmony and texture. Essentially an eclectic, Koechlin is skillful with metrically free, long modal lines reminiscent of ancient organum. This is quite noticeable in *Esquisses Opus 41* (Sketches, 1905–1915) and the *Sonatines Opus 59* (1915–1916) and *Opus 87* (1923–1924). Among Koechlin's musically mature collections is *Paysages et Marines Opus 63* (Landscapes and Seascapes), two books of six pieces each. These landscapes and marine sketches often contain diffuse chord structures and sometimes monotony develops from overuse of simple devices; yet despite the textural complexity the sonorities are surprisingly clear and refreshing.[2]

Florent Schmitt

In 1946 the author had an interesting conversation with the late Alfred Cortot, eminent concert pianist and scholar. When asked whom he considered to be France's greatest living composer, Cortot unhesitatingly answered, "Without any doubt, Florent Schmitt." History will probably disprove M. Cortot's assertion, for **Florent Schmitt** (1870–1958) is largely forgotten today. A student of both Massenet and Fauré, he never succeeded in equaling his masters' expressionistic abilities. But he was prolific and his huge quantity of piano music is scattered over twenty-five opus numbers.[3] The early works are quasi-impressionistic, bearing some external likenesses to the music of Debussy and Chabrier, but only superficially. His later works are laden with superfluous detail. The few positive qualities sprinkled here and there among his many compositions—vigor, a facile eloquence, and a spark of passion—do not compensate for the lack of invention and the heavy-handed textural inadequacies.

Jacques Ibert

Jacques Ibert (*b*. 1890) has won the universal recognition unmerited by Schmitt. Ibert's style leans to the Impressionist school but only in its Ravel derivations and not those of Debussy. Clarity, precision, wit, and elegance—all qualities admired by the French—abound in his large repertoire. As a keyboard composer he is essentially a skillful miniaturist. His two best-known piano collections are *Histoires* (1922) and *Petite Suite en 15 Images* (1943). The former—ten delightfully descriptive pieces—is in

[2] Koechlin's principal music editor is Salabert (catalogues of Mathot and Senart).
[3] Durand of Paris publishes a voluminous amount of Florent Schmitt's music.

turn gay, humorous, brilliant, and meditative. The individual titles provide clues to the often quaint musical content: *Le Petit Âne Blanc* (The Little White Donkey); *A Giddy Girl; Le Cage de Cristal* (The Crystal Cage); *La Marchande d'Eau Fraîche* (The Fresh-Water Vendor).[4]

The Six

As charming as it sometimes is, the music of Koechlin and Ibert gives little indication of the future. Their music is fundamentally an extension of Romantic tendencies coupled with out-of-context procedures appropriated from the Impressionists. Reaction was bound to come, and it did. After the First World War, opposition arose against Wagnerian Romanticism, Debussy Impressionism, and the Ravel dilettantism. Several young composers active in the opposition were placed by the musicologist Henri Collet into a theoretical group called *Les Six* (The Six). Collet was trying to create an organism similar to the *Russian Five*. The Six—Milhaud, Honegger, Poulenc, Auric, Durey, and Tailleferre—strove for quick success and gained it, but their cause suffered from the effects of their achievement. Despite the exalted phrases and lofty ideals of their manifesto (as conjured up later by Jean Cocteau), the music created by this enthusiastic group did little to raise French musical standards—at least in the keyboard idiom. With two exceptions—Honegger (who rather quickly disassociated himself from the group) and Poulenc—these composers typically produced overly facile, undisciplined music, frequently lacking the very qualities that have always distinguished good French music.

Of *Les Six*, **Francis Poulenc** (1899–1963) was the one composer who wrote worthwhile keyboard pieces. The origins of his style go back to music from the late nineteenth and early twentieth century; his approach, especially in keyboard music, is traceable directly back to the clavecinists: it unashamedly proclaims that its sole purpose is pleasure, often the pleasure of the moment. This is a refreshing attitude, all the more so in a composer who had so much inherent compositional talent. Naturally, critical examination uncovers the flaws in Poulenc's music: a mixture of incongruous elements, basically undistinguished ideas hidden in handsome garb, an overt sentimentality. But these "faults" may be exactly the reason why Poulenc's music is immediately accessible—and enjoyable.

Poulenc has written a quantity of piano music. After the early *Mouvements Perpétuels* (1918) established him as a significant keyboard composer, he consistently turned out series of keyboard works substantiating this initial positive impression: *Suite* (1920); *Napoli* (1922–1925); *Huit*

---

[4] The complete set of *Histoires* is published by Alphonse Leduc.

Nocturnes (1929–1938); *Les Soirées de Nazelles* (1930–1936).[5] The last is one of his most important keyboard writings. It consists of a *Préambule* (with cadenza), eight *Variations, Cadence,* and *Final;* and Poulenc himself supplies an explanation: "The variations which form the center of this work were improvised at Nazelles during the course of long soirées in the country where the author played at 'portraits' with friends grouped around the piano.

"We hope today that, presented between a *Préambule* and a *Final,* they will evoke the memory of this game played in the setting of a Touraine salon, a window opening on to the night." The "memories" evoked are distinctly delightful: echoes of the music hall, flashes of parody, impudent dissonances, and a masterful lyric quality (Ex. 1).

Ex. 1. Poulenc: *Les Soirées de Nazelles: Le comble de la distinction*

Arthur Honegger (1892–1955) is undoubtedly the greatest "pure" musician among *Les Six*. Structure was always important to him and he handled it with wonderfully disciplined imagination. His style is dominated by a contrapuntal texture applied in such a manner as to produce a harsh and often uncompromising polytonality.

Honegger's comparatively few piano works usually have more musical substance than any produced by his French contemporaries, but unfortunately they are largely unpianistic, which may explain their infrequent appearance in concert. The early *Toccata et Variations* (1916) is one of his finest piano works. The theme for the variations is slow and solemn, akin to Chopin's *Prelude in C Minor,* and the succeeding variations are continuous, all in different textures and tempos. Brief collections comprise most of his piano music: *Trois Pièces* (1910); *Sept Pièces Brèves* (1919–1920); *Le*

---

[5] Poulenc has written a great quantity of piano music. This is mostly divided among the publishers Durand, J. & W. Chester, and Salabert: *Suite Française, Les Soirées de Nazelles* (Durand); *Mouvements Perpétuels, Suite in C, Five Impromptus* (Chester); *Improvisations, Napoli, Villageoises* (Salabert).

Cahier Romand (1921–1923); *Deux Esquisses* (1941). The only serious later work is the *Prélude, Arioso et Fughetta* (on the name B.A.C.H.) dating from 1932.[6]

Faced with a catalogue of works by **Darius Milhaud** (*b.* 1892), one cannot help thinking that here is enough material for several composers; but quantity and quality are indeed two different things. As a pupil of Dukas and d'Indy, Milhaud should have quickly realized the necessity for self-criticism and the need for caution in approaching compositional forms, both large and small. Instead, Milhaud attempted more than ten operas, a dozen or so ballets, music for a score of films, dozens of choral works, orchestral pieces, etc. This overabundance is also apparent in the somewhat extensive list of piano works. In all media, Milhaud displays an extraordinary skill in handling polytonal counterpoint and a capacity for assimilating musical influences essentially foreign to his own Gallic culture.

It is difficult to choose the best of his keyboard music. Some of the most pleasing music comes in the two-volume *Saudades do Brazil*, an early (1920) collection of sophisticated dances in the tango or rumba category. The pieces—*Sorocabo, Botofago, Tijuca*, etc.—are named for different sections in and around Rio de Janeiro. Two more serious works date from a later period. *Sonata No. 2* (1949) is a fairly difficult work in Milhaud's typical linear style—contrapuntal lines in two or three parts. An even later work (1951), *Le Candélabre à Sept Branches* (The Seven-Branched Candelabrum), has seven pieces inspired by the seven festivals of the Jewish calendar.[7]

Jeune France

As if one manifesto (synthetic or otherwise) were not enough, another appeared some years later to challenge the somewhat unfulfilled tenets of the earlier *Six*. In June, 1936, several French composers, calling themselves *Jeune France*, presented a concert featuring their own works. Notes attached to the program announced their avowed purpose: to create a fundamentally humanistic outlook in music to counteract life's tendency to be uncompromising, mechanical, and impersonal. This statement is sufficiently vague to withstand many interpretations; therefore, a certain *succès d'estime* will probably come no matter what music emerges, as long as some semblance of musicianship is maintained.

André Jolivet (*b.* 1905) develops a series of symbolic images from his

---

[6] Salabert publishes the piano music of Honegger.

[7] Milhaud's keyboard music is distributed among many publishers. Following is a representative list: *Saudades do Brazil* in two volumes (Eschig); *Le Candélabre à Sept Branches* (Israeli Music Publications); *Suite* (Durand).

interest in the mystical, magical propensities of music. His harmonic language is extremely free, basically atonal, stressing rhythmic and dynamic details. His two most characteristic piano works are powerfully influenced by his interest in the primitive religions expressing their beliefs through magic. Jolivet's fantastic suite *Mana* was composed in 1935. In an introductory note by Olivier Messiaen, the term *Mana* is explained as "that force which projects us into our familiar fetishes." These "familiar fetishes"— *Beaujolais* (a little copper doll), *The Bird, The Bali Princess, The Goat, The Cow, Pegasus*—are described, or rather the mystical energy flowing from them is commented upon, in Jolivet's sensitive and often diffuse language. Complex rhythmic designs, percussive effects, and atonal harmony all unite to fashion a truly unique work.

A further set entitled *Cinq Danses Rituelles* (1947) presents five exciting, exotic dances in an overpowering blend of primitivism and modernism. Jolivet's two piano sonatas, on the other hand, are not convincing examples of his full potential, although the second is commendable for its musical substance extracted from the full and partial tone rows.[8]

Olivier Messiaen (*b*. 1908), another member of *Jeune France*, has the same basic attitude except that it is propelled by orthodox Roman Catholicism rather than pagan primitivism. And his musical language is of course different. A highly organized and personal aestheticism (he has written a book on the subject) enables him to create ideas that clearly translate his mysticism into comprehensive tonal patterns. His principle of "exact repetition" and "varied repetition"—too complex to be treated here—should be looked into to get an exact perception of his aims and purposes.

The solo-keyboard work that focused attention upon Messiaen was *Vingt Regards sur l'Enfant Jésus* (1944) with three musical motives representing God, the Star and the Cross, and a "theme of Chords." These motives are used in conjunction with canonic treatment, polymodality, and other complexities to present an extremely lengthy collection (177 pages) of contemplations about the Infant Jesus by the Father, the Star, the Virgin, angels, etc. Each contemplation is described and analyzed by the composer, who explains at the beginning, "I have sought here a language of mystic love, simultaneously varied, powerful, and tender, elsewhere brutal in multicolored arrangements."[9]

Although both Jolivet and Messiaen design music with pronounced modernistic tendencies, this is by no means the last word. One of Messiaen's disciples, **Pierre Boulez** (*b*. 1926), has stretched twelve-tone music to the

---

[8] Durand publishes *Cinq Danses Rituelles*. *Mana* suite is issued by Editions Costallat. Jolivet's first sonata is published by Universal, the second by Heugel.

[9] Durand is Messiaen's publisher for keyboard music. In addition to the *Vingt Regards*, Messiaen has written many other piano works.

straining point. His three piano sonatas (1946, 1948, 1957) offer nearly insurmountable obstacles for the pianist and an equally perplexing sonorous experience for the listener. Although his finished product has fewer elements of chance than Stockhausen's, it is equally as difficult to understand. Here tone rows of notes, of rhythm, and of dynamics all join hands in an unbelievably complex *mélange*.[10]

Jean Françaix

At the opposite end of the spectrum is **Jean Françaix** (*b*. 1912), a pupil of Nadia Boulanger (*b*. 1887), the famous Parisian teacher who has shaped the musical destinies of so many composers. Although this invigorating tonalist might be considered a Neo-Classicist because of his penchant for traditional forms—trio, quartet—he does not consistently follow this path in his piano music. At the keyboard he excels in anecdotal, humorous, and sometimes sly musical descriptions, admirably illustrated in two fine collections. In *Cinq Portraits de Jeunes Filles* (Five Portraits of Young Ladies) of 1936, he realistically recreates the motivating spirit of five "eternal feminine" types—*La Capricieuse, La Tendre, La Prétentieuse, La Pensive, La Moderne*. In 1957 the first performance of his second collection, the highly diverting harpsichord suite *L'Insectarium*, revealed a series of six sketches that indelicately evoke the "personalities" of such insects as the centipede, the ladybug, ants, etc.

In the *Sonate pour Piano* (1960) Françaix bestows his graceful chromaticisms on both harmony and melody. Dancelike rhythms are sprinkled throughout the four movements *Prélude, Elégie, Scherzo*, and *Toccata*, which are really more like a suite than a sonata.[11]

HUNGARY

For most of the present century the course of Hungarian art music has been determined by three fine composers—Dohnányi, Kodály, and Bartók —and it would appear that this will remain true for some years to come. Although both Kodály and Bartók have guided their compositional temperaments solely in the path of folk music—stylized though it may be—Bartók still emerges as one of the master composers in the twentieth century.

Ernö Dohnányi

Ernö Dohnányi (1877–1960) was first of all an excellent concert pianist, a facility that is a great boon to a keyboard composer. His style springs from

[10] Universal publishes Boulez' third sonata. Theodore Presser handles the second one.
[11] All three Françaix works are issued by Schott.

the fount of German Romanticism, notably Johannes Brahms, a fact that accounts for his resourceful craftsmanship; but a less fortunate offshoot of the same background makes his music weak in individuality and originality. Dohnányi's style first impresses one as glib and "slick" rather than sincerely expressive, but it can be pleasing if not taken too seriously.

Unlike Bartók and Kodály, Dohnányi never earnestly studied the genuine Hungarian folk idiom; therefore, his attempts to use it prove artificial. Authentic or not, his personal interpretation of that idiom can be charming, as he so well proves in *Ruralia Hungarica Opus 33a* of 1926 (there is also an orchestral version). Dohnányi's most frequently played piano works are the four *Rhapsodies Opus 11*, but the *Clavierstücke Opus 23* are also worthy of note.[12]

Zoltán Kodály

Zoltán Kodály (*b*. 1882) began by assimilating Impressionist factors into his compositions in a highly entertaining manner. Later he became interested in Hungarian folk music, eventually becoming an expert in this field. Magyar folk music affected his writings so much that it remains the dominant influence. The conspicuous element in this music is a characteristic melodic line.

Unlike Bartók, Kodály is not an innovator. There is nothing really new in his seemingly unconventional approach; it merely grew out of the dormant elements of different traditions, which he first absorbed and then logically took for his own. Although Kodály prefers other media, he has written two convincing keyboard collections. *Zongora Muzsika Opus 11* (Piano Music, 1910–1918) offers seven piano pieces bearing the first signs of his interest in the Magyar idiom: the quasi-popular melodic types and piquant rhythms announce his preoccupation with folk music. The dance series *Marosszéki táncok* (Marosszék Dances, 1930), based on peasant tunes, also appears in an orchestral version.[13]

Béla Bartók

Next to Stravinsky and Schönberg, **Béla Bartók** (1881–1945) has been the most influential composer of the twentieth century. He has demonstrated to a younger generation that new expressive means within traditional confines are still possible; that musical ideas can be reshaped

---

[12] Most of Dohnányi's piano music is published by Ludwig Doblinger; *Ruralia Hungarica* is available at Boosey & Hawkes.

[13] Boosey & Hawkes handles most of Kodály's keyboard music: *Marosszék Dances, Piano Variations, Children's Dances*. Leeds Music Corp. lists the *Zongora Muzsika*.

and restated in countless ways; that nationalism can be energizing; and that rhythmic transformations can be accomplished by infinite variation.

Bartók's early keyboard music recalls other composers—Brahms, Liszt, Ravel—but it changed gradually as he became aware of the need for expressive resources. His personal contact with Hungarian folk music brought about a decided change in his writing. His ultimate musical language is terse and the harmonic framework is condensed to bare essentials, resulting in fine transparent textures. Above all, he creates vibrant rhythms breathing life and excitement.

Bartók enjoyed writing for the piano, perhaps because it could be simultaneously a melodic, harmonic, *and* percussive instrument. Even the early *Two Rumanian Dances* (1909–1910) are marked by his interest in indigenous Hungarian music. These melodies sound like folk tunes but they are pure Bartók; the music is alive, full of contrasts, and the spacious structural framework contains finely etched part writing. In his first large-scale virtuoso work, *Allegro barbaro* (1911), Bartók blends passages of Phrygian and Lydian modes with primitive, percussive rhythms, molding them into a beautifully concentrated whole.

As Bartók continued to search for new tonal vistas, he pushed his harmonies to the threshold of atonality. This can be seen in three *Études Opus 18* (1918), which deal with specific problems in technique. These problems are generally concerned with the extension and contraction of the hand, and in this respect they are highly effective. Harmonically the *Études* show Bartók's determination to reach toward new frontiers of sound, a determination evident again in the *Sonata* (1926), whose unorthodox formal aspects mirror his personal idiom. This, his largest work for keyboard, challenges the finest available techniques. The piano is treated as a percussion instrument: one looks in vain for a truly lyric section. As a whole the sonata is based on rhythmic repeated figures with tone clusters playing an important role. The structure housing this most original creation is, strangely enough, rather conventional; the first movement shows the elements of sonata-allegro form, the second is a ternary structure, and the third combines elements of the rondo and variations.

Bartók's keen interest in native folk music was bound to have a direct consequence. He made many settings of actual folk tunes, giving them more exotic dress in his keyboard paraphrases. *For Children* (1908–1909) is a collection of eighty-five settings of Hungarian and Slovakian melodies. In these the melodies are kept intact; they are merely repeated once or twice with varied accompaniments derived from the melodies themselves.

For Children was followed by other collections. *Rumanian Christmas Songs of Hungary* (1915) contains two series of ten pieces each, each series to be played without pause. Here there is interest created by the considerable metrical variety employed. *Fifteen Hungarian Peasant Songs* (1914–1917) contains settings of songs from Bartók's ethnological collections. The eight *Improvisations on Hungarian Peasant Songs* (1920) represent a departure from the rather straightforward settings previously encountered. Here the composer treats the songs as original themes; he improvises on his *own* creations.

Sometimes the titles to Bartók's music belie the actual debt to folk song. The *Sonatina* (1915) is a short three-movement suite based on Rumanian folk dances (in 1931 the composer transcribed the *Sonatina* for orchestra, calling it *Transylvanian Dances*). The dances used here are usually extended by repetition, sometimes broken up by episodes. The movements are: *Bagpipers, Bear Dance,* and *Finale.*

After Bartók had finished these numerous "songs without words," he began the mighty task of composing the *Mikrokosmos* he originally intended for his son Péter. For eleven years (1926–1937) he worked diligently to produce the 153 pieces in the sets. The series includes every element proper to his keyboard style; it is the essence of Bartók—ranging from his easiest writing to the most complex, from elementary harmonic structures to bitonality (Ex. 2). The *Mikrokosmos* almost provides one with a textbook of twentieth-century devices used in musical composition. There are excellent examples of the whole-tone scale (*No. 136*), of chords built in fourths (*No. 131*), of major and minor seconds (*Nos. 140, 142, 144*), of tone clusters (*No. 107*), of bitonality (*Nos. 70, 105, 142*). Contrapuntal devices are also evident: canon (*No. 91*), inversion (*No. 34*), mirror (*No. 121*). Exercises in rhythm are provided in the delightful *Six Dances in Bulgarian Rhythm* (*Nos. 148–153*). The *Mikrokosmos* is a remarkable collection, a keyboard epic so fine that it alone could perpetuate the name of Béla Bartók.[14]

Ex. 2. Bartók: *Mikrokosmos Vol. III: Melody against Double Notes*

MIKROKOSMOS (No. 70) by Béla Bartók. Copyright 1940 by Hawkes & Son (London) Ltd. Reprinted by permission of Boosey & Hawkes, Inc.

[14] The most complete collection of Bartók's piano music is issued by Boosey & Hawkes. In fact, apart from three early unpublished works, all the rest are found here.

HOLLAND

Twentieth-century Holland is undergoing a musical renaissance unlike anything that has happened there since the era of the fifteenth-century Flemish masters. Credit must be given to the contemporary composers and to a public that enjoys new music, but the outstanding work of the Donemus Foundation must also be recognized. Since 1947 this benevolent organization has made it possible for talented Dutch composers to have their music published, and in addition it issues a periodical, *Sonorum Speculum,* listing current musical events in Holland and performances of Dutch music elsewhere.

Bernhard van den Sigtenhorst Meyer

One of the early figures in twentieth-century Dutch music, **Bernhard van den Sigtenhorst Meyer** (1888–1953), began his career under the spell of Impressionism. A journey to the Far East resulted in several series of piano pieces, such as *Het oude China* (Ancient China) of 1916 and *Zes gezichten op de Fuji* (Six Views of Fuji) of 1919. Once again in Holland, he looked to the beauties of his own country, composing *De Maas* (The Meuse) in 1920 and also *Oude Kastelen* (Ancient Castles) in 1920. But he abandoned tonal mood painting when he became interested in Jan Sweelinck's music; instead he tried to achieve in his works the clarity inherent in that great Dutch organist's music. Sigtenhorst Meyer's later piano works —*Sonatinas, Sonata No. 2, Opus 23* (1926), *Capriccios Opus 42*—are the result of the Sweelinck influence; they are somewhat devoid of sentiment, somewhat contrived, but they are nonetheless quite distinguished.[15]

Alexander Voormolen

Another composer who initially approached his art via French influences is **Alexander Voormolen** (b. 1895), who at twenty settled in Paris where he became friends with Ravel and Roussel. During his Parisian sojourn he produced *Tableaux des Pays-Bas* (1919–1924), two Impressionist collections of Dutch landscapes translated into sound, and *Suite de Clavecin* (1921) in homage of the spirit of eighteenth-century French keyboard composers. But Voormolen returned to Holland in 1923, broke with his French models, and studied the works of Haydn. Thereafter he worked to

[15] The music of Sigtenhorst Meyer is, with few exceptions, published by G. Alsbach & Co. of Amsterdam.

develop contrapuntal skill, which he then applied more often to orchestral music than piano music.[16]

Willem Pijper

The strongest force in contemporary Dutch music to date has been **Willem Pijper** (1894–1947). Because of his widespread influence, Dutch music has regained its reputation in European musical society. Pijper's pupils have preserved the integrity of his principles—derived basically from the polyphony of the old Dutch masters—while presenting them in modern attire.

Debussy and Mahler were Pijper's early idols and from both he appropriated those elements he liked. His eventual polished style indicates an aversion to the "tyranny of the bar line," which he furthers by using polymetric and polyrhythmic figures. A sworn opponent of atonality, he saw in polytonality a logical unfolding of traditional monotonality. This polytonality is prominent in his mature keyboard compositions (Ex. 3).

Ex. 3. W. Pijper: *Sonatina No. III*

Reproduced by permission of Oxford University Press.

Within this textural framework Pijper evolved his own procedures. He was convinced that "a musical work blossoms out of the germ force of only a few elements which may be called the composer's 'ideas.'" He believed that the composer's first duty was to develop this germination process. Apart from this, he seldom explained himself, resorting instead to such generalities as "We make music as composers whenever we feel the need to make the forces which are flowing in us into a reality existing outside ourselves." The results of Pijper's superorganized theories may be seen in piano *Sonatinas Nos. II* and *III* (1925) and the later *Sonata* (1930).[17]

[16] Voormolen's *Suite de Clavecin* and piano sonata (1947) are published by Alsbach. The *Tableaux des Pays-Bas* come from Rouart, Lerolle et Cie. (Salabert).

[17] The *Sonata* and first *Sonatine* are published by Donemus; the other two *Sonatines* by Oxford University Press.

Henk Badings

Henk Badings (*b.* 1907) worked briefly with Pijper but by and large he is self-taught. His seven large *Sonatas* (1934–1947) seem to be modeled on Beethoven's motivic construction principles, although their style continues the Brahms-Reger-Hindemith development sequence. The *Sonatas* and other keyboard works—*Sonatinas* (1936–1950), *Suite* (1930)—visibly demonstrate his working principle: an expansive melodic line developed contrapuntally.[18]

Other Dutch Composers

As a skilled piano virtuoso, **Léon Orthel** (*b.* 1905) would be expected to write effective keyboard music. So it is, for in his numerous piano works—*Preludes, Sonatinas*—the original musical language is skillfully presented.[19]

Marius Flothuis (*b.* 1914) is the most widely discussed Dutch composer of the younger generation. Logical formal construction expressed in complex polyphonic textures give meaning to his compositions. External influences—Pijper, Mozart, Schubert—have helped him to shape his own interesting style. Fortunately, he applies this style in his comparatively few keyboard works: *Suite Opus 4* (1938), *Zes Moments Musicals Opus 31* (1947), *Variations Opus 12* (1941).[20]

The Dutch school is rather conservative compared with activity in Germany and the United States. Nevertheless, it is outstanding for the consistently high quality of the solid, musicianly works produced these last twenty-five years.

SPAIN

It is difficult to predict the future of Spanish contemporary music or, for that matter, to describe the present scene. During and after the Spanish Civil War, many composers and performing musicians left Spain never to return, a cultural exodus that has created a deplorable void. Some composers went to France, others to Mexico or South America, and a few reside in the United States. The nationalist trend so beneficial during the early twentieth

---

[18] The majority of Badings' keyboard compositions are distributed thusly: *Sonatas I, II,* and *Sonatine 1936* (Schott); *Sonatas III, VI,* and *Sonatine II* (Ed. Jeannette); *Sonata IV* (W. Hansen); *Sonata V* (Alsbach); *Sonatine III, Suite 1930* (C. C. Bender); *Tema con variazioni* (Universal).

[19] Various short pieces by Orthel are published by Donemus, Albersen & Co., and Alsbach.

[20] Most of Flothuis' piano works come from Donemus. The *Variations Opus 12* are published by Broekmans & Van Poppel.

century has run its course. In the past few decades Spanish nationalism, contrary to Hungarian nationalism, has not provided incentive for imaginative composition. The Spanish composers who have risen above the superficial folk-song potpourris are to be commended indeed.

Joaquín Nin (1879–1949) was Cuban by birth but always a Spaniard in spirit. His music, tinged with Romanticism, is impregnated with distinctly Spanish flavors. *Chaîne de Valses* (1929) contains musical tributes to various masters of the waltz—Schubert, Ravel, Chopin.[21]

The Catalan composer **Federico Mompou** (*b.* 1893) composes music reminiscent of French Impressionism—pure chamber music, intimate, even fragile at times—yet he writes with such clarity and style that he is one of Spain's best composers of piano music. Mompou remains a Spaniard in spite of his dependency on French Impressionism. His *Canciones y Danzas* (1921–1946) as well as other works—*Dialogues* (1923–1941) and *Charmes* (1921)—are atmospheric, colorful sketches in a style uniquely his own.[22]

One of the best-known Spanish composers is the prolific **Oscar Esplá**, who was born in Alicante in 1886. He is a Romantic, but an intellectual Romantic who mingles elements of German scholasticism and the disciplines of the *Schola Cantorum* with more popular sources. His published piano music includes *Tres Movimientos* (1930), *Evocations Espagnoles* (1936), and the *Sonata Española* (1949) written in homage to Chopin.[23]

Another composer originating from the Spanish Levante (Valencia and environs) is without reservation Spain's finest contemporary composer. **Joaquín Rodrigo** (*b.* 1902) was a student of Paul Dukas in France, and he creates keyboard works with impressive substance: *Serenata Española* (1931), *Danzas de España* (1936, 1941), *Sonatas de Castilla* (1952).[24] Any "Spanish" influence usually appears only incidentally and then very naturally in matters of rhythm. In other words, he is an excellent example of the international musician. His works exhibit a free use of quartal harmony, modality, polytonality, and a sure awareness of innate formal logic.

The *Avant-Garde*

Dodecaphony has only recently made noticeable inroads in conservative Spain. In 1958 a group of modernists calling themselves *Grupo Nueva*

---

[21] Nin's *Chaîne de Valses* is published by Eschig, who also issues Nin's two splendid editions of early Spanish keyboard music.

[22] Mompou's piano music is handled by the following: *Canciones y Danzas 1–4, Impresiones Intimas, Cantos Mágicos* (Union Musical Española); *Charmes, Dialogues, Trois Variations* (Max Eschig); *Scènes d'Enfants, Suburbis, Chansons et Danses 5–10* (Salabert [Senart]); *Four Preludes* (Presser).

[23] Practically all of Esplá's music is published by Union Musical Española.

[24] Salabert (Rouart-Lerolle) edits most of Rodrigo's music: *Bagatelle, Sérénade, Suite pour Piano.* The *Sonatas de Castilla* were brought out privately in an Edición del autor.

Música presented a concert at the Conservatory of Madrid. Although the organization lasted only a year, it was able to initiate many changes. In 1959 an *Aula de Música* (more or less an institute) was established in the hallowed *Ateneo de Madrid* (Madrid Athenaeum), and it is here that recitals and lectures on serial music and *avant-garde* music are presented.

There are only a few Spanish atonalists, but they are enthusiastic and their cause is growing. **Cristóbal Halffter** (*b.* 1930) is the nephew of two well-known musicians, Ernesto and Rodolfo Halffter, neither of whom has written any important piano music. Cristóbal began his career writing little pieces in neo-Scarlatti style—like his one-movement *Sonata para Piano*—but during the past several years he has become increasingly interested in twelve-tone technique. Halffter's *Introducción, Fuga y Final Opus 15* (1957) uses a carefully worked out, stylized serial technique.

Luis de Pablo (*b.* 1930) is Spain's answer to Karlheinz Stockhausen. A musical extremist, he forces the keyboard to its end limits in his *Libro para el Pianista Opus 1*. In the last movement—similar to Stockhausen's *Klavierstück XI*—the pianist may match four right-hand segments with four left-hand passages in a completely arbitrary manner. Another convinced dodecaphonist, **Ramón Barce** (*b.* 1928) tries to infuse a lyric quality into his pieces. His music is not strictly atonal but he uses the system as a basis for composition, as illustrated in his early *Sonata No. 1, Opus 3*.

Finally, there are the *Cuatro Piezas Breves* (Four Short Pieces, 1960) written by **Manuel Carra** (*b.* 1931). This eminently pianistic collection—the composer himself is a fine pianist—uses Webern for a model and achieves highly effective results.[25]

ENGLAND

Few substantial creative works appeared in England in the one hundred and fifty years that followed the Purcell era. There was of course an interest in music—the oratorios and operas of Handel's time, the distinguished teaching and playing of Clementi and Cramer, the influence of John Field and his *Nocturnes*—but the British tradition of excellence in composition was at a standstill.

An interest in keyboard composition, as well as other media, was revived toward the latter part of the nineteenth century. One finds composers like **William Sterndale Bennett** (1816–1875) writing sonatas and salon

---

[25] Union Musical Española publishes both the *Sonata* and *Introducción, Fuga y Final Opus 15* by Halffter; also Manuel Carra's *Cuatro Piezas Breves*. Three movements from Luis de Pablo's *Libro para el Pianista* are published by Edition Tonos.

pieces in the style of the German Romantics but withal showing some signs of personal originality.

One talented composer, **Charles Villiers Stanford** (1852–1924), had an Irish background. While conducting in England, he gave many performances of Brahms's works. His friendship with the German master noticeably influenced him. Stanford is known primarily as a choral-music composer—particularly Anglican church music—but his keyboard music is not negligible.[26]

Most English keyboard music from *ca.* 1900 to 1930 is quite undistinguished: a somewhat tired Romanticism with overtones of Impressionism often prevents so-called "contemporary" music from being contemporary. **Cyril Scott** (*b.* 1879), being a pianist, writes effectively for his instrument, but his language is neither outstanding nor unique. His earlier works are often played—*Chimes Opus 40, No. 3* (1904), *Lotus Land Opus 47, No. 1* (1905)—but the piece revealing the most outward attempt at consistent contemporary writing is the one-movement *Sonata Opus 66*. The finest collection of short pieces is *Poems* (1912) which—despite some quasi-mystical titles such as "The Garden of Soul-Sympathy"—shows dexterity and genuine inspiration.[27]

John Ireland

The most prolific keyboard writer of the early twentieth century was **John Ireland** (1879–1962). Essentially a miniaturist, he fashioned his colorful pictures with delicacy and sensitivity. Many of them are grouped in collections. *Decorations* (1912–1913) includes the atmospheric *Island Spell*, lyric *Moon-Glade,* and brilliantly virtuoso *Scarlet Ceremonies.* In an entirely different spirit, the *London Pieces* (1917–1920) are three striking explorations of life in the great city. Ireland's large-scale *Sonata* (1918–1920) is a three-movement work whose ebullient initial movement and brilliant finale frame a central slow movement of great expression.[28]

Arnold Bax

In 1937 **Arnold Bax** (1883–1953) was knighted for his musical services and in 1942 was appointed "Master of the King's Musick," tributes that acknowledge his superior musical talents. He remained a conventional

---

[26] Stainer and Bell publishes a series of *Four Irish Dances* and *Three Rhapsodies* by Stanford.

[27] Schott handles the *Poems* and numerous light pieces by Scott. *Lotus Land,* the three sonatas, a *Passacaglia,* and two *Études* are listed by Galaxy Music Corp.

[28] Augener publishes a good collection of Ireland—*Decorations, London Pieces, Sonata in E Minor.* Boosey & Hawkes fills out the list with the four *Preludes* and the *Rhapsody.*

musician whose basic interest lay in music as an emotional medium. In expressing himself his solid technique held him in good stead, although it cannot be claimed that he remained a consistently original composer. His short piano compositions are essentially salon pieces, yet many are rather difficult. The three sonatas are more fully developed and more interesting: the first is unashamedly romantic, while the second and particularly the third display unusual rhythms and chromatic harmony.[29]

The *Second Sonata in G,* for example, is a one-movement work conforming rather closely to sonata-allegro form. There are two themes, one of which is in complete character with Bax's expressive indication: *Gloomy and menacing in mood.* The second theme is marked *Brazen and glittering* and it is just that. The development is imaginative, and Bax uses a variety of techniques—counterpoint, dotted rhythms, syncopation, meter change —before returning to his thematic restatement. The *Sonata* is effective, interesting, and written with apparent skill and pianistic know-how.

Later English Composers

Brief mention is due several composers of the next generation who have won recognition from their compatriots although they are not necessarily well known elsewhere.

Nadia Boulanger (see page 373) claims **Lennox Berkeley** (*b.* 1903) as one of her pupils. Like John Ireland, Berkeley specializes in small forms where sectional contrast is preferable to learned developmental procedures. A certain melodic charm—often superficial—envelops his six *Preludes* (1948), and he has written an excellent *Scherzo* (1950). Although the mildly dissonant harmonic texture lends interest, it is not always sustained throughout because of the facile, frequently monotonous accompaniment figures.[30]

A special sympathy for the piano is apparent in *Bagatelles* by **Alan Rawsthorne** (*b.* 1905). His consistent style, though emotionally restrained, is founded on a constantly shifting chromaticism that is usually expressed in contrapuntal texture.[31]

Michael Tippett (*b.* 1905) has renewed English melodic principles. His personal rhythmic concept pervades *Piano Sonata* (1938); its second movement is quite reminiscent of folk song and the final movement boasts ornamentation derived from the harmonic figures. His *Sonata No. 2* is recent, having received its first performance in 1962 at the Edinburgh In-

---

[29] Chester issues some light pieces by Bax, but the more serious *Sonatas* are published by Chappell & Co., Ltd.

[30] Berkeley's piano music is published by J. & W. Chester.

[31] The *Bagatelles* and a *Sonatina* by Rawsthorne are published by Oxford University Press.

ternational Festival. This sonata is in one movement and is highly original. He lays out (not consecutively) a series of eight different tempos related to eight distinctive types of pianistic writing—parallel octaves, arpeggios, declamatory chords, etc. These tempos are alternated, and their corresponding textures are paraphrased to form a type of structure that seems to be a product of the composer's search for new approaches to composition.

Tippett's *Sonatina* is a serious four-movement work; the first three movements are disciplined in both emotion and movement but the last, *Allegro con brio*, flashes with unrestrained gaiety.[32]

EPILOGUE

Chapters 29 and 30 by no means exhaust the list of competent twentieth-century European composers of keyboard music. Many others have contributed at least a part of their generous talents to keyboard writing. For example, the late **Fartein Valen** (1887–1952) of Norway employed his advanced musical idiom in two piano sonatas and the *Variations Opus 23* (1936). **Marcel Mihalovici** (*b*. 1898), a native of Bucharest, has written a masterful set of free variations called *Ricercari Opus 46*. Belgium has produced at least two fine composers in this century. **Joseph Jongen** (1873–1953) was a highly prolific composer whose compositions show his admiration for César Franck and the Impressionists. For piano he wrote miniature pieces such as the *24 Little Preludes Opus 116* (1941), as well as the larger *Suite en Forme de Sonata Opus 60* (1919). A more contemporary composer, **Marcel Poot** (*b*. 1901), also teaches and writes criticisms for musical journals. The majority of his work has been orchestral, but he has written a few piano pieces—*Sonate, Six Easy Pieces,* and *Six Recreational Pieces*.

A Polish-born composer who has spent most of his life in Paris, **Alexandre Tansman** (*b*. 1897) has become an eclectic who blends utterly disparate elements into a basically lyric style. He has written innumerable piano works; in fact, his entire output is so vast that it requires a separate catalogue arranged by his editor Max Eschig. **Alexander Tcherepnin** (*b*. 1899) is theoretically a Russian composer, but he has traveled most of his life: to Paris, China, Japan, the United States, etc. Although he has written considerable piano music, his best-known collection is *Opus 5, Bagatelles.* More recent works—*Twelve Preludes* and *Polka*—are on an equally small scale. In these pieces chromatic decoration and construction by evolving motives preserve the charm first evidenced in the *Bagatelles*.

[32] Tippett's two *Sonatas* are published by Schott.

The Polish-born Parisian **Antoni Szalowski** (*b.* 1907) has written a refreshingly uncomplicated *Suite for Harpsichord or Piano.* In its three movements—*Moderato, Tranquillo,* and *Animato*—the linear style is fitted into a sonorous texture which is dominantly tonal.[33]

This list could grow and grow; however, even such a brief survey proves the strength and durability of European keyboard music in the first half of the twentieth century.

BIBLIOGRAPHY

Austin, William. "Satie before and after Cocteau." *Musical Quarterly,* April, 1962.

Bela Bartok. A Memorial Review. New York: Boosey & Hawkes, 1950.

Chase, Gilbert. *The Music of Spain,* second revised edition. New York: Dover Publications, 1959.

Collet, Henri. *L'Essor de la Musique Espagnole au XXᵉ Siècle.* Paris: Editions Max Eschig, 1950.

Ewen, David. *European Composers Today.* New York: The H. W. Wilson Co., 1954.

Fenyo, Thomas. *The Piano Music of Béla Bartók.* Dissertation. University of California, Los Angeles, 1956.

Hartog, Howard, ed. *European Music in the Twentieth Century.* New York: F. A. Praeger, 1957.

Hell, Henri. *Francis Poulenc* (translated and edited by E. Lockspeiser). New York: Grove Press, Inc., 1959.

Mersman, Dr. Hans. *Die Moderne Musik.* Wildpark-Potsdam: Akademische Verlagsgesellschaft Athenaion, 1929.

Myers, Rollo H. *Erik Satie.* London: Dennis Dobson Ltd., 1948. Dover reprint

---

[33] Following is a list of publishers for those composers mentioned in the Epilogue. Fartein Valen: *Variations Opus 23, Prelude and Fugue Opus 28, Sonata No. 2, Opus 38* (Peters); Marcel Mihalovici: *Ricercari* (Heugel); Joseph Jongen: *Deux Pièces Opus 33, Deux Rondes Wallonnes* (Durand), *Sérénade Opus 19* (Salabert), *Suite en Forme de Sonata, Sonatine* (Chester); Marcel Poot: *Sonate* (Eschig), *Suite, Variations* (Universal); Alexandre Tansman: Complete piano works (Eschig); Alexander Tcherepnin: *Bagatelles Opus 5* (G. Schirmer), *Six Concert Études Opus 52* (Schott), *Quatre Préludes, Sonatine Romantique* (Durand), *Twelve Preludes* (E. B. Marks), *Polka* (Templeton); Antoni Szalowski: *Suite for Piano or Harpsichord* (Augener). There are also some collections which are useful: *Fifty-One Piano Pieces from the Modern Repertoire* (Schirmer); *Collection Moderne,* 2 vols. (E. B. Marks); *Album des "6"* (Eschig); *Contemporary British Composers* (Schott); *Antologia Pianistica di Autori Italiani Contemporanei,* ed. Montani (Suvini Zerboni); *The U. E. Piano Book* (Universal).

Reeser, Eduard, ed. *Music in Holland*. Amsterdam: J. M. Meulenhoff, n.d.

Rostand, Claude. *French Music Today* (translated by Marx). New York: Merlin Press, n.d.

Sopeña, Federico. *La Música Europea Contemporánea*. Madrid: Union Musical Española, 1953.

Stevens, Halsey. *The Life and Music of Bela Bartok*. New York: Oxford University Press, 1953.

Suchoff, Benjamin. *Guide to the Mikrokosmos*. Silver Spring, Maryland: Music Services Corporation of America, 1956.

31

CONTEMPORARY PIANO MUSIC

IN THE AMERICAS:

CANADA

Canadian music faced a situation similar to that of her neighbor the United States during the nineteenth century. In the first place, with her people spread over a vast country, Canada had problems more urgent than the creation of serious art music. Secondly, any good music written in Canada at that time was inevitably secondhand, a product whose immediate roots lay in Europe. Finally, most nineteenth-century Canadian musical compositions were oratorios, Masses, operas (only a few) or else practical, secular music, like marches. Piano composition was sporadic and relatively unimportant.

Canada's prominent nineteenth-century musician, **Calixa Lavallée** (born in Quebec in 1842, died in Boston, Mass., in 1891), has had this written about him: "Lavallée must be regarded as the first native-born Canadian creative composer—first in time, in genius, in versatility of achievement and in meritorious musicianship."[1] From 1873 to 1875 he studied at the *Conservatoire de Paris* under Adrien Louis Boieldieu and Marmontel, but he eventually migrated to the United States. He composed a huge amount of salon music for piano, now mostly out of print.[2]

Although **Alexis Contant** (1858–1918) also wrote salon music that is now forgotten, this Montreal musician was a competent teacher. He helped to develop other Canadian musicians such as Wilfred Pelletier and Claude Champagne.

Wesley Octavius Forsyth (1863–1937), from Ontario, studied composition and piano in both Leipzig and Vienna. Forsyth worked chiefly in Canada, but he became well known abroad: at least seventeen publishers in Canada, Germany, England, and the United States have issued his music, although it is now out of print. A few of his some fifty published piano pieces are virtuoso; most are short lyrical compositions whose style has been likened to Cyril Scott's.

---

[1] D. J. Logan, "Canadian Creative Composers," in *Canadian Magazine*, 1913, p. 489.
[2] G. Schirmer publishes an *Étude de Concert* by Lavallée called *Le Papillon*.

Clarence Lucas (1866–1947) preferred living in London, New York, or Paris so that he actually spent only a few of his active years in Canada; nevertheless for many decades he was regarded as the outstanding Anglo-Canadian composer of his time. He must have been a composer of stature, for respectable houses like Boosey & Hawkes, Schott, Simrock, G. Schirmer, Breitkopf & Härtel, and Chappell & Co. all published his music. His Canadian contemporary Forsyth wrote of him, "His piano pieces have the real piano idiom. They not only require from the pianist fine technical resources, but they sound well—rich, harmonious blends of tone effectively and beautifully contrasted."[3] A goodly share of his piano works definitely belongs to the category of serious music: *Fantasy and Fugue*, *Preludes and Fugues*, *Epithalamium* (*Impromptu*) *Opus 24*, *Ariel* (*Scherzo*) *Opus 55*.

By the time World War I began, Canada had produced a number of competent composers. Yet no one paid much attention to music education in the country because these native composers had gone away from home for their advanced instruction, usually to Germany or France.

CLAUDE CHAMPAGNE

One of the first twentieth-century composers to exert a long-lasting influence is **Claude Champagne** (*b.* 1891),[4] who studied in Montreal and Paris. His catholic outlook—he is a composer, pianist, violinist, violist, teacher, and conductor—and his knowledge of his country's musical heritage have led him to a lectureship at Rio de Janeiro Conservatory as well as to participation in European folk-music conferences.

Since much of Champagne's music is orchestral the few piano pieces provide an incomplete picture of his talents. The theme of *Quadrilha Brasileira*—a work commissioned in 1942 by the Canadian Ambassador to Brazil—is a melody from the island of Marajo, but as a folk-tune fantasy the piece is only moderately successful. Someone like Villa-Lobos would have been better equipped (through his nationality if nothing else) to undertake such a work. Another of Champagne's piano works unites two short pieces—*Prélude et Filigrane*—romantically tinged miniatures reminiscent of an earlier musical era. The second of the two pieces does contain modern-sounding dissonances, but they seem out of place—unoriented and frequently inconsistent.

---

[3] W. O. Forsyth, "Clarence Lucas," in *Canadian Journal of Music*, I (May 1914).
[4] The piano music of Champagne as well as that of most twentieth-century Canadian composers is published by BMI Canada Limited.

JEAN COULTHARD

The pianist-composer Miss **Jean Coulthard** (*b.* 1908) took advanced studies with Kathleen Long and Ralph Vaughan Williams at the London Royal College of Music as well as training in Paris and her native Canada. She has concertized a great deal and won many honors and prizes for her compositions; she writes truly contemporary piano music.

Her piano works now in print steadily maintain high standards of musicianship. They are contemporary—she likes to use dissonance, linear counterpoint, polytonality, and intricate rhythmic patterns—and yet they heed the lessons of the past. Particularly attractive are *Four Études*, which explore important pianistic problems. In the first étude an incessant pattern of right-hand triplets is played against contrasting left-hand figures. Subdivisions of note values are accented in the second étude; the quarter-note unit is alternately broken into groups of two, three, four, and five fractional values. The third piece, *Toccata*, is a bravura study in syncopation. The last étude is the finest; it brings to mind several of Brahms's *Capriccios*, in which passionate emotions are condensed into a framework that nearly bursts in its attempts to confine them.

Miss Coulthard has other delightful works. Three *Preludes for Piano* form a suite of contrasting moods: *Leggiero* is a light, wispy piece with seven-note arabesques rippling in harmonious grace; *Torment* alternates toccata-style passages with keyboard recitative; and the final *Quest* consists of an introduction and an *Allegro moderato*.

Although her grandly conceived *Sonata* is commendable, Miss Coulthard has more affinity for the short, idiomatic piano piece. The three-movement *Sonata* stresses contrasting and alternating tempos and textures. The first movement is especially expressive because the composer has carefully indicated every nuance, every slight change in spirit and tempo.

BARBARA PENTLAND

Another Canadian composer, **Barbara Pentland** (*b.* 1912), has written original, tastefully designed music. She graduated from the Julliard Graduate School of Music in New York and studied privately with Aaron Copland. Like Miss Coulthard, she has won several prizes and commissions and has concertized in America and Europe. Her most unique piano collection is called *Studies in Line* (1941). To quote from the explanatory notes, "The four 'Studies' are fashioned from single ideas developed in four short movements. Each is headed by a sketch rather than a verbal title. The contours of each sketch are descriptive not only of the general contour of the following 'Study' but of the emotional effect as well. Thus the first fluctuates like a graph, in the pattern of its title; the second goes in circles; the third is level and tranquil as a straight line; and the last is zigzag." Another work, *Dirge*, is noteworthy for the paucity of notes involved and its graphically stark atmosphere. Her *Toccata* has also been published.

JEAN PAPINEAU-COUTURE

Jean Papineau-Couture (*b.* 1916) received his musical education almost exclusively in the United States: Longy School in Boston (Nadia Boulanger) and the New England Conservatory (Quincey Porter). The style of his numerous compositions might be characterized as Neo-Romantic. His *Suite pour Piano* shows that he can fashion charming epigrammatic pieces: it includes two *Bagatelles, Prelude, Aria,* and concluding *Rondo.* The *Bagatelles* sparkle with wit and elfin grace while the *Aria* is an uncompromising bit of melodic writing.

OTHER CANADIAN COMPOSERS

The list of Canadian composers of the younger generation is growing longer. Born in the nine years from 1918 to 1927, they are just getting settled in their respective careers. **Gerald Bales** (*b.* 1919)—organist, conductor, and composer—has as yet published only one piano work, a *Toccata* whose expansive chord progressions attest to his preoccupation with the organ keyboard. Though quite short the piece has a very direct expression and a certain imagination.

Although **George Hurst** (*b.* 1926) is Edinburgh-born, he studied at Toronto's Royal Conservatory. For a time he taught at the Peabody Conservatory in Baltimore but is now in Britain. To date he is represented by an effective *Toccata,* modestly proportioned; a romantic *Masque* in the style of a nocturne; and four *Dance Preludes* that are short essays in contrasting moods. The first prelude creates impressive simplicity with its two-part counterpoint; the second, *Allegro,* is too repetitive to be successful; the third returns to the transparency of the first; and the set closes with a rhythmic *Allegro molto e vivace.*

Rhené Jaque is actually **Sister M. Jacques-René** (*b.* 1918), a theory teacher at the *Ecole Vincent d'Indy* in Montreal. She is both pianist and violinist as well as composer and has studied composition with Claude Champagne. Her *Suite pour Piano Opus 11* suggests that she has skill, imagination, and a special feeling for the picturesque. The initial movement is marked *de l'aurore au plein midi;* then follows the dirgelike *heure* *d'angoisse* with augmented intervals adding to the severity. Number three, *dans le sentiment d'une joie enfantine,* dispels the preceding sadness with toccata-like jubilation. Two more movements conclude the suite: *pour danser modérément,* a gracious dance primarily in 5/4 meter, and a sparkling finale inscribed as *dans le caractère de la gigue.*

Another of Claude Champagne's numerous pupils, **Maurice Dela** (*b.* 1919), for several years taught literature, history, and music at Holy Cross Normal School in Montreal. His suite *La Vieille Capitale* leads one to believe that he studied with Gabriel Fauré rather than Claude Champagne, but even though it could have been written fifty years ago, this is a pleasant triptych: *Prélude—Veille sous la Porte Saint-Jean; Chanson—Ballade des Petites Rues; Divertissement—Danse sur la Terrasse.* In his short *Hommage,* full of saccharine harmonies, he tries too hard to develop a popular style.

Harry Somers (*b.* 1925) has been fortunate in that his music has been widely performed beyond his native Toronto. He studied piano with E. Robert Schmitz in San Francisco and worked for a year in Paris with Darius Milhaud. Like Milhaud, he writes copiously: many works for orchestra (including two piano concertos and one symphony), songs, choral music, and piano music, including several fine works. His collection *12 x 12 Fugues for Piano* contains twelve distinctive fugues as delightful as they are ingenious; they are remarkable examples of contemporary fugal writing. Each of Somers' *Three Sonnets* is built around a single musical idea, which is then commented upon: the prevailing approach in *Prelude* is derived from a broken arpeggiated figure; the second *Sonnet* has the lugubrious title *Lullaby to a Dead Child;* the third is a rambunctious virtuoso study titled *Primeval.*

This brief summary outlines Canada's status in the field of contemporary piano music. There are in addition several young composers who have as yet produced comparatively little. **Frederick Karam** (*b.* 1926) has Syrian parents but he was born in Ottawa. His brief *Scherzo* was perhaps intended as a teaching piece, for it is not difficult. An unpretentious *Sonatina Opus 1* by Ukranian-born **George Fiala** (*b.* 1922) also calls for minimum technical skill. It has three movements: a lightly sketched *Andantino melancolico; Larghetto espressivo,* an essay in intervals of the fourth; and a polytonal *Tarantella.*

To conclude on a note of excellence one might mention **John Beckwith's** (*b.* 1927) *Novelette,* a superior piece of music disclosing the influence of his teacher Nadia Boulanger in the carefully worked-out details and formal design. Of the three-part form, the first and third sections are dominated by an initial rhythmic figure. Dissonant counterpoint plays an important role. The contemporary folk-song style of the second section is very like Béla Bartók's sketches.

In attempting to summarize today's Canadian keyboard music, one realizes that Canadian composers are mainly conservative. Few have experimented with twelve-tone technique and many seem reluctant to relinquish the rich harmonies of nineteenth-century Romanticism.

BIBLIOGRAPHY

Archer, Thomas. "Claude Champagne." *Canadian Musical Journal*, II, Winter, 1958.

Composers of the Americas. Washington, D.C.: Pan American Union, 1955–1961, Vols. 5 and 6.

George, Graham. "Canada's Music 1955." *Culture*, Spring, 1955 (XVI).

Kallmann, Helmut, ed. *Catalogue of Canadian Composers*. Toronto: Canadian Broadcasting Corp., 1952.

Kallmann, Helmut. *A History of Music in Canada 1534–1914*. Toronto: University of Toronto Press, 1960.

Walter, Arnold. "Canadian Composition." *Music Teachers National Association*, Vol. of Proceedings, Ser. 40, Pittsburgh, 1946.

32

CONTEMPORARY PIANO MUSIC
IN THE AMERICAS:
LATIN AMERICA

Any analysis of Latin-American keyboard music almost automatically turns into a discussion of *contemporary* piano music in the various countries south of the United States, because Latin America has only a short history of keyboard music. To be sure, composers in these countries wrote keyboard music in the nineteenth century, but although some of it was good, the majority was bad. The Italianism then sweeping through Spain carried over into Latin America; the public wanted to hear Rossini's music, and even the native composers who attempted to write operas followed Italian models.

In retrospect it seems that keyboard composition should have fared better at that time. While it was natural for Latin-American composers to imitate the Europeans, it is surprising that their imitations were so badly done. Most of Latin-America's nineteenth-century piano repertoire can be described only as salon music; unfortunately, not music inspired by models like Schumann and Chopin but patterned after sentimental types which themselves have long since mercifully disappeared.

With the coming of the twentieth century, Latin-American art music began to improve on its own merits. In addition to Romanticism's more attractive aspects, four other trends arose when native composers seriously tackled the task of making a place for themselves in contemporary music. The nationalists preferred to use native folk arts—song and dance—as basic components in their musical language. Another group favored a more or less international style, using standard techniques—quartal harmony, polytonality—within rather classical frameworks. The atonalist composers leaned to the precepts laid down by Arnold Schönberg, the spiritual father of Expressionism. And finally, experimentalists such as Julián Carrillo used microtones.

It is impossible to place each composer neatly into one of these four categories. He may, for instance, have begun as a Romanticist, then later changed his style by setting melodic folk elements into a contemporary musical texture. Musically speaking, Latin America is young, and her energetic composers are receptive to diverse musical currents and cultural trends. A good healthy atmosphere exists in South America, where contemporary music is avidly cultivated by an informed public. In general, four Latin-American nations stand out for their intense, superior musical activity: Argentina, Brazil, Chile, and Mexico. In these countries the quality of compositions matches that of the finest European or American repertoire.

ARGENTINA

The man looked upon as the father of twentieth-century Argentine music really had several careers: composer, author, teacher, lecturer, and musical organizer. **Alberto Williams** (1862–1952) studied with César Franck, and his style exhibits more than one Franck trait. Early in the twentieth century, after Williams had accepted the tenets of Impressionism, he worked various impressionistic elements into his early techniques. The Williams catalogue lists over a hundred piano works, all the more impressive because one single listing is sometimes a suite including as many as twenty-six smaller pieces. His seven collections of children's piano pieces reveal him in the role of educator. Important as Williams was in fostering an Argentine national school of composers, his own piano music—faded echoes of other eras—is rarely played.[1]

Floro Ugarte (*b*. 1884) studied in Paris and the French influence can be traced in his music. He has a more positively Romantic approach than Williams. *Cinco Preludios* is a series supplied with individual titles hinting at the musical content: *Sad, Festive, Romantic, Dramatic, Cheerful*. In a nostalgic vein, he composed *De mi Tierra* (1923), a suite of three quasi-improvisatory pieces.[2]

Three Castro brothers in Argentina have made their name synonymous with superior musical intelligence and sound workmanship, and two of them have enhanced piano repertoire with some attractive pieces. **José María Castro** (*b*. 1892) underwent several stylistic changes—from Romanticism up to an approach that is best described as Neo-Classic—with the result that his textures range from lush, traditional sonorities to bitonality, polytonality, and atonality. His collection *Diez Piezas Breves* (Ten Short Pieces) is a good example of his approach to piano composition. *Estudio*, for instance, gives the impression of a contemporary two-part invention

---

[1] Most of Williams' music was published by Editorial "La Quena" S. R. L., Calle Viamonte 859, Buenos Aires.

[2] Both *Cinco Preludios* and *De mi Tierra* are published by Ricordi. The latter is a piano version which the composer himself made from an orchestral work.

using mostly eighth and sixteenth notes. *Canción de Cuna*, a cradle song, sets a simple melody against a predominantly chromatic texture. An exuberant rhythmic study is outlined in *Circo*; *Campanas* employs a 5/4 meter. Castro's *Sonata* (1931) in three movements is more ambitious: an *Allegro moderato*, an *Arietta* with six variations, and a *Finale*.[3] The entire work is notable for its clarity and musical logic.

José María's younger brother **Juan José Castro** (*b.* 1895) began his career with works whose improvisational nature betray their creator's youth. But studies with Vincent d'Indy in Paris served to tighten the framework of Castro's music. He does not hesitate to use an effective polyphonic style when required, and he usually achieves a clarity that makes his compositions musically satisfying. His virtuoso *Toccata* (1940) exploits an effective technical idiom; and *Sonatina Española* contains three movements, the last of which is an *Allegro* based on a *Rondo* by Weber.[4]

Russian-born **Jacobo Ficher** (*b.* 1896), violinist, composer, and orchestral conductor, has lived forty-three years in Buenos Aires. He was one of the founders of the 1930 *Grupo Renovación*, whose purpose was to assimilate European techniques into contemporary Latin-American musical composition. Understandably, not much of his music is inspired by Latin America, any more than it has roots in his native Russia. He has composed a number of noteworthy piano pieces, among them *Tres Piezas Opus 19*, *Tres Preludios Opus 23*, two sets of *Seis Fábulas*, *Seis Danzas Opus 66*, *Tres Danzas* (polytonal dances in popular Argentine style). His *Sonata Opus 44* in three movements won the Municipal Prize offered by the city of Buenos Aires in 1943. A later *Cuarta Sonata Opus 72* consists of only one movement but that movement has infinite variety in tempos and rhythms.[5]

Another founding member of *Grupo Renovación*, **Juan Carlos Paz** (*b.* 1897) has explored all facets of twentieth-century techniques. In his youth he advocated post-Romantic ideals, later investigated Neo-Classic trends, and finally passed into Expressionism. His *Cinco Piezas Características* (1937) include several delightful piano compositions. *Junto al Parana* (The Coast of Parana) has variations on an eight-measure theme in tango rhythm; and one of his few excursions into descriptive music—the slow moving *Pampeana* (The Pampas)—creates a distinctive mood picture. A fine example of Paz's atonality appears in No. 2 of his *Canciones y Baladas*; the whole piece is based on a complete tone row found in the first two

---

[3] *Diez Piezas Breves* are published by Barry y Cía. Numbers 1, 3, 6, and 10 are also found in the collection *Latin-American Art Music for the Piano*, ed. Lange (G. Schirmer). The *Sonata* (1931) is available through Ricordi.

[4] Castro's *Toccata* is available through C. Fischer. The *Sonatina Española* is published by Universal Edition.

[5] Ficher's *Sonata Opus 44* may be obtained at C. Fischer; *Seis Fábulas* is published by Axelrod. Ricordi handles the *Sonata Opus 72* and *Tangos y Milongas para Piano Opus 66*, and *Tres Danzas* are published by Editorial Argentina de Música.

measures. Other atonal works for piano occur in *Diez Piezas sobre una Serie de doce Tonos Opus 30* and the *Sonatina, No. 3, Opus 25.*[6]

Both Impressionist and Romantic tendencies mingle in the works of **Carlos Suffern** (*b.* 1905). Most of his piano music—*Sonata* in one movement, *Leyenda de Flores,* and *Danza*[7] with its eighth-note triplets accompanying a quasi-folk melody—suggests that he tries to be economical with material and is reluctant to relinquish the techniques and ideas of fifty years ago.

Early works by **Roberto García Morillo** (*b.* 1911) point to an admiration for Scriabin's techniques, but this style gradually gave way to a contemporary idiom with biting harmonic texture and inner intensity. Morillo is no folklorist but his music bears a primitive imprint—strong rhythms and insistently repeated accompanimental figures, especially the suite *Conjuros* (Incantations) and *Variaciones Opus 13* (1944).[8] Dedicated to Aaron Copland, Morillo's nineteen variations on a three-measure theme are conceived in stark, bold sonorities demanding much from the listener.

Although he is an excellent pianist and accompanist, **Carlos Guastavino** (*b.* 1912) has directed his composing talents chiefly to vocal music. What piano music he has produced is quite agreeable: forthright, outgoing, and written in a mildly contemporary idiom. Guastavino composed several works in classic form, including *Tres Sonatinas* (1949), three one-movement works based on popular Argentine rhythms: *Movimiento, Retama,* and *Danza.* In a freer vein, his little suite *La Siesta* contains three pieces: *El Patio, El Sauce* (The Willow), and *Gorriones* (Sparrows). He has also written some enchanting works based on children's songs: the *Diez Preludios sobre canciones populares.*[9]

In the younger generation of Argentine composers, **Alberto Ginastera** (*b.* 1916) ranks first. Blessed with superior musical intelligence, Ginastera is able to employ whatever techniques seem momentarily appropriate, transforming them into personal tools to carry out his musical dictates. Although he borrows occasionally from native melodies, he typically uses them thematically, enveloping them in his own highly refined harmonic and rhythmic apparatus.

Danzas Argentinas, an early work, is a suite with three dances: the first is polytonal with the right hand playing on white keys, the left hand

---

[6] C. Fischer publishes both *Junto al Parana* and *Pampeana. Balada No. 2* is in *Latin-American Art Music, op. cit.* Ediciones Musicales Politonia publishes the *Diez Piezas sobre una Serie de doce Tonos Opus 30.* Southern Music Publishing Co. issues the *Sonatina Opus 25.*

[7] Suffern's *Danza* is included in *Latin-American Art Music, op. cit.* Ricordi publishes *Leyenda de Flores.*

[8] Morillo's *Conjuros* and *Variaciones Opus 13* are available through Southern Music Publishing Co. and his *Canción Triste y Danza Alegre* is in *Latin-American Art Music, op. cit.*

[9] Guastavino's piano works are published by Ricordi.

on black notes; the second is lilting and immensely charming; by contrast, the final dance is all verve and motion.

Ginastera's *Tres Piezas* appeared in 1940: *Cuyana* uses arpeggio treatment to sustain the folklike melody; complex rhythmic material prevails in *Nortena;* driving rhythm also animates the last piece *Criolla*. *Twelve American Preludes* (1944) is a kind of Pan-American suite, a series of very brief but enormously effective pieces in different styles, textures, and tempos. Other works by this talented composer are *Suite de Danzas Criollas* and the extremely difficult *Sonata para Piano*.[10]

The *Sonata* was commissioned for the 1952 Pittsburgh International Contemporary Music Festival. It is difficult to play and makes no concessions to the listener. The first of the four movements, *Allegro marcato*, is fashioned on multiple meters. The alternating sections in different textures remind one somewhat of the classic toccata. The opening motive is dramatic (Ex. 1).

Ex. 1. Ginastera: *Sonata: Allegro marcato*

SONATA FOR PIANO by Alberto Ginastera, Copyright 1954 by Barry & Cía; Sole Agents: Boosey & Hawkes Inc. Reprinted by permission.

In the *Presto misterioso*, passages three octaves apart, in double octaves, and in single melodic lines succeed each other in a relentless 6/8 meter. The third movement, *Adagio molto appassionato*, has three sections. The first and third sections are dominated by an ascending seven-note figure alternated with cadenza-like figures. The middle portion is more harmonic with its pungent, acrid chords. This *Sonata*, so characteristic of Ginastera's art, closes with a movement marked *Rudivo ed ostinato*. The composer alternates his rhythmic accents; what emerges is a brilliant finale in hemiola rhythm—i.e., the first measure 1–2–3–4–5–6, the next 1–2–3–4–5–6.

---

[10] Durand publishes *Danzas Argentinas* and Ricordi the *Tres Piezas*. The *Twelve American Preludes* are issued by C. Fischer. Barry y Cía publishes the *Sonata para Piano*. The *Suite de Danzas Criollas* is available through Boosey & Hawkes.

BRAZIL

Brazilian composers have achieved a distinction equal to that of their Argentine colleagues. For many years Brazilian music was dominated by the personality of **Heitor Villa-Lobos** (1887–1959). His death deprived Brazil of one of her most dedicated sons and Latin America of one of its most vital composers. Although Villa-Lobos' musical vocabulary was inborn, he took some inspiration from Milhaud and, as a matter of fact, from French music in general, for he lived in France for awhile.

As a composer, Villa-Lobos was an ardent nationalist and folklorist. Realizing that rich material lay in his country's indigenous music, he set out to make this treasure serve in his own compositions; and because he passed through many stylistic phases, he employed multiple technical means to accomplish his ends. He began, logically enough, as a Romanticist, later turned to a style similar to Impressionism; and then his passion for Bach led him into a kind of classicism. Eventually he was able to assimilate all his earlier approaches into a mature—and decidedly complex—personal idiom, remarkably expressive. This last style depends heavily on chromaticism, polyrhythm, and polytonality—frequently applied with forcefulness and authority. One must stress the word "frequently," for Villa-Lobos was neither a cautious nor a critical composer; he saved everything he wrote and there is little evidence that he was interested in revision. As a result, banality and triteness are often evident.

Villa-Lobos' large output includes many piano works, but only the most representative can be discussed here. He made a unique contribution to piano repertoire with his collections pertaining to children and their surroundings. There are three collections of pieces jointly called *Prole do Bebe* (Baby's Playthings): the first describes dolls—porcelain, paper, clay, rubber, wooden, rag, Punch (the popular *Polichinelle*), and a little witch doll; the second deals with little toy animals—cardboard cat, toy mouse, rubber dog, wooden horse, tin ox, cloth bird, cotton bear, and glass wolf. Needless to say, these are not pieces children can play; although they vary, the majority demand an exceptional pianist. Another attractive suite *As Tres Marias* (The Three Maries) was freely inspired by a Brazilian children's tale about three little girls who wander through life together. All three pieces are written in the treble clef.

Villa-Lobos also composed two series of instrument and voice combinations with the general titles *Bachianas Brasileiras* and *Choros*. The first title substantiates his admiration for the cantor of St. Thomas; the second title denotes any work inspired by folk song or dance. Number four in the *Bachianas Brasileiras* is a piano solo containing four pieces: *Preludio*, *Coral*, *Aria*, and *Dança*. Written in song form, *Choros No. 5—*

subtitled *Alma Brasileira*—is also for keyboard; the first section has a nostalgic, lyrical line, a mood changed by the rhythmic middle section.

Villa-Lobos' seldom performed concert piece *Rudepoema* is full of savage fury and is wickedly hard for the pianist. It is a brilliant illustration of virtuoso technique abetted by superior musical substance.[11]

Octavio Pinto (1890–1950) also liked to compose pieces centered around the world of children, and his works in this category are perhaps better known outside Brazil than are any piano pieces by his contemporaries. Most frequently heard are pieces from the suite *Scenas Infantis* (Memories of Childhood) whose five compositions—*Run, Run; Ring around the Rosy; March, Little Soldier; Sleeping Time;* and *Hobby Horse*—can actually be played by children. Though not as difficult as Villa-Lobos' pieces, they require certain facility; and if the pianist has an imaginative touch this little suite can be a delight. Another collection can also be played by children: *Children's Festival* includes *Prelude, Minuet, Little March, Serenade,* and *Playing Marbles.*[12]

One Brazilian composer has taken advantage of folk material from the very beginning of his career. **Francisco Mignone** (*b.* 1897) uses native rhythms, predominantly Negro, in his powerfully expressive, emotional music. His harmonies are often tinged with Italianisms, the result of advanced studies at Milan, Italy. There are numerous waltzes among his more than seventy-five piano works—sonorous, Romantic pieces, not important examples of serious music. More significant is the series collectively titled *Lenda Brasileira, lenda* being the Brazilian equivalent of ballade. Charged with dramatic contrasts, No. 3 of this series sustains vitality in recitative-like passages alternating with complicated rhythmic sections. A study in atonality, No. 4 is based on the legend of *Jara,* the Brazilian symbol of good and evil.

In 1930 Mignone presented *Quatro Peças Brasileiras,* four studies in rhythm and lilting melody: a song without words is called *Maroca;* a lively dance is delineated in *Maxexando;* mirth and sparkle distinguish *Nazareth;* and the fourth piece, *Toada,* goes along at a comparatively subdued, sentimental pace. Along classic lines, Mignone has written an effective three-movement *Sonata* and some *Sonatinas* having either one or two movements. Every one of the *Sonatinas* accents sharply contrasted rhythms accompanied by ever changing atmospheres and emotions.[13]

Camargo Guarnieri (*b.* 1907) is one of the top modern composers in

---

[11] Max Eschig publishes a quantity of Villa-Lobos music: *Choros No. 5, Bachianas Brasileiras No. 4, Rudepoema, Prole do Bebe* (the first series of this last work is also issued by E. B. Marks). C. Fischer publishes *As Tres Marias.*

[12] Pinto's two collections are published by G. Schirmer.

[13] E. B. Marks handles Mignone's four *Lendas Brasileiras,* and Ricordi publishes his *Quatro Peças Brasileiras, Four Sonatinas,* and *Sonata.*

Brazil. His father was Sicilian and Guarnieri himself studied for two years
in Europe. In addition, he has conducted in the United States. This acquaintance with other musical cultures has served to strengthen his musical
vocabulary, though it has barely influenced his ultimate style. Nationalism
is the driving spirit behind his music, a desire to weave material from the
songs and dances of Brazilian folklore into a strong web of competent
musicality. The music often requires three staves, and is frequently without
a key signature.

There are worthwhile additions to keyboard repertoire to be found in
his piano music. The dance has always been a favorite keyboard idiom,
and Guarnieri has enhanced that tradition. Samba rhythms vibrate throughout the colorful *Dansa Brasileira,* accompanied by sudden shifts of tonal
intensity. The passionate, primitive *Dansa Selvagem* imitates drumbeats
through bare fifths and seventh chords. Another rhythmic study in dance
style is *Dansa Negra.*

The dance is only one outlet for Guarnieri's agile imagination. *Toada
Triste,* a sad, songlike melody expressed in thirds and sixths, requires three
staves as it is etched with its filigree accompaniment. *Choro Torturado*
portrays a succession of moods. *Toccata* is a sparkling virtuoso work whose
chromaticism and double-note technique necessitate mature pianism. Like
most Latin-American composers, Guarnieri has written sonatinas and preludes. Only the treble clef is used for the third *Sonatina,* whose movements
are titled *Allegro, Con tenerezza,* and *Fugue Ben Ritmico.* His series of
Ponteios (Preludes) occupies several volumes.[14]

CHILE

Despite the fact that Chile has not produced many internationally
known composers, she still is an active musical center. Instead of being
nationalistic, most Chilean composers have been affected by European styles
and techniques.

Alfonso Leng (*b.* 1884) belongs to the older generation. Almost wholly
self-taught, he at times writes with an invigorating freshness and spontaneity; on the other hand, his music sometimes falls short in discipline,
causing slack construction and vagueness. Leng's *Sonata,*[15] published in
1959, has many qualities to recommend it. The first movement, *Allegro
con brio,* is in brief song form with a condensed coda; the technique is

---

[14] Associated Music Publishers publishes several Guarnieri works: *Dansa Brasileira, Dansa
Negra, Choro Torturado, Sonatina No. 3.* Ricordi issues *Dansa Selvagem* and three volumes of
Ponteios. A *Toada Triste* is included in *Latin-American Art Music, op. cit.*

[15] Leng's *Sonata para Piano* is published by the Pan American Union (sold through Peer
International Corporation).

predominantly polytonal. The lyricism usually associated with slow movements is absent from this sonata; its sparsely written *Lento* is also in A B A form. The *Final*—less successful than the first two movements—seems to be based on fragmentary ideas and too often uses dissonance merely for its own sake.

Enrique Soro (*b*. 1884) embraced two careers: composer and concert pianist. He attended the Conservatory of Milan for six years—his parents were Italian—then embarked on an extended concert tour before he settled down for nine years as director of the National Conservatory in Chile. He has collected many prizes and honors for his works. The following piano compositions deserve mention: *Andante Appassionato, Cuatro Piezas para Piano, Cuatro Piezas de Concierto,* and *Dos Tonadas Chilenas. Tonada* (similar to the Portuguese *Toada*) is a song or short instrumental piece based on Chilean folk music.[16]

Pedro Humberto Allende (*b*. 1885), composer and teacher, prefers that irregular metric patterns accompany his often biting, crisp harmonies. His *Six Études* seem to be not true studies in technique but rather attempts to explore other interpretative pianistic problems. Twelve *Tonadas* run the gamut of major and minor keys. They are all attractive and usually contain two sections: a lento followed by a fast passage conceived somewhat in a dance spirit.[17]

One of the busiest Chilean musicians is **Domingo Santa Cruz** (*b*. 1899). As an educator he has taught music history, served as Dean of Fine Arts at the University of Chile, supervised the publication of pieces by Chilean composers, and also supervised recordings at RCA Victor's Chilean branch. As a composer he is somewhat Neo-Classical. Sometimes called the Chilean Hindemith, he does share common traits with the German composer: rich harmonic style that admits the superposition of polyphony; and a refreshing, vital concept of rhythmic elements. Despite their descriptive titles, Santa Cruz's four *Viñetas* of 1927—*Galante, Desolada, Clásica, Grotesca*—are conceived in the spirit of the early suite; his five *Poemas Trágicas* at times border on atonality.[18]

Juan Orrego-Salas (*b*. 1919), a recipient of Rockefeller and Guggenheim grants, is another important Chilean musical figure. Advanced studies with Randall Thompson and Aaron Copland have strengthened his musical apparatus and shaped his mature musical style. Comparatively few of his piano compositions are available except for the following: *Suites Nos. 1* and *2, Variaciones y Fuga sobre un Pregón* (dedicated to Alberto Ginastera).[19]

[16] G. Schirmer publishes Soro's *Andante Appassionato* and *Cuatro Piezas para Piano.* Ricordi handles *Cuatro Piezas de Concierto* and *Dos Tonadas Chilenas.*

[17] Salabert (Senart) lists the *Six Études* (*Estudios*) and *12 Tonadas* of Allende.

[18] Casa Amarilla of Santiago publishes Santa Cruz's *Viñetas* and *Poemas Trágicas.*

[19] Barry y Cía publishes *Suites 1* and *2* and Hargail Music Press the *Variaciones.*

MEXICO

Mexico rates fourth in order of appearance in this chapter not because there is less musical activity in that country but because most Mexican composers do not concentrate on keyboard music. This is true even of the father of twentieth-century Mexican music, **Manuel Ponce** (1882–1948) —the man who introduced nationalism to Mexican music. Ponce, at least in his early phase, was self-taught. Then at forty, feeling himself inadequate and in need of further grounding in compositional principles, he went to the *École Normale* in Paris to study with Paul Dukas.

Ponce did not produce any solid piano music. There are a few salon pieces but they cannot be taken seriously. *Deux Études* are two contrasted studies: one for crossed hands, the other exploiting a technique in double notes and octaves. *Four Pieces for Piano* (1929) are pleasing enough. The basic technique in these short sketches calls for one hand on all white keys, the other on all black.[20]

Although Ponce is recognized as the father of twentieth-century Mexican music, **Carlos Chávez** (*b.* 1899) is Mexico's outstanding living composer. He inaugurated the era of actual contemporary music in Mexico. His music is energetic and resourceful, reflecting the age which engendered it; and he has made a deep, durable impression upon younger composers. As one who shuns sensationalism and "snobbism" in art, he is able to offer his pupils examples of music that gets its vitality from its own Mexican heritage. It is music that is often difficult to fathom at first hearing because the harmonic outlines are harsh and acrid, the tone color percussive; in short, the music seems to be as austere as some Mexican landscapes. But perseverance is rewarded, and repeated hearings disclose the composer's logic. As the music unfolds it reveals the single-minded purpose of the means and technique employed, and it makes the listener aware of the role that music can assume in highlighting Mexico's cultural treasures.

Such a superior musical intellect has naturally produced fine compositions. Several of Chávez' sonatas and sonatinas, though written quite early, display some of his most idiomatic writing. In *Sonata No. 3* (1928) all four movements center primarily on the white keys, and Chávez' biting, vigorous style is evident in every phrase. Sometimes abstract pieces are found side by side with their opposites. This is true of the *Seven Pieces for Piano* in which some—*Fox, Blues*—are based on dance idioms and others such as *Polígonos* (Polygons) emphasize the abstract. The ten *Preludes* of 1937 are highly attractive works based primarily on modal scales.[21]

---

[20] *Deux Études* by Ponce appear in *Latin-American Art Music, op. cit.* Salabert (Senart) publishes *Quatre Pièces pour Piano.*

[21] Several Chávez works are published by New Music Editions (through American Music Center): *Sonata No. 3* and *Seven Pieces for Piano.* G. Schirmer publishes *Ten Preludes.* A more recent work is *Invención para Piano* (Boosey & Hawkes).

OTHER LATIN-AMERICAN COUNTRIES

Argentina, Brazil, Chile, and Mexico are the Latin-American countries which have steadily fostered interest in piano composition, but of course composers in other Latin-American countries have written—and are now writing—piano music along with works in other media. This chapter should also look at these other composers.

Colombia is the home of the talented young composer **Luis Antonio Escobar** (*b.* 1925), whose fine musical background includes studies in the United States at the Peabody Conservatory, in Europe with Boris Blacher, and at the Berlin *Hochschule für Musik*. His *Sonatina No. 2 para Piano*[22] is very good, written in an easy, contemporary idiom accessible to all. The opening *Allegro* is rhythmically alive, with a basic theme consisting of a lyric phrase followed by a knocking motive. The central *Andantino* is simply achieved with a melody that appears in both hands. And the clear-textured *Allegro-Finale* is full of happiness.

Cuba has two composers of merit. **Harold Gramatges'** (*b.* 1918) *Tres Preludios*[23] are essays in contrasting moods and techniques. *Allegro* consistently changes its rhythm and meter, and its interesting harmonic texture comes from chords in thirds, fourths, and fifths. The second prelude, *Andante e molto espressivo*, dispenses a long lyric melody whose contour depends on rhythm. This melody appears sometimes in the right hand, sometimes in the left. The final *Allegro* is like a toccata, with eighth-note triplets in various combinations. An andante middle section in this final movement contains some imitative treatment.

Alejandro García Caturla (1906–1940), a student of Nadia Boulanger in Paris, blends all musical Cuban traditions within his own idiom, emphasizing the Negro element. When he uses an extremely modern harmonic approach, he becomes obsessed with recreating native coloristic effects. *Son en Fa Menor* consists of a four-measure theme with variations. *Dos Danzas Cubanas* is typical of his approach to folkloric composition: he uses drumlike imitations and effective cross rhythms in *Danza del Tambor*; *Danza Lucumi* delights in complicated rhythms in the spirit of an Afro-Cuban dance.[24]

Guatemala also has a pair of first-rate composers. **Ricardo Castillo** (*b.* 1894) spent more than two years in Paris, studying and observing the contemporary musical scene. Since 1938 he has taught composition at the National Conservatory in Guatemala City. The opening *Presto* of his *Suite en Re para Piano* (published 1957)[25] is like a toccata, with an insistent

---

[22] Peer International handles Escobar's *Sonatina No. 2 para Piano.*
[23] Gramatges' *Tres Preludios* are available through Peer.
[24] C. Fischer publishes Caturla's *Son en Fa Menor*, and Salabert lists *Dos Danzas Cubanas.*
[25] Castillo's *Suite en Re* is handled by Peer.

rhythm in eighth and sixteenth notes. In *Giocoso* the composer traces an unusual pattern of 6/8 meter in the left hand against 3/4 in the right hand; in *Espressivo* (written in song form) he uses a melody stated two octaves apart and a rapid middle section. The *Cantabile* is like a folk song and is followed by the concluding *Malinconico*.

Manuel Herrarte, also from Guatemala, graduated from the National Conservatory in 1944 and then received a scholarship to the Eastman School of Music, where he studied with Howard Hanson and Robert Casadesus. Herrarte is a fine pianist, a fact mirrored in his gratefully written music for that instrument. Although *Tres Danzas* (published 1957)[26] demand much of the performer, the end result is worth the effort. The first dance, *Allegro (rítmico, con mucho fuego)*, consists of two short melodic motives, which in repetition are built into a stunning interplay of rhythm and melody. In contrast, *Andantino* is mostly polytonal, with a consistent rhythm based on eighth-note triplets. The third dance, *Presto*, emphasizes glissandos and the extreme registers of the piano.

The Nicaraguan Luis A. Delgadillo (*b.* 1887) has studied at Milan and conducted in the United States and Latin America. A nationalist, he borrows from Nicaraguan folk art for inspiration. His piano compositions include *Sonata en Re Menor, Cinco Estudios, Veinticuatro Preludios,* and *Sonatina en La Menor.*[27]

Although he was born in Paris and lived many years in Brussels, Andres Sás (*b.* 1900) is considered a Peruvian composer—in 1933 he founded his own conservatory in Peru. He has also studied violin under Eugene Ysaye and concertized extensively. Both French and Peruvian musical cultures influence him. France has provided the principles for his harmony and texture; Peru's native music influences the melodic and rhythmic elements. Two piano sets, each with two pieces, are worthy of mention: *Hymno y Danza* and *Arrulo y Tondero. Hymno*—a march written mostly on three staves and using a full-chord texture—possibly recalls the ancient Inca culture. *Danza* is a *huayno*—a type still danced in certain sections of Peru—in which a basic rhythmic figure accompanies the dramatic climax ending the dance. In the second set, *Arrulo* is a kind of berceuse: a tender melody with an unobtrusive accompaniment, all fitted into a 5/4 meter. An exciting Creole dance is delineated in *Tondero*, a work of effective proportions.[28]

The young Peruvian José Carlos Malsio (*b.* 1924) shows promise of becoming an outstanding composer. He has studied mostly in the United States: at Eastman Conservatory and at Yale University with Hindemith.

[26] Peer also carries *Tres Danzas* by Herrarte.
[27] Delgadillo's works mostly remain in manuscript at the present time.
[28] *Latin-American Art Music, op. cit.,* contains a *Hymno y Danza* by Sás; his *Arrulo y Tondero* was published by Elkan-Vogel.

In 1952 he won Peru's National Music Prize. *Preludio y Toccata* decries the abstract quality of his work. The *Preludio* is intricate, having a dissonant linear texture in its three sections: *Recitativo, Arioso,* and *Tempo primo.* In *Toccata,* which is built on a one-measure ostinato figure with a compass of a major third, the composer uses sections in two-part counterpoint as melodic material.[29]

Nadia Boulanger, Irving Fine, and Aaron Copland all helped to mold the style and musical vocabulary of Puerto Rican **Heitor Campos-Parsi** (*b.* 1922). In 1954 his *Sonata en Sol*[30] was awarded a prize at the first Festival of Latin-American Music at Caracas. The first movement opens with an episodic introduction followed by an *Allegro* in sonata-allegro form. A diatonic melodic line pervades the atmosphere of the second movement, *Mesto,* and a brief four-part *Corale* interrupts the energetic drive of the final *Vivo.*

Finally, there is **Juan Bautista Plaza** (*b.* 1898) in Venezuela. Having studied for three years at the Pontifical Institute of Sacred Music, he concentrates on vocal music. A scholar as well as composer, Plaza has transcribed a lot of colonial music. He is a folklorist, evident in his one-movement *Sonatina Venezolana,*[31] which is in Baroque sonata form but has a style based on native themes and rhythms.

This discussion of Latin-American piano music,[32] necessarily cursory and incomplete, can serve merely as a starting point for further research. The brief outline, however, points out several facts. First, Latin America in general is keeping pace with the United States and continental Europe in musical activity and atmosphere. Second, the Latin-American musical scene presents mixed styles and approaches: some music is based on European traditions; some is nationalistic; and some falls into an international, abstract category. Finally, we can conclude that Latin America's many gifted composers have made lasting contributions to contemporary music.

BIBLIOGRAPHY

Chase, Gilbert. *A Guide to the Music of Latin America.* Washington, D.C.: Pan American Union, 1962.

[29] Malsio's *Preludio y Toccata* appears through Peer.
[30] Peer handles the *Sonata en Sol* by Campos-Parsi.
[31] Plaza's *Sonatina Venezolana* is published by G. Schirmer.
[32] Two representative collections are the *Album of Six Modern Cuban Composers* (Elkan-Vogel) and *Album of Six Modern Guatemalan Composers* (Elkan-Vogel).

Composers of the Americas. Washington, D.C.: Pan American Union, 1955–1961. 7 Vols.

Meyer-Serra, Oscar. *Música y Músicos de Latinoamerica.* Mexico: Editorial Atlante, S.A., 1947. 2 Vols.

Orrego-Salas, Juan. "The Young Generation of Latin American Composers." *Inter-American Music Bulletin,* November, 1963.

Slonimsky, Nicolas. *Music of Latin America.* New York: Thomas Y. Crowell Co., 1945.

33

CONTEMPORARY PIANO MUSIC
IN THE AMERICAS:
THE UNITED STATES

During the course of this present century, piano composition in the United States has become vigorous, developing a degree of perfection that very nearly challenges Europe. This is remarkable in view of the fact that comparatively speaking this is a young nation, one that is still choosing from the old and the new as it establishes the foundations of its artistic tradition. Although prospects are bright, tradition takes time.

Early-twentieth-century American composers faced the difficult task of reconciling Romanticism's last embers with the oncoming modern avenues of expression. Jazz seized American musical thought in the twenties when composers like **George Gershwin** (1898–1937) managed to work the stable elements of jazz into something approaching respectability. Gershwin's unpretentious *Preludes* for piano are *con tempore* but they also have substance. Some aspects of the jazz age endured: as in Aaron Copland's *Four Piano Blues* (1948) and Herbert Haufrecht's excellent *Études in Blues* (1956). For the last thirty years piano composition has advanced steadily. Today's styles and methods of approach are too varied to be grouped together categorically, but on the whole modern composers have identical goals: clarity and succinctness uncluttered by extraneous details, the use of dissonant counterpoint, and experiments with untried rhythmic formulas.

To be more specific, some present-day composers are basically Romanticists, although they usually adjust this attitude to the contemporary idiom. There is also a fairly large nationalist group which tries—with varying degrees of enthusiasm—to write "American" music. Some composers, especially during the earlier years, were strongly influenced by Impressionism. In direct contrast to them stand the atonalists, or at least the writers who appropriate elements of twelve-tone technique. But the largest group of United States composers—native-born or otherwise—may be called Classicists or Neo-Classicists. Their language is definitely in tune with the times but the scaffold on which it relies usually reverts to some Baroque or Classic form: sonata, suite, prelude and fugue, toccata.

Since this century has already produced countless keyboard composers (or rather composers who have written some keyboard music), we can deal only with the ones who now appear to have won a permanent reputation. Although each composer is placed into one of several categories— which could not be done in the previous chapter because of the numerous countries involved—it must be understood that such classification is not immutable. Each composer is grouped according to what seems to be his conspicuous trait or quality, in some cases merely his attitude toward musical art.

IMPRESSIONISTS

The term impressionist aptly applies to the early works of **Charles Tomlinson Griffes** (1884–1920), the most typical being *Four Roman Sketches Opus 7* (1915–1916). In these piano pieces—*The White Peacock, Nightfall, The Fountain of Acqua Paola,* and *Clouds*—Griffes proves that he has a remarkable feeling for tone color and atmospheric re-creation. The first, based on the poem "The White Peacock" by Fiona Macleod (William Sharp), is widely known; Griffes also arranged it for orchestra.

In 1918 Griffes finished his *Sonata* (revised in 1919), which visibly bespeaks a new attitude on his part. Combinations of diversified elements —oriental-type scale patterns, Scriabinesque chromaticisms, deliberate experimentation in new harmonies—announce Griffes' *Sonata* to be one of the earliest works written in what is now known as the contemporary idiom. It has three movements: *Feroce-Allegretto con moto, Molto tranquillo,* and *Allegro vivace.*[1]

There are other American composers whose works lean considerably on French Impressionist models: **John Alden Carpenter** (1876–1951), **Arthur Shepherd** (1880–1958), **Edward Burlingame Hill** (*b.* 1872). However, the piano music offered by these gentlemen is not distinctive.

NATIONALISTS

There is more than one definition for "nationalist composer." It may mean that a composer enjoys appropriating actual folk tunes and using them openly, or it may indicate that he employs melodic material which sounds authentic even though he has fashioned it himself. Again it may

---

[1] Griffes' piano music is published by G. Schirmer.

apply to a composer who builds his music around characteristic folk-song rhythms and folk-dance types. American history supplies a rich lode of source material for the nationally oriented composer: Indian themes, Negro spirituals, white spirituals, songs of the early West.

Arthur Farwell

Arthur Farwell (1872–1952) was a pioneer in this field. In 1901 he founded the Wa-Wan Press with the following declaration: "The Wa-Wan Press, at Newton Center, Massachusetts, is an enterprise organized and directly conducted by composers, in the interest of the best American composition. It aims to promote by publication and public hearings, the most progressive, characteristic, and serious works of American composers, known or unknown, and to present compositions based on the melodies of American folk-songs."

Farwell himself liked to delve into historical Indian music, taking either a mood or an actual melody as the foundation for his work: *American Indian Melodies* (1901), *From Mesa and Plain* (1905), *Impressions of the Wa-Wan Ceremony of the Omahas* (1906). Other composers added to the Wa-Wan Press catalogue of Indian paraphrases: **Harvey Worthington Loomis** (1865–1930) contributed *Lyrics of the Red-Man* (1903), and **Carlos Troyer** (1837–1920) offered a *Ghost Dance of the Zuñis* (1904).[2]

Charles Ives

Charles Ives (1874–1954) has finally been recognized as the true pioneer in American contemporary music. His superior compositions are not easy from any viewpoint: the printed page confronts the performer with endless—and seemingly aimless—notes, chromatics, just about every configuration imaginable. But Ives was able to write as he pleased, free of any anxiety about public acceptance, because he had a successful insurance business to support him. At first his works were privately printed, but now many of them are issued by professional publishing houses. They are harshly dissonant and rhythmically complex and occasionally need a second performer to lend a helping hand. Ives was indeed a pioneer. Even before Schönberg and Stravinsky evolved their respective idioms, he was working with polytonality, atonality, polyrhythms, and other techniques that later became so essential to modern musical language. Yet, paradoxically, he was

---

[2] After eleven years of activity, the Wa-Wan Press was absorbed by G. Schirmer, which now publishes a few pieces by Farwell. His *Navajo War Dance Opus 29, No. 2* is available from Music Press.

devoted to simple folklike music and to this end he relied heavily upon hymn tunes for source material.

Ives's first sonata, a mammoth fifty-page production, was written mostly in 1902. It has two *scherzos* in ragtime style, a slow rhapsodic section, and two other movements, making a total of five. He interpreted his work as "in a way a kind of impression, remembrance, and reflection of the country life in some of the Connecticut villages in the 1880's and 1890's." Echoes of gospel songs—"Bringing in the Sheaves" and "What a Friend We Have in Jesus"—measurably vivify the atmospheric picture.

His second sonata—the *"Concord Sonata"*—is the best example of his fully ripened style. In an attempt to clarify, or justify, this iconoclastic keyboard symphony, Ives wrote a set of *Essays before a Sonata* to accompany the musical score. In a playful spirit of almost prophetic humor he writes, "These prefatory essays were written by the composer for those who can't stand his music—and the music for those who can't stand his essays; to those who can't stand either, the whole is respectfully dedicated." In the Prologue he goes on to describe his piano work as "a group of four pieces called sonata for want of a more exact name. The whole is an attempt to present one person's impression of the spirit of transcendentalism that is associated in the minds of many with Concord, Mass., of over a half century ago . . . impressionistic pictures of Emerson and Thoreau, a sketch of the Alcotts, and a scherzo supposed to reflect a lighter quality which is often found in the fantastic side of Hawthorne."

In addition to the explanatory essays, Ives provided his music with a complement of performance and interpretative suggestions. He also utilizes other instruments—viola and flute—for an occasional melodic line. Thematically the entire sonata is based on two motives: one a descending five-note figure initially stated in octaves; the other is the same four-note motive which opens Beethoven's *Fifth Symphony!*

Certain of the musical passages from the first movement, *Emerson,* are associated with (unspecified) corresponding poetical and prose writings of the transcendentalist. In the second movement, *Hawthorne,* Ives evokes only too clearly his childhood memories: the gospel hymn, the circus parade, the camp meeting—each interrupting rather brazenly the ultra-dissonant language of the composer. In the *Essays* he gives a clue to at least one aspect of the third movement: "and there sits the little old spinet-piano Sophia Thoreau gave to the Alcott children, on which Beth played the old Scotch airs, and played at the *Fifth Symphony.*" Here Charles Ives does indeed "play at the *Fifth Symphony.*" *Thoreau,* the concluding part of the *Concord Sonata,* has no key signatures, no time signatures, and no bar lines. Here the composer returns to the quasi-impressionistic sketching introduced in *Emerson.*

Ives's two sonatas are formidable works equal to the finest productions of the twentieth century. However, Ives has a much lighter side, as in the *Three Page Sonata*. And *The Anti-Abolitionist Riots in Boston in the 1850's* and *Some Southpaw Pitching* give further evidence of his often enigmatic (tongue-in-cheek?) attitude.[3]

Roy Harris

Roy Harris (*b.* 1898) has one of the best reputations among today's American composers. He is respected by his fellow musicians and earnestly appreciated by a public that has ample opportunity to hear his music. A deft craftsman, he can maneuver twentieth-century techniques with enough moderation to render his music readily accessible. Although his rhythms are varied and at times involved, they are never so complex as to be obscure; and although his harmonies—built by preference in fourths—are dissonant and sometimes polytonal, they remain logical.

Harris' *Piano Suite* (1942) presents three fairly difficult pieces. *Occupation,* first in the suite, is principally "occupied" with unrestrained clashing sounds. In the middle piece *Contemplation* a folklike theme is submitted to several textures, one of which holds the melody in the left hand while the right hand plays an obbligato accompaniment in another tonality. *Recreation,* the last piece, might well be called "Children at Play." In the midst of its bouncy tones, one hears snatches of "London Bridge is Falling Down" along with singsong motives belonging to other children's games (Ex. 1). A more candid attempt at integrating folk material and also less successful, *American Ballads* (1946) sets folk tunes like "Black Is the Color of My True Love's Hair" in rather dull paraphrases.

Ex. 1. Harris: *Piano Suite: Recreation*

Copyright 1944 Mills Music, Inc. Used by Permission.

[3] Ives's *First Sonata* is published by Peer International, the *"Concord"* Sonata by Arrow Music Press; Mercury Music (Presser) handles most of the short pieces. The *Essays before a Sonata* may be found in a volume titled *Three Classics in the Aesthetic of Music* issued by Dover Publications.

Harris' first published work—*Sonata Opus 1* (1928) in four movements —is his most serious piano work, and it is a superior composition. The grandeur in the opening *Prelude* is followed by a quiet *Andante Ostinato*; then a bright and quasi-contrapuntal *Scherzo* leads to a *Coda* similar to the *Prelude*.[4]

Aaron Copland

Aaron Copland (*b.* 1900), one of America's best-known composers, has created movie and ballet music besides working independently. Copland's compositions range from quasi-Romantic French sounds to strident, uncompromising tones, and he is alert to all currents in musical vocabulary. His initial style is well underscored in *Scherzo Humoristique: The Cat and the Mouse* (1920), a witty package of pianistic tomfoolery that is absolutely disarming. *Piano Variations* (1930) is an excellent example of Copland's seasoned, disciplined, and discerning writing. The variations are cumulative, built entirely on the initial statement. The music summons many moods, from dignified sobriety to playfulness; but whatever the atmosphere, the fabric is stark and brittle. This austere quality lingers on in the piano *Sonata* (1939–1941) although it is greatly softened. In the expertly constructed *Four Piano Blues*, written intermittently from 1926, Copland successfully injects a jazz element into serious music. In contrast to the relaxed, easygoing pieces of the *Blues* stands *Piano Fantasy* (1957) —a long, through-composed work in one movement with contrasting sections alternating between acidity, sensuous tonal colors, brilliantly fashioned rhythmic designs. Copland uses Expressionistic devices, basing his *Fantasy* on a "row" of ten notes (Ex. 2). A difficult piece for both pianist and listener, *Piano Fantasy* is also one of this century's distinctive keyboard pieces.[5]

Ray Green

If any present-day music can be said to sound "American" it is that of **Ray Green** (*b.* 1908). His buoyant piano pieces are clearly meant to be heard and enjoyed, and they are irresistibly enjoyable. The *Short Sonata in F Major* (published 1951) is almost wholly built in fourths, with some sections in blues style; that is, an alternate raising and lowering of the third. Green's *Festival Fugues* are a pleasant bit of Americana, with folk

---

[4] Arrow Music Press publishes Harris' *Sonata Opus 1*, C. Fischer the *American Ballads*, and Mills Music the *Suite for Piano*.

[5] Salabert publishes the Copland *Passacaglia*. Boosey & Hawkes handles the following: *Cat and the Mouse, Variations* (1930), *Sonata* (1941), *Four Piano Blues* (1948), *Fantasy* (1957).

Ex. 2. Copland: *Piano Fantasy*

PIANO FANTASY by Aaron Copland, copyright 1957 by Boosey & Hawkes
Inc. Copyright assigned to Aaron Copland. Reprinted by permission of Aaron
Copland, copyright owner, and Boosey & Hawkes Inc., sole agents.

materials included in the various sections: *Prelude Promenade, Holiday
Fugue, Fugal Song, Prelude Pastorale,* and *Jubilant Fugue.*[6] They prove that
fugues do not necessarily have to be dry, pedantic exercises.

NEO-ROMANTICS

Virgil Thomson

The closest approach to an American Erik Satie is **Virgil Thomson** (*b.*
1896), a pupil of the famous Nadia Boulanger. For many years (1925–
1940) he made his home in Paris, where he found his true approach via
Satie and *Les Six.* This contact with French music and French musicians
explains some of the qualities that are now an integral part of his music:
lucid expression and an impeccable taste in the creation of musical materials.
Thomson's irreverent façade, his attitude of self-spoofing, is merely part of
his witty, sophisticated nature. In his many piano works—sonatas, études,
inventions, portraits—he avoids excessive dissonance. He obtains variety by
abrupt key changes, by using short forms (even the sonata movements are
brief to the point of terseness), and by rhythmic imaginativeness. He is
not ashamed to be frankly sentimental and there lies one factor of the immediate charm of his music.

A great deal of Thomson's music is easy to play. *Piano Sonata No. 3*
(1930), dedicated to Gertrude Stein, requires only five pages for its four
movements. It is a delightful, nonchalant work with simplicity as its chief
technical device. The fourth *Sonata* (1940) is slightly harder but equally
brief and witty.

---

[6] American Music Edition is the publisher for Ray Green.

His *Ten Études* (1943) are eminently worthwhile for they combine technical problems—repeated tremolos, parallel chords, fingered glissandos, etc.—with highly diverting keyboard writing. In 1928 Thomson began a series of musical "portraits" now numbering over a hundred. As he explains, "The subject sits for his likeness as he would for a painter. An effort has been made to catch in all cases a likeness recognizable to persons acquainted with the sitter." Many are sketches of his personal friends, some widely known personalities like Pablo Picasso and the composer Lou Harrison. Other piano works by Thomson include the *Five Two-Part Inventions* (1926).[7]

Ernest Bloch

Ernest Bloch (1880–1959) spent more than thirty years in the United States (1916–1927, 1938–1959) and always kept a close tie with Hebraic culture. This feeling of oneness with his traditional past has indelibly stamped his music; however, this does not mean he used Jewish folk melodies in his music—it was much subtler than that. The very core of his music is emotion, musically expressed with exaltation bordering on mysticism and rhapsodic freedom often amounting to sensuous abandon.

Bloch's best works are the early ones written *ca.* 1910 to 1925. Ingredients from his French-Swiss-Hebraic backgrounds and schoolings are mixed within a quasi-Romantic, quasi-Classic frame of reference. His piano music is good but does not represent him at his best. *Poems of the Sea* (1922) is a collection of three pieces—*Waves, Chanty,* and *At Sea*—each piece bearing a motto from Walt Whitman. The next year he composed *Five Sketches in Sepia,* a partially impressionistic suite comprised of *Prélude, Fumées sur la Ville, Lucioles, Incertitude,* and *Epilogue.*

A later composition, the *Sonata* (1935), deserves mention as an attractive, neglected work. It is a brief but compact sonata, romantic but not sentimental. The three movements are of equal interest and importance: a freely flowing, texturally complicated *Pastorale* framed by two robust pieces with sonorous harmonic designs.[8]

Samuel Barber

Samuel Barber (*b.* 1910) has written only two important solo-piano compositions to date, neither one typical of his romantically inclined style

---

[7] Elkan-Vogel publishes *Sonata No. 4* and the *Inventions.* Mercury Music publishes *Sonata No. 3* and the *Portraits.* C. Fischer publishes *Ten Études.*

[8] Bloch's *Sonata* is listed by Carisch & Co. Most of the shorter pieces are published by G. Schirmer.

(a style that is becoming less romantic all the time). During the last twenty years, Barber has built up an enviable reputation as one of today's most elegant craftsmen. His basically tonal works—characterized by a shifting of major and minor tonality—display a wonderful lyric talent. His refined taste is reflected in the interesting counterpoint.

The suite *Excursions* (1944) contains the following explanation in the score: "These are 'Excursions' in small classical forms into regional American idioms. Their rhythmic characteristics, as well as their source in folk material and their scoring, reminiscent of local instruments, are easily recognized." Such folklore research is not typical of Barber but certainly not beyond him. The first piece, *Un poco Allegro*, has boogie-woogie style and the second stipulates "In slow blues tempo." These are followed by a set of variations on a cowboy song and a concluding *Allegro* that might be considered a stylized barn dance.

Barber's *Piano Sonata Opus 26* (1948)—commissioned by the League of Composers for its twenty-fifth anniversary—may well be the prime American sonata written in the last three decades or so. A very difficult work in four movements, the *Sonata* has an affinity with similar Beethoven works in its dramatic impact and skillful motivic development. Barber uses twelve-tone technique here but the handling is all his own.

In the first movement, *Allegro energico*, Barber uses motives extracted from series of twelve-note melodies; however, this is not a slavish attempt at strict dodecaphonic writing, for Barber infuses other expressive means with personal dexterity. *Allegro vivace e leggero*, the second movement, is a little scherzo with a humorous touch (Ex. 3). The third movement, *Adagio mesto*, is based on two twelve-note rows employed somewhat like a passacaglia but parceled into three sections A B A. The finale is a *Fuga* in toccata style.[9]

Ex. 3. Barber: *Piano Sonata: Allegro vivace e leggero*

p leggerissimo

etc.

Copyright, 1950, by G. Schirmer, Inc. Reproduced by permission.

[9] G. Schirmer publishes for Barber: *Excursions, Sonata,* and a *Nocturne* (Homage to John Field).

Paul Creston

Paul Creston (*b.* 1906) is largely a self-taught musician. His approach to composition is methodical and his music has a lively, vibrant quality. He stresses musical content in an atmosphere mingling romanticism, impressionism, and archaism (use of modal harmony). *Six Preludes Opus 38* are examples meant to show his methods of rhythmic structure. One prelude is devoted to each of the following: regular subdivision, irregular subdivision, overlapping, regular subdivision overlapping, irregular subdivision overlapping, and a mixture of the five methods. On the other hand, the *Prelude and Dance Opus 29, No. 1* is an effective work using simple means and particularly sparse writing.[10]

Paul Bowles

Paul Bowles (*b.* 1911) is a genuine eclectic. He has studied with Virgil Thomson and traveled considerably. His numerous trips through Africa and Latin America have given an exotic cast to his music, which at some time or other reflects almost every trend of contemporary idiom. Bowles' most exceptional pieces—at least outwardly—are those spiced with extramusical flavor. One of these is the *Carretera de Estepona* (The Highway to Estepona). Other extramusical elements are found in *El Indio* (1941), a short dance taken from his ballet *Pastorelas,* and *El Bejuco* (1943), the latter derived from a *chilena,* a popular Mexican song type. Another Mexican type, the *huapango,* is vividly sketched in two brilliant dances. Moving closer to home, Bowles has made tasteful keyboard settings of several English-American folk tunes. *Folk Preludes* contains seven of these tunes—*Peter Gray, Ching A Ring Chaw, Whar Did You Cum From, Oh! Potatoes They Grow Small Over There, Cape Ann, Ole Tare River,* and *Kentucky Moonshiner.* In addition to his folk-song and dance music, Bowles has written a *Sonatina* in three well-designed movements: *Allegro ritmico, Andante cantabile,* and *Allegro.*[11]

Norman Dello Joio

Contrasting textures and a predilection for the very old and the very new—these elements identify the music of **Norman Dello Joio** (*b.* 1913).

---

[10] *Six Preludes Opus 38* is published by Leeds Music Corp. *Prelude and Dance Opus 29, No. 1* is published by Mercury Music. *Prelude and Dance Opus 29, No. 2* is published by Axelrod Publications.

[11] Paul Bowles has a variety of publishers: *Carretera de Estepona* (E. B. Marks); *El Indio, El Bejuco, Folk Preludes* (Mercury Music); *Six Preludes* (Music Press); *Sonatina* (Elkan-Vogel); *Huapango Nos. 1* and *2* (Templeton).

Quite often he weaves Gregorian themes into a clear, precise contemporary fabric. (In *Sonata No. 3* [1948] he submits a Gregorian theme to five variations.) Although Dello Joio admittedly writes in a modern spirit, his music shows a need for emotional expression that is decidedly romantic. His writing can be easy and relaxed or it can overflow with dissonant harmony and exuberance. The early works are not too significant. *Suite for Piano* (1940) contains four partly effective short pieces of contrasting character.

One of Dello Joio's first important keyboard works is *Sonata No. 1* composed in 1943. It is unconventional, avoiding the forms ordinarily associated with sonata structure: the movements are *Chorale-Prelude, Canons,* and *Capriccio*. The *Second Piano Sonata* dates from the same year and although it also has three movements, they are more elaborately worked out. Each movement is in freely conceived A B A form. His third keyboard sonata (1948) has four movements: the Gregorian Kyrie *De Angelis* is submitted to five variations with simplicity the keynote (Ex. 4); then follows a vivacious scherzo, *Presto leggiero,* a lyrical slow movement, and a boisterous *Allegro vivo e ritmico*.[12]

Ex. 4. Dello Joio: *Piano Sonata No. 3: First Movement*

William Bergsma

The final romantically inclined composer to be mentioned here is a product of the Eastman School of Music at Rochester, N.Y. **William Bergsma** (*b.* 1921) is basically traditional although nationalism intrudes from time to time. To be exact, he is neither Neo-Romantic nor Neo-Classic; he takes

[12] The *Suite for Piano* was brought out by G. Schirmer, also *Sonata No. 2* (1943). The first sonata was issued by Hargail and the third by C. Fischer.

whatever path seems appropriate for musical expression at the moment. His *Three Fantasies* of 1943 are short and the rhythmic elements are deftly controlled. Although there are bar lines and time signatures, the music gives the impression of having complete freedom. *Tangents* is a rather whimsical suite: a fanfare-like *Prologue*, two improvisatory *Prophecies*, a triptych called *De Rerum Natura* (*Unicorns, Fishes, Mr. Darwin's Serenade*), two *Masques*, three short *Pieces for Nickie*, and finally an *Epilogue*. Bergsma states in an explanatory note that "*Tangents* is like an old-time vaudeville show, in which an excerpt from high tragedy might be followed by acrobats or a slapstick farce. The complete work is designed as a series of contrasts which balance into a good show. The work can be played as a whole, or separate groups or pieces may be taken from it."[13]

NEO-CLASSICISTS

Ernst Toch

Ernst Toch (*b.* 1887) is Vienna-born but has spent many years in the United States. His *Third Symphony* won a Pulitzer Prize, testimony to his competent musicianly equipment. Toch is a chromaticist whose linear approach resembles Hindemith's. *Five Times Ten Studies Opus 55–59* (1931) are pieces in a dissonant idiom, which scrutinizes various aspects of contemporary piano style. Toch's most popular piano pieces are five *Capricetti Opus 36*.[14]

Walter Piston

Walter Piston (*b.* 1894) has written only a small amount of piano music, but in all the pieces he displays fine workmanship, an especially fortunate quality in a musician whose textbooks on music theory are widely used in American colleges and universities. This does not imply that his compositions are pedantic; far from that, their solidity and concentrated thought make them durable. Piston's *Passacaglia* (1943)[15] is one of the best extant. Although it is short, skillful craftsmanship makes it an impressive variation treatment.

[13] Hargail issued Bergsma's *Three Fantasies* and C. Fischer publishes *Tangents*.
[14] Schott publishes Toch's piano music. This includes *Five Capricetti Opus 36, Five Times Ten Studies*, and the *Sonata Opus 47*.
[15] *Passacaglia* by Piston is published by Mercury Music. A small *Improvisation* is included in the album *U.S.A. Vol. 1* handled by Leeds Music Corp.

Roger Sessions

Roger Sessions (*b.* 1896) writes distinctive music dominated by intellectualism and a firm command of technical problems. Endowed with an ability to absorb elements in order to make them part of his own temperament, Sessions composes in a style distilled from Bloch, Stravinsky, and Schönberg influences. To understand his sometimes abstract, architectural language, the listener must listen to his works often and intensively. *Sonata No. 1* (1931), a large work with four connected movements, features multiple textures and uncompromising harmonies. Complete chromaticism dominates *Sonata No. 2* (1946). Violent mood contrasts pervade its three movements—played without pause—and the technical difficulties present unusual rhythmic problems for even the best pianists. Easier from a listening point of view, the little suite *From My Diary* (1940) has four successfully contrasting pieces.[16]

David Diamond

David Diamond (*b.* 1915) has written several rather easy works, a welcome relief since so much contemporary music is overrun with formidable technical obstacles. Diamond's *Sonatina* (1935) has three short movements: a serious *Largo assai*, a fluid *Allegretto*, and a scherzo-like *Allegro*. Athough not technically difficult, *Tomb of Melville* (1949) needs a mature approach and musicianly execution. An example of Diamond's more involved writing lies in his expansive *Sonata* (1947).[17]

Vincent Persichetti

Vincent Persichetti (*b.* 1915) seems to favor piano composition: ten piano sonatas, six sonatinas, and a sonata for harpsichord. His music is a joy for pianists because he writes in a supremely pianistic idiom. At his best in large instrumental forms, Persichetti employs a mainly tonal, homophonic language strong in lyricism and expressiveness. Classic rhythms add to the impression of clarity. His *Third Piano Sonata* (published 1945) has three rather unusual movements: *Declaration*, which keeps changing tempo and explores the entire keyboard; *Episode*, where two broad melodic lines alternate in an essentially homophonic texture; and a *Hymn* whose organ-like sonorities introduce a deceiving simplicity—a rapidly moving section acts as a coda to this last movement. The *Fourth Piano Sonata*, one of

[16] *From My Diary* and *Sonata 2* are listed by E. B. Marks, *Sonata 1* by Schott.
[17] Southern Music publishes the Diamond *Sonata*, Mercury Music the *Sonatina*, Leeds the *Tomb of Melville*, and G. Schirmer *Eight Piano Pieces*.

Persichetti's most difficult compositions, is broad in scope but possesses his regular clear style. This lucid texture is still apparent in the four-movement *Sixth Piano Sonata Opus 39.*[18]

Gail Kubik

Oklahoma-born **Gail Kubik** (*b.* 1914) brings to the piano keyboard a talent for sparkling sonorities and scintillating rhythms. The music of this Pulitzer Prize winner has consistent musicianly qualities, yet it is as easily assimilated as Mendelssohn's. Kubik has written a long four-movement *Sonata* whose obvious American idiom is immediately identifiable, but his choicest piano works are found elsewhere. The *Sonatina* (1941) has four short movements: *Moderately fast,* an especially pleasing piece in rapidly changing meters; *Lively, with spirit,* brief with passages of repeated notes giving a percussive effect; *Very slowly;* and *Toccata: Fast, hard and brittle.* *Dance Soliloquy* (1942) is a short rhythmic study attractive in every detail. Between 1938 and 1950 he composed a really unique work entitled *Celebrations and Epilogue:* two slow, atmospheric pieces come first, followed by seven "celebrations" such as *Birthday Piece, Wedded Bliss* (a sly parody on the traditional wedding march?), *A Gay Time, Movies—Saturday Night,* etc. The set closes with a coda-type *Epilogue.*[19]

William Schuman

William Schuman (*b.* 1910) is primarily a symphonic composer. This former student of Roy Harris is a flexible musician even though he at times resembles Roger Sessions in his uncompromising approach. This latter characteristic is not evident in *Voyage,* a cycle of five rhythmically vital piano pieces. The work also exists in an orchestral version as music for a Martha Graham ballet, and it was only after seeing the dance that Schuman affixed the individual titles: *Anticipation, Caprice, Realization, Decision,* and *Retrospection.*[20]

Halsey Stevens

Halsey Stevens (*b.* 1908) is a musician's musician. A brilliant teacher and scholar—his book on Bartók is the first definitive work devoted to that

---

[18] Elkan-Vogel Co. is the music publisher for Persichetti.

[19] Kubik's *Sonata* and *Celebrations and Epilogue* are handled by Southern Music. Mercury Music publishes his *Sonatina.*

[20] Schuman's most serious piano work *Voyage* is published by Howard Music Co. (selling agent G. Schirmer). Schirmer publishes *Three-Score Set.* Presser has brought out three rather easy pieces called *Three Piano Moods.*

composer—Stevens' preoccupation with all things musical is reflected in his own compositions. When he uses so-called music artifices, they are no longer artifices but become vehicles for expressing a profoundly musical temperament.

Sonata No. 3 (1947–1948) is traditional in form: a first movement in sonata-allegro form, a slow movement in large ternary form, and a rondo. Practically all motivic material stems from the first three measures of the first movement (Ex. 5). One of his happiest works (which this writer had the pleasure of premiering), *Nepdalsvit* (1950) is a series of eight short settings of Magyar folk songs from the Bartók collection. The *Scherzo* written in 1949 is most impressive.[21]

Ex. 5. Stevens: *Sonata No. 3: Allegro non troppo*

Used by permission. Copyright 1952 by American Music Edition.

COMPOSERS USING
TWELVE-TONE TECHNIQUES

Wallingford Riegger

Wallingford Riegger (1885–1961) began experimenting with atonality in 1927. In the thirties he theoretically adopted the principle of tone rows but applied this with his own singular approach. Even in his mature works he does not bind himself stringently to serial procedures but reverts to tonality whenever he feels impelled to do so. Basically, he creates key motives from the tone row and then develops these motives traditionally. Riegger was not only one of America's prominent composers, he was also highly esteemed by his fellow musicians. His music is original, clear-textured, and enriched with natural integrity. *New and Old* (1945) is a collection of twelve instructive piano pieces supplied with analyses and explanations. A favorite piece with both performer and audience is *Finale*

---

[21] The *Sonata No. 3* is published by American Music Edition. The *Scherzo* and *Nepdalsvit* may be obtained through the American Composers Alliance Library.

from the New Dance (1942). This fascinating exploration into Latin-American rhythms is not written in Riegger's atonal style. *Toccata* for piano is less popular than the *Finale*. It relies on polyharmony, with right-hand sonorities on white notes played against chords on black notes in the left. At the climax it proceeds gradually up to the highest register of the keyboard.[22]

Ernst Krenek

Ernst Krenek (*b.* 1900) is Vienna-born. He evolved his style from several sources: stark rhythms from primitive music, elements from jazz music, and patterns based on abstract expression. He bases his mature style on the "aggressive idiom of atonality, whose main organizing agency was elemental rhythmic force." His music—intensely and successfully abstract—is too severely intellectual to be universally popular, but Krenek seems unwilling to sacrifice his musical ideals for any reason. He has written many piano works. *Twelve Short Piano Pieces Opus 83* (1938) provides a very interesting introduction to twelve-tone technique; Krenek adds a Preface illustrating his basic material. Also effective are *Eight Piano Pieces* (1946). Generally speaking, his six sonatas are arduous for any pianist.[23]

Ross Lee Finney

Ross Lee Finney (*b.* 1906) has been writing twelve-tone music since 1950, but prior to that he fitted better into the nationalist category. His first contact with dodecaphony was in 1931 when he studied with Alban Berg. Most of his piano works are early so they are not written in his advanced, dissonant idiom. These early works include *Fantasy* (1939) and four *Sonatas* (1932, 1933, 1942, 1945). *Piano Sonata No. 4 in E Major*, subtitled *Christmastime 1945*, consists of a broadly expansive *Hymn* followed by three derivative movements—*Invention*, *Nocturne*, and *Toccata*—then a return to the *Hymn* material.[24]

Elliott Carter

One of Nadia Boulanger's talented pupils is **Elliott Carter** (*b.* 1908). Three piano sonatas and a work called *Music for Piano* (1947) show that he

---

[22] Arrow Music brought out the *Four Tone Pictures* and *Finale from the New Dance*. Boosey & Hawkes publishes *New and Old* and the *Toccata*.

[23] Krenek's first two sonatas are published by Universal, number three by Associated Music Publishers, and number four by Bomart. Schirmer issues the *Twelve Short Piano Pieces Opus 83*. Mercury Music issues the *Eight Piano Pieces*.

[24] Arrow Music brought out Finney's *Fantasy*, Valley Music the *Sonata No. 3*, and Mercury Music *Sonata No. 4*.

has absorbed a number of influences: Copland, Piston, Stravinsky, Hindemith. However, Carter continues to be a notably original composer. Clashing tonalities (approaching atonality), fugal writing, intricate harmonic patterns, all make his music slightly remote at first hearing, but it is well worth closer examination. The *Sonata* of 1946 is a work of large proportions written while he held a Guggenheim Fellowship. The first movement is quite lengthy and has irregular meters; the second movement, *Andante misterioso*, leads into a powerful *Allegro giusto* in fugal style and finally returns to the andante tempo.[25]

Ellis Kohs

Ellis Kohs (*b.* 1916) has proved to be adaptable to all currents in music. His writing has direct expression and consistency. Although the variation form is not favored by contemporary composers, Kohs has written two very effective sets: *Variations on l'Homme armé* (1946–1947) show resourceful invention and skill in this particular form; *Piano Variations* (1946) is more abstract. His *Toccata* (1949) for harpsichord or piano employs elements of twelve-tone technique with contrasted passages of varied texture.[26]

Irwin Bazelon

The young atonalist **Irwin Bazelon** (*b.* 1922) so far has given special attention to piano music: three piano sonatas, a *Sonatina*, and the *Five Pieces for Piano*.[27] His music is primarily polyphonic, as might be expected from a musicianly dodecaphonist. Widely spaced leaps design disjunct melodic patterns, and the additional complication of fluid rhythmic patterns makes this bright music hard to play.

CODA

This brief sketch of contemporary keyboard composers in the United States is by no means definitive. The list could be greatly expanded, for almost every composer resident in this country has written some piano music.[28] For example, the Cape Cod composer **Carl Ruggles** (*b.* 1876) has a set of *Evocations* (1937–1943) written in his intricate atonal style. And although her recent opera *Alcestis* (1959) is written in twelve-tone idiom, the piano music of **Louise Talma** (*b.* 1906) is compactly tonal. Her *Alleluia*

[25] Elliott Carter's *Sonata* is published by Mercury Music.

[26] Kohs's piano music is published by Mercury Music (Merrymount Press).

[27] Both the *Sonatina* and *Five Pieces for Piano* are published by Weintraub Music Co.

[28] A brief panorama of American piano music may be seen in *USA Vol. I* and *USA Vol. II* (Leeds Music Corp.), which contain pieces by eighteen contemporary composers.

in Form of Toccata is a beautifully fashioned rhythmic étude, and *Piano Sonata No. 1* (1943) is equally charming.

Henry Cowell (*b.* 1897) has written many piano pieces, some in traditional style, others employing experimental procedures such as forearm tone clusters and plucked strings. Typical of the latter approach are *Three Irish Legends,* which use clusters of two octaves, white notes separately, black notes separately, and a combination of the two. **George Antheil** (1900–1959)—his *Ballet Méchanique* calling for eight pianos and a pianola created a furor in the twenties—has written a number of piano compositions in which satire, irony, and parody play important roles. **Leonard Bernstein** (*b.* 1918), that universal musician of unquenchable energy and immense talent, has some lovely miniatures, which he calls *Anniversaries* (two collections).

Another fine addition to the constantly expanding repertoire of contemporary American piano music is the collection *Five Pieces for Piano* (published 1951) by **Peter Mennin** (*b.* 1923), a young man who writes vibrant, energetic, *musical* music. Another younger-generation composer **Harold Shapero** (*b.* 1920) has written three sonatas for piano, music that utilizes certain traditional substances within today's fresh, spontaneous idiom. A distinguished contribution to harpsichord literature has been provided by **John Lessard** (*b.* 1920) with his *Toccata in Four Movements* (1951).

Alan Hovhaness (*b.* 1911), the American-born composer of Armenian parents, has written a quantity of music during each of his successively individualistic style periods, and each stage is markedly derived from the exotic. The one objection to his keyboard music is that it tries to be something else. The piano is not an exotic instrument; it cannot produce any timbres but its own, so the bell effects and other Eastern-instrument effects that Hovhaness wishes to reproduce would be better left to the original instruments. Much of his music, like *Jhala,* calls for keyboard accessories, such as a timpani stick. Myriad repeated notes, rhapsodic melody, and static harmony contribute to his music which, at the least, employs an odd approach to keyboard composition.[29]

[29] Following are the publishers for those composers mentioned in the Coda. Carl Ruggles: *Evocations* (American Music Edition); Louise Talma: *Alleluia in Form of Toccata, Sonata No. 1* (C. Fischer), and *Six Études* (G. Schirmer); Henry Cowell: *Piano Music by Henry Cowell* (Associated Music) is a good collection of nine pieces written over a forty-year span, and in addition Associated Music publishes almost all of Cowell's music; George Antheil: *Sonata No. 4* (Weintraub) and *Suite, Two Toccatas* (G. Schirmer); Leonard Bernstein: *Four Anniversaries* (G. Schirmer) and *Seven Anniversaries* (M. Witmark); Peter Mennin: *Five Piano Pieces* (C. Fischer); Harold Shapero: *Three Sonatas* (G. Schirmer); John Lessard: *Toccata for Harpsichord* (ACA Library); Alan Hovhaness: *Bardo Sonata Opus 192, Lake of Van Sonata Opus 175, Madras Sonata Opus 176, Poseidon Sonata Opus 191, Shalimar Suite Opus 177, Sonata Opus 145* (Peters) and *Orbit No. 2, Jhala, Hymn to a Celestial Musician, Fantasy on an Ossetin Tune* (Peer International), and *Suite Opus 121 in G* (ACA Library).

It would be impossible even to mention all of the piano music written in the past twenty years or so, but one conclusion seems obvious. Although some of this music cannot endure and will no doubt quickly disappear, a large bulk of it has unusually high quality, so much in fact that one can see the emerging outlines of a tradition in keyboard composition, a slowly evolving tradition of excellence and integrity that is rapidly assuming an aura of permanence.

Concerning today's music, the distinguished composer and critic **Virgil Thomson** feels that a merger of the various styles is in process: "The Late Romantics have all died. The eclectical Romantics, with no conservative support left them, have moved into the neo-classical and neo-Romantic neighbourhoods. And these neighbourhoods are in constant flirtation with both the chromatic composers of the former middle-left and with the arithmetical constructors from music's engineering or factory suburbs. The result is a melting pot, where everybody practises at least a little bit all the techniques and where everybody's music begins to sound more and more alike."[30]

BIBLIOGRAPHY

Broder, Nathan. *Samuel Barber.* New York: G. Schirmer, 1954.

Chase, Gilbert. *America's Music.* New York: McGraw-Hill Book Co., Inc., 1955.

Composers of the Americas. Washington, D.C.: Pan American Union, 1955–1961. 7 Vols.

Cowell, Henry and Sidney. *Charles Ives and His Music.* New York: Oxford University Press, 1955.

Downes, Edward. "The Music of Norman Dello Joio." *Musical Quarterly,* April, 1962.

Machlis, Joseph. *American Composers of Our Time.* New York: Thomas Crowell Co., 1963.

McKeon, Sister Mary de La Salle. *Stylistic Tendencies in Mid-Twentieth-Century American Piano Music.* Dissertation. Eastman School of Music, 1957.

Schreiber, Flora Rheta and Vincent Persichetti. *William Schuman.* New York: G. Schirmer, 1954.

Tischler, Hans. "Barber's Piano Sonata Opus 26." *Music and Letters,* 1952 (XXXIII).

[30] Virgil Thomson, "Music Now," in *The London Magazine* (March, 1962).

GLOSSARY

(The asterisks ° indicate reference to other items in the glossary.)

ACCIACCATURA

(*It. "crush"*) A harpsichord ornament° of the eighteenth century used chiefly with chords. A lower second of a chord member is struck simultaneously with the chord itself.

AIR

(*Aria*) A term synonymous with song, theme, melody. It is applied to instrumental as well as vocal music.

AIR DE COUR

A seventeenth- and eighteenth-century strophic song for one or more voices with lute accompaniment.

ALLEMANDE

(*Alemanda, Alman*) A seventeenth- and eighteenth-century dance type in duple or quadruple meter, leisurely tempo.

ANACRUSIS

An unaccented note or note group at the beginning of a musical phrase or motive.

APPOGGIATURA

An ornament° or nonharmonic° tone connected melodically (usually the interval of a second) with the main note.

ARABESQUE

This term may indicate: (1) a melodic flourish, with characteristic embellishment; (2) a title used by Robert Schumann for a graceful type of character piece.°

ARPEGGIO

A term applied to a chord when its notes are played consecutively instead of sounded simultaneously.

ASSUMPTION OF KEY

A quasi-modulation° procedure whereby a new tonality is introduced without any previous preparation.

ATONALITY

Literally "without tonality"; applied to compositions of the Expressionist° school.

AUGMENTATION

A contrapuntal° device by which the note values of a theme or melodic line are lengthened.

BAGATELLE

Literally a "trifle," applied to short characteristic pieces in harpsichord (Couperin) and piano (Beethoven) music.

BALLADE

An extended piece for the piano, usually in ternary form, supposedly inspired by literary models.

427

BARCAROLLE

A boat song. The title was used by Romantic composers for character pieces in moderate 6/8 or 12/8 meter with a reiterated accompaniment figure.

BAROQUE

A name for the artistic era that flourished *ca.* 1600–1750. See Chapter 3 for a discussion of Baroque musical forms.

BASSE DANSE

A popular court dance in France during the fifteenth and sixteenth centuries. It was in slow tempo.

BERCEUSE

A lullaby or cradle song. In piano music it is usually in 6/8 meter with a patterned accompaniment.

BOURRÉE

An animated French dance in quadruple meter from Auvergne.

BRANLE

A French dance similar to the *Gavotte.**

CADENCE

A harmonic pattern at the end of a composition, phrase, or section to give the impression of repose, either momentary or permanent.

CANARIS

(*Canario*) A seventeenth-century dance. Its origins are perhaps Spanish (Canary Islands). It is usually in 6/8 meter with a dotted note occurring on each strong beat.

CANON

A polyphonic* composition, similar to a round, wherein each voice line has the same melody, yet starts at a different point.

CANTE FLAMENCO

Cante flamenco is a term used with *Cante jondo* to designate Andalusian folk music.

CANZONE

(*Canzona*) An instrumental piece of the sixteenth and seventeenth centuries derived from the Franco-Flemish polyphonic chanson.

CAPRICCIO

(1) In the seventeenth century the name of a contrapuntal keyboard form less complicated than the *Ricercar** or *Canzone**; (2) in the nineteenth century the title is found with short piano pieces of whimsical or restless character.

CEBELL (CIBEL)

A type of gavotte* used by several English composers.

CHACONNE	A keyboard form that employs a type of continuous variation. The only apparent "theme" is the harmonic pattern established by the initial chords.
CHARACTER PIECE	A short piano piece of the nineteenth century, which may have a quasi-programmatic content or merely hint at an atmosphere or mood.
CHORALE (CHORAL)	A hymn tune of the German Lutheran church. The term is used also to designate keyboard paraphrases on chants from the Roman Catholic repertoire.
CHORD	The sounding together of several notes usually spaced a third apart—i.e., G B D. A seventh chord would be G B D F, a ninth chord G B D F A, etc. Certain of these intervals may be altered, producing so-called augmented or diminished chords.
CHROMATICISM	The use of tones extraneous to a given tonality.*
CLASSICISM	The Classic or Neo-Classic movement of the eighteenth century. See Chapter 11 for a discussion of musical Classicism.
CLAVICHORD	For a discussion of the clavichord (monachord, clavichordium, manichordion) see Chapter 1.
CLAVIER	A term that refers to the keyboard of an organ, piano, or any stringed instrument that has a keyboard.
COLORIST SCHOOL	An early German organ school whose composers gave special attention to ornamentation.*
CONCERTO (GROSSO)	A musical form for soloists and orchestra. (1) In the Baroque period the concerto grosso was a very important form. A work for a small group of soloists and orchestra, its essential style is that of solo passages interspersed with orchestral ritornellos. (2) During the Classic period the typical solo concerto evolved and was usually in sonata* form.
CONTRAPUNTAL	In the style of counterpoint.*
COPLA	A Spanish word meaning refrain.
COUNTERPOINT	The technique of combining several individual lines of melody into a single musical fabric.

COURANTE	(*Corante, Coranto*) One of the standard dances of the seventeenth- and eighteenth-century suite. There were two basic rhythmic types of courante—the Italian and French.
CRESCENDO	A gradual increase in dynamics.
CROSS RELATION	See False relation.
CYCLIC FORM	The binding more closely together (by means of similar thematic material or other procedures) of individual movements or sections in a large-scale composition.
DANCES	See individual dance names. Most dances of the seventeenth and eighteenth centuries are in bipartite form.
DECEPTIVE CADENCE	A cadence* which, instead of initiating a feeling of repose, extends the phrase line or melodic section.
DIFERENCIAS	A type of variation indigenous to Spain in the sixteenth and seventeenth centuries.
DIMINUENDO	A gradual decrease in dynamics.
DIMINUTION	A contrapuntal* device by which the note values of a theme or melodic line are shortened.
DIVERTIMENTO	In piano music, a composition whose several movements (2–5) blend elements of the suite* and sonata.*
DIVERTISSEMENT	See *Divertimento*.
DODECAPHONY	The use of twelve-tone* technique in composition.
DOMINANT	A chord built on the fifth degree of a scale—i.e., the dominant in the key of C is G B D.
DULCIMER	A stringed instrument similar in shape to the Psaltery.* The strings are struck with hammers or mallets held in the hand.
ECHIQUIER	The echiquier (*exchaquier, echequier*) is an obsolete stringed instrument. See Chapter 1.

ECHO	A keyboard piece utilizing an echo effect (Bach's French Overture in B Minor). The echo effect itself is usually accomplished on the harpsichord or organ by playing a phrase on one keyboard, then by sounding an identical phrase on a softer manual.
ENHARMONIC	Modulation° using the same sound (or chords) two different ways (G♭ becomes F♯, etc.).
ENTRÉE	A title used by some Belgian and Dutch keyboard composers for a composition similar to a two-part invention. See Bach's Inventions in Chapter 10.
ESCAPEMENT	A mechanism which facilitates note repetition in a stringed keyboard instrument.
ESTAMPIE	An instrumental form of the thirteenth and fourteenth centuries. It consisted of four to seven sections called *puncta,* each provided with an *ouvert* and *clos* cadence, corresponding somewhat to the more familiar first and second endings.
ÉTUDE	A study piece whose basic purpose is the development of technical proficiency.
EXPRESSIONISM	See Chapter 29 (section on Germany and Austria).
FALSE RELATION	Harmonically, a note in one voice which is immediately followed by its alteration (or vice versa) in a different voice.
FANDANGO	A Spanish dance in triple meter characterized by varied rhythms. It is danced by a single couple to the accompaniment of a guitar and castanets.
FANTASIA	(*Fantasy*) Usually a piece of quasi-improvisatory character with several sections in different tempos and textures. In the sixteenth century the fantasia was of a more strict contrapuntal° nature.
FAUXBOURDON	(*Faburden*) Literally a "false bass." Actually a series of parallel sixth chords (chords with the third in the bass or lower voice).

FIGURED BASS	A Baroque practice where a bass line is supplied with numbers indicating the harmony, which the performer is to fill in.
FIORITURA	A musical embellishment or ornament.°
FIRST INVERSION	A chord whose third (second member) is placed in the lowest position or bass.
FLAMENCO	See Cante flamenco.
FORLANE	(*Forlana*) An Italian dance of popular origin, usually in 6/8 meter.
FORM	The manner in which a musical composition is constructed. See Chapters 3 and 11 for discussions of the different musical forms.
FUGATO	A passage in fugal style.
FUGHETTA	A little fugue or a short fugue.
FUGUE	See Chapter 3.
GALLIARD	(*Gaillard, Gallardus*) A seventeenth-century dance, moderately fast, in triple meter.
GAVOTTE	A dance of French origin that reached its zenith during the time of Lully. In moderate 4/4 meter, usually beginning on the third beat.
GIGUE	One of the four standard dances of the late seventeenth- and eighteenth-century keyboard suite. It is in rapid compound triple meter.
GLISSANDO	In piano music a slide, usually from the top register of the keyboard to the bottom, taking in a large area of white or black notes.
GREGORIAN CHANT	The ritual plainsong, named after Pope Gregory I, used in the Roman Catholic Church; it is unaccompanied, unharmonized, and without meter.
GROUND	An English term for the ostinato°; a short phrase that is repeated over and over in the bass with changing superstructures. A type of variation.

HABANERA	A dance similar to the *tango*. Although considered a Cuban dance, it is probably of Spanish origin.
HARPEGEMENT	A French term for arpeggio° or spreading out of chords.
HARPSICHORD	See Chapter 1 for a discussion of the harpsichord (flugel, clavecin).
HEMIOLA	A term applied to the use of combinations of triple and duple rhythm. It is found in the French courante where the accents vary from $\underline{1}\ 2\ \underline{3}\ 4\ \underline{5}\ 6$ to $\underline{1}\ 2\ 3\ \underline{4}\ 5\ 6$.
HOMOPHONIC	A musical texture with a dominant melodic line supported by a chordal accompaniment.
HOQUETUS	(*Hocket*) Literally a "hiccough." A device (from the Middle Ages) by which the notes of a melody were interspersed with rests.
HORNEPYPE	A popular English dance from 1500 to about 1900.
HUMORESQUE	A whimsical or fanciful musical composition.
IMITATION	The restatement of an initial theme or motive in another contrapuntal° voice of a vocal or instrumental composition.
IMPRESSIONISM	A school of art, predominantly French, which flourished in the late nineteenth century and early twentieth century. See Chapter 27 for a discussion of musical Impressionism.
IMPROMPTU	A character piece° for piano popular in the nineteenth century. See Schubert's Impromptus in Chapter 16 and those of Chopin in Chapter 17.
IN NOMINE	A contrapuntal° keyboard piece usually based on a plainsong fragment.
INTAVOLATURA	See Tablature.
INTERMEZZO	A nineteenth-century character piece° for piano.
INVENTION	A short keyboard piece written in imitative counterpoint. See Bach's Inventions in Chapter 10.

JOTA	A dance originating in Aragón, Spain. It is in fast triple meter, usually accompanied by castanets.
LEADING TONE	The seventh degree of the scale.
LESSONS	A seventeenth-century English term for suite (Suite of Lessons).
LIED	A German art song.
LUTE	A pear-shaped instrument popular in Europe and England during the sixteenth and part of the seventeenth century. It usually had six strings.
MALAGUEÑA	A Spanish dance from Málaga, a variety of the *fandango*.* It is in moderately fast triple meter.
MARCHA TORERA	Literally a "march of the bullfighter."
MASQUERADE	Music inspired by or written for the English Masque.
MAZURKA	A popular Polish dance in moderate triple meter with the accent usually on the second or third beat.
MENSURAE	Compositions based on a song tenor in measured rhythms.
MICROTONES	Intervals smaller than semitones—i.e., intervals smaller than that from C to C-sharp.
MINUET	(*Menuet*) A French dance of the seventeenth century. It was the only dance to retain popularity in the Classic period where it was incorporated into the Sonata.* It is in ternary form—Minuet, Trio or contrasting section, Minuet repeated.
MODALITY	A term used to indicate opposition to tonality.* It refers specifically to the use of old church modes (Dorian, Lydian, etc.).
MODULATION	The process of changing from one key to another within a given piece.
MOMENT MUSICAL	A title used by Schubert for a short character piece* for piano.

MORDENT	An ornament° (𝄽) popular in the Baroque period indicating the principal note, its lower neighbor, and a return of the principal note.
MOTET	In the sixteenth century, a polyphonic° sacred work with Latin words. This became the basis for the instrumental *Ricercar.*°
MYSTIC CHORD	A type of chord built in fourths, a favorite of Scriabin. See Chapter 21 under Scriabin.
NOCTURNE	An introspective character piece° created by John Field and further developed by Chopin. See Chapter 17.
NONHARMONIC TONES	Tones foreign to a given harmony.
ORGAN	A keyboard instrument whose sound is produced by means of pipes, activated by a bellows or blower.
ORGAN POINT	A sustained note, usually in the bass, accompanied by changing harmonic progressions.
ORNAMENTS	Decorations or embellishments of the melody or harmonies of a composition.
OSTINATO	A short melodic phrase that is repeated, usually in the bass, and accompanied by changing superstructures.
OVERTURE	(*Ouverture*) In harpsichord music, a keyboard piece that imitates the style of the operatic French overture (slow-fast-slow) or Italian overture (fast-slow-fast).
PANTALEON	A dulcimer-type musical instrument invented by a German named Pantaleon Hebenstreit.
PASO-DOBLE	A dance of Spanish origin, usually in moderate 2/4 meter.
PASSACAGLIA	A form consisting of continuous variations based on a repeated melodic pattern. It belongs to the category of the ostinato.°
PASSAMEZZO	A sixteenth-century Italian dance in leisurely 4/4 meter with a steady rhythm of quarter or eighth notes.

PASSEPIED | (*Paspié*) A dance of lively character in 3/8 or 6/8 meter. It was popular in France under Louis XIV and Louis XV.

PASSING TONES | Tones that do not belong to the harmony but which serve to connect those that are essential.

PAVANE | (*Pavan, Paduana*) A sixteenth-century court dance, probably Spanish in origin. It is in moderate duple meter and was usually followed by a *galliard.*

PIANO | See Chapter 1.

PLAINSONG | The monophonic chant of the Catholic Church (Gregorian Chant*).

PLECTRUM | A piece of quill or leather inserted in a harpsichord jack to activate the string.

POLKA | A nineteenth-century Bohemian dance in duple meter, a dance that was stylized into art music by Smetana.

POLO | A Spanish dance written in moderately fast 3/8 meter. It makes some use of hemiola* rhythm.

POLONAISE | A Polish dance of noble character in moderate triple meter, with distinctive rhythmic patterns. It originated in the seventeenth century.

POLYPHONY (POLYPHONIC) | A texture made up of two or more voices heard simultaneously. The technique used is counterpoint.*

POLYTONALITY | The simultaneous use of several tonalities.*

PRALLTRILLER | An inverted mordent* found in the works of the Pre-Classic period (after 1750).

PRELUDE | A keyboard piece in free style used as the preface to a fugue or suite in the Baroque period. In the Romantic era, the prelude became an entity unto itself.

PSALTERY | A medieval stringed instrument whose strings were plucked with the fingers.

QUARTAL HARMONY | A harmonic idiom based on chords constructed in intervals of fourths (D G C) rather than thirds.

QUODLIBET	A quasi-contrapuntal work (see *Goldberg Variations* in Chapter 10) where several well-known folk songs or tunes are combined.
RECITATIVE	Originally a speechlike declamation in opera, oratorio, and cantata. This was later transferred to keyboard music by Beethoven and others.
RETROGRADE	One of the basic elements of twelve-tone° technique where the tone row is used starting with the last note and ending with the first. By inverting the intervals in the tone row and employing retrograde, another possibility, retrograde inversion, is obtained.
RHAPSODY	A title used for nineteenth-century piano pieces of a dramatic or national cast. The style is free, quasi-improvisatory, and spontaneous.
RICERCAR	A sixteenth- and seventeenth-century keyboard composition derived from the vocal *motet.°* It consists of a series of fugal expositions. Each exposition usually has its own distinctive theme.
RIGAUDON	A seventeenth-century dance from Provence in France. It is in a lively 4/4 meter.
RITORNELLO	Literally a "return." It may denote a recurring refrain or an orchestral tutti in a concerto.
ROMANTICISM	The Romantic movement of the nineteenth century. See Chapter 15 for a discussion of musical Romanticism.
RONDEAU	A favorite form of the French *clavecin* school. It consists of a basic refrain that alternates with contrasting sections called *couplets.*
RONDEÑA	A Spanish dance originating in Ronda in southern Spain. It is one of several varieties of the *fandango.°*
RONDO	A favorite form of the Classic period, used as the final movement of sonatas. It is derived from the *rondeau°* by limiting the *couplets* to three, of which the first and third are similar.

ROOT POSITION — A chord position wherein the first note of the original chord spelling is found in the bass.

SALON MUSIC — A somewhat deprecatory term used to describe a light and rather frivolous variety of piano piece popular in the nineteenth and early twentieth century.

SALTARELLO — A lively Italian dance in triple meter.

SARABANDE — One of the standard dances of the Baroque suite, in slow triple meter with an accent on the second beat. It is frequently highly ornamented.

SCHERZO — A movement used in the nineteenth century to replace the minuet in the sonata. The form, though considerably expanded, is essentially like the minuet (A B A). With Beethoven the scherzo is whimsical, humorous. Chopin, who lifted it from its sonata framework, endowed the scherzo with tragic overtones.

SEQUENCE — The restatement of a motive or phrase (both melody and harmony) at different pitches.

SERENADE — In keyboard music, a light-textured work similar to a divertimento.*

SERIAL MUSIC — Music constructed from the manipulation of a tone row—i.e., dodecaphonic music.

SEVILLANAS — A typical dance of Andalusia, in animated ternary meter.

SICILIANA — A type of pastoral music originating in Sicily. It is in leisurely 6/8 or 12/8 meter. Sometimes it is in bipartite form, other times not.

SON — A highly rhythmic composition based on native folk music, principally that of Cuba and Central America.

SONATA — A term that denotes different forms at different periods: (1) for the Baroque sonata, see Chapter 3; (2) for the Classic sonata, see Chapter 11.

SONATA-ALLEGRO — A term designating the usual form of the first movement of a Classic sonata. It contains three basic sections: Exposition (statement of themes), Development, and Recapitulation.

SONATINA	A short sonata.
SPAGNOLETTA	An ancient dance of Spanish origin. In the sixteenth century, examples are found in both binary and ternary meter.
SPINET	A small harpsichord. See Chapter 1.
STYLE BRISE	A lutenist technique passed on to the French clavecinists. It consists of making a slow arpeggio* of the final chord in a cadence.*
STYLE GALANT	A decorative style of music characteristic of certain composers in the eighteenth century (F. Couperin, Daquin, Telemann, etc.). Rococo is the term used to name this period, which encompasses parts of the Baroque and Pre-Classic periods.
SUITE	(*Partie, Partita, Ordre, Lesson*) See Chapter 3.
SUSPENSION	A nonharmonic tone* created by delaying one of the notes in a chord progression.
SYNCOPATION	The displacement of the normal accent in a composition (or a section thereof).
TABLATURE	A system of notation (used for organ and some stringed instruments) with letters or figures used instead of notes.
TANGENT	The piece of metal that comes in contact with the clavichord string, thus producing a sound.
TEMPERAMENT	A general term for systems of tuning, one of which is *equal temperament* (see *Well-Tempered Clavier* in Chapter 10).
TEMPO RUBATO	Literally "stolen time." An interpretative device, consisting of a relaxation of strict tempo (see Chapter 17).
TIENTO	(*Tento*) A contrapuntal* instrumental form of sixteenth- and seventeenth-century keyboard music in Spain and Portugal. It is similar to the *Ricercar.**
TOCCATA	A keyboard piece in free style with contrasting textures and tempos.

TONADA

(*Toada*) A composition based on an indigenous folk or popular song of Latin America.

TONADILLA

Originally songs sung to several stock tunes, later a miniature cantata (Spain).

TONALITY

The term designating the use of major and minor scales in contrast to modal* scales.

TONIC

The first degree of a given major or minor scale, or a chord built on that degree.

TOYE

A title used by English virginal composers for a piece of playful character.

TRILL

A musical ornament* consisting of a rapid alternation of a given note and its upper neighbor.

TUNING

See Temperament.

TWELVE-TONE

A system developed by Arnold Schönberg as a compositional procedure (see Germany and Austria in Chapter 29).

VARIATION SUITE

A suite in which the succeeding dances (Courante, Sarabande, etc.) are variations of the initial dance (usually Allemande).

VERISMO

This term refers to the Italian school of operatic realism, which had its roots in the music of Mascagni and Leoncavallo.

VIHUELA

An early type of Spanish guitar. A *vihuelista* is one who plays the vihuela.

VIRGINAL

A small harpsichord. See Chapters 1 and 4.

VOICE LEADING

Contrapuntal* principles that govern the progression of the various voice parts.

VOLTA

A vivacious dance popular around 1600. It is in dotted 6/8 meter.

VOLUNTARY

A keyboard piece that gives the impression of an improvisation.

WALTZ

A dance in moderate triple meter, which began *ca.* 1800 and has continued in popularity ever since.

WHOLE-TONE

A scale composed entirely of whole steps—i.e., C–D–E–F♯–G♯–A♯–C.

ZAPATEADO

A Spanish dance in quick triple meter with rhythmic variety. It features the stamping and tapping of the feet.

GENERAL BIBLIOGRAPHY

Aguettant, Louis. *La Musique de Piano*. Paris: Editions Albin Michel, 1954.

Apel, Willi. "Early German Keyboard Music." *Musical Quarterly*, April, 1937.

Apel, Willi. *Harvard Dictionary of Music*. Cambridge: Harvard University Press, 1944.

Apel, Willi. *Masters of the Keyboard*. Cambridge: Harvard University Press, 1947.

Auerbach, Cornelia. *Die deutsche Clavichordkunst des 18. Jahrhunderts*. Kassel: Bärenreiter Verlag, 1953.

Bach, Carl Philipp Emanuel. *Essay on the True Art of Playing Keyboard Instruments* (translated by Wm. Mitchell). New York: W. W. Norton & Co., Inc., 1949.

Bachs, A. Miró. *Cien Músicos Célebres Españoles*. Barcelona: Ediciones Ave, 1955.

Bacon, Ernst. *Notes on the Piano*. Syracuse: Syracuse University Press, 1963.

Bedbrook, Gerald Stares. *Keyboard Music from the Middle Ages to the Beginnings of the Baroque*. London: Macmillan & Co., Ltd., 1949.

Beer, R. "Ornaments in Old Keyboard Music." *Music Review*, Vol. 13, No. 1, 1952.

Bie, Oscar. *Das Klavier*. Berlin: Paul Cassirer, 1921.

Blom, Eric, ed. *Grove's Dictionary of Music and Musicians*, fifth edition. London: Macmillan & Co., Ltd., 1954. 9 Vols.

Blom, Eric. *The Romance of the Piano*. London: Foulis, 1928.

Blom, Friedrich, ed. *Die Musik in Geschichte und Gegenwart*. Kassel: Bärenreiter Verlag, 1949–   . 10 Vols. and 4 Fascicles, A–SCHAE.

Bosquet, Emile. *La Musique de Clavier, et par Extension de Luth*. Bruxelles Dépositaire: Les Amis de la Musique, 1953.

Bücken, Dr. Ernst. *Die Musik des 19. Jahrhunderts bis zur Moderne*. Wildpark-Potsdam: Akademische Verlagsgesellschaft Athenaion, 1928.

Bukofzer, Manfred. *Music in the Baroque Era*. New York: W. W. Norton & Co., Inc., 1947.

Calvocoressi, M. D. and Gerald Abraham. *Masters of Russian Music*. New York: Alfred A. Knopf, 1936.

Casella, Alfredo. *Il Pianoforte*. Milan: G. Ricordi, 1954.

Casella, Alfredo. *Music in My Time* (translated by S. Norton). Norman: University of Oklahoma Press, 1955.

Closson, E. and Ch. van den Borren, eds. *La Musique en Belgique du Moyen Age à Nos Jours*. Bruxelles: La Renaissance du Livre, 1950.

Collaer, Paul. *A History of Modern Music* (translated by Sally Abeles). New York: Grosset & Dunlap, 1961.

Coon, Leland. "The Distinction between Clavichord and Harpsichord Music." Papers read at the annual meeting of the *American Musicological Society*, 1936.

Cortot, Alfred. *La Musique Française de Piano.* Paris: Presses Universitaires de France, 1944. 3 Vols.

Dale, Kathleen. *Nineteenth-century Piano Music.* London: Oxford University Press, 1954.

Dannreuther, Edward. *Musical Ornamentation.* London: Novello & Co., Ltd., n.d. 2 Vols. Reprint in 1 Vol. by Kalmus.

Davison, A. and W. Apel. *Historical Anthology of Music.* Cambridge: Harvard University Press, 1946, 1950. 2 Vols.

Debaar, Mathieu. *Le Piano, son Historique, ses Maîtres et sa Littérature.* Pepinster: H. Thoumsin, 1945.

Demuth, Norman. *French Piano Music.* London: Museum Press Ltd., n.d.

Dolmetsch, Arnold. *The Interpretation of the Music of the XVII and XVIII Centuries.* London: Novello & Co., Ltd., 1946.

Donington, Robert. *The Interpretation of Early Music.* London: Faber & Faber, 1963.

Dufourcq, Norbert. *La Musique Française.* Paris: Librairie Larousse, 1949.

Dufourcq, Norbert. *Le Clavecin.* Paris: Presses Universitaires de France, 1949.

Einstein, Alfred. *Music in the Romantic Era.* New York: W. W. Norton & Co., Inc., 1947.

Eitner, Robert. *Quellen-Lexikon der Musiker und Musikgelehrten.* Graz: Akademische Druk-U. Verlagsanstalt, 1959. 11 Vols. in 6.

Ellis, Mildred Katharine. *The Piano Character-Piece and Its Treatment by French Composers of the Nineteenth Century.* Dissertation (in progress). Indiana University.

Farrenc, Louise. *Traité des Abréviations, Signes d'agrément et Ornements employés par les Clavecinistes du XVII et XVIII Siècles.* Paris: Alphonse Leduc, 1895.

Ferguson, Donald. *The Piano Music of Six Great Composers.* New York: Prentice-Hall, Inc., 1947.

Fétis, F.-J. *Biographie Universelle des Musiciens*, second edition. Paris: Firmin-Didot et Cie., 1878. 8 Vols.

Friskin, J. and I. Freundlich. *Music for the Piano.* New York: Rinehart & Co., Inc., 1954.

Gabeaud, Alice. *Histoire de la Musique.* Paris: Librairie Larousse, 1930.

Ganz, Peter Felix. *The Development of the Étude for Pianoforte.* Dissertation. Northwestern University, 1960.

Gaudefroy-Demombynes, J. *Histoire de la Musique Française*. Paris: Payot, 1946.

Georgii, Walter. *Klaviermusik*. Zurich: Atlantis-Verlag, 1950.

Goléa, Antoine. *Vingt Ans de Musique Contemporaine*. Paris: Editions Seghers, 1962. 2 Vols.

Grout, Donald Jay. *A History of Western Music*. New York: W. W. Norton & Co., Inc., 1960.

Hamilton, Clarence G. *Piano Music*. Boston: Oliver Ditson Co., 1925.

Hansemann, Marlise. *Der Klavier-Auszug von den Anfängen bis Weber*. Borna: Meyer, 1943.

Hansen, Peter S. *An Introduction to Twentieth Century Music*. Boston: Allyn and Bacon, Inc., 1961.

Hewitt, Helen, ed. *Doctoral Dissertations in Musicology*. Philadelphia: American Musicological Society, 1961.

Hoffmann-Erbrecht, Lothar. *Deutsche und italienische Klaviermusik zur Bachzeit*. Leipzig: Breitkopf & Härtel, 1954.

Hutcheson, Ernest. *The Literature of the Piano*, second edition. New York: Alfred A. Knopf, 1949.

Jean-Aubry, Georges. *An Introduction to French Music*. London: Palmer & Hayward, 1917.

Kenyon, Max. *Harpsichord Music*. London: Cassell & Co., Ltd., 1949.

Landowska, Wanda. *Music of the Past* (translated by W. A. Bradley). New York: Alfred A. Knopf, 1924.

Lang, Paul Henry. *Music in Western Civilization*. New York: W. W. Norton & Co., Inc., 1941.

Leonard, Richard Anthony. *A History of Russian Music*. New York: The Macmillan Co., 1957.

Le Piano. Bruxelles: Revue Internationale de Musique, 1939.

Lockwood, Albert. *Notes on the Literature of the Piano*. Ann Arbor: University of Michigan Press, 1940.

Loesser, Arthur. *Men, Women and Pianos*. New York: Simon and Schuster, 1954.

Machlis, Joseph. *Introduction to Contemporary Music*. New York: W. W. Norton & Co., Inc., 1961.

Mooser, Robert Aloys. *Annales de la Musique et des Musiciens en Russie au XVIIIe Siècle*. Genève: Mont-Blanc, 1948-51. 3 Vols.

Newman, Wm. S. "A Checklist of the Earliest Keyboard Sonatas." *Music Library Association Notes*, XI (1954). Correction in XII (1954).

Newman, Wm. S. *The Sonata in the Baroque Era*. Chapel Hill: The University of North Carolina Press, 1959.

Newman, Wm. S. *The Sonata in the Classic Era.* Chapel Hill: The University of North Carolina Press, 1963.

Niecks, Frederick. *Programme Music in the Last Four Centuries.* London: Novello & Co., Ltd., *ca.* 1906.

Parrish, Carl G. *The Early Piano and Its Influence on Keyboard Technique and Composition in the Eighteenth Century.* Dissertation. Harvard University, 1939.

Pena, Joaquín and Higinio Anglés. *Diccionario de la Música Labor.* Barcelona: Editorial Labor, S. A., 1954. 2 Vols.

Perle, George. *Serial Composition and Atonality.* Los Angeles and Berkeley: University of California Press, 1962.

Pirro, André. *Les Clavecinistes.* Paris: Laurens, 1925.

Riemann, Hugo. *Musik Lexikon,* twelfth edition. Mainz: B. Schott's Söhne, 1959, 1961. 2 Vols. of biography, 1 Vol. of encyclopedic material.

Rolland, Romain. *Essays on Music.* New York: Allen, Towne & Heath, Inc., 1948.

Rostand, Claude. *Les Chefs-d'Oeuvre du Piano.* Paris: Librairie Plon, 1950.

Scholes, Percy A., ed. *Dr. Burney's Musical Tours in Europe.* London: Oxford University Press, 1959. 2 Vols.

Scholes, Percy A. *The Oxford Companion to Music,* ninth edition. London: Oxford University Press, 1955.

Schünemann, Georg. *Geschichte der Klaviermusik,* revised by Herbert Gerigk. Münchberg: Bernhard Hahnefeld Verlag, 1953.

Seiffert, Max. *Geschichte der Klaviermusik.* Leipzig: Breitkopf & Härtel, 1899. Vol. 1.

Selva, Blanche. *Quelques Mots sur la Sonate.* Paris: Librairie Paul Delaplane, 1914.

Shedlock, John S. *The Pianoforte Sonata.* London: Methuen & Co., 1895. Reprint by Da Capo Press, N.Y., 1964.

Subirá, José. *Historia de la Música.* Barcelona: Salvat Editores, S. A., 1951. 2 Vols.

Torrefranca, Fausto. *Le Origini Italiane del Romanticismo Musicale: I Primitivi della Sonata Moderna.* Torino: Fratelli Bocca, 1930.

Ulrich, Homer and Paul Pisk. *A History of Music and Musical Style.* New York: Harcourt, Brace & World, Inc., 1963.

Villanis, Luigi Alberto. *L'Arte del Piano in Italia de Clementi a Sgambati.* Torino: Fratelli Bocca, 1907.

Walker, Ernest. *A History of Music in England,* third edition, revised by J. A. Westrup. London: Oxford University Press, 1952.

Weitzmann, C. F. *A History of Pianoforte Playing and Pianoforte Literature* (translated by Theodore Baker). New York: G. Schirmer, 1897.

Westerby, Herbert. *The History of Pianoforte Music*. London: Kegan Paul, Trench, Trubner & Co., Ltd., 1924.

Wolf, Henry S. *The Twentieth-Century Piano Sonata*. Dissertation. Boston University, 1957.

LIST OF MUSIC PUBLISHERS

I. Publishers of keyboard music in the United States. Location of parent houses is indicated in parentheses.

American Composers' Alliance Library, New York, N.Y.
Associated Music Publishers, Inc., New York, N.Y.
Bärenreiter Music, New York, N.Y. (Kassel, Germany)
M. Baron Co., Oyster Bay, N.Y.
Big 3 Music Corp., New York, N.Y.
Boosey & Hawkes, Inc., New York, N.Y. (London, England)
Boston Music Co., Boston, Mass.
Broude Bros., New York, N.Y.
Chappell & Co., Inc., New York, N.Y.
Franco Colombo, New York, N.Y.
Elkan-Vogel Co., Inc., Philadelphia, Pa.
Carl Fischer, Inc., New York, N.Y.
J. Fischer & Bros., Glen Rock, N.J.
Galaxy Music Corp., New York, N.Y.
Hargail Music Press, New York, N.Y.
International Music Co., New York, N.Y.
E. F. Kalmus, New York, N.Y.
Leeds Music Corp., New York, N.Y.
McGinnis & Marx, New York, N.Y.
E. B. Marks Music Corp., New York, N.Y.
Mercury Music Corp., New York, N.Y.
Mills Music, Inc., New York, N.Y. (London, England)
Music Publishers Holding Corp., New York, N.Y.
Novello & Co., New York, N.Y. (London, England)
Oxford University Press, Inc., New York, N.Y. (London, England)
C. F. Peters Corp., New York, N.Y.
Theodore Presser Co., Bryn Mawr, Pa.
E. C. Schirmer Music Co., Boston, Mass.
G. Schirmer, Inc., New York, N.Y.
Shawnee Press, Inc., Delaware Water Gap, Pa.
Southern Music Publishing Co., Inc., New York, N.Y.
Summy-Birchard Publishing Co., Evanston, Ill.
Weintraub Music Co., New York, N.Y.
Willis Music Co., Cincinnati, Ohio

II. Foreign music publishers and subsidiaries of American companies. American agents or parent companies are indicated in parentheses.

Alpeg Editions, New York, N.Y. (Peters)
Alsbach, Amsterdam, Netherlands (Peters)

Editorial Argentina de Música, Buenos Aires, Argentina (Southern Music)

Arno Volk Verlag, Cologne, Germany (Leeds)

Arrow Press (Boosey & Hawkes)

Artia, Prague, Czechoslovakia (Boosey & Hawkes)

Assoc. Board of the Royal Schools of Music, London, England (Mills)

Augener, Ltd., London, England (Galaxy)

Axelrod Publications (Shawnee Press)

Barry & Cía, Buenos Aires, Argentina (Boosey & Hawkes)

M. P. Belaieff, Paris, France (Boosey & Hawkes)

C. C. Bender, Amsterdam, Netherlands

F. Bongiovanni, Bologna, Italy

Bote & Bock, Berlin, Germany (Associated Music Pub.)

Breitkopf & Härtel, Leipzig and Wiesbaden, Germany (Associated Music Pub.)

Broadcast Music Inc. of Canada, Toronto, Canada (Associated Music Pub.)

Broekmans & Van Poppel, Amsterdam, Netherlands (Peters)

Carisch, Milan, Italy (Mills)

Casa Amarilla, Santiago, Chile

J. & W. Chester, London, England (Marks)

Choudens, Paris, France (Peters)

Costallat, Paris, France (Baron)

Edizioni Curci, Milan, Italy (Big 3)

"De Ring," Antwerp, Belgium

Ludwig Doblinger, Vienna, Austria (Associated Music Pub.)

Donemus, Amsterdam, Netherlands (Peters)

Enoch & Cie., Paris, France (Associated Music Pub.)

Max Eschig, Paris, France (Associated Music Pub.)

Forlivesi & C., Florence, Italy (Colombo)

Gutheil Edition, Moscow, Russia (Boosey & Hawkes)

Hamelle & Cie., Paris, France (Elkan-Vogel)

Wilhelm Hansen, Copenhagen, Denmark (G. Schirmer)

G. Henle, Munich, Germany (Novello)

Edition Heuwekemeijer, Amsterdam, Netherlands (Elkan-Vogel)

Hinrichsen Edition, London, England (Peters)

Israeli Music Publications, Tel Aviv, Israel (Leeds)

Alphonse Leduc, Paris, France (Marks)

F. E. C. Leuckhart, Munich, Germany (Associated Music Pub.)

Collection Litolff, Brunswick, Germany (Peters)

Edizioni R. Maurri, Florence, Italy

Merrymount Music, Inc. (Presser)

Ediciones Mexicanas de Música, Mexico City (Leeds)

Willy Mueller, Suddeutsche Musikverlag, Heidelberg, Germany (Peters)

Murdoch & Murdoch, London, England (Chappell)

Music Press, Inc. (Presser)

Nagel's Musik-Archiv, Mainz, Germany (Associated Music Pub.)
Editions de l'Oiseau-Lyre, Monaco
Peer International (Southern Music)
G. Ricordi, Milan, Italy (Colombo)
Rouart, Lerolle & Cie., Paris, France (Colombo)
Salabert, Paris, France (Colombo)
Editions Musicales de la Schola Cantorum (Elkan-Vogel)
Schott Edition, London and Mainz (Associated Music Pub.)
N. Simrock, Berlin, Germany (Associated Music Pub.)
Stainer & Bell, London, England (Galaxy)
Edizioni Suvini Zerboni, Milan, Italy (Associated Music Pub.)
Templeton Publishing Co. (Shawnee Press)
Edition Tonos, Darmstadt, Germany (McGinnis)
Union Musical Española, Madrid, Spain (Associated Music Pub.)
Universal Edition, Vienna, Austria (Presser)
Vieweg, Berlin, Germany (Peters)
M. Witmark and Sons Co., New York, N.Y. (Music Pub. Holding)
Zimmerman, Frankfurt am Main, Germany (Peters)

INDEX

A CATALOG OF SELECTED DOVER
BOOKS IN ALL FIELDS OF INTEREST

CONCERNING THE SPIRITUAL IN ART, Wassily Kandinsky. Pioneering work by father of abstract art. Thoughts on color theory, nature of art. Analysis of earlier masters. 12 illustrations. 80pp. of text. 5⅜ × 8½. 23411-8 Pa. $3.95

ANIMALS: 1,419 Copyright-Free Illustrations of Mammals, Birds, Fish, Insects, etc., Jim Harter (ed.). Clear wood engravings present, in extremely lifelike poses, over 1,000 species of animals. One of the most extensive pictorial sourcebooks of its kind. Captions. Index. 284pp. 9 × 12. 23766-4 Pa. $11.95

CELTIC ART: The Methods of Construction, George Bain. Simple geometric techniques for making Celtic interlacements, spirals, Kells-type initials, animals, humans, etc. Over 500 illustrations. 160pp. 9 × 12. (USO) 22923-8 Pa. $8.95

AN ATLAS OF ANATOMY FOR ARTISTS, Fritz Schider. Most thorough reference work on art anatomy in the world. Hundreds of illustrations, including selections from works by Vesalius, Leonardo, Goya, Ingres, Michelangelo, others. 593 illustrations. 192pp. 7⅛ × 10¼. 20241-0 Pa. $8.95

CELTIC HAND STROKE-BY-STROKE (Irish Half-Uncial from "The Book of Kells"): An Arthur Baker Calligraphy Manual, Arthur Baker. Complete guide to creating each letter of the alphabet in distinctive Celtic manner. Covers hand position, strokes, pens, inks, paper, more. Illustrated. 48pp. 8¼ × 11.
24336-2 Pa. $3.95

EASY ORIGAMI, John Montroll. Charming collection of 32 projects (hat, cup, pelican, piano, swan, many more) specially designed for the novice origami hobbyist. Clearly illustrated easy-to-follow instructions insure that even beginning papercrafters will achieve successful results. 48pp. 8¼ × 11. 27298-2 Pa. $2.95

THE COMPLETE BOOK OF BIRDHOUSE CONSTRUCTION FOR WOOD-WORKERS, Scott D. Campbell. Detailed instructions, illustrations, tables. Also data on bird habitat and instinct patterns. Bibliography. 3 tables. 63 illustrations in 15 figures. 48pp. 5¼ × 8½. 24407-5 Pa. $1.95

BLOOMINGDALE'S ILLUSTRATED 1886 CATALOG: Fashions, Dry Goods and Housewares, Bloomingdale Brothers. Famed merchants' extremely rare catalog depicting about 1,700 products: clothing, housewares, firearms, dry goods, jewelry, more. Invaluable for dating, identifying vintage items. Also, copyright-free graphics for artists, designers. Co-published with Henry Ford Museum & Greenfield Village. 160pp. 8¼ × 11. 25780-0 Pa. $9.95

HISTORIC COSTUME IN PICTURES, Braun & Schneider. Over 1,450 costumed figures in clearly detailed engravings—from dawn of civilization to end of 19th century. Captions. Many folk costumes. 256pp. 8⅜ × 11¾. 23150-X Pa. $10.95

STICKLEY CRAFTSMAN FURNITURE CATALOGS, Gustav Stickley and L. & J. G. Stickley. Beautiful, functional furniture in two authentic catalogs from 1910. 594 illustrations, including 277 photos, show settles, rockers, armchairs, reclining chairs, bookcases, desks, tables. 183pp. 6½ × 9¼. 23838-5 Pa. $8.95

AMERICAN LOCOMOTIVES IN HISTORIC PHOTOGRAPHS: 1858 to 1949, Ron Ziel (ed.). A rare collection of 126 meticulously detailed official photographs, called "builder portraits," of American locomotives that majestically chronicle the rise of steam locomotive power in America. Introduction. Detailed captions. xi + 129pp. 9 × 12. 27393-8 Pa. $12.95

AMERICA'S LIGHTHOUSES: An Illustrated History, Francis Ross Holland, Jr. Delightfully written, profusely illustrated fact-filled survey of over 200 American lighthouses since 1716. History, anecdotes, technological advances, more. 240pp. 8 × 10¾. 25576-X Pa. $11.95

TOWARDS A NEW ARCHITECTURE, Le Corbusier. Pioneering manifesto by founder of "International School." Technical and aesthetic theories, views of industry, economics, relation of form to function, "mass-production split" and much more. Profusely illustrated. 320pp. 6⅛ × 9¼. (USO) 25023-7 Pa. $8.95

HOW THE OTHER HALF LIVES, Jacob Riis. Famous journalistic record, exposing poverty and degradation of New York slums around 1900, by major social reformer. 100 striking and influential photographs. 233pp. 10 × 7⅞.
22012-5 Pa $10.95

FRUIT KEY AND TWIG KEY TO TREES AND SHRUBS, William M. Harlow. One of the handiest and most widely used identification aids. Fruit key covers 120 deciduous and evergreen species; twig key 160 deciduous species. Easily used. Over 300 photographs. 126pp. 5⅜ × 8½. 20511-8 Pa. $3.95

COMMON BIRD SONGS, Dr. Donald J. Borror. Songs of 60 most common U.S. birds: robins, sparrows, cardinals, bluejays, finches, more—arranged in order of increasing complexity. Up to 9 variations of songs of each species.
Cassette and manual 99911-4 $8.95

ORCHIDS AS HOUSE PLANTS, Rebecca Tyson Northen. Grow cattleyas and many other kinds of orchids—in a window, in a case, or under artificial light. 63 illustrations. 148pp. 5⅜ × 8½. 23261-1 Pa. $3.95

MONSTER MAZES, Dave Phillips. Masterful mazes at four levels of difficulty. Avoid deadly perils and evil creatures to find magical treasures. Solutions for all 32 exciting illustrated puzzles. 48pp. 8¼ × 11. 26005-4 Pa. $2.95

MOZART'S DON GIOVANNI (DOVER OPERA LIBRETTO SERIES), Wolfgang Amadeus Mozart. Introduced and translated by Ellen H. Bleiler. Standard Italian libretto, with complete English translation. Convenient and thoroughly portable—an ideal companion for reading along with a recording or the performance itself. Introduction. List of characters. Plot summary. 121pp. 5¼ × 8½.
24944-1 Pa. $2.95

TECHNICAL MANUAL AND DICTIONARY OF CLASSICAL BALLET, Gail Grant. Defines, explains, comments on steps, movements, poses and concepts. 15-page pictorial section. Basic book for student, viewer. 127pp. 5⅜ × 8½.
21843-0 Pa. $3.95

BRASS INSTRUMENTS: Their History and Development, Anthony Baines. Authoritative, updated survey of the evolution of trumpets, trombones, bugles, cornets, French horns, tubas and other brass wind instruments. Over 140 illustrations and 48 music examples. Corrected and updated by author. New preface. Bibliography. 320pp. 5⅜ × 8½. 27574-4 Pa. $9.95

HOLLYWOOD GLAMOR PORTRAITS, John Kobal (ed.). 145 photos from 1926–49. Harlow, Gable, Bogart, Bacall; 94 stars in all. Full background on photographers, technical aspects. 160pp. 8⅜ × 11¼. 23352-9 Pa. $9.95

MAX AND MORITZ, Wilhelm Busch. Great humor classic in both German and English. Also 10 other works: "Cat and Mouse," "Plisch and Plumm," etc. 216pp. 5⅜ × 8½. 20181-3 Pa. $5.95

THE RAVEN AND OTHER FAVORITE POEMS, Edgar Allan Poe. Over 40 of the author's most memorable poems: "The Bells," "Ulalume," "Israfel," "To Helen," "The Conqueror Worm," "Eldorado," "Annabel Lee," many more. Alphabetic lists of titles and first lines. 64pp. 5³⁄₁₆ × 8¼. 26685-0 Pa. $1.00

SEVEN SCIENCE FICTION NOVELS, H. G. Wells. The standard collection of the great novels. Complete, unabridged. First Men in the Moon, Island of Dr. Moreau, War of the Worlds, Food of the Gods, Invisible Man, Time Machine, In the Days of the Comet. Total of 1,015pp. 5⅜ × 8½. (USO) 20264-X Clothbd. $29.95

AMULETS AND SUPERSTITIONS, E. A. Wallis Budge. Comprehensive discourse on origin, powers of amulets in many ancient cultures: Arab, Persian, Babylonian, Assyrian, Egyptian, Gnostic, Hebrew, Phoenician, Syriac, etc. Covers cross, swastika, crucifix, seals, rings, stones, etc. 584pp. 5⅜ × 8½. 23573-4 Pa. $12.95

RUSSIAN STORIES/PYCCKNE PACCKA3bl: A Dual-Language Book, edited by Gleb Struve. Twelve tales by such masters as Chekhov, Tolstoy, Dostoevsky, Pushkin, others. Excellent word-for-word English translations on facing pages, plus teaching and study aids, Russian/English vocabulary, biographical/critical introductions, more. 416pp. 5⅜ × 8½. 26244-8 Pa. $8.95

PHILADELPHIA THEN AND NOW: 60 Sites Photographed in the Past and Present, Kenneth Finkel and Susan Oyama. Rare photographs of City Hall, Logan Square, Independence Hall, Betsy Ross House, other landmarks juxtaposed with contemporary views. Captures changing face of historic city. Introduction. Captions. 128pp. 8¼ × 11. 25790-8 Pa. $9.95

AIA ARCHITECTURAL GUIDE TO NASSAU AND SUFFOLK COUNTIES, LONG ISLAND, The American Institute of Architects, Long Island Chapter, and the Society for the Preservation of Long Island Antiquities. Comprehensive, well-researched and generously illustrated volume brings to life over three centuries of Long Island's great architectural heritage. More than 240 photographs with authoritative, extensively detailed captions. 176pp. 8¼ × 11. 26946-9 Pa. $14.95

NORTH AMERICAN INDIAN LIFE: Customs and Traditions of 23 Tribes, Elsie Clews Parsons (ed.). 27 fictionalized essays by noted anthropologists examine religion, customs, government, additional facets of life among the Winnebago, Crow, Zuni, Eskimo, other tribes. 480pp. 6⅛ × 9¼. 27377-6 Pa. $10.95

FRANK LLOYD WRIGHT'S HOLLYHOCK HOUSE, Donald Hoffmann. Lavishly illustrated, carefully documented study of one of Wright's most controversial residential designs. Over 120 photographs, floor plans, elevations, etc. Detailed perceptive text by noted Wright scholar. Index. 128pp. 9¼ × 10¾.
27133-1 Pa. $11.95

THE MALE AND FEMALE FIGURE IN MOTION: 60 Classic Photographic Sequences, Eadweard Muybridge. 60 true-action photographs of men and women walking, running, climbing, bending, turning, etc., reproduced from rare 19th-century masterpiece. vi + 121pp. 9 × 12. 24745-7 Pa. $10.95

1001 QUESTIONS ANSWERED ABOUT THE SEASHORE, N. J. Berrill and Jacquelyn Berrill. Queries answered about dolphins, sea snails, sponges, starfish, fishes, shore birds, many others. Covers appearance, breeding, growth, feeding, much more. 305pp. 5¼ × 8¼. 23366-9 Pa. $7.95

GUIDE TO OWL WATCHING IN NORTH AMERICA, Donald S. Heintzelman. Superb guide offers complete data and descriptions of 19 species: barn owl, screech owl, snowy owl, many more. Expert coverage of owl-watching equipment, conservation, migrations and invasions, etc. Guide to observing sites. 84 illustrations. xiii + 193pp. 5⅜ × 8½. 27344-X Pa. $7.95

MEDICINAL AND OTHER USES OF NORTH AMERICAN PLANTS: A Historical Survey with Special Reference to the Eastern Indian Tribes, Charlotte Erichsen-Brown. Chronological historical citations document 500 years of usage of plants, trees, shrubs native to eastern Canada, northeastern U.S. Also complete identifying information. 343 illustrations. 544pp. 6½ × 9¼. 25951-X Pa. $12.95

STORYBOOK MAZES, Dave Phillips. 23 stories and mazes on two-page spreads: Wizard of Oz, Treasure Island, Robin Hood, etc. Solutions. 64pp. 8¼ × 11.
23628-5 Pa. $2.95

NEGRO FOLK MUSIC, U.S.A., Harold Courlander. Noted folklorist's scholarly yet readable analysis of rich and varied musical tradition. Includes authentic versions of over 40 folk songs. Valuable bibliography and discography. xi + 324pp. 5⅜ × 8½. 27350-4 Pa. $7.95

MOVIE-STAR PORTRAITS OF THE FORTIES, John Kobal (ed.). 163 glamor, studio photos of 106 stars of the 1940s: Rita Hayworth, Ava Gardner, Marlon Brando, Clark Gable, many more. 176pp. 8⅜ × 11¼. 23546-7 Pa. $10.95

BENCHLEY LOST AND FOUND, Robert Benchley. Finest humor from early 30s, about pet peeves, child psychologists, post office and others. Mostly unavailable elsewhere. 73 illustrations by Peter Arno and others. 183pp. 5⅜ × 8½.
22410-4 Pa. $5.95

YEKL and THE IMPORTED BRIDEGROOM AND OTHER STORIES OF YIDDISH NEW YORK, Abraham Cahan. Film Hester Street based on Yekl (1896). Novel, other stories among first about Jewish immigrants on N.Y.'s East Side. 240pp. 5⅜ × 8½. 22427-9 Pa. $5.95

SELECTED POEMS, Walt Whitman. Generous sampling from *Leaves of Grass*. Twenty-four poems include "I Hear America Singing," "Song of the Open Road," "I Sing the Body Electric," "When Lilacs Last in the Dooryard Bloom'd," "O Captain! My Captain!"—all reprinted from an authoritative edition. Lists of titles and first lines. 128pp. 5³⁄₁₆ × 8¼. 26878-0 Pa. $1.00

MY BONDAGE AND MY FREEDOM, Frederick Douglass. Born a slave, Douglass became outspoken force in antislavery movement. The best of Douglass' autobiographies. Graphic description of slave life. 464pp. 5⅜ × 8½. 22457-0 Pa. $8.95

FOLLOWING THE EQUATOR: A Journey Around the World, Mark Twain. Fascinating humorous account of 1897 voyage to Hawaii, Australia, India, New Zealand, etc. Ironic, bemused reports on peoples, customs, climate, flora and fauna, politics, much more. 197 illustrations. 720pp. 5⅜ × 8½. 26113-1 Pa. $15.95

THE PEOPLE CALLED SHAKERS, Edward D. Andrews. Definitive study of Shakers: origins, beliefs, practices, dances, social organization, furniture and crafts, etc. 33 illustrations. 351pp. 5⅜ × 8½. 21081-2 Pa. $7.95

THE MYTHS OF GREECE AND ROME, H. A. Guerber. A classic of mythology, generously illustrated, long prized for its simple, graphic, accurate retelling of the principal myths of Greece and Rome, and for its commentary on their origins and significance. With 64 illustrations by Michelangelo, Raphael, Titian, Rubens, Canova, Bernini and others. 480pp. 5⅜ × 8½. 27584-1 Pa. $9.95

PSYCHOLOGY OF MUSIC, Carl E. Seashore. Classic work discusses music as a medium from psychological viewpoint. Clear treatment of physical acoustics, auditory apparatus, sound perception, development of musical skills, nature of musical feeling, host of other topics. 88 figures. 408pp. 5⅜ × 8½. 21851-1 Pa. $9.95

THE PHILOSOPHY OF HISTORY, Georg W. Hegel. Great classic of Western thought develops concept that history is not chance but rational process, the evolution of freedom. 457pp. 5⅜ × 8½. 20112-0 Pa. $8.95

THE BOOK OF TEA, Kakuzo Okakura. Minor classic of the Orient: entertaining, charming explanation, interpretation of traditional Japanese culture in terms of tea ceremony. 94pp. 5⅜ × 8½. 20070-1 Pa. $2.95

LIFE IN ANCIENT EGYPT, Adolf Erman. Fullest, most thorough, detailed older account with much not in more recent books, domestic life, religion, magic, medicine, commerce, much more. Many illustrations reproduce tomb paintings, carvings, hieroglyphs, etc. 597pp. 5⅜ × 8½. 22632-8 Pa. $9.95

SUNDIALS, Their Theory and Construction, Albert Waugh. Far and away the best, most thorough coverage of ideas, mathematics concerned, types, construction, adjusting anywhere. Simple, nontechnical treatment allows even children to build several of these dials. Over 100 illustrations. 230pp. 5⅜ × 8½. 22947-5 Pa. $5.95

DYNAMICS OF FLUIDS IN POROUS MEDIA, Jacob Bear. For advanced students of ground water hydrology, soil mechanics and physics, drainage and irrigation engineering, and more. 335 illustrations. Exercises, with answers. 784pp. 6⅛ × 9¼. 65675-6 Pa. $19.95

SONGS OF EXPERIENCE: Facsimile Reproduction with 26 Plates in Full Color, William Blake. 26 full-color plates from a rare 1826 edition. Includes "The Tyger," "London," "Holy Thursday," and other poems. Printed text of poems. 48pp. 5¼ × 7. 24636-1 Pa. $3.95

OLD-TIME VIGNETTES IN FULL COLOR, Carol Belanger Grafton (ed.). Over 390 charming, often sentimental illustrations, selected from archives of Victorian graphics—pretty women posing, children playing, food, flowers, kittens and puppies, smiling cherubs, birds and butterflies, much more. All copyright-free. 48pp. 9¼ × 12¼. 27269-9 Pa. $5.95

ANATOMY: A Complete Guide for Artists, Joseph Sheppard. A master of figure drawing shows artists how to render human anatomy convincingly. Over 460 illustrations. 224pp. 8⅜ × 11¼. 27279-6 Pa. $9.95

MEDIEVAL CALLIGRAPHY: Its History and Technique, Marc Drogin. Spirited history, comprehensive instruction manual covers 13 styles (ca. 4th century thru 15th). Excellent photographs; directions for duplicating medieval techniques with modern tools. 224pp. 8⅜ × 11¼. 26142-5 Pa. $11.95

DRIED FLOWERS: How to Prepare Them, Sarah Whitlock and Martha Rankin. Complete instructions on how to use silica gel, meal and borax, perlite aggregate, sand and borax, glycerine and water to create attractive permanent flower arrangements. 12 illustrations. 32pp. 5⅜ × 8½. 21802-3 Pa. $1.00

EASY-TO-MAKE BIRD FEEDERS FOR WOODWORKERS, Scott D. Campbell. Detailed, simple-to-use guide for designing, constructing, caring for and using feeders. Text, illustrations for 12 classic and contemporary designs. 96pp. 5⅜ × 8½. 25847-5 Pa. $2.95

OLD-TIME CRAFTS AND TRADES, Peter Stockham. An 1807 book created to teach children about crafts and trades open to them as future careers. It describes in detailed, nontechnical terms 24 different occupations, among them coachmaker, gardener, hairdresser, lacemaker, shoemaker, wheelwright, copper-plate printer, milliner, trunkmaker, merchant and brewer. Finely detailed engravings illustrate each occupation. 192pp. 4⅝ × 6. 27398-9 Pa. $4.95

THE HISTORY OF UNDERCLOTHES, C. Willett Cunnington and Phyllis Cunnington. Fascinating, well-documented survey covering six centuries of English undergarments, enhanced with over 100 illustrations: 12th-century laced-up bodice, footed long drawers (1795), 19th-century bustles, 19th-century corsets for men, Victorian "bust improvers," much more. 272pp. 5⅜ × 8¼. 27124-2 Pa. $9.95

ARTS AND CRAFTS FURNITURE: The Complete Brooks Catalog of 1912, Brooks Manufacturing Co. Photos and detailed descriptions of more than 150 now very collectible furniture designs from the Arts and Crafts movement depict davenports, settees, buffets, desks, tables, chairs, bedsteads, dressers and more, all built of solid, quarter-sawed oak. Invaluable for students and enthusiasts of antiques, Americana and the decorative arts. 80pp. 6½ × 9¼. 27471-3 Pa. $7.95

HOW WE INVENTED THE AIRPLANE: An Illustrated History, Orville Wright. Fascinating firsthand account covers early experiments, construction of planes and motors, first flights, much more. Introduction and commentary by Fred C. Kelly. 76 photographs. 96pp. 8¼ × 11. 25662-6 Pa. $7.95

THE ARTS OF THE SAILOR: Knotting, Splicing and Ropework, Hervey Garrett Smith. Indispensable shipboard reference covers tools, basic knots and useful hitches; handsewing and canvas work, more. Over 100 illustrations. Delightful reading for sea lovers. 256pp. 5⅜ × 8½. 26440-8 Pa. $7.95

FRANK LLOYD WRIGHT'S FALLINGWATER: The House and Its History, Second, Revised Edition, Donald Hoffmann. A total revision—both in text and illustrations—of the standard document on Fallingwater, the boldest, most personal architectural statement of Wright's mature years, updated with valuable new material from the recently opened Frank Lloyd Wright Archives. "Fascinating"—The New York Times. 116 illustrations. 128pp. 9¼ × 10¾. 27430-6 Pa. $10.95

AUTOBIOGRAPHY: The Story of My Experiments with Truth, Mohandas K. Gandhi. Boyhood, legal studies, purification, the growth of the Satyagraha (nonviolent protest) movement. Critical, inspiring work of the man responsible for the freedom of India. 480pp. 5⅜ × 8½. (USO) 24593-4 Pa. $7.95

CELTIC MYTHS AND LEGENDS, T. W. Rolleston. Masterful retelling of Irish and Welsh stories and tales. Cuchulain, King Arthur, Deirdre, the Grail, many more. First paperback edition. 58 full-page illustrations. 512pp. 5⅜ × 8½. 26507-2 Pa. $9.95

THE PRINCIPLES OF PSYCHOLOGY, William James. Famous long course complete, unabridged. Stream of thought, time perception, memory, experimental methods; great work decades ahead of its time. 94 figures. 1,391pp. 5⅜ × 8½. 2-vol. set.
Vol. I: 20381-6 Pa. $12.95
Vol. II: 20382-4 Pa. $12.95

THE WORLD AS WILL AND REPRESENTATION, Arthur Schopenhauer. Definitive English translation of Schopenhauer's life work, correcting more than 1,000 errors, omissions in earlier translations. Translated by E. F. J. Payne. Total of 1,269pp. 5⅜ × 8½. 2-vol. set.
Vol. 1: 21761-2 Pa. $10.95
Vol. 2: 21762-0 Pa. $11.95

MAGIC AND MYSTERY IN TIBET, Madame Alexandra David-Neel. Experiences among lamas, magicians, sages, sorcerers, Bonpa wizards. A true psychic discovery. 32 illustrations. 321pp. 5⅜ × 8½. (USO) 22682-4 Pa. $8.95

THE EGYPTIAN BOOK OF THE DEAD, E. A. Wallis Budge. Complete reproduction of Ani's papyrus, finest ever found. Full hieroglyphic text, interlinear transliteration, word-for-word translation, smooth translation. 533pp. 6½ × 9¼. 21866-X Pa. $9.95

MATHEMATICS FOR THE NONMATHEMATICIAN, Morris Kline. Detailed, college-level treatment of mathematics in cultural and historical context, with numerous exercises. Recommended Reading Lists. Tables. Numerous figures. 641pp. 5⅜ × 8½. 24823-2 Pa. $11.95

THEORY OF WING SECTIONS: Including a Summary of Airfoil Data, Ira H. Abbott and A. E. von Doenhoff. Concise compilation of subsonic aerodynamic characteristics of NACA wing sections, plus description of theory. 350pp. of tables. 693pp. 5⅜ × 8½. 60586-8 Pa. $13.95

THE RIME OF THE ANCIENT MARINER, Gustave Doré, S. T. Coleridge. Doré's finest work; 34 plates capture moods, subtleties of poem. Flawless full-size reproductions printed on facing pages with authoritative text of poem. "Beautiful. Simply beautiful."—*Publisher's Weekly*. 77pp. 9¼ × 12. 22305-1 Pa. $5.95

NORTH AMERICAN INDIAN DESIGNS FOR ARTISTS AND CRAFTSPEOPLE, Eva Wilson. Over 360 authentic copyright-free designs adapted from Navajo blankets, Hopi pottery, Sioux buffalo hides, more. Geometrics, symbolic figures, plant and animal motifs, etc. 128pp. 8⅜ × 11. (EUK) 25341-4 Pa. $7.95

SCULPTURE: Principles and Practice, Louis Slobodkin. Step-by-step approach to clay, plaster, metals, stone; classical and modern. 253 drawings, photos. 255pp. 8⅛ × 11. 22960-2 Pa. $9.95

THE INFLUENCE OF SEA POWER UPON HISTORY, 1660–1783, A. T. Mahan. Influential classic of naval history and tactics still used as text in war colleges. First paperback edition. 4 maps. 24 battle plans. 640pp. 5⅜ × 8½.
25509-3 Pa. $12.95

THE STORY OF THE TITANIC AS TOLD BY ITS SURVIVORS, Jack Winocour (ed.). What it was really like. Panic, despair, shocking inefficiency, and a little heroism. More thrilling than any fictional account. 26 illustrations. 320pp. 5⅜ × 8½.
20610-6 Pa. $7.95

FAIRY AND FOLK TALES OF THE IRISH PEASANTRY, William Butler Yeats (ed.). Treasury of 64 tales from the twilight world of Celtic myth and legend: "The Soul Cages," "The Kildare Pooka," "King O'Toole and his Goose," many more. Introduction and Notes by W. B. Yeats. 352pp. 5⅜ × 8½.
26941-8 Pa. $7.95

BUDDHIST MAHAYANA TEXTS, E. B. Cowell and Others (eds.). Superb, accurate translations of basic documents in Mahayana Buddhism, highly important in history of religions. The Buddha-karita of Asvaghosha, Larger Sukhavativyuha, more. 448pp. 5⅜ × 8½.
25552-2 Pa. $9.95

ONE TWO THREE . . . INFINITY: Facts and Speculations of Science, George Gamow. Great physicist's fascinating, readable overview of contemporary science: number theory, relativity, fourth dimension, entropy, genes, atomic structure, much more. 128 illustrations. Index. 352pp. 5⅜ × 8½.
25664-2 Pa. $8.95

ENGINEERING IN HISTORY, Richard Shelton Kirby, et al. Broad, nontechnical survey of history's major technological advances: birth of Greek science, industrial revolution, electricity and applied science, 20th-century automation, much more. 181 illustrations. ". . . excellent . . ."—Isis. Bibliography. vii + 530pp. 5⅜ × 8¼.
26412-2 Pa. $14.95

Prices subject to change without notice.

Available at your book dealer or write for free catalog to Dept. GI, Dover Publications, Inc., 31 East 2nd St., Mineola, N.Y. 11501. Dover publishes more than 500 books each year on science, elementary and advanced mathematics, biology, music, art, literary history, social sciences and other areas.